MVS Control Blocks

J. Ranade IBM Series

In order to receive additional information on these or any other McGraw-Hill titles, in the United States please call 1-800-822-8158. In other countries, contact your local McGraw-Hill representative.

MVS Control Blocks

Hank Murphy

McGraw-Hill, Inc.

New York San Francisco Washington, D.C. Auckland Bogotá
Caracas Lisbon London Madrid Mexico City Milan
Montreal New Delhi San Juan Singapore
Sydney Tokyo Toronto

ESA/390, ESA/370, MVS/ESA, IBMLink, ImagePlus, and OpenMVS are trademarks of the International Business Machines Corporation. DEC and VAX are trademarks of the Digital Equipment Corporation. All other trademarks used are the property of their respective holders.

Library of Congress Cataloging-in-Publication Data

Murphy, Hank (Hank A.)
    MVS control blocks / by Hank Murphy.
      p.   cm.

    Includes index.
    ISBN 0-07-044309-2
    1. IBM MVS.   I. Title.
    QA76.6.M866   1994
    005.4'3—dc20   94-34416
                                             CIP

1 2 3 4 5 6 7 8 9 0   DOC/DOC   9 9 8 7 6 5 4

The sponsoring editor for this book was Jerry Papke, the book editor was Kellie Hagan, and the executive editor was Robert E. Ostrander. The director of production was Katherine G. Brown. This book was set in ITC Century Light. It was composed in Blue Ridge Summit, PA.

Printed and bound by R.R. Donnelley & Sons Company.

0443092
MH94

Contents

Acknowledgments

The creation of this book involved assistance from many people. I must first thank the long-suffering students who sat through my "MVS Control Blocks" and other classes at UCLA Extension, and who reviewed or contributed information that improved my efforts. Thanks to (in no special order) Jerry Bronner (Sterling Software), Randy Green and Harry Bogosian (Great Western Bank), Chris Cook, Alex Kamajian, Sharokh Nezamzadeh, and Wai Yin Wong (Candle), Bruce Coyle (Litton), Art Moore (UCLA), Michael Smith (L.A. Times), Michael Cernyar, Walter Hamilton, Steve Ishii, Steve Johnson, Romeo Rili, Andrew Robinson, John Trainor, and Jim Woodward. Special thanks go to Margaret Daugherty for XA GQSCAN research and to Henry Ransons for the IDLI tip.

UCLA Extension has many competent professionals who make good programs great. Special thanks go to Don Hausnecht for his support in the development of this book, and to Shoreh for her assistance.

I've been lucky to have worked with some exceptional talents, and would like to thank Ray Walker, Thom Hillman, Dan Yum, John Maher, Eric Jackson, Mark Durman, and Bill Ek for taking the time to review pieces of this manuscript at Candle Corporation. Tom Bird, president of Innovative DP Designs and coauthor of *The Dynamics of Data Base* (Prentice-Hall, 1986), deserves thanks for understanding an author on deadline.

McGraw-Hill is lucky to have Jay Ranade as editor of this series. I have to thank both Jay and Jerry Papke, sponsoring editor, for their patience in waiting for this book, which must have seemed like waiting for Godot. Kellie Hagan did a good job adapting my random scribblings into their current form, and Dawn Bowling whipped the manuscript into final production form with a speed that outpaced my own. I'd also like to commend Jodi Tyler for a yeoman's job of patient indexing.

Speaking of patience . . . words cannot express my feelings for my wife Barbara and long-suffering offspring Joe, Jennifer, Jessica, and Matthew. In addition to love and understanding, I am also relieved that they didn't hit me when I started talking about writing another book.

In any event, I also have to thank the literally dozens of other people who helped me with information or advice along the way. I apologize for forgetting anyone, and, everyone else's assistance notwithstanding, any omissions or errors are my own.

If you want to contact me, you can do so through CompuServe at 70033,1174, or through the National Systems Programmers Assocation (NaSPA) bulletin board at user ID MurpJosV.

Preface

If you have to create or maintain assembler language programs that use the facilities of IBM's MVS operating system, if you need an overall understanding of the internal logic of MVS, or if you want to be able to make sense of an MVS dump, this book is for you.

IBM's MVS (Multiple Virtual Storage) system predecessors appeared almost 30 years ago, with the release of the OS/360 operating system. MVS has grown substantially through the years, both in size and complexity. This makes learning how it works a Herculean struggle for the neophyte; understanding how new features work is often equally difficult for even experienced MVS programmers.

The Purpose of This Book

I didn't write this book to make you an expert in every nuance of MVS internal logic (hereafter called *internals*). With a self-imposed limit of 400 pages, comprehensive coverage of every MVS component is impossible. As one measure of the size of that task, there are 714 separate control blocks in the MVS version 4 data areas manuals. If you were to sit down and learn one per day at work, it would take about three years to cover them all . . . by which time many would have changed.

This book, instead, has two complementary goals. The first is to provide an understanding of the basic control blocks within MVS, and the second is to show how to research MVS features using MVS control blocks. (This research is sometimes complicated by fields that are still defined but no longer used.)

The basic control blocks within MVS comprise those used to describe the computer itself, the addresses of various MVS component services and related control blocks, the work being run on the machine at any point in time, and the use of the machine's resources.

Researching MVS features requires several techniques, which vary based on the facilities available. At the most elementary level, a programmer can access only the standard IBM-supplied macro libraries; other resources include access to actual MVS listings, either on microfiche or through the IBMLink system. This book starts with the assumption that you have only limited access, and discusses additional information sources when needed.

One problem with teaching (or learning about) MVS control blocks is how to place the information in its proper context. In many cases, control blocks are visible only as part of a storage dump. To make the information in the book as immediately relevant as possible, appendix C is annotated to include references to the chapters that discuss the control blocks as they appear in a storage dump.

Another problem with learning about MVS control blocks is what to do with the information. To make this book as relevant as possible, most chapters will have a section (or sections) devoted to specific uses of information from the control blocks in that chapter. With luck, this will be a meaningful and useful source of information over time.

Finally, you might note that many parts of MVS are not discussed in any detail in this book. There are several reasons for this. One is that I had to draw the line somewhere; a complete discussion on modifying the Open/Close/End-Of-Volume component of MVS to provide your own access method isn't one of the goals for this book. Another reason for limiting the MVS elements covered in the book relates to the changes in IBM's MVS documentation—which leads into a discussion of the history of MVS and how systems programmers used it in general.

Background

IBM announced the System/360 family of processors in 1964. At the same time, they announced several operating systems for these new computers—one of which was OS/360, the original ancestor of today's MVS.

OS/360 was a tremendous undertaking by the software project standards of the day. It encountered many problems by virtue of its complexity, size, and new concepts. (Frederick P. Brooks used his experience in managing the OS/360 development project to write the classic software engineering text, *The Mythical Man-Month*; I highly recommend it for any professional programmer.)

The numerous problems in OS/360 development led to rapid changes. (I began programming in 1967 using OS/360, release 17.)

In addition to rapid releases, OS/360 installations were often forced to develop their own extensions to the operating system. This was possible because IBM made the source code to the operating system available, which was necessary because there were many things in OS/360 that didn't work as well as they should have.

The greatest example of a user modification to OS/360 came in the area of spooling. OS/360 originally created temporary data sets that were eventually spun off to separate "writer" jobs that deleted the disk space after printing the file in question. The process was slow; in addition to scattering temporary data sets throughout the system, the printers also paused noticeably when the writer program was deleting the old data sets, selecting the next print file, and so forth.

To alleviate this printer delay problem, an IBM systems engineer (SE) named Tom Simpson at the NASA Houston space center developed an alternate program: the Houston Automatic Spooling Program, or HASP. It was the most popular OS/360 modification for a long time. It was so popular, in fact, that it eventually became part of the operating system itself—although it had to be renamed Job Entry System/2 (JES2) along the way.

One other common modification was to add the job name to messages on the master console; this eventually made it into MVS as well.

OS/360 had three implementation options; the one of most interest to this book was the Multiprogramming with a Variable number of Tasks (MVT) option, which allowed up to 15 jobs of varying sizes to run simultaneously. This was transformed around 1972 to OS/VS2, or Operating System/Virtual Storage 2. OS/VS2 in this period started out with one 16-megabyte view of virtual storage that was later called Single Virtual Storage, or SVS. (SVS was sometimes called "the operating system that combined the worst features of MVT and MVS.") SVS was supplanted by an OS/VS2 version that allowed multiple views of part of its 16-megabyte virtual storage area. It was called Multiple Virtual Storage, or MVS.

In its early implementation, MVS was—to put it mildly—less than optimum where performance was concerned. As a result, it was still modified by its customer installations; modifications were freely distributed among IBM customers, and IBM still provided access to the source code for MVS.

However, mainframe competition for IBM appeared during the late 1970s. Firms such as Amdahl and Itel sold many machines to formerly captive IBM mainframe customers, and caused IBM to begin rethinking some of its business practices. As a result, IBM began charging for its operating systems, which had previously been provided at no charge. To the best of my knowledge, this began in 1977 with a product called MVS/Systems Extensions (MVS/SE).

The changes in IBM's business practices continued, and around 1981 IBM announced a policy for new products called Object Code Only (OCO). This was the beginning of the end of an IBM customer's ability to modify MVS. While OCO didn't completely bar access to existing IBM source code, it did preclude access to new products and major new releases and versions of existing products.

Concurrent with OCO, IBM began changing its documentation. In OS/360 and previous versions of MVS, each major component included something called a *logic manual*. Logic manuals described the programs in a product or component, and included things like flowcharts and HIPO diagrams to describe the overall logic of each program. Logic manuals were often out of date and sometimes glossed over important details, but they provided a starting point for programmers who wanted to learn how the code worked.

Contemporary IBM products now tend to have a different type of manual, called a *component diagnosis* manual. These include much less information—often none—about the program's internal logic, data areas, and other information previously available. Additionally, IBM's diagnosis manuals that documented the layout of data areas became licensed material rather than being generally available manuals.

These changes were controversial within many IBM user groups. It would take several chapters to fairly present all sides of the OCO discussion. In IBM's defense, many installations had stopped modifying MVS for some time and their management had no intent of doing so in the future. The point is that the reasons for learning MVS internals have changed over the life of the product. At the same time, the resources for learning about MVS internals have also changed. Enough said.

The effect on the presentation in this book is that no IBM-licensed material will be used. To the degree possible, the information in this book will be drawn only from the basic data areas distributed by IBM as part of the operating system. These take the form of assembler language dummy sections (DSECTs) within IBM macro instructions. Licensed manuals (for data areas, etc.) aren't essential for understanding most of the material in this book, although some will benefit from it. References to licensed material will be provided for those who have access to it.

What You Should Know to Use This Book

At a fairly high, overview level, you might be able to benefit just from the fact that the control blocks within a storage dump are identified in this book. Programmers who don't know assembler language will benefit from this.

Programmers who know assembler language will be able to access information they previously couldn't. To do this, you should be familiar with how DSECTs are used. If you don't, I recommend you read my previous book, *Assembler for COBOL Programmers*.

In general, the more assembler language you know the more you'll benefit from the book. However, I assume no special prior knowledge and most chapters will have examples or explanations of how services are invoked.

The audience for this book is intended to be both systems programmers and advanced assembler language applications programmers. However, I encourage anyone who can benefit from it to read this book. It's what you learn that counts.

Recommended Manuals

Plan on reading the appropriate manuals for your environment. You'll need the Principles of Operation, which most assembler programmers will have used previously. This might be the S/370, XA, or ESA version; I'll attempt to keep things straight among the various versions. You should also have a 370 reference summary: the yellow, pink, or blue card (the XA or ESA versions is preferable). These have been booklets for some time, but the OS/360 terminology—as in "green card"—still survives.

If available, you should have the data area manuals for the version of MVS that you run. These manuals are licensed material, and might be difficult to obtain. Additionally, they're currently in five volumes. As a result, I'll also refer to the older MVS 3.8 data area handbooks, which are composed of three small-format manuals and are still available from IBM. (Manual numbers are listed at the end of the Introduction.) While obsolete, the manuals' portability makes them useful when compared to the 17-pound, seven-inch-thick current manual set.

Additionally, you'll be expected to research data areas using the SYS1.MACLIB and SYS1.MODGEN libraries. These will supplant the data area manuals, but access to both is desirable. You might also want to refer to the Supervisor SPL manuals (or their renamed equivalents) from time to time. The Initialization and Tuning Guide and Reference might be useful if you have access to the SYS1.PARMLIB library. Order numbers for some recommended manuals are listed in the Introduction.

Development of This Book

This book grew from a UCLA extension course called "Operating System Internals: IBM's MVS" that I began teaching in 1990. The assistance of many long-suffering students has been inestimable in developing the topics addressed herein.

The course originated in the mid-1970s. Reflecting the needs of the times, it concentrated somewhat more on modifying MVS than is the case for this book. The original developer of the course was William Finkelstein, a well-known and highly regarded member of the Los Angeles systems programming community, who served at that time in various positions at Security Pacific National Bank.

In the early 1980s, the second instructor for the course was the talented Alan Feinstein, an early staff member at Candle Corporation. During Alan's ten years of teaching the course, he concentrated on teaching MVS internals and dump reading.

My contributions pale by comparison. I updated the course to include selected MVS/ESA topics, while reducing the stress on the RSM and ASM topics. Additionally, the course covered more how to use internal knowledge to extract useful information, used more programming examples, and the like.

One problem that arose quickly was what to do for a text book. There are several computer science texts on operating system design; extensive coverage of MVS internals (and IBM operating systems in general) has been the exception rather than the rule. To make a long story short, I wrote this book in response to that need.

"Bon appetit!"

Introduction

Getting Started

A *control block* is "a storage area, used by both MVS and programs running within MVS, to hold or specify information needed in using and providing MVS services." You don't need to memorize that, but a few points about control blocks are in order.

First, control blocks are just another data structure, like a 01-level COBOL record layout or C structure. There's no magic to storage containing a control block, although MVS uses several methods to protect many control blocks from accidental changes and prying eyes. Control blocks are just data areas, used in most cases by more than one program. The format of control blocks is normally documented in the form of assembler language "dummy sections," or DSECTs.

Another characteristic of control blocks is that they usually exist only within main storage, rather than being written to I/O devices. There are a few examples where this isn't true, as you'll see, but control blocks generally exist only within MVS, not outside.

Another characteristic is that DSECTs are normally accessed by their address, rather than being copied into your program as a record might be. There are several reasons for this. One is that copying a control block uses both CPU time and memory; neither is desirable for frequently executed operating system components. Another is that, by their nature, control blocks are used by several programs—in MVS, often by two programs running simultaneously on separate processors. This means that control blocks have to be in one place, and they stay in one place for their lifetime.

(There are some notable exceptions to this rule. For example, many services provide access to a copy of the Unit Control Block (UCB) rather than to the control block itself. This practice will probably expand to other control blocks in the future.)

Within MVS, control blocks are created almost exclusively by the operating system. There are, of course, several notable examples of control blocks created within user programs, the Data Control Block (DCB) being the most common example. Many operating system parameter lists are defined by IBM-supplied DSECTs much like control blocks, and are also created within your program. However, the majority are created by unseen hands.

Another characteristic of control blocks, common to both MVS and other operating systems, is the use of different techniques to store them. MVS control blocks are frequently "chained" in "linked lists." Chaining, much like a chain letter, means that each control block must contain the address of the next control block in the series. A data structure (control block) that uses this technique is said to be in a linked list. If control blocks contain the addresses of both the next and preceding control blocks in the series, they are said to be in a doubly linked list. You'll see an example of this with the control block named the Address Space Control Block in chapter 3, and I'll discuss it more fully there.

Control blocks, in particular instances, have several other unique characteristics. Sometimes these arise from a need to store information as compactly as possible. You'll read about these when I discuss specific examples later in the book.

Finding Control Blocks

Since control blocks are usually referenced or updated by more than one program, it follows that there have to be common ways of locating specific control blocks. There are many such ways, and they're described in the following sections.

In the simplest case, the control block can be part of your program. The Data Control Block (DCB) is again the common example. Parameter lists and feedback areas provide other examples. (A *feedback area*, as used here, is simply an area in your program where MVS passes back information; it might be a control block.)

Another fairly straightforward approach is to pass the address of a control block to a program when it's called by MVS. (Programs that MVS calls for specific situations are *exits*; you'll see examples later on.)

More commonly, however, the address of a control block is obtained from another control block. For example, the DCB contains the address of the Data Extent Block (DEB) and the DEB in turn contains the address of the Unit Control Blocks (UCBs) for the devices used for a particular DD statement—and so on.

However, getting the address of a control block from another control block begs the question of how to get the address of the first control block in the first place. This leads to a method of locating a control block that's both the rarest and most common: putting the control block's address in a fixed location. This is the rarest form because it's reserved for use only by the most important control blocks in MVS. At the same time, it's the most common way to locate control blocks since the most frequent access to MVS information is through the Communications Vector Table (CVT), which uses this approach.

Examples of control blocks that follow this approach begin with something called the PSA (Prefixed Save Area). This is always at location zero in the CPU. The PSA in turn points to other important MVS control blocks. The most important of these is the CVT (Communications Vector Table), whose address is always at location X'10' and at location X'4C' in the PSA. The instructions to access the CVT are:

```
L       R1,X'10'
USING CVT,R1
```

These are ubiquitous in MVS assembler language programs that refer to MVS control blocks. (You'll see an example of a C language program that accesses the CVT in chapter 2.)

Other control blocks whose addresses are kept in the PSA include the current ASCB, the current Task Control Block (TCB), and several control blocks that need to be commonly addressable for a variety of reasons. One such control block is the VTAM ATCVT (Advanced Telecommunications CVT). Others include control blocks used during interruption processing. You'll see further examples of this when I discuss the PSA in detail in chapter 1.

The requirement for commonly addressable storage areas isn't unique to MVS. For example, the CICS Common Storage Area (CSA) holds addresses and constants needed by many or all CICS programs. Indeed, this requirement appears in almost all IBM program products, and systems software from many different sources for many different types of computer systems.

Information about Control Blocks

Locating control blocks is often simpler than determining how they're used. To assist in this, you should start investigating the following sources of information:

IBM manuals

Many—perhaps too many—IBM manuals contain reference information that you'll find useful throughout this book. The first is the *ESA/370 Reference Summary*, commonly known as the "blue card." (It previously existed in green, yellow, and pink forms.) This will be useful when you're reading about the hardware interface that supports MVS, which includes both data areas and special instructions.

The more detailed reference for this material is the *Principles of Operations*. The contents of this manual provide the most comprehensive, if not the most understandable, explanation of how IBM mainframe processors really work.

The best reference for the control blocks discussed in this book is a series of licensed IBM manuals. They document the contents of a number of data areas. At one point, this information was in one handbook (MVT), then in three handbooks (MVS 3.8); it's currently in five volumes (ESA), along with a few supporting manuals that are also indispensable.

The data area manuals used to prepare this book were entitled *MVS/ESA Diagnosis: Data Areas*, and were a part of a five-volume set. The order numbers for these were LY28-1043 through LY28-1047. Note that these are marked as "Licensed Materials—Property of IBM" and you can't order them without being an IBM customer running the appropriate version of MVS. The 17-pound, five-volume set is in marked contrast to the compact, eight-ounce, 363-page MVT handbook (S229-3169-3), which shows how far MVS development has come since the 1960s.

If you don't have access to this information, you might find the three-volume handbook set from MVS release 3.8 to be useful. It's the *OS/VS2 System Programming Library: Debugging Handbook*, and the order numbers are GC28-0708 through GC28-0710. These manuals, strictly speaking, are obsolete for many MVS/ESA purposes; much of their content still has value, however, and they're certainly more portable than the more recent versions.

Additional control block and MVS internal information can be gleaned from various MVS component diagnosis manuals, and from older programming logic manuals where they're still available. As a general rule, this book doesn't require them. Another source of information is programming manuals, such as the *ESA Application Development Guide*. These will be mentioned throughout the book where useful; they're handy to have, but aren't essential.

I recommend that you refer to the following manuals for MVS/ESA version 4:

- *MVS/ESA Diagnosis: Data Areas*, volumes 1 through 5, IBM form numbers LY28-1821 through LY28-1825

- *MVS/ESA Diagnosis: System Reference*, LY28-1820

- *MVS/ESA Diagnosis: Using Dumps and Traces*, LY28-1813

- *MVS/ESA Diagnosis: Component Reference*, LY28-1814

- *MVS/ESA Initialization and Tuning Guide*, GC28-1634

- *MVS/ESA Initialization and Tuning Reference*, GC28-1635

- *MVS/ESA System Management Facilities (SMF)*, GC28-1628

- *MVS/ESA Application Development Guide: Authorized Assembler Language Programs*, GC28-1645

- *MVS/ESA Application Development Reference: Services For Authorized Assembler Language Programs*, volumes 1 through 4, GC28-1647 through GC28-1650

- *MVS/ESA Application Development Guide: Assembler Language Programs*, GC28-1644

- *MVS/ESA Application Development Reference: Services For Assembler Language Programs*, GC28-1642

- *ESA/390 Principles of Operations*, SA22-7200

Note that not all of these are essential; your own interests will lead you to use of some of them more often, while others gather dust. This is the typical pattern of IBM manual usage. As a co-worker at Amdahl, Tom Lyon, once remarked, "you don't read IBM manuals, you collect them."

If you don't have access to the licensed data area manuals, the old MVS 3.8 data area handbooks might be useful, although obsolete for many uses. They are *OS/VS2 System Programming Library: Debugging Handbook*, volumes 1 through 3, GC28-0708 through GC28-0710.

Another source of MVS programming information is McGraw-Hill's Jay Ranade Series of mainframe programming books. Titles from this series that are useful include:

- *IBM Mainframes*, Prasad

- *MVS Concepts and Facilities*, Johnson

- *DASD: IBM's Direct Access Storage Devices*, Johnson and Johnson

- *MVS I/O Subsystems: Configuration, Management, and Performance Analysis*, Houtekamer and Artis

- *MVS Performance Management*, Samson

- *MVS Power Programming*, Marx and Davis

These are available by calling 1-800-822-8158.

Macro libraries

If you don't have access to the IBM manuals and other listed resources, you might be feeling a rising sense of panic. Don't worry. Most of the control blocks discussed in this book are also documented in various IBM macro libraries. The two most important of these are SYS1.MACLIB and SYS1.MODGEN. (SYS1.MODGEN was previously called SYS1.AMODGEN, and you might find it under that name.) This book will refer to both of those libraries. Other libraries of interest include:

- SYS1.AMACLIB (should be on distribution library volume)

- SYS1.AGENLIB (should be on distribution library volume)

- SYS1.PVTMACS (rare and old)
- SYS1.SAMPLIB
- Other product-related libraries (e.g., SYS1.DFP370.MACLIB)

Finally, while SYS1.PARMLIB isn't a macro library, this book will refer to members in that library that affect how control blocks are built. This library is useful, but access to it is restricted in some installations.

Microfiche

Another research source is the various forms of IBM-distributed microfiche, containing program source for selected base products and PTF tapes. IBM announced during the preparation of this book that they were discontinuing this product, but diehard MVS hackers might still want to keep their old fiche.

Online services

The replacement for access to selected IBM source programs through microfiche is access through IBMLink.

Non-IBM sources

In addition to the documentation and other sources of information listed previously, there are numerous other valuable resources for those who want to learn more about MVS. The most valuable of these are IBM user groups such as Share and Guide, and selected local MVS user groups. The National Systems Programmer's Association (NaSPA) is especially valuable. Non-IBM product user groups and outside education comprise other sources.

How This Book Is Organized

The sections in the book are arranged as follows:

Chapter 1: The Prefixed Save Area. Chapter 1 discusses the fundamental CPU resource control block called the Prefixed Storage Area (PSA), along with some related control blocks. This section also introduces some coverage of how IBM multiprocessor computer complexes operate, and discusses some specific techniques.

Chapter 2: The Communications Vector Table. Chapter 2 introduces what Saddam Hussein might call "the mother of all control blocks"—the Communications Vector Table, or CVT. You can use the CVT to find the location of almost anything in the MVS operating system. This chapter will also cover some related system-wide control blocks.

Chapter 3: Control Blocks for Dispatching. Chapter 3 introduces the control blocks that MVS actually uses to perform useful work. These are used by a part of MVS called the *dispatcher*. The control blocks included are the Address Space Control Block (ASCB), the Task Control Block (TCB), the Service Request Block (SRB), and various flavors of Request Blocks (RBs).

These first three chapters should provide a solid foundation for understanding how MVS works. They also introduce acronym overload—a common problem with IBM software products.

Chapter 4: Virtual Storage Management. This begins a section that covers the control blocks for particular areas within MVS. Chapter 4 examines virtual storage management. In addition to control blocks, this chapter includes some discussion of how MVS and its predecessors have mapped virtual storage, and explains the concept of an *address space*.

Chapter 5: Real Storage Management. Chapter 5 builds on the previous chapters to discuss how real storage management and auxiliary storage management work. This chapter also explains how paging works within MVS at a general level.

Chapter 6: System Measurement. Chapter 6 covers the general area of resource measurement. This topic and system tuning have been thoroughly addressed by another book in the Jay Ranade series, *MVS Performance Management*, by Stephen L. Samson of the Candle Corporation. As a result, this chapter is somewhat less detailed than the rest of the book. If your only interest is in tuning, I advise you to start with that book before investing the time needed to understand MVS internals. In addition, chapter 6 addresses selected control blocks used by the Systems Management Facility (SMF), which seemed most appropriate here.

Chapter 7: Resource Serialization. Chapter 7 addresses the component in MVS called Global Resource Serialization. This chapter explains the concept of serialization and the MVS services associated with it. It provides somewhat less coverage of the control blocks involved, and more on the services used to extract GRS information.

Chapter 8: Input/Output System Control Blocks. The next topic area is that of I/O control blocks. Chapter 8 discusses the process involved in executing an I/O operation, and details the control blocks created as part of I/O processing in general. This chapter includes a fair amount of detail, and might not be suitable for all viewers.

Chapter 9: Cross-Memory and Data Space Control Blocks. Chapter 9 introduces the concept of Cross-Memory Services, which is a technique frequently
used to provide new services in MVS. I'll also analyze several of the services
covered in preceding chapters to show how they use Cross-Memory Services.
This chapter also covers the 370 instructions (e.g., Program Call) used in this
process, and selected ESA/390 addressing and data space concepts.

Chapter 10: Recovery and Diagnostic Control Blocks and Services. Chapter
10 examines diagnostic tools and techniques in general, and introduces the
MVS component called the Recovery/Termination Manager (RTM) and provides information useful in evaluating ABEND dumps.

Chapter 11: MVS Tracing Services. Chapter 11 continues the discussion of
diagnostic tools with an overview of the MVS trace table. The trace table is
often invaluable for backtracking through a program's execution prior to an
error. It's also rarely understood and can provide a useful debugging skill.

Chapter 12: Contents Supervision. The book concludes with an introduction to Contents Supervision. This includes coverage of both the control
blocks for this feature and program information retrieval facilities.

Appendix A: The TSO Test Command. The material included in the 12 chapters of the book is augmented by several appendices. Appendix A provides
an elementary discussion of how to use the TSO Test Command. If you
haven't used this facility, I highly recommend it for developing and debugging assembler language programs. It's also excellent for control block research, although TSO Test can't display control blocks in protected storage.

Appendix B: SYS1.MODGEN Members. Appendix B provides a complete
list of the macro instructions in the MVS/ESA SYS1.MODGEN macro library.
This includes the title of the data area associated with each macro. This information isn't available from any other source to the best of my knowledge.

Appendix C: An Annotated MVS SYSUDUMP. Appendix C provides a complete MVS SYSUDUMP storage dump, along with the assembler programs
that created it. This is referenced by several of the book's chapters.
   Each chapter, to some degree, will contain the following:

- A brief overview of the MVS function associated with the control blocks,
  such as the MVS dispatcher, I/O supervisor, etc.

- Where appropriate, a description of the area's services, such as the
  macros provided to invoke the service and/or the MVS supervisor calls
  (SVCs) associated with the service

- Where appropriate, a list of the control blocks used with the service, usually with diagrams to show relationships among the control blocks

- A list of the service's data areas, intended to be used with the appropriate "data areas" manual

- Sample programs showing how you can use the control blocks to extract useful information

Sample Programs

A disclaimer about the sample programs is essential at this point. MVS is constantly changing. A comparison of the MVS 3.8 data area handbooks to the MVS/ESA data areas will give you some idea of just how much MVS can change over the course of 10 years. The sample programs are explicitly *not* guaranteed to work forever—not even until the next release of MVS or in your particular installation. IBM can move data around in control blocks, between control blocks, or into a separate address space. It can also encrypt the information or make any number of changes that could invalidate the sample programs supplied in this book.

Consequently, you must use your own judgment in applying the samples to your own installation's needs. IBM has attempted to identify what control blocks and fields it expects to remain available in the future. This is in a manual called the *Directory of Programming Interfaces*, which describes the services and data that should remain stable as MVS evolves. I haven't attempted to strictly observe the limits of that manual in the programs in this book. Thus, I urge you to carefully evaluate your application of the techniques discussed in this book.

Miscellanous Rambling

There are several other concepts I need to mention before addressing the individual sets of control blocks in successive chapters.

One of these is the PL/S language. PL/S was introduced at IBM around 1970; to the best of my recollection, the IEBDG utility program was the first IBM code shipped using PL/S for development. PL/S has been used extensively since then for development within many IBM components.

IBM never released the PL/S compiler to the outside world. A manual was prepared describing how to read PL/S listings, but PL/S appeared only in microfiche program listings. The main exception to this is that the PL/S and assembler language versions of MVS control blocks coexist in the same members in many cases. Thus, when browsing SYS1.MACLIB or SYS1.MODGEN, you might see the entire set of fields in a control block repeated at the end of the assembler description. In some cases, only the PL/S version of a data area is distributed. For the most part, you can ignore the presence of PL/S versions of a data area, although the comments in the PL/S version might be different and are sometimes enlightening.

Another term I've used throughout the book is *control block anchor*. An *anchor* is used to indicate how a control block's address can be obtained; it's typically used when describing access to a linked list of control blocks.

Enough rambling—onward.

1

The Prefixed Save Area and Other Control Blocks

This chapter covers the Prefixed Save Area (PSA), as well as several other fundamental control blocks. Three other related control blocks are also discussed; they're used, along with the PSA, by various MVS services and in machine check handling. These are the PCCA (Physical Configuration Communication Area), the LCCA (Logical Configuration Communication Area), and the PCCAVT (PCCA Vector Table). The CSD (Common System Data area) is also examined.

1.1 The Prefixed Save Area (PSA)

The Prefixed Save Area (PSA) is unique in several ways among MVS control blocks. It's the first example you'll see of a global control block, i.e., one that's used by many programs or jobs. Indeed, the PSA is used by every job or TSO user, and by all of MVS.

The global nature of the PSA means that it must be commonly addressable. Thus, it always starts at location zero in each CPU. Because the PSA contains CPU-specific information relating to interruptions, there must be one PSA for each processor in a multiprocessor complex. However, to your program, it always looks as if there's one PSA, and it's always at location zero.

In a multiprocessor system (such as the IBM 3090, model 400), there's one central memory coupled to several processors. Since memory is shared among all the processors, all of them use the same addresses to access the same area in storage. (This is sort of like saying that people travelling to the same street address from different directions all use the same address. Thus, 1234 Elm Street is the same house whether you're driving north, south, east, or west. Similarly, location X'5000' is the same spot in storage for CPU 1 or CPU 3.)

This brings up a problem, however, because locations 0 through 511 (decimal) on 370 computers have specific purposes. They're listed in the *Reference Summary* under the heading of Fixed Storage Locations, and they're directly related to the workings of a specific processor. Thus, to have all the processors in a multiprocessor configuration share location zero would introduce all sorts of problems and delays. Instead, IBM multiprocessor designs add a facility called *prefixing*.

Prefixing allows the operating system to fool each processor into thinking it has exclusive use of location zero, when in fact it's using another address. To accomplish this, IBM added some instructions called Set Prefix and Store Prefix to the 370 instruction set. Set Prefix (opcode SPX) sets up an address of a 4096-byte (4K) area that the processor uses instead of location zero. The processor then executes all instructions that refer to the low-order 4K of storage by referring to the 4K of storage at the address provided by the SPX instruction. As the magicians might say, it's all done with mirrors.

The Store Prefix instruction (opcode STPX) is used to determine what location a processor is using instead of location zero. Both SPX and STPX are privileged instructions.

One of the responsibilities of the MVS Initial Program Load (IPL) component is to set up the prefix for each of the processors in a multiprocessing system. See Fig. 1.1 for a diagram illustrating the prefixing process. Normally, it's not important to know where the PSA is really located. It might be useful when debugging operating system dumps, however.

The PSA has several purposes. The first is to describe the low-order 4K (4096 bytes) of storage in each processor. It contains CPU-related information. The layout of the PSA is as follows:

Locations 0-511.   Hardware-related data

Locations 512-2047.   Software-related data

Locations 2048-4095.   Software-related data (fetch-protected)

PSA mapping is available in the IHAPSA macro, located in SYS1.MACLIB. Note that the PSA is the only control block in MVS that can use register zero as a base register, since it's at location zero.

The fields in the PSA follow several different naming conventions. Most IBM MVS DSECTs follow the practice of starting field names with the acronym of the control block. Most fields in the PSA are thus PSA*xxxxx*,

Memory:

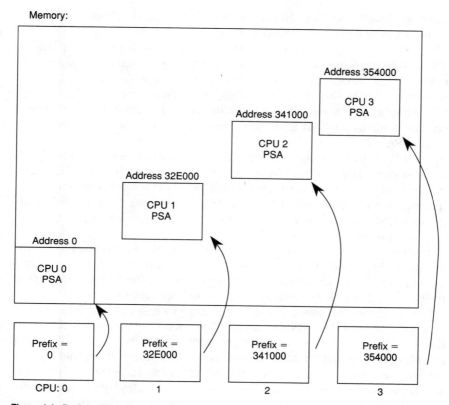

Figure 1.1 Prefixing PSAs for multiprocessors.

where *xxxxx* is a unique field name. However, since the PSA has been around for a long, long time by MVS standards, there are a few other historical uses. Some fields are FLC*xxxxx*, where FLC stands for Fixed Low Core, dating from the OS/360 period. Some others have long-standing historical uses—for example, the IEATCBP field.

Now we'll examine some of the PSA fields in detail, but first let's examine how the PSA is stored.

1.1.1 PSA storage protection

Since the contents of the PSA are essential to successful system execution, it must be protected against accidental alteration. As you'll see, MVS has two main methods for protecting storage. The first is to put the data that needs protection in a separate address space, i.e., make it invisible to the rest of the system. (This approach is somewhat like confiscating all the maps to the parts of the city you don't want people visiting.) This approach won't work with the PSA, though, because it's at location zero and is commonly addressable by everybody.

The second approach is to use the System/370 fetch protection facility. This will be explained in detail when you examine virtual and real storage; essentially, it allows 2K chunks of storage to be unreadable based on the protection key in the PSW. This facility has been used since the days of OS/360; its only drawback is that it doesn't protect overlays from accidental storage by programs that have valid access. This approach is used for part of the PSA.

The PSA is placed in what's called Key 0 Storage. This can't be modified by most user tasks in MVS. The specific implementation for the PSA makes the low-order 2K (address zero through X'7FF') not fetch-protected—thus, this part of the PSA is readable by any task. The upper 2K of the PSA (addresses X'800' to X'FFF') is fetch-protected, i.e., not accessible to most user tasks unless they're authorized.

The reason for fetch-protecting the last half of the PSA relates to the integrity of the overall system. This prevents access by most tasks to a number of fields that might provide a security exposure; the general rule is that no job should be able to see another job's register contents.

However, the PSA was still at risk in the early versions of MVS because it was still susceptible to MVS routines. There were several bugs relating to the way MVS code stored data using an address of zero; this usually forced an IPL fairly quickly! To address this problem, IBM added another special type of storage protection for the PSA only. This was added about 1980, and was called *low-address protection control*. This feature prohibited alteration of low storage, specifically locations zero through 511 (hexadecimal X'1FF'), regardless of the PSW protection key. It was enabled or disabled by the setting or clearing of control register 0, bit 3.

(This is the first appearance of control registers in this book. Each processor has 16 of them, which determine how certain hardware options operate. The *Reference Summary* has a listing of what each control register bit or field does; the *Principles of Operation* manual describes them in more exhaustive detail. I'll discuss them at various places in the book.)

IBM provided an additional instruction, called TPROT, to test the state of low-address protection. This is usable only by supervisor-state programs. MVS also provides the PROTPSA macro to turn protection on or off for privileged programs. I suggest that you not plan on using either of these.

1.1.2   PSA contents, hardware-related areas

The hardware-related storage areas of the PSA are listed in the Fixed Storage Locations section of the *Reference Summary*. These include the Old and New PSWs for each of the interrupt classes (I/O, Program, Supervisor Call, External, Machine Check, and Restart). This part of the

PSA also holds interruption-related information, e.g., the Instruction Length Code and the Translation Exception Address. It also contains fixed logout areas used for machine check interruptions.

The PSWs are processed during interruptions as follows. There are three types of PSWs when an interruption occurs: Old, New, and Current. The Current PSW is constantly updated by the processor and contains the instruction address field (i.e., where you are in the program). When an interruption condition arises, the PSW must be changed. The things that cause an interruption are grouped into the six interruption classes provided in the System/370 design. Table 1.1 lists different events that cause interruptions.

The process of swapping PSWs begins by saving the Current PSW. This is done so that MVS can start up whatever program was running at the time of the interruption. To save the current PSW, it's stored in the appropriate Old PSW location. The current PSW is then replaced by the appropriate New PSW value. Figure 1.2 represents this process.

For example, if a program tries to open a file, it will eventually issue an MVS OPEN macro. This results in a Supervisor Call (SVC) instruction, which causes an SVC interruption. The processing for this is:

The processor hardware stores the current PSW in the SVC old PSW location (Location X'20' in the PSA, field name FLCSOPSW). The processor then copies the SVC new PSW into the current PSW. The processor hardware then starts up the program whose address is in the current PSW.

Thus, the interruption process saves where you are and then starts up a different program to handle the interruption. Eventually, MVS will be ready to restart the program that was running when the interruption originally occurred. To do this, as well as handle certain other conditions in interruption processing, IBM provides several special instructions for PSW manipulation.

The first of these is LPSW (Load PSW). LPSW loads the current PSW from a doubleword location. This instruction acts like the second part of the previously described interruption process. This instruction is used by MVS to restart a program after it has been interrupted.

TABLE 1.1 Examples of System/370 Interruption Classes

Interruption class	Event causing interruption
I/O	An I/O operation completing
Supervisor Call (SVC)	A program requesting an MVS service (such as the OPEN macro)
Program Check	A program error, such as an OC7
External	A time period expiring
Machine Check	A real hardware error
Restart	Console Restart key or command

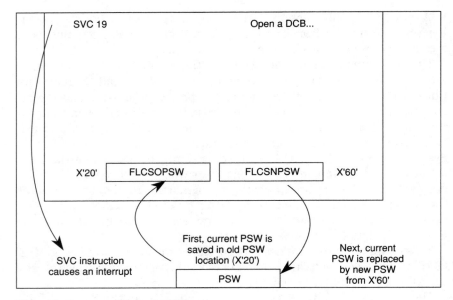

Figure 1.2 The process of swapping PSWs.

Some additional PSW manipulation instructions are provided to control the state of the system during interruption processing. These include:

STOSM. Store then OR system mask

STNSM. Store then AND system mask

SSM. Set system mask (an older instruction)

These instructions change the state of the system mask part of the PSW. The system mask is basically the first byte of the PSW. It contains two bits that control the processing of I/O and external interruptions.

One complicating factor for MVS, and any System/370 operating system, is what to do about interruption conditions that happen while another interruption is being processed. The normal approach for these is to not allow a second interruption until the first is handled completely. Thus, the 370 architecture provides a way to hold off (disable) interruptions. A program that allows interruptions during its processing is considered to be enabled for interruptions; this is how almost all MVS programs run. A program that doesn't allow interruptions is said to be disabled. In general, a disabled state slows down the overall system, and is avoided wherever possible.

STOSM, STNSM, and SSM allow a program to allow interrupts (STOSM) or prevent interrupts (STNSM). (SSM changes the whole program mask; the first two instructions are preferable.) If you review the IHAPSA DSECT, you should find several examples of these instructions. Additionally, the PSA DSECT contains several PSW mask definitions. (These are the FLCxNPSW equates in the IHAPSA macro.)

Each of the interruption classes also stores specific information relating to that type of interruption. This extended interruption information is stored at locations X'80' through X'100'. One useful field, PSAPIILC, contains the Instruction Length Code (ILC). The ILC indicates how long the instruction was that was being executed when the interruption occurred. (Note that this is a three-bit field in the PSA, which defines the actual length of the instruction.)

Another field of some value is the Translation Exception Address (FLCTEA) at location X'90'. This is often useful for page and segment faults, which appear as 0C4 ABENDs. Fortunately, both of these fields also are available in MVS SYSUDUMP storage dumps, so it isn't necessary to go to the PSA to obtain this information.

This leads to a caveat about the PSA. Since it can be updated by an interruption at literally almost any time, you shouldn't make a practice of using the hardware-related fields in the PSA directly. In almost all cases, the information needed is stored somewhere else by MVS to preserve it.

Other fields of occasional interest in the PSA include those holding machine check information. One is FLCMCIC, and holds the machine check interruption code (location X'E8'). Another is FLCFSA, and holds the failing storage address when a machine check interruption occurs. It's at location X'F8'. The important thing to note is that this is *not* the same as the FLCTEA field discussed previously.

A discussion of all of the other fields within the hardware section is probably not of interest to most of you. However, I'll be covering the use of some fields in the PSA in later chapters, so you'll be revisiting this part of the PSA several times.

There is a macro located in SYS1.MACLIB, IHAPSW, that describes the PSW layout.

1.1.3 PSA contents, software-related areas

The software-related areas in the PSA are those defined by MVS, rather than in the *Principles of Operation*. With one exception, these are all stored in locations X'200' through X'FFF'.

The one exception is the most-used control block pointer in MVS, the address of the Communication Vector Table, or CVT. This is stored at location X'10'. (It's also stored at location X'4C', although this is less commonly used.) The code sequence to access this is usually coded as:

```
L       R1,X'10'
USING   CVT,R1
```

and this sequence appears in many MVS assembler language programs. (I'll discuss the CVT extensively in the next chapter.)

The PSA contains the addresses of several other control blocks. For example, the current Task Control Block address can be found in the field PSATOLD at location X'218'. (Note that this field is also redefined as label IEATCBP, which is the old OS/360 name for it.) This is the fastest way to get your own TCB address, which has numerous uses. Also, the current Address Space Control Block address is in field PSAAOLD at location X'220'.

Other useful control blocks can be located through the PSA, and will be discussed further at various places in this book.

Location X'200' contains the character value 'PSA', and the label PSAPSA. This can be used to show that you have the address of a valid PSA.

The PSA also has two fields that identify which processor it describes. The label PSACPUPA contains the physical CPU number within the processor complex. This number is defined as ranging from zero to 15, although the highest physical CPU number is five (for an IBM 3090-600) or seven (for the larger ES/9000 models). The format of the CPU number is a one-byte hexadecimal field.

Note that the physical CPU number is *not* the same as the CPU serial number. I'll discuss how to get the serial number later. The difference might best be explained by an automotive analogy. Cars have a serial number on their engine. Engines, in turn, contain several cylinders that produce power to drive the car. The cylinders are all numbered, but there's no relationship between the serial number on the engine and the numbers of its cylinders. So the cylinder numbers are like the physical CPU numbers, and the engine serial number is like the CPU serial number.

IBM provides an instruction, STAP (Store CPU Address), that gives the physical CPU number. This is a privileged instruction, but there's no need to execute it because the PSACPUPA field already provides the same information. There's also a PSACPULA (logical CPU number) field. This is stored in a slightly different format (X'4n' instead of X'0n').

There are several other significant fields within the software segment of the PSA, which I'll mention again later in the book. These include:

- PSASUPER (CPU-wide status indicators)
- PSACLHT (lock table)
- PSAHLHI (highest lock held indicator)
- PSASTOR (segment table real address for master ASCB)
- FRR (Functional Recovery Routine) stacks
- PSAATCVT (VTAM ATCVT address)
- PSATBVTV (trace buffer virtual address)

I'm not going to describe the fetch-protected area in the PSA in detail. If you want information on this, review the IHAPSA DSECT contents for further information when you've completed the book.

One PSA coding convention deserves further mention. Some of the addresses coded in the PSA are 31-bit addresses (i.e., above the 16-megabyte address line). The coding convention followed in IHAPSA for these is:

```
DC      A(X'80000000' + routine name)
```

This signifies that the routine name represents a 31-bit address. This way of coding 31-bit addresses will appear again in several control blocks.

1.2   The Physical Configuration Communication Area (PCCA)

The PCCA contains CPU-related information mostly related to hardware status. The PSA contains two address fields for the PCCA. The first one, and the one that should normally be used, is PSAPCCAV (the PCCA virtual address). The second is PSAPCCAR and holds the real address of the PCCA. The real address is provided for cases where it's needed, such as machine check processing.

The PCCA holds hardware status information, mostly for error recovery. It also contains the CPU serial number and model in EBCDIC. The serial number begins at four bytes past the start of the PCCA (field name PCCACPID), and is eight bytes long.

The CPU model type begins at 12 bytes past the start of the PCCA (PCCACPID+8), and is four bytes long (e.g., '3090'). The format of the information is taken from the STIDP (Store CPU ID) privileged instruction, but it's converted from hexadecimal to EBCDIC format and is thus immediately displayable. For example, the following is a real CPU serial number extracted from a PCCA:

```
A64112999021
```

Referring to the description of the Store CPU ID (STIDP) instruction in the *Principles of Operation*, the CPU type is 9021 (the last four bytes). The processor complex has a serial number of 11299 (the five bytes before 9021). So the job that extracted this was running on processor number 4 in this complex. (Note that the STIDP instruction includes the processor number in the serial number; the last five bytes seem to be reliable, in my experience.) The version code for the processor is A6, but this is model-dependent information, not germane to identifying a particular processor.

You can use the PCCACPID field to validate that a software product is actually being run on a particular machine.

The PCCA also contains a physical CPU number bit mask in field PCCA-CAFM at offset X'12'. This is a two-byte field with one bit set on, corresponding to the physical CPU number within a processor complex. The coding of this has a value of X'8000' for physical CPU zero, X'4000' for physical CPU 1, X'2000' for physical CPU number 2, and so forth.

The PCCA also contains the virtual address of the PSA. Remember that, in a multiprocessor configuration, the PSA can be located at other than location zero. This allows a program to examine the PSA for CPUs other than the one on which it's running, which might be used to gather system-wide status information. The PSA virtual address is in field PCCAPSAV. The PCCA is documented as the IHAPCCA macro.

1.3 The Physical Configuration Communication Area Vector Table (PCCAVT)

One requirement that occasionally arises in a multiprocessor system is how to determine the status of each of the processors in the complete processor complex. Two control blocks help provide this information. One is the Common System Data area (CSD), which we'll examine later in this chapter. The other is the PCCA Vector Table.

There's one PCCAVT per MVS system, and it's accessed via an address field in the CVT (CVTPCCATV) at offset X'2FC'. The PCCAVT contains the addresses of each PCCA in the processor complex (one per processor). The PCCAVT is mapped by DSECT IHAPCCAT.

The layout of the PCCAVT can be determined from the system data area manuals. The first 16 words (64 bytes) of the PCCAVT contain the virtual addresses of the PCCA control blocks for processors zero through 15. See Fig. 1.3, which shows the relation between the CVT, PCCAVT, and PCCAs for a four-processor MVS system.

The main use for the PCCAVT is to determine the status of processors within the MVS system; it allows a program running on one processor to determine the location of the PCCAs for other processors.

1.4 The Logical Configuration Communication Area (LCCA)

Each processor needs to have unique areas for processor-specific work areas. To a large degree, these are provided by the Logical Configuration Communication Area (LCCA). The LCCA contains numerous fields related to the software configuration of the processor, just as the PCCA holds hardware-related information. Examples of LCCA fields include several register save areas used in processing interruptions.

The registers at the time of an interruption can be used to deduce a great deal of information about the program causing the interrupt. (I'll show examples of this when discussing the trace table.) Because this provides a pos-

Memory:

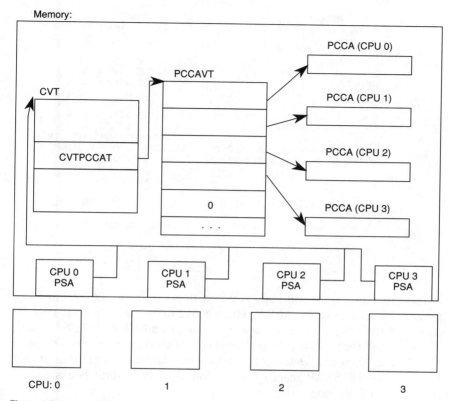

Figure 1.3 Relationship of PSAs, CVT, PCCAVT, and PCCAs.

sible security exposure, the LCCA is placed in fetch-protected storage. Since many of you won't be able to access it, I won't discuss it in great detail.

One field that might be of interest if you're writing your own performance monitoring software is LCCAWTIM. This is a doubleword field that's documented as containing the accumulated CPU wait time for the processor. This can be used to compute the processor percentage busy, etc. The field is stored in TOD clock format. The LCCA DSECT is IHALCCA. There's a corresponding LCCA Vector Table, addressed through the CVT field CVTLCCAT at offset X'300'.

If you're able to run authorized programs, the following is a sequence of code used to display selected LCCA fields with the MVS SNAP macro:

```
*          WE MUST BE AUTHORIZED TO SWITCH TO PROTECT KEY ZERO.
*          ISSUE A TESTAUTH MACRO TO VERIFY THAT WE ARE. IF IT
*          FAILS, WE SHOULDN'T GO ANY FURTHER.
           TESTAUTH  FCTN=1,AUTH=1        TEST AUTHORIZATION
           LTR    R15,415                 CHECK RETURN CODE
```

```
          BZ     MODEOK                        ZERO - GOOD
          ABEND  1,DUMP,STEP                   NOT ZERO - ABEND

MODEOK    EQU    *
          USING  PSA,R0                        SET UP ADDRESSABILITY
          L      R4,PSALCCAV                   GET ADDRESS OF LCCA
          USING  LCCA,R4                       SET UP ADDRESSABILITY

LOOP      EQU    *
          MODESET  KEY=ZERO,MODE=SUP           SET SUPVR STATE/KEY 0
          LH     R5,LCCACPUA                   GET CPU ADDRESS
          MVC    AREA+8(8),LCCAWTIM            GET ACCUMULATED WAIT TIME
          MVC    AREA+16(LCCAEND-LCCATTSC),LCCATTSC   COPY FIELDS
          MODESET  MODE=PROB,KEY=NZERO         RETURN TO PROBLEM MODE

          STCK   AREA                          SAVE TIME OF DAY

          SNAP   PDATA=(REGS),STORAGE=(AREA,AREA+512),DCB=SNAPFILE

          STIMER  WAIT,BINTVL=F100             WAIT ONE SECOND

          AP     TIMES,=P'1'        ADD TO RECORD COUNT
          CP     TIMES,=P'5'        COMPARE TO LIMIT
          BL     LOOP               NOT OVER - CONTINUE
```

The preceding code will copy selected fields from the LCCA into your program in an area called AREA, which is 512 bytes long. This will then be displayed with the SNAP macro, which refers to a DCB called SNAPFILE. The code will repeat this process five times, limited by the packed decimal field TIMES, then end. Details on how to create an authorized program and how to use the SNAP macro can be found in preceding books in the McGraw-Hill J. Ranade series.

The MVS data areas needed by the code are created by the following DSECT macros (the program's data areas are also shown):

```
          CNOP   0,8                           DOUBLEWORD ALIGNMENT
AREA      DS     CL512                         WORK AREA
F100      DC     F'1.00'                       1.00 SECONDS
TIMES     DC     PL1'0'                        LOOP COUNTER
*                DEFINE PREFIXED STORAGE AREA DSECT
          IHAPSA
*                DEFINE LCCA DSECT
          IHALCCA
```

1.5 The Common System Data Area (CSD)

One other control block is related to the PSA/PCCA/PCCAVT complex in terms of containing processor status data. The CSD contains summary information about the number of processors, timing facilities, and important system-wide flags.

The CSD is documented as DSECT IHACSD and is SYS1.MACLIB. Its address is contained in the CVT in field CVTCSD at offset X'294'.

Field CSDCPUOL is a halfword containing the number of CPUs online in this MVS system. Additionally, the CSD contains several count fields for valid CPUs, working timers, and similar items.

The CSD also contains a bit switch labelled CSDSYSND. This is the system-wide nondispatchability bit, which will appear again later.

1.6   Uses for Chapter Control Blocks

The PSA will be used most often to access the CVT, TCB, and ASCB. Later chapters will show examples of this.

The other unique use of this set of control blocks is to determine what specific processor serial number is running software. The following shows an example of a program to verify the CPU serial number:

```
          TITLE 'VERIFY CPU NUMBER'
FIG0104  CSECT
FIG0104  AMODE 24
FIG0104  RMODE 24
         BAKR  R14,0                   SAVE REGS
         LR    R12,R15                 SET UP
         USING FIG0104,R12             BASE REGISTER
         LA    R13,MYSAVE              SET UP SAVE AREA
         USING PSA,R0                  ESTABLISH ADDRESSABILITY
         L     R3,PSAPCCAV             GET ADDRESS OF PCCA
         USING PCCA,R3                 ESTABLISH ADDRESSABILITY
         CLC   PCCACPID+8(4),CPUTYPE   CHECK CPU TYPE
         BNE   NOT_LICENSED            NOT EQUAL - ERROR MSG
         CLC   PCCACPID+3(5),SERIALNO  CHECK SERIAL NUMBER
         BNE   NOT_LICENSED            NOT EQUAL - WRONG CPU

RETURN   EQU   *
         L     R15,RETURN_CODE
         PR


*        DOCUMENT LICENSE INFORMATION
NOT_LICENSED     EQU    *
         LA    R2,LIC_WTO1             GET WTO ADDRESS
         USING WPL,R2                  USE WTO PARM LIST DSECT
         MVC   WPLTXT+5(4),PCCAPCCA    MOVE 'PCCA' EYECATCHER TO WTO
         MVC   WPLTXT+18(12),PCCACPID  MOVE CPU ID FIELD
         LA    R2,LIC_WTO2             GET NEXT WTO ADDRESS
         MVC   WPLTXT+16(5),SERIALNO   MOVE EXPECTED SERIAL NO
         MVC   WPLTXT+27(4),CPUTYPE    MOVE EXPECTED CPU TYPE
LIC_WTO1         WTO   '____ CPU ID: _____',           X
                 ROUTCDE=(2,11)
LIC_WTO2         WTO   ' EXPECTING: _____ ON A ____',          X
                 ROUTCDE=(2,11)
         MVC   RETURN_CODE,SIXTEEN
         DROP  R2
         B     RETURN
*        DATA AREAS
MYSAVE   DC    F'0',C'F1SA',16F'0'     ESA FORMAT SAVE AREA
RETURN_CODE  DC    F'0'
SIXTEEN      DC    F'16'               ERROR RETURN CODE
CPUTYPE  DC    C'3090'                 EXPECTED CPU TYPE
```

```
SERIALNO DC    C'02345'                    EXPECTED SERIAL NUMBER

         LTORG

         PRINT ON,NOGEN
*        DEFINE PREFIXED STORAGE AREA DSECT
         IHAPSA

*        DEFINE PCCA DSECT
         IHAPCCA

*        DEFINE WTO PARAMETER LIST
         IEZWPL

*        REGISTER EQUATES NOT SHOWN
```

The IEZWPL macro produces a DSECT that describes the parameter list for a WTO macro instruction, which includes the label WPLTXT for the WTO message text.

1.7 Summary

System/370 operating systems interface with the underlying hardware through the Prefixed Save Area, along with the set of control registers for that processor. The PSA contains 512 bytes of hardware-defined fields, whose functions are strictly defined in the *Principles of Operation* manual. This is followed by 3584 bytes of MVS-defined fields. This latter part of the PSA contains pointers for processor-unique values, such as the address space currently executing on that processor.

The PSA is accompanied by two related control blocks: the Physical Configuration Communication Area (PCCA) and the Logical Configuration Communication Area (LCCA). The PCCA contains the processor serial number, along with additional processor-specific hardware status information, such as the fields relating to timing facilities errors. The LCCA contains several interruption-related fields (e.g., register save areas) and is fetch-protected to prevent possible unauthorized access to register contents. Both the PCCA and the LCCA have corresponding vector tables that can be used to locate them for specific processors.

Finally, the Common System Data area (CSD) contains additional count and status fields related to the entire system's status.

1.8 Things to Do

- Use the TSO TEST command to determine the following information for your organization's CPU(s). See appendix A for a brief overview of the TSO TEST command if you haven't used it before.

  ~ The CPU serial number from the PCCA. If you have access to a multi-processor, try checking this field several times while the system is busy to see if any part of the serial number changes.

~ The number of CPUs running MVS in the complex. To determine this information, examine the PCCAVT; each of the PCCA pointers (PCCAT00P, etc.) that's nonzero represents a processor in the MVS system.

~ The number of CPUs available in the complex. To determine this, locate the CSD and then check the CSDCPUOL field.

- The SIGP instruction is used to communicate between processors. Review the *Principles of Operation* description of this instruction, along with the MVS DSGNL macro that implements it.

- If you want to understand the contents of CPU ID fields, obtain the appropriate functional characteristics manual for your specific processor type. (Two examples are *IBM 3090 Processor Complex Functional Characteristics*, SA22-7121 and *IBM 4381 Dual Processor Functional Characteristics*, GA24-4021.) Try the STIDP and CPU ID index entries.

- When determining processor type, one factor that affects the CPU's performance is use of the Logical Partition (LPAR) facility. To determine this, you'll need access to the manual *Resource Management Facility: Data Areas*, form number LY28-1303. Review the STGST control block. The address of this can be found in the CVT field CVTMFCTL. The CVT is discussed in the next chapter. You might also want to review the RMF macros, which begin with the prefix ERB (for example, ERBSTGST) and might be in a separate library.

2

The Communications Vector Table

This chapter introduces the fundamental MVS control block called the Communications Vector Table (CVT), and also some related data areas. These, and their uses, include:

Global Data Area. Virtual storage mapping

Secondary CVT. Additional CVT-type information

System Function Table. Cross-memory service directory

SVC Table. Describes Supervisor Call modules

The common thread among the control blocks discussed in this chapter is that they provide access to, and communication with, services that are common throughout MVS. Additionally, they provide access to a number of system-wide constants (e.g., the default region size).

2.1   The Communication Vector Table (CVT)

The CVT can clearly be termed the most important control block in MVS. It provides a commonly addressable area that contains the addresses of specific MVS data areas and routines. While the CVT originally contained a number of actual data values, its primary use is now mainly as an anchor for other control blocks. (The term *anchor* refers to a control block or field that allows multiple routines to get the address of other control blocks.)

The CVT has existed since the beginning of OS/360. As a result, it permeates MVS and is a repository for system-wide addresses and values. This longevity has also resulted in the CVT containing a number of historical artifacts in the form of fields that are no longer used, but still kept around for compatibility. (This condition arises for several other control blocks, as will be seen occasionally throughout the book.)

The CVT actually comprises several separate sections, which have been added from time to time when it seemed like a good idea. These include the:

CVT prefix. MVS product and version IDs, and the release number

CVT basic section. The original CVT

CVT extension. OS-OS/VS common extension

CVT OS/VS1-OS/VS2 extension. Virtual storage extension

CVT extended addressing extension. OS/VS2 extension with 31-bit XA addresses

The reason for this separation of the CVT is that the various extensions were added for specific reasons, some of which are historical. For example, the CVT OS & OS/VS common extension was created to support both OS/360 and OS/VS (what we call SVS). The only field left in this extension is one used by ISAM—the Indexed Sequential Access Method, now obsolete. Figure 2.1 shows the relationship among these sections of the CVT.

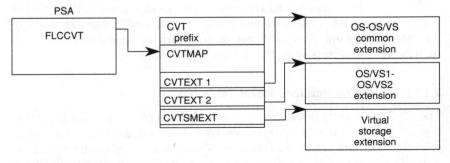

Figure 2.1 Relationships of CVT extensions.

The mapping macro used to access the CVT is called, oddly enough, CVT. The recommended coding is:

```
CVT DSECT=YES,LIST=YES
```

Addressing the CVT can be messy due to the various extensions. The correct addressing for each extension will be discussed along with the fields in each extension. The CVT macro is located in SYS1.MACLIB.

2.1.1 CVT prefix

The CVT prefix is a 256-byte area immediately ahead of the CVT proper. It contains mostly character fields with MVS-level information. The examples shown here are those found in the UCLA Office of Academic Computing's (OAC) IBM 3090 as of January 1993. As with most of the examples, your mileage may vary . . .

The field called CVTPROD contains the IBM MVS software product ID. (At OAC, this was HBB4410.) You can use this field to determine the exact version of MVS your installation uses. Its technical name is the FMID. This is used by IBM-supplied programs (SMP) to update MVS.

The CVTVERID field identifies the version of the CVT in use. The UCLA value was UY90705—this refers to a specific IBM-supplied Programming Temporary Fix (PTF). The CVTMDL field contains the CPU model number in unsigned decimal (hexadecimal). This is the same value as found in the PCCA, discussed in chapter 1. The UCLA value was X'3090'. The CVTRELNO field contains the eight-byte release name in version (release) modification level format. The value at UCLA was SP4.1.0. To access these fields, code:

```
L     R3,X'10'     GET CVT ADDRESS
SH    R3,=H'256'   SUBTRACT TO GET PREFIX ADDRESS
USING CVTFIX,R3    ESTABLISH ADDRESSABILITY
```

2.1.2 The CVT proper

The CVT proper is 1280 bytes in length, and contains numerous fields. This section will highlight some of them and mention some possible uses. The CVT is so central to accessing MVS internal data and services that a complete description exceeds the size of a reasonable chapter. Note that you'll be revisiting the CVT in most of the subsequent chapters in the book, so most of its contents will have been discussed by the end.

The CVT fields of interest follow. Refer to an assembly listing of the CVT for offsets and lengths.

CVTTCBP. Contents of IEATCBP in PSA. This is the address of your Task Control Block (the current TCB). This is possibly the most frequently referenced field in the CVT and will be discussed in chapter 3. PSATOLD can be used instead.

CVTLINK. Address of the SYS1.LINKLIB Data Control Block. This is the DCB used to load programs from the link list libraries. These libraries are listed in member LNKLST*xx* of the SYS1.PARMLIB data set.

CVTSYSAD. The IPL UCB address. This can be used to determine the volume serial of the pack containing the running MVS system. Chapter 9 discusses the UCB and other I/O control blocks.

CVTEXIT. An SVC 3 instruction. This is where your program returns when it issues a BR 14 instruction.

CVTBRET. A BR 14 instruction, sometimes used by MVS routines.

CVTVPRM. Vector parameters, two halfwords. These determine the availability and size of the vector facility. Few MVS installations have this installed; it will be mentioned again in chapter 4 as part of the trace facility discussion.

CVTCUCB. UCM (console) address. It can be used to determine the master MVS console.

CVTDCBA. SYS1.LOGREC DCB address. This is used for hardware error recording. This isn't of special interest to most MVS programmers, but the first byte of this field contains bits that can be tested to determine the version of MVS being run, and also if you're running in an MVS or VM environment. I'll show an example of this later in the chapter. The CVTNLOG bit indicates that there's no LOGREC recording, which could be of assistance to those using this to record software errors.

CVTSMCA. The address of the System Management Facility data area; this will be discussed in chapter 6.

CVTUSER. This field is identified as available to MVS installations for their own enhancements. Many non-IBM products have used this over the years. In general, it's best to avoid using this field to avoid conflicts.

CVTTSAF. Address of the RACF Security Access Facility Router; see the RACROUTE macro instruction for background information.

CVTEXT1. Address of the first extension to the CVT, discussed in a later section.

CVTDMSRF. This field contains bits that, when set, produce extensive dumps for Open/Close/EOV ABENDs ($x13$, $x14$, and $x37$ ABENDs).

CVTREAL. The highest V=R address; it marks the largest REGION parameter allowed with the ADDRSPC=REAL in JCL.

CVTJESCT. Address of the JES Control Table; this can be used to determine which subsystems are present in your MVS system.

CVTEORM. Potential high real storage address—the MVS storage limit. Compare to CVTRLSTG.

CVTEXT2. Address of the second CVT extension.

CVTSNAME. The 8-byte system ID. The UCLA value is 'OAC1 '.

CVTPVTP. Address of the Real Storage Manager Page Vector Table. Chapter 7 will cover this in more detail.

CVTSHRVM. Address of the beginning of the Common Storage Area.

CVTGVT. Global Resource Serialization vector table, used for ENQ and DEQ macro processing. This will be discussed in more detail in chapter 9.

CVTMAXP. Maximum number of CPUs supported.

CVTAUTHL. Contained the address of the authorized library list in earlier versions of MVS. Currently zero.

CVTGDA. Address of the Global Data Area, described later in this chapter.

CVTASCBH, CVTASCBL. Addresses of highest- and lowest-priority ASCBs in the system—the ASCB chain anchors.

CVTRTMCT. Recovery/Termination Control Table; this can be used to determine the default dump options for your system. Your program could then provide an alternate parameter list (via the SETRP macro, as one example) if needed. See the IHARTCT mapping macro.

CVTOPCTP. Resource Manager Control Table for SRM; this will be covered in chapter 7.

CVTGSMQ, CVTLSMQ. Service Request Block (SRB) pointers for the MVS dispatcher, a list of the SRBs waiting to execute.

CVTCSD.   CSD pointer, as described in chapter 1.

CVTSPSA.   Global work area/save area pointer; see DSECT IHAWSAVT.

CVTASMVT.   Address of the Auxiliary Storage Manager Vector Table, used for paging services. Chapter 8 will cover this.

CVTPCCAT.   Address of the PCCA Vector Table, discussed in chapter 1.

CVTXSFT.   Address of the System Function Table, used for cross-memory services. This is part of the interface to MVS services that use the Program Call (PC) instruction rather than the older Supervisor Call (SVC) instruction.

CVT0TC0A.   Address of the routine that gives you C0D ABENDs; this occurs when your program destroys a DCB, as one example.

CVTRLSTG.   Real Storage online in K.

CVTRAC.   RACF CVT address.

CVTXCPCT.   EXCP limit for this MVS system; the default is 500. If your address space issues more than this number of I/O requests in a row (before the first intervening WAIT), it will receive a C22 ABEND.

CVTUCBA.   Address of the first UCB in the system; chapter 9 will discuss the I/O control blocks. This was often used to scan all devices in an MVS system; the UCBSCAN service should be used from MVS 4.2 and up.

The CVT has many, many other fields, some of which will be discussed in later chapters. Note that there are several fields in the CVT proper that are kept around for compatibility, but which have no current function. For example, CVTNUCB is listed as the first address past the end of the nucleus in older CVT DSECTs, but is zero in SP4.1 and later versions.

2.1.3 CVT OS & OS/VS extension

This area contained fields common to MVT and virtual storage operating systems. The only current field in this is CVTFACHN, used as an ISAM extension field.

2.1.4 CVT OS/VS2 common extension

This segment of the CVT contains data that was common between MVS and older versions of OS/VS. It's accessed by the following code (assuming that your program has addressability to the CVT):

```
L       R4,CVTEXT2      Get address of CVT Extension 2
USING CVTXTNT2,R4       Establish addressability
```

Fields within this extension include:

CVTNUCLS. The currently IPLed nucleus member ID. This is a one-byte field, appended to IEANUC0x to form the full member name.

CVTATCVT. A VTAM ATCVT pointer. An earlier one was mentioned in chapter 1. The leftmost bit can be tested to determine if VTAM is active.

CVTIOCID. The current IOCDS identifier (two bytes).

There are several other fields in this extension, mostly used for branch entry services for various MVS components. A review might be useful.

2.1.5 OS/VS2 Virtual Storage Address extension

This extension contains information about the beginning and ending addresses for various parts of the MVS system storage map. It can be used to determine the size of various areas in MVS for holding programs, e.g., the Pageable Link Pack Area (PLPA). This area is accessed by:

```
L       R6,CVTSMEXT     Get extension address
USING R6,CVTVSTGX       Establish addressability
```

This extension contains the starting and ending addresses of the modifiable, fixed, and pageable LPA; the nucleus (read/write and read-only); and the extended LPA addresses for common MVS modules above the 16MB storage line. Each separate area is described by two fields, which have the starting and ending addresses for the area in question. The size can be determined by subtracting one from the other.

I recommend that you review the CVT DSECT listing for these fields. Note that the Global Data Area, discussed later, has similar information for other MVS memory. Figure 2.2 provides an overview of the MVS/ESA storage layout.

2.2 The Global Data Area

This control block is closely tied to the subject of virtual storage management, which is covered in chapter 4. However, the contents are somewhat related to those of the CVT OS/VS2 virtual storage extension, and are discussed here.

The function of the GDA is to contain the size and starting address of certain MVS storage areas. These, along with the CVT extension, can be used

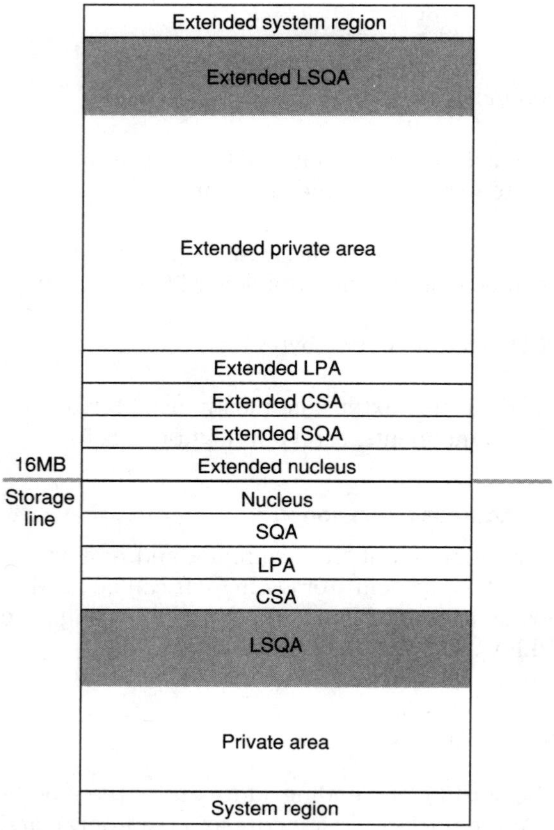

| Extended system region |
| Extended LSQA |
| Extended private area |
| Extended LPA |
| Extended CSA |
| Extended SQA |
| Extended nucleus |
| Nucleus |
| SQA |
| LPA |
| CSA |
| LSQA |
| Private area |
| System region |

16MB
Storage
line

Figure 2.2 Overview of ESA storage layout.

to produce a complete storage map of your MVS system. The mapping macro, IHAGDA, is located in the SYS1.MODGEN library. You can address this control block with the following code:

```
L  R7,CVTGDA
USING GDA,R7
```

An example of the fields of interest include:

PASTRT. The starting address of the private area (your region).

PASIZE. The size of the private area. This is a proxy for the largest RE-GION parameter in JCL.

These fields have been included since MVS release 3.8. Note that each succeeding release of MVS has added functionality to this control block, so it also contains the following sets of starting addresses and sizes:

GDACSA, GDACSASZ. Starting address and size of the CSA.

GDASQA, GDASQASZ. Starting address and size of SQA.

GDAESQA, GDAESQAS. Starting address and size of extended SQA (31 bits).

GDAPVT, GDAPVTSZ. Starting address and size of private area (these are alternate names for PASTRT and PASIZE).

GDAEPVT, GDAEPVTS. Starting address and size of extended private area.

The GDA also contains numerous fields that support tracking CSA utilization. The quantity of fields used in this endeavor is too large to provide a full discussion here; I suggest you review the mapping macro.

2.3 The Secondary CVT

MVS also includes a secondary CVT, which contains some additional useful information. The mapping macro for this control block is IHASCVT. Its address is in the CVT field CVTABEND. One useful pointer is SCVTSVCT, which contains the address of the MVS SVC table although it isn't an IBM-defined programming interface.

The MVS SVC table is used to map Supervisor Call instructions, issued by programs to request MVS services. Many MVS macros, such as OPEN and CLOSE, generate Supervisor Call instructions. A list of MVS SVCs is in the *MVS/ESA Diagnosis: System Reference* manual, LY28-1011.

The SVC table contains 256 entries, one for each SVC number from zero to 255. These are mapped by the macro IHASVC. (There's also an SVCTABLE macro, distributed in SYS1.AGENLIB, which was used to create the SVC table.)

MVS conventions assign SVC numbers from zero to 200 for MVS services. The SVC numbers from 201 through 255 are available for an installation to customize MVS. As part of a common trend in MVS services, this control block can be updated through a service, SVCUPDTE, rather than requiring direct (and risky) alteration by anyone who wants to make later changes.

The SVCUPDTE macro allows dynamic changes to the SVC table; with proper planning, you can use this to add an SVC to MVS. A more common usage among some third-party software is to "front-end" an existing IBM-supplied SVC, for example, replacing the WTO SVC (35) with a routine to examine, change, or suppress console messages before they're issued.

2.4 The System Function Table

There's no IBM-distributed DSECT for the System Function Table (SFT) to the best of my knowledge. The SFT provides a common location for the Program Call (PC) numbers used in cross-memory MVS services. While the table isn't intended as a programming interface, a list of these services is in the *MVS/ESA Diagnosis: System Reference* manual, LY28-1011. Access to this information is useful when interpreting the system trace table in a dump. Examples will be provided in appendix C.

2.5 CVT Usage Examples

The CVT will be used many times in examples throughout the book, but I'll include one here that relies only on information in the CVT. This C program will determine the operating system from the CVTDCBA field, and display it along with the CPU model number from the CVT prefix.

```
#include <stdio.h>
#define CVTDCB 0x74
main()
{
/* Define pointers to use in accessing the CVT                        */
    char    *pCVT, **pWork1, *pWork3;
    unsigned short *pWork2;
/* Define integer value to receive CPU model number                   */
    unsigned short uCPU = 0;
    short uVMindicator = 0;
/* Get CVT address                                                     */
    pWork1 =   0;
    pWork1 += 4 ;                    /* address 16 divided by 4 = 4... */
    pCVT   = *pWork1 ;
/* Get CPU model number address — it's at CVT - 6                      */
    pWork2 =   pCVT-6;
    uCPU   = *pWork2 ;
/* Test to determine if we are running under VM or MVS                 */
    pWork3 = pCVT + CVTDCB;          /* offset to CVTDCB field         */
    uVMindicator = 0x40 & *pWork3; /* AND CVT1SSS with CVTDCB value */
/* Display operating system and CPU type                               */
    if (uVMindicator != 0)
    {
      printf("Welcome to VM on the %4x", uCPU);
    }
    else
    {
      printf("Welcome to MVS on the %4x", uCPU);
    }
    return 0; }
```

Note that this example uses a specific offset (X'74') into the CVT to compute an address. This works, but a better technique is to generate a C structure that redefines the DSECT. An example of this is provided in chapter 6.

2.6 Summary

The Communication Vector Table (CVT) is the common access point for
other control blocks within MVS. Usage of the CVT literally permeates MVS
services, and it's the first MVS control block used for most services. While a
few data elements remain in the CVT, mostly in the prefix portion, MVS currently uses the CVT only as an anchor point to get to other control blocks.

The Secondary CVT is an example of another control block accessed
through the CVT. It contains pointers to generally newer services than the
CVT. One major control block accessed through the SCVT is the MVS SVC
Table; this can be updated through the SVCUPDTE service.

The Global Data Area is used by MVS Virtual Storage Management
(VSM), and will be discussed further in chapter 4. The System Function
Table provides a common cross-memory service directory for MVS-pro-
vided services.

2.7 Things to Do

The Extended CVT provides a further extension to the CVT, much like the
Secondary CVT. Review the IHAECVT DSECT in SYS1.MODGEN.

3

Control Blocks for Dispatching

This chapter discusses the control blocks used by the MVS dispatching service. Dispatching means giving control of the CPU to a specified program to do some work. Dispatching is based on three control blocks:

- Task Control Block (TCB)
- Address Space Control Block (ASCB)
- Service Request Block (SRB)

The TCB and ASCB also have several associated control blocks, such as the Secondary TCB (STCB), Address Space Vector Table (ASVT), ASCB Extension (ASXB), and Address Space Secondary Block (ASSB). Each of these will be discussed as well.

3.1 A Little History

In OS/360, the predecessor to MVS, the TCB was the original dispatching element. OS/360 maintained a "System TCB chain" anchored in the CVT (field CVTHEAD), as shown in Fig. 3.1. The TCB chain could be scanned by any program in OS/360, providing an easy way to locate all the running jobs in the system, etc. OS/VS1 maintained a similar structure.

The development of the MVS addressing structure made this approach impossible to maintain. The TCB is located in the storage area for each job called Local System Queue Area (LSQA). Remember that the MVS address space structure allows only each job's or TSO user's own region to be addressed. This, in turn, meant that the MVS dispatcher needed a globally ad-

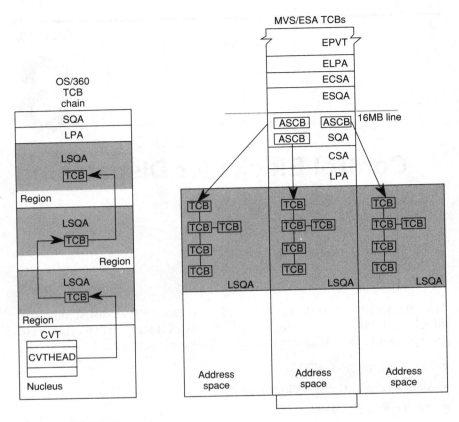

Figure 3.1 OS/360 TCB chain.

dressable control block to access and dispatch the running tasks in the system. Rather than choosing to move the TCB out of LSQA, IBM instead opted to add another control block to represent each address space. This led to the development of the ASCB.

This, however, wasn't entirely sufficient. Switching from one address space to another affected system performance. Several MVS components—the I/O Supervisor being the easiest example—needed an independent, cross-memory dispatchable unit. In the case of I/O, this allows the results of interrupts to be promptly posted to the original I/O requester without the need to immediately dispatch the address space. (This process will be discussed in further detail in chapter 8.) The need for this independent, cross-memory dispatchable unit led to development of the Service Request Block for cross-memory work.

While the TCB actually came first, the ASCB is the foundation for dispatching through MVS 4.3, so I'll discuss it first.

3.2 Address Space Control Block (ASCB)

The ASCB provides a commonly addressable control block throughout all address spaces in an MVS system. Each ASCB represents a job, a TSO user, or a started task in MVS. (For brevity, I'll usually specify *job* when all three types could be possible.) The ASCB helps the MVS dispatcher keep track of which tasks are ready to run, which are running, and which aren't ready for some reason (e.g., waiting for I/O).

ASCBs are chained together in doubly linked lists. Within each ASCB, there are two fields that can be used to scan through the chain of ASCBs:

- ASCBFWDP, which represents the next ASCB address
- ASCBBWDP, which represents the previous ASCB address

The ASCB anchors most job-related control blocks. The mapping macro is called IHAASCB. You can locate the ASCB for your job from the PSAAOLD and PSAAANEW fields in the Prefixed Save Area. You can locate the address of ASCBs for other jobs by chaining through the ASCBs, or by using the ASVT. The CVT fields CVTASCBH and CVTASCBL provide access to the chain of ASCBs, if you want. I'll show an example using the ASVT, which is the preferred method.

Note that the ASCB, ASSB, ASVT, and ASXB all have their mnemonic names included as a four-byte character field at the start of the respective control blocks.

3.2.1 ASCB fields

The ASCB has several fields of interest, some of which will be discussed in this section. The ASCB will reappear at various times throughout the book, so I'm intentionally deferring discussion of some important fields until later. Many of the ASCB fields illustrate how the MVS dispatcher works with the control blocks discussed so far, however. Some of the control blocks that apply to the dispatching service are:

ASCBAFFN. This field represents the CPU affinity bit mask for the job represented by this ASCB. CPU affinity represents the condition wherein a job must run on a particular processor within an MVS system. There are numerous reasons for this need; one is for access to the System/370 Vector Facility, which is a feature that might not be installed on all processors within a processor complex. If this is the case, the MVS dispatcher can test if a given ASCB can run on a given processor by comparing this field to the physical CPU bit mask. (This was a field in the PCCA named PCCACAFM.) CPU affinity is also invoked for systems that include the Integrated Cryptographic Facility, which should not be installed on all processors within a processor complex.

ASCBASID. This is a two-byte field that represents the address space identifier. This field, or more specifically the value it contains, is very frequently used to identify an address space in other control blocks. You'll see several places where this value is used, such as in creation of SRBs and in the MVS trace table. The value is usually referred to as the ASID.

ASCBCPUS. This is a count of the number of CPUs active in the address space. (The term *memory* is sometimes used.) Remember that, on a multiprocessor system, more than one CPU can be active at a time for the same job. This field will indicate that condition; if it's more than one, multiple CPUs are running in the address space. It's present through MVS 4.3.

ASCBSTOR. This is the Control Register 1 value for this address space. (Control Register 1 holds the segment table address, which I'll discuss in chapter 5.)

ASCBCSCB. This is a pointer to the Command Scheduling Control Block (CSCB). The CSCB is used to signal MVS operator commands such as MODIFY and STOP. (These are usually abbreviated to F and P, respectively.) I won't cover this process in the book; you might want to review the QEDIT macro to gain more understanding of this process.

ASCBTSB. This is the TSO control block address; a nonzero value implies that this address space is a TSO user.

ASCBTCBS. A count of the number of TCBs ready to run in this address space. I'll go into this further when discussing TCBs.

ASCBFMCT. Allocated frame count—the number of 4K pages (*frames*) being used by this address space.

ASCBJBNI. Address of an eight-byte job name field for initiated jobs. This will be zero if the ASCB represents a TSO user or started task.

ASCBJBNS. Similar to ASCBJBNI, but for TSO users and started tasks.

ASCBSRBT. The accumulated step SRB time for the address space. (You'll see the ending value for this field in MVS message IEF374I, which contains the step starting and ending times, etc.)

The ASCB contains the address of numerous other control blocks, along with other information. I'll mention these fields when discussing the associated control blocks.

3.2.2 Related data areas

These related control blocks contain information that, for one reason or another, isn't part of the ASCB. There are two directly related control blocks for each ASCB:

- ASCB Extension (ASXB)
- Address Space Secondary Block (ASSB)

Additionally, the Address Space Vector Table (ASVT) relates to the ASCB much as the PCCAVT related to the PCCA, as discussed in chapter 1. Figure 3.2 shows the relationship between the ASCB, ASXB, and ASSB.

3.2.2.1 ASCB Extension (ASXB)

The ASCB was designed to contain the information regarding an address space that needs to be commonly addressable. However, since the ASCB was commonly addressable, it required common memory, and enlarging it to contain all the required information could lead to unnecessary storage constraints. As a result, IBM provides a related control block called the Address Space Extension Block, or ASXB.

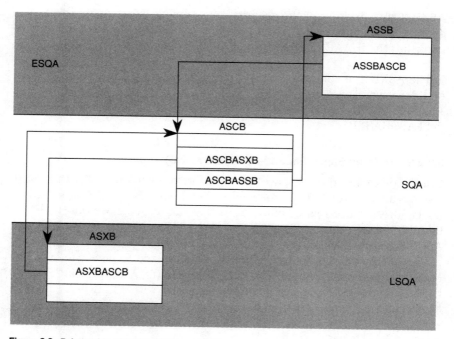

Figure 3.2 Relationship of ASCB, ASXB, and ASSB.

The ASXB provides a separate control block, one per address space, which holds information that's used only when that address space is dispatched (running). Since the address space is running when it's used, the ASXB is located in the user region's Local System Queue Area (LSQA). This is at the upper address end of the user region. As a result, while you can write a program to investigate your own job's ASXB, you can't do the same for another address space without authorization. Some fields of interest within the ASXB include:

TCB pointers. These are in the fields ASXBFTCB and ASXBLTCB, which have the first and last TCB addresses in your address space.

ASXBTCBS. A count of the TCBs in the address space.

ASXBOMCB. The address of the Object Access Method control block, which is used with the ImagePlus product.

ASXBUSER. This is the seven-byte TSO User ID associated with the job. This field can be used to determine who submitted the JCL that's running a program.

ASXBSENV. Address of the security environment information; this is the address of the RACF ACEE control block. I won't be covering this in the book, but the IHAACEE DSECT maps the information.

The ASXB also contains a variety of control block pointers used by several MVS services, such as the SRB queue pointers (ASXBFSRB and ASXBLSRB). The ASXB DSECT is IHAASXB; its address is in the ASCB field ASCBASXB.

3.2.2.2 Address Space Secondary Block (ASSB)

In addition to the address-space-unique information in the ASXB, the ASCB also has another related control block called the ASSB. The ASSB is used to hold address-space-related information that can reside above the 16MB 24-bit address line. The ASSB DSECT is IHAASSB, and its address is in the ASCB field ASCBASSB.

The ASSB contents tend to be more often related to newer features of MVS than do those of the ASCB and ASXB. Since the ASSB is located above the 24-bit storage line, it can be increased in size without affecting storage constraints in the first 16MB of virtual storage, and as such is the preferred spot to put any new address-space-related information. Fields in the ASSB relate to MVS facilities such as:

- ESA/370 data spaces
- Cross-memory services
- Vector facility usage

and so forth. Additionally, the ASSB contains fields used by a variety of other components. Some fields of possible interest include:

ASSBVSC and ASSBNVSC. The Auxiliary Storage Manager (paging) VIO and non-VIO slot counts.

ASSBSTKN. The address space STOKEN value, used to identify ESA/370 data spaces (Refer to *MVS Power Programming* for further information).

ASSBBALV. The data space access list.

ASSBTSQN. The next TTOKEN sequence number.

3.2.2.3 Address Space Vector Table (ASVT)

One problem with using the chain of ASCB addresses is the number of control blocks you must examine to find the ASCB for a given address space ID (ASID). To speed up this type of search, IBM provides an additional control block called the ASVT.

The ASVT is located with the address in the CVTASVT field of the CVT. It comprises a header with various pieces of control information, followed by an array of ASCB pointers. The first 480 bytes are marked as "reserved for future expansion." The DSECT name is IHAASVT and there's one ASVT per MVS system.

The ASVT has a field called ASVTMAXU, which contains the total number of address spaces in the system. This can be used as a counter for loop control when scanning the entire set of ASCBs in the system.

The field ASVTENTY occurs ASVTMAXU times. Each occurrence contains either an ASCB address, zero, or a pointer to the next free entry. The last entry has the leftmost (high-order) bit set to one. Thus, to determine if an ASVTENTY occurrence contains an ASCB address, you could use the following code:

```
          L     R3,ASVTMAXU    Get number of entries
          LA    R4,ASVTENTY    Get first address
LOOP1     EQU   *
          L     R5,0(,R4)      Get address of first ASCB
          LTR   R5,R5          Test for zero
          BZ    RUNLOOP        Yes -- skip this entry
          USING ASCB,R5        Set ASCB addressability
```

```
          B      DO_ASCB        Yes -- go process ASCB
                        RUNLOOP  EQU   *
          L      R4,4(,R4)      Next ASVTENTY address
          BCT    R3,LOOP1       And continue loop
```

See Fig. 3.3 for the relationship of the ASVT and ASCBs. The following is a program to scan the ASCBs in an MVS system and report CPU time for started tasks using the ASVT (the OUCB control block is discussed in chapter 6):

```
ASCB        TITLE 'UCLA X414.371 4/93 ASCB SCAN PROGRAM'
*           R3     CVT ADDRESS
*           R4     ASVT ADDRESS
*           R5     CURRENT ASCB ADDRESS
*           R6     POINTER WITHIN ASVT
*           R7     LOOP COUNTER FROM ASVTMAXI
*           R8     JOB NAME ADDRESS FROM ASCB
*           R12    PROGRAM BASE REGISTER
ASCBSCAN CSECT
ASCBSCAN AMODE 24
ASCBSCAN RMODE 24
          BAKR   R14,0                 SAVE REGISTERS
          LR     R12,R15               ESTABLISH
          USING  ASCBSCAN,R12              ADDRESSABILITY
          LA     R13,SAVEAREA          SAVE AREA
          SPACE 3
          OPEN   (SYSPRINT,OUTPUT)     OPEN PRINT FILE
          LA     R1,SYSPRINT
          USING  IHADCB,R1
          LA     R15,16                SET UP RETURN CODE
          TM     DCBOFLGS,X'10'        TEST FOR GOOD OPEN
          BZ     RETURN2               GIVE UP IF NOT
          SPACE 1
*           DISPLAY CURRENT TIME AND DATE
          STCK   DOUBLEWD              STORE CLOCK
          STCKCONV    STCKVAL=DOUBLEWD,CONVVAL=CPU_TIME,TIMETYPE=DEC, X
                 DATETYPE=MMDDYYYY
          MVC    PH_TIME,=X'4020207A20207A2120'
          ED     PH_TIME,CPU_TIME      EDIT CURRENT TIME
          MVC    PH_DATE,=X'40202061202061212020'
          ED     PH_DATE,CPU_TIME+8    AND DATE
          PUT    SYSPRINT,PH_HEADING   WRITE LINE
          SPACE 1
*           INITIALIZE FOR ASCB SCAN
          L      R3,X'10'              GET CVT ADDRESS
          USING  CVT,R3                ESTABLISH ADDRESSABILITY
          L      R4,CVTASVT            GET ASVT ADDRESS
          USING  ASVT,R4               ESTABLISH ADDRESSABILITY
          L      R7,ASVTMAXU           GET MAX USER COUNT
          LA     R6,ASVTENTY           SET UP ADDRESS OF FIRST ENTRY
SCAN_ASCBS   EQU   *
          TM     0(R6),ASVTRSAV        TEST FOR VALID ASCB ADDRESS
          BZ     PROCESS_ASCB          PROCESS ASCB INFO
          AP     UNUSED_ASIDS,=P'1'    ADD TO COUNT OF UNUSED ASIDS
          B      SCAN_ASCB_CONT        CONTINUE LOOP
PROCESS_ASCB   EQU   *
          L      R5,0(R6)              GET AN ASCB ADDRESS
          USING  ASCB,R5               ESTABLISH ADDRESSABILITY
```

```
          AP     USED_ASIDS,=P'1'          ADD TO COUNT OF USED ASIDS
          SPACE 1
*         DETERMINE IF THIS ASCB IS A STARTED TASK OR NOT
          L      R8,ASCBOUCB              GET OUCB ADDRESS
          USING  OUCB,R8                  ESTABLISH ADDRESSABILITY
          L      R14,TEST_ADDR            GET 31-BIT ADDR OF TEST_OUCB
          BSM    0,R14                    SET 31-BIT MODE FOR OUCB
TEST_OUCB EQU    *
          SR     R0,R0                    CLEAR R0
          IC     R0,OUCBYFL               SAVE FLAG
          ICM    R0,2,OUCBMFL3            SAVE FLAG
          TM     OUCBYFL,OUCBSTT          TEST STARTED TASK FLAG
          BNO    SCAN_ASCB_CONT             NOT ON - CONTINUE
          TM     OUCBMFL3,OUCBINIT        IS THIS AN INITIATOR?
          BO     SCAN_ASCB_CONT             YES - BYPASS IT
          MVI    PL_NSWAP,C' '            CLEAR NON-SWAP FLAG
          TM     OUCBSFL,OUCBNSW          NON-SWAPPABLE?
          BZ     SHOW_ASCB                  NO - SHOW ASCB INFO
          MVI    PL_NSWAP,C'N'            SET NON-SWAP FLAG
SHOW_ASCB EQU    *
          LA     R14,SHOW_ASCB_2          GET ADDRESS
          BSM    0,R14                    SET 31-BIT MODE FOR OUCB
SHOW_ASCB_2 EQU  *
          L      R8,ASCBJBNS              GET STARTED TASK NAME
          MVC    PL_JBNS,0(R8)            MOVE TO PRINT LINE
          LA     R1,ASCBASID              GET ASID
          BAS    R14,HEXCONV              CONVERT TO HEXADECIMAL
          MVC    PL_ASID,EBCDICEQ         MOVE TO PRINT LINE
          LA     R2,ASCBEJST              CPU TIME
          STCKCONV STCKVAL=(2),CONVVAL=CPU_TIME,TIMETYPE=DEC
          OI     CPU_TIME+4,X'0F'         SET SIGH
          MVC    PL_CPUTIME,=X'4020207A20207A21204B202020'
          ED     PL_CPUTIME,CPU_TIME      EDIT CPU TIME VALUE
          LA     R2,ASCBINTS              START TIME
          STCKCONV     STCKVAL=(2),CONVVAL=CPU_TIME,TIMETYPE=DEC,   X
               DATETYPE=MMDDYYYY
          OI     CPU_TIME+4,X'0F'         SET SIGN
          MVC    PL_STARTED,=X'4020207A20207A2120'
          ED     PL_STARTED,CPU_TIME      EDIT CPU TIME VALUE
          MVC    PL_DATE,=X'402020612020612120202020'
          ED     PL_DATE,CPU_TIME+8       EDIT CPU TIME VALUE
          PUT    SYSPRINT,PL_ASCB         WRITE LINE
SCAN_ASCB_CONT EQU *
          LA     R6,4(,R6)                POINT TO NEXT ENTRY
          BCT    R7,SCAN_ASCBS            CONTINUE PROCESSING
          SPACE 3                         LISTING CONTROL CARD - SPACE 3
*         ALL DONE - DISPLAY TOTALS, ET CETERA
          OI     UNUSED_ASIDS+3,X'0F'     SET SIGN
          OI     USED_ASIDS+3,X'0F'       BITS
          UNPK   PT_USED,USED_ASIDS       UNPACK
          UNPK   PT_UNUSED,UNUSED_ASIDS    TOTALS
          PUT    SYSPRINT,PL_ASCB         WRITE LINE
          SPACE 1
*         RETURN TO CALLING PROGRAM
RETURN    EQU    *
          CLOSE (SYSPRINT,)
          SR     R15,R15                  SET RETURN CODE
RETURN2   EQU    *
          PR                              RETURN TO OS
          SPACE 1
          CNOP   0,4
```

```
HEXCONV   EQU   *
          UNPK  EBCDICEQ(9),0(5,R1)      UNPACK
          TR    EBCDICEQ,TRTAB-240       TRANSLATE
          BR    R14                      RETURN
EBCDICEQ DC     CL8' ',C' '              8 DATA BYTES, 1 FILLER BYTE
          EJECT
*         DATA AREAS
SAVEAREA DC     F'0',CL4'F1SA',16F'+0'
UNUSED_ASIDS   DC    PL4'0'
USED_ASIDS     DC    PL4'0'
CPU_TIME DS    2D
DOUBLEWD DS    D
PH_HEADING     DC    C'1ASCB SCAN FOR:'
PH_PREFIX      DC    CL8' ',C' AT'
PH_TIME        DC    CL9' ',C' ON '
PH_DATE        DC    CL11' '
          DC    CL(PH_HEADING+133-*)' '    FILLER
PL_ASCB  DC    C'0==ASCB FOR:'
PL_JBNS  DS    CL8
          DC    C' ASID:'
PL_ASID  DC    CL4' ',C' '
PL_NSWAP DC    C' ',C' '
PL_CPUTIME     DC    CL13' ',C' '
PL_STARTED     DC    CL09' ',C' '
PL_DATE  DC    CL11' ',C' '
          DC    CL(PL_ASCB+133-*)' '       FILLER
          SPACE 1
PT_ASCB  DC    C'0*** TOTAL ACTIVE:'
PT_USED  DS    CL8
          DC    C' INACTIVE:'
PT_UNUSED      DS    CL8
          DC    CL(PT_ASCB+133-*)' '       FILLER
TEST_ADDR      DC    A(TEST_OUCB+X'80000000')  31-BIT ADDRESS
TRTAB    DC    C'0123456789ABCDEF'        HEX CONVERSION TABLE
          SPACE 3
*         REGISTER EQUATES
*
R0        EQU   0
R1        EQU   1
R2        EQU   2
R3        EQU   3
R4        EQU   4
R5        EQU   5
R6        EQU   6
R7        EQU   7
R8        EQU   8
R9        EQU   9
R10       EQU   10
R11       EQU   11
R12       EQU   12
R13       EQU   13
R14       EQU   14
R15       EQU   15
          SPACE 3
*         DATA CONTROL BLOCK FOR PRINT OUTPUT FILE
SYSPRINT DCB   DDNAME=SYSPRINT,DEVD=DA,DSORG=PS,MACRF=(PM),RECFM=FBA, X
               LRECL=133
          CVT   DSECT=YES,LIST=NO
          PRINT NOGEN
          DCBD  DSORG=PS,DEVD=(DA)
          IHAASCB
```

```
IHAASVT
IRAOUCB
END    ASCBSCAN
```

The size of the ASVT is controlled by entries coded in the SYS1.PARMLIB data set. Member IEASYS*xx* contains a parameter called MAXUSER=. This is the number of ASVT entries. Another parameter, RSVSTRT, contains an added count for operator START commands. Finally, the SYS1.PARMLIB IEASYS*xx* parameter RSVNONR specifies the number of entries to be supplied as additional replacements for failing address spaces. These counts are in the fields ASVTMAXU, ASVTSTRT, and ASVTNONR, respectively.

MVS provides a macro instruction, LOCASCB, which will locate an ASCB if given an ASID as input. This is simpler than coding an ASVT scan if the ASID is known.

3.3   Task Control Block (TCB)

The TCB was the original basic OS/360 control block that represented a unit of work for the CPU. The TCB, in its OS/360 form, was addressable by all programs running in MVT. This structure wasn't tenable with the MVS address space layout.

TCBs are created by the ATTACH macro and deleted by the DETACH macro after the program completes. The mapping macro is IKJTCB. Each address space contains several TCBs, even if the program being executed doesn't create any additional tasks. The standard TCBs within an address space for normally executing jobs include:

The Region Control Task (IEAVAR00).   Essentially responsible for starting and ending the address space.

The SVC Dump Task for the address space (IEAVTSDT).   This task is usually inactive, but starts up for storage dumps.

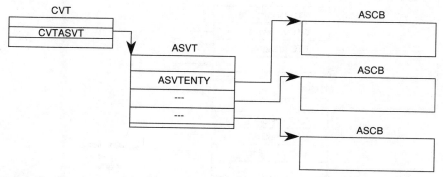

Figure 3.3 Relationship of ASVT and ASCBs.

The Allocation Task (IEFSD060). This, among other things, serves as the owner of data set names within each address space, and will be discussed in chapter 7.

The Initiator TCB (IEFIIC). This selects each job running in the address space for execution and starts it.

Your program's TCB. This is what appears in SYSUDUMP storage dumps.

The relationship of these tasks is shown in Fig. 3.4. Note that the relationship is somewhat different when running under TSO. For example, the TSO TEST command inserts an additional TCB for the TEST command itself.

TCBs are chained together to reflect various relationships with other TCBs in the address space. If a task issues the ATTACH macro to create an-

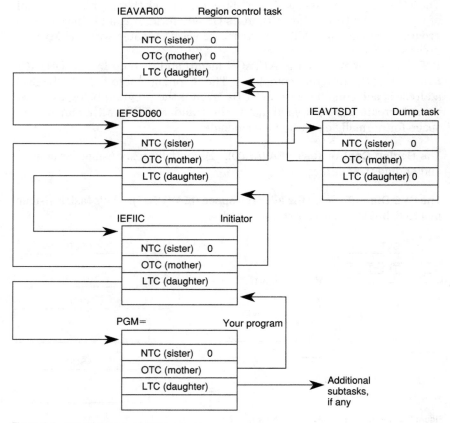

Figure 3.4 TCB structure in an address space.

other TCB, the new one is called the daughter TCB. The task that issued the ATTACH is called the mother TCB. If the mother TCB issues ATTACH again to create another daughter TCB, this is called a sister TCB to the first. The field names that support these relationships are:

TCBLTC. Address of a daughter TCB. This is the result of the most recent ATTACH macro.

TCBOTC. Address of the mother (owning) TCB.

TCBNTC. Address of the next newest sister TCB. This is zero in the first daughter TCB.

The TCB includes numerous pointers to other control blocks, as well as the following fields of interest:

TCBCMPC. TCB completion code in ABEND SVC format.

TCBPKF. The task's storage protection key.

TCBJLB. Address of the JOBLIB DCB.

TCBFSA. Address of the first save area for the task.

TCBUSER. "A word available to the user"—the same cautions apply as discussed for the CVTUSER field.

TCBAFFN. CPU affinity.

The TCB also contains numerous flags that describe the task's dispatchability. (See the TCBFLGSx, TCBNDSP, and TCBXSCTx fields for examples.) Unfortunately, due to the age of the TCB, there are also a few bits that are obsolete, such as the OS/VS1 flag bits. The TCB also serves as an anchor for many other task-related MVS control blocks. These include:

TCBRB. Current Request Block pointer.

TCBSTAB. Current STAE Control Block.

TCBTCT. SMF Timing Control Table.

TCBEXCPD. EXCP Debugging area—for Sx00 ABENDs.

TCBs can be controlled by the STATUS macro, which changes a task's dispatchability. The START and STOP options will respectively make a TCB dispatchable or mark it as nondispatchable. The TCB field TCBFLGS4 contains a bit, TCBHNDSP, that indicates this. Note that it's meaningful to interrogate this only for other tasks; if you can check it for your own TCB, your TCB is obviously running!

The CHAP macro can be used to change the dispatching priority of TCBs in your address space. Other information regarding task dispatchability can be found beginning at the byte labeled TCBNDSP.

The TCB DSECT also includes an extension with a DSECT name of TCBXTNT2. The address of this extension is in the field named TCBEXT2. Use of the TCB, like the ASCB and CVT, permeates MVS, and I'll be referring to it often.

3.3.1 Secondary Task Control Block (STCB)

The Secondary TCB (STCB) became both possible and necessary with the advent of 31-bit addressing in MVS/XA. Its purpose is to retain various task-related information that need not be kept below the 16MB address line.

The DSECT for the STCB is in the macro IHASTCB; USING directives should refer to label STCB. The STCB itself is stored in Extended LSQA storage. It exists for the duration of the related TCB.

The fields within the STCB tend to relate to the more recent MVS services. Some of the fields of interest include:

STCBVSSA. Vector Status Save Area.

STCBDUCV. Address of the Dispatchable Unit Control Table, used to access MVS/ESA data spaces.

STCBARS. Save area for ESA access registers.

STCBLSDP. Address of the Linkage stack entry descriptor, used with the ESA/370 Branch and Stack instruction.

STCBTTKN. The TTOKEN for this TCB, used with MVS/ESA data spaces.

There are numerous other fields used with newer MVS services, such as System Managed Storage, OpenMVS, data-in-virtual, and so forth. The STCB is worth investigating, as it will probably be the location for task-related information in new MVS functions.

3.4 Service Request Block (SRB)

The MVS addressing structure created a need for commonly addressable control blocks, which led to the ASCB, as previously discussed. This also created a need for a service that allowed one address space to run a program in another address space. This interaddress-space communication was needed by several system services (e.g., the I/O supervisor). In response to this need, MVS includes cross-memory services. This provides the ability to run programs in another address space. The control block used to support this facility is the Service Request Block, or SRB.

SRBs can run with the addressability and dispatching elements of another address space (segment and page tables, ASCB, etc.), and they're used whenever an authorized program needs to access memory in another address space, for example.

IBM also provided a later implementation of cross-memory services, using several specialized instructions (e.g., Program Call) to provide a similar function. This is discussed in *MVS Power Programming*.

The Service Request Block itself is a user-created control block analogous to a request block (PRB, SVRB, etc.). However, SRBs are dispatched by MVS before any other work in an address space. SRBs can have either global or local priority; global means they precede any other work and local SRBs are dispatched first within that address space. Several macros and DSECTs are provided to support the use of SRBs:

SCHEDULE. A macro used to pass an SRB to the MVS dispatcher, which will schedule it for later execution in the requested address space.

SRBTIMER. A macro that sets a loop timer limit for SRBs.

SRBSTAT. A macro used to save and restore a running SRB's status.

PURGEDQ. A macro used to cancel an SRB before or during its execution.

SETFRR. Used for recovery and the IHASRB mapping macro, which provides a DSECT used to create an SRB or to access its fields.

MVS Power Programming includes a complete example of running an SRB for those who need a full explanation of the process. This includes a discussion of the SETFRR macro, which I very strongly recommend when coding any SRB. You can also consult the IBM documentation; a few details will be included here.

Creating SRBs requires MVS authorization; a program that issues the SCHEDULE macro must be in supervisor state and protect key 0. The SRB code itself cannot issue SVCs; however, branch entry is permitted to those services (e.g., GETMAIN) that also provide it. The format of the SCHEDULE macro follows:

```
label      SCHEDULE  SRB= address,  X
                     SCOPE={GLOBAL|LOCAL},    X
                     LLOCK={YES|NO},          X
                     FRR={YES|NO},            X
                     DISABLED
```

The SCHEDULE operand values are:

SRB=. Points to the SRB itself.

SCOPE. Sets priority when the SRB is dispatched (global or local).

LLOCK=YES. Automatically gets the local lock before the SRB is dispatched (locking will be discussed in chapter 7).

FRR=. Specifies if a functional recovery routine is available for this SRB.

DISABLED. Indicates that the program issuing the SCHEDULE macro is disabled for interrupts.

3.4.1 Constructing an SRB

The SRB is also unique in being created by the caller of the SCHEDULE macro rather than by MVS, as the ASCB, TCB, and most other control blocks are. Several rules that apply to construction of an SRB are that the SRB must be in page-fixed storage and it must be in a commonly addressable area, such as CSA or SQA. After obtaining the appropriate type of storage, the following fields must be filled in:

SRBASCB. Address of the target address space's ASCB.

SRBPKF. The SRB's protect key.

SRBEP. Address of the program to be run under SRB.

SRBPARM (optional) parameters for SRBEP program. This address is placed in register 1 when the program executes.

SRBCPAFF (optional) CPU affinity. Set to zeroes if this isn't needed.

SRBRMTR resource manager termination routine. Address of a cleanup routine; the PURGEDQ macro uses this.

SRBPASID ASID of 'target' address space. This can be used by PURGEDQ, otherwise set to zero.

SRBID. An EBCDIC eye catcher with a value of SRB.

SRB programs, called *service routines*, get control in supervisor state, with the protect key specified in SRBPKF. When they execute, register 0 at entry points to the SRB control block itself, and register 1 contains the SRBPARM field. Register 14 contains the return address, and register 15 contains the service routine entry point address. Service routines can't issue SVCs (e.g., OPEN and WTO), although ABEND is an exception to this rule. Service routines are interruptible, but nonpreemptible. This means that the service routine's execution can be interrupted (for example, due to an I/O event or timer expiration), but the SRB won't be preempted to allow another program to run. (Use the SRBTIMER macro to avoid loops in SRB service routine code.) This nonpreemptible characteristic means that SRBs can't wait for external events.

Note that several other cross-memory facilities exist besides those provided via the SRB. Examples include the cross-memory option of the POST macro, and the cross memory ABEND function via the CALLRTM macro.

3.5 Request Blocks

Another control block that's useful for understanding the dispatching process and flow of control in MVS is the Request Block, or RB. RBs were part of the original OS/360 design. An RB, oversimplifying somewhat, is created whenever a program transfers control to another program using MVS services. Thus, while it's far more common to pass control to another program without involving MVS (via a static call, BALR or BASR instruction, etc.), MVS needs a method of keeping track of the linkage when it's involved.

Thus, an RB is created when a program issues certain MVS service requests. These include LINK, SVC service requests, and certain program exits. RBs are destroyed when a program returns control following one of these situations.

Strictly speaking, RBs are not an MVS dispatcher control block. They're created by MVS Contents Supervision, or by the SVC first-level interrupt handler (FLIH). However, this is a reasonable point at which to introduce them.

RBs come in several forms. The first is the Program Request Block, or PRB. This exists for a program invoked by JCL (EXEC PGM=). PRBs are also created when a LINK macro instruction is issued. The next is the Supervisor Request Block, or SVRB. SVRBs are created as a result of issuing an SVC for some operating system service, such as OPEN. (Not all SVCs generate an SVRB; small SVCs called Type 1 or Type 6 SVCs don't.) The RB representing the program that currently has control can be located through the TCBRB (Current Request Block Pointer) field.

Familiarity with the RB is extremely useful for debugging, because the chain of RBs holds a record of the register contents at each transfer of control. You can also use RBs to track back through each SVC or program call, building a history of who called who, and so forth.

The mapping macro for the RB is IKJRB. This DSECT is somewhat complicated due to the variety of included RB types, prefix information, and so forth. The label RBBASIC is recommended as the name for the USING statement. Fields of interest include:

RBOPSW. The PSW when linkage made.

RBGRSAVE. Registers at time of linkage.

RBLINK. Address of previous RB, or of TCB if first RB.

RBINTCOD. Halfword interruption value; this holds the SVC number or program check identifier.

RBINLNTH. Instruction length (useful for program checks).

Note that RBINTCOD and RBINLNTH are in the RB prefix, ahead of RBBASIC. Interpreting the RB chain in a dump takes a little practice. The typical sequence for an OPEN SVC-related ABEND (e.g., 013) in a batch program will be:

- PRB for the batch program; the RBINTCOD will contain the SVC number issued, which is X'0013' (decimal 19). The RBOPSW field contains the address in the program where the OPEN was issued. RBGRSAVE will be the registers when the batch program received control.

- SVRB for the SVC (OPEN); RBGRSAVE will contain the register contents when the OPEN SVC was issued. Since OPEN processing decided to fail your request and issue an ABEND, RBOPSW will contain an address somewhere in OPEN macro processing code. RBINTCOD will contain X'000D' (decimal 13), which is the number for the ABEND SVC.

- SVRB for the ABEND SVC; RBGRSAV will contain the registers at the time the ABEND SVC was issued. Register 1 contains the ABEND code and dump parameters (X'A0013000', for example). Since ABEND will have requested that a dump be printed, RBINTCOD will contain X'0000033'—the SVC number for the SNAP macro, which prints dumps.

- SVRB for the SNAP SVC (which is printing the dump); this isn't of much interest here. RBINTCOD will contain whatever was the last SVC issued by SNAP; for example, X'0078' would represent a GETMAIN SVC.

This example didn't require use of RBINLNTH, since every transfer of control was due to an SVC. If there had been a program check in the sequence (0Cx), the length of the failing instruction would have been in RBINLNTH. Another type of RB, the Interruption Request Block (IRB), is created to support certain types of user exits. The CIRB macro creates these.

3.6 Summary

The three fundamental control blocks used in MVS dispatching are ASCB, TCB, and SRB. The ASCB provides a commonly addressable control block that represents the address space to MVS, and also serves to anchor numerous other job-related control blocks. The TCB fulfills a similar need for tasks within an address space. Both of these have related control blocks, which include the ASSB, ASXB, and STCB. Additionally, MVS provides the ASVT vector table to locate ASCBs quickly.

Finally, the SRB provides a method of executing programs (service routines) within another address space for properly authorized callers. RBs, while not created by the MVS dispatcher, also provide related information.

3.7 Things to Do

- The following are dispatcher macro instructions:
CALLDISP
T6EXIT
INTSECT
SUSPEND
RESUME
PURGEDQ

- Look at the macro instructions mentioned in the text, specifically LOCASCB and STATUS.

4

Virtual Storage Management

This chapter begins a discussion of the three types of storage in MVS: virtual storage, auxiliary storage, and real storage. Virtual storage is what you typically use as an MVS applications programmer, and almost all MVS interfaces that involve specifying storage deal with virtual storage.

Real storage, by contrast, is what the processor really uses to carry out your program's instructions. Since there's usually an imbalance between real storage resources and virtual storage needs, MVS needs to store some of the virtual storage on disk (paging), which is the role of auxiliary storage management.

Real storage in MVS/ESA has two parts: central storage, where most of the real work is done, and extended storage (or expanded storage), which is used for ESA data spaces and a number of other functions. I'll discuss these concepts in more detail later, but you need to consider a few points about real storage now, because they affect how virtual storage services are provided.

Real storage in the System/370 architecture is organized into chunks of 4096 bytes each, called *pages*. The original 1964 System/360 design was organized into chunks of 2048 bytes; this affected the design of much of IBM's operating systems, and you still see references to "2K pages" for this older size, perhaps along with references to "4K pages." I'll use the larger size whenever I use the word *page*. *IBM Mainframes* and *MVS: Concepts And Facilities* both have discussions on this topic.

Each page has a storage protection mechanism called a *storage key*. The storage key is a four-bit value, ranging from zero to 15, which classifies the storage into some type. The value of the key is often used in referring to the type, such as in key 0 storage. Unless otherwise authorized, MVS application programs use key 8 storage. The other keys have varying uses, to be discussed later.

And now, on to virtual storage. Virtual storage management is usually abbreviated VSM, so I'll use that abbreviation henceforth.

4.1   Virtual Storage Management Services

VSM provides a number of services to assembler programmers. These are typically invoked via a macro, which might translate into various methods of actually performing the service. The VSM macros and services are each discussed in the following sections.

4.1.1   GETMAIN and FREEMAIN

The GETMAIN and FREEMAIN macros are the oldest form of VSM services, originally comprising part of OS/360. GETMAIN is used to request virtual storage; FREEMAIN releases it. GETMAIN and FREEMAIN are supported by four SVCs: 4, 5, 10, and 120. Each of these can be invoked depending on the options of the GETMAIN or FREEMAIN macro.

GETMAIN has several parameters, some of which are listed in Table 4.1. A full discussion of GETMAIN and FREEMAIN can be found in the appropriate assembler language development manuals, so I won't cover all the options in detail.

GETMAIN and FREEMAIN can also be invoked without the use of an SVC. This is necessary in certain circumstances, such as within an SRB service routine or in code that runs disabled for interruptions. The macros will use branch entry if the operand BRANCH=YES is coded. *Branch entry* means that your program will use the BASR instruction to transfer control to VSM. (This requires that you be authorized and running with protection key 0. *MVS Power Programming* provides an example.)

TABLE 4.1   Selected GETMAIN/FREEMAIN Options

Parameter	Description
MODE	Type of request (Register, List, etc.)
LV	Length of storage requested
LA	Address of a list of lengths
SP	The subpool requested (see text)
BNDRY	Boundary for the storage, doubleword or page
KEY	Storage protection key requested
BRANCH	YES specifies branch entry option
LOC	Requested location of the storage (below or above 16MB)
OWNER	Owning address space

One concept that's essential to understanding how VSM works is that of sub-pools. *Subpools* are a method MVS uses to subdivide virtual storage into related groups. This groups areas with similar characteristics together, which reduces the total storage requirement. There are 256 subpools, ranging from zero to 255. Subpools in the range of zero to 127 are available for any MVS program, and are kept within the user region of your address space. There's no intermixing of storage between two jobs or TSO users, even if they use the same subpools within the range of 0–127.

Subpools 128 and above are reserved for MVS (131 and 132 are an exception). In actual use, MVS groups related types of control blocks in different subpools based on how the storage is used. If authorized, your program can also acquire storage in these subpools—for example, when creating an SRB.

A complete list of subpools is provided in the *Diagnosis: System Reference and Application Development Guide: Authorized Assembler Language Programs* manuals, and you should rely on those for specific details. For an older list, see pages 5–72 of the *Debugging Handbook, vol. I*. If you don't have access to these manuals, an abbreviated list of storage subpools is shown in Table 4.2. (This information is also available in the Subpool Translation Table control block, albeit in less accessible form.) Some notes on this table:

- Subpools 128–232, 238, 242, 243, 244, 246, and 249 are reserved for compatibility with VS1, SVS, and MVT.

- The nucleus, PLPA, FLPA, and MLPA are not assigned to any subpool.

- Subpools 129–202, 202–212, and 216–222 are undefined. (This can change with subsequent releases of MVS, of course.)

- Some subpools can be either above or below the 16MB line; this is indicated by an (E) preceding the location name, such as (E)LSQA.

- FPROT indicates fetch protection.

- DREF indicates disabled reference storage; this will be discussed in the next chapter, along with fetch protection.

- SWA stands for Scheduler Work Area.

Note that subpools provide MVS with an easy method of grouping control blocks together that have unique characteristics (e.g., fixed). Also, please remember that subpool zero is not the same as key zero storage!

4.1.2   The STORAGE macro

STORAGE is a newer macro than GETMAIN and FREEMAIN. It uses MVS cross-memory facilities to receive control, rather than the SVCs of GETMAIN and FREEMAIN. (This takes the form of a Program Call instruction—refer to

TABLE 4.2 Storage Subpools

Subpool #	Location	Key	Freed	Attributes
0-127	Private	Job	Freed at step end	
203	ELSQA	0	Freed at TCB end	DREF
204	ELSQA	0	Freed at step end	DREF
205	ELSQA	0	Freed explicitly	DREF
213	ELSQA	0	Freed at TCB end	DREF, FPROT
214	ELSQA	0	Freed at step end	DREF, FPROT
215	ELSQA	0	Freed explicitly	DREF, FPROT
223	ELSQA	0	Freed at TCB end	FPROT
224	ELSQA	0	Freed at step end	FPROT
225	ELSQA	0	Freed at TCB end	FPROT
226	SQA	0		Fixed
227	(E)CSA	User		Fixed, FPROT
228	(E)CSA	User		Fixed
229	Private	User	Freed at TCB end	FPROT
230	Private	User	Freed at TCB end	
231	(E)CSA	User		FPROT
233	(E)LSQA	0	See 253	Fixed
234	(E)LSQA	0	See 254	Fixed
235	(E)LSQA	0	See 255	Fixed
236	Private	1	Freed at TCB end	SWA
237	Private	1	Freed at TCB end	SWA
239	(E)SQA	0	Freed explicitly	FPROT
240	Private	Job	See 250/Step end	FPROT
241	(E)CSA	User		
245	(E)SQA	0	Freed explicitly	Fixed
247	ESQA	0	Freed explicitly	DREF
248	ESQA	0	Freed explicitly	DREF
250	Private	Job	User key storage acquired by key 0 tasks	FPROT
251	Private	Job	Programs/step end	
252	Private	0	Auth'd reentrant modules/step end	
253	(E)LSQA	0	Freed at TCB end	
254	(E)LSQA	0	Freed at step end	
255	(E)LSQA	0	Freed at TCB end	

MVS Power Programming for an example.) STORAGE is essentially a GET-MAIN/FREEMAIN replacement; any new VSM services might be expected to show up in this macro.

Like many newer macros, STORAGE includes extensive information as comments within the macro source itself. Thus, even if you don't have the appropriate manual handy, you can just browse SYS1.MACLIB(STORAGE) and determine what each operand of the macro requires. I highly recommend this as a research method.

As a general point, wherever GETMAIN is used in an explanation in this chapter, you can assume that the explanation also applies to STORAGE. The same will be true for FREEMAIN.

4.1.3 Cell pool services

One of the recurring performance problems in many software environments is the time spent acquiring and releasing storage. This applies to both GET-MAIN and FREEMAIN, as well as to the equivalent services in other environments, such as malloc in C. The performance "hit" can be especially severe when small blocks of storage are rapidly and repetitively acquired and freed.

The early deliveries of MVS were no stranger to this effect, and IBM developed a separate set of VSM services to address this. These provide access to a type of storage called a *cell pool*. The characteristics of a cell pool are:

- Storage is frequently acquired and released.
- Storage requests are always for the same size area.
- A common storage area is available to anchor the cell pool.

Ideally, a common routine will also be available to release the entire pool when it's no longer needed, but this doesn't always happen.

Invocation of cell pool services is through a macro called CPOOL. CPOOL has operands to specify the number and size of the individual "cells" within the pool, along with other normal VSM data, such as subpool number. CPOOL also provides services such as getting a new cell, freeing a previously gotten cell, getting pool usage information, and so forth.

Cell pools appear fairly regularly in MVS, although not all use CPOOL. The ASCBSVRB field in the ASCB is an example of MVS usage of a cell pool—in this case for SVC request blocks, which tend to be frequently needed and short-lived.

The performance advantage of CPOOL for assembler programs can't be overstated. Storage management is the most frequently used system service in most assembler programs. The CPU time advantage of CPOOL compared to a GETMAIN-FREEMAIN pair is roughly 20 to one.

There are also two macros, GETPOOL and FREEPOOL, that might seem to be related to cell pool services. In fact, they're related to I/O buffer services and aren't part of VSM.

4.1.4 VSM miscellaneous services

VSM also provides three macros that replace the functions of scanning all the VSM control blocks to extract information: VSMREGN, VSMLIST, and VSMLOC.

These macros are especially useful in implementing code to meet some common requirements. For example, VSMLOC can be used to validate addresses. It can also be used to determine the subpool and protection key of a control block. Although VSMLOC runs in either 24-bit or 31-bit mode, it assumes that all addresses are 31 bits.

You can use VSMREGN to determine your program's region size, and possibly prevent a storage-related ABEND (e.g., 80A). And you can use VSMLIST to locate all the storage in a specified subpool; this is often useful to determine what storage needs to be freed.

The VSMLIST macro can be used to obtain detailed storage usage information. VSM supplies a mapping macro, IGGVSMD, discussed later in this chapter. An example of VSMLOC is as follows:

```
VSMLOC    CSECT
VSMLOC    AMODE   31
VSMLOC    RMODE   ANY
          BAKR    R14,0
          LR      R10,R15
          USING   VSMLOC,R10
          USING   PSA,R0
          LA      R13,ASAVE
          SPACE 1
*******************************************************************
*                                                                 *
*         THE FOLLOWING CODE SETS UP ADDRESSES TO SHOW HOW THE     *
*         'TESTADDR' ROUTINE WORKS.                                *
*                                                                 *
*******************************************************************
*         GET A VALID ADDRESS IN SQA
          L       R1,PSAAOLD          GET ASCB ADDRESS
          BAS     R11,TESTADDR        LINK TO ADDRESS TEST ROUTINE
          SPACE 1
*         DISPLAY RESULTS
          CVD     R15,DWD1            CONVERT RETURN CODE TO DECIMAL
          OI      DWD1+7,X'0F'        SET SIGN
          UNPK    WTO1+22(2),DWD1     UNPACK INTO WTO
          N       R0,=X'000000FF'     ZERO ALL BUT ONE BYTE
          CVD     R0,DWD1             CONVERT SUBPOOL TO DECIMAL
          OI      DWD1+7,X'0F'        SET SIGN
          UNPK    WTO1+34(3),DWD1     UNPACK INTO WTO
WTO1      WTO     ' RETURN CODE: __ SUBPOOL: ___      ',ROUTCDE=(2,11)
          SPACE 1
*         GET AN INVALID ADDRESS (NOT IN SQA)
          L       R1,=X'40404040'     BLANKS TO SIMULATE AN ERROR
          BAS     R11,TESTADDR        LINK TO ADDRESS TEST ROUTINE
          SPACE 1
*         DISPLAY RESULTS
          N       R0,=X'000000FF'     ZERO ALL BUT ONE BYTE
          CVD     R0,DWD1             CONVERT TO DECIMAL
          OI      DWD1+7,X'0F'        SET SIGN
          UNPK    WTO2+34(3),DWD1     UNPACK INTO WTO
          CVD     R15,DWD1            CONVERT TO DECIMAL
          OI      DWD1+7,X'0F'        SET SIGN
          UNPK    WTO2+22(2),DWD1     UNPACK INTO WTO
WTO2      WTO     ' RETURN CODE: __ SUBPOOL: ___      ',ROUTCDE=(2,11)
```

```
          SPACE 1
*         RETURN TO MVS
          PR   ,                        RETURN TO CALLER
          SPACE 3
*********************************************************************
*                                                                   *
*         ROUTINE TO VALIDATE ADDRESS IN SQA                        *
*                                                                   *
*********************************************************************
          SPACE 3
TESTADDR  EQU    *
          SR     R0,R0                  CLEAR REGISTER ZERO
          L      R2,X'10'               GET CVT ADDRESS
          USING  CVT,R2                 ESTABLISH ADDRESSABILITY
          L      R3,CVTGDA              GET GLOBAL DATA AREA ADDRESS
          USING  GDA,R3                 ESTABLISH ADDRESSABILITY
          DROP   R2                     END CVT ADDRESSABILITY
          L      R4,GDASQA              GET STARTING ADDRESS OF SQA
          LA     R15,8                  SET UP BAD RETURN CODE
          CR     R1,R4                  COMPARE ADDRESSES
          BL     DONE                   ADDRESS BELOW CSA — DONE
          A      R4,GDASQASZ            ADD SIZE OF SQA
          CR     R1,R4                  COMPARE ADDRESSES
          BNL    DONE                   ADDRESS PAST END OF SQA...
          SPACE 1
*         WE KNOW THE ADDRESS IS IN SQA — ISSUE VSMLOC TO SEE IF
*         IT'S STILL VALID
          LR     R2,R1                  ADDRESS CANT BE IN REG 1
          VSMLOC SQA,AREA=((2),256),  TEST ADDRESS IN REG 2 LENGTH 256 X
                 LINKAGE=SYSTEM          USES PROGRAM CALL
DONE      EQU    *
          DROP   R3
          BR     R11                    RETURN TO CALLER
          SPACE 1
*         DATA AREAS
          CNOP   0,4
DWD1      DC     D'0'
ASAVE     DC     F'0',C'F1SA',16F'0'
R0        EQU    0
R1        EQU    1
R2        EQU    2
R3        EQU    3
R4        EQU    4
R5        EQU    5
R6        EQU    6
R7        EQU    7
R8        EQU    8
R9        EQU    9
R10       EQU    10
R11       EQU    11
R12       EQU    12
R13       EQU    13
R14       EQU    14
R15       EQU    15
          SPACE 1
*         DSECT MACROS
          CVT    DSECT=YES
          IHAPSA
          IHAGDA
          END    VSMLOC
```

4.2 VSM Data Areas

VSM involves a large number of control blocks; I'll outline the purpose of 15 of them here. The control block names are shown in the following list. For our purposes, they're organized into those used throughout MVS, those that apply only to a particular address space or task, and those that might appear in either area. This organization is fairly arbitrary; several other logical groupings are possible. In addition to these, MVS/ESA 4.3 added VSM services and data areas used to support monitoring of common storage usage; these are discussed separately later.

- System-wide data areas
  - ~ Global Data Area (GDA), previously covered
  - ~ Region Request Element (RGR), for V=R
  - ~ Subpool Table (SPT); describes CSA
  - ~ Subpool Translation Table (SPTT), subpool characteristics
- Address-space-associated control blocks
  - ~ Local Data Area (LDA), like GDA for ASCB
  - ~ Address Queue Anchor Stack (AQST); see description
- Task-associated control blocks
  - ~ Subpool Queue Element (SPQE); describes a subpool
  - ~ Subpool Queue Anchor (SPQA), addresses of SPQE chains
- Common control blocks
  - ~ Free Queue Element (FQE); describes free areas under 4K
  - ~ Free Block Queue Element (FBQE); describes free 4K chunks
  - ~ Cell Pool Anchor Block (CPAB), cell pool characteristics
  - ~ Descriptor Queue Element (DQE); describes allocated pages
  - ~ Address Queue Anchor Table (AQAT); used with GDA and LDA
  - ~ Size Queue Anchor Table (SQAT); used with GDA and LDA
  - ~ Double Free Element (DFE); used with AQAT and SQAT

4.2.1 System-wide VSM data areas

These control blocks are useful in determining storage sizes and usage for an entire MVS system.

4.2.1.1 Global Data Area (GDA)

This control block was discussed in chapter 2, but will be covered here again because of its position in VSM. The GDA describes the SQA and CSA storage queues, so it's an anchor for several other VSM control blocks for these storage areas. The GDA specifically covers subpools 226, 239, 245, 247, and 248.

As an anchor point, the GDA contains the addresses of the AQAT and SQAT control blocks, which are described later in this chapter. It also contains the addresses of the DFE queues for the AQAT and SQAT, also described later.

As a repository for information, the GDA has several fields of interest. One is GDACSARE—the remaining CSA/SQA storage value. This is useful when monitoring storage availability; running out of CSA or SQA storage is generally pretty grim. Another field is GDAPVTSZ, which is the maximum size of the private area. Several other fields were covered in chapter 2. Figure 4.1 shows the mapping of storage by the GDA.

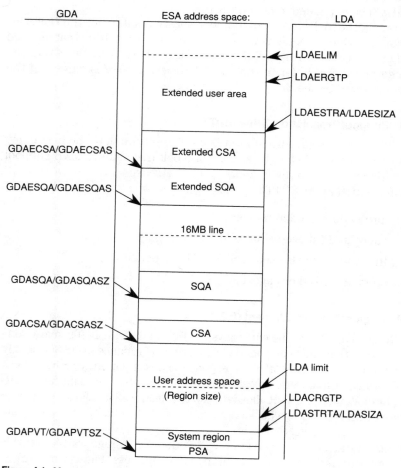

Figure 4.1 Mapping of storage by the GDA.

4.2.1.2 Subpool Table (SPT)

The subpool table is accessed through the GDA. It describes the allocated areas within the CSA. This includes pointers to the appropriate DQE and FQE control blocks, which will be discussed later in this chapter.

The SPT also provides a mechanism to separate storage by its underlying real storage requirement. GETMAIN and STORAGE provide a LOC operand, which specifies the location—above or below the 16MB line—of the requested storage. These macros also provide LOC options to specify the actual real storage used to implement or "back" the virtual storage.

The reasons for this lie in the not-so-distant past. When MVS/XA introduced 31-bit addressing, some software products couldn't handle addresses above the 24-bit 16MB line. (Typical reasons for this related to I/O processing, and will be explained in chapter 8.)

As a result, the SPT has to maintain two sets of pointers for the DQEs for CSA subpools. One list anchors the page descriptions for those that must be backed by storage below the 16MB line, and the other covers those that can be placed anywhere. Refer to the IHASPT macro for a description of the subpools covered by the SPT.

4.2.1.3 Subpool Translation Table (SPTT)

The SPTT doesn't have a distributed DSECT description, to the best of my knowledge. The SPTT is a global control block that defines MVS subpool characteristics. Refer to the *Diagnosis: Data Areas* manuals for a description. Information in the SPTT includes:

- Fetch protection characteristics.
- Where allocated (above/below 16MB).
- What the storage key is used (PSW, TCB, or specific).
- If the storage is fixed or pageable.

4.2.1.4 Region Request Element (RGR)

The RGR is an artifact of the early days of MVS. In the late 1970s, many software packages that had been coded to optimize performance in OS/360 simply performed unacceptably in MVS. In response to this situation, MVS included a service termed virtual=real, or V=R. This is implemented through the ADDR-SPC= parameter in JCL. V=R allowed a job to execute all its allocated storage addresses with real storage backing, which essentially eliminated page faults for the programs running there.

The disadvantage to this service was that the real storage wasn't available for the other users of the system. This could lead to less-than-optimal (okay, dismal) performance for the rest of the MVS work. As a result, it's probably not a practice to be encouraged in the future.

V=R regions needed contiguous real storage. This means that all the real storage had to be together, rather than spread randomly throughout the total storage of the machine. Large quantities of contiguous real pages usually weren't available, however, which led to the need for the RGR.

The RGR represents waiting V=R requests. It contains information such as the ASCB pointer for the waiting address space and the requested region size. The RGR queue address is located in the GDA; its DSECT is IHARGR. There's a related control block called the Get Region Work Table, with a DSECT macro name of IHAGWT.

4.2.2 Address-space-related VSM control blocks

VSM also retains a series of related control blocks describing storage within each address space. These are mostly common to other VSM uses, and will be described elsewhere. The one control block that's related to address spaces is the Local Data Area.

4.2.2.1 Local Data Area (LDA)

The LDA contains information relating to regions and address spaces. Some selected fields include:

- LDAREGRQ (region size requested)
- LDALIMIT (region size limit)
- LDAVVRG (high used value, also called "high water mark")
- LDAELIM and LDAEVVRG for extended region

The LDA also includes several subpool anchors. The pointers are to VSM control blocks, described later. The DSECT macro is IHALDA. The LDA information fields are useful in setting up GETMAIN requests when the maximum size available is needed.

4.2.3 Task-associated VSM control blocks

VSM maintains a far more numerous set of control blocks to hold task-related storage management information. Most of these are very old control blocks, and were present in OS/360.

4.2.3.1 Subpool Queue Element (SPQE)

The SPQE is used to describe each storage subpool used by a TCB. The SPQEs are chained together in a singly linked list. The beginning address of the chain is in the TCBMSS field of the TCB. An SPQE is built for a task's storage requests when one is needed. There's one SPQE per combination of subpool number and storage key used by the task. Thus, each GETMAIN for a new combination of subpool and storage key results in an SPQE being constructed. The SPQE contains the address of the SPQA.

Additionally, the SPQE contains a flag that indicates if the subpool and key combination is shared with another task, or if it's unique. Subpools of storage are normally freed by VSM when the owning task ends; "shared" subpools aren't freed until the last TCB using them ends. The DSECT for the SPQE is IHASPQE.

4.2.3.2 Subpool Queue Anchor (SPQA)

This control block is addressed by the SPQE. Its purpose is to hold the addresses of the DQEs for the specific combination of subpool and key described by the SPQE. The SPQA actually describes three sets of DQEs.

The first set of DQEs is for storage with virtual addresses below 16MB that must be backed by real storage below the 16MB line. The next is for storage with virtual addresses below 16MB that can be backed anywhere. The final set is for virtual storage above the 16MB line that can be backed anywhere. The mapping macro for the SPQA is IHASPQA.

4.2.3.3 Descriptor Queue Element (DQE)

The Descriptor Queue Element describes allocated pages of virtual storage. Its mapping macro is IHADQE. VSM creates a DQE whenever a GETMAIN request needs a new 4K page. Thus, if you issue a GETMAIN for 4096 bytes, you'll probably cause a new DQE to be created or an existing DQE to change.

Since many GETMAIN requests are for less than 4K of storage, VSM maintains a separate control block called the FQE to keep track of the unused space within each partially used page. The DQE contains a pointer to the FQEs for the free space within its area.

The DQE includes two fields that define the pages it maps. The first is DQEAREA—the virtual address of the allocated pages. The other, DQE-SIZE, contains the size of the allocated area. DQEs are chained in a singly linked list. The mapping macro is IHADQE.

4.2.4 Common VSM control blocks

The control blocks within this final section are referred to, or contained in, the control blocks listed previously.

4.2.4.1 Free Queue Element (FQE)

The FQE describes an area of free space within pages already described by a DQE. The FQE includes two fields that describe the free area. FQESIZE holds the size of the free storage and FQEAREA has the address of the free storage area. FQEs are maintained in a doubly linked list.

Since FQEs are used to describe free space within a virtual page, the total free space amount in FQESIZE is limited. The theoretical maximum should be 8176 bytes; this would arise if an 8K area was gotten and then all but the first and last eight bytes were freed. If the free space includes a complete page, the FQE and DQE should be split and the complete page made available for other subpools. The mapping macro for the FQE is IHAFQE.

4.2.4.2 Free Block Queue Element (FBQE)

The DQE and FQE describe virtual pages allocated by GETMAIN requests. However, pages not currently in use are described by another control block, the Free Block Queue Element. The FBQE describes free pages within a private area (region) of the CSA. It's pointed to by the GDA (for the CSA) or the LDA (for private areas), and it includes the field FBQESIZE, the size of the free pages(s) in bytes, and FBQEAREA, the address of the free pages(s).

The combination of DQEs and FBQEs should completely describe a private area. FBQEs are kept in a singly linked list. The mapping macro is IHAFBQE. Having described the DQE, FQE, and FBQE, I'll describe how VSM actually uses these control blocks when allocating storage.

The combination of the FQE and DQE is used for any storage allocations of less than one page. VSM allocates storage by searching for a DQE with the combination of subpool and key that's being requested. If none is found, VSM will create a new DQE, scan the FBQEs to locate a page, update the FBQE to reflect that a page is being used, and create an FQE to describe the unused space.

For storage requests requiring several pages, VSM scans the FBQEs to locate the needed virtual storage. It then scans the SPQEs for the combination of subpool and key in the request. If none is found, VSM will create a new SPQA and SPQE and add them to the chain of DQEs. If one is found, VSM will update the chain of DQEs from the SPQA.

If possible, an existing DQE will be used. If pages are allocated whose address happens to be adjacent to the end of the area mapped by an existing DQE, that existing DQE will be updated. If the new storage isn't next to any existing storage within the chain of DQEs for that SPQA, a new DQE will be constructed. An FQE is similarly added or updated as appropriate. Figure 4.2 shows the relationship of the DQE, FBQE, FQE, SPQA, and SPQE.

4.2.4.3 Address Queue Anchor Table (AQAT)

One performance problem within MVS has been the CPU time spent in acquiring and releasing storage within the SQA. This storage area is heavily used, so wasted time during a GETMAIN affects the performance of the

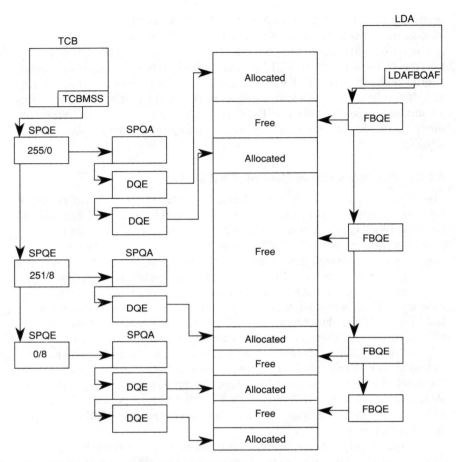

Figure 4.2   Relationship of DQE/FBQE/FQE/SPQA/SPQE.

complete MVS system. At the same time, storage in the SQA is a limited resource, and running low is highly undesirable.

In general, storage allocation follows one of two strategies: first fit or
best fit. *First fit* means that the storage manager allocates the first storage large enough to meet the size requested. *Best fit* means that the storage manager searches all free storage, looking for an exact size match; if
none is found, the smallest free area that will hold the requested size is
chosen.

First-fit strategies are usually faster, but use memory less efficiently.
Best-fit strategies are usually slower, but make the best use of the available
memory. The problem with choosing a strategy for the SQA was that the
method had to be both fast and efficient.

To accomplish these contradictory goals, IBM created three control blocks to manage the free storage within SQA: the AQAT, SQAT, and DFEs. (The same technique is used for LSQA.)

When allocating storage with a best-fit algorithm, the closest-sized free storage area must be chosen. Normally, this requires that—on average—half the free storage areas must be examined. (Sometimes the right size is found early in the scan and sometimes later, but the average tends to be halfway through.) IBM enhanced the performance of this step by describing SQA-free storage with DFEs.

DFEs are maintained as a doubly linked list. Each DFE describes the starting address and size of a free area. To optimize search performance, the DFEs are in order by size. Thus, if a perfect match isn't found, the closest match will be next on the list. Smaller requests tend to find their storage quickly, and only the largest-sized requests will need to scan the entire chain. The index into the DFEs for this search is the SQAT control block.

When the time comes to free storage, however, this strategy isn't optimum. When storage is released, the newly freed area should be merged with an existing area to make a larger free area if possible. To do this, the beginning and ending addresses of the newly freed area are compared to every other free area. If the starting address is adjacent to an existing free area, the two are merged into one larger free area. If the ending address is adjacent to an existing free area, the two are also merged into a larger area. Since this strategy must also handle where the freed area is between two existing free areas (i.e., three free areas must be merged), this requires a complete scan of the free area list.

IBM's design also addresses this potential problem. It does so by keeping a duplicate chain through the DFEs. This duplicate chain is ordered by address, rather than by size. The effect of this design choice is that free space can be merged quickly, without having to scan the complete list. In general, lower free storage addresses are found and merged earlier than higher ones. This effect is useful for the LSQA, where storage allocation starts from the top of the region. The AQAT control block serves as the anchor for the free area address scan.

The AQAT is addressed through the GDA or the LDA. The GDA contains three AQATs; one each for subpools 239, 247, and 248. Its mapping macro is IHAAQAT.

4.2.4.4   Size Queue Anchor Table (SQAT)

The SQAT is similar to the AQAT described previously, but it maintains the chain of free areas ordered by the size of the free storage. This allows storage to be allocated on a best-fit basis more efficiently. It includes two fields of interest in addition to the DFE addresses. The first, SQATMAX, holds the size of the largest free storage area. This avoids the need to scan the entire

DFE chain if a request is too large for the available free space. The second field, SQATCNT, holds the number of free storage areas, thus providing a loop counter. The SQAT DSECT is IHASQAT.

4.2.4.5 Double Free Element (DFE)

The DFE is used with the AQAT and SQAT. It describes free areas within SQA and LSQA subpools. DFEs are maintained on a double doubly linked list. Each DFE contains forward and backward chain pointers for the storage address queue (AQAT). Each DFE also holds forward and backward chain pointers for the storage size queue (SQAT). The DFE includes the fields DFESIZE (size of the free storage) and DFEAREA (the address of the free storage). The DFE DSECT name is IHADFE.

4.2.4.6 Region Descriptor (RD)

The Region Descriptor serves two functions. One is to describe the size and starting address of a user region. (There's also an RD for the CSA.) The second is to provide an anchor point for the FBQEs describing the free space within the region. The mapping macro is named IHARD. The RD contains two fields that define a region. The first holds the region starting address (RDSTART). The second holds the region size (RDSIZE).

The RD is actually located within the LDA control block, and the LDA contains three Region Descriptors. The first is for the actual region address space, beginning at label LDAFBQAF. The extended address space (above 16MB) is described beginning at label LDAEFBAF. Finally, the LDA contains an RD for the system region beginning at label LDAFBQSF. The CSA is described by an RD within the GDA. This begins at label GDAFBQCF.

4.2.4.7 Cell Pool Anchor Block (CPAB)

The CPAB contains cell pool characteristics information. There might be more than one CPAB for a cell pool if it has been extended, i.e., has had more cells added. The cell pool was discussed earlier with the CPOOL macro. The mapping macro name is IHACPAB.

4.2.5 VSM data areas used to monitor CSA usage

A recurring problem in MVS has been management of the common storage areas, particularly the CSA. A number of third-party monitors have been developed over time to address this requirement; most have needed to modify VSM code to track what jobs requested CSA storage. IBM modified VSM in MVS/ESA release 4.3 to provide a cleaner interface for this. The following five control blocks are provided in support of this service:

- Common Area User Block (DSECT IGVCAUB)
- GQE Getmained Queue Element (IGVGQE)
- GQE Anchor (DSECT IGVGQAT)
- VSM Address Space Block (IGVVAB)

The function of this code is to keep track of the storage requirements of individual jobs and of the system as a whole for both SQA and CSA. Due to the frequent use of CSA and SQA, tracking storage usage involves additional CPU time; many installations won't want to use this at all times. Thus, CSA and SQA tracking is controlled through the SYS1.PARMLIB (DIAG*xx*) member, rather than being a full-time feature of VSM.

VSM will categorize each storage request into type, such as job related or MVS system related. If jobs terminate without releasing the CSA or SQA storage they have acquired, the storage is moved to the unknown queue.

The IGVCAUB DSECT contains extensive information regarding use of this feature, and should be consulted. The following shows a simple example of this feature:

```
         TITLE 'DISPLAY CSA/SQA USAGE INFO'
FIG0404  CSECT
FIG0404  AMODE 31
FIG0404  RMODE ANY
         BAKR  R14,0                 SAVE REGS
         LR    R12,R15               SET UP
         USING FIG0404,R12             BASE REGISTER
         LA    R13,MYSAVE              SET UP SAVE AREA
         SPACE 1
         USING PSA,R0                  ESTABLISH ADDRESSABILITY
         L     R3,FLCCVT               GET CVT POINTER
         USING CVT,R3                  ESTABLISH ADDRESSABILITY
         L     R4,CVTGDA               GET GLOBAL DATA AREA ADDRESS
         USING GDA,R4                  ESTABLISH ADDRESSABILITY
         SPACE 1
*        DISPLAY AMOUNT OF CSA AND SQA IN USE
         LA    R1,MSG0403A             ADDRESS OF MESSAGE
         USING WPL,R1                  ESTABLISH ADDRESSABILITY
         L     R0,GDACSASZ             GET CSA SIZE
         CVD   R0,DOUBLEWD             CONVERT TO DECIMAL
         OI    DOUBLEWD+7,X'0F'        SET SIGN BITS
         UNPK  WPLTXT+26(8),DOUBLEWD   UNPACK INTO MESSAGE
         L     R0,GDASQASZ             GET SQA SIZE OF BYTES USED
         CVD   R0,DOUBLEWD             CONVERT TO DECIMAL
         OI    DOUBLEWD+7,X'0F'        SET SIGN BITS
         UNPK  WPLTXT+40(8),DOUBLEWD   UNPACK INTO MESSAGE
MSG0403A WTO   'MVSCB0403A TOTAL CSA: 26...... SQA: 40...... ',   X
               ROUTCDE=(11)
         LA    R1,MSG0403B             ADDRESS OF MESSAGE
         L     R0,GDA_CSA_ALLOC        GET NUMBER OF BYTES USED
         CVD   R0,DOUBLEWD             CONVERT TO DECIMAL
         OI    DOUBLEWD+7,X'0F'        SET SIGN BITS
         UNPK  WPLTXT+30(8),DOUBLEWD   UNPACK INTO MESSAGE
         L     R0,GDA_SQA_ALLOC        GET NUMBER OF BYTES USED
```

```
              CVD    R0,DOUBLEWD                  CONVERT TO DECIMAL
              OI     DOUBLEWD+7,X'0F'             SET SIGN BITS
              UNPK   WPLTXT+44(8),DOUBLEWD        UNPACK INTO MESSAGE
MSG0403B WTO   'MVSCB0403B ALLOCATED CSA: 30...... SQA: 44...... ',X
              ROUTCDE=(11)
              DROP   R1                           END MESSAGE ADDRESSABILITY
              SPACE 1
*             CHECK THAT CSA AND/OR SQA TRACKING ARE BEING USED.
              TM     GDAFLGS,GDACSATR+GDASQATR    TEST BITS
              BO     CHECK_STG                    ON -- GO DISPLAY A USER
MSG0403C WTO   'MVSCB0403C CSA/SQA TRACKING NOT IN USE',ROUTCDE=(11)
              B      CHECK_DONE                   STOP
              SPACE 1
CHECK_STG     EQU   *
              L      R5,GDASCAUB                  GET ADDRESS OF SYSTEM CAUB
              USING CAUB,R5                        ESTABLISH ADDRESSABILITY
              LA     R1,MSG0403D                  ADDRESS OF MESSAGE
              USING WPL,R1                         ESTABLISH ADDRESSABILITY
              L      R0,CAUB_CSA_BELOW            GET BYTES OF SYSTEM CSA STG
              CVD    R0,DOUBLEWD                  CONVERT TO DECIMAL
              OI     DOUBLEWD+7,X'0F'             SET SIGN BITS
              UNPK   WPLTXT+24(8),DOUBLEWD        UNPACK INTO MESSAGE
              L      R0,CAUB_SQA_BELOW            GET BYTES OF SYSTEM SQA STG
              CVD    R0,DOUBLEWD                  CONVERT TO DECIMAL
              OI     DOUBLEWD+7,X'0F'             SET SIGN BITS
              UNPK   WPLTXT+38(8),DOUBLEWD        UNPACK INTO MESSAGE
MSG0403D WTO   'MVSCB0403D   SYSTEM CSA: 24...... SQA: 38...... ',X
              ROUTCDE=(11)
              LA     R1,MSG0403E                  ADDRESS OF MESSAGE
              TM     CAUB_DATAINCOMPLETE,CAUB_CSADATAINCOMPLETE
              BZ     CHK_SQA_INCOMPLETE           OK -- CHECK SQA BIT
              MVC    WPLTXT+15(3),=C'CSA'         NO -- SET IN MESSAGE
              MVI    INCOMPLETE_FLAG,1            AND SET OUR OWN FLAG
CHK_SQA_INCOMPLETE    EQU   *
              TM     CAUB_DATAINCOMPLETE,CAUB_SQADATAINCOMPLETE
              BZ     MSG0403D                     OK -- CHECK SQA BIT
              MVC    WPLTXT+18(3),=C'SQA'         NO -- SET IN MESSAGE
              MVI    INCOMPLETE_FLAG,1            AND SET OUR OWN FLAG
CHK_MESSAGE_FLAG    EQU   *
              CLI    INCOMPLETE_FLAG,1            CHECK OUR FLAG
              BNE    CHECK_DONE                   NOT ON -- NO MESSAGE
MSG0403E WTO   'MVSCB0403E    COUNT MAY BE IN ERROR',      X
              ROUTCDE=(11)
CHECK_DONE    EQU   *
              SPACE 1
RETURN        EQU   *
              L      R15,RETURN_CODE
              PR
              EJECT
*             DATA AREAS
MYSAVE   DC    F'0',C'F1SA',16F'0'   ESA FORMAT SAVE AREA
RETURN_CODE   DC   F'0'
DOUBLEWD DC    D'0'
INCOMPLETE_FLAG    DC   X'00'
              SPACE 1
              LTORG
              SPACE 1
              PRINT ON,NOGEN
*             DEFINE PREFIXED STORAGE AREA DSECT
              IHAPSA
              SPACE 2
```

```
*             DEFINE CVT DSECT
              CVT  DSECT=YES
              SPACE 2
*             DEFINE GDA DSECT
              IHAGDA
              SPACE 2
*             DEFINE CAUB DSECT
              IGVCAUB
              SPACE 2
*             DEFINE WTO PARAMETER LIST
              IEZWPL
              SPACE 2
*             REGISTER EQUATES
*
R0            EQU  0
R1            EQU  1
R2            EQU  2
R3            EQU  3
R4            EQU  4
R5            EQU  5
R6            EQU  6
R7            EQU  7
R8            EQU  8
R9            EQU  9
R10           EQU  10
R11           EQU  11
R12           EQU  12
R13           EQU  13
R14           EQU  14
R15           EQU  15
              END  FIG0404
```

4.3 Summary

Virtual storage management provides several services to MVS programs, including GETMAIN, FREEMAIN, STORAGE, CPOOL, and VSMLIST/VSM-LOC/VSMREGN. VSM manages both system-wide (global) and address-space-specific (local) storage.

Among VSM control blocks, the GDA and LDA serve as the main global and local starting points. A large number of control blocks for allocated and free storage can be located from these.

The concept of subpools is fundamental to understanding VSM. Subpools are arbitrarily numbered from 0 to 255. The range of 0–127 is reserved for application programs. Subpools 128 and above are assigned to MVS system usages, and can be in the requester's private area or in commonly address-able storage (CSA/SQA).

4.4 Things to Do

- Write a program to determine if an address is in SQA, CSA, LSQA, ESQA, or ECSA. Use the GDA and LDA address fields to determine where an address falls. Base this on the sample code shown previously in the chapter.

- Review the *System Diagnosis: Reference* manual listing of MVS sub-pools.
- Modify the program in the first item to display the size of the private and extended private areas, along with the current size of SQA and CSA.

Chapter

5

Control Blocks for
Real Storage Management

This chapter continues the discussion of storage management in general. With the virtual storage overview in mind, we can now turn to the MVS services and data areas needed to support the underlying central storage, in the MVS component called real storage management.

Since real storage management (henceforth called RSM) must periodically save and retrieve virtual pages, it works closely with another component of MVS, which is actually responsible for the paging. This is auxiliary storage management, or ASM.

5.1 Real Storage Management Overview

RSM isn't as well documented as several of the other components discussed in this book. It is, however, characterized by its services, its data areas, and the System/370 hardware features used to implement it. RSM (and ASM) require that you access licensed IBM material for a full explanation; thus, in the data area discussion I'll direct you to selected data areas that aren't documented in one of the SYS1 libraries.

5.1.1 RSM services

RSM services are implicit in MVS, specifically in assigning real storage in response to program exceptions (page faults). This service must release unused real storage (paging out) and provide information to the MVS Systems

Resource Manager. RSM also provides some macro instructions for explicit services.

5.1.1.1 Virtual storage overview

The virtual storage feature in IBM's System/370 processors was first made available in 1971, in the S/370 models 155-II and 165-II. IBM used a two-level virtual storage approach. First, virtual memory was divided into segments, which were either 64K or 1MB in size. Each segment was then divided into pages of 2K or 4K. Various flavors of IBM operating systems (OS/VS2, OS/VS1, DOS/VSE, and VM) used different combinations of segment and page sizes. For MVS, the current values are 1MB segments and 4K pages. Pages are also called frames in some RSM contexts.

The S/370 hardware can translate a virtual address into the corresponding real address. To do so, the hardware must know where the segments and pages are. The starting point for all this information is control register 1, which holds the address of the current segment table. In turn, each segment table consists of an array of four-byte entries that are pointers to page tables. The page tables contain the real storage address of the actual page being referenced.

The actual process is much more complicated than the preceding paragraph implies. Both the segment tables and page tables have numerous switch bits, which further describe the status and type of the page. An additional characteristic is that the addresses are all real storage addresses, rather than the virtual storage addresses you're familiar with. This is a complicating factor, as you've seen before. (For example, the PSA stores both virtual and real addresses for the PCCA and LCCA.)

Since RSM services are so central to MVS, RSM has appeared in the control blocks I've previously discussed. For example, the ASCBSTOR field holds the contents of control register 1 for each address space. This can be used to locate segment table information, although it contains a real storage address rather than a virtual storage address. Similarly, the LDARSVPT field contains the address of the page table for its associated address space.

RSM is responsible for maintaining the segment table and page table for each address space. RSM updates these tables in response to two types of events. The first is an explicit request to allocate real storage, either through a branch-entered service or through an RSM page services macro. The second is an unanticipated storage request, i.e., a page fault.

The term *page fault* actually covers two types of events. Both arise when a program uses an address for which there's no corresponding real storage frame. This condition is indicated by a bit in a page table entry that marks the page as invalid. (The specific layout of segment and page table entries will be discussed in section 5.1.3.)

When this occurs, RSM must allocate a page frame to provide real storage to match the virtual storage being used. Once this is done, RSM must then determine if the page was previously used or if it's new. If it was previously used, the page must be brought in (paged in) by ASM. If it's being used for the first time (for example, immediately after a GETMAIN), RSM just has to allocate the page.

To allocate a page, the RSM must usually take back a page that was previously allocated to another address space (called *page stealing*). This requires that the RSM have some way of determining which pages are the best to steal. The RSM uses a least recently used (LRU) algorithm for this, which steals the pages that haven't been used for the longest time.

The LRU algorithm requires that RSM periodically look at each real storage frame to determine if it has been used. If it hasn't been used since the last time the RSM checked, RSM updates the unreferenced interval count (UIC). When RSM needs to steal a page, it can just search for the frame with the highest UIC value, page out that frame, and then reallocate it to the address space that had the original page fault.

Information regarding each page is retained in a data area called the Page Frame Table Entry, or PFTE. Unfortunately, I couldn't find any documentation for this process in MVS/ESA. (This control block is documented as going OCO in the *MVS/XA Data Areas* manuals.) The layout for an older version is available in the *Debugging Handbook*, if you have access to it.

5.1.1.2 RSM macro services

RSM provides a number of assembler language macros to invoke various RSM services. These include:

PGLOAD. Brings a page into real storage.

PGOUT. Allows RSM to page out a frame.

PGFIX. Fixes a page in real storage.

PGSER. General page service macro, incorporating previous services.

The *Assembler Development Reference* manual describes these macros.

5.1.2 Real storage management data areas

MVS/ESA doesn't document all the RSM data areas. However, the ones that are documented provide a good source of information regarding the overall real storage picture of the MVS system. The data areas documented by mapping macros in the SYS1 macro libraries are:

- Page Vector Table (IHAPVT)
- RSM Control and Enumeration Area (IARRCE)
- RSM Address Space Block Extension (IARRAX)

Additionally, the *Principles of Operation* manual describes the format of the page and segment tables. It's important to understand these data areas in order to understand RSM concepts. I know of no other SYS1.MODGEN or SYS1.MACLIB data area macros.

5.1.2.1 Page Vector Table

The Page Vector Table (PVT) is described by the IHAPVT macro. There's one PVT per MVS system, and its address is in field CVTPVTP. The PVT holds information that's essential to the operation of RSM, such as the addresses of callable RSM routines, e.g., Page Fix.

Additionally, the PVT contains several fields of interest, which are all related to paging and swapping counts. I suggest that you review the macro itself due to the volume of fields included.

5.1.2.2 RSM Control and Enumeration Area

The RSM Control and Enumeration Area is mapped by DSECT macro IARRCE. There's one RCE per MVS system, and its address is in CVTRCEP. The RCE holds flag, count, and limit fields relating to RSM and ASM activity. These are mainly for use by the System Resources Manager, but are commonly available. The count fields of interest in the RCE include:

RCEPOOL. Number of frames usable in the system.

RCEBELPL. Usable frames below the 16MB line.

RCETOTFX. Total page fix count.

RCEAFC. Total available pages.

RCECOMAL. Total pages allocated to common.

RCECOMPO. Common pages paged out.

The RCE includes numerous other counts, e.g., page reclaims. As with the PVT, the IARRCE macro is well worth investigating. Some limit fields of interest include:

RCEMAXFX. Fix threshold.

RCEDEFFX. Defers page fixes if RCEAFC isn't greater.

RCEAFCLO. Available page low threshold.

RCEAFCOK. Available page OK threshold.

The SRM is notified when any of these limits are exceeded.

5.1.2.3 RSM Address Space Block Extension

The Address Space Block Extension is created by RSM when it sets up the storage for the related address space. The mapping macro is IARRAX, and its address is in ASCBRSME. The purpose of the RSM is to hold address-space-related information and to retain certain address-space-related count fields. Fields of interest include:

RAXFMCT. The count of frames currently in use by this address space.

RAXBELFX. The count of page-fixed frames backed by real storage below 16MB.

RAXDSHWM. The high-water-mark of data space memory allocated to this address space in megabytes.

As with the RCE and PVT, I advise that you review the DSECT macro.

5.1.2.4 Page Service List

The Page Service List is mapped by macro IHAPSL. This DSECT describes a parameter list used in processing PGSER and related macros by RSM. This might be of interest when using or debugging page services macros.

5.1.3 Instructions and CPU features used with RSM

RSM uses several specialized instructions in managing real storage. This section presents an overview of these, along with the System/390 facilities used to support virtual storage.

MVS/ESA virtual storage requires specific virtual storage characteristics. These are controlled by the Translation Format subfield in control register zero, bits 8–12. MVS/ESA requires a value of binary 10110, which specifies 4K pages and a 1MB segment size.

As covered earlier, the basis for virtual storage addressing is the segment table. This is addressed by control register 1, bits 1–19. Since System/390 requires 31-bit addressing, these 19 bits are expanded to 31 bits by adding 12 zero bits on the right. This means that segment tables must always begin on a page boundary. Figure 5.1 shows the layout of control register 1, and Fig. 5.2 illustrates the translation process.

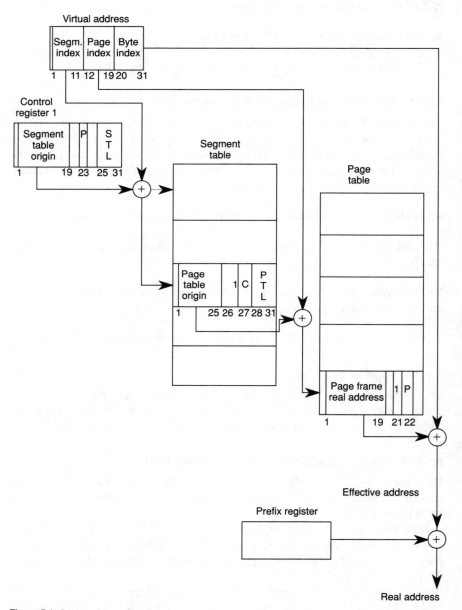

Figure 5.1 Layout of control register 1.

Control register 1:

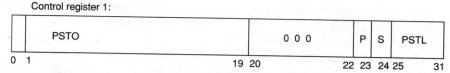

Figure 5.2 Virtual address translation process.

When hardware processes a virtual address, it uses bits 1 through 11 of the virtual address as the segment table index. This is multiplied by four to get the actual segment table entry. Each segment table entry is four bytes long. Within each segment table entry, bits 1 through 25 point to a page table, with zeros appended on the right to make a complete 31-bit address. There's only one segment table per address space. Figure 5.3 shows the layout of a segment table entry.

Within each segment table entry, additional bit settings provide added functions. Bit 26 is the "segment invalid" bit. This indicates that the 1MB of virtual addresses that map to that entry aren't valid. You'll see this when running with a region size more than 2MB less than the actual maximum within a region. For example, if your MVS system's maximum private area size is eight megabytes and you run a program that uses 1.5MB of virtual storage, the segment table would have bit 26 set off in the first two entries, since that storage is used, and the segments would be valid. The next five entries would have bit 26 set on because they represent virtual addresses not accessed during the program's execution. Finally, the next segment table entry would have bit 26 set off; MVS would use part of it for LSQA, even if your program doesn't.

Segment table entry bit 27 is the "common segment" bit. This is used with the segments for SQA, CSA, the nucleus, and LPA—in other words, any storage that's commonly addressable within the MVS storage map.

Finally, segment table entry bits 28 through 31 are the page table length. This is a multiple of 16, so the hardware adds four zero bits on the right to compute the actual address of the page table entry. Figure 5.6, later in this chapter, shows a program to display the beginning part of a segment table.

One characteristic of MVS/ESA that results from this segment table construction is that each MVS/ESA segment table is 8K long. (Two gigabytes divided by 1MB yields 2K segment table entries; each is four bytes long, hence 8K.)

Segment table entry

0	Page table origin		I	C	Page table length
0	1		25 26	27	28 31

Figure 5.3 Format of segment table entry.

After the segment table has provided the page table address, System/390 hardware then uses bits 12–19 of the virtual address as the page table index. Within each page table entry, bits 1 through 19 are real 4K block addresses. Finally, bits 20 through 31 of the original virtual address are added to this to develop the actual real storage address that corresponds to the virtual address. (Storage prefixing, as discussed in chapter 1, alters this process somewhat; refer to the *Principles of Operation* manual for further details.)

Also within each page table entry, bit 21 is the "page invalid" bit. This indicates that the page isn't within an area already processed with the GETMAIN macro. An attempt to access such a page will result in a page-translation program exception, otherwise known as a *page fault*.

Bit 22 of the page table entry is the "page protected" bit, which disallows alteration of the page. Its purpose is to protect selected programs from accidental overlay due to program error or bad addresses, and to enforce reentrance. Figure 5.4 shows the format of a page table entry.

The casual user might wonder how anything ever gets done in IBM mainframes, given the cumbersome number of steps that have to be taken just to translate one address from virtual to real. The answer is that it doesn't really happen every time. System/390 hardware maintains a special storage area called the Translation Lookaside Buffer (TLB). The TLB's function is to keep track of previous virtual-to-real address computations, and to bypass the previous steps if the particular page address has already been computed. Thus, these steps are taken only when a new page address has to be translated. They also happen simultaneously with instruction decoding, and this overlap avoids some of the potential delays.

The TLB is the only example within IBM mainframe architecture of associative memory. *Associative memory* is addressable by both its location, as in normal memory, as well as by its contents. This means that segment table entries and page table entries can be located in the TLB by using the virtual address as a search argument.

Management of the TLB requires a little further planning in MVS. The actual search for previous translations in the TLB is based on the combination of control register 1's contents and the virtual address. Without the addition of control register 1, the entire TLB would have to be erased, with predictable performance effects. Earlier versions of MVS used an instruction called Purge TLB (opcode PTLB) to do this.

Page table entry

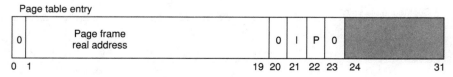

Figure 5.4 Format of page table entry.

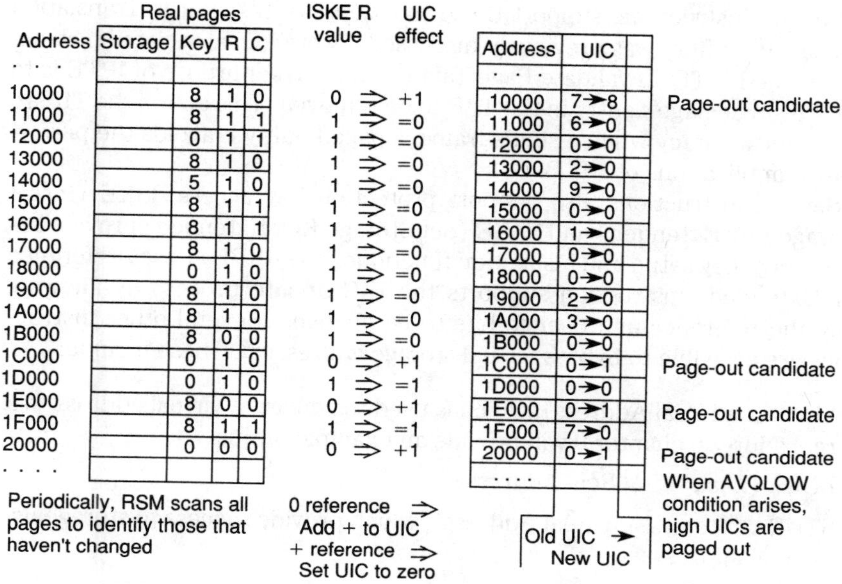

Figure 5.5 content:

Address	Real pages Storage	Key	R	C	ISKE R value		UIC effect		Address	UIC	
. . .									. . .		
10000		8	1	0	0	⇒	+1		10000	7→8	Page-out candidate
11000		8	1	1	1	⇒	=0		11000	6→0	
12000		0	1	1	1	⇒	=0		12000	0→0	
13000		8	1	0	1	⇒	=0		13000	2→0	
14000		5	1	0	1	⇒	=0		14000	9→0	
15000		8	1	1	1	⇒	=0		15000	0→0	
16000		8	1	1	1	⇒	=0		16000	1→0	
17000		8	1	0	1	⇒	=0		17000	0→0	
18000		0	1	0	1	⇒	=0		18000	0→0	
19000		8	1	0	1	⇒	=0		19000	2→0	
1A000		8	1	0	1	⇒	=0		1A000	3→0	
1B000		8	0	0	1	⇒	=0		1B000	0→0	
1C000		0	1	0	0	⇒	+1		1C000	0→1	Page-out candidate
1D000		0	1	0	1	⇒	=1		1D000	0→0	
1E000		8	0	0	0	⇒	+1		1E000	0→1	Page-out candidate
1F000		8	1	1	1	⇒	=1		1F000	7→0	
20000		0	0	0	0	⇒	+1		20000	0→1	Page-out candidate
. . . .									. . . .		

Periodically, RSM scans all pages to identify those that haven't changed

0 reference ⇒ Add + to UIC
+ reference ⇒ Set UIC to zero

Old UIC ➤ New UIC

When AVQLOW condition arises, high UICs are paged out

Figure 5.5 RSM page stealing.

Note that this description of the TLB is abbreviated; refer to the *Principles of Operation* manual for the precise definition. Note also that the TLB segment table entries with the "common" bit set are usable by all address spaces, which changes the description. The private space feature (bit 23 of control register 13) also alters these rules.

Another hardware element essential to the operation of RSM is the System/390 storage key facility. OS/360 provided a four-bit storage key, along with a fetch-protection bit for each 2K page in storage. System/370 virtual storage facilities add a reference indicator bit and a change indicator bit. These two bits are set to 1 whenever the associated page is referenced (read from) or changed (written to).

The reference and change information is essential to RSM being able to determine which pages have actually been used recently. Remember that RSM must update the UIC (Unreferenced Interval Count, or the number of intervals a page has not been used) value for unreferenced pages; the reference and change bits allow easy access to this information. The change bit, in particular, indicates if the frame must be paged out. Figure 5.5 shows an overview of this process.

When selecting pages during the page-stealing process, RSM determines if a given page can be stolen without being paged out based on the setting of the change bit. If the page has been accessed in previous UIC update cycles but no storage has been altered, the change bit will be off. This means that the page hasn't changed and the page-out can be avoided.

Several instructions support these functions. PTLB (Purge Translation Lookaside Buffer) was previously discussed. There's an associated instruction named IPTE (Invalidate Page Table Entry). The purpose of IPTE is to allow a single page's entry in the TLB to be removed. This allows the TLB to retain its accuracy when a single frame is paged out, yet avoids the performance implications of PTLB.

Several instructions also support protection key access. ISKE (Insert Storage Key Extended) and SSKE (Set Storage Key Extended) provide basic storage key setup and inspection functions. The RRBE (Reset Reference Bit Extended) instruction supports the UIC update process by allowing only the reference and change bits to be changed. Several other instructions are available to bypass virtual storage addressing. These include:

- LRA (Load Real Address), which is used to convert a virtual address to a real address; chapter 9 will provide an example of this.
- LURA (Load using Real Address).
- STURA (Store Using Real Address), which provides access to storage using real addresses.

See Fig. 5.6 for an example of LURA. RSM will appear again in the SRM discussion in chapter 6.

5.2 Auxiliary Storage Manager

The Auxiliary Storage Manager (ASM) operates mostly in response to RSM requests. Only one data area of the many included within ASM is documented within a macro, so access to licensed documentation is necessary for a full discussion. The one documented data area is the Address Space ASM Header (ILRASMHD); I know of no other SYS1.MODGEN data areas.

5.2.1 Auxiliary storage management data areas

The licensed *Data Areas* manuals show numerous data areas for ASM, which will be outlined here. The ASM Address Space Header will be discussed first.

5.2.1.1 Address space ASM header

The ASMHD is documented in macro ILRASMHD. Its function is to contain status and count information for ASM operations in an address space. Fields of interest include the swap-out flag, which is the ASHWSPOT bit of the ASHFLAG1 byte. Field ASHSWPCT contains the swap-out I/O count. There are a number of other fields that relate to the other ASM data areas, as described in the following section.

```
                    DISPLAY SEGMENT AND PAGE TABLES                                                      PAGE    1

 LOC    OBJECT CODE    ADDR1  ADDR2  STMT  SOURCE STATEMENT                                   ASM H V 02 17.29 05/06/91

000000                                                                                                       00000070
                                      2  SEGMENT  CSECT                                                      
                                      3  SEGMENT  AMODE 31                                                   
                                      4  SEGMENT  RMODE 24                                                   
000000 B240 00E0                      5           BAKR  R14,0                 SAVE REGISTERS                  00000080
000004 18CF                           6           LR    R12,R15              ESTABLISH                       00000090
                00000                 7           USING SEGMENT,R12            ADDRESSABILITY                00000100

                                      9  *  SET UP SAVE AREA ADDRESSABILITY                                  00000120
000006 41D0 C488       00488         10           LA    R13,SAVEAREA          GET SAVE AREA ADDRESS          00000130
                00000                11           USING IHADCB,R1             DCB DATA AREA DSECT             00000180
                                     12           PRINT ON,NOGEN                                             00000190

                                     14  *  OPEN THE OUTPUT PRINT FILE                                       00000210
                                     15           OPEN  (SYSPRINT,OUTPUT),MODE=31                            00000220
00001E 4110 C4F4       004F4         24           LA    R1,SYSPRINT           GET ADDRESS OF DCB             00000230
000022 9110 1030  00030              25           TM    DCBOFLGS,X'10'        TEST FOR SUCCESSFUL OPEN       00000240
000026 47E0 C198       00198         26           BNO   BADOPEN                 OPEN FAILED - END JOB        00000250
                                     27           PRINT ON,GEN                                               00000260

                                     29  *  MAIN LINE PROCESSING                                             00000280
                       0002A         30  MAINLINE EQU   *                                                    00000290
                                     31  *  DETERMINE IF WE ARE AUTHORIZED BEFORE ISSUING MODESET           00580001
                                     32           TESTAUTH  FCTN=1,AUTH=1                                    00590003
00002A 4110 0001       00001         33+          LA    1,1(0,0)              SPECIFY FUNCTION CODE        YM1995 01-TESTA
00002E 4100 0001       00001         34+          LA    0,1(0,0)              SPECIFY AUTHORIZATION CODE   YM1995 01-TESTA
000032 0A77                          35+          SVC   119                                                        01-TESTA
000034 12FF                          36           LTR   R15,R15               TEST RETURN CODE               00600000
000036 4780 C05E       0005E         37           BZ    GET_CR1               IF RC ZERO, CONTINUE           00610001
00003A 50F0 C4E0       004E0         38           ST    R15,MACR15            SAVE RETURN CODE               00620003
00003E 4110 C4E0       004E0         39           LA    R1,MACR15             CONVERT                        00630003
000042 4DE0 C1CC       001CC         40           BAS   R14,HEXCONV            TO HEXADECIMAL                00640000
000046 D207 C318 C1DA  00318  001DA  41           MVC   ERRRC,EBCDICEQ        MOVE TO PRINT                  00650000
00004C D207 C2FF C558  002FF  00558  42           MVC   ERRMACRO,=CL8'TESTAUTH'  SHOW MACRO USED            00660001
000052 4100 C2D2       002D2         43           LA    R0,ERRLINE            GET ADDRESS OF PRINT LINE      00670001
000056 4DE0 C1A2       001A2         44           BAS   R14,PRINT31           INVOKE PUT SUBROUTINE          00680000
00005A 47F0 C182       00182         45           B     RETURN                END EXECUTION                  00690001
```

Figure 5.6 Displaying segment tables.

Figure 5.6 Continued

```
00005E                    47  *        GET OUR CONTROL REGISTER 1          00710001
0005E                     48  GET_CR1  EQU  *                              00720001
                          49           MODESET  MODE=SUP        CHANGE MODE        @D1A
00068                     50+* MACDATE Y-3 81030
00005E 0700               51+          CNOP  0,4
000060 4510 C068          52+          BAL   1,*+8
000064 0000003C           53+          DC    B'00000000000000000000000000111100'
000068 5810 1000          54+          L     1,0(0,1)
00006C 0A6B               55+          SVC   107                                   YM1995
                          56           PRINT ON,NOGEN          DON'T PRINT AGAIN   0000190
00006E B611 C240    00240 57           STCTL 1,1,MY_CR1        GET CONTROL REGISTER 1
                          58           MODESET  MODE=PROB      BACK TO NORMAL MODE
                          66  *        GET ADDRESS OF SEGMENT TABLE
000082 D208 C244 C240 00244 00240 67   MVC   SEG_PTR,MY_CR1    COPY CR1
```

DISPLAY SEGMENT AND PAGE TABLES

```
LOC    OBJECT CODE     ADDR1  ADDR2   STMT  SOURCE STATEMENT            ASM H V 02 17.29 05/06/91    PAGE    2

                                        68  *        COPY FIRST ENTRY FROM SEGMENT TABLE
000088 D403 C244 C560  00244  00560     68           NC    SEG_PTR,=X'7FFFF000'   GET ADDRESS PART
00008E 5830 C244       00244            69           L     R3,SEG_PTR             GET SEGMENT TABLE ADDRESS
                                        71  *        COPY FIRST ENTRY FROM SEGMENT TABLE
                                        72           MODESET  MODE=SUP            CHANGE MODE
0000A2 B24B 0043                        79           LURA  R4,R3                  GET SEGMENT TABLE ADDRESS
                                        80           MODESET  MODE=PROB           BACK TO NORMAL MODE
0000B6 5040 C248       00248            87           ST    R4,COPY_SEG_TAB        SAVE ENTRY
                                        89  *        DISPLAY CR1 CONTENTS, SEGMENT TABLE ADDRESS, FIRST ENTRY
0000BA 4110 C240       00240            90           LA    R1,MY_CR1
0000BE 4DE0 C1CC       001CC            91           BAS   R14,HEXCONV
0000C2 D207 C384 C1DA  00384  001DA     92           MVC   PL1,CR1,EBCDICEQ
0000C8 4110 C244       00244            93           LA    R1,SEG_PTR
0000CC 4DE0 C1CC       001CC            94           BAS   R14,HEXCONV
0000D0 D207 C3A3 C1DA  003A3  001DA     95           MVC   PL1_SEG_PTR,EBCDICEQ
0000D6 4110 C248       00248            96           LA    R1,COPY_SEG-TAB
0000DA 4DE0 C1CC       001CC            97           BAS   R14,HESCONV
```

```
0000DE D207 C3C0 C1DA 003C0 001DA   98         MVC   PL1_SEG_ENTRY,EBCDICEQ
0000E4 4100 C370            00370    99         LA    R0,PL1               GET ADDRESS OF PRINT LINE
0000E8 4DE0 C1A2            001A2   100         BAS   R14,PRINT31          INVOKE PUT SUBROUTINE

                                    102   *          COPY PAGE TABLE ENTRIES
0000EC 5440 C564            00564   103         N     R4,=X'FFFFFFC0'      TURN OFF I/C/LENGTH BITS
0000F0 4150 0010            00010   104         LA    R5,16                LOOP COUNTER
0000F4 4160 C24C            0024C   105         LA    R6,COPY_PAGE_TAB     ADDRESS OF COPIED ENTRIES

000F8                               107   PAGE_TAB_LOOP   EQU   *
                                    108         MODESET  MODE=SUP          CHANGE MODE
000106 B24B 0074                    115         LURA  R7,R4                GET SEGMENT TABLE ADDRESS
                                    116         MODESET  MODE=PROB         BACK TO NORMAL MODE
00011A 5070 6000           00000    123         ST    R7,0(,R6)            SAVE ENTRY
00011E 4140 4004           00004    124         LA    R4,4(,R4)            POINT TO NEXT ENTRY
000122 4160 6004           00004    125         LA    R6,4(,R6)            AND TO NEXT COPY AREA
000126 4650 C0F8           000F8    126         BCT   R5,PAGE_TAB_LOOP     REPEAT SIXTEEN TIMES

                                    128   *          DISPLAY PAGE TABLE
00012A 4150 0010           00010    129         LA    R5,16                SET UP DISPLAY LOOP COUNTER
00012E 4160 C24C           0024C    130         LA    R6,COPY_PAGE_TAB     ADDRESS OF COPIED ENTRIES
000132 F810 C2D0 C56A 002D0 0056A   131         ZAP   OFFSET,=P'0'         RESET OFFSET COUNTER
000138 92F0 C3F5           003F5    132         MVI   PL2,C'0'             SET UP CARRIAGE CONTROL

0013C                               134   DISPLAY_PAGE_TAB   EQU   *
00013C 4110 C000           00000    135         LA    R1,0(,R6)            GET ADDRESS OF ENTRY
000140 4DE0 C1CC           001CC    136         BAS   R14,HEXCONV          CONVERT TO DISPLAYABLE
000144 D207 C41C C1DA 0041C 001DA   137         MVC   PL2_ENTRY,EBCDICEQ   MOVE TO PRINT AREA
00014A 960F C2D1           002D1    138         OI    OFFSET+1,X'0F'       SET SIGN
00014E F321 C412 C2D0 00412 002D0   139         UNPK  PL2_OFFSET,OFFSET    UNPACK OFFSET
000154 4100 C3F5           003F5    140         LA    R0,PL2               GET ADDRESS OF PRINT LINE
000158 4DE0 C1A2           001A2    141         BAS   R14,PRINT31          INVOKE PUT SUBROUTINE
00015C 9240 C3F5           003F5    142         MVI   PL2,C' '             RESET CARRIAGE CONTROL
000160 FA10 C2D0 C56B 002D0 0056B   143         AP    OFFSET,=P'4'         ADD TO OFFSET
000166 4160 6004           00004    144         LA    R6,4(,R6)            AND TO NEXT COPY AREA
00016A 4650 C13C           0013C    145         BCT   R5,DISPLAY_PAGE_TAB  REPEAT SIXTEEN TIMES
```

Figure 5.6 Continued

```
                      DISPLAY SEGMENT AND PAGE TABLES                                ASM H V 02  17.29  05/06/91    PAGE    3

LOC    OBJECT CODE       ADDR1  ADDR2  STMT  SOURCE STATEMENT

                                        147  *                  RETURN TO CALLING PROGRAM                              00001220
                         0016E           148  ENDEXEC  EQU  *                                                          00001230
                                         149           CLOSE (SYSPRINT),MODE=31                                        00001240
                                                                                                                       00001250
                         00182  004E4    158  RETURN   EQU  *                                                          00001260
000182  48F0 C4E4                        159           LH   R15,RETCODE        GET RETURN CODE VALUE
                                         160           ABEND 333,DUMP          FOR TESTING
000196  0101                             167           PR                     RETURN TO OS                            00001280

                                         169  *        FAILURE OPENING A FILE - ISSUE BAD RETURN CODE AND QUIT.       00001300
                         00198           170  BADOPEN  EQU  *                                                         00001310
000198  D201 C4E4 C568   004E4  00568    171           MVC  RETCODE,=H'16'     SET BAD RETURN CODE                    00001320
00019E  47F0 C182               00182    172           B    RETURN            RETURN TO OS WITH CC = 16               00001330

                                         174  *        SUBROUTINE TO SWITCH INTO 24-BIT MODE, THEN SWITCH BACK
                                         175  *        TO CALLER'S MODE AFTER ISSUING A PUT MACRO.  R0 = PRINT AREA.
                         001A2           176  PRINT31  EQU  *
0001A2  5000 C1C4               001C4    177           ST   R0,PRINT31_LINE_ADDRESS SAVE DATA ADDRESS
0001A6  50E0 C1C8               001C8    178           ST   R14,PRINT31_RETURN_ADDRESS SAVE CALLER'S ADDRESS
0001AA  4110 C1B0               001B0    179           LA   R1,*+6             LOAD ADDRESS, ZERO MODE BIT
0001AE  0B01                             180           BSM  0,R1               BRANCH AND SET MODE=24
0001B0  5800 C1C4               001C4    181           L    R0,PRINT31_LINE_ADDRESS
                                         182           PUT  SYSPRINT          WRITE ERROR LINE                        00001200
0001BE  58E0 C1C8               001C8    186           L    R14,PRINT31_RETURN_ADDRESS
0001C2  0B0E                             187           BSM  0,R14             RETURN AND SET MODE
0001C4                                   188  PRINT31_LINE_ADDRESS   DS  F
0001C8                                   189  PRINT31_RETURN_ADDRESS DS  F

                                         191  *        ROUTINE TO CONVERT TO DISPLAYABLE EBCDIC FROM HEXADECIMAL      00001480
                         001CC           192  HEXCONV  EQU  *                                                         00001490
0001CC  F384 C1DA 1000   001DA  00000    193           UNPK EBCDICEQ(9),0(5,R1)  UNPACK DATA                          00001500
0001D2  DC07 C1DA C0F3   001DA  000F3    194           TR   EBCDICEQ,HEXTAB-240   TRANSLATE                           00001510
0001D8  07FE                             195           BR   R14               RETURN TO CALLER                        00001520
0001DA  4040404040404040                 196  EBCDICEQ DC   CL8' ',C' '        EIGHT DATA + 1 GARBAGE BYTE            00001530
0001E3  F0F1F2F3F4F5F6F7                 197  HEXTAB   DC   C'0123456789ABCDEF'                                       00001540
```

```
                DISPLAY SEGMENT AND PAGE TABLES                              ASM H V 02  17.29  05/06/91     PAGE  4

LOC     OBJECT CODE      ADDR1 ADDR2  STMT  SOURCE STATEMENT

                                       199         PRINT ON,GEN                                               00001350
                                       200  *       DATA AREAS                                                00001360

0001F3  00
0001F4  07000700                       202  SPIESAV2      CNOP  0,8
0001F8  0000000000000000               203                DC    18F'0'
000240  00000000                       204  MY_CR1        DC    F'0'       CONTROL REGISTER 1 FROM STCTL
000244  00000000                       205  SEG_PTR       DC    F'0'       SEGMENT TABLE ADRESS PART OF CR1
000248  00000000000000000000           206  COPY_SEG_TAB  DC    16F'0'     COPY OF FIRST SEGMENT TABLE ENTRY
00024C  0000000000000000               207  COPY_PAGE_TAB DC    F'0'       COPY OF SIXTEEN PAGE TABLE ENTRIES
00028C  00000000                       208  COPY_SEG_TAB2 DC    16F'0'     COPY OF ANOTHER ENTRY
000290  0000000000000000               209  COPY_PAGE_TAB2 DC   F'0'       COPY OF ANOTHER PAGE TABLE
0002D0  000C                           210  OFFSET        DC    PL2'0'     OFFSET INTO PAGE TABLE

0002D2  605C5C5C5C5C5C5CC5             212  ERRLINE       DC    CL45'-*******ERROR ISSUING:'                  01490001
0002FF                                 213  ERRMACRO      DS    CL8                                           01500001
000307  40D9C5E3E4D9D5C540             214                DC    C' RETURN CODE IS :'                          01510001
000318  4040404040404040               215  ERRRC         DC    CL8' ',CL80' '                               01520000

000370  F0C3D6D5E3D9D6D3               217  PL1           DC    C'0CONTROL REGISTER 1:'
000384                                 218  PL1_CR1       DS    CL8
00038C  40E2C5C7D4C5D5E3               219                DC    C' SEGMENT TABLE ADDRESS:'
0003A3                                 220  PL1_SEG_ENTRY DS    CL8
0003AB  40E2C5C7D4C5D5E3               221                DC    C' SEGMENT TABLE ENTRY:'
0003C0                                 222  PL1_SEG_ENTRY DS    CL8
0003C8  4040404040404040               223                DC    CL(PL1+133-*)' '       FILLER

0003F5  40D7C1C7C540E3C1               225  PL2           DC    C' PAGE TABLE ENTRY AT OFFSET +'
000412                                 226  PL2_OFFSET    DS    CL3
000415  40E5C1D3E4C57A                 227                DC    C' VALUE:'
00041C                                 228  PL2_ENTRY     DS    CL8
000424  4040404040404040               229                DC    CL(PL2+133-*)' '       FILLER

                                       231  *       OTHER DATA AREAS                                          00001560
00047A  00000000000000                 232  DOUBLEWD      DC    D'0'                                          00001570
000480  0000000000000000000            233  SAVEAREA      DC    18F'+0'                                       00001580
000488  0000000000000000000            234  SAVER14       DC    F'+0'      USED TO SAVE REGISTER 14 CONTENTS  00001590
0004D0  00000000
```

Figure 5.6 Continued

```
0004D4 0000000000000000
0004E0 00000000
0004E4 0000

0004E6 F0F561F0F661F9F1


235 SAVER24  DC   3F'+0'               USED TO SAVE REGISTERS 2, 3, 4   00001600
236 MACR15   DC   F'+0'                REGISTER 15 AFTER MACRO ERROR    00001600
237 RETCODE  DC   H'0'                                                 00001610
238 EYE_INFO DC   C'&SYSDATE &SYSTIME'                                  00001610
   +EYE_INFO DC   C'05/06/91 17.29'

240          PRINT ON,NOGEN    DON'T PRINT MACRO EXPANSIONS             00001820
241 *        DATA CONTROL BLOCK FOR PRINT OUTPUT FILE                   00001830
242 SYSPRINT DCB  DDNAME=SYSPRINT,DEVD=DA,DSORG=PS,MACRF=(PM),RECFM=FBA,X00001840
                  LRECL=133,BLKSIZE=1330                                 00001850


CONTROL REGISTER 1:002307F SEGMENT TABLE ADDRESS:00A23000 SEGMENT TABLE ENTRY:053AB00F

PAGE TABLE ENTRY AT OFFSET +000 VALUE:00000001
PAGE TABLE ENTRY AT OFFSET +004 VALUE:00000400
PAGE TABLE ENTRY AT OFFSET +008 VALUE:00000400
PAGE TABLE ENTRY AT OFFSET +012 VALUE:00000400
PAGE TABLE ENTRY AT OFFSET +016 VALUE:00000400
PAGE TABLE ENTRY AT OFFSET +020 VALUE:03889001
PAGE TABLE ENTRY AT OFFSET +024 VALUE:00F0B001
PAGE TABLE ENTRY AT OFFSET +028 VALUE:05796011
PAGE TABLE ENTRY AT OFFSET +032 VALUE:00000400
PAGE TABLE ENTRY AT OFFSET +036 VALUE:00000400
PAGE TABLE ENTRY AT OFFSET +040 VALUE:00000400
PAGE TABLE ENTRY AT OFFSET +044 VALUE:00000400
PAGE TABLE ENTRY AT OFFSET +048 VALUE:00000400
PAGE TABLE ENTRY AT OFFSET +052 VALUE:00000400
PAGE TABLE ENTRY AT OFFSET +056 VALUE:00000400
PAGE TABLE ENTRY AT OFFSET +060 VALUE:00000400
```

5.2.1.2   Other ASM data areas

Several other data areas can be investigated for a better understanding of ASM's internal operation. The primary control block for ASM is the ASM Vector Table, referred to as the ASMVT. Field CVTASMVT provides its address.

The ASMVT provides access to the other ASM control blocks. The PART (Paging Activity Reference Table) describes page data sets. The PART includes a series of PART Entries, or PARTEs, for each page data set in the system. There's a corresponding PAT (Page Allocation Table) that describes the utilization of frames within the page data set. A separate series of control blocks cover individual page requests. The AIA (ASM I/O Request Area) represents an individual page in or out request.

The following lists the ASM control blocks documented in the licensed *Data Areas* manual for further research. The ASMVT and PART are the best starting points.

- ACA (ASM Control Area), which is used when setting up a logical group.
- ACE (ASM Control Element).
- AIA (ASM I/O Request Area).
- ATA (ASM Tracking Area).
- DEIB (Dataset Extent Information Block).
- EQSRD (see QSRCD).
- LGE (Logic Group Element).
- LGVT (Logical Group Vector Table), which is used to group page activity within an address space.
- OPSPL (ASM Operations Parameter List).
- PART (Paging Activity Reference Table); describes page data sets.
- PCCW (Paging CCW Area), for individual page I/O operations.
- PCT (Performance Characteristics Table); describes page data sets.
- QSRCD (Quick Start Record), for IPL.
- SART (Swap Activity Reference Table), which is like PART for swap.
- SAT (Swap Allocation Table), which is like PAT for swap.
- SCCW (Swap CCW Area).
- SDCT (Swap Device Characteristics Table), like PCT for swap.
- XQSRD (Quick Start Record Extension); see QSRCD.

5.3   Uses for RSM/ASM Control Blocks

The primary uses for these control blocks are in performance monitoring and resource utilization measurement. In contrast, there are many uses for RSM and ASM services within MVS. Dispatching an SRB was the initial case discussed in this book that needed fixed storage, available through the PG-FIX or PGSER macros. This need will arise again in other MVS components.

5.4   Things to Do

- If you have access to IPCS, use the ASMCHECK and RSMDATA commands to display ASM and RSM information from your own running system.

- If you have access to a software performance monitor, such as RMF or OMEGAMON, review the system paging and real storage screens. As an exercise, pick one or two fields at random, then try to determine that ASM or RSM control block hold that information.

- Review the REFPAT macro. This provides a cooperative paging interface that allows RSM to preallocate large areas of storage (over 4K) when specific reference patterns are known. (This macro was added in MVS/ESA 4.2.)

6

System Measurement

This chapter addresses the control blocks for the two components of MVS used in measuring performance and resource utilization. The first of these is the Systems Resource Manager, or SRM. The other is the Systems Management Facility, or SMF. Both of these provide a wealth of useful information. This chapter, however, can only scratch the surface in terms of coverage.

The definitive reference for a better understanding of the SRM is *MVS Performance Management* second edition, by Steve Samson. I recommend it for insight into using the SRM. To avoid duplication of material covered within that book, this chapter will primarily concentrate on the control blocks used by SRM, rather than providing examples of their use.

SMF is essentially a straightforward record logging service. Complexity within SMF comes less from the control blocks used than from the extensive set of records it supports. I recommend that you refer to the appropriate level of SMF manual. In this chapter, I'll discuss some control blocks that are available within individual address spaces.

6.1 Systems Resource Manager

The SRM provides a method of automating system tuning and performance management. It allows the MVS performance specialist a method of specifying certain performance goals, or objectives, along with resource usage classes, or domains. SRM uses several unique terms in defining the workload it controls. One of these is *service*—the amount of resources consumed by a job, started task, or TSO user. (I'll use *job* to refer to all three in this chapter.)

Service defines the amount of CPU time, storage, and I/O utilization for a given job. Time is measured over SRM measurement summarization intervals. The measurement of CPU time is an SRM second—about 1 second of CPU time on an IBM 370/155-II. (Allegedly, this was because SRM was developed on one of these CPUs.) The actual speed of whatever processor is in use is adjusted to this unit. For example, there are about 19.6078 SRM seconds per wall clock second on an IBM 3090-600E.

Since many small programs and individual TSO commands take less than one second, CPU time for TCBs is counted in service units rather than in actual CPU time. A CPU service unit was originally established as the time to execute about ten thousand instructions on an IBM 370/155-II. The *Initialization Guide* contains a table describing the service units per wall clock second possible for various IBM CPUs. SRB service units are similarly tracked.

Another area measured by the SRM is storage utilization, or Main Storage Occupancy (MSO). MSO units are the use (occupancy) of one page for one second.

I/O operations have been measured in varying ways as the I/O facilities of MVS have changed. Initially, SRM measured the raw rate of I/O resource utilization by counting EXCPs (Execute Channel Program, which will be covered in chapter 8). This changed to counting the number of blocks transferred in MVS/XA and MVS/ESA. Since this was still not a true measure of I/O resource utilization, the SRM now measures the I/O connect time for the greatest accuracy.

SRM's mission is to meet service objectives for various classes of MVS work. As a job uses more resources in the various services classes, it moves through various domains. In some cases, SRM uses a smaller unit of work for measurement, called a *transaction*. Work can also be classified in various performance groups.

A full understanding of the interoperation of all of these factors is beyond the scope of this book; refer to the *Initialization Reference* manual and *MVS Performance Management*.

6.1.1 SRM external interfaces

SRM's external interfaces, in contrast to the MVS components discussed earlier in the book, aren't generally delivered via macros. There's one macro interface to SRM, the SYSEVENT macro, which is used both to retrieve and to provide information to the SRM regarding the status of workload and system elements. SRM interfaces include entries in SYS1.PARMLIB, operator commands, and JCL.

6.1.1.1   SYS1.PARMLIB

SYS1.PARMLIB holds numerous system definition and control entries. SRM uses several of these, including:

IEAOPT*xx* member.   Controls the "optimizer" processing of SRM.

IEAICS*xx* member.   Installation Control Specification.

IEAIPS*xx* member.   Installation Performance Specification.

These specify the performance groups, domains, and objectives for SRM's processing. SYS1.PARMLIB specifications directly affect the quantities of some SRM control blocks. For example, the IEASYS*xx* CMB parameter affects the number of Channel Measurement Blocks.

6.1.1.2   JCL and operator commands

You can indicate to SRM which performance group applies to a given job through the JCL PERFORM= parameter. (See the *JCL Reference* manual for coding details.) The performance group for a specified job can then be changed by a console RESET (E) command. The SET (T) command can also change the SRM IPS specification. See the *System Commands Reference* manual for details of these.

6.1.1.3   SYSEVENT macro

For SRM to respond effectively to changes in the system workload, it must be able to gather information from all parts of MVS. The method used to provide this is the SYSEVENT macro. SYSEVENT generates either SVC 95 or branch entry to the SRM, depending on its coding. It includes a variable number of parameters, depending on what information is being reported to or requested from SRM.

The primary parameter is the system event mnemonic. This is the name of the condition being reported (or the type of information request). For example, the completion of a job results in a JOBTERM SYSEVENT being reported to SRM. Another example lies in VSM processing when the amount of free space in SQA falls below the value in the GDASQALO field, which generates an SQALOW SYSEVENT.

Information can also be requested from the SRM. The REQSERVC SYSEVENT requests resource service unit utilization information from SRM. (The TSO TIME command uses this SYSEVENT; use it for an example of REQSERVC values.)

The SYSEVENT macro is documented in *Authorized Assembler Language Reference* manual; this includes a comprehensive list of SYSEVENT codes. The SYSEVENT macro also validates the event code keyword, and can be researched without this manual. An older list is also included in the *Debugging Handbook*, vol. I.

6.1.2   SRM internal control blocks

For the purposes of this discussion, I'll divide SRM control blocks into those predominantly used in controlling SRM's overall processing, and those that hold primarily address-space-related data. This section covers the internal control blocks.

SRM's internal control blocks are located mostly in a CSECT named IRARMCNS, which is located in the MVS nucleus. The control blocks in IRARMCNS then contain the address of other control blocks, usually with multiple occurrences. Most of these control blocks are documented only in the *Data Areas* manuals. Those that have mapping macros available are covered in more detail later in this chapter. Table 6.1 shows a summary of SRM internal control blocks. Figure 6.1 shows the internal control block relationship.

6.1.2.1   SRM Control Table (RMCT)

The RMCT is located in nucleus module IRARMCNS. Its primary purpose is to hold addresses of SRM routines and pointers to other SRM control

TABLE 6.1 SRM Internal Control Blocks

Name	DSECT	Description
CCT	IRACCT	SRM CPU Management Control Table
CMB	IRACMB	SRM Channel Measurement Block
CMCT	IRACMCT	SRM Channel Measurement Control Table
CPMT	IRACPMT	SRM Channel Path Measurement Table
DMB	IRADMB	Device Measurement Control Block
DMDT	IRADMDT	Domain Descriptor Table
ICT	IRAICT	SRM I/O Management Control Table
LPBT	IRALPBT	Table of Logical Path Control Blocks
MCT	IRAMCT	SRM Storage Management Control Table
RCT	IRARCT	SRM Resource Control Table
RMCA	IRARMCA	SRM Control Area
RMCT	IRARMCT	SRM Control Table
RMEP	IRARMEP	SRM Entry Point Block
RMEX	IRARMEX	SRM External Entry Point Description Table
RMPT	IRARMPT	SRM Parameter Table
RRPA	IRARRPA	SRM Recovery Parameter Area
WAMT	IRAWAMT	SRM Workload Activity Measurement Table
WMST	IRAWMST	SRM Workload Manager Specifications Table

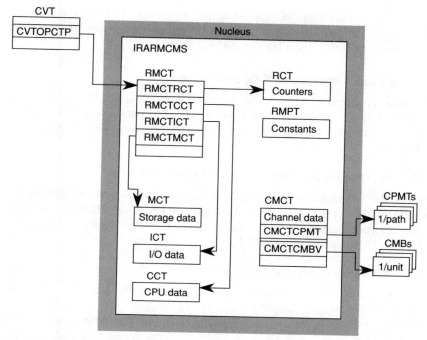

Figure 6.1 Internal SRM control block relationship.

blocks. CVT field CVTOPCTP has the address of the RMCT. Its DSECT macro is IRARMCT.

One field of interest within the RMCT is the CPU speed adjustment value in field RMCTADJC. This can be used to approximate the relationship between SRM computations and actual CPU time. (Normally, SRM's actual values are accessible through the address-space-related control blocks.)

6.1.2.2 SRM Channel Measurement Control Table (CMCT)

The CMCT essentially provides the root control block for SRM's I/O measurement. Its address is in RMCTCMCT, and its DSECT name is IRACMCT. It provides pointer fields, with selected limit values added. (For example, see the field named CMCTCMBT, which relates back to the SYS1.PARMLIB CMB entry.) The CMCT field CMCTCPMB contains the address of the CPMB, discussed in the next section.

6.1.2.3 SRM Channel Path Measurement Block (CPMB)

The CPMB provides an array of path usage time counts. The DSECT, macro name IRACPMB, includes both a header and entry description, requiring different USING statements. Note that the time value is in units of 128 microseconds. The DSECT states that this time value will wrap around after 35.79 minutes of utilization for the path in question.

6.1.3   Address-space-related SRM control blocks

SRM maintains four control blocks for each address space that provides a complete picture of the address space's resource usage and SRM status. These are listed in Table 6.2. Figure 6.2 shows the relationship among some of these control blocks.

6.1.3.1   RM User I/O Management Control Block (IMCB)

The IMCB contains information relating to an individual address space's I/O connect time for individual paths. As discussed previously, this time is kept in 128 microsecond increments. To the best of my knowledge, there's no distributed macro for the DSECT for this control block.

6.1.3.2   SRM User Control Block (OUCB)

The OUCB is the main address-space-level SRM control block. Its address is in ASCBOUCB, and its mapping macro is IHAOUCB.

The OUCB contains many flags relating to the performance characteristics of an address space. It also contains flags for several other pieces of information. As examples, the OUCBLOG flag indicates a LOGON-created user, and the OUCBOMVS flag indicates that the address space is processing an OpenMVS transaction.

Information fields in the OUCB include OUCBSPG, the performance group number for the address space. (This is only one of several performance group fields.) The OUCBTRXN field contains the transaction name (as far as SRM is concerned), the OUCBUSRD field contains the user ID, and so forth.

Due to the number of fields in the OUCB and the two control blocks described in the following section, I suggest that you review the DSECT for a good understanding of its possible uses.

6.1.3.3   SRM User Swappable Block (OUSB)

The OUSB contains further information regarding an address space's SRM characteristics. Unlike the OUCB and OUXB, however, it resides

TABLE 6.2   Address-Space-Related SRM Control Blocks

Name	DSECT	Description
IMCB	IRAIMCB	SRM User I/O Management Control Block
OUCB	IRAOUCB	SRM User Control Block
OUSB	IRAOUSB	SRM User Swappable Block
OUXB	IHAOUXB	SRM User Extension Block

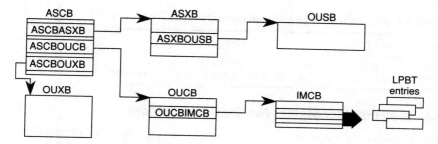

Figure 6.2 Relationship among address-space SRM control blocks.

within the address space's LSQA, and can thus be swapped out with the address space. Its address is in field ASXBOUSB, and its mapping macro is IHAOUSB.

Fields of interest include OUSBPIN, the session page-in count, and OUSBPOUT, the session page-out count. There are similar fields named OUSBSPIN and OUSBSPOT for swap I/O counts, which have equivalent fields named OUXBSPIN and OUXBSPOT in the OUXB.

6.1.3.4 SRM User Extension Block (OUXB)

The OUXB contains SRM information that isn't required while the address space is swapped out. It resides in ESQA, and is addressed by the ASCBOUXB field. The mapping macro is IHAOUXB. The OUXB contains many accumulation fields recording event counts for the address space. Examples of these include:

OUXBSWCT. The address space's swap count.

OUXBJBS. The address space's session service accumulation; this is CPU time expressed in SRM CPU service units.

OUXBFLGS. This flag byte includes a bit, OUXBCLST, indicating that the address space is currently in CLIST mode.

I suggest that you review the OUCB, OUSB, and OUXB DSECTs.

6.1.4 SRM parameter lists

The SYSEVENT macro provides two forms of parameter lists (listed in Table 6.3), for which IBM provides corresponding mapping macros. The purpose for these is to support passing dynamic SYSEVENT information. If you want to pursue this topic, review the macros for background information on how SYSEVENT operates.

TABLE 6.3 SRM Parameter Description Control Blocks

Name	DSECT	Description
TRBP	IHATRBPL	Transaction-Reporting Basic Parm List
TREP	IHATREPL	Transaction-Reporting Extended Parm List

6.2 Systems Management Facility Control Blocks

SMF provides the majority of its information via SMF records written to the SMF data sets. These records come from both MVS and other components (e.g., RMF and DB2). This section won't describe these in any detail, however, due to the sheer volume of information.

SMF implements a separate address space in MVS to manage the SMF data sets, etc. Many of the SMF control blocks exist only in that address space, and I won't discuss them since many of you won't have an occasion to inspect them closely.

6.2.1 SMF macro services

SMF provides macros to write SMF records to the current SMF data set, to describe SMF record layouts, and to display or extract SMF parameters. Table 6.4 lists these macros and their functions.

SMFWTM and IFASMFR existed in the initial OS/360 implementation of SMF. The others have been added at various points in MVS history, as control blocks migrated into the SMF address space from globally addressable control blocks.

6.2.2 SMF SYS1.PARMLIB controls

SMF is controlled by the SMFPRM*xx* member of SYS1.PARMLIB. SMF parameters can also be updated by the SET SMF operator command. SMF provides several exit points at which installations can insert their own code. These

TABLE 6.4 SMF Macro Instructions

Name	Function
SMFWTM	Write a record to the current SMF data set
SMFEWTM	Branch Entry Version of SMFWTM
SMFRTEST	Test current SMF recording options
SMFEXIT	Branch to an installation-written SMF exit
SMFINTVL	Determine the current SMF interval for Type 30 records
SMFDETAL	Determine SMF detail record recording options
SMFSUBP	Determine SMF parameters for a subsystem
SMBCHSUB	Change SMF parameters for a subsystem
IFASMFR	Generate SMF record DSECTs

are named IEFU*xx* (for example, IEFUJV) and are documented in the SMF manual. Writing your own SMF exit continues to be a low-level rite of passage for many systems programmers, and has been the start of many careers.

6.2.3 SMF control blocks

Many SMF control blocks are OCO and exist only within the SMF address space. However, there are two SMF-specific control blocks documented in the *Data Areas* manuals that I'll cover here. They are the System Management Control Area (SMCA) and the SMF Timing Control Table (TCT). Additionally, the SMF records themselves are defined by the IFASMFR mapping macros.

6.2.3.1 System Management Control Area

The SMCA is a globally addressable control block that holds selected system-wide information for SMF processing. The mapping macro is IEESMCA. Key fields in the SMCA include:

SMCAJWT. The system wait time limit.

SMCASID. The system ID from the SMFPRM*xx* member.

SMCAASID. The SMF address space ID.

SMCAPCNO. The SMF Program Call number.

SMCAITME. Time of the most recent IPL.

SMCAIDTE. Date of the most recent IPL.

These fields have several uses. The SMCAJWT is particularly useful to avoid 622 ABENDs. The field holds the maximum amount of time a task can wait before a 622 ABEND occurs. When you write programs that intentionally wait for a given period, 622 ABENDs cannot occur as long as the wait time doesn't exceed this value. SMCAJWT holds the time in seconds.

The SMCAITME and SMCAIDTE fields are similarly useful. The time field is kept in hundredths of seconds. (Refer to the IBM documentation on the TIME macro for an explanation of the time and date formats.)

6.2.3.2 SMF Timing Control Table (TCT)

The SMF Timing Control Table contains detailed count fields for most resource consumption for a particular job. The TCT is the basis for the SMF type 4 record, which is written at step termination time, along with the type 30 records. The TCT DSECT is IEFTCT.

The TCT comprises four separate areas. It can be addressed through the TCBTCT field. The first TCT area is the TCT common section. It contains fields like TCTPPST (the time the step's program was loaded, i.e., the time that the program actually started), TCTTJLM (remaining job CPU time), and numerous service usage counts.

The TCT common section also contains the addresses of the TCT storage table (TCTCRTBL field), the TCT I/O table (TCTIOTBL), and the extended TCT I/O table (TCTFETIO).

The TCT storage table (also called the *core table*) contains counters of the total virtual storage used by the step. This is subdivided into the total storage in user subpools and in LSQA below and above the 16MB line, the starting region address, and the region size request, among other fields.

The TCT I/O table contains one entry for each DD statement in the step, preceded by a short header section. The TCTSZLKP field holds the count of DD entries. Each entry includes an offset into another control block (the Task I/O Table, or TIOT) and the address of an I/O counter entry. The TIOT offset is added to the TIOT address (available in the TCB field TCBTIOT) to get the DD name for the entry. The I/O counter entry contains the number of EXCPs, the device connect time, and the block size for the DD statement. (Chapter 8 explains what an EXCP is.)

Finally, the Extended TCT I/O Table includes an equivalent series of entries, one for each I/O table entry. These contain a pointer to a control block called the Data Set Association Block, or DSAB, which can be used to locate the data set name associated with the DD statement. Figure 6.3 attempts to show the relationship between the four sections of the TCT.

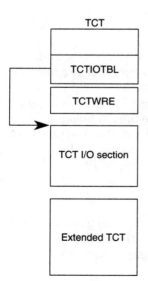

Figure 6.3 Relationship among four sections of TCT.

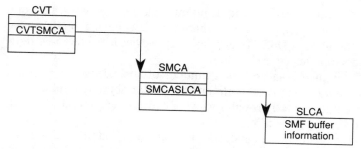

Figure 6.4 Relationship between SMCA and SLCA.

6.2.3.3 SMF records

The eventual output of SMF is a series of SMF records on an SMF data set. These records are widely used for job accounting, chargeback, and performance and capacity planning purposes. SMF provides a DSECT that describes each record in detail, generated by the IFASMFR macro. This macro accepts a series of SMF record numbers as its parameter, then generates the fields for each record type. (Due to the number of record types, IFASMFR actually calls in several other macros to generate the needed DSECT information.)

6.2.3.4 SMF Local Communications Area

For those interested in delving further into the internal structure of the SMF address space, SMF includes a control block called the SMF Local Communications Area, or SLCA. This is pointed to by the SMCA field SM-CASLCA. The SLCA contains further information about SMF's internal buffers, etc. Note that this isn't a formal IBM-supplied programming interface. Figure 6.4 shows the relationship between the SMCA and SLCA.

6.2.3.5 Uses of SMF data

The wide use of SMF data makes it impossible to give a comprehensive list of all the possible uses for SMF records. At the end of this section is a simple reporting program that uses SMF type 4 records. Note that this example is in C, and makes use of an IFASMFR DSECT converted into a C header file.

The conversion of assembler DSECTs into C language equivalent structs is tedious if performed manually. However, the SAS C compiler provides a utility program, DSECT2C, which automates the conversion. The input to this utility is an assembler source program that generates the DSECT. The output is the source code for an equivalent C struct.

Running this with the IFASMFR macro, in particular, raises some problems. Unlike most DSECTs discussed elsewhere in this book, IFASMFR generates several record layouts at once using one DSECT statement; this can cause difficulties with C addressing using multiple record types. I recommend separate struct creation for each record type, which can be time-consuming as the number of DSECTs increases. However, it needs to be done only once, and simplifies later C coding.

The SAS C compiler also defines a number of special data types, e.g., BL3, whose definition might be counterintuitive for some assembler programmers. I recommend a thorough review of everything generated by this approach before you proceed.

Having created a separate header file through some manual editing, a C program to read SMF type 4 records is as follows:

```
#pragma inline
#include <stdio.h>
#include <osio.h>
/* The SMF record DSECT equivalent in C is not shown   */
typedef struct {
char stg [256];
} stg_str;
static DCB_t *infile;
int main()
{
MYSMFREC* rec; /* SMF record type pointer */    union ADDR1
   {
   void* curbyte;
   int    addrof1;
   } addr1;
   float secs;
   int* p2;
   stg_str* p3;
   char work1[37] ;
   char workj[ 9] ;
   int err, len, i, j, k, type4 = 0;
   infile = osdcb("infile", 0, 0, 0);
   if (osopen(infile, "input", 0)== 0) {
     for (j = 0;           ; j++)
       {
         /* processing loop */
         err = osget(infile, &rec, &len);
         /* verify no errors and a complete record − if length
           negative, it's a segment other than the last */
         if ((err == 0) && (len > 0)) {
            addr1.curbyte = rec;
            addr1.addrof1 -= 4;
          rec =  addr1.curbyte;
           if (rec->smf4rty == 0x04) { /* step termination record */
              type4++;
              addr1.curbyte = (void*)&rec->smf4lenn;
              addr1.addrof1 += rec->smf4lenn.BF; /* add smf4lenn */
              p2 = (int*)addr1.curbyte;
              i = *p2 & 0x00FFFFFF ; /* zero high-order bits */
              secs = i;
              secs /= 100.0;
              i = strlen(rec->smf4pgnm);
              printf("Program: %8s CPU: %06.2f, Job:%s   \n",
                   rec->smf4pgmn, secs, rec->smf4jbn  );
              p3 = (stg_str*) rec;
          }
```

```
      if (rec->smf4rty == 0x03) { /* dump trailer */
        /* add any termination code desired here */
        }
    }
     else {
       if (err != 0) {
             printf("error on get: %d length:%d\n", err, len);
             break;
       }
       else { /* partial record - read until end */
             do {
                 err = osget(infile, &rec, &len);
             } while ((err == 0) && (len < 0));
       }
     }
   }
 else {
    printf("error on open: %d\n", err);
 }
 printf("Done... %d records processed\n", j);
 return(0);
}
```

6.3 Summary

There are two system reporting services, SRM and SMF.

SRM's intent is to provide performance management services, ensuring that higher-priority workloads receive better service, while also allowing overall system tuning. The key SRM control blocks discussed in this book are RMCT, OUCB, OUSB, and OUXB. The RMCT can be located through the CVT, and provides addresses for SRM system-wide routines and control blocks. The OUCB, OUSB, and OUXB can be located by starting with the ASCB. These three control blocks hold the specific resource usage information for specific address spaces.

SMF's intent is to provide primarily accounting data, with performance and audit data also available. This chapter discussed two SMF control blocks, SMCA and TCT. The SMCA includes various system-wide SMF fields of interest, such as IPL time and date. The TCT includes numerous items of information regarding resource utilization.

6.4 Things to Do

- Review the SMF records defined in the IFASMFR macro. Note that, since IFASMFR calls several other macros, you'll have to browse several different members to review this.

- Browse your installation's SYS1.PARMLIB library and review the SRM control members (IEAOPT*xx*, IEAICS*xx*, and IEAIPS*xx*). Try to determine the relative service associated with the performance groups open to you.

7

Control Blocks for Resource Serialization

All multiprogramming operating systems need to be able to coordinate between separate units of work. This requirement appears in MVS in the following areas:

- Multitasking among several TCBs within an address space.
- Inter-address-space processing (between several jobs, TSO users, or started tasks).
- Multiprocessing with multiple tightly coupled processors.
- Multiprocessing between loosely coupled CPUs (multiple copies of MVS).

Other operating systems (e.g., DEC's VMS) have similar requirements, and most operating systems provide services that allow serialization among multiple processes. *Serialization* means that processes (like TCBs) doing the same thing at the same time follow certain conventions to ensure that they don't destroy each other's work.

A simple analogy is a street intersection with four-way stop signs. When stopping at one of these, you look for other traffic and proceed when it's safe. Problems arise, of course, if other drivers ignore the stop sign and fail to yield the right-of-way to that large truck over there.

Because MVS provides several different environments, it has several common services for serialization. These are implemented in the MVS component Global Resource Serialization (GRS), and in the MVS service Lock Management. These are covered in the following two major sections.

7.1 Global Resource Serialization

GRS is the current implementation of a service that dates back to the original OS/360 operating system. GRS provides services through four macros:

ENQ. Requests control of a resource.

DEQ. Releases control of a resource previously obtained with ENQ.

RESERVE. Used with shared DASD devices.

GQSCAN. Used to obtain information about current resource holders.

Additionally, GRS provides an exit for resource control by an installation. Up to this point, I've used the term *resource* without defining what it means. A resource, oversimplifying somewhat, is something that must be updated by only one process at a time. Resources are defined by GRS in three parts. The first is a major resource name (QNAME), which is an eight-byte value representing the general type of the resource. The second part is the minor resource name (RNAME), which defines the specific resource to be controlled. An RNAME can be up to 255 bytes long. The third is the scope of the resource, which I'll explain in section 7.1.1.1.

What are the rules for defining a resource of your own? Essentially, it's whatever you want, except for certain combinations reserved for IBM use. You could specify a QNAME of MASTER and RNAME of UPDATE, for instance. Any combination is legitimate. The key element is not what you pick for a QNAME and RNAME combination, but that all programs to be serialized use the same name. Since the RNAME designates a specific resource, both the QNAME and the RNAME must be the same to ensure that only one process at a time updates a particular resource.

The reserved IBM names are listed in the *System Diagnosis: Reference* manual. A list is also provided in the *MVS/ESA Version 4 Planning: General Resource Serialization* manual. Some of the more common examples are:

- QNAME=SYSDSN and RNAME=*data set name* are used to control access to data sets; this is the enforcement mechanism for the JCL DISP= parameter.

- QNAME=SYSVSAM and RNAME=*data set name*, catalog name, and other indicators for VSAM cluster serialization.

- QNAME=SPFEDIT and RNAME=*data set name* and member name for ISPF edit serialization (the "member in use" message).

- QNAME=SYSVTOC and RNAME=*volume serial* for disk space updates and data set creation or deletion.

Numerous other QNAME and RNAME combinations exist for MVS use. In general, any QNAME beginning with SYS cannot be used unless authorized. I strongly advise you to review the listed sources for a fuller understanding of this requirement. With this overview of the QNAME and RNAME structure, we now turn to the GRS macro services.

7.1.1   GRS macro services

GRS provides four macro services (ENQ, DEQ, RESERVE, and GQSCAN). However, ENQ and RESERVE are implemented with the same SVC and will be discussed together.

7.1.1.1   ENQ/RESERVE macros

ENQ is used to request control of a specified resource. It generates SVC 56. The operands of ENQ include:

- QNAME and RNAME, as discussed earlier.
- Scope of the request; the choices are STEP, SYSTEM, or SYSTEMS.
- Type of control requested: exclusive (E) or shared (S).
- Type of request (RET=): NONE, HAVE, CHNG, USE, or TEST.
- A Step Must Complete (SMC) indicator.
- An ECB address.
- A TCB address associated with the request.
- A matching ASID and TCB to be associated with the request.
- MASID and MTCB.

The last four operands aren't specified for typical requests. The scope of the request indicates how much control is desired. STEP implies that you're in a multitasking environment and want to serialize something only within your own address space. SYSTEM implies that you want to serialize something within the copy of MVS under which you're running, but not within other copies of MVS. Finally, SYSTEMS implies that the resource should be serialized across all copies of MVS known to GRS; this applies only to a multi-CPU environment. (This oversimplifies the case somewhat; LPAR configurations with multiple copies of MVS also fit this situation, among other examples.)

I can best illustrate the type of control operand (exclusive or shared) by describing its use with the JCL DISP= parameter. A DISP value of OLD, NEW, or MOD implies that exclusive use is needed; SHR implies shared control.

The type of request operands specify what ENQ is to do with the request. For example, USE implies that your task is requesting control of the resource. HAVE indicates that you want the resource if it's available, but don't want to wait for it. TEST indicates that you want to determine the status of the resource, but don't want to seize it if it's available. ENQ provides several return codes for all the request types to indicate precisely what happened with the request. Refer to the *Assembler Programming Reference* manual for a description of the other operands.

The RESERVE macro is a special case of ENQ. Originally, RESERVE was used with shared disk devices (a disk control unit attached to two or more CPUs). RESERVE caused a special channel program (called Reserve) to be executed that locked out all other systems from the disk unit. This remained true until the same system issued another channel program called Release. This was a brute-force approach to serializing access to data sets on the disk pack in question, and led to suboptimal performance in many cases. (Refer to the *Johnson & Johnson DASD* for details.)

The operands of RESERVE included the Unit Control Block address of the shared DASD device. (The other operands were as described with ENQ.) GRS was developed, among other reasons, to reduce the impact of RESERVE processing.

7.1.1.2   The DEQ macro

DEQ is used to release control of a resource after it's seized by ENQ. DEQ generates SVC 48. The operands of DEQ include:

Reset Step Must Complete (RMC).   The opposite of Step Must Complete (SMC) above.

Generic DEQ indicator.   Releases all the RNAMESs related to the QNAME; releases the data set names at the end of a step.

Other operands are as described in ENQ and RESERVE, previously.

7.1.1.3   The GQSCAN macro

The GQSCAN service was not originally provided in MVS 3.8. When a program needed to know what data sets were in use, for example, the information was available by scanning several control blocks named Queue Control Blocks (QCBs) and Queue Elements (QELs). The QCB represents a specific QNAME from an ENQ request; the QEL, which was chained from the

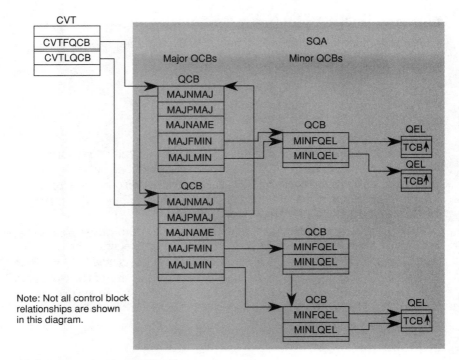

Figure 7.1 MVS 3.8 QCB and QEL structure.

corresponding QCB, represents the RNAME portion of the request. Figure 7.1 shows this structure.

The QCB and QEL were stored in SQA, so they were generally available. However, common storage was required for ENQs, leading to storage constraints. To resolve this, MVS/370 introduced a new, separate address space for serialization. This (called the GRS address space) then held the QCBs and QELs, thus reducing SQA requirements. Figure 7.2 shows this revision to the structure of Fig. 7.1.

Unfortunately, moving the QCBs and QELs meant they couldn't be freely scanned, so programs that scanned these control blocks would no longer work. (It would be possible to scan QCBs and QELs by dispatching an SRB, but this is more difficult.) To resolve this dilemma, IBM introduced the GQSCAN service.

The purpose of GQSCAN is to extract information regarding current resource ENQ status. The operands of the GQSCAN macro are:

- A work area (1024 bytes minimum).
- Request limit—number of entries to return.

- Scope (as in ENQ).
- Resource identifier (Qname/Rname, UCB, System ID).
- GENERIC or SPECIFIC keyword indicator.
- Request/owner/wait count limits.
- Token (fullword returned by GQSCAN as an ID).
- Quit indicator.

GQSCAN then returns the current status for the specified resource. The status information is returned in the work area in a control block called a Resource Information Block, or RIB. The individual resources or resource users are described in subsections following the RIB, named RIB Entries, or RIBEs. The ISGRIB DSECT describes these two.

GQSCAN is fairly well documented in the *Assembler Language Reference*, so refer to that manual for details. Note, however, that executing the GQSCAN macro multiple times for the same set of search parameters might not work for all versions of MVS. You want to be able to increase the size of the work area so it can hold all the expected RIBEs. See item E366713 for an example if you have access to IBM's Info/System database. See APAR OY34580 if you have access to the IBMLink system.

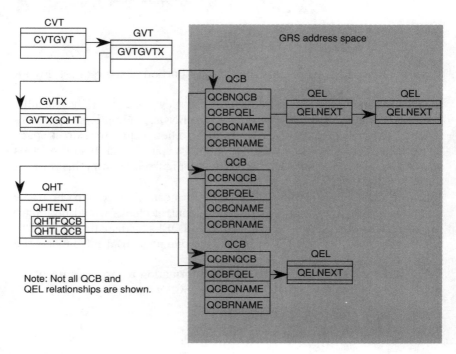

Figure 7.2 GRS QCB and QEL structure.

GQSCAN can determine which jobs or TSO users are holding a resource, which address spaces are waiting for a given resource, and any other ENQ-related information. The following is a sample program that determines which TSO user is editing a specified ISPF data set. (This could be executed after an ISPF "member in use" message, for example. The QNAME and RNAME format can be found in the IBM manual *ISPF and ISPF/PDF Version 2 Release 2 Diagnosis*, form number SC34-4020.)

```
AGQSCAN   CSECT
AGQSCAN   AMODE  31
AGQSCAN   RMODE  24
          BAKR   R14,0
          LR     R10,R15
          USING  AGQSCAN,R10
          LA     R13,ASAVE
          SPACE 1
*                ISSUE GQSCAN FOR THE SELECTED QNAME AND RNAME TO SEE
*                IF ANYONE ALREADY HAS IT.
          LA     R4,WORK1          ADDRESS OF GQSCAN AREA
          LA     R6,TOKEN          ADDRESS OF TOKEN AREA
          GQSCAN AREA=((R4),L'WORK1),REQLIM=1,                         X
                 SCOPE=ALL,QUIT=NO,                                    X
                 RESNAME=(Q,R,6,GENERIC),TOKEN=(6)
          ST     R15,RETCODE       SAVE RETURN CODE
          CH     R15,=H'0'         CHECK FOR ALL ENTRIES FOUND
          BE     DISPLAY           NO DATA -- END
          CH     R15,=H'4'         CHECK FOR NO DATA
          BE     RETURN            NO DATA -- END
          CH     R15,=H'8'         CHECK FOR OTHER ERRORS
          BH     RETURN            ERRORS -- END
          SPACE 1
*                IF MULTIPLE RESPONSES WERE RETURNED, CODE TO LOOP THROUGH
*                THEM SHOULD GO HERE.
          SPACE 1
*                END THE GQSCAN OPERATION (IF MULTIPLE REQUESTS WERE MADE)
          GQSCAN QUIT=YES,TOKEN=(6)
          SPACE 1
*                DISPLAY THE DATA WE GOT BACK
DISPLAY   EQU    *
          USING  RIB,R4            ESTABLISH ADDRESSABILITY
          L      R0,RIBNTO         GET NUMBER OF OWNERS
          CVD    R0,DOUBLEWD       CONVERT TO DECIMAL
          MVC    OWNERCNT,MASK1    MOVE EDIT MASK
          ED     OWNERCNT,DOUBLEWD+5   EDIT COUNT
          L      R0,RIBNTWE        GET NUMBER WAITING (EXCLUSIVE)
          CVD    R0,DOUBLEWD       CONVERT TO DECIMAL
          MVC    WAITECNT,MASK1    MOVE EDIT MASK
          ED     WAITECNT,DOUBLEWD+5   EDIT COUNT
          L      R0,RIBNTWS        GET NUMBER WAITING (SHARED)
          CVD    R0,DOUBLEWD       CONVERT TO DECIMAL
          MVC    WAITSCNT,MASK1    MOVE EDIT MASK
          ED     WAITSCNT,DOUBLEWD+5   EDIT COUNT
          MVC    QNAME,RIBQNAME    MOVE QUEUE NAME
          LA     R6,RIBEND         POINT TO VARIABLE SECTION START
          USING  RIBVAR,R6         ESTABLISH ADDRESSABILITY
          LA     R6,RIBRNAME       GET ADDRESS OF RNAME
          DROP   R6                END ADDRESSABILITY
          LR     R3,R6             SAVE FOR LATER
          XR     R7,R7             SET UP
```

```
          IC    R7,RIBRNMLN              FOR
          LA    R8,RNAME                  MVCL
          LA    R9,L'RNAME
          MVCL  R8,R6                   MOVE RNAME
          TPUT  MSG1,80                 DISPLAY
          TPUT  MSG2,80                  INFORMATION
          IC    R7,RIBRNMLN             GET LENGTH AGAIN
          LA    R7,0(R7,R3)             COMPUTE RIB ENTRY ADDRESS
          TM    RIBRNMLN,X'03'          IS LENGTH A MULTIPLE OF 4?
          BZ    LEN_DONE                  YES -- CONTINUE
          LA    R7,4(,R7)                 NO -- ADD 4,
          N     R7,=X'FFFFFFFC'           THEN AND OFF LAST TWO BITS
LEN_DONE  EQU   *
          USING RIBE,R7                 ESTABLISH ADDRESSABILITY
          MVC   OWNER,=C'WAITING'
          MVC   JOBNAME,RIBEJBNM        COPY JOB NAME
          MVC   SYSNAME,RIBESYSN        AND SYSTEM NAME
          TM    RIBESFLG,RIBESTAT       OWNER?
          BZ    CHKDISP                   NO -- CHECK EXCLUSIVE/SHARED
          MVC   OWNER,=C'OWNER)'
CHKDISP   EQU   *
          MVC   DISP,=C'SHARED   '
          TM    RIBERFLG,RIBETYPE       EXCLUSIVE?
          BZ    SHOWMSG3                  NO -- DISPLAY
          MVC   DISP,=C'EXCLUSIVE'
SHOWMSG3  EQU   *
          TPUT  MSG3,80
          DROP  R7                      END RIBE ADDRESSABILITY
          SPACE 1
RETURN    EQU   *
          L     R15,RETCODE             SET RETURN CODE
          PR
          SPACE 3
*         DATA AREAS
          CNOP  0,8
WORK1     DS    XL1024                  GQSCAN WORK AREA
RETCODE   DC    F'0'                    GQSCAN RETURN CODE
TOKEN     DC    D'0'                    TOKEN RETURNED HERE
DOUBLEWD  DC    D'0'                    WORK AREA
ASAVE     DC    F'0',C'F1SA',16F'0'
Q         DC    CL8'SPFEDIT'             ISPF EDIT Q NAME
R         DC    CL6'USERID'              LIBRARY DSNAME PREFIX
MSG1      DC    C' OWNERS:'
OWNERCNT  DS    CL6
          DC    C' WAITING (EXCLUSIVE):'
WAITECNT  DS    CL6
          DC    C' WAITING (SHARED):'
WAITSCNT  DS    CL6
          DC    C' FOR:'
QNAME     DS    CL8
          DC    C'/'
          DS    CL(MSG1+80-*)' '    FILLER
MSG2      EQU   *
RNAME     DS    CL80' '
MSG3      DC    C' '
OWNER     DC    CL7' ',C' '
JOBNAME   DC    CL8' ',C' ON:'
SYSNAME   DC    CL8' ',C' '
DISP      DC    C'             '
          DC    CL(MSG3+80-*)' '        FILLER
```

```
MASK1     DC    X'402020202120'    BZZZZ9 EDIT MASK
          SPACE 3
R0        EQU   0
R1        EQU   1
R2        EQU   2
R3        EQU   3
R4        EQU   4
R5        EQU   5
R6        EQU   6
R7        EQU   7
R8        EQU   8
R9        EQU   9
R10       EQU   10
R11       EQU   11
R12       EQU   12
R13       EQU   13
R14       EQU   14
R15       EQU   15
          ISGRIB
          END   AGQSCAN
```

Since there are no rules for specifying the QNAME and RNAME, one occasional use for this MVS facility is to pass addresses from one task or address space to another. The method for doing this is to agree on some unique QNAME (for example, MVSCB93) and then specify the address to pass as a four-byte RNAME value. The task that creates the data area in question issues the ENQ; the tasks or address spaces that want to retrieve the address issue a GQSCAN macro to locate all the entries under QNAME MVSCB93. This permits an authorized address space to create a work area in CSA, then issue ENQ. Unauthorized address spaces can then locate the CSA work area without the need for authorization, cross-memory services, or more demanding methods.

7.1.2 GRS controls

GRS is controlled by two members of SYS1.PARMLIB. The GRSRNL*xx* member allows redefinition of the scope or type of ENQ and RESERVE requests. It defines Resource Name Lists (RNLs) for system inclusion, system exclusion, or RESERVE conversion. A site can identify specific QNAMEs and RNAMEs, or resource name lists to be processed specially. Use of the GRSRNL*xx* options allows an installation to reduce the scope of an ENQ or RESERVE to a lower level, which can presumably reduce GRS CPU time. A site should have fairly detailed knowledge of how local applications use ENQ or RESERVE before proceeding with this.

The second SYS1.PARMLIB entry is the GRSCNF*xx* configuration member. This defines the multiple-CPU environment for GRS, as well as GRS startup options. Refer to the *GRS Planning* manual for details on these two GRS controls.

7.1.3 Global Resource Serialization data areas

GRS uses numerous data areas, which are listed in Table 7.1. However, only three DSECTs are provided by IBM for GRS data areas:

ISGRIB. For the information returned by GQSCAN.

ISGPEL. For the parameter list created by ENQ, etc.

ISGRNLE. Created from SYS1.PARMLIB GRSRNLxx information.

The others are documented in the *Data Areas* manuals, for those who want to research this area further.

7.2 MVS Locking Facilities

ENQ and DEQ provided reliable serialization from OS/360 onwards, but extracted an unacceptable performance price when frequently used. To provide other, faster serialization options, IBM developed both hardware and software solutions.

The hardware solutions began with the System/360 Test and Set instruction (opcode TS). This instruction provided limited serialization capability. It essentially operated like a Test under Mask instruction combined with a Move Immediate. The equivalent code would be:

```
TM      BYTE,X'80'
MVI     BYTE,X'FF'
```

However, the condition code was set differently. The advantage to using TS was that you could detect if another process (TCB) was in the middle of updating some common area.

The System/370 added the Compare and Swap instructions—opcodes CS and CDS. These offered an operation that might best be described as "store if unchanged." CS requires that the old value of a fullword be placed into the first register operand, and the desired new value into the second register operand. The old value is then compared to the current contents of the fullword. If the values are equal, the fullword will be replaced by the new value. If the values aren't equal, the current value will be placed in the first operand register. The condition code reflects what actually happened. (Opcode CDS (Compare Double and Swap) provides the same function for a doubleword, using even-odd register pairs.)

CS and CDS can update any field that could conceivably be updated simultaneously by two different TCBs or SRBs. CS should be used, for example, to update the forward pointer in an entry in a linked list. (CDS should be used similarly to update a doubly-linked list.) CS can also be used to by-

TABLE 7.1   GRS Data Area List By Name and Function

Name	DSECT	Description
CEPL	ISGCEPL	Command ESTAE Parm List
CPEP	ISGCPEP	Command Parser Exit Parms
CRB	ISGCRB	Command Request Block
CRWA	ISGCRWA	Command Recovery Work Area
DSPL	ISGDSPL	Dump Sort Parm List
GCB	ISGGCB	GRS CTC Driver Request Block
GCC	ISGGCC	GRS CTC Driver Control-card Table
GCL	ISGGCL	GRS CTC Driver Link Control Block
GCQ	ISGGCQ	GRS CTC Driver Queueing Element
GCT	ISGGCT	GRS CTC Driver Branch Table
GCV	ISGGCV	GRS CTC Driver Vector Table
GCX	ISGGCX	GRS CTC Driver Extract Table
GVT	ISGGVT	GRS Vector Table
GVTX	ISGGVTX	GRS Vector Table Extension
MRB	ISRMRB	Message Request Block
PARS	ISGPARS	GRS Parse Setup Macro
PEL	ISGPEL	Parameter Element List
PEXB	ISGPEXB	Pool Extent Block
PQCB	ISQPQCB	Placeholder Queue Control Block
QCB	ISGQCB	Queue Control Block
QEL	ISGQEL	Queue Element
QFPL	ISGQFPL	ENQ/DEQ FRR Parm List
QFPL1	ISGQFPL1	GRS Queue Scanning Services FRR Parm List
QHT	ISGQHT	Queue Hash Table
QPL	ISGQPL	Queue Work Block Parm List
QWA	ISGQWA	Queue Work Area
QWB	ISGQWB	Queue Work Block
QXB	ISGQXB	Queue Extension Block
REPL	ISGREPL	Ring-Processing ESTAE Parm List
RIB	ISGRIB	Resource Info Block
RIBE	ISGRIB	Resource Info Block Element
RNLE	ISGRNLE	Resource Name List Entry
RPT	ISGRPT	Resource Pool Table
RSA	ISGRSA	Ring-processing System Authority Message
RSC	ISGRSC	Ring Status Change Parm List
RSL	ISGRSL	Ring-processing System Link Block
RSP	ISGRSP	Ring-processing Permutation Work Area
RST	ISGRST	Ring-processing Status Table
RSV	ISGRSV	Ring-processing System Vector Table
SAHT	ISGSAHT	System/ASID Hash Table
SMPL	ISGSMPL	Storage Mgmt Parm List Entry

pass the WAIT and POST macros—*Principles of Operation* includes examples in an appendix.

MVS also provides a software serialization function called *locking*. Locking provides an MVS service to control and serialize various MVS functions using fullword data areas called locks. Each lock protects a category of work, such as the MVS dispatcher, I/O Supervisor, and even ENQ/DEQ.

There are several different lock types. A spin lock lets the lock holder prevent other CPUs from doing the category of work. Other CPUs or TCBs requesting the lock will loop (or spin) until the lock is available. Examples of events requiring this include page fixing and updating the ASVT. Spin locks can be shared or exclusive. A suspend lock stops the process that requests it, but allows the CPU to do other work. The CMSEQDQ lock, which serializes ENQ and DEQ, is an example of a suspend lock. Finally, the CPU lock (a special category) is used to disable the processor for interrupts.

MVS updates locks differently, based on their type. For example, the CPU ID (processor number) that holds a lock is stored in the lock when it's held for spin locks. (Other types are updated differently.) The *Diagnosis: System Reference* manual contains a list of locks, along with their type and contents when held. The IHACMS macro describes the layout of a lock word.

Locks are not created equal, and MVS enforces a lock hierarchy. The lowest-level lock is called the local lock. You will often need to obtain this lock when requesting some MVS services. Table 7.2 shows some of the documented MVS locks.

There's one local lock per ASCB, one IOSUCB lock per Unit Control Block, and one CPU lock per processor in a complex. The others are unique within an MVS system.

In Table 7.2, "global" and "local" refer to the scope of the lock. Global locks are used to serialize a function across all processors and address spaces in an MVS system. Local locks are used to serialize MVS functions within one address space.

Locking services are provided through the SETLOCK macro. SETLOCK has several operands, including:

OBTAIN/RELEASE/TEST.   The type of processing desired.

MODE.   Conditional or unconditional.

REGS.   Save or use R11-R14.

TABLE 7.2   Selected MVS Locks

Name	Purpose	Type
Local	Serializing within an address space	Local suspend
CML	Used to serialize in another address space	Local suspend
CMSEQDQ	ENQ/DEQ cross-memory lock	Global suspend
CPU	Provides disablement; multiple holders	Special
SRM	System Resource Manager lock	Global spin
IOSUCB	Control UCB update	Global spin
DISP	Dispatcher control block update	Global spin
ASM	Auxiliary storage manager	Global spin

TYPE. The lock ID.

DISABLED. Return control in disabled state.

The following is a section of code that uses SETLOCK to obtain the local lock, uses branch entry GETMAIN to obtain some storage, then uses SET-LOCK again to release the lock:

```
LOCK       TITLE 'UCLA X414.371 9.93 SETLOCK EXAMPLE'
*          R4     TCB ADDRESS
*          R7     ASCB ADDRESS
*          R12    PROGRAM BASE REGISTER
SETLOCK    CSECT
           BAKR   R14,0                   SAVE REGISTERS
           LR     R12,R15                 ESTABLISH
           USING  SETLOCK,R12               ADDRESSABILITY
           LA     R13,SAVEAREA            SAVE AREA
           SPACE 3
*          GET INTO SUPERVISOR STATE, PROTECT KEY ZERO
           MODESET KEY=ZERO,MODE=SUP
           SPACE 1
*          GET LOCAL LOCK PRIOR TO DOING BRANCH ENTRY GETMAIN
           SETLOCK  OBTAIN,TYPE=LOCAL,                                X
                  MODE=UNCOND,REGS=STDSAVE
           SPACE 1
*          NOW ISSUE BRANCH ENTRY GETMAIN
           L      R4,PSATOLD-PSA(,R0)     GET TCB ADDRESS
           L      R7,PSAAOLD-PSA(,R0)     AND ASCB ADDRESS
           GETMAIN RC,LV=72,BRANCH=YES,KEY=0,LOC=(ANY,ANY),SP=231
           LTR    R15,R15                 TEST RETURN CODE
           BNZ    ERROR1                     NOT ZERO -- GIVE UP...
           ST     R1,HOLDADDR             SAVE ADDRESS OF STORAGE
           SPACE 1
*          RELEASE LOCAL LOCK
           SETLOCK  RELEASE,TYPE=LOCAL,                               X
                  REGS=STDSAVE
           SPACE 1
*          RELEASE THE STORAGE NOW (DON'T NEED LOCAL LOCK UNLESS USING
*          BRANCH ENTRY)
           L      R1,HOLDADDR             GET STORAGE ADDRESS
           STORAGE  RELEASE,LENGTH=72,ADDR=(1),SP=231
           SPACE 1
*          RETURN TO CALLING PROGRAM
RETURN     EQU    *
           SR     R15,R15                 SET RETURN CODE
           PR                             RETURN TO OS
           SPACE 1
*          FORCE AN ABEND IF ERRORS ARISE
ERROR1     EQU    *
           EX     0,*                     ABEND 0C3
           SPACE 1
HEXCONV    EQU    *
           UNPK   EBCDICEQ(9),0(5,R1)     UNPACK
           TR     EBCDICEQ,TRTAB-240      TRANSLATE
           BR     R14                     RETURN
EBCDICEQ   DC     CL8' ',C' '             8 DATA BYTES, 1 FILLER BYTE
```

```
          EJECT
*         DATA AREAS
SAVEAREA  DC    F'0',CL4'F1SA',16F'+0'
HOLDADDR  DC    F'0'
TRTAB     DC    C'0123456789ABCDEF'       HEX CONVERSION TABLE
          SPACE 3
*         REGISTER EQUATES
*
R0        EQU   0
R1        EQU   1
R2        EQU   2
R3        EQU   3
R4        EQU   4
R5        EQU   5
R6        EQU   6
R7        EQU   7
R8        EQU   8
R9        EQU   9
R10       EQU   10
R11       EQU   11
R12       EQU   12
R13       EQU   13
R14       EQU   14
R15       EQU   15
          SPACE 3
          PRINT NOGEN
          CVT   DSECT=YES,LIST=NO
          DCBD  DSORG=PS,DEVD=(DA)
          IHAASCB
          IHAPSA
          END   SETLOCK
```

MVS locking uses several data areas for which there are no mapping macros, to the best of my knowledge. However, locks appear frequently in other data areas. For example, the local lock for each address space is kept in the ASCB, in the field named ASCBLOCK.

The MVS lock manager code also uses a Lock Manager Parameter List Table. This defines nucleus lock information, but there's no distributed mapping macro.

7.3 Summary

Serialization is a necessary service for any multitasking operating system. MVS and the S/370 instruction set provide several tools for serialization. Chief among these are the ENQ and DEQ macros, which provide serialization based on two fields called QNAME and RNAME, along with the scope of the request. ENQ and DEQ are extensively used within MVS, and a list of system ENQ QNAME and RNAME combinations is provided in the *System Diagnosis: Reference* manual.

The System/370 architecture provides three instructions for serialization: TS, CS, and CDS. CS or CDS should be used for any linked list insertions or deletions, and have numerous other uses for multitasking and multiprocessing situations.

MVS locking services provide a faster serialization service intended for MVS internal use only. The SETLOCK macro is used to invoke locking services.

7.4 Things to Do

- If you can execute MVS console commands, try the D GRS,CONTENTION command.

- If you have access to the SYS1.PARMLIB library, review the GRS controls for your installation.

- If you maintain any assembler language programs, research them for use of the ENQ/DEQ macros.

- If you have access to SYS1.SAMPLIB, review the GRS sample exits in that library (for example, ISGECMON).

8

MVS Input/Output System Control Blocks

The topics in this chapter cover the process through which an application program's I/O requests are executed. This process actually comprises three elements, which will be addressed separately. The first is MVS access methods, which represent the normal assembler language I/O interface. The second is the MVS EXCP processor, which performs the actions needed to execute low-level channel commands. And the third is the MVS I/O Supervisor (IOS), which actually issues the I/O instructions and handles I/O completion interrupts.

It would require several books to provide full coverage of access methods, so this chapter isn't comprehensive. However, it does cover the primary interface control blocks to the extent that IBM provides DSECTs to access them.

The EXCP processor essentially provides a simple service, but the complexity of channel programming makes it a much more difficult topic. I won't attempt to explain I/O programming for the EXCP in complete detail; I will, however, take a working example through the entire process. Two recommended resources for more in-depth coverage of I/O devices and their performance are *IBM DASD*, by Robert Johnson, and *I/O* by Pat Artis and Gilbert Houtemaker.

The I/O supervisor itself provides the essential services needed to complete I/O processing at a very low level. While direct IOS services aren't frequently used (unless you're writing your own access method or supporting special non-IBM devices, for example), IOS control blocks are frequently useful sources of information.

8.1 Access Method Control Blocks

The collection of software that supports specific combinations of I/O devices and patterns of access to data from those devices is called an access method. IBM has provided numerous examples through the years, including many that are obsolete at present. The access methods most frequently used in MVS are the Queued Sequential Access Method (QSAM), the Virtual Access Method (VTAM). Additionally, the Basic Partitioned Access Method (BPAM) provides support for partitioned data sets (PDSes).

The control blocks for these access methods are documented to varying levels. DSECTs for many of the internal VSAM and VTAM control blocks are no longer distributed by IBM; some of those for VSAM will be discussed here, but you'll have to figure out how to use them. The following sections describe a few of the commonly used access method control blocks:

8.1.1 Sequential Access Method control blocks

The fundamental control block for QSAM, BPAM, and the other older access methods is the Data Control Block, or DCB. The DCB is coded within each application program using it and initialized with an OPEN macro, at which point the access method OPEN executors fill in various pieces of information. The DCB is accessed through the DCBD macro, which produces the DSECT IHADCB. Fields of frequent interest within the DCB include the following:

DCBBLKSI. The block size of the file being processed.

DCBLRECL. The record length of the file being processed.

DCBRECFM. Bit flags describing the record format (fixed, variable, etc.).

DCBDDNAM. The JCL DD name (before the OPEN macro is issued).

DCBTIOT. The TIOT offset to the DD name after the OPEN macro is issued.

DCBOFLGS. Bit flags describing if the DCB was opened successfully.

The DCB DSECT listing is about 20 pages long, and there are numerous other fields of interest. The DCB is complicated in that it was used for many years by a number of access methods, most of which are now obsolete. The DCB also comprises five sections, and its layout changes when the OPEN and CLOSE macros process it. Thus, for example, DCBDDNAM is valid before the OPEN macro, but disappears after the DCB is open (i.e., the storage is reused to save space). Similarly, the DCBBLKSI field isn't valid before

OPEN (unless the BLKSIZE parameter was coded on the DCB, which usually isn't a recommended practice). The DSECT identifies which fields are changed by OPEN.

Another DSECT that holds informative data is IHAPDS. This DSECT provides information on the fields within a PDS directory entry. The data within the directory can be retrieved with the BLDL macro, which is described in the appropriate MVS DFP manuals. The IHAPDS DSECT maps the directory information for load modules, which contain information such as module length and alias indicator.

8.1.2 Virtual Storage Access Method control blocks

Both VSAM and VTAM share certain application-program-level control blocks, although their use of these is markedly different. The common control blocks include the following:

- Access Method Control Block (ACB), DSECT name IFGACB
- Request Parameter List (RPL), DSECT name IFGRPL
- Exit List (EXLST), DSECT name IFGEXLST

These three control blocks are generated by macros ACB, RPL, and EXLST. The ACB is similar to the DCB, and includes a DD name field (ACB-DDNAM) and open flags (ACBOFLGS) at the same offsets. It also provides an error field (ACBERFLG) that contains an error code from the OPEN or CLOSE macros. The RPL contains information related to a specific I/O request; some of the fields of interest are:

RPLAREA. The address of the data area for this request.

RPLRTNCD. Return code for failing requests.

RPLFDB2. Additional error recovery information.

RPLERRCD. Error code for failing requests.

The RPLRTNCD field's value is also returned in register 15 after a request completes. For a complete description of the three error fields, refer to the appropriate DFP macro reference manual. (You can also get a good understanding of the type of information returned in these three fields by looking at the information for message IEC161; the data in this message comes from these fields.)

IBM provides several macros for inspecting and changing VSAM and VTAM control blocks: TESTCB, SHOWCB, and MODCB. For examples of their use, refer to my *Assembler for COBOL Programmers* book.

IBM formerly provided DSECTs for many additional VSAM control blocks, which allowed access to much statistical information about VSAM clusters. One valuable control block was the Access Method Data Statistics Block, or AMDSB. This holds the statistical information about a VSAM cluster in the user's address space while the cluster is open. Fields of interest within this include the number of control interval splits and free space percentages. (The AMDSB holds the information available through the ID-CAMS utility program LISTCAT function.) Access to the AMDSB is through another control block named the AMBL, whose address is kept in the ACB.

While the AMDSB is no longer distributed as a DSECT, the information within it is frequently quite useful. For most purposes, the layout in the debugging handbooks will serve as a useful introduction. Note that the SHOWCB macro can be used to access the information from the AMDSB, albeit with more instructions.

8.2 EXCP Processor Control Blocks

The EXCP processor receives low-level I/O requests directly from application programs, or indirectly through access methods. Then it translates them into requests suitable for IOS. The interface to EXCP is through several macros, which have unique SVC numbers associated with them:

- EXCP, SVC 0
- ERREXCP, SVC 15
- EXCPVR, SVC 114
- PURGE, SVC 16
- RESTORE, SVC 17

There's another macro, XDAP, that provides a simplified interface to EXCP and also uses SVC 0.

The input to EXCP is the Input/Output Block, or IOB. This is a user-constructed control block, like the DCB. However, unlike the DCB, it has no associated macro to construct it automatically. The DSECT macro is IEZIOB. The IOB is built by access methods for individual I/O requests (e.g., to read in a block of data). Direct EXCP users are, in essence, their own access method, and have to construct this control block themselves. The IOB holds the address of the DCB associated with the file being accessed; it also holds the address of the channel program to be executed.

A *channel program* is a series of machine commands called channel command words, or CCWs. These are all eight-byte (doubleword) fields, and contain a command code, data area address, data length, and various flag bits. There are two types of CCWs: Format-0 CCWs, which are the old style, used to access data below the 16MB line, and Format-1 CCWs, used to access data for 31-bit addressing mode. The layout of these can be found in the *ESA Reference Summary* (blue card).

Because the Format-0 CCW dates back to the initial System/360 design, there's still a large quantity of old programs coded to use it. Even the EXCP processor still expects Format-0 CCWs as input. This frequently requires that I/O-related blocks be placed below the 16MB line, which you saw in the discussion of VSM and V\RSM components. There's also a facility that allows Format-0 CCWs to use buffers above the 16MB line, called a "virtual IDAW."

The role of the EXCP processor is to translate the IOB-based I/O request and its associated CCWs into a request suitable for direct execution by IOS. To do this, the EXCP processor must first page-fix the data areas used by the request into real storage. It must then translate the addresses in the original CCW chain into real storage addresses, and create a new copy of the original CCW chain with the revised (real) addresses. (The EXCP processor might also need to add additional CCWs to the original set, which is done at this point.) To complete the process, EXCP uses the Begin End Block (BEB) and Translated CCW (TCCW), among others.

Along with this CCW translation and page-fixing, EXCP builds a control block named the Request Queue Element (RQE). The RQE originally served as the main I/O scheduling element in OS/360; in MVS, its main use is to find the original IOB when the I/O is complete.

Normally, EXCP users don't have to concern themselves with this series of control blocks, and direct access isn't normally needed. However, when an error arises in preparing the channel program for execution, the EXCP processor will create a separate area for debugging called the EXCP Debugging Area, or XDBA. The XDBA is addressed through the TCB (field name TCBEXCPD). When constructed, the XDBA contains a copy of the RQE, TCCW, and BEB, along with other information. This control block is present whenever the EXCP processor produces an ABEND with system codes of 200, 400, or 800. The DSECT macro name is IECDXDBA.

Users of the EXCPVR macro follow a similar path, but are responsible for the CCW translation and page-fixing themselves. (As a result, programs using EXCPVR must be authorized.) For both EXCP and EXCPVR macros, the EXCP processor constructs an IOS Block (IOSB) and passes the request to IOS. Table 8.1 lists EXCP-related control blocks.

When the request is complete, EXCP updates the IOB with the status of the request, releases the translated CCW copies, and posts the ECB associated with the request to indicate that it was completed. (IBM advises in *System Data Administration* that use of EXCP isn't recommended. Since it's the only way to execute nonstandard CCWs, however, this represents a problem if you're using nonstandard devices. Each situation is unique, so be careful if you're already using EXCP. This discussion will be continued later.)

TABLE 8.1 EXCP-Related Control Blocks

Name	DSECT	Description
BEB	IECDBEB	TCCW Beginning-End Block
DEB	IEZDEB	Data Extent Block
EPCB	IECDEPCB	EXCP Purge Control Block
FIX	IECDFIX	TCCW Translator Fix List
IDAL	IECDIDAL	TCCS Translator Indirect Address List
IOB	IEZIOB	Input/Output Block
RQE	IECDRQE	EXCP Request Queue Element
TCCB	IECDTCCW	Translation Control Block
XCPS	IECDXCPS	Channel Program Scan Program List/Work Area
XDBA	IECDXDBA	EXCP Debugging Area

8.2.1 Data Extent Block (DEB)

The DEB isn't specifically an EXCP-related control block, since it's also used by the VSAM access method. The DEB is created by an OPEN macro, and serves to retain various information about the I/O devices and file areas associated with the DCB being opened. However, I'll cover it before proceeding to the MVS I/O supervisor proper.

The IEZDEB macro documents the DEB's layout. DEBs are organized as a singly linked list, chained from the TCB field TCBDEBA. Additionally, the DCB field DCBDEBA holds the address of the DEB associated with that DCB.

The DEB contains several types of fields. The basic section of the DEB contains the address of the TCB that opened the DCB. This section also has a field, DEBOFLGS, that provides bit fields indicating the JCL DISP= value (NEW, OLD, or MOD). The DEB basic section begins at the label DEBBASIC; this field name is what the TCB and DCB fields address.

Following this, for disk files there's a direct-access storage device section. This contains repeating elements, one for each extent in each data set assigned to the DCB. Each element contains the address of the Unit Control Block (UCB, described later) for the device holding this extent. The beginning and ending disk addresses for the extent are also kept, along with the number of tracks in the extent. All this information begins at label DEBDASD.

There are also a number of other sections in the DEB. These include sections to support various access methods and EXCP, etc. I recommend that you review the IEZDEB macro.

Because the DEB is addressable through the TCB, you can use it to locate an open DCB or ACB without knowing the address. The technique to do this relies on another control block called the Task I/O Table (TIOT). The TIOT, oversimplifying somewhat, contains one entry for each DD statement in a step. Each DCB, when open, contains a field named DCBTIOT, containing the offset (not the address!) of the first DD entry for that DCB. Figure 8.1 shows the control block relationships involved. This technique is useful when writing subroutines for high-level languages, which might not permit the DCB address to be passed as a parameter.

8.3 I/O Supervisor Control Blocks

The I/O supervisor is responsible for scheduling and starting I/O operations, notifying the requester when the I/O operations complete, and recovering from I/O errors when required. IOS control blocks are listed in Table 8.2.

Most IOS control blocks are of interest only to those writing their own access methods or custom database systems, or supporting unique non-IBM devices. The IOS control blocks of most general interest are the Unit Control Block (UCB) and IOS Block (IOSB). The numerous other IOS control blocks are usually of less interest to most assembler programmers, unless they're writing their own access methods.

8.3.1 Unit Control Block (UCB)

The UCB has existed since OS/360. Its represents a specific, individually addressable I/O device, and can also serve to represent a different path or exposure to a previously defined I/O device.

Several terms are key to understanding UCBs and how IOS uses them. An individual I/O device is frequently termed a *unit*. Typically, several I/O devices are connected to *control units* or *controllers*. An IBM 3380 or 3390 disk is an example of a unit; units, in turn, connect to an IBM 3880 or 3990

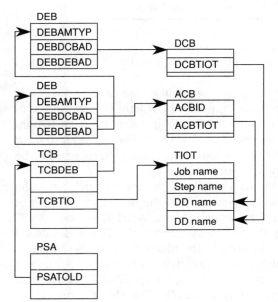

Figure 8.1 Finding VSAM ACBs using the DEB chain.

TABLE 8.2 IOS Control Blocks

Name	DSECT	Description
CRW	IHACRW	Channel Report Word
CRWQ	IOSDCRWQ	Channel Recovery Word Queueing Element
CWR	IOSDCWR	Channel Recovery Word LOGREC Record
DCE	IECDDCE	
DCQ	IHADCQ	Device Class Queue
DDT	IECDDT	Device Descriptor Table
ERPMSG	IECDLMSG	IOS/ERP Error Message Mapping
ESW	IHAESW	Extended Status Word
ESWL	IHAESWL	Extended Status Word Long
EWA	EWAMAP	ERP Work Area
FMTP	IOSDFMTP	IOS Formatter Parameters
HIDT	IOSDHIDT	Hot I/O Detection Table
ICHPT	IHAICHPT	Installation Channel Path Table
IOCOM	IECDIOCM	I/O Communications Area
IOQ	IECDIOQ	IOS Queue Element
IOSB	IECDIOSB	IOS Block
IPIB	IECDIPIB	IOS Purge Interface Block
IPWA	IOSDIPWA	IOS Purge Work Area
IRB	IHAIRB	Interruption Response Block
MIR	IOSDMIR	Missing Interrupt LOGREC Record
ORB	IHAORB	Operation Request Block
SCD	IOSCSCD	Status Collector Data
SCHIB	IHASCHIB	Subchannel Information Block
SLR	IOSDSLR	Subchannel Logout Record
TICW	IOSDTICB	MIH Time Interval Control Block
UCB	IEFUCBOB	IOS Unit Control Block
UCBCX	IECUCBCX	TCB Tape Class Extension
URLB	IOSDURLB	Unconditional Reserve Mapping Macro

controller. Control units, in turn, connected to a *channel* in the original System/360 architecture.

A channel was essentially a limited-capability computer, whose only function was to process I/O requests from the CPU. Channels have access to the same central memory as the CPU. However, instead of regular 370 instructions, channels process special commands called *channel command words* (CCWs). CCWs could be completed by the channel itself, or could be passed on to the controller and unit for execution.

The CPU had special instructions for "talking" to each channel. Thus, the Start I/O (SIO) instruction told the channel to begin processing a series of CCWs, whose address was in the channel address word at location X'48'. The channel also could notify the CPU that a series of CCWs had finished execution. This was via an I/O interrupt. The channel could also cause an I/O interrupt if it received status information from a controller.

This description held true roughly through MVS/370. The advent of MVS/XA changed the I/O structure dramatically. The set of channels attached to a CPU was replaced by an independent unit called an external data controller, or EXDC. (Current processors call it the channel subsystem (CSS).) The I/O instructions were all replaced by new ones; SIO was replaced by the Start Subchannel (SSCH) instruction, for example. A new CCW format was also made available for 31-bit addressing, but the old format was still acceptable.

However, in spite of these significant changes, the old System/360 names still appear frequently. Thus, *channel* is often used where *EXDC* or *channel path* would be more precise. Similarly, *SIO* might still be used as a term for an individual I/O operation, although *SSCH* would be proper. For a fuller discussion of the nuances of IBM mainframe I/O configurations, refer to the Prasad *IBM Mainframes* or Johnson and Johnson *DASD* books.

With this background, the purpose of the UCB is to represent an individual I/O device. The UCB holds the current status of the device, along with some device-specific characteristics. It's organized into a prefix, a common segment, an extension, and device-dependent segments. Fields of interest in the UCB include:

- UCBSTAT and UCBSFLS, containing the current device status.
- UCBNAME, the device ID in EBCDIC.
- UCBTYP, a coded device type field.
- UCBVOLI, the volume serial currently mounted on the device (for DASD and tape).
- UCBSTAB, a volume status flag (public/private/storage).

Numerous device-dependent fields exist in the varying device-dependent segments. Segments are defined for DASD, tape, unit record, and other types. The unit record segment, in turn, incorporates several types of printer information.

Several methods are available for accessing the UCB. One is to use the beginning address of the UCB chain, found in the CVTUCBA field, and to locate all subsequent UCBs using the UCBNXUCB field. This is typically used in older programs. The second is to use the IOSLOOK macro, which provides a UCB lookup service. IOSLOOK, however, requires the user to be in the supervisor state and to provide the device number.

The third technique uses the UCBSCAN macro. This service removes the requirements of IOSLOOK, and is more suited for scanning all UCBs in the system. An example using the UCBSCAN service is shown in the following. (This example also uses the LSPACE macro, which returns the free space on a disk volume.) This example shows using a copy of the UCB rather than accessing the actual UCB itself; this will probably be a desirable technique for future MVS products.

```
LSPA      TITLE 'UCLA X414.371 12/93 LSPACE EXAMPLE'



*         R11   TERMINAL LINE SIZE
*         R12   PROGRAM BASE REGISTER
LSPACE    CSECT
LSPACE    AMODE 31
LSPACE    RMODE 24
          BAKR  R14,0                     SAVE REGISTERS
          LR    R12,R15                   ESTABLISH
          USING LSPACE,R12                  ADDRESSABILITY
          LA    R13,SAVEAREA              SAVE AREA
          SPACE 1
*         GET PARM=INFO
          L     R2,0(,R1)                GET PARM= ADDRESS
          CLC   0(2,R2),=H'0'            ZERO LENGTH?
          BNH   CHECKTSO                   YES - NO SPACE MINIMUM
          LH    R3,0(,R2)                GET LENGTH
          BCTR  R3,0                     SUBTRACT ONE FOR EXECUTE
          EX    R3,PACK1                 PACK AMOUNT
          MVC   PH_LIMIT,=CL4' '         CLEAR 'NONE'
          EX    R3,MOVE1                 AND MOVE LIMIT TO HEADING
          CVB   R4,DOUBLEWD              CONVERT LIMIT TO BINARY
          ST    R4,MYLIMIT               AND SAVE FOR LATER USE
          SPACE 1
*         GET TERMINAL LINE SIZE
CHECKTSO  EQU   *
          GTSIZE
          LR    R11,R1                   SAVE LINE SIZE
          SPACE 3
*         DISPLAY CURRENT TIME AND DATE
          STCK  DOUBLEWD                 STORE CLOCK
          STCKCONV STCKVAL=DOUBLEWD,CONVVAL=CPU_TIME,TIMETYPE=DEC, X
                DATETYPE=MMDDYYYY
          MVC   PH_TIME,=X'4020207A20207A2120'
          ED    PH_TIME,CPU_TIME    EDIT CURRENT TIME
          MVC   PH_DATE,=X'40202061202061211202020'
          ED    PH_DATE,CPU_TIME+8       AND DATE
          TPUT  PH_HEADING,(11)          DISPLAY LINE
          SPACE 1
*         INITIALIZE FOR UCB SCAN
SCAN_UCBS     EQU   *
          MVC   MACTYPE,=CL8'UCBSCAN'    SET UP MACRO NAME IF ERROR
          UCBSCAN COPY,                  GET COPY OF UCB            X
                WORKAREA=WORK1,          WORK AREA FOR UCBSCAN MACRO X
                UCBAREA=MYCOPY,          UCB COPY RETURNED HERE      X
                DYNAMIC=YES,             BOTH STATIC AND DYNAMIC UCBSX
                NONBASE=NO,              ONLY FIRST IF MULTIPLE PATHSX
                DEVCLASS=DASD,           DISK DEVICE CLASS           X
                IOCTOKEN=WORK2,          I/O CONFIGURATION TOKEN     X
                RETCODE=RC1,             RETURN CODE AREA            X
                RSNCODE=RS1              REASON CODE AREA
          LTR   R15,R15                  TEST RETURN CODE
          BNZ   CHECK_STOP                 NONZERO - CHECK REASON, END
          LA    R2,MYCOPY                GET UCB COPY ADDRESS
          USING UCBCMSEG,R2              ESTABLISH ADDRESSABILITY
          TM    UCBSTAT,UCBONLI          DEVICE ONLINE?
          BZ    SCAN_UCBS                  NO -- BYPASS IT
          TM    UCBSTAT,UCBSYSR          SYSTEM RESIDENCE DEVICE?
          BO    SCAN_UCBS                  YES -- BYPASS IT
          MVC   DISP_VOL,UCBVOLI         MOVE VOLUME ID
```

```
        DROP  R2                          END ADDRESSABILITY
        SPACE 1
*       ISSUE LSPACE TO DETERMINE FREE SPACE AVAILABLE
        MVC   MACTYPE,=CL8'LSPACE'        SET UP MACRO NAME IF ERROR
        LA    R2,MYCOPY                   GET UCB ADDRESS
        LSPACE MF=I,                      INLINE FORM OF MACRO            X
               UCB=(2),                   UCB ADDRESS                     X
               DATA=MYDATA,               RETURNED DATA AREA             X
               F4DSCB=MYDSCB              RETURNED FORMAT-4 DSCB
        ST    R15,RC2                     SAVE RETURN CODE
        ST    R0,RS2                      AND REASON CODE
        LTR   R15,R15                     TEST RETURN CODE
        BNZ   CHECK_STOP                    NONZERO - CHECK REASON, END
        SPACE 1
*       DETERMINE IF THIS VOLUME IS SMS CONTROLLED
        MVC   DISP_SMS,=C'    '           CLEAR INDICATOR
        LA    R2,MYDSCB                   GET DSCB ADDRESS
        USING IECSDSL4,R2                 ESTABLISH ADDRESSABILITY
        TM    DS4SMSFG,DS4SMSTS           TEST SMS BITS
        BZ    SHOW_SPACE                    NOT ON -- NO SMS
        MVC   DISP_SMS,=C'(SMS)'            ON - MOVE IN INDICATOR
        SPACE 1
*       SHOW SPACE AVAILABLE
SHOW_SPACE    EQU   *
        LA    R2,MYDATA                   GET DATA AREA ADDRESS
        USING LSPDRETN,R2                 ESTABLISH ADDRESSABILITY
        ICM   R0,15,LSPDTCYL              GET TOTAL FREE CYLINDERS
        C     R0,MYLIMIT                  COMPARE TO LOW LIMIT
        BL    SCAN_UCBS                     IF ZERO, IGNORE THIS PACK
        CVD   R0,DOUBLEWD
        OI    DOUBLEWD+7,X'0F'
        UNPK  DISP_CYLS,DOUBLEWD
        L     R0,LSPDLCYL                 GET LARGEST FREE AREA
        CVD   R0,DOUBLEWD
        OI    DOUBLEWD+7,X'0F'
        UNPK  DISP_LARGEST,DOUBLEWD
        DROP  R2
        TPUT  DISP_DATA,(11)              DISPLAY LINE
        B     SCAN_UCBS                   AND CONTINUE
        SPACE 1
CHECK_STOP    EQU   *
        CLC   RC1,=F'4'                   RETURN CODE 4 FROM UCBSCAN?
        BNE   SHOW_STOP                     NO -- DISPLAY INFO
        CLC   RS1,=F'1'                   REASON CODE 1 FROM UCBSCAN?
        BNE   SHOW_STOP                     NO -- DISPLAY INFO
        TPUT  DONE_MSG,(11)               DISPLAY 'DONE'
        B     RETURN                      AND END
SHOW_STOP     EQU   *
        L     R0,RC1                      SET UP RETURN CODES
        CVD   R0,DOUBLEWD
        OI    DOUBLEWD+7,X'0F'
        UNPK  STOP_RC1,DOUBLEWD
        L     R0,RS1
        CVD   R0,DOUBLEWD
        OI    DOUBLEWD+7,X'0F'
        UNPK  STOP_RS1,DOUBLEWD
        L     R0,RC2
        CVD   R0,DOUBLEWD
        OI    DOUBLEWD+7,X'0F'
        UNPK  STOP_RC2,DOUBLEWD
        L     R0,RS2
```

```
            CVD   R0,DOUBLEWD
            OI    DOUBLEWD+7,X'0F'
            UNPK  STOP_RS2,DOUBLEWD
            TPUT  STOP_MSG,(11)             DISPLAY LINE
            SPACE 1
*           RETURN TO CALLING PROGRAM
RETURN      EQU   *
            SR    R15,R15                   SET RETURN CODE
            PR                              RETURN TO OS
            SPACE 1
HEXCONV     EQU   *
            UNPK  EBCDICEQ(9),0(5,R1)       UNPACK
            TR    EBCDICEQ,TRTAB-240        TRANSLATE
            BR    R14                       RETURN
EBCDICEQ DC       CL8' ',C' '               8 DATA BYTES, 1 FILLER BYTE
            EJECT
*           EXECUTED INSTRUCTIONS
PACK1    PACK     DOUBLEWD,2(0,R2)          *** EXECUTED INSTRUCTION ***
MOVE1    MVC      PH_LIMIT(0),2(R2)         *** EXECUTED INSTRUCTION ***
*           DATA AREAS
DOUBLEWD DS       D
SAVEAREA DC       F'0',CL4'F1SA',16F'+0'
CPU_TIME DC       5F'0'
WORK1    DC       XL100'00'
MYCOPY   DC       XL48'00'
WORK2    DC       XL48'00'
RC1      DC       F'0'
RC2      DC       F'0'
RS1      DC       F'0'
RS2      DC       F'0'
MYDSCB   DC       24F'0'
MYDATA   DC       10F'0'
MYLIMIT  DC       F'0'                      MINIMUM FREE SPACE TO DISPLAY
STOP_MSG DC       C' ERROR IN:'
MACTYPE  DC       CL8'********'
         DC       C' RETURN CODES:'
STOP_RC1 DC       CL4' ',C'('
STOP_RS1 DC       CL4' ',C'),'
STOP_RC2 DC       CL4' ',C'('
STOP_RS2 DC       CL4' ',C')'
         DC       CL(STOP_MSG+133-*)' '  FILLER
DISP_DATA DC      C' VOLUME:'
DISP_VOL DC       CL6'******'
         DC       C' TOTAL CYLINDERS:'
DISP_CYLS DC      CL6' ',C' (LARGEST:'
DISP_LARGEST DC   CL6' ',C') '
DISP_SMS DC       CL5' '
         DC       CL(DISP_DATA+133-*)' '  FILLER
DONE_MSG DC       CL132' ---------- VOLUME DISPLAY DONE ----------'
PH_HEADING DC     C' SPACE SCAN AT'
PH_TIME  DC       CL9' ',C' ON '
PH_DATE  DC       CL11' ',C' LIMIT:'
PH_LIMIT DC       C'NONE'
         DC       CL(PH_HEADING+133-*)' '  FILLER
TRTAB    DC       C'0123456789ABCDEF'    HEX CONVERSION TABLE
         SPACE 3
*           REGISTER EQUATES
*
R0       EQU      0
R1       EQU      1
R2       EQU      2
```

```
R3          EQU    3
R4          EQU    4
R5          EQU    5
R6          EQU    6
R7          EQU    7
R8          EQU    8
R9          EQU    9
R10         EQU    10
R11         EQU    11
R12         EQU    12
R13         EQU    13
R14         EQU    14
R15         EQU    15
            SPACE  3
MYUCB       DSECT
            IEFUCBOB   DEVCLAS=DA
            IECSDSL1 (4)
            LSPACE MF=(D,DATA)              GENERATE DSECT AREA
            END    LSPACE
```

The address of an individual UCB is also available from the DEB (DE-BUCBAD) and the TIOESRTF field of a TIOT entry. UCBs are located in the MVS nucleus.

8.3.2 IOS Block (IOSB)

The IOSB represents the lowest-level control block for an I/O request. It exists for the duration of the request, and is normally freed on completion of the I/O operation. Like the IOB, the IOSB is created by the requestor rather than by MVS. It's normally in SQA below the 16MB line, but could be in other commonly addressable fixed storage.

The EXCP processor creates an IOSB from information in the IOB, DEB, and other control blocks. The IOSB is used in conjunction with the macro STARTIO. (This is, unfortunately, a homonym for the SIO opcode, which can lead to misunderstandings. It's advisable to say "STARTIO macro" rather than "start I/O" to keep the context clear.)

The STARTIO macro allows programmers to code their own CCWs for a device. However, these must be coded using with addresses, so the STARTIO macro is closer to EXCPVR than to EXCP. (STARTIO also requires authorization.) Unfortunately, STARTIO isn't documented by IBM to the best of my knowledge, but the macro itself contains several hundred lines of comments describing how to use it. Thus, should EXCP support be withdrawn in the future, STARTIO might provide an acceptable backup for authorized users.

When the STARTIO macro is issued, IOS receives control and builds a separate control block called an IOQ (IOS Queue Element). The UCB contains the address of the chain of IOQs for requests queued to that device.

When the I/O operation completes, IOS transfers control to the EXCP processor. The EXCP processor then translates the status information in the IOSB back to the old Channel Status Word format expected in the IOB.

The EXCP processor then frees the storage associated with the request and posts the IOB's ECB as complete.

This description of how the IOSB is used assumes that the I/O operation was requested by the EXCP processor. This isn't always the case. Users of the STARTIO macro are called *drivers* or *direct drivers* of IOS. These drivers include several other MVS components, such as ASM and VTAM. Refer to the IECDIOSB DSECT for a list of these.

8.3.3 Other IOS control blocks

The other IOS control blocks listed in Table 8.2 usually apply only to special facets of IOS. For example, the EWA (ERP Work Area) is necessary if you're writing programs called Error Recovery Procedures (ERPs). ERPs are typically needed only for non-IBM device support. Similar specialized areas, such as hot I/O detection and missing interrupt handler, also have related control blocks. (Both of these refer to situations involving I/O ending status returned from a device. In the case of a hot I/O, there are too many status messages; missing interrupts implies that a device hasn't sent in a status response when expected.)

One control block is of somewhat general use within this list, however. The IOCOM control block contains addresses for most IOS internal routines, along with some activity counters and status flags. This control block DSECT must be included to use some macros (for example, IOSLOOK).

8.4 Uses for IOS Control Blocks

Numerous uses exist for the IOS control blocks. For the purposes of this discussion, I'll divide them into EXCP users and general information extraction, which doesn't begin to cover the total set of uses. (Note that the examples given here are all in 24-bit mode.)

8.4.1 Using EXCP

The use of EXCP requires extensive knowledge of the device being used for the channel programming. To simplify this requirement, I'll present examples using the simple command Sense ID. Sense ID is supported across all recent IBM devices. (The only exception that affects most readers is the IBM 3420 tape drive.)

Sense ID returns seven bytes of data in its normal form. The System/390 architecture defines further fields that describe the ESCON channel path to the device. To simplify the discussion, these will be ignored; refer to the *Common I/O Commands* manual for details. The seven bytes of Sense ID data include:

- Byte zero is always X'FF' for identification.

- Bytes 1–2 are the controller identification (e.g., X'3880').

- Byte 3 is the controller model (this requires interpretation).

- Bytes 4–5 are the device identification (e.g., X'3380').

- Byte 6 is the device model (this requires interpretation).

The model information requires interpretation because the common model descriptions for several types of controller or device don't fit within one byte in hexadecimal. You must refer to the appropriate component description manual for an explanation of what is returned for these values. (You need one of these manuals for channel programming in general, anyway.)

While the device type can be determined from the UCB, the controller type isn't easily available. Thus, one use for the sample program in this section is to determine the controller type. Refer to the following for an example of EXCP (note that some of this information is available in the DASD Class Extension, or DCE):

```
          TITLE 'UCLA X414.334 EXAMPLE OF DISK EXCP '

EXCPDISK CSECT
          STM   R14,R12,12(R13)         SAVE REGISTERS
          LR    R12,R15                 ESTABLISH
          USING EXCPDISK,R12               ADDRESSABILITY
          SPACE 3
*         CHAIN SAVE AREAS
          LA    R2,SAVEAREA
          ST    R2,8(R13)
          ST    R13,4(R2)
          LR    R13,R2
          USING SAVEAREA,R13            PROGRAM DATA AREAS BASE
          USING IHADCB,R1               DCB DATA AREA DSECT
          PRINT ON,NOGEN
          SPACE 1
*         OPEN FILES
          SPACE 1
*         OPEN THE OUTPUT PRINT FILE
          OPEN  (SYSPRINT,OUTPUT)
          LA    R1,SYSPRINT             GET ADDRESS OF DCB
          TM    DCBOFLGS,X'10'          TEST FOR SUCCESSFUL OPEN
          BNO   BADOPEN                    OPEN FAILED - END JOB
          SPACE 1
*         OPEN THE DISK DATA SET
          OPEN  (DISK1,INPUT)
          LA    R1,DISK1                GET ADDRESS OF DCB
          TM    DCBOFLGS,X'10'          TEST FOR SUCCESSFUL OPEN
          BO    MAINLINE                   OKAY - CONTINUE
          DROP  R1                      END DCB DSECT ADDRESSABILITY
          SPACE 1
```

```
*          ERROR IN OPEN OF DISK DCB - ISSUE ERROR MESSAGE AND END
           PUT   SYSPRINT,OPENLINE
           MVC   RETCODE,=H'16'             SET BAD RETURN CODE
           B     ENDEXEC2                   GO END EXECUTION
           SPACE 3
*          MAIN LINE PROCESSING
MAINLINE EQU     *
           SPACE 1
*          BEFORE WE CAN DO ANYTHING WITH A DISK DATA SET, WE MUST
*          SET UP A SEEK ADDRESS. TO DO THIS, WE WILL PASS THE ADDR
*          OF THE FIRST BLOCK IN TTR FORMAT TO THE CONVERSION ROUTINE.
           BAS   R14,CALL_IECPCNVT    GO SET UP FULL DISK ADDRESS
           SPACE 1
           PRINT ON,GEN
*          ISSUE EXCP MACRO - SENSE ID
           EXCP  SIDIOB
           SPACE 1
*          WAIT FOR I/O TO COMPLETE
           WAIT  1,ECB=SIDECB
           BAL   R14,SHOWIT                 GO DISPLAY RESULTS
           SPACE 1
           PRINT ON,NOGEN
*          RETURN TO CALLING PROGRAM
ENDEXEC  EQU     *
           CLOSE (DISK1)                     CLOSE TAPE DCB
ENDEXEC2 EQU     *
           CLOSE (SYSPRINT)                  CLOSE PRINTER DCB
RETURN   EQU     *
           LH    R15,RETCODE                GET RETURN CODE VALUE
           L     R13,4(R13)                 GET ADDRESS OF OLD SAVE AREA
           RETURN (14,12),T,RC=(15)         RETURN TO OS
           SPACE 1
*          ROUTINE TO DISPLAY RESULTS
SHOWIT   EQU     *
           ST    R14,SAVER14                SAVE CALLER'S ADDRESS
           LA    1,SIDECB                   POINT TO ECB
           BAL   R14,HEXCONV                GO CONVERT TO HEXADECIMAL
           MVC   ECBDATA,EBCDICEQ           MOVE TO OUTPUT LINE
           PUT   SYSPRINT,ECBLINE           WRITE LINE
           LA    R4,SIDIOB                  SET
           LA    R2,4                         UP
           LA    R3,SIDIOBND-1                 FOR
           LA    R5,IOBDATA                      BXLE
DISPLP1  EQU     *                          LOOP TO DISPLAY IOB IN HEX
           LA    R1,0(R4)                   POINT TO A FULLWORD IN IOB
           BAL   R14,HEXCONV                GO CONVERT TO EBCDIC
           MVC   0(8,R5),EBCDICEQ           MOVE TO PRINT AREA
           LA    R5,9(R5)                   POINT TO NEXT PRINT AREA SLOT
           BXLE  R4,R2,DISPLP1              CONTINUE HEX DISPLAY OF IOB
           PUT   SYSPRINT,IOBLINE
           L     R14,SAVER14                RESTORE RETURN ADDRESS
           BR    R14                        RETURN TO CALLER
           SPACE 1
*          FAILURE OPENING A FILE - ISSUE BAD RETURN CODE AND QUIT.
BADOPEN  EQU     *
           MVC   RETCODE,=H'16'             SET BAD RETURN CODE
           B     RETURN                     RETURN TO OS WITH CC = 16
           SPACE 1
*          ROUTINE TO CONVERT TO DISPLAYABLE EBCDIC FROM HEXADECIMAL
HEXCONV  EQU     *
           UNPK  EBCDICEQ(9),0(5,R1)        UNPACK DATA RN CODE
```

```
          TR    EBCDICEQ,HEXTAB-240      TRANSLATE
          BR    R14                      RETURN TO CALLER
EBCDICEQ  DC    CL8' ',C' '              EIGHT DATA + 1 GARBAGE BYTE
HEXTAB    DC    C'0123456789ABCDEF'
          CNOP  0,4
          SPACE 1
*         THE FOLLOWING ROUTINE CALLS NUCLEUS ROUTINE IECPCNVT,
*         WHICH CONVERTS A TTR INTO AN MBBCCHHR ADDRESS. NOTE
*         THAT IECPCNVT USES NON-STANDARD LINKAGE CONVENTIONS.
CALL_IECPCNVT EQU  *
          LR    R7,R13             HOLD SAVE AREA ADDRESS TEMPORARILY
          STM   R0,R15,SAVE_ALL_REGS  SAVE ALL REGISTERS
          LA    R1,DISK1           GET DCB ADDRESS
          USING IHADCB,R1          ESTABLISH ADDRESSABILITY TO DCB DSECT
          L     R1,DCBDEBAD        GET DEB ADDRESS
          DROP  R1                 END DCB ADDRESSABILITY
          LA    R2,SIDCCHHR        SET UP ADDRESS OF FULL DISK ADDRESS
          L     R0,TTR1            GET RELATIVE TRACK AND RECORD - REC 1
          L     R3,X'10'           GET CVT ADDRESS
          L     R15,28(,R3)        GET CONVERSION ROUTINE ADDRESS
          BASR  R14,R15
*         AT THIS EXACT POINT, REGISTERS 9-13 ARE INVALID.
          LR    R13,R7             GET OLD SAVE AREA ADDRESS
          LM    R0,R15,SAVE_ALL_REGS  RESTORE ALL REGISTERS
          BR    R14                RETURN TO CALLER
          SPACE 3
*         DATA AREAS
DOUBLEWD  DC    D'0'
SAVEAREA  DC    18F'+0'
SAVE_ALL_REGS DS    16F            SAVE REGISTERS WHEN CALLING IECPCNVT
SAVER14   DC    F'+0'              USED TO SAVE REGISTER 14 CONTENTS
TTR1      DC    X'00000100'        TTR OF RELATIVE TRACK 0 RECORD 1
RETCODE   DC    H'0'
          SPACE 1
SENSECCW  CCW   X'E4',SENSE_DATA,X'20',256
          SPACE 1
SENSE_DATA    DC    XL256'00'
          SPACE 1
SIDECB    DC    F'0'               EVENT CONTROL BLOCK
          SPACE 1
SIDIOB    EQU   *
SIDFL1    DC    X'C2'              FLAGS (1)
          DC    X'00'              FLAGS (2)
          DC    XL2'00'            IOS SENSE GOES HERE
          DC    XL1'00'            RESULT OF I/O (X'7F' = OK)
          DC    AL3(SIDECB)        ADDR OF EVENT CONTROL BLOCK
          DC    X'00'              FLAGS (3)
          DC    XL7'00'            CSW GOES HERE
          DC    XL1'00'            START I/O CONDITION CODE
SIDIOCCW  DC    AL3(SENSECCW)      ADDRESS OF CCW TO RUN
          DC    X'00'
          DC    AL3(DISK1)         ADDRESS OF DCB
          DC    X'00'              RESERVED
          DC    AL3(0)             POINTS TO CHAIN OF RELATED IOBS
          DC    H'1'               TAPE BLOCK COUNT INCREMENT
          DC    XL2'00'            RESERVED - ERROR RETRY COUNTER
SIDCCHHR  DC    XL8'00'            DISK ADDRESS PUT HERE
SIDIOBND  EQU   *                  MARKS END OF IOB FOR LOOP
          SPACE 3
OPENLINE  DC    CL133'-*********OPEN FAILED FOR DISK DCB - ENDING EXX
                ECUTION***************'
```

```
           SPACE 1
IOBLINE    DC    C'-****** IOB CONTENTS:'
IOBDATA    DC    CL111' '
           SPACE 1
ECBLINE    DC    C'-****** ECB CONTENTS:'
ECBDATA    DC    CL8' ',CL104' '
           SPACE 3
           PRINT ON,GEN
*          DATA CONTROL BLOCK FOR DISK FILE
DISK1      DCB   DDNAME=DISK1,                                       X
                 MACRF=(E),    EXCP ACCESS METHOD                    X
                 DEVD=DA,      MAGNETIC DISK                         X
                 IOBAD=SIDIOB ADDRESS OF INPUT/OUTPUT BLOCK
           EJECT
           PRINT ON,NOGEN
*          DATA CONTROL BLOCK FOR PRINT OUTPUT FILE
SYSPRINT DCB  DDNAME=SYSPRINT,DEVD=DA,DSORG=PS,MACRF=(PM),           X
                 RECFM=FBA,LRECL=133,BLKSIZE=1330
           SPACE 3
*          DEFINE IOB DSECT MACRO
           IEZIOB
           EJECT
           PRINT ON,NOGEN
           SPACE 3
*          REGISTER EQUATES
*
R0         EQU   0
R1         EQU   1
R2         EQU   2
R3         EQU   3
R4         EQU   4
R5         EQU   5
R6         EQU   6
R7         EQU   7
R8         EQU   8
R9         EQU   9
R10        EQU   10
R11        EQU   11
R12        EQU   12
R13        EQU   13
R14        EQU   14
R15        EQU   15
           SPACE 3
*          DEFINE DCB DSECT MACRO
           DCBD  DSORG=(PS),DEVD=(DA,TA)
           END   EXCPDISK
```

EXCP can be executed with no special authorization. If a program can run in supervisor state, the EXCPVR macro might be more efficient. EXCPVR requires the program to page-fix all data areas and control blocks involved in the I/O request. It also requires that the CCWs being passed use real addresses in place of virtual addresses. These two requirements can be met by using the PGSER macro (see chapter 5) and the Load Real Address (LRA) instruction.

Note that using EXCP isn't a performance panacea; if you aren't doing something very unique with the channel programs, you should probably avoid it.

Approach EXCPVR with caution; unless you can avoid the page-fix processing and CCW translation for each EXCPVR, there's no real performance advantage over EXCP. Avoid using EXCP, in general, unless a comparable function is completely unavailable in MVS. There are places where it's the only solution.

8.4.2 Extracting IOS information

This section describes several unrelated uses of the IOS control blocks.

8.4.2.1 Locating a VOLSER from the DEB

It's occasionally useful to know the volume for a disk or tape data set. This can be obtained in several ways. If the data set is open, the DCB contains the DEB address in DCBDEBAD. The DEB's UCB extension contains a field, DEBUCBAD, which in turn points to the UCB. Field UCBVOLI contains the volume serial.

This method works for data sets on a single volume, but multivolume data sets aren't accurately reported. If you want to determine when a new volume is mounted, there's a DCB exit called the EOV (End Of Volume) exit.

Concatenated data sets pose a slightly different problem, requiring a loop through the DASD extensions.

8.4.2.2 Locating a VOLSER from the TIOT

Using the TIOT to locate the current volume serial has an advantage over the DEB method because it's possible to do so before the data set is opened. The TIOEFSRT field contains the UCB address, allowing access to the UCB-VOLI field. Note that the same restrictions regarding multivolume data sets and concatenated data sets still apply.

8.4.2.3 JCL DISP information from the DEB

The DEB contains the one-byte field DEBOFLGS. Within this, two bits are used to indicate if the related data set's disposition is NEW, OLD, or MOD.

8.4.2.4 Block size and record length

You can determine the block size and record length of an open data set from the DCB fields DCBBLKSI and DCBLRECL, respectively. See my *Assembler for COBOL Programmers* book for further details.

8.4.2.5 Determining device type

When you want to determine the device type that a UCB represents, test the UCBDVCLS byte. This allows you to determine the general class of device. For example, X'80' indicates tape and X'20' indicates disk. Following this, you could examine the UCBUNTYP byte to determine the specific model of the device. Refer to the IEFUCBOB DSECT for details.

Note that there's a macro, DEVTYP, that can be used to obtain the same information. DEVTYP also describes disk-specific information, such as track size. Refer to *System Data Administration* for details.

8.5 Summary

I/O processing in MVS includes three general areas: access methods, the EXCP processor, and the I/O supervisor itself. The DCB or ACB control blocks form the primary interface to the access methods for a program, and are used with macros such as GET or PUT. The OPEN macro prepares a DCB or ACB for processing, and also creates the DEB. The process of actually issuing an I/O request leads to use of the EXCP processor (although not in all cases). The EXCP processor uses an additional control block, the IOB, which in turn contains the address of channel command words (CCWs) for the actual request.

The EXCP processor builds an RQE to track the request, translates the CCWs, and builds an IOSB. It then issues the request with the STARTIO macro. This actually drives IOS to start the I/O operation. IOS builds a control block called an IOQ to track the request, and issues the actual SSCH instruction when the desired I/O device is available. Upon completion, IOS notifies the EXCP processor, which in turn posts its original requestor.

IOS uses numerous other control blocks. The most important of these are the UCB, which represents individual I/O devices, and the IOCOM, which contains the addresses of common IOS routines.

8.6 Things to Do

- Modify the program shown earlier in the chapter to accept other parameters, such as volume serial patterns or device types.

- If you have access to IMS/VS or IMS/ESA macro libraries, review the IDLIVSAM macro instruction. This provides DSECTs for a number of VSAM control blocks that are otherwise not available, like the AMDSB. The macro libraries can be named GENLIB, GENLIBA, or GENLIBB, depending on the release of IMS.

9

Cross-Memory and
Data Space Control Blocks

This chapter covers the preferred methods for communicating between two
address spaces and the ESA/390 data space facility. While the functions of
these two MVS features are distinct, some of the related control blocks are
in common. This chapter's brief presentation of these services isn't intended to be a comprehensive explanation of how to use cross-memory services or data spaces; I urge you to obtain *MVS Power Programming* for
details.

9.1 Cross-Memory Services

Cross-memory services were introduced in MVS/370, circa 1981. The cross-
memory facility was introduced in response to two requirements. First, the
only prior method for communication between two address spaces involved
the use of SRBs, as discussed in chapter 3. This required authorization and
lowered the performance level. The second reason was to relieve virtual
storage constraints.

Cross-memory services have become the preferred implementation for
new MVS services in place of SVCs. The benefits include:

- No required SVC number
- Dynamically installed service
- Potential performance improvement, in comparison to SVC interrupt

Cross-memory services, in comparison to SVCs, allow synchronous processing by another address space, while SRBs are asynchronous. (SRBs have to be allocated (scheduled) and dispatched in the target address space; then an ECB must be posted to signal completion. By comparison, the Program Call instruction branches directly to the service routine.) Cross-memory services are applicable for any situation where:

- You're writing a program or subsystem that must provide services to several address spaces.

- You must provide services to an unknown address space.

- You want to provide authorized services to unauthorized address spaces.

Use of cross-memory services allows you to keep your subsystem's data in a separate address space. This provides virtual storage constraint relief by reducing the amount of data that must be kept in CSA, SQA, ECSA, or ESQA. The disadvantage is a proliferation of address spaces, since each subsystem has its own address space to provide its own services, its own private storage, etc.

9.1.1 Hardware support for cross-memory services

The advent of cross-memory services brought many changes to the System/370 architecture, including 13 new instructions, changes to control register usage, and several new hardware-supported data areas. The instructions associated with cross-memory services are shown in Table 9.1. ASN in the table stands for Address Space Number (another term for ASID). These instructions are, generally speaking, used to:

- Manage cross-memory services setup (EPAR, ESAR, IAC, LASP, SAC, and SSAR).

- Move data between address spaces (MVCDK, MVCK, MVCP, MVCS, and MVCSK).

- Transfer control between address spaces (PC and PT).

Control registers were also affected. The layouts of control registers 0, 3, 4, 5, 7, 8, 13, 14, and 15 were changed. Control register 0 holds added flag bits. Control registers 3 and 4 contain the secondary and primary ASNs, along with the PSW-key mask and authorization index. Control register 5 holds the ASN second table entry (ASTE) pointer in ESA; in XA, it held the linkage table origin and length. Control registers 7 and 13 hold the secondary and home segment table addresses. (Control register 1 already held what is now called the *primary segment table origin*.) Control register 14 holds the ASN first table origin.

TABLE 9.1   Cross-Memory Instructions

Instruction	Description
EPAR	Extract Primary ASN
ESAR	Extract Secondary ASN
IAC	Insert Address Control
LASP	Load Address Space Parameters
MVCDK	Move With Destination Key
MVCK	Move With Key
MVCP	Move To Primary
MVCS	Move To Secondary
MVCSK	Move With Source Key
PC	Program Call
PT	Program Transfer
SAC	Set Address Control
SSAR	Store Secondary ASN

(Note that some of these control register assignments occurred in 1981, and some weren't changed until 1987 with the advent of ESA. A comparison of the S/370, XA, and ESA reference summaries will give some idea of the evolution of the changes.)

Because so many cross-memory services are implemented in hardware rather than through straight MVS services, most of the data areas I'll discuss are hardware related.

9.1.1.1   The Program Call instruction

Now I'll describe one of the cross-memory instructions in some detail in order to illustrate the reasons behind the underlying data areas. The Program Call instruction (PC) was developed to provide an alternative linkage for system services to the Supervisor Call (SVC) instruction. Program Call is used for almost all new MVS services, and examples can be found in many macros. (For examples, see the STORAGE and VSM-LIST macros previously discussed.)

Program Call allows a program running in one address space to transfer control to a program in another address space. To do this, the instruction must provide enough information for the segment table—pointed to by control register 1—to change from the calling address space to the called address space. To accomplish this, IBM has provided many new hardware features, making cross-memory services the most complicated System/370 service.

The operand of Program Call is a number, called the *program call number* or *PC number*. This number is usually loaded into a register and is a 20-bit number, zero filled on the left. The 20-bit number is in turn broken down into a 12-bit linkage index and an eight-bit entry index. Figure 9.1 shows the layout of the PC number in a register.

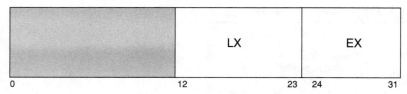

Figure 9.1 Layout of the PC number.

The PC instruction first uses the linkage index to locate an entry in a linkage table. This is a series of four-byte entries, each holding a valid/invalid bit (I), the address of the entry table for this linkage table, and an entry table length (ETL). See the ESA reference summary for the layout of an entry in the linkage table.

Having obtained the address of the appropriate entry table, the PC instruction next looks up the entry designated by the entry index in the PC number. The ESA entry table entries are 32 bytes long and contain:

- The authorization key for the program being called
- The ASN for the program being called
- The address of the program within the called address space
- An entry parameter for the called program
- The entry key mask for the called program
- The address of the ASN second table entry for the called address space
- Several other flags and fields

(The XA version of the entry table was 16 bytes long, and is still supported for compatibility.)

At this stage, the PC instruction has determined the address of the program being called. The other piece of information needed is the segment

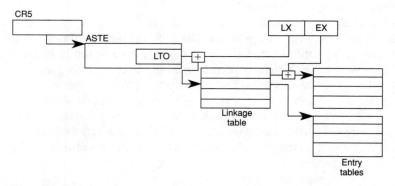

Figure 9.2 Linkages between the entry table and PC number.

table address of the called address space; this is in the ASN second table entry, whose address is in the entry table entry. At this point, the PC instruction can now branch to the called program.

The only loose end in this explanation is the linkage table address. This is kept in the ASN second table entry for the calling address space. The address of this is in control register 5. Figure 9.2 shows the linkages between these data areas and the PC number.

Since the PC structure defined so far would allow security exposures, IBM also includes authorization checking as part of the PC instruction. This involves use of an authorization index, carried in control register 4 and compared against the authorization table in the ASN second table entry.

The foregoing is only a brief summary of the factors that affect the processing of the Program Call instruction. If you want to fully grasp the complexity of this instruction, I urge you to review the four-page flowchart in the *Principles of Operation* manual, which shows the full logic.

9.1.2 MVS macros for cross-memory services

The MVS services associated with cross-memory services include 13 macro instructions, listed in Table 9.2. These macros are used to update various parts of the hardware-related data areas used for cross-memory services. For example, ETDEF defines an entry table entry, LXRES reserves an entry in the linkage table, ETCRE creates an entry table from a series of ETDEF macros, ETCON then connects this to the specified linkage table entry, ETDIS and ETDES provide the ending service equivalents for ETCON and ETCRE respectively, and LXFRE provides the ending equivalent for LXRES. PCLINK is used to save and restore selected registers within a PC routine. It has two functions: STACK and UNSTACK.

**TABLE 9.2 MVS Macro
Instructions for Cross-Memory Services**

Instruction	Description
ATSET	Authorization Table Set
AXEXT	Authorization Index Extract
AXFRE	Authorization Index Free
AXRES	Authorization Index Reserve
AXSET	Authorization Index Set
ETCON	Entry Table Connect
ETCRE	Entry Table Create
ETDEF	Entry Table Definition
ETDES	Entry Table Destroy
ETDIS	Entry Table Disconnect
LXFRE	Linkage Index Free
LXRES	Linkage Index Reserve
PCLINK	Register Preservation For PC Routines

For a full explanation and examples of the cross-memory services macro instructions, refer to *MVS Power Programming* or the *Application Development Reference: Services for Authorized Assembler Language Programs* series of manuals.

9.1.3 MVS data areas for cross-memory services

The data areas associated with cross-memory services are listed in Table 9.3. In addition, several other MVS data areas hold information related to cross-memory operations, although they aren't dedicated to that function.

Unfortunately, IBM provides only three mapping macros for these (ASTE, ETD0/1, and XSB). The others are kept in the PC/Auth address space. Figure 9.3 shows the relationship of these data areas within the PC/Auth address space. The starting point for this is the Supervisor Vector Table (SVT), addressed from either the PSA or CVT. Within Fig. 9.3, the AXAT is updated in response to AXRES, AXSET, and AXFRE macros. The LXAT is updated by LXRES and LXFRE macros.

The XMD serves as the primary anchor point within the PC/Auth address space for other cross-memory control blocks. The XMD layout in volume 5 of the *Data Areas* manual also identifies the storage subpools used in the PC/Auth address space for the various cross-memory data areas. The PCRA and SRRA are used for internal PC/Auth error recovery. The other control blocks are discussed in the following sections.

9.1.3.1 ASN Second Table Entry (ASTE)

The ASTE is predominantly a hardware control structure. The mapping macro is IHAASTE. While the ASTE contains several key fields, such as the addresses of the linkage table and authorization table, these are in the form of real addresses. As such, direct use is difficult, although you could use the LURA instruction (see chapter 5) to access them.

TABLE 9.3 MVS Data Areas
Used in Cross-Memory Services

Area	Description
AXAT	Authorization Index Allocation Table
ETD0	Entry Table Descriptor (Format 0 - old)
ETD1	Entry Table Descriptor (Format 1 - ESA)
ETE	Entry Table Entry
ETIB	Entry Table Information Block
LXAT	Linkage Index Allocation Table
PCRA	Program Call Recovery Area
SRRA	Service Routine Recovery Area
XMD	Cross Memory Directory
XSB	Extended Status Block

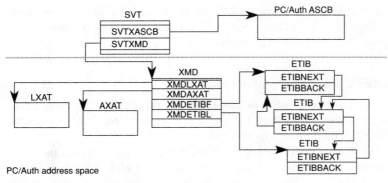

Figure 9.3 Relationship of XMD and PC/Auth address space.

The *Principles of Operation* manual defines the layout and fields of the ASTE; use it in conjunction with the ASTE DSECT.

9.1.3.2 Entry Table Descriptor (ETD)

The ETD comes in two formats. The version used with MVS/SP and MVS/XA is 16 bytes long and is called the Format-0 ETD or ETD0. The MVS/ESA version is 32 bytes long, and is called the Format-1 ETD or ETD1. The ET-DEF macro creates each one, and can create either format. (Format 1 should be used for any new applications, although Format 0 is still available for compatibility.)

The fields in the ETD are all generated as a direct result of operands on the ETDEF macro. As a result, you can more easily research the contents of the ETD by reviewing the documentation for the ETDEF macro than by studying the DSECT.

The mapping macro is IHAETD. The type of ETD generated is controlled by the FORMAT= operand (0 or 1), and there's a LIST=YES operand.

9.1.3.3 Extended Status Block (XSB)

The Extended Status Block will be the most familiar of the cross-memory control blocks for many of you because it appears in dumps. The XSB is used to hold cross-memory status information at the time of an interrupt and, as such, it's associated with a TCB, SRB, or RB, depending on the type of routine in control when the interrupt occurred. (It's also referenced from interrupt handlers.) The information in the XSB includes:

- The contents of control registers 3, 4, and 8 (fields XSBXMCR3, XS-BXMCR4, and XSBEAX)
- Authorization index (XSBAX)
- Protection key mask (XSBKM)

In addition, the XSB holds several fields related to MVS/ESA data spaces, which I'll discuss later in this chapter. The mapping macro for the XSB is IHAXSB and there's a LIST=YES operand.

9.1.3.4 Other cross-memory information

In addition to the entries listed in Table 9.3, several previously covered data areas contain information that can be useful in tracking PC/Auth status. These are primarily defined elsewhere in the book.

The System Function Table (SFT) discussed in chapter 2 contains cross-memory service information related to the Program Call instruction. This is also listed in the *Diagnosis: System Reference* manual. The Supervisor Vector Table (SVT) contains several fields of interest relating to cross-memory services, including:

SVTXASCB. The address of the PC/Auth ASCB.

SVTXMD. The address of the XMD within the PC/Auth private area.

SVTCSI. A flag byte indicating the status of PC/Auth services.

The DSECT macro is IHASVT. It can be addressed by fields PSASVT or CVTSVT in the PSA or CVT, respectively. If you're deeply interested in the matter, you can research the SVTAFTR, SVTAFTB, SVTNSLX, and SVTCBLS fields.

The Address Space Secondary Block (ASSB) discussed in chapter 3 contains cross-memory information for a specific address space. Its address is in the ASCB field ASCBASSB. Fields of interest include ASSBXMF1, a flag byte indicating if the address space has added entries to its entry table, and ASSBXMCC, the halfword count of connections made. The mapping macro is IHAASSB. The ASSBXEAX, ASSBXMCC, and ASSBBALV fields might merit further research.

Finally, the ASCB field ASCBASTE contains the address of the ASN second table entry for the address space.

9.2 Data Spaces

The announcement of MVS/ESA in 1987 included several dramatic new processor features. The single most exciting new element in the S/390 architecture was the data space feature. A data space provides an entirely separate address space, usable for data only. Up to 15 data spaces, of 2 gigabytes each, can be addressed at one time by a program. Thus, up to 32GB of storage is theoretically available to a properly coded application program.

In addition, data spaces can be configured as commonly addressable or private. The ability to address a common 2GB storage area from many address spaces allows a reduction of common storage requirements, and provides further virtual storage constraint relief.

Data space support was added in MVS/ESA for several reasons. One was the limited life span of the address space extension provided by MVS/XA. Hennessy and Garcia, in their text *Computer Architecture: A Quantitative Approach*, identified that the address space requirements for typical operating systems grow at a rate of one-half bit per year. Since MVS/SP was undergoing severe virtual storage constraints in large installations by around 1980, it would have been reasonable to predict that MVS/XA, without modification, would approach saturation around 1994. While it's easy to doubt needing more than 2 gigabytes, remember how big 640K of memory seemed to early PC developers.

Another reason was the limiting size of a 31-bit address in a decade of plummeting real memory costs. A typical large MVS/ESA shop has tens or hundreds of gigabytes of real memory; remaining with the original 2GB MVS/XA limit for real memory wouldn't allow the larger sizes of contemporary machines without hardware changes.

Like cross-memory service, data space support is implemented in hardware rather than being a straight MVS service. Data space support was also developed from the beginning as an OCO feature. Thus, no control blocks are documented in the sense that I've used them in this book. However, many control blocks have been expanded or changed to support data spaces. For an example, look at STCB.

The remainder of this section will outline the hardware and MVS services that support MVS/ESA data spaces.

9.2.1 Hardware support for data spaces

The hardware support for implementing data spaces includes new instructions, a new type of register (called *access registers*) for data space addressing, a new addressing mode, changes to control registers, an improved method of program linkage using stacks, and hardware-supported data areas. The instructions added for data space support are shown in Table 9.4. These instructions can roughly be classified as follows:

- Access register manipulation (CPYA, EAR, LAM, SAR, and STAM)
- Linkage stack manipulation (BAKR, EREG, ESTA, MSTA)
- Load address in access register mode (LAE)
- Revised cross-memory linkage (PR)

TABLE 9.4   Data Space Support Instructions

Instruction	Description
BAKR	Branch and Stack
CPYA	Copy Access
EAR	Extract Access
EREG	Extract Stacked Registers
ESTA	Extract Stacked State
LAE	Load Address Extended
LAM	Load Access Multiple
MSTA	Modify Stacked State
PALB	Purge Access Lookaside Buffer
PR	Program Return
SAR	Set Access
STAM	Store Access Multiple

Access registers were also added for the express purpose of accessing data spaces. There are 16 access registers, and they can be updated only with the access register manipulation instructions. (LAM and STAM are the equivalents of LM and STM for regular registers, CPYA is the equivalent of LR for access registers, and EAR and SAR are used to copy data between general-purpose registers and access registers.)

Access registers were used to "shadow" the associated general-purpose register. This was done to allow existing programs to use data spaces without introducing entirely new instructions. The effect of access registers is to select a data space, which is done with a special value called an Access List Entry Token, or ALET. This is a 32-bit value that identifies a specific data space, which I'll cover in detail later, along with the other data areas.

When an instruction—for example, MVI 0(R3),C'*'—is executed, its operation can now change depending on the addressing mode in force when it's executed. If the processor is operating in one of the "normal" modes, the instruction will operate just as it always had.

However, if the processor is in access register mode, the processing is different. The base register and displacement in the instruction ("0(R3)") is still used to determine the virtual storage address of the byte being changed. However, simultaneously, hardware now checks the contents of the associated access register to determine which address space or data space is being used. The associated access register is simply the access register with the same number as the base register—in this case, since the base register was R3, the hardware would check the contents of access register 3. The ALET in the register would then be used to select the address space or data space to be used.

The selection of the addressing mode is done through a change to the Set Address Control (SAC) instruction, originally added for cross-memory support. This now provides four addressing modes (primary, secondary, home, and access register). The addressing mode is stored in bits 16 and 17 of the PSW. (Note that this is separate from the 24/31 bit addressing mode, which is in bit 32 of the PSW.)

The implementation of access register mode also introduced the need for different programming conventions by assembler programmers. Since data spaces are associated with the base register in an instruction, the match of base and access registers has to be considered when updating a program.

Additionally, one certain programming habit completely acceptable in prior versions of IBM mainframe architecture became a problem. This problem was due to the differing processing of base and index registers when in access register mode. In prior implementations, the contents of the base and index registers were added together to determine the desired address (along with the displacement). Thus, if only one register was involved, it didn't matter if it was specified in the index or base register position. For example:

```
L     R2,0(R3)
```

specifies an index register of R3. Since no base register is coded in the instruction, zero is assigned as the base register. If register 3 contained an ALET, the above instruction should have been coded as:

```
L     R2,0(,R3)
```

to force the assembler to assign R3 into the base register portion of the instruction. (Review the format of RX format instructions if this isn't clear.) It's confusing, since on some instructions (such as MVI, an SI format instruction) there's no index register anyway, and the issue doesn't arise. The upshot is that if you're programming in assembly language, exercise caution when coding RX format instructions in programs that use access register addressing.

Another modification to support data spaces properly in existing programs has to do with address determination. The LA instruction still operates as before, but a new instruction, Load Address Extended (LAE), has been added. LAE operates just as LA does, but it also updates the access register associated with the first operand.

Another entirely new feature in ESA/390 is the linkage stack feature. This was developed to simplify the function of saving a caller's state when transferring control between programs. With ESA, there are too many individual elements that need to be saved by a called program, such as access registers, cross-memory ASNs and authorization, and addressing modes. IBM thus implemented a new instruction, Branch and Stack (BAKR), which performs the function of saving all the individual pieces that make up a program's state. The linkage stack is also used in some cross-memory transfers, depending on the entry table setup.

When a program completes after saving the caller's state with BAKR, it must use another new instruction—Program Return (PR)—to unstack the caller's information and return control. The combination of BAKR and PR effectively replace the STM and LM/BR instructions at the beginning and end of most assembler language programs, and ends the need for save area chaining. (However, since many older services still expect a save area, programs using the linkage stack and BAKR still have to provide a save area. The save area, however, should contain the characters FMT1 in the second fullword when you use the linkage stack and BAKR.)

Programs using this combination of BAKR, PR, and the new save area format are said to use *ESA linkage*. The hardware-supported data areas for data space support include the following:

- The ALET (mentioned earlier)
- The Dispatchable Unit Control Table
- Access List Entries
- Linkage Stack Entries

The ALET describes a data space or address space. The format of an ALET is shown in Fig. 9.4. The P in the figure represents the primary data space bit (a zero indicates that the data space is associated with a specified TCB rather than being available to the entire system). The ALESN is the access list entry serial number. The access list entry number is explained further in the following paragraphs.

The Dispatchable Unit Control Table is a hardware data area associated with an individual TCB. There are two ways to locate an access list in ESA. The first, which applies to commonly-addressable data spaces, is through the Primary Access List Designator (PALD), whose address is in control register 14. This is used when the P bit in the ALET is 1. The second, which applies to private data spaces for use by a single TCB, is through the Dispatchable Unit Control Table, or DUCT. Hardware uses the DUCT when the P bit in the ALET is zero.

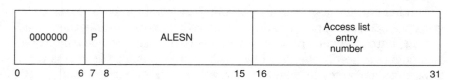

Figure 9.4 Format of an ALET.

Both of these paths lead to the Access List Entry, or ALE. The ALET includes an access list entry number, which is used to index in the access list (pointed to by either the DUCT or the PALD) to the specific entry for the data space. Access list entries are 16 bytes long.

Another hardware data area, included in ESA but entirely unrelated to the above, is the linkage stack. The linkage stack is a storage area used to store program linkage data, generated at the time of a BAKR or stacking PC instruction. The format of the linkage stack is described fully in the *Principles of Operation* manual. Control register 15 contains the real storage address for the next stack entry.

Due to the large number of linkage stack entry formats and fields, refer to the *Principles of Operation* manual for full descriptions. *MVS Power Programming* also contains descriptions of their use.

9.2.2 MVS macros for data space support

MVS/ESA provides many macros that are used to support data spaces. Some of these are dedicated to data space support and others are extensions of existing services, modified to operate in the ESA environment. Finally, some new ESA services are applicable both to data space support and other processing.

The ESA macros directly related to data space support are listed in the following sections. Examples of ALESERV and DSPSERV will be provided later.

9.2.2.1 ALESERV (Access List Entry Services)

The access list defines all the data spaces that a task or address space can reference at one time. Access list entries (ALEs) are created for each data space defined for a task. Since a task might create many data spaces but not use them simultaneously, there needed to be some way to manage the contents of the access list entries. This led to the ALESERV macro.

ALESERV can be used to add or delete access list entries. It also provides services for translating data space identifiers, called STOKENs, to ALETs and vice versa. These are the ADD, DELETE, and SEARCH functions.

The SEARCH function, when given a STOKEN and an ALET of minus 1, will return the ALET value for that STOKEN. If the STOKEN is legitimate, register zero will contain 0 for a public (global) entry and 4 for a private entry.

9.2.2.2 DSPSERV (Data Space Services)

The DSPSERV macro is used to create and delete address spaces. When making the request, you can specify the size requested (in 4K blocks), along with a number of other characteristics for authorized programs (for example, storage key). The following shows a fragment of code to obtain a data space:

```
*     SET ADDRESS CONTROL TO GET INTO ACCESS REGISTER MODE
            SAC   512                THIS GETS AR MODE
*     ISSUE A DSPSERV MACRO TO CREATE THE DATA SPACE
            DSPSERV  CREATE,         MAKE A NEW ONE               X
            NAME=MY_NAME,            A CHARACTER NAME             X
            TYPE=BASIC,              (VERSUS HIPERSPACE)          X
            STOKEN=MY_STOKEN,        STOKEN RETURNED HERE         X
            ORIGIN=MY_ORIGIN,        STARTING ADDRESS IN THE D.S. X
            BLOCKS=MY_MAX,           MAXIMUM NUMBER OF PAGES      X
            NUMBLKS=MY_PAGES         NUMBER OF PAGES TO START
```

The data areas referenced in the above code are:

```
MY_STOKEN   DC   D'0'              STOKEN RETURNED HERE
MY_ORIGIN   DC   F'0'              ORIGIN OF DATA SPACE GOES HERE
MY_PAGES    DC   F'20'             NUMBER OF PAGES IN DATA SPACE
MY_MAX      DC   F'1024'           MAXIMUM SIZE = 4MB (1K * 4K)
MY_NAME     DC   CL8'EXAMPLE1'     NAME OF THIS DATA SPACE
```

The following code deletes the data space.

```
* ISSUE A DSPSERV MACRO TO DISPOSE OF THE DATA SPACE
      DSPSERV  DELETE,        DONE WITH IT                X
      STOKEN=MY_STOKEN        STOKEN RETURNED BY CREATE
```

In addition, DSPSERV also provides an EXTEND service to enlarge an existing data space, subject to installation limits. It uses the STOKEN and NUMBLKS parameters.

9.2.2.3 Other macros related to data spaces

A number of other macros are related to the data space feature or other features of MVS/ESA. Some of these are outlined in the following paragraphs.

LSEXPAND is used to expand the linkage stack. If your program exceeds the size of the linkage, it will eventually cause a program interruption with code X'0030'. LSEXPAND allows your program to increase the size of its linkage stack.

The TCBTOKEN macro can be used to extract a 16-byte TCB identifier. IBM will begin using this to identify tasks rather than relying on TCB address for most new MVS services. To extract your task's token, specify TYPE=CURRENT, along with the label of a 16-byte area for the TTOKEN= parameter.

TESTART can be used to check the validity of an ALET. This will help avoid various program checks related to invalid ALET conditions (such as program interruption codes X'0028', X'0029', and X'002A'). Note, however, that the macro will eventually generate a TAR (Test Access) instruction and that use of TAR will be a little bit faster.

The system completion code related to these ALET and linkage stack program checks is S0E0. The underlying program interruption code, e.g., x'28' or x'30', appears in register 15 when this ABEND is issued. Refer to the *System Codes* manual for details.

In addition to these ESA-specific macros, many other existing MVS macros have been enhanced to work in the cross-memory and data space environment. Generally, this has been accomplished by defining a new macro and appending X to the name. Examples include LINKX, SNAPX, and ESTAEX.

9.3 Summary

This chapter has presented a truly abbreviated description of some aspects of the cross-memory and data space facilities of MVS/ESA. Since both of these methods were developed under OCO guidelines, many control blocks used in these services aren't documented, thus limiting the extent to which I can discuss them. If you want to delve into these topics more comprehensively, I urge you to read *MVS Power Programming* before starting any further research.

10

Recovery and Diagnostic Control Blocks and Services

This chapter covers several topics, some of which stray from the strict control block orientation of preceding chapters. The topics all share the common theme of debugging; these are data areas and services that readers can use frequently. The first MVS component covered is the Recovery/Termination Manager, which is the part of MVS that supports recovery from errors and termination of the offending TCB or SRB. The second is synonymous with the first in many reader's eyes, dump services, which produces the evidence. Additionally, I'll discuss various uses for SYS1.LOGREC error recording.

10.1   Recovery/Termination Manager Control Blocks

The MVS Recovery/Termination Manager (RTM) is responsible for the initial processing of program errors and for invoking the appropriate recovery routine where possible. If recovery isn't successful, RTM will cause the problem to be documented via MVS dump services and then handle the termination of the failing TCB or SRB.

Several of these terms need to be defined for the RTM context. *Program errors* mean errors in the execution of a program (in contrast to errors in the execution of a processor or I/O device, which are the responsibility of the MVS Machine Check Handler, MCH, or I/O Error Recovery Procedures, ERPs). Program errors can arise from two causes.

The first is a program check, detected by the processor when an instruction can't be executed due to an error in its coding, its data, or the machine state. (Program checks result in the familiar $0Cx$ ABENDs.) The second cause of program errors is software detection, resulting in a request by the detecting program or MVS component to abnormally end (ABEND) the task in question. This latter category includes most other types of ABENDs (213, 806, 80A, etc.).

A *recovery routine* is a program or subprogram that's never executed by itself. Instead, a recovery routine functions as a subroutine of RTM and is called when the associated type of error occurs. Two types of recovery routines are generally available in the context of RTM. The first, the ESPIE exit, is used to intercept and recover from program checks. The second, the ESTAE exit, is used to intercept and recover from ABENDs; this includes program checks, which are a subset of the general ABEND case. (RTM also provides several other types of error recovery, such as Functional Recovery Routines and Resource Managers, which I'll also be covering.)

Termination is another responsibility of RTM. This includes closing any files still open, and releasing any memory allocated to the TCB. While not obvious, this type of cleanup must be invoked for normal termination, in case the programmer forgets to close a file; it also means that parts of RTM receive control when a TCB ends normally.

The initial processing of errors takes place in two areas. For program checks, the Program Check First-Level Interrupt Handler (FLIH) receives control when the processor detects an instruction problem. This results in RTM receiving control after the program check is determined to be a real error. (Remember that page faults are also reported as program checks and they aren't necessarily errors.)

The other interface to RTM is via the ABEND macro, which also invokes RTM. ABEND is used to terminate a task. It provides the mechanism by which other MVS components report software-detected errors, such as an 806 ABEND.

10.1.1 RTM macro interfaces

RTM provides macro instructions in three general categories. The first contains macros to terminate a task or SRB abnormally, such as ABEND or CALLRTM. The second category comprises the macros used to set up a recovery environment (to identify a recovery routine to RTM); examples of this include ESPIE, ESTAE, and SETFRR. The third category are those macros used when recovering from an error, such as SETRP. Table 10.1 lists RTM macro instructions.

**TABLE 10.1 Recovery/Termination
Management Macro Instructions**

Macro instruction	Description
ABEND	Abnormally End a Task
CALLRTM	Call RTM (extended ABEND functions)
ESPIE	Extended Specify Program Interrupt Element
ESTAE	Extended Specify Task ABEND Exit
FESTAE	Branch Entry ESTAE
RESMGR	RTM Resource Manager Services
SETFRR	Low-level recovery for SRBs, etc.
SPIE	Older version of ESPIE
STAE	Older version of ESTAE

Comments on ABEND, ESTAE, and RESMGR follow. For a discussion of ESPIE, refer to *Assembler for COBOL Programmers*. SPIE and STAE are basically obsolete subsets of ESPIE and ESTAE. For a discussion of SET-FRR, refer to *MVS Power Programming*.

10.1.1.1 ABEND

My favorite macro instruction generates a SVC 13 (and also has a branch entry option). It allows its invoker to specify the code for the ABEND, dump options, and to indicate the scope of the ABEND. The ABEND code is a 12-bit value; separate values are maintained for system and user ABEND codes. The scope can be coded as STEP; the default is the affected TCB.

A dump is requested by the DUMP keyword option. You can also specify the dump options to be used by specifying the DUMPOPT keyword. This allows you to create dump options by generating a parameter list for the SNAP macro, then passing it to the ABEND macro with the DUMPOPT keyword. Finally, the RETURN= operand allows you to code a return code value to be used with the ABEND.

The format of the ABEND parameter list is shown in Fig. 10.1. In most cases, programmers don't get involved in the details of SVC parameter lists. ABEND should be an exception to this, however, because its parameter list appears in several other places. For example, the TCBCMPCD field contains a copy of the ABEND parameter list for an abending task. Take care in coding user ABEND codes; if a code greater than the maximum (4095) is specified, the ABEND could appear with a system completion code, which would lead to confusion at best.

The DUMP and STEP parameters for ABEND are straightforward, but the DUMPOPT parameter needs a little clarification. This option requires

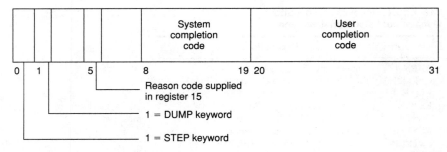

Figure 10.1 Format of ABEND parameter list.

that you code both the ABEND and a separate SNAP macro. The SNAP macro should use the MF=L list form. You can specify parameters in the SNAP macro coding to control exactly what's printed.

10.1.1.2 CALLRTM

CALLRTM provides a service that can be viewed as a super ABEND. CALL-RTM stands for CALL Recovery/Termination Manager. Programs must be in supervisor state and key zero to use CALLRTM.

CALLRTM provides the mechanism to cancel a task in another address space. (It can also abnormally end tasks in the same address space, but ABEND will usually suffice for that case.) CALLRTM allows the user to specify generally the same options as for the ABEND macro. The ASID of the affected address space is also an option. CALLRTM also disallows retry—thus, any ESTAE routines in the terminated TCB's recovery environment cannot bypass the CALLRTM-invoked termination of the TCB.

CALLRTM also provides two levels of termination: ABTERM and MEMTERM. The ABTERM option operates like the ABEND macro; it's also the option used for the console operator CANCEL command. MEMTERM terminates the address space; it's the option used for the operator FORCE command.

Keyword options for CALLRTM include TYPE (ABTERM and MEMTERM), COMPCOD (completion code), ASID, TCB, DUMPOPT, and REASON, the last two being similar to the DUMPOPT and RETURN operands of ABEND.

10.1.1.3 ESTAE

ESTAE stands for Extended STAE, and STAE means Specify Task Abnormal End Exit. STAE was developed early in OS/360, and ESTAE originated in MVS 3.0 if my memory serves me correctly. The purpose of ESTAE is to allow a program or set of programs to intercept an ABEND. ESTAE allows a program to specify an exit routine, which operates as a subroutine of the operating system when an ABEND occurs for the specified task. The exit routine might allow the ABEND to continue or be corrected through a retry routine. Operands of ESTAE include:

- The name of the exit routine.
- I/O processing options (purge, halt, or quiesce I/O operations in process at the time of an ABEND).
- $x22$ ABEND options (TERM=YES).
- Applicability across module transfers (XCTL macros).

An example of ESTAE is provided in appendix C, program 1. ESTAE is a particularly valuable error recovery tool, since it can receive control for a wide variety of situations. In general, if you take the time to develop a comprehensive ESTAE exit and retry routine, it will pay good dividends. However, writing code for an ESTAE exit or retry routine is philosophically different from writing other types of programs. An ESTAE routine receives control when the associated base program has failed in some way. This might be due to just plain dumb outside factors (B37), invalid parameters, poor editing, or possibly a catastrophic event, such as a storage overlay.

The ESTAE routine is coded some time—possibly even years—before a particular error arises. At the time of coding, you must avoid certain assumptions. First, there can't be any dependency on register contents. Because a program can fail at many points—some of which are outside the program in MVS service routines—register contents at the time of a failure will vary widely. Second, there can't be any dependency on values in storage; storage overlays can cause the exit routine to fail in this case. Third, the exit routine can't rely on any subroutines of the failing program, since these might also be destroyed by a storage overlay. Rely on nothing outside the code and data in the exit routine itself.

If the exit routine determines that the program can continue, the retry routine must then determine where to continue from. There are several ways to approach this. I favor identifying some higher-level service, e.g., an input command, next record, or some similar unit of work, and then proceeding with the next command, record, or unit of work. Attempts to fix up a failing unit of work often lead to further problems; if you knew exactly how to fix a failure, you'd also know how to avoid it in the first place.

ESTAE processing comes in several other guises. A macro called FESTAE (Fast ESTAE) is provided for authorized branch-entry callers. The ATTACH macro provides operands, STAI= and ESTAI=, which specify an exit routine for a subtask ABEND when the subtask is created. The ESTAEX macro is provided for access-register-mode users.

ESTAE processing involves a concept called *percolation*, which I'll discuss along with the SCB later in this chapter.

10.1.1.4 SETRP (Set Recovery Parameters)

The ESTAE exit routine has the option to retry or continue with the ABEND. Numerous options are associated with each of these courses of action. The SETRP macro is provided to simplify coding them. SETRP is used to leave an ESTAE exit routine. SETRP includes options to specify:

- Recovery actions (retry, ABEND, or pass to other ESTAE exits)
- Retry routine address
- SYS1.LOGREC error recording option
- Register updates for retry or termination options
- Control of dump options

An example of using SETRP to control dump options is shown in appendix C, program 1.

10.1.1.5 RESMGR

ESTAE routines are useful for recovering from errors related to a particular program or TCB. Occasionally, however, you'll need an ESTAE-like function for a task in another address space. The typical scenario for this is when you're writing a program or system that provides services to other address spaces. The original method of dealing with this situation was to dispatch an SRB into the address space to be monitored and use branch entry ESTAE. Older methods of accomplishing the same thing usually relied on changes ("hooks") to MVS itself.

The RESMGR services provides a simpler method of handling this situation. RESMGR allows you to establish an exit that receives control when ASCBs or TCBs end. The scope of the exit can be limited to a specific TCB or ASCB, or to every ASCB and TCB in the MVS system. Also, unlike ESTAE, RESMGR exits receive control for both normal and abnormal termination.

RESMGR stands for *resource manager*. The intent of a resource manager exit is different from that of an ESTAE exit. While both can receive control at the time of an ABEND, only the ESTAE exit can intercept the ABEND. RESMGR exits are restricted to performing cleanup actions when a task or address space has ended. This cleanup is typically for resources in the main (service-providing) address space—releasing storage, freeing connections, issuing DEQ macros, etc. The *MVS/ESA Application Development Guide: Authorized Assembler Language Programs* manual lists some general cases where RESMGR is appropriate.

Unlike the ESTAE exit, RESMGR exits need to be placed in common storage so they're addressable from all address spaces that invoke them. Your program must be authorized to use RESMGR.

An installation might also create global resource manager exits, which will receive control on all terminations. Up to three such exits can be identified in CSECT IEAVTRML. It's essential that you're extremely careful when testing global exits in general, and these in particular! Errors in setup or coding can result in IPL failures, all tasks or address spaces failing on normal terminations, and similar events. Operands of RESMGR include:

- Function (DELETE or ADD).

- TOKEN, a fullword token returned to identify the specific RESMGR exit just established (for ADD) or to be removed (for DELETE).

- Type of termination to be monitored—either address space (ADDRSPC) or task (TASK).

- ASID, the address space to be monitored by this exit; options include CURRENT, ALL, or a specific ASID number.

- TCB, the task to be monitored by this exit; choices include CURRENT, ALL, or a specific TCB address.

- TTOKEN, an alternative to specifying a TCB address.

- ROUTINE, which specifies the method of access and the identifier of the resource manager exit being established. The LINK option uses the exit name, which must be a separate program or entry point. The BRANCH option specifies an address and the PC option requires a Program Call number.

- ECB specifies the address of an Event Control Block to be posted when DELETE processing for an exit has completed.

- PARAM specifies an eight-byte set of parameters to be passed to the resource manager exit when it's invoked; see Fig. 10.2 for the relationship.

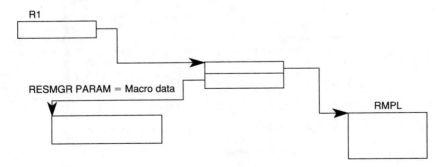

Figure 10.2 Relationship of RMPL and RESMGR exit parameters.

An example of a trivial RESMGR invocation is shown following this paragraph. Note that it moves the resource manager exit into common storage. This is an acceptable technique, although placement in LPA would be preferable in many cases. This example doesn't delete the common storage used for the exit, which isn't advisable for any exit that's frequently used.

```
RESM      TITLE 'UCLA X414.371 12/93 RESOURCE MANAGER SAMPLE '
RESMGR1   CSECT
RESMGR1   AMODE 31
RESMGR1   RMODE ANY
          BAKR  R14,0                 SAVE REGISTERS
          LR    R12,R15               ESTABLISH
          USING RESMGR1,R12               ADDRESSABILITY
          LA    R13,SAVEAREA          SAVE AREA
          SPACE 3
*         GET INTO SUPERVISOR STATE, PROTECT KEY ZERO
          MODESET  KEY=ZERO,MODE=SUP
          SPACE 1
*         GET COMMON STORAGE FOR EXIT ROUTINE
          LA    R3,EXITLEN            GET LENGTH OF EXIT CODE
          STORAGE  OBTAIN,            GET STORAGE                    X
               LENGTH=(3),            LENGTH IN R3                   X
               SP=241,                A COMMON SUBPOOL               X
               LOC=(ANY,ANY),         ABOVE THE 16MB LINE           X
               KEY=0,                 KEY ZERO                       X
               COND=YES               CONDITIONAL REQUEST
          ST    R1,ADDR1              SAVE STORAGE ADDRESS
          LTR   R15,R15               TEST RETURN CODE
          BNZ   RETURN2                  NOT ZERO — GIVE UP FOR NOW
          SPACE 1
*         COPY EXIT ROUTINE TO COMMON STORAGE
          L     R2,ADDR1             GET STORAGE ADDRESS
          LA    R3,EXITLEN           AND LENGTH
          LA    R4,RESEXIT1          GET EXIT ADDRESS
          LR    R5,R3                AND LENGTH
          MVCL  R2,R4                COPY EXIT INTO CSA AREA
          SPACE 1
*         ISSUE RESMGR MACRO TO SET UP OUR EXIT.                    *
          L     R4,ADDR1             GET EXIT COPY ADDRESS
          RESMGR  ADD,                                               X
               TOKEN=RESTOKEN,       RESMGR EXIT ID TOKEN           X
               TYPE=TASK,            SPECIFY EXIT FOR TASKS ONLY X
               TCB=CURRENT,          SPECIFY FOR THIS TASK ONLY  X
               ROUTINE=(BRANCH,(4)), BRANCH TO COPY OF RESEXIT1  X
               PARAM=EXITPARM        ADDRESS OF PARAMETERS FOR EXIT
          LTR   R15,R15              TEST RETURN CODE
          BNZ   RETURN2                 NOT ZERO -- GIVE UP FOR NOW
          SPACE 1
*         DRIVE RESMGR EXIT -- FORCE 0C3 ABEND                      *
          SPACE 1
          EX    0,*                  FORCE 0C3 ABEND
          SPACE 3
*         RETURN TO CALLING PROGRAM
RETURN    EQU   *
          SR    R15,R15              SET RETURN CODE
```

```
RETURN2    EQU    *
           PR                                RETURN TO OS
           CNOP   0,8                        ALIGNMENT
           EJECT
*******************************************************************
*          RESOURCE MANAGER EXIT                                 *
*******************************************************************
RESEXIT1   EQU    *                          RESOURCE MANAGER EXIT
           STM    R14,R12,12(R13)            SAVE REGISTERS
           LM     R2,R3,0(R1)                GET RMPL AND PARAM ADDRESSES
           USING  RMPL,R2                     ESTABLISH ADDRESSABILITY
           LM     R4,R5,0(R3)                GET SPARE AND CSECT ADDRESS
           LR     R12,R15                    GET EXIT ADDRESS
           USING  RESEXIT1,R12                ESTABLISH ADDRESSABILITY
           LA     R5,EXITSAVE                GET ADDRESS OF EXIT SAVE AREA
           ST     R5,8(,R13)                 CHAIN
           ST     R13,4(,R5)                   SAVE
           LR     R13,R5                         AREAS
           SPACE 1
*          WE WOULD TAKE ANY CLEANUP ACTIONS DESIRED AT THIS POINT
           SPACE 1
*          RETURN TO RECOVERY/TERMINATION MANAGER
           L      R13,4(,R13)                GET OLD SAVE AREA ADDRESS
           LM     R14,R12,12(R13)            RESTORE OLD REGISTERS
           SR     R15,R15                    SET RETURN CODE ZERO
           BR     R14                        RETURN TO RTM
EXIT SAVE  DC     18F'0'                     SAVE AREA FOR EXIT USE ONLY
DOWDY      DS     D                          CPU TIME AT RESMGR EXIT ENTRY
D3         DS     D                          AT RESMGR EXIT ENTRY
EXITPARM   DC     A(0,RESMGR1)               EXIT PARAMETERS - 1ST IS SPARE
           DC     CL16'*END RESEXIT1*'       EYECATCHER
EXITLEN    EQU    *-RESEXIT1                 LENGTH OF EXIT AND DATA AREAS
           EJECT
*          DATA AREAS
SAVEAREA   DC     F'0',CL4'F1SA',16F'+0'
ADDR1      DC     F'-1'                      ADDRESS OF GOTTEN STORAGE
RESTOKEN   DC     F'0'                       RESMGR TOKEN FOR OUR EXIT
           SPACE 3
*          REGISTER EQUATES
*
R0         EQU    0
R1         EQU    1
R2         EQU    2
R3         EQU    3
R4         EQU    4
R5         EQU    5
R6         EQU    6
R7         EQU    7
R8         EQU    8
R9         EQU    9
R10        EQU    10
R11        EQU    11
R12        EQU    12
R13        EQU    13
R14        EQU    14
R15        EQU    15
           SPACE 3
           PRINT NOGEN
           IHARMPL
           END    RESMGR1
```

10.1.2 RTM control blocks

Table 10.2 lists the documented RTM and dump service control blocks. The RTM control blocks can generally be categorized as RTM internal control blocks and RTM exit interface control blocks. I'll concentrate on the exit interface elements here. In addition, a number of control blocks are listed that are used by dump services; some of these are used by both RTM and dump services, so classification as one or the other can be hazy.

TABLE 10.2 Recovery/Termination Manager and Dump Services Control Blocks

Control block	Description
ADSR	Symptom Record
DSVCB	Dump Services Control Block
EED	Extended Error Descriptor
EPIE	Extended Program Interruption Element
ESA	RTM2 Extended Save Area
ESPI	Extended SPIE Parameter List
ESTA	Extended STAE Parameter List
FRRS	FRR Stack
NSSA	RTM Normal Stack Save Area
PIE	Program Interrupt Element
RBCB	Recording Buffers Control Block
RCB	RTM Recording Control Block
RCBE	RTM Record Control Block
RMPL	Resource Manager Parameter List
RTCT	Recovery Termination Control Table
RTM2WA	RTM2 Work Area
RTSD	RTCT SDUMP Extension
RT1W	RTM RT1W Work Area
SCB	STAE Control Block
SCE	SLIP Control Element
SCVA	SLIP Control Element Variable Area
SDDSQ	SDUMP Data Set Queue
SDEPL	SDUMP Exit Parameter List
SDMPX	SVC Dump Parameter List
SDRSN	SDUMP Partial Dump Reason Codes
SDST	SVC Dump Status Area
SDUMP	SVC Dump Parameter List
SDWA	System Diagnostic Work Area
SDWORK	SVC Dump Work Area
SHDR	SLIP Header
SLFP	RTM SLIP FRR Parameter Area
SLPL	SLIP Parameter List
SLWA	SLIP Work Area
SMDLR	Summary Dump Work Area
SMEW	RTCT SDUMP Extension
SMWKRSCB	Summary Dump Real Storage Control Block
SNAPX	SNAP Parameter List
VRAMAP	Variable Recording Area Mapping Macro

10.1.2.1 SPIE and ESPIE macro control blocks

The SPIE and ESPIE macros use a number of control blocks from the list in Table 10.2. These include the EPIE, ESPI, and PIE. Of these, the EPIE is the most useful.

The IHAEPIE macro provides mapping of this control block. It's presented to an ESPIE exit when a program check occurs of a type that's being tracked by the exit. It contains the following information from the time of the program check:

- General-purpose registers
- PSW
- Instruction length and interruption code
- Translation Exception Address
- Access registers

An example of an ESPIE exit using the EPIE will be shown in chapter 12 in the discussion of the CSVQUERY macro.

10.1.2.2 SCB (STAE Control Block)

Each issuance of the ESTAE macro in its various forms (STAE, ESTAE, ESTAEX, FESTAE, or ATTACH with ESTAI) will create a STAE Control Block. The SCB represents an active ESTAE exit, which can receive control when an error arises.

The SCBs are kept in a singly linked list chain, with the address of the first SCB in the TCBSTABB field. The SCBCHAIN field within each SCB then documents each succeeding ESTAE exit. Figure 10.3 shows the layout of the SCB chain.

Each SCB contains the address of the exit routine, along with the address of parameters supplied at the time of the ESTAE issuance, if any. Each SCB also contains a full set of flags that identify each of the options specified on the ESTAE macro. The mapping macro for the SCB is IHASCB.

SCBs are dumped along with the RTM2WA control block. This allows users to identify all ESTAE exits that are active at the time of an ABEND. This is a useful practice if you encounter an ABEND in a system service, which might have its own ESTAE exit active at the time of the error.

The processing of an ABEND by RTM involves a practice called *percolation*, by which multiple exits are allowed to assess and attempt recovery from a particular ABEND. The idea behind this concept is that not all exit routines are written to recover from all errors. Thus, if the most recent SCB's exit routine indicates that the ABEND should continue, RTM will pass control to the exit routine in the next SCB. This process continues until an exit routine indicates that it wants to drive a retry routine, or until all SCBs have been checked.

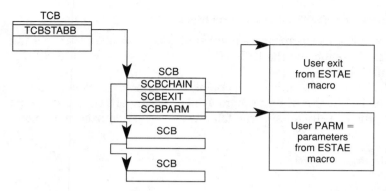

Figure 10.3 Layout of SCB chain.

The complete process of percolation is somewhat more complex. The *MVS/ESA Application Development Guide: Authorized Assembler Language Programs* manual describes the complete percolation process. The key element is that, if you add an ESTAE exit to an existing program or system, the recovery processing in that should be coordinated with other ESTAE exits if they exist in the program or system being modified.

The SCB also contains the address of an SCB extension, mapped by the same DSECT. The SCB extension contains the cross-memory and data space support information for the exit (control register settings, an ALET, and linkage stack information). Additionally, the SCB extension contains the ESTAE token for this exit.

The token is used to remove all SCBs and exits prior to a particular SCB, and is done with the cancel form of the ESTAE macro. Removal of SCBs created after yours is necessary to avoid some possible complications of having invalid ESTAE exits around. For example, if your program brings in a program that uses the LOAD macro, BASRs to the other program, then deletes it upon its return to your program, you can experience problems if an ABEND occurs after that. RTM will still attempt to pass control to the exit that's no longer there, usually resulting in an 0C4. Use of the ESTAE token to delete the prior exits avoids this type of problem. In general, it is good practice to cancel your own ESTAE exits before returning to a caller.

Another control block related to the SCB is the ESTA (ESTAE Parameter List), which maps the input to SVC 60 (ESTAE).

10.1.2.3 RTM2WA (Recovery/Termination Manager Work Area)

The RTM2WA is a useful control block for two reasons. The first is that it summarizes almost all information about a particular ABEND in one control block. The second is that it's printed in SYSUDUMP dumps in most cases, and thus provides the most constant problem information available.

The RTM2WA begins with a description of itself that includes an eye-catcher: its own address, subpool, and length. It also includes information about the specific error environment, including TCB, ASCB, CVT, and RB addresses. Field RTM2CC contains the ABEND code from register 1. (The dump formatting routine prints the field names without the RTM2 prefix, so this appears as CC in the formatted RTM2WA.) Field RTM2CCF contains the ABEND flags.

Several fields of significant interest are formatted directly under the heading RTM2WA SUMMARY, including completion code, name and address of the program suffering the ABEND, registers and PSW at the time of the error, and selected control block addresses. As a result, you don't need to memorize a list of RTM2WA field names to glean information from the RTM2WA. However, a few fields aren't individually listed. Thus, the label EC PSW AT TIME OF ERROR within the RTM2WA summary also includes the instruction length code, interruption code, and a copy of the FLCTEA page fault address field at the time of the error.

Some other fields are not described in the summary, but are useful from time to time. Some of them are:

RTM2MCHI. Machine check flags; if nonzero, a machine check might be involved in the ABEND.

RTM2FLGS. A four-byte flags area, relabeled as RTM2ERRA through RTM2ERRD in the full description. Flags of interest include:

> **RTM2STAF.** A flag in RTM2ERRC that indicates that a previous ESTAE exit failed.

> **RTM2PERC.** A flag in RTM2ERRC that indicates that percolation is in progress, i.e., that another ESTAE exit hasn't been able to retry the error.

RTM2SCBN, RTM2SCBO, RTM2SCBC. Addresses of the newest, oldest, and current SCBs.

RTM2FLAG. A byte of flags defining which resource manager exits are being driven at present.

RTM2SNPL. Address of SNAP macro parameters; this is followed by several related fields describing what is to be dumped.

RTM2DD. The DD name to be used for the dump.

RTM2PREV. Address of the previous RTM2WA, which means you have to review two of them, one for the original failure and one for the current failure. There can be more than two RTM2WAs, depending on the circumstances leading up to the ABENDs.

RTM2TRF1. Two bytes of flags indicating that an external routine is in control (e.g., GETMAIN); this will normally have one bit on when the RTM2WA is printed, since SNAP is in control at that point.

RTM2RECT. Exit routine recursion count; it implies failures in exit routines or retry routines.

RTM2SDW1. Address of the SDWA.

The list goes on and on. In most cases, you'll be reviewing a copy of the RTM2WA as part of a dump. Most of the fields of greatest interest are also in the SDWA, described later. If you want a program to access the RTM2WA during recovery, the TCBRTWA field in the TCB will provide the address.

The RTM2WA summary is usually the fastest way to get information about a specific ABEND; remember to check the translation exception address for 0C4s.

10.1.2.4 SDWA (System Diagnostic Work Area)

The SDWA is provided to ESTAE exit routines, and contains almost all the information previously discussed in the section on RTM2WA. The address of the SDWA is provided to the exit routine in register 1 at entry.

(There's one special case where the SDWA isn't provided. If storage isn't available for the SDWA—for example, during an 80A ABEND—no SDWA would be provided. In this case, register 0 would contain the value 12 and register 1 would contain the ABEND code. Always test the register zero value before accessing the SDWA to avoid 0C4s in the exit routine itself.)

The DSECT for the SDWA is in macro IHASDWA. This is a relatively large DSECT, generating over 20 pages when expanded. Fields of interest include:

SDWAPARM. Parameters for the exit from the ESTAE macro.

SDWAABCC. ABEND code from register 1 at the time the ABEND macro was issued.

SDWAGRSV. Registers 0 through 15 at the time of the error.

SDWANAME. Eight-byte name of the abending program (from RB).

SDWAEPA. Entry point address of the abending program; this and the preceding field aren't always available.

SDWAEC1. EC-mode PSW at the time of the failure; this is broken down into several smaller fields in the DSECT.

SDWAILC1. Instruction length code for the failing instruction (from PSA field FLCPIILC).

SDWAINC1. Program interruption code (from PSA field FLCPICOD).

SDWATRAN. Address causing page fault (for 0C4s—from PSA field FLCTEA).

SDWAEC2. EC-mode PSW of the last interrupt from the RB; this PSW usually represents the last "normal" interrupt, such as a GETMAIN, before the error represented by SDWAEC1. It isn't always present or meaningful. This PSW also has fields following it that are the instruction length, etc., as listed previously (SDWAILC2, SDWAINC2, SDWATRN2).

SDWARSRV. Registers 0 through 15 associated with SDWAEC2.

SDWAFLGS. Four bytes of flags (SDWAERRA through SDWAERRD) defining the type of error (program check, machine check, etc.), previous ESTAE exit information (percolation and failures), and similar information.

SDWAIOFS. I/O status (quiesced, halted, etc.).

SDWARTYA. Retry routine address (provided by exit).

SDWARECA. Address of Variable Recording Area (VRA), described later.

SDWAMODN, SDWACSCT, SDWAREXN. Eight-byte fields where the exit can store the module, CSECT, and exit name for later recording.

Many other fields of interest for special situations are present, and the SDWA merits a full review. Figure 10.4 shows the relationship between the RTM2WA and SDWA.

10.1.2.5 RTCT (Recovery/Termination Control Table)

The RTCT contains common information used by all RTM processes. In addition to module addresses, the RTCT contains the default dump options for all types of MVS-generated dumps (SYSUDUMP, SYSMDUMP, SYS-

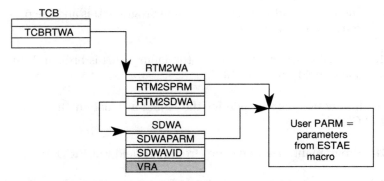

Figure 10.4   Relationship between RTM2WA and SDWA.

ABEND, and SVC dumps). These default dump options are controlled through members of SYS1.PARMLIB, as shown in Table 10.3. The corresponding RTCT field names are shown in parentheses where applicable.

You can change these parameters with the operator CHNGDUMP command, so the consider the RTCT as holding the current options rather than a copy of the SYS1.PARMLIB options.

The RTCT also contains status information about SVC dumps in progress and the installation's SVC dump data sets. These data sets all are named SYS1.DUMP*xx*, where *xx* is a two-digit number beginning with 00. The status of each dump data set is kept in the SDDSQ (SDUMP Dump Data Set Queue) control blocks. These are kept in a doubly linked list, with the beginning address kept in the RTCTSDDS field. Figure 10.5 shows the relationships of these control blocks. The RTCT DSECT is IHARTCT; its address is in the CVT field CVTRTMCT.

10.1.2.6   RMPL (Resource Manager Parameter List)

The RMPL is provided to resource manager exits created by the RESMGR macro for each invocation of the exit. The RMPL contains the following fields of interest:

TABLE 10.3   SYS1.PARMLIB
Members Controlling Dump Options

Dump option	Description
ADYSET00	Dump analysis and elimination
BLSCECT	Dump formatting exit routines
IEAABD00	SYSABEND dump parameters (RTCTSAO)
IEADMP00	SYSUDUMP dump parameters (RTCTSUO)
IEADMR00	SYSMDUMP dump parameters (RTCTSYO)

RMPLFLG1. A flag byte describing the type of termination (normal or abnormal, task or address space) and other environmental conditions.

RMPLASID. The address space ID for the terminating TCB or ASCB.

RMPLASCB. The ASCB for the address space in which the termination is occurring.

RMPLTCBA. The address of the TCB being terminated, if applicable.

RMPLRBPA. The address of the Request Block associated with the previous TCB.

The mapping macro for the RMPL is IHARMPL. Its address is passed to the resource manager exit using register 1; it's also available through the RTM2WA RTM2RMPL field.

10.2 Dump Control Blocks

Due to the substantial overlap between RTM and dump services, I've already covered several control blocks that might otherwise be considered here.

10.2.1 Dump macro interfaces

The two major interfaces for dump services are the SNAP and SDUMP macros. SNAP produces a dump of specified storage areas and classes of control blocks to one of the standard MVS dump output destinations, like SYSUDUMP. SDUMP's mission is to produce an SVC dump, whose destination is a system SVC dump data set. Both macros have extended forms (SNAPX and SDUMPX) for preparing dumps in cross-memory and access register mode.

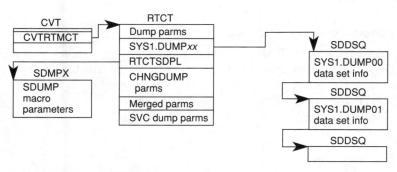

Figure 10.5 RTCT and SDDSQ relationship.

10.2.1.1 SNAP

SNAP is used to prepare formatted output dumps both by MVS and by problem state programs. This means that you can produce the functional equivalent of a SYSUDUMP or other dump from the comfort and privacy of your own program. This isn't normally necessary, but SNAP provides the same facilities to all its invokers. SNAP generates SVC 51 (hexadecimal 33). Its parameters take several forms, including:

DCB. The address of the DCB to be used by SNAP; it must have the characteristics of RECFM=VB, MACRF=(W), LRECL=125, and BLKSIZE=1632.

SDATA. The system data areas and control blocks to be dumped.

PDATA. The problem program data areas and control blocks to be dumped.

ID. An optional ID number for the SNAP output.

Additionally, there are numerous options for specifying storage areas to be dumped.

10.2.1.2 SDUMP

The SDUMP macro is restricted to authorized callers. Its function is to copy storage and control blocks to a specified dump data set. When invoked by RTM, this will be one of the SYS1.DUMPxx data sets tracked through the RTCT and SDDSQ control structures. However, any data set with parameters equivalent to these data sets can be used.

SDUMP differs from SNAP in that it doesn't produce formatted output in the sense of being human-readable. Instead, SDUMP produces a data set for later formatting with the IPCS TSO service. SDUMP parameters mirror those of SNAP to a degree, but they also include facilities for dumping multiple address spaces and providing a dump title.

10.2.2 Dump service control blocks

This section introduces only the control blocks not covered earlier as part of the RTM topics. Other than the SNAP and SDUMP parameter lists, the primary use of the remaining control blocks is to support exits for dump control and customization. Table 10.4 lists these exits.

TABLE 10.4 Installation Dump-Processing Exits

Dump service exit	Description
IEAVADFM	Format dump exit (SYSUDUMP, etc.)
IEAVADUS	Select and format dump data exit
IEAVTABX	Change options/suppress dump exit
IEAVTSEL	Post dump exit

These aren't the names of the individual exits, but rather the names of CSECTs into which an installation can place the names of its own exits. (IEAVADUS is the exception to this.)

IEAVADFM-specified exits are used to format special control blocks. They receive control during the control block formatting phase of SNAP processing, before programs or subpools are dumped. Each exit receives the address of the dump parameter list, mapped by the IHAABDPL DSECT.

IEAVADUS operates much like the IEAVADFM exits, but there's only one IEAVADUS exit, versus multiple formatting exits with IEAVADFM. IEACADUS receives the address of the Common Exit Parameter List, mapped by the BLSABDPL macro.

IEAVTABX exits are invoked before the SNAP dump formatting processing begins. They're used to control the dump options based on the specific ABEND code being presented or to suppress printing a dump entirely. These exits receive the ABDUMP Exit Parameter List (ABEP) data area as a parameter, which is mapped by the IHAABEPL macro. This data area in turn contains the address of the SNAP parameter list, mapped by the IHASNAPX macro.

IEAVTSEL exits are invoked following completion of dump processing for SVC dumps and SYSMDUMPs. Modules in this list of exits are used to provide post-dump processing actions, such as updating a central log of SVC dumps. These exits receive the address of the SDUMP Exit Parameter List (SDEPL), which is mapped by the IHASDEPL macro.

10.3 SYS1.LOGREC Error Recording

I referred to the facility of recording error information to the SYS1.LOGREC data set earlier in this chapter. This facility is invoked through the SETRP macro instruction, which has a RECORD=YES option. When SETRP RECORD=YES is selected, RTM will automatically make a record of the ABEND in the SYS1.LOGREC data set.

SYS1.LOGREC is normally associated with hardware error recording. It's also used to record crucial software errors, for which a specific record type is reserved. Records in LOGREC are usually associated with an SVC dump, but can be entered there without an associated dump.

Indiscriminate use of this facility isn't recommended. The first concern is the possibility of flooding SYS1.LOGREC with extraneous software records, thus hampering or preventing recording of genuine hardware or software errors. The second is the difficulty in accessing SYS1.LOGREC; a special formatting program, IFCEREP1, must be run to produce reports of the records. SYS1.LOGREC error recording is extensively used by IBM to record symptom information about errors, however, simplifying the reporting and lookup of these. The main advantage of SYS1.LOGREC as a recording facility is that it's usually reliable; while SYSUDUMP dumps can be misplaced or canceled, SYS1.LOGREC is normally safer.

For third-party software developers, SYS1.LOGREC can provide a stable method of recording summary information about program errors. This technique can reduce the number of problems that need to be re-created at customer sites because documentation is lost.

In addition to specifying RECORD=YES, the other key to using SYS1.LOGREC software error recording is preparing the SDWA at the time of the error. RTM records the entire SDWA to SYS1.LOGREC; to make best use of it, selected fields should be filled in within the ESTAE exit routine.

One set of fields that's needed is the failing module ID (SDWAMODN, SDWACSCT, and SDWAREXN). Another is the Variable Recording Area, documented as the IHAVRA data area and actually located in the SDWAVRA field of the SDWA. The VRA can be used for any type of desired data, all of which will be written to SYS1.LOGREC with the record. Figure 10.6 provides an overview of the structure of the data in the VRA.

10.4 Summary

This chapter has covered the control blocks and associated techniques used in intercepting ABENDs and printing dumps. The main macros involved in

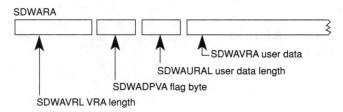

Figure 10.6 Overview of VRA data area.

this process are ESTAE, SETRP, and SNAP. The primary data areas are the SDWA and RTM2WA. Resource managers provide a useful cleanup option for programs that provide services or maintain connections across multiple address spaces. The RESMGR macro and RMPL data areas implement this service. Finally, installation dump exits and SYS1.LOGREC software error recording provide specialized facilities for controlling and documenting problems.

10.5 Things to Do

If you're interested in using SYS1.LOGREC for software error recording, I advise you to investigate the creation of symptom records. The SYMREC and SYMRBLD macros are good starting points. Note that, if you're considering this for a product, an installation's ASREXIT exit might affect what's logged.

11

MVS Tracing Services

MVS provides a fundamental trace service that can be extremely helpful in many debugging situations. This is the MVS trace table, the prime topic of this chapter.

11.1 The MVS Trace Table

The concept behind the trace can be illustrated by comparison to watching a football game on TV. For example, if you find out about game results by reading the newspaper, you might see a picture of a linebacker crossing the goal line. If you actually attend, you'd see the entire play rather than the picture. If you're watching the game on TV, you can view each play again in instant replay and see details of certain plays in slow motion.

This serves as an analogy for some of the debugging tools MVS programmers have available. Storage dumps are similar to photos in the newspaper; they show what was happening when the picture was taken. The events leading up to the dump are often masked. By comparison, a trace table is like an instant replay; it allows the programmer to review the events leading up to the ABEND.

11.1.1 Trace hardware implementation

From the origin of OS/360 through MVS 3.8, the trace table was implemented purely by software. This was achieved by having the major MVS service routines add one or more calls to trace routines at crucial points in their processing. Since the crucial points tended to be the most heavily used parts of MVS, turning off the system trace was a frequent strategy for those installations looking for five percent more CPU time.

With MVS/System extensions in 1978, IBM began providing trace functionality through hardware rather than strictly through software, and this trend has continued. The advantages of providing the trace in hardware were two-fold: first, there was less performance overhead by having one instruction do the work of several in a separate routine and, second, the trace service was somewhat less subject to storage overlays by failing programs.

The instruction provided is the TRACE instruction, which builds a trace entry based on its operands. The trace entry includes:

- A trace operand, coded to indicate to MVS dump services what type of event is being traced.
- Selected registers, specified as a range in the TRACE instruction.
- Part of the Time Of Day clock (bits 16–63).

The presence of the TOD clock value allows the trace table in a dump to be used for limited performance measurements and tuning. The benefit of this varies widely from one application to another. In addition to the TRACE instruction, System/390 hardware also traces certain specific instructions and events. Four instructions are explicitly traced as part of their execution:

- Program Call
- Program Transfer
- Program Return
- Set Secondary ASN

In addition, branch instructions can also be traced, although the large number of them tends to crowd out other types of trace entries.

Trace processing is controlled by the contents of control register 12. The layout of this control register is shown in Fig. 11.1. Bit 0 is used to control branch tracing, and is normally off. Bits 1 through 29 form the trace entry address. This is the storage location where the next trace entry should be constructed by the hardware. Hardware trace support uses 4K trace buffers, aligned on a page boundary.

As TRACE instructions are executed, the trace data is stored at the real address in control register 12. The address portion of control register 12 is then updated. If the new ending address crosses a page boundary, the buffer is recognized as being full and a special type of program check occurs called a trace table exception. (This is program check code X'0016'.) MVS trace services then allocate a new buffer and save the 4K buffer that was just filled until all other buffers have been reused.

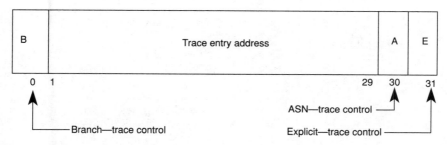

Figure 11.1 Layout of control register 12.

Two more trace control bits round out the contents of control register 12. (Since all trace entries are multiples of four bytes, the low-order two bits can be used without affecting the address.) Bit 30 (A) is the ASN-trace control bit, which controls trace processing of the PC, PR, PT, and SSAR instructions. Bit 31 (E) is the explicit trace control bit; this enables or disables the function of the TRACE instruction.

Bits 30 and 31 are normally on and bit zero is normally off in ESA/390. You can determine the trace control bits at the time of an ABEND by reviewing the contents of control register 12 in the RTM2WA.

11.1.2 MVS trace table support

MVS provides services to prepare and control hardware trace processing. The trace support must initialize tracing, provide new trace buffers as they're filled, and provide information on request to dump services. Additionally, MVS provides a macro to allow you to add your own user trace entries to the trace table.

The PTRACE (Processor TRACE) macro provides a way of formatting your own trace entries for use with the TRACE instruction. The TRACE instruction should not be issued by other than MVS components, because dump processing of the entries is based on the trace operand ID value.

PTRACE is coded with three operands. The first is a user trace type, which is a value ranging from 0 to 15. This is coded as a keyword in the range of USR0 through USRF. Next is a range of registers to be traced (up to a maximum of six). The final, optional operand is the type of save area provided. A short fragment of code to use the PTRACE macro follows:

```
*****************************************************************
*                                                               *
*          EXAMPLE OF PTRACE MACRO INSTRUCTION                  *
*                                                               *
*****************************************************************
          LA    R2,SNAPDCB1          GET DCB ADDRESS
          OPEN  ((2),OUTPUT)
```

```
         SPACE 1
*        GET INTO SUPERVISOR STATE, PROTECT KEY ZERO
         MODESET  KEY=ZERO,MODE=SUP
         SPACE 1
*        SET UP SOME REGISTER CONTENTS TO TRACE
         LR   R3,R12                  COPY PROGRAM BASE REGISTER
         SPACE 1
*        ISSUE PTRACE MACRO
         PTRACE   TYPE=USR5,           TYPE = USER 5              X
                  REGS=(2,3),          TRACE REGISTERS 2 AND 3    X
                  SAVEAREA=STANDARD    NORMAL MVS SAVE AREA
         SPACE 3
*        SNAP TO DISPLAY TRACE TABLE ENTRIES...
         SNAP  DCB=(2),                                           X
               SDATA=(TRT)
```

Obviously, your program must be authorized to use the PTRACE macro. Other trace services are tailored to the requirements of specific MVS components, and aren't intended for end users.

Trace options can be controlled by the console operator TRACE command with the ST option. The command TRACE ST,OFF turns off the system trace. It can be reinstated with the TRACE ST command; this also provides the option of varying the trace buffer size. (The SCHED*xx* member of SYS1.PARMLIB sets the default trace buffer size.)

11.1.3 Trace control blocks

The provision of trace services requires four primary control blocks, along with the trace entries themselves. The following sections will provide additional parameter lists for the MVS services that use trace services, and also discuss the layout of the trace entries themselves.

11.1.3.1 System Trace Option Block (TOB)

The TOB contains the starting options for the system trace. The TOB is located in the nucleus as CSECT IEAVETOB; its address is also carried in the TRVT, described later. Fields of interest in the TOB include:

TOBTRFG1. A flag byte with the system trace facility status; bit TOB-STACT indicates that the system trace is active.

TOBTROPT. Trace options in the same format as in control register 12.

TOBTRBUF. The number of 4K trace buffers per processor.

The options in the TOB are those at the time of system initialization.

11.1.3.2 System Trace Vector Table (TRVT)

The TRVT is the main control block for system trace activities. It holds most commonly needed addresses, but doesn't contain any trace buffer addresses. It contains the address of the TOB, along with the addresses of numerous trace service routines to format trace entries and to provide dump services of various types. The TRVT is addressable through the PSA, using field PSATRVT. Its mapping macro is IHATRVT.

11.1.3.3 System Trace Buffer (TBVT)

One TBVT exists for each trace buffer. TBVTs are organized in a circular doubly linked list. The TBVT holds buffer status information, including a copy of the control register 12 setting to start using the associated buffer. A 4K buffer is associated with each TBVT. The mapping macro for the TBVT is not distributed, to the best of my knowledge. Figure 11.2 shows the relationship of the TBVTs, trace buffers, and control register 12.

11.1.3.4 System Trace Operand Table (TOT)

The TOB is included in the nucleus as CSECT IEAVETOT. Its purpose is to hold model trace entries for each type. There's no distributed mapping macro, to the best of my knowledge. Figure 11.3 shows the relationship between the TRVT, TOB, and TOT.

11.1.3.5 Other trace control blocks

A number of other control blocks are provided for routines that interface directly to trace services. These are shown in Table 11.1. No mapping macros are distributed for these, to the best of my knowledge, except for IHATROB. This maps the System Trace Table Formatter Output Buffer, which is used by user exits in dump printing to format user trace entries. Writing one of these is a sure sign of too much spare time.

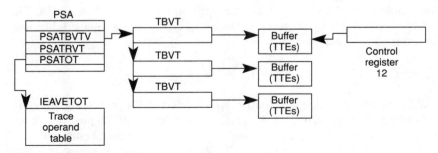

Figure 11.2 TBVT and trace buffer relationship.

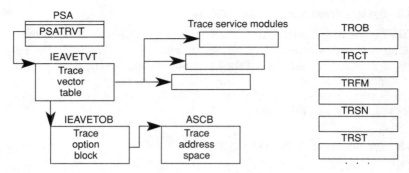

Figure 11.3 TRVT, TOT, and TOB relationship.

TABLE 11.1 Trace Service Parameter List

Trace control block	Description
TRCT	COPYTRC Parameter List
TRFM	Trace Format Request Parameter List
TROB	Trace Table Formatter Output Buffer
TRSN	SNAPTRC Parameter List
TRST	Status Parameter List
TTCH	Trace Table Snapshot Copy Header

11.1.4 Trace Table Entries (TTEs)

The whole purpose of the system trace is to record trace entries. While these are usually formatted for you in a dump, it's essential to understand the type of entries and their contents in order to obtain the most value from the trace table.

The MVS trace table format is described by the IHATTE macro. IHATTE's purpose is to map all the possible trace table entries. Since many of the trace table entry types are of interest only in special situations, IHATTE provides options that will generate the entry types only for selected types. For example, coding:

```
IHATTE IO=YES
```

would generate the trace table entry types related to I/O processing. To generate all possible types, use the ALL=YES option. The IHATTE macro defined 42 different entry types and associated keywords the last time I counted.

The generated DSECT name is TTE. Within this DSECT, there's a separate entry name for each type, such as TTE005 for SVC interrupts. Table 11.2 lists a few typical trace entries and their associated TTE*xxx* numbers.

TABLE 11.2   Selected MVS Trace Entry Types

Mnemonic	TTE #	Description
SSCH	001	Start Subchannel
EXT	003	External Interrupt
SVC	005	SVC Interrupt
PGM	007	Program Interrupt
DSP	00F	Task Dispatch
IO	00B	I/O Interrupt
SVCR	105	SVC Return
SRB	10F	SRB Dispatch
SSRB	20F	Suspended SRB Dispatch
SSRV	205	PC or Branch Entered System Service

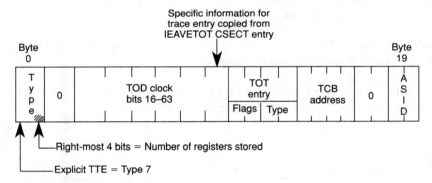

Figure 11.4   General format of trace entries.

Trace table entries follow a specific hardware-defined layout. Figure 11.4 shows the general format of explicit trace table entries. (This shows the fixed segment only; each trace type adds other fields at the end.) Note that the TOT control block initializes the four-byte flags and type field.

Each type of entry, however, is customized differently based on the contents of the general-purpose registers at the time the TRACE instruction was executed. Some entries have formats defined by hardware. For example, Fig. 11.5 shows the layout of a Program Call (PC) trace table entry.

By contrast, other trace entries are larger and more complex. Figure 11.6 shows the layout of a Program Check (PGM) trace entry. (This figure shows only the variable part of the trace entry; the fixed portion from Fig. 11.4 will precede it.)

The contents of some of the more frequently used trace table entries are discussed in the following sections. When printed in a dump, the trace table has the following headings:

PR. The processor number (CPU number) on which the event happened.

ASID. The address space ID number either related to the event or that had control at the time of an interrupt.

TCB-ADDR. The Task Control Block address for the current task.

IDENT. The mnemonic for the type of trace entry, such as is listed in Table 11.2 (SSCH, PGM, etc.).

CD/D. A code field with various meanings for different types of interrupts or trace entries.

PSW. The Program Status Word at the time of an interrupt; this field is used differently for some entry types.

UNIQUE *n*. The fields unique to this trace entry; type n varies from 1 to 6. This is explained later for selected entries.

PSACLHS. The current contents of PSACLHS (the current lock status for the processor); see the four bytes described as PSAHLHI.

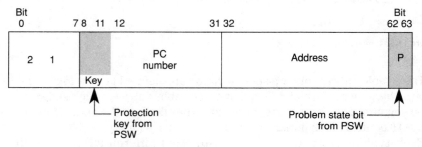

Figure 11.5 Layout of PC (Program Call) trace entry.

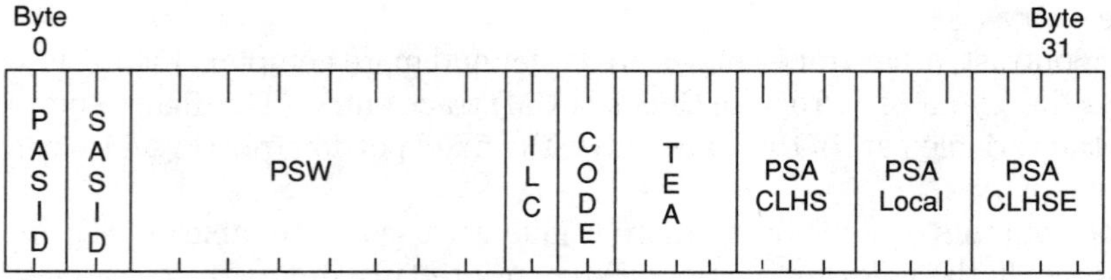

Figure 11.6 Layout of the PGM (Program Check) trace entry.

PSACLHSE. The current contents of PSACLHSE (extended lock information).

PSALOCAL. The current contents of PSALOCAL (local address space lock information).

PASD. The current primary address space designator.

SASD. The current secondary address space designator.

TIMESTAMP. The time of the trace entry; follows the format of the STCK instruction output.

Because the beginning and ending fields within a trace entry usually follow the same format, the descriptions of individual TTEs that follow will cover only the middle portion of the TTE. The fields listed are IDENT, CD/D, PSW ADDRESS, and UNIQUE.

11.1.4.1 PC (Program Call TTE)

Program Call entries are made automatically by hardware when a PC instruction is executed. PC comes in two formats: space switching, called PC-ss in the *Principles of Operation* manual, and current primary, called PC-cp. The PC-ss variant is associated with service requests to a different address space. These are often made by MVS when executing some service request for your program.

The PC number is shown in the left side of the PSW fields. To determine which service is being requested, refer to chapter 2 of the *MVS/ESA Diagnosis: System Reference* manual.

One disconcerting characteristic of both Program Call and Program Return trace entries is that the instruction address field might be an odd number. Since only even addresses are valid for instructions, this seems like an error at first glance. The explanation is that the current setting of the problem state (P) bit of the PSW is placed in the right-most bit of the address. This allows the trace to track changes from problem state to supervisor state through PC instructions. Subtract one before using the address if the PC entry was made in problem state. The following shows a PC entry:

```
PC   ... 0   85C5EDA2   01600
```

The field meanings are:

PC. Program Call identifier.

0. The PSW key.

85C5EDA2. Address at which the PC instruction was issued.

01600. Program Call (PC) number; refer to the *Diagnosis: System Reference* manual to decode. This entry was made during dump processing.

11.1.4.2 PR and PT (Program Return and Program Transfer TTEs)

PR and PT are the flip side of the PC instruction; they represent the return from completion of a system service. Each PC trace entry should eventually have a matching (ending) PR or PT trace entry.

Items traced for these two are identical, with one exception. The identical items traced include the PSW key and the return address being transferred to. The PR entry records the address being branched from; PT records the ASID being branched to. An example of a PT is:

```
PT   ... 0   85C5EDA2   0321
```

The field meanings are:

PT. Identifier for Program Transfer TTE.

0. Current PSW key.

85C5EDA2. New (branch to) instruction address.

0321. New ASID from the PT instruction.

11.1.4.3 DSP (Task Dispatch TTE)

Dispatch TTEs indicate that a TCB is being given control of the CPU by the MVS dispatcher. This usually occurs after a preceding interruption of some type has caused the dispatcher to give control to another task. It might also happen following I/O or external interruptions when there's no higher-priority work waiting for the interruption before proceeding.

Elements recorded for the DSP TTE include the new PSW to be dispatched, the PSAMODEW field, and the contents of registers 0 and 1. The PSAMODEW field includes four bytes, one of which is labeled PSAMODE. This byte indicates what mode is being dispatched (task, SRB, dispatcher, or wait). Refer to the IHAPSA macro for bit meanings. Registers 0 and 1 are included on the chance that a prior service had set them before entering the dispatcher. Depending on the event that caused the dispatch entry, they might have no intrinsic meaning.

An example of a DSP trace entry, which comes after the EXT TTE sample in the next section, follows:

```
DSP   070C0000 8540D1B4   00000000 009E084C 009E06E0
```

The meanings of these fields are:

DSP. Identifier for a Dispatch TTE.

070C0000 8540D1B4. The new PSW to be dispatched.

00000000. PSAMODEW; X'00' in the last byte indicates task mode dispatch.

009E084C. Register 0 at the time of the original interrupt.

009E06E0. Register 1 at the time of the original interrupt.

11.1.4.4 EXT (External Interrupt TTE)

External interrupts are related to a number of outside sources. These include other processors in the same processor complex, the operator interrupt key (or hardware console command), and the various processor timing facilities. Processor timing (the clock comparator and CPU timer) is the most frequent cause of external interrupts.

External interrupts are of interest in two cases. The first is when your program (or the one you're debugging) is waiting for some time period to end. This is usually tied to an STIMER macro with the WAIT option. In this case, the EXT TTE signals that the time period has ended. The second case is when the program in question has gone into a loop. In this case, the loop is marked in the trace table by repetitive EXT and DSP entries until an $x22$ ABEND terminates the job. The value of the EXT entries in the second case is that you can use them to determine the scope of the loop. (To do this, just list all the PSW addresses in the EXT entries. These addresses will reflect the parts of the program involved in the loop.)

The outside cause of an external interrupt is identified by the external interruption code stored as part of the interrupt. A list of these is contained in the *ESA/370 Reference Summary*.

Elements stored as part of the EXT TTE include the external interrupt code, PSW, and the fullword from location X'84' in the PSA, which will contain the CPU address causing the external interruption and interrupt code if appropriate. The following is an example of the middle portion of an EXT trace table entry:

```
EXT   1005 070C0000 8540D1B4   00001005
```

The meanings of the fields are:

EXT. External TTE identifier.

1005. External interrupt code (CPU timer).

070C0000 8540D1B4. PSW stored at the time of the interrupt.

00001005. Location X'84' of the PSA—just has the external interrupt code for this particular case.

11.1.4.5 IO (I/O Interrupt TTE)

IO TTEs usually mark the completion of an I/O event, and are normally related to a preceding SSCH TTE. (Alternatively, they can be preceded by an RSCH TTE.) I/O event status is communicated by hardware in the form of an Interruption Response Block. The IRB is defined by the IHAIRB DSECT, but the first 12 bytes of this are the hardware data structure called the Subchannel Status Word, or SCSW.

The SCSW is stored as the first three fullwords of the UNIQUE-1-2-3 areas. It contains flags in the first fullword and the ending CCW address in the second fullword. (The ending CCW address usually points past the last CCW executed, much as the PSW points past the last instruction executed.) The third fullword contains the device status and subchannel status in the first two bytes and the residual count in the last halfword.

The two status bytes contain 16 flags, but you can check for a few recurring patterns without examining all 16 bits. Normal completion is coded as X'0C00', which represents the flags called Device End and Channel End. X'0D00' normally represents the end of file. This adds the Unit Exception bit (X'0100') to normal ending status; if this bit is on, an end-of-file marker has generally been read on disk or tape. Any response including the X'0200' bit (Unit Check) usually represents an I/O error, although this might only be an incorrect block size.

The residual count halfword is best interpreted as the number of bytes not read. Thus, if you attempt to read a block size of 4096 bytes but the block is only 3072 bytes long, the residual count will be 1024 bytes, or X'0400'. A residual count of zero, coupled with the X'0040' bit (Incorrect Length) in subchannel status, indicates that you specified a block size that's too small. If the residual count is nonzero and this bit is on, subtract the residual count from your block size to determine the actual block size.

The UNIQUE-4 entry of the IO TTE is the first fullword of the extended status word section of the IRB. This contains additional error logout information; it's valid only in the context of bit 5 of the first fullword of the IRB (the UNIQUE-1 field) being set on.

The *ESA/370 Reference Summary* defines the meanings of each bit in the IRB; consult it for any detailed questions. The definitive reference is the *ESA/370 Principles of Operation*.

The final fullword of IO TTE information (UNIQUE-5) is the UCB address associated with the interruption. Note that some I/O interruptions arise independently of a preceding SSCH. Examples of this include pressing the

Enter key on a locally attached 3270 terminal, which generates an attention interrupt. This causes VTAM to issue a read command to the terminal, generating an SSCH TTE. When the I/O completes, there's another IO TTE. Another example would be when an operator makes a tape drive ready. The following shows an example of the middle portion of an IO TTE:

```
I/O  2CA 078D1000 89F7280C   00004007 00323368 0C000000
                             0040000A 00F24D90
```

The meanings of the fields are:

I/O. Identifier for an IO TTE.

2CA. The device number associated with the interrupt.

078D1000 89F7280C. The PSW stored at the time of the interrupt; note that this doesn't have to be in your address space.

00004007. The first fullword of the IRB. The 4 bit indicates that the interruption was as the result of an SSCH; the 7 bits are normal status control settings.

00323368. The ending CCW address; this is a real address.

0C000000. The ending device and subchannel status; 0C00 is normal completion and the last halfword is a residual count of zero.

0040000A. The first fullword of the extended status word; this isn't applicable because the logout bit (X'04000000') of the first IRB fullword isn't on.

00F24D90. The address of the UCB for device 2CA.

IO TTEs record a great deal of information into their entries, much of which isn't immediately obvious to those not experienced in EXCP programming. Thus, it might seem unlikely that you'll be able to glean the full meaning from these entries. Note, however, that the trace formatting routines flag any IO entries suspected of having errors with an asterisk. Just checking for this will identify whether further research is appropriate.

The following is the IO TTE for an I/O operation that detected an end-of-file mark. Note that it's flagged with an asterisk and that the unit and subchannel status is X'0D00'.

```
*I/O  2CA 078D1200 8A49CE62   00804017 12E02098 0D000000
                              0020003A 00F24D90
```

11.1.4.6 PGM (Program Check TTE)

Program check entries are usually the last entry in a trace of a 0Cx-type ABEND immediately before RTM and dump processing. These are normally flagged with an asterisk to mark them as being some sort of problem.

However, program check entries will also occur naturally as a matter of normal program operation. This is true for page faults, which is the most common example of this situation.

Details recorded for PGM TTEs include the interruption code, PSW, instruction length code and condition code, and translation exception address. A typical page fault entry is:

```
PGM  011 070C2000 860A9FD0  00020011 7F741000
```

The field meanings are:

PGM. Identifier for Program Check TTE.

011. Interruption code (see ESA/390 Reference Summary).

070C2000 860A9FD0. The PSW stored for the program check.

00020011. A two-part field; the first is the instruction length code (0002), and the second is the interruption code (0011).

7F741000. The translation exception address; the program that encountered the program check was trying to use storage with a virtual address of 7F741000.

Note that the translation exception address, which comes from the FLCTEA field in the PSA, is not always exactly the address the program was trying to access. The stored address depends on the specific implementation of page faults in the processor on which the program is running. You might encounter the addresses of the next lower fullword, doubleword, and so on.

PGM TTEs are normally found near the end of the trace table for 0Cx ABENDs. For page faults and other recoverable errors, there should eventually be a matching DSP (Dispatch) TTE when the program is restarted. Note that numerous page faults are detrimental to performance; you can estimate the cost by subtracting the time field of the DSP entry from that of the PGM entry. Expect this to vary widely, depending on where a page is located.

11.1.4.7 SRB (Initial SRB Dispatch TTE)

An SRB TTE records the initial dispatch of an SRB. SRBs can be sent for any number of reasons; the most common is to post completion of an I/O event.

Information recorded for an SRB TTE includes the new PSW, the LC-CASAFN field, registers 0 and 1, and a flag byte. The LCCASAFN field contains the CPU affinity to be used for the dispatch, if any, and the ASID into which the SRB is to be dispatched. According to the IHATTE mapping, the flag byte is a copy of the SRBFLGS field.

The following is the middle portion of an SRB TTE. This one follows an IO TTE and performs completion processing when the I/O operation is finished.

```
SRB    070C0000 8100F960   00000321 00FC19D4 00FC1968   80
```

The field meanings for this entry are:

SRB. Identifier for an SRB dispatch TTE.

070C0000 8100F960. New PSW to be used to dispatch the SRB.

00000321. LCCASAFN field; no affinity, ASID 0321.

00FC19D4. Register 0 for the SRB routine.

00FC1968. Register 1 for the SRB routine.

80. SRBFLGS; X'80' indicates that a local lock is required.

11.1.4.8 SSCH (Start Subchannel TTE)

SSCH is the opcode for the Start Subchannel instruction, discussed in chapter 8. SSCH signifies the commencement of an input/output operation, which involves an I/O unit. The TTE operands displayed for SSCH are:

- Device number associated with the I/O; you can correlate this to the devices your own program is using by referring to the IEF237 device allocation messages in JCL listings (or IGD100 messages for SMS-controlled data sets).
- Condition code for the SSCH instruction (refer to the *ESA/390 Reference Summary* for meanings).
- IOS driver ID (see the IECDIOSB DSECT field IOSDVRID for a list of these values).
- Address of the IOSB for the request, also described by IECDIOSB; this control block is often released by the time dump processing starts, so it might be hard to trap except for x00-code ABENDs.

- UCB address.

- Operation Request Block (ORB) words 2 and 3. Refer to the *ESA/370 Reference Summary* to decode; word 3 is the real storage CCW address for the request.

The SSCH entry should be paired with an IO TTE entry marking the end of the I/O request. If none appears in the trace table, the I/O was in progress at the time the dump was processed. SSCH follows an EXCP operation, so an SVC 0 (or 114) should appear ahead of many SSCH entries; for VSAM clusters, an SVC 121 should be found. Note, however, that many other MVS operations (such as a page fault) result in SSCH without an EXCP, so this is a flexible rule.

The RSCH (Resume Subchannel) TTE is similar to SSCH, but omits the ORB. The following shows the middle segment of an SSCH trace entry:

```
SSCH   2CA 00   02   00F1552C   00F24D90 0000F000 00323120
```

The field meanings for this entry are:

SSCH. TTE mnemonic.

2CA. Device number.

00. SSCH condition code.

02. IOS driver ID (from IOSB); 02 is the EXCP driver.

00F1552C. IOSB address.

00F24D90. UCB address.

0000F000. ORB words 2 and 3.

11.1.4.9 SSRB (Suspended SRB Dispatch TTE)

SSRB entries represent the redispatch of a suspended SRB. This is normally done after a page fault in the SRB routine. There should be a preceding SRB entry in the trace, along with an entry for the event (PGM TTE in the case of a page fault) that caused the SRB to stop running.

SSRB entries record a subset for the original SRB entry. This includes only the new PSW, LCCASAFN field, and register 1. Refer to the SRB discussion earlier for details of the LCCASAFN field.

11.1.4.10 SSRV (System Service TTE)

In the interest of efficiency, many MVS macros have a branch entry facility for authorized (key zero, supervisor state) callers. This allows faster service execution when used in place of an SVC. It also allows use of the service by code that can't issue SVCs, such as SRBs, code running with interruptions disabled, or code that holds certain locks. The SSRV trace entry provides a method of documenting these for debugging.

The contents of the SSRV-unique fields varies greatly depending on the service being requested. Normally, there's a correspondence between the SSRV identifier number and the SVC that would have been issued, although this isn't true for all services.

The most frequently seen entry is probably the SSRV for branch entry GETMAIN and FREEMAIN, which replaces SVC 120. The parameters for this are listed in the *Diagnosis: System Reference* manual.

The following shows the middle portion for a FREEMAIN branch entry. Refer to the *Diagnosis: Using Dumps and Traces* manual to decode the entries.

```
SSRV 78   860A9F9C   00000003 00000160 00009EA0   A91BE664525FD102
                     03210000
```

11.1.4.11 SVC (Supervisor Call TTE)

Supervisor Call instructions are issued by programs requesting service from MVS. OPEN and CLOSE are typical examples of macros that generate SVCs to complete their service. SVC TTEs record the fact that a program has requested a service.

The salient information recorded for an SVC entry includes the SVC number. The PSW at the time the SVC was issued, and the contents of registers 15, 0, and 1. The following shows an SVC entry in the trace table:

```
SVC  1 070C0000 8106EDE0  00000000 00000001 009DD53C  A91BE66451FD8802
```

The field meanings are:

SVC. Identifier for an SVC TTE.

1. The SVC number (1 is the WAIT macro).

070C0000 8106EDE0. The PSW stored as part of the SVC interruption.

00000000. Register 15 contents at SVC issuance.

00000001. Register 0 contents at SVC issuance.

009DD53C. Register 1 contents at SVC issuance.

Refer to the *MVS/ESA Diagnosis: System Reference* manual to interpret the SVC trace entries. Even without that manual, however, you should be able to relate an SVC entry back to a macro in your program based on the PSW. (The old *Debugging Handbook* manuals will also be useful because many SVC parameters haven't changed for a long time.)

In the case of a WAIT macro, register 1 will contain the address of an Event Control Block (ECB) to be waited on, or the address of a list of ECBs. (The list address is made into a negative number to differentiate it from the single entry.) Register 0 contains a count of the number of events needed to complete the wait operation, in this case 1. Register 15 has no meaning in the case of a WAIT macro. Thus, this entry is waiting for one ECB at location 009DD53C to be posted.

I strongly recommend that you access some reference that lists the SVCs and their associated register contents, in order to get the most benefit from SVC trace entries.

11.1.4.12 SVCR (SVC Return TTE)

Eventually, SVCs must either complete or ABEND. If they complete, they'll produce an SVC Return TTE. Expect an SVCR TTE to follow each SVC entry at some point. Note, however, that their appearance in the trace table is in a last-in, first-out (LIFO) order. Thus, if an OPEN macro issues SVC 13 (hex), which in turn issues SVC 0 (EXCP), the SVCR for the SVC0 must appear before the SVCR for the SVC 13.

The trace information for SVCR is the same as for SVC entries. Note, however, that the registers reflect the results of the SVC. Thus, register 15 normally contains a return code (if provided by the SVC), register 0 contains a reason code for those SVCs that provide them, and register 1 normally contains the address of some storage area, depending on the specific SVC.

The following is the SVCR entry that corresponds to the SVC entry in section 11.3.6.11. None of the values have changed, except for register 15. This happens to hold the current request block address, which is placed into an ECB at the time a WAIT SVC is issued.

```
SVCR  1 070C0000 8106EDE0  809FF6B8 00000001 009DD53C
```

11.1.4.13 TTE Summary

This section has given an overview of the more common trace table entry types. You'll be able to effectively use trace tables with practice. As your familiarity with trace tables grows, you might want to consult the *MVS/ESA Diagnosis: Using Dumps and Traces* manual. This describes all the trace entry types, and contains a great deal of related debugging lore.

11.2 Other MVS Trace Services

MVS provides two other trace services that I won't cover in this book. The first is the MVS Generalized Trace Facility (GTF). GTF provides tracing services using external trace data sets, and allows larger entries than the MVS system trace table. The second is the MVS Component Trace Service.

11.2.1 GTF

GTF trace entries can be created with the GTRACE macro, which uses the Monitor Call (MC) instruction to invoke GTF. However, GTF must be explicitly started and stopped for tracing to occur.

GTF has several drawbacks. It has the reputation of requiring extensive system resources when in operation. GTF traces tend to produce voluminous output unless the trace print process is carefully planned. (The IPCS facility is used to format GTF traces.) For these two reasons, many people prefer to avoid GTF usage.

On the other hand, GTF has several key advantages. The first is that it can record far more information than the MVS system trace. It can also record data from several MVS components (VTAM, VSAM, and Open/Close/EOV, as three examples) that can't be recorded in the MVS system trace. And it does a better job of recording events that are separated by more than a second; the MVS system trace table tends to "wrap" quickly in a busy system.

GTF includes a few data areas. MCHEAD is the Monitor Call Head control block. Its address is in CVT field CVTGTFA, and its purpose is to control the operation of the GTRACE macro.

The GTRACE macro generates a Monitor Call instruction after building a parameter list. The Monitor Call (MC) instruction includes a 16-bit mask field. This mask field is ANDed with the right-most 16 bits of control register 8. If the bits resulting from the AND operation are all zeros, nothing happens. If any of these bits are on, the MC instruction generates a program interruption with a code of X'0040' (monitor event). GTF then eventually gets control from the program check interrupt handler, records the user's information, and passes control back to the program that included the GTRACE macro.

To control this operation, GTF must set and reset control register 8 as its trace options change. This is one mission of the MCHEAD control block, although it also contains other fields used in recording the GTF trace entries.

Note that this implementation effectively reduces the amount of CPU time needed to support GTF tracing when GTF isn't active. Unless control register 8 is appropriately set for the trace class in the GTRACE macro, no interruption occurs, and hence no formatting routines are invoked. The CVT field CVTGTF contains a flag bit indicating if GTF is active.

GTF also includes two other entries in the *Data Areas* manuals: the FFAP (GTF Appendage Parameters) and the WKAL (GTF Trace Work Area List). Both of these are used in IPCS formatting, rather than in the actual GTF tracing operation.

11.2.2 MVS component trace

To address some of the performance and usability concerns related to GTF, IBM developed the MVS Component Trace service. Component Trace allows detailed tracing of a single part of MVS. Examples of MVS elements that support Component Trace include RSM, GRS, and Contents Supervision, which I'll cover in the next chapter.

Component Trace includes a macro, CTRACE, which you can use to define (add) your own component trace. Component Trace includes several *Data Areas* manual entries. In addition to the CTRACE macro, the ITTCTE mapping macro defines the layout of user Component Trace entries (CTEs). The CTSS data area defines the parameter list passed to a Component Trace start/stop routine (ITTCTSS macro).

The Component Trace buffer area is defined by the ITTTBWC mapping macro. Each component is responsible for acquiring its own buffers. The ITTSTAB macro defines a subname mapping area.

The CTRACE macro also includes other options beyond DEFINE. The CS option sets up fields in the TBWC trace buffer. The WR option writes trace buffers. Finally, the CTRACE DELETE option stops the Component Trace.

Additionally, you can use the ITTFMTB macro to define the layout of user CTEs for formatting by IPCS. The ITTCTXI macro defines the information passed to the IPCS Component Trace formatting exit.

11.3 Summary

MVS system trace table information is valuable in dump reading and debugging. The IHATTE mapping macro can serve as a useful source of information for the contents of individual trace entries. There are two additional trace services: GTF and MVS Component Trace.

12

Contents Supervision

This final chapter deals with the MVS component responsible for managing executable programs—MVS Contents Supervision. Contents Supervision provides several services and control mechanisms, which will be described as an introduction to the topic. Contents Supervision also includes a number of programmer-visible control blocks, such as the Contents Directory Entry, that are useful both for debugging and development. Finally, Contents Supervision provides several services that it has traditionally provided by scanning its control blocks; an example will be provided of these.

12.1 Contents Management Services

The original contents management mission in OS/360 was directly related to bringing programs into storage (program fetch) and deleting them. Facilities were provided to search for programs in commonly addressable storage rather than loading them for each request.

Programs have several characteristics that affect their management. The most desirable characteristic is *reentrancy*, which means that multiple TCBs (or SRBs) can execute the same copy of a program at the same time, and that reentrant programs don't hold any variable data (they don't modify themselves). Another type of program is said to be *serially reusable*; in this case, only one task can use a copy of the program but another task can reuse that copy after the first has finished. Serially reusable programs can modify data fields within the program, but they must reinitialize these fields each time the program is executed.

Readers might also see references to *refreshable* as a third characteristic, usually associated with reentrant programs, which means that the program can be reloaded in the event of a machine storage problem without affecting the program's execution. This is no longer tracked in the Contents Directory Entry.

You can place reentrant programs in commonly addressable storage so multiple address spaces share the same copy. The PUT module, IGG019DJ, provides one example. Programs can reside in either the Job Pack Area (JPA), which is within your own address space, or in the Link Pack Area (LPA), which is in common storage. Because effective selection of modules for the LPA has a significant effect on overall system performance, it has typically been the systems programmer's duty, for the last 30 years or so, to tune the Link Pack Area.

The LPA is further divided into three types of LPA: Pageable LPA (PLPA), Modifiable LPA (MLPA), and Fixed LPA (FLPA). The addresses of these three areas are kept in the CVT, as discussed in chapter 2. There are above-the-line extended variants of these three as well.

To optimize program management even further, IBM has added facilities called Virtual Fetch and Library Lookaside (LLA) to Contents Supervision. Virtual Fetch provides improved performance over normal program loading. LLA provides more efficient loading of selected programs, which allows the most frequently used programs in an installation to be staged into a data space for faster loading, among other features. I'll be discussing control blocks associated with both of these.

With this background information, on to the macros. *MVS Power Programming* provides more details.

12.1.1   Program management macros

This section groups selected macros together, as does the next. The common characteristic of the macros discussed here is that they're used solely to bring programs into storage and dispose of them.

12.1.1.1   LINK

The LINK macro generates SVC 6 to invoke its service. LINK loads in a new copy of the requested program, then passes control to it. LINK processing will also create a new Program Request Block and add it to the RB chain for the current TCB.

Operands for LINK include the name of the desired program (EP or EPLOC operands), an optional DCB address, and an optional error routine (ERRET=) that receives control if the operation can't be completed normally. You can also supply the directory entry for the desired program, which is the DE operand. Additionally, LINK provides a LINKX form for access register environments.

Note that, since LINK builds a PRB for each execution, overuse tends to impair performance. If you use the LOAD macro along with BASR, you'll need slightly less resources.

12.1.1.2 LOAD

LOAD generates SVC 8, and its function is to load a copy of a program into storage. Unlike LINK, LOAD passes control back to its invoker rather than to the loaded program. The invoker of LOAD is then responsible for passing control, typically by way of a BASR or BALR instruction, with a CALL macro specifying the loaded program's address in a register rather than by name, or with a BASSM instruction if you're changing addressing modes.

LOAD's operands are similar to those of LINK. In addition, LOAD provides several operands for authorized callers. The GLOBAL operand allows a program to be loaded into globally addressable storage for use by multiple address spaces. The ADDR (or ADDRNAPF) options allow a program to be loaded to a specific address, which can be useful for SRB routines, for example. If you use this option, you're responsible for freeing the storage yourself. By contrast, the EOM option allows authorized LOAD macro users to acquire program storage with the GLOBAL option, to be released at the end of memory.

Misuse of any of these options can result in common storage overallocation.

12.1.1.3 XCTL

XCTL stands for Transfer Control, and is a combination of LINK and the DELETE and EXIT macros, which will be discussed later. XCTL generates a SVC 7. Its operation is as follows:

1. Operate as though the program that issued XCTL ended with the EXIT macro, sort of.

2. Delete the program that issued XCTL.

3. Link to the program requested by the XCTL macro.

XCTL is somewhat like a "branch and destroy self" instruction, if there were such a thing. Its big advantage is that it doesn't need the XCTLing program to hang around in storage until the XCTLed-to program finishes. This minimizes total storage needs. A more practical solution, in many cases, is to move programs or data above the 16MB line, or to move data to a data space.

12.1.1.4 DELETE

DELETE's purpose is to dispose of programs that are no longer in use. As a rule of thumb, DELETE should always be used after a loaded program isn't needed any more. DELETE generates a SVC 9. It doesn't always delete the specified program. Reentrant or serially reusable programs are permitted to hang around the JPA until MVS needs the storage for other requests.

12.1.1.5 IDENTIFY

IDENTIFY adds a new entry point to an existing program. It generates SVC 41. The purpose of IDENTIFY is to allow programs to create new program names on the fly, or to add program names to intercept another program's calls. IDENTIFY is a fairly specialized macro.

12.1.2 Contents management macros

Contents Supervision provides three macros whose purpose is to retrieve load module and library information, and one additional macro for interaction with the LLA function. A related macro that isn't, strictly speaking, part of Contents Supervision will also be covered.

12.1.2.1 CSVQUERY

The most commonly coded use of Contents Supervision control blocks has been to determine which load module is at a given address. This information seems to be constantly needed in MVS program products, in my experience. To resolve this, numerous assembler programmers have written code to scan the CDE chains for their local TCB, then scan the CDEs and LPDEs for the link pack area.

This is all great fun, but IBM provided a macro in MVS/ESA 3.1 that removes the need to code the CDE scan. The CSVQUERY macro can retrieve essentially any desired information about a program (location, size, attributes, load module name, etc.) based on either a name or a location, so it handles all the typical requirements for program information.

CSVQUERY is helpful in several situations. First, many applications need to locate a common control block or storage area. This has traditionally been accomplished in several ways, each of which has its own drawbacks. The CVTUSER and TCBUSER fields can be used to anchor a common control block, unless another application or product needs to use them for the same thing. A special SVC can be coded and its number included in each program that needs it, but it creates a great deal of work if the SVC number needs to change.

Rather than relying on any of these methods, a simpler solution is to create a separate load module containing the data area (or its address) and use CSVQUERY to locate it.

Another typical situation is determining where a program check occurred. This arises in ESTAE or ESPIE exits in order to document which program was involved in a failure. An example of a program to do this will be provided later in the chapter.

I'm not going to give a full description of the CSVQUERY macro syntax due to its size. As an overview, it has operands to specify the name (INEPNAME) or address (INADDR) to be used as the search argument. CSVQUERY then provides various output fields (OUTLENGTH, OUTEPNM, OUTLOADPT, OUTATTR1, etc.) that can receive information about the module in question.

CSVQUERY's drawback is that it provides information only about a single load module. You can use the CSVINFO macro to inquire about all programs within the Job Pack Area.

12.1.2.2 CSVAPF

Another, less frequent use of Contents Supervision control blocks is to determine which libraries are authorized in an MVS/ESA system. You can do this by browsing the IEAAPF*xx* member of SYS1.PARMLIB, but this might present practical difficulties when done in a program. The CSVAPF macro provides additional services to assist in managing the authorized library list.

CSVAPF has several parameters. The REQUEST parameter defines the general type of processing to be done. Selections here include LIST, ADD, and DELETE, along with QUERYFORMAT. QUERYFORMAT is used to determine which format of APF list the system is using, and the CHANGEFORMAT option allows a program to alter it. The LIST option presents a list of the current authorized libraries, up to the capacity of a programmer-supplied work area. ADD and DELETE allow a program to add and remove their own selections to the authorized library list. CSVAPF users must be authorized to use the ADD, DELETE, and CHANGEFORMAT options. The QUERYFORMAT and LIST options can be performed in problem state.

CSVAPF uses two additional parameters, ANSAREA= and ANSLEN=, to specify the size and address of a work area. The CSVAPFAA macro describes the contents of the work area.

The authorized assembler language development macro reference manual contains a coded example of CSVAPF. Because of the crucial nature of an installation's authorized libraries and the implicit security exposure, you must carefully plan, control, and test your use of CSVAPF.

12.1.2.3 LLACOPY

The Library Lookaside (LLA) feature of Contents Supervision provides faster program fetch operations. To do so, however, LLA must be made aware of changes to load libraries since it might save an older copy of a load module to an intermediate area. LLACOPY provides a way of updating LLA's internal directories to reflect new or changed load modules.

LLACOPY generally follows the operation of the BLDL macro. Its operands include the DCB address to be used for the library, a parameter list in the same format as used with BLDL, and return code and reason code operands.

12.1.2.4 NUCLKUP

NUCLKUP is not a Contents Supervision macro; instead, it's part of the nucleus mapping service. I'm discussing it here, however, because its function is similar to that of the CSVQUERY macro.

NUCLKUP is used to determine the name and address correspondence of CSECTs in the MVS nucleus. It has three operands. The first is a key word, BYADDR or BYNAME, which indicates what type of lookup is to be performed. The second, NAME=, specifies the name to be searched for or the location where the name is to be placed when searching by address. The third, ADDR=, specifies the address to be searched for or the location where the address is to be placed when searching by name.

The following includes usage of the NUCLKUP macro. See *Assembler for COBOL Programmers* for another example of NUCLKUP.

```
               TITLE 'UCLA X414.334 EXAMPLE OF ESPIE EXIT
AND CSVQUERY'
SPIESAMP CSECT
SPIESAMP AMODE 31                         31-BIT MODE
SPIESAMP RMODE 24                         24-BIT RESIDENCY
         STM   R14,R12,12(R13)            SAVE REGISTERS
         LR    R12,R15                    ESTABLISH
         USING SPIESAMP,R12                 ADDRESSABILITY
         ST    R12,REALBASE               SAVE REAL BASE REGISTER VALUE
         SPACE 1
*        CHAIN SAVE AREAS
         LA    R2,SAVEAREA
         ST    R2,8(R13)
         ST    R13,4(R2)
         LR    R13,R2
         USING IHADCB,R1                  DCB DATA AREA DSECT
         PRINT ON,NOGEN
         SPACE 1
*        OPEN THE OUTPUT PRINT FILE
         OPEN  (SYSPRINT,OUTPUT),MODE=31
         LA    R1,SYSPRINT                GET ADDRESS OF DCB
         TM    DCBOFLGS,X'10'             TEST FOR SUCCESSFUL OPEN
         BNO   BADOPEN                    OPEN FAILED - END JOB
         PRINT ON,GEN
         SPACE 2
*        MAIN LINE PROCESSING
MAINLINE EQU   *
*        ISSUE ESPIE MACRO TO IDENTIFY EXIT ROUTINE ADDRESS
         LA    R2,EXITPARM     GET ADDRESS OF EXIT PARAMETERS
         ESPIE SET,            INDICATE WE ARE CREATING A SPIE EXIT   X
               SPIEEXIT,       EXIT NAME                              X
               (1,(3,5),15),   EXIT CLASSES 0C1, 0C3-0C5, 0CF         X
```

```
            PARAM=(2)        PARAMETER LIST ADDRESS IN REGISTER 2
     LTR    R15,R15          TEST RETURN CODE
     BNZ    SPIEERR          IF RC NOT ZERO, PRINT RETURN CODE AND END
     ST     R1,TOKEN1        SAVE 'TOKEN' IDENTIFYING THE EXIT
     SPACE  1
*    PRINT R15 AND R1 HERE
     ST     R15,SETR15       SAVE RETURN CODE
     LA     R1,SETR15        CONVERT
     BAS    R14,HEXCONV       TO HEXADECIMAL
     MVC    SETRC,EBCDICEQ MOVE TO PRINT
     LA     R1,TOKEN1        CONVERT
     BAS    R14,HEXCONV       TO HEXADECIMAL
     MVC    SETTOKEN,EBCDICEQ MOVE TO PRINT
     LA     R0,SETLINE         GET ADDRESS OF PRINT LINE
     BAS    R14,PRINT31        INVOKE PUT SUBROUTINE
     SPACE  3
*    ISSUE ESPIE 'TEST' OPTION TO SEE WHAT WAS ESTABLISHED
     ESPIE  TEST,            INDICATE WE ARE TESTING CURRENT ESPIE  X
            TESTPARM         4-WORD RESULT AREA
     LTR    R15,R15          TEST RETURN CODE
     BNZ    SPIEERR          IF RC NOT ZERO, PRINT RETURN CODE AND END
     SPACE  3
*    PRINT R15 AND 'TESTPARM' HERE
     ST     R15,SETR15       SAVE RETURN CODE
     LA     R1,SETR15        CONVERT
     BAS    R14,HEXCONV       TO HEXADECIMAL
     MVC    TESTRC,EBCDICEQ MOVE TO PRINT
     LA     R1,TESTPARM      CONVERT
     BAS    R14,HEXCONV       TO HEXADECIMAL
     MVC    TESTW1,EBCDICEQ MOVE TO PRINT
     LA     R1,TESTPARM+4    CONVERT
     BAS    R14,HEXCONV       TO HEXADECIMAL
     MVC    TESTW2,EBCDICEQ MOVE TO PRINT
     LA     R1,TESTPARM+8    CONVERT
     BAS    R14,HEXCONV       TO HEXADECIMAL
     MVC    TESTW3,EBCDICEQ MOVE TO PRINT
     LA     R1,TESTPARM+12   CONVERT
     BAS    R14,HEXCONV       TO HEXADECIMAL
     MVC    TESTW4,EBCDICEQ MOVE TO PRINT
     LA     R0,TESTLINE        GET ADDRESS OF PRINT LINE
     BAS    R14,PRINT31        INVOKE PUT SUBROUTINE
     SPACE  1
     LA     R1,PGMADDR       POINT TO PROGRAM ADDRESS
     BAS    R14,HEXCONV      GO CONVERT TO HEX
     MVC    PGMHEX,EBCDICEQ MOVE TO PRINT LINE
     PRINT  ON,NOGEN
     LA     R0,PGMLINE         GET ADDRESS OF PRINT LINE
     BAS    R14,PRINT31        INVOKE PUT SUBROUTINE
     SPACE  3
*    NOW THAT THE ESPIE EXIT HAS BEEN ESTABLISHED, FORCE AN 0C3
*    ABEND TO DRIVE THE EXIT.
     LA     R3,AFTER         R3 SHOULD MATCH PSW ADDRESS
     EX     0,*              THIS SHOULD FORCE AN 0C3 ABEND
AFTER EQU    *
     SR     R6,R6            CLEAR REGISTER 6
     ICM    R6,7,SYSPRINT+DCBPUTA-IHADCB  PUT ROUTINE ADDRESS
     DC     XL2'00EE'        THIS SHOULD FORCE AN 0C1 ABEND
     L      R4,X'10'         GET CVT ADDRESS
     L      R5,CVTPCNVT-CVT(R4) GET CONVERSION ROUTINE ADDRESS
     LE     R0,=E'100.0'     SET UP FOR AN 0CF ABEND
```

```
          DE    R0,=E'0.0'     FORCE FLOATING POINT DIVIDE EXCEPTION
          B     ENDEXEC        ENOUGH OF THIS FRIVOLITY
          SPACE 3
*         ESPIE EXIT ROUTINE
SPIEEXIT  EQU   *
          USING *,R15                SET UP TEMPORARY ADDRESSABILITY
          STM   R0,R15,SPIESAV1  SAVE REGISTERS
          L     R12,REALBASE     GET ORIGINAL BASE REGISTER
          DROP  R15              END TEMPORARY ADDRESSABILITY
          SPACE 1
*         CHAIN SAVE AREAS
          LA    R13,SPIESAV2     SET UP OUR OWN SAVE AREA
          SPACE 1
*         NOW PRINT THE PARAMETERS PASSED TO US
          ST    R1,SPIEDATA                 SAVE ADDRESS FOR LATER USE
          SPACE 1
          LA    R0,TITLE1          GET ADDRESS OF PRINT LINE
          BAS   R14,PRINT31        INVOKE PUT SUBROUTINE
          SPACE 1
          L     R5,SPIEDATA    GET EPIE ADDRESS
          USING EPIE,R5          ESTABLISH ADDRESSABILITY
          LA    R1,EPIEPARM      GET PARAMETER ADDRESS
          BAS   R14,HEXCONV      CONVERT TO HEXADECIMAL
          MVC   ELPARM,EBCDICEQ MOVE TO PRINT
          LA    R1,EPIEPSW       GET PSW ADDRESS
          BAS   R14,HEXCONV      CONVERT TO HEXADECIMAL
          MVC   ELPSW1,EBCDICEQ MOVE TO PRINT
          LA    R1,EPIEPSW+4     GET PSW ADDRESS (SECOND HALF)
          BAS   R14,HEXCONV      CONVERT TO HEXADECIMAL
          MVC   ELPSW2,EBCDICEQ MOVE TO PRINT
          LA    R1,EPIEINT       GET INTERRUPTION CODE/ILC
          BAS   R14,HEXCONV      CONVERT TO HEXADECIMAL
          MVC   ELILC,EBCDICEQ    MOVE INSTRUCTION LENGTH CODE
          MVC   ELINTCOD,EBCDICEQ+4 MOVE INTERRUPTION CODE
          LA    R0,EL            GET ADDRESS OF PRINT LINE
          BAS   R14,PRINT31      INVOKE PUT SUBROUTINE
          SPACE 1
*         NOW USE THE CSVQUERY MACRO TO GET THE FAILING PGM NAME
          MVC   HOLD_ADDR,EPIEPSW+4 MOVE ADDRESS
          NI    HOLD_ADDR,X'7F'  TURN OFF 31-BIT MODE BIT
*         MVC   HOLD_ADDR,SYSPRINT+48 MOVE PUT ROUTINE ADDRESS
*         NI    HOLD_ADDR,X'00'   TURN OFF EXTRA BITS
*         LA    R2,EPIEPSW+4      GET FAILING ADDRESS FROM PSW
          LA    R2,HOLD_ADDR      GET FAILING ADDRESS FROM PSW
          PRINT ON,GEN
          SPACE 1
*         PRINT REGISTER VALUES
          LA    R4,EPIEGPR     SET UP  (POINT TO REGISTERS)
          LA    R3,16          SET LOOP COUNT
          ZAP   REG_NUMBER,=P'0'  SET REGISTER NUMBER
PRNTGR1   EQU   *
          MVC   REG_NUM,=X'40202120'  EDIT MASK
          ED    REG_NUM,REG_NUMBER
          AP    REG_NUMBER,=P'1'        SET UP NEXT REGISTER NUMBER
          LA    R1,0(,R4)               POINT TO REGISTER VALUE   {
          BAS   R14,HEXCONV    CONVERT TO HEXADECIMAL
          MVC   REG_VALUE,EBCDICEQ    MOVE PRINTABLE VALUE
          L     R2,0(R4)                BXLE
          BAS   R14,LOCATE_ADDRESS GET MODULE NAME IF ANY
          LA    R0,REG_LINE      GET ADDRESS OF PRINT LINE
          BAS   R14,PRINT31      INVOKE PUT SUBROUTINE
```

```
              LA     R4,4(,R4)          POINT TO NEXT REGISTER VALUE
              BCT    R3,PRNTGR1         LOOP THROUGH REGISTERS
              SPACE 3
*             FOR THIS EXAMPLE, WE WILL DRIVE A RETRY ROUTINE. TO DO
*             THIS, WE MODIFY THE PSW ADDRESS IN THE EPIE CONTROL BLOCK.
              AP     PROG_CHK_CTR,=P'1'      COUNT PROGRAM CHECKS
              CP     PROG_CHK_CTR,=P'5'      IF OVER FIVE, STOP
              BL     DO_RETRY                UNDER 5, START AT NEXT INST
              L      R5,SPIEDATA             GET EPIE ADDRESS AGAIN
              LA     R15,RETRYIT             GET RETRY ROUTINE ADDRESS
              ST     R15,EPIEPSW+4           STORE INTO EPIE PSW FIELD
DO_RETRY      EQU    *
              LM     R0,R15,SPIESAV1         GET OLD REGISTER CONTENTS
              BR     R14                     RETURN TO OS
              SPACE 1
*             ROUTINE TO DISPLAY RESULTS
SHOWIT        EQU    *
              ST     R14,SAVER14     SAVE RETURN REGISTER
              STM    R2,R4,SAVER24   SAVE CURRENT BXLE REGISTERS
              LA     R2,4            UP
              LA     R3,31(R4)          FOR
              LA     R5,RESHEX            BXLE
DISPLP1       EQU    *
              LA     R1,0(R4)        POINT TO A FULLWORD IN IOB
              BAS    R14,HEXCONV     GO CONVERT TO EBCDIC
              MVC    0(8,R5),EBCDICEQ MOVE TO PRINT AREA
              LA     R5,9(R5)        INCREMENT TO NEXT SLOT IN PRINT AREA
              BXLE   R4,R2,DISPLP1   CONTINUE DISPLAYING IOB IN HEX
              LM     R2,R4,SAVER24   RESTORE CALLER'S BXLE REGISTERS
              L      R14,SAVER14     RESTORE RETURN ADDRESS
              BR     R14             RETURN TO CALLER
              SPACE 3
*             ROUTINE TO SHOW SPIE MACRO ROUTINE CODE
SPIEERR       EQU    *
              ST     R15,SPIER15     SAVE RETURN CODE
              LA     R1,SPIER15      CONVERT
              BAS    R14,HEXCONV      TO HEXADECIMAL
              MVC    ERRRC,EBCDICEQ  MOVE TO PRINT
              BAS    R14,ERRLINE     GO CONVERT TO HEX
              LA     R0,RESULTLN      GET ADDRESS OF PRINT LINE
              BAS    R14,PRINT31      INVOKE PUT SUBROUTINE
              SPACE 3
*             RETURN TO CALLING PROGRAM
ENDEXEC       EQU    *
              CLOSE (SYSPRINT)
RETURN        EQU    *
              LH     R15,RETCODE             GET RETURN CODE VALUE
              L      R13,4(R13)              GET ADDRESS OF OLD SAVE AREA
              RETURN (14,12),T,RC=(15)       RETURN TO OS
              SPACE 3
*             ESPIE RETRY ROUTINE
RETRYIT       EQU    *
              LA     R0,RESULTLN     GET ADDRESS OF PRINT LINE
              BAS    R14,PRINT31     INVOKE PUT SUBROUTINE
              B      ENDEXEC             GO END
              SPACE 1
*             FAILURE OPENING A FILE - ISSUE BAD RETURN CODE AND QUIT.
BADOPEN       EQU    *
              MVC    RETCODE,=H'16'          SET BAD RETURN CODE
              B      RETURN                  RETURN TO OS WITH CC = 16
              SPACE 3
```

```
*          SUBROUTINE TO SWITCH INTO 24-BIT MODE, THEN SWITCH BACK
*          TO CALLER'S MODE AFTER ISSUING A PUT MACRO. R0 = PRINT AREA.
PRINT31  EQU   *
         ST    R0,PRINT31_LINE_ADDRESS SAVE DATA ADDRESS
         ST    R14,PRINT31_RETURN_ADDRESS SAVE CALLER'S ADDRESS
         LA    R1,*+6              LOAD ADDRESS, ZERO MODE BIT
         BSM   0,R1                BRANCH AND SET MODE=24
         L     R0,PRINT31_LINE_ADDRESS
         PUT   SYSPRINT            WRITE ERROR LINE
         L     R14,PRINT31_RETURN_ADDRESS
         BSM   0,R14               RETURN AND SET MODE
PRINT31_LINE_ADDRESS   DS F
PRINT31_RETURN_ADDRESS DS F
         SPACE 1
*          ROUTINE TO LOCATE AN ADDRESS USING THE CSVQUERY OR
*          NUCLKUP MACROS. INPUT ADDRESS SHOULD BE IN REGISTER 2.
*          OUTPUT IS A 90-BYTE AREA CALLED 'ADDRESS_INFO'. LINKAGE
*          IS VIA  'BAS R14,LOCATE_ADDRESS'.
LOCATE_ADDRESS DS  0H
         ST    R14,LOCATE_ADDRESS_RETURN   SAVE CALLER ADDRESS
         ST    R2,HOLD_ADDR_2              STORE ADDRESS
         NI    HOLD_ADDR_2,X'7F'           TURN OFF MODE BIT
         CSVQUERY INADDR = HOLD_ADR_2                                   X
               OUTLENGTH=MODULE_LENGTH,                                 X
               OUTEPA=MODULE_EPA,OUTEPNM=MODULE_NAME,                   X
               OUTLOADPT=MODULE_LOAD,                                   X
               OUTMJNM=MODULE_LOADNAME,                                 X
               OUTATTR1=ATTR_1,                                         X
               OUTATTR2=ATTR_2,OUTATTR3=ATTR_3,                         X
               OUTVALID=CSV_VALID,RETCODE=CSV_RETCD,SEARCH=JPALPA
         PRINT ON,NOGEN
         CLC   CSV_RETCD,=F'0'     CHECK RETURN CODE
         BNE   LOCATE_NUCLKUP         NO GO - TRY NUCLEUS
         MVC   CSMODNM,MODULE_LOADNAME
         MVC   CSEPNM,MODULE_NAME
         LA    R1,MODULE_LENGTH
         BAS   R14,HEXCONV    CONVERT TO HEXADECIMAL
         MVC   CSLEN,EBCDICEQ
         LA    R1,MODULE_EPA
         BAS   R14,HEXCONV    CONVERT TO HEXADECIMAL
         MVC   CSEPA,EBCDICEQ
         LA    R1,ATTR_1
         BAS   R14,HEXCONV    CONVERT TO HEXADECIMAL
         MVC   CSATTR,EBCDICEQ
         L     R1,HOLD_ADDR_2     GET REGISTER ADDRESS
         S     R1,MODULE_LOAD     CALCULATE OFFSET
         ST    R1,HOLD_R2         SAVE OFFSET
         LA    R1,HOLD_R2
         BAS   R14,HEXCONV    CONVERT TO HEXADECIMAL
         MVC   CSOFFSET,EBCDICEQ  MOVE TO PRINT
         MVC   ADDRESS_INFO,CSV_LINE  MOVE DATA FOR CALLER
         L     R14,LOCATE_ADDRESS_RETURN   GET CALLER ADDRESS
         BR    R14                RETURN TO CALLER
LOCATE_NUCLKUP EQU    *
*          THE ADDRESS WAS NOT IN A LOADED MODULE. CHECK THE NUCLEUS
*          BY USING 'NUCLKUP' TO FIND THE ADDRESSES
         NUCLKUP BYADDR,NAME=NUC_MODNAME,ADDR=HOLD_ADDR_2
         LTR   R15,R15            TEST RETURN CODE
         BNZ   LOOK_UP_DONE       NOT ZERO - FORMAT AS DECIMAL
         LR    R1,R2              GET REGISTER ADDRESS
         S     R1,HOLD_ADDR_2     GET OFFSET
```

```
        ST    R1,HOLD_R2           SAVE OFFSET
        LA    R1,HOLD_R2
        BAS   R14,HEXCONV     CONVERT TO HEXADECIMAL
        MVC   NUC_OFFSET,EBCDICEQ  MOVE TO PRINT
        LA    R1,HOLD_ADDR_2  POINT TO MODULE ADDRESS
        BAS   R14,HEXCONV     CONVERT TO HEXADECIMAL
        MVC   NUC_MOD_ADDR,EBCDICEQ    MOVE ADDRESS
        MVC   ADDRESS_INFO,NUC_MOD_INFO  MOVE FOR CALLER
        L     R14,LOCATE_ADDRESS_RETURN   GET CALLER ADDRESS
        BR    R14                  RETURN TO CALLER
LOOK_UP_DONE   EQU    *
*       ADDRESS OF A MODULE NOT FOUND. FORMAT AS DECIMAL NUMBER.
        CVD   R2,DOUBLEWD
        OI    DOUBLEWD+7,X'0F'     SET SIGN BITS
        MVC   DEC_VALUE,=X'40202020202020202020202120'
        ED    DEC_VALUE,DOUBLEWD+2     EDIT
        LTR   R2,R2                NEGATIVE NUMBER?
        BNM   DEC_POSITIVE         NO - NO MINUS SIGN
        MVI   DEC_VALUE,C'-'       SET MINUS SIGN
DEC_POSITIVE EQU *
        MVC   ADDRESS_INFO,DECIMAL_DATA
        L     R14,LOCATE_ADDRESS_RETURN   GET CALLER ADDRESS
        BR    R14                  RETURN TO CALLER
        SPACE 1
        SPACE 1
*       ROUTINE TO CONVERT TO DISPLAYABLE EBCDIC FROM HEXADECIMAL
HEXCONV EQU    *
        UNPK  EBCDICEQ(9),0(5,R1)      UNPACK DATA
        TR    EBCDICEQ,HEXTAB-240      TRANSLATE
        BR    R14                  RETURN TO CALLER
EBCDICEQ DC   CL8' ',C' '          EIGHT DATA + 1 GARBAGE BYTE
HEXTAB   DC   C'0123456789ABCDEF'
        EJECT
        PRINT ON,GEN
*       DATA AREAS FOR SPIE EXAMPLE
        SPACE 1
SPIESAV1 DC   18F'0'
SPIESAV2 DC   18F'0'
SETR15   DC   F'0'            REGISTER 15 FROM ESPIE SET
REALBASE DC   F'0'            SAVE PROGRAM BASE REGISTER
TESTPARM DC   4F'0'           RESULTS OF ESPIE TEST
EXITPARM DC   A(SYSPRINT)
SPIEDATA DC   F'0'            SAVE R1 AT ENTRY TO EXIT ROUTINE
TOKEN1   DC   F'0'            'TOKEN' FROM ESPIE SET MACRO
SPIER15  DC   F'0'            STORE R15 HERE IF SPIE DOESN'T WORK
PROG_CHK_CTR DC P'0'                 PROGRAM CHECK LOOP COUNTER
        SPACE 1
SETLINE  DC   C'0 ESPIE SET RESULTS - REGISTER 15:'
SETRC    DC   CL8' ',C', REGISTER 1 (TOKEN):'
SETTOKEN DC   CL8' '
         DC   CL80' '
        SPACE 1
TESTLINE DC   C'0 ESPIE TEST OUTPUT - REGISTER 15:'
TESTRC   DC   CL8' ',C' TEST PARAMETERS:'
TESTW1   DC   CL8' ',C' '
TESTW2   DC   CL8' ',C' '
TESTW3   DC   CL8' ',C' '
TESTW4   DC   CL8' ',C' '
         DC   CL60' '
        SPACE 1
PGMADDR  DC   A(SPIESAMP)     ADDRESS OF PROGRAM
```

```
          SPACE 1
*         DATA AREAS
DOUBLEWD  DC    D'0'
SAVEAREA  DC    18F'+0'
SAVER14   DC    F'+0'            USED TO SAVE REGISTER 14 CONTENTS
SAVER24   DC    3F'+0'           USED TO SAVE REGISTERS 2, 3, 4
LOCATE_ADDRESS_RETURN DS F
RETCODE   DC    H'0'
          SPACE 1
ERRLINE   DC    CL45'-******ERROR ISSUING SPIE -  RETURN CODE IS :'
ERRRC     DC    CL8' ',CL80' '
          SPACE 1
PGMLINE   DC    CL45'-*************PROGRAM BEGINNING ADDRESS IS :'
PGMHEX    DC    CL8' ',CL80' '
          SPACE 1
RETRYLN   DC    CL133'0*** RETRY ROUTINE HAS RECEIVED CONTROL - ENDING'
          SPACE 1
TITLE1    DC    CL133'-************* ESPIE EXIT INFORMATION AREA DUMP INX
               HEX:'
          SPACE 1
EL        DC    C'0 EPIE FIELDS: PARM:'
ELPARM    DC    CL8' ',C' PSW:'
ELPSW1    DC    CL8' ',C' '
ELPSW2    DC    CL8' ',C' INTERRUPTION CODE:'
ELINTCOD  DC    CL4' ',C' ILC:'
ELILC     DC    CL4' ',CL50' '
          SPACE 1
RESULTLN  DC    C'-*'
RESDATA   DC    CL32' ',C'* '
RESHEX    DC    CL72' ',CL24' '
          SPACE 1
MODULE_LENGTH DS    F
MODULE_EPA    DS    F
MODULE_LOAD   DS    F
MODULE_LOADNAME DS  CL8
MODULE_NAME   DS    CL8
ATTR_1        DS    X
ATTR_2        DS    X
ATTR_3        DS    X
CSV_VALID     DS    X
CSV_RETCD     DS    F
HOLD_R2   DS    F
HOLD_ADDR DS    F
HOLD_ADDR_2   DS    F
HOLD_ADDR_3   DS    F
MODULE_NAME_2 DS    CL8
          SPACE 1
CSV_LINE  DC    C' OFFSET:'
CSOFFSET  DC    CL8' ',C' IN MODULE:'
CSMODNM   DC    CL8' ',C' AT ADDR:'
CSEPA     DC    CL8' ',C' E/P:'
CSEPNM    DC    CL8' ',C' LEN:'
CSLEN     DC    CL8' ',C' ATTR:'
CSATTR    DC    CL8' '
          DC    CL(CSV_LINE+95-*)' '  FILLER
          SPACE 1
NUC_MOD_INFO DC    C' OFFSET:'
NUC_OFFSET DC    CL8' ',C' IN MODULE:'
NUC_MODNAME DS    CL8
          DC    C' AT ADDR:'
```

```
NUC_MOD_ADDR DC   CL8' '
            DC    CL(NUC_MOD_INFO+95-*)' '
            SPACE 1
DECIMAL_DATA DC C'(DECIMAL VALUE:'
DEC_VALUE DC    CL12' ',CL68')'
            SPACE 1
REG_LINE DC     C' REGISTER'
REG_NUM DS      CL4
            DC    C' '
REG_VALUE DC    CL8' ',C' '
ADDRESS_INFO DS CL95
            SPACE 1
            DC    CL(REG_LINE+133-*)' '   FILLER
REG_NUMBER DC   PL2'0'
            SPACE 1
            PRINT ON,NOGEN        DON'T PRINT MACRO EXPANSIONS
*           DATA CONTROL BLOCK FOR PRINT OUTPUT FILE
SYSPRINT DCB   DDNAME=SYSPRINT,DEVD=DA,DSORG=PS,MACRF=(PM),RECFM=FBA,   X
               LRECL=133,BLKSIZE=1330
            EJECT
            PRINT ON,GEN
*           'IHAEPIE' DSECT MAPS THE EXTENDED PIE USED WITH 'ESPIE'
            IHAEPIE
            EJECT
*           DEFINE DCB DSECT MACRO
            PRINT ON,NOGEN
            DCBD  DSORG=(PS),DEVD=(DA)
            SPACE 2
            CVT   DSECT=YES
            SPACE 2
*           REGISTER EQUATES
*
R0          EQU   0
R1          EQU   1
R2          EQU   2
R3          EQU   3
R4          EQU   4
R5          EQU   5
R6          EQU   6
R7          EQU   7
R8          EQU   8
R9          EQU   9
R10         EQU   10
R11         EQU   11
R12         EQU   12
R13         EQU   13
R14         EQU   14
R15         EQU   15
            END   SPIESAMP
```

12.2 Contents Management Interfaces

Contents Supervision provides two other general control mechanisms beyond the macros discussed previously. The first is a set of six members of
SYS1.PARMLIB, which define global programs and libraries and control
Contents Supervision. The second is a pair of installation exits that influence the operation of the LLA facility.

12.2.1 PARMLIB members for contents management

Six members of SYS1.PARMLIB control Contents Supervision. The prime
function of these is to manage link pack contents, the link and authorized library lists, and the LNKLST Lookaside facility. Table 12.1 lists the
SYS1.PARMLIB members and their function. All of these can be suffixed.

The CSVLLA member updates the libraries and members used in the
LNKLST Lookaside facility. This can be invoked only through the console
operator MODIFY LLA,UPDATE=xx command. IEAFIXxx lists programs
within the Link Pack Area that should be page-fixed in storage.

The IEAAPFxx entry defines which libraries can contain authorized programs. Programs that are link-edited with authorization (the SETCODE AC
command) will be authorized if and only if they're loaded from a library in
this list.

IEALPA's mission is to define modified members in LPA. These are members that must be tested, are temporary replacements for an existing member, and so forth.

The IEAPAKxx member is used to minimize paging in the pageable link
pack area. It specifies how members in PLPA should be grouped, i.e., placed
adjacent to one another in storage. LNKLSTxx defines the libraries that
make up the system link list. This allows commonly used programs to be invoked without a JOBLIB or STEPLIB DD statement.

LPALSTxx lists the libraries to be included as part of the Link Pack Area
load libraries. This allows an installation to include third-party products or
the installation's own common modules in LPA without needing to place
them in SYS1.LPALIB.

12.2.2 Contents management exits

Contents Supervision provides two exits that can affect processing of the
Library Lookaside feature (LLA). With LLA in effect, Contents Supervision
maintains statistics regarding the frequency of requests for individual programs. As time passes, LLA performs module staging analysis to determine

**TABLE 12.1 Contents Supervision
SYS1.PARMLIB Members**

Member	Function
CSVLLAxx	LNKLST Lookaside Directory Refresh List
IEAAPFxx	Authorized Program Facility Library List
IEAFIXxx	Fixed Link Pack Area List
IEALPAxx	Modified Link Pack Area List
IEAPAKxx	Link Pack Area Pack List
LNKLSSTxx	Link List Libraries
LPALSTxx	Link Pack Area Libraries

which are the most frequently requested programs. The highest-used programs can then be migrated to a Virtual Lookaside Facility (VLF) data space, and copied from there on future requests.

You might want to influence LLA operation to favor moving certain programs into VLF for faster loading, or you might want other programs loaded anew for each request. To address these needs, Contents Supervision provides two exits at important points in LLA processing.

The first, the LLA module fetch exit (named CSVLLIX1), receives control each time a program is loaded (from either VLF or the appropriate load library). It receives a parameter list described by the LLP1 data area (see macro IHALLP1), and can specify that LLA should trigger staging by its return code setting.

The second, the LLA module staging exit (CSVLLIX2), is invoked by LLA for each program that LLA is evaluating for staging to VLF. The exit receives a parameter list described by the LLP2 data area (IHALLP2). This contains statistics regarding the number of times the program was loaded, the resource cost to load it, and a number of related items. The exit can then either instruct LLA to stage the module or not, or the exit can amend selected weighting values in LLP2 to allow LLA to increase or decrease the likelihood of staging the module.

Since program fetch is a comparatively time-consuming activity, using these exits can provide good dividends if your program reference patterns are well defined. Balancing this is the frequency of program loading, which means that poorly coded exits can adversely affect overall system performance.

12.3   Contents Management Control Blocks

For the purposes of this discussion, I'll arbitrarily divide Contents Supervision control blocks into two categories. The first, which I'll call local address-space control blocks, includes those that a programmer would normally see as part of a formatted SYSUDUMP. These will generally be created as a direct result of some action in a user's program. The second category, which I'll term global Contents Supervision control blocks, covers those that would exist as part of normal MVS operation, including those resulting from installation customization efforts. These are entirely my own distinctions, and aren't common MVS parlance.

12.3.1   Local address-space control blocks

This category covers the control blocks created as a result of the LINK or LOAD macros. They're also modified by the XCTL and IDENTIFY macros, and removed where appropriate by the DELETE or EXIT services.

12.3.1.1 Contents Directory Entry (CDE)

The CDE is created by a LINK or LOAD macro. These can be issued by an explicit action in your program, or used as part of another operating system service (for example, ATTACH). The CDE contains the following fields of interest:

CDRRBP.   Address of the RB related to this CDE for programs invoked via LOAD.

CDENTPT.   The entry point address of the program, i.e., the address that receives control when the program starts.

CDXLMJP.   Address of the extent list control block for this program. (Note that this can also be the address of another CDE instead for the case of a "minor" CDE.)

CDUSE.   The "use count" of the program, which is basically the sum of all the LINK and LOAD requests for the program, minus the DELETEs.

CDATTR.   Module attribute flag byte, with flags for reentrant and serially reusable modules, the minor CDE flag (for entry points created by IDENTIFY), and the Job Pack Area flag, among others.

CDSP.   Storage subpool in which the program resides.

CDATTRB.   CDE attributes; review for further information.

The mapping macro for the CDE is IHACDE. The CDE is printed in the formatted part of a SYSUDUMP; unfortunately, not all fields are shown, so further research might be useful. CDEs are chained together with the CDCHAIN field. The starting address of the CDE chain for your TCB can be found in TCBJPQ. Another nettlesome characteristic of CDE formatting is that not all CDEs are shown in the SYSUDUMP; only those with nonzero use counts are formatted.

The CDE is often used to locate programs other than the one in which an ABEND occurred. When doing this, note that the CDENTPT field isn't the same as the starting address of the program, which is carried in the XTLST. To determine the true starting address of a module, use the XTLST MSBAD field. Figure 12.1 shows the relationship between a program and the CDE and XTLST that describe it.

CDE addresses are carried in several places. Besides TCBJPQ, the RBCDE field in the PRB contains a CDE pointer. The CDE chain for the Link Pack Area is addressed through the CVT field CVTQLPAQ.

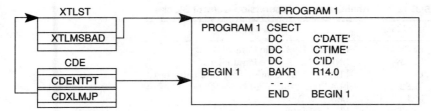

Figure 12.1 Relationship of a program, CDE, and XTLST.

12.3.1.2 Load List Element (LLE)

The LLE is used when a program attempts to load another program that's defined in the Link Pack Area. LLEs are chained from the TCBLLE field. Each LLE contains the address of the corresponding Link Pack Directory Entry (CDE or LPDE) for the loaded module. The same control block structure also covers LINK requests, and the LLE includes use counts.

12.3.1.3 Link Pack Directory Entry (LPDE)

The LPDE is used to identify modules loaded into the pageable Link Pack Area at IPL. It generally follows the format of the CDE, but has a different interpretation of its flag bits. Additionally, the LPDE contains fullword module address and length fields. (Note that CDEs are still used for programs in the fixed and modifiable Link Pack Areas.)

12.3.1.4 Extent List (XTLST)

An Extent List entry is associated with every program described by a major CDE. The purpose of the XTLST is to define the size and location of a program. Field XTLMSBAD contains the address of the program being described. Field XTLMSBLA contains the four-byte length. There's also a three-byte field called XTLMSBLN that defines a subset of XTMSBLA; this is satisfactory for all uses unless the load module length exceeds 16 megabytes.

12.3.2 Global Contents Supervision control blocks

The control blocks in this arbitrary grouping are those that are less likely to be seen by programmers in their address spaces, although usage isn't strictly global for all of these control blocks. Table 12.2 provides a list.

The LLT address can be found through the CVT field CVTLLTA. It contains the DSNAMEs of the link list libraries. The LPAT is in a similar format, but contains the data set names as specified in the LNKLST*xx* member of

TABLE 12.2 Global Contents Supervision Control Blocks

Control block	Description
LLCB	LNKLST Lookaside Control Block
LLPM	LNKLST Lookaside Parameter List
LLP1	LLA Fetch Installation Exit Parameter List
LLP2	LLA Staging Installation Exit Parameter List
LLT	Link List Table
LPAT	LPALST Table
VFCB	Virtual Fetch Control Block
VFDE	Virtual Fetch Directory Entry
VFPM	Virtual Fetch Parameter List
VFVT	Virtual Fetch Vector Table
VFWK	Virtual Fetch Work Area

SYS1.PARMLIB. Its address is in CVT field CVTEPLPS. I suggest that you review the *Data Areas* manual for these.

The VFVT and VFWK are control blocks used for virtual fetch in each address space. The VFVT is located through ASXB field ASXBVFVT.

12.4 Example of Contents Management Services

As mentioned previously, ESTAE and ESPIE exits commonly need to match addresses up with programs. This is useful when writing code to be used in your own installation, because it can format addresses in a more usable fashion. It's also extremely useful when writing a product for use by other people. One of the common problems vendors have when responding to customers is in getting all the information about an ABEND at one time.

As an example of the CSVQUERY macro, I developed the program in section 12.2.2.4 for one of my UCLA classes. It sets up an ESPIE exit to handle program checks, then forces several.

The ESPIE exit, in turn, documents the problem by formatting the PSW and registers. The contents of each register are used as arguments to CSVQUERY to produce the module address and displacement in each. If the address can't be resolved by CSVQUERY, it's then checked using NUCLKUP; if this doesn't produce any result, the register contents are displayed as a decimal number. The format of the output is similar to that of a popular debugging product.

If you want to use the code shown previously in your own programs, you might want to add further checking for addresses not found in a program by either CSVQUERY or NUCLKUP. The VSMLOC service might be a useful addition.

12.5 Summary

This chapter has presented an outline of the services and data areas used with MVS Contents Supervision. The data areas of most value to most people will probably be CDE and XTLST. The Contents Supervision services are used widely through MVS. The information retrieval services of CSV-QUERY and CSVAPF will be of interest for special situations.

The TSO Test Command

Many of you will likely want to examine various MVS control blocks on your system. While a SYSUDUMP dump provides a good starting point, many of the control blocks I discuss aren't printed in SYSUDUMPs. Some of these are in common areas, such as CSA or SQA, which aren't printed as part of SYSUDUMP processing. Others can be printed, but not formatted. Some are created as part of nucleus CSECTs, but aren't printed by SYSUDUMP.

An alternative approach is to print a SYSABEND dump. This will print the nucleus, LSQA, CSA, SQA, and above-the-line equivalents. However, the size of a SYSABEND dump is probably excessive at most MVS installations, running to 5,000 pages in some cases.

A simpler method is to use the TSO TEST command to look at storage. This won't allow access to everything; many of the control blocks discussed in this book are in fetch-protected storage. However, it will provide access to many and will be a good starting point for further research.

The TEST command was provided in the initial implementation of the OS/360 Time Sharing Option; it has been a part of MVS for a long time. TEST is an interactive debugging package. It allows TSO users to stop a program while it's executing in order to examine and change storage and registers, and set breakpoints to make the program stop at various points in its execution. Once you learn it, TEST is very effective for many application debugging situations.

However, TEST isn't as easy to learn as some other TSO facilities. Because of its need for complete control of its environment, TEST doesn't run under ISPF. You must exit ISPF and get to the TSO READY prompt before invoking it.

To start TEST, you must specify a load module to be tested. You can specify the load module as a fully qualified data set name (with member) in quotes, or using your high-level qualifier as the default. In this case, TEST assumes a lowest-level type of LOAD. Thus, if your user ID were TSO4104 and you had a library named TSO4104.PDS.LOAD with a member named TRY1, the command to start TEST would be:

```
TEST PDS(TRY1)
```

Alternatively, you could enter:

```
TEST 'TSO4104.PDS.LOAD(TRY1)'
```

If parameters were to be supplied to the program (e.g., PARM= in JCL), enter:

```
TEST PDS(TRY1) 'PARMS GO HERE'
```

This will accomplish the same thing as the following JCL:

```
//    EXEC PGM=TRY1,PARM='PARMS GO HERE'
```

TSO will set things up for a bit, then respond with a TEST prompt. At this point, you have several options. You can start the program with the GO command. (You should have allocated any DD statements the program will need with the TSO ALLOC command beforehand.) The program will run normally, just as though it were executed through JCL. A second option is to set a breakpoint. This is done with the AT subcommand of TEST. The syntax is:

```
AT location (commands)
```

Location can have many values in the TSO TEST environment. Table A.1 shows some types of locations, examples of syntax, and explanations of the statements. Note that not all of these are possible at all times. To use qualified labels, you must have assembled the program with the TEST option. You must then have link-edited the module with the TEST option as well.

Qualified addressing won't apply to most of the elements you research while reading this book. Almost all the control blocks I discuss are outside of any programs you might assemble, so you'll have to apply labels some other way.

TEST provides another way to create labels: the EQUATE subcommand. The format of EQUATE is:

```
EQUATE label location
```

TABLE A.1   TSO TEST Location Examples

Type	Example	Explanation
Symbolic	TRY1	Program TRY1
Relative	TRY1+4	Four bytes past the start of program TRY1
Absolute	10.	Location X'10' in storage (the CVT pointer)
Register	5R	General purpose register 5
Register	2A	Access register 2
Register	4E	Floating-point register 4 (short format)
Register	4D	Floating-point register 4 (long format)
Register	0M	Vector Mask Register
Register	6V	Vector register 6
Register	6V(2)	Vector register 6 element 2
Indirect	5R%	The 24-bit address in register 5
Indirect	5R?	The 32-bit address in register 5
Indirect	7E8.?	The 32-bit address at location X'7E8'
Qualified	TRY1.FLD1	Label FLD1 in CSECT TRY1

where *label* is any eight-byte name and *location* follows the rules shown in Table A.1. TEST will display the contents of storage using the LIST command, abbreviated L. The format of LIST is:

```
L location format length multiple
```

Where:

- L is the LIST command.
- *location* is a location as previously discussed.
- *format* is the format in which you want the area displayed (C for character, default is hexadecimal, XC for both).
- *length* is the length in decimal, coded as L(*number*). The maximum allowed is 256; the default is 4.
- *multiple* is the number of areas you want to display.

Thus, the command:

```
L 10.
```

will list the four-byte address of the CVT in hexadecimal. The command:

```
L 200. l(4) C
```

will list the PSA eye-catcher. The commands:

```
EQUATE CVT 10.%
L CVT-6 L(2)
```

will display the model number of the CPU on which you're running. You could also have entered:

```
L 10.
```

and received back a value like 00FD4C20; you could then have used this absolute address as a location for EQUATE by entering:

```
EQUATE CVT FD4C20.
L CVT-6 L(2)
```

and achieved the same result. (Absolute addresses are identified with a period at the end, and consist of only valid hex digits.) To finish TSO TEST, enter the END command. If you're having problems with any of the commands, TEST supports the HELP subcommand.

As you read the book, attempt to look at some of the control blocks in each chapter using TSO TEST. At a minimum, try to view the PSA, PCCA, CVT, your ASCB and TCB, GDA and LDA, SMCA, a UCB, TIOT, and a CDE chain. If you practice with TSO TEST, you'll be rewarded with faster debugging in the end.

SYS1.MODGEN Members

Member	Type	Description
ADJTCBQ	Macro	Adjusts ASCB TCB chain
ADYDSPD	DSECT	DAE predump/postdump parm list
ADYDSX	DSECT	DAE symptom extraction routine parm list
ADYPRD	DSECT	DAE Dump header
ADYSRCD	DSECT	DAE dataset record format
AIA2ASCB	Macro	Convert AIA address to ASCB address
AMDDATA	DSECT	Dump Records Mapping
AMDSADM2	Macro	SADMP stage 2 code generation
AMDSAPRD	DSECT	Stand-alone Dump CPU Status record mapping
AUSREQ	Macro	Assign/unassign service request
BLDCPOOL	Macro	Build cell pool
CALLAVM	Macro	Call availability manager
CBPYDIP	DSECT	Device Information Parameters (for UIMs)
CVAFDIR	Macro	CVAF direct VTOC access
CVAFDSM	Macro	Set up CVAF parm list
CVAFFILT	Macro	CVAF filtering
CVAFSEQ	Macro	CVAF sequential VTOC access
CVAFTST	Macro	CVAF test for indexed VTOC
CVAFVOL	Macro	Build volume information block
CVAFVRF	Macro	Set up VRF data
DEBCHK	Macro	Verify a DEB
DELCPOOL	Macro	Delete cell pool
DFPCPYRT	Macro	Define copyright for DFP

Member	Type	Description
DMABCOND	Macro	ABEND replacement for O/C/EOV modules
DSECALL	Macro	Device dependent services (e.g., VARY)
ENFREQ	Macro	Event Notification Facility
EWAMAP	DSECT	ERP Work Area
EWDMAP	DSECT	ERP Work Area DASD Dependent map
EWDURMAP	DSECT	ERP Unconditional Reserve Mapping Macro
FREECELL	Macro	Release Cell Pool entry
GETCELL	Macro	Get Cell Pool entry
GETIX	Macro	VSAM Get Index
HOOK	Macro	Used with IEC/IEA/IRA/ (PMP DSECTs— Code AHL)
HRTPB360	Macro	HASP workstation program
HRTPOPTS	Macro	Global variables for previous
IARRAX	DSECT	RSM Address Space Block Extension
IARRCE	DSECT	RSM Control and Enumeration area
ICHACHKL	DSECT	RACF Auth Chking Intf RACHECK Parm list
ICHPAUL	DSECT	RACF RACAUDIT Parm list
ICHPCGRP	DSECT	RACF Connect Group Name Table Def
ICHPMDEL	DSECT	RACF Data Set Model Name Table Def
ICHRDDFL	DSECT	RACF RACDEF Parm List
ICHSAFV	DSECT	RACF SAF Router Vector Table Map
ICHSAFW	DSECT	RACF SAR Router Work Area (RACROUTE macro)
ICVAFBFL	DSECT	CVAF Buffer List Mapping Macro
ICVAFMAP	DSECT	CVAF VIXM, VPSM, VMDS Mapping Macro
ICVAFPL	DSECT	CVAF Parm List
ICVFCL	DSECT	CVAF Filter Criteria List
ICVVIER	DSECT	CVAF VIER Mapping Macro
ICYMMIB	DSECT	Media Manager Interface Block
ICYMMRE	DSECT	Media Manager Request Element
IDAELEM	DSECT	VSAM Element Argument Control Entry (GENCB, etc.)
IDAGENC	DSECT	VSAM GENCB Header Argument Control Entry
IDAMODC	DSECT	VSAM MODCB Header Argument Control Entry
IDASHOW	DSECT	VSAM SHOWCB Header Argument Control Entry
IDATEST	DSECT	VSAM TESTCB Header Argument Control Entry
IDAVSERR	Macro	VSAM Internal Macro Error Messages

Member	Type	Description
IEAPMP	DSECT	Symbolic names for HOOK macro
IEAVBK	Macro	Produce message during sysgen—no source for IEAVBK00
IEAVM172	DSECT	WPL to WPX conversion routine parm list
IEAVM173	DSECT	MLWTO extract routine parameter list
IECANWA	DSECT	Maps ANSI labels work area
IECCRSA	DSECT	O/C/EOV Component Recovery Save Area (SDWACOMP has pointer)
IECDATB	DSECT	I/O Attention Table
IECDDCE	DSECT	UCB DASD Extension Mapping Macro
IECDDPCT	DSECT	Device Performance Capabilities Table
IECDDT	DSECT	Device Descriptor Table Mapping
IECDERWA	DSECT	ERP Work Area—invokes EWAMAP, EWDMAP, EWTCMAP, etc.
IECDIOCX	DSECT	IOCOM Extension
IECDIOSB	DSECT	I/O Service Block
IECDIPIB	DSECT	I/O Purge Information Block
IECDSECS	DSECT	O/C/EOV generate DSECTs—invokes IKJTCB, IHAASCB, etc.
IECDSECT	DSECT	O/C/EOV Work Area
IECDUCBC	DSECT	UCB CTC device dependent section
IECDUCBD	DSECT	UCB DASD device dependent section
IECDUCBE	DSECT	UCB Comm Equipment device-dependent section
IECDUCBG	DSECT	UCB Graphics device-dependent section
IECDUCBT	DSECT	UCB Mag Tape device-dependent section
IECDUCBU	DSECT	UCB Unit Record device dependent section
IECDXCPS	DSECT	Channel Program scan parm list/work area
IECEQU	DSECT	O/C/EOV SVC module equates
IECIEPRM	DSECT	ANSI Labels Exit Parm List
IECIEXPL	DSECT	DADSM Installation Exit Parm List
IECOENTE	DSECT	O/C/EOV Non-spec Vol Req User Exit Parm List
IECOEVSE	DSECT	O/C/EOV Volume Security Verification Exit Parm List
IECOIEXL	DSECT	O/C/EOV Installation Open Exit Parm List
IECPDINI	DSECT	O/C/EOV Abend Interpretation Table (internal code to abend)
IECPDSCB	DSECT	Partial DSCB Mapping Macro
IECPDSCT	DSECT	O/C/EOV Problem Determination Work Area
IECPMP	DSECT	HOOK macro info
IECRES	Macro	O/C/EOV Common Service Routine Macro
IECSDSL1	DSECT	DSCB mapping macro

Member	Type	Description
IECUCBCX	DSECT	UCB Tape Class Extension
IECVRFDA	DSECT	VTOC Recovery Facility Parm List
IECVTCWA	DSECT	DADSM VTOC Conversion Work Area (old format to indexed)
IECVUCB	Macro	Generate UCB Common section
IEEBASEA	DSECT	Master Scheduler Resident Data Area—CVTMSER has address
IEECDCM	Macro/	Generate Console TDCM area; DOM info DSECT, others DSECTs
IEECHAIN	DSECT	Command Scheduling Control Block
IEECUCM	DSECT	Console Unit Control Module
IEEMIATB	DSECT	Instruction Address Trace Buffer (IATB)—used with SCCB
IEETRACE	Macro	Invoke trace service
IEEXSA	DSECT	SVC 34 Extended Save Area
IEEZB806	DSECT	Master Trace Table Mapping Macro
IEEZB822	DSECT	Input Parm List for PARMLIB Read Routine
IEFALLCT	DSECT	Job Management/Alloc Linkage Control Table
IEFASIOT	DSECT	Step I/O Table—looks like DD stmt entry
IEFAUIPM	DSECT	Assignable Device Initialization Parm list
IEFAUSCB	DSECT	Assign/Unassign Service Control Block
IEFAUSPM	DSECT	Assign/Unassign Service Parm List
IEFCMAUP	DSECT	Common Authorization Check Parameter List
IEFCNMB	DSECT	Converter Message Buffer Mapping
IEFCOMWA	DSECT	Common Work Area (for converter and interpreter)
IEFDOCNP	DSECT	Dynamic Output SVC Parm List (SVC 109)
IEFDSNT	DSECT	Data Set Name Table
IEFENFCT	DSECT	Event Notification Facility Control Table
IEFENFPM	DSECT	Event Notification Facility Parm List
IEFJCTX	DSECT	Job Control Table Extension
IEFJFCBE	DSECT	JFCB Extension for 3800 Printer
IEFJICA	DSECT	JES/Interpreter Communications Area
IEFJMR	DSECT	Job Management Record
IEFJSSVT	DSECT	Subsystem Vector Table
IEFJSSWA	DSECT	Subsystem Scheduler Work Area (used with SUBSYS DD statement)
IEFNEL	DSECT	Interpreter Entrance List
IEFPCCB	DSECT	Private Catalog Control Block
IEFQMDIP	DSECT	SWA Manager Diagnostic Routine Parm List

Member	Type	Description
IEFQMIOP	DSECT	QMNGRIO Macro Parm List
IEFQMST	DSECT	SWA Manager Storage Table
IEFRSTB	DSECT	Restart Codes Table
IEFSCTX	DSECT	Step Control Table Extension
IEFSDBAR	DSECT	Tables needed when using EXCP— IEFSDXYZ, IEFSD081
IEFSDDSB	DSECT	Data Set Block (Sysout Writer IEGSD085)
IEFSDPAR	DSECT	Sysout Writer Common Parm List
IEFSDSDR	DSECT	Sysout Writer Work Areas
IEFSDSET	DSECT	External Writer Work Fields
IEFSDSMF	DSECT	SMF Work Table For Sysout Writer
IEFSDWKT	DSECT	Sysout Writer Work List
IEFSDWKX	DSECT	Sysout Writer Spanning Control Area
IEFSJACP	DSECT	Scheduler JCL Access Function Parm List
IEFSJDFP	DSECT	Scheduler JCL Facility Define JCVT Parm List
IEFSJDLP	DSECT	Scheduler JCL Facility Delete Scheduler Work Block Parm List
IEFSJERP	DSECT	SJF Erase SWB Parm List
IEFSJEXP	DSECT	SJF Extract Parm List
IEFSJFNP	DSECT	SJF Find SWB Chain Parm List
IEFSJGEP	DSECT	SJF Get SWB Parm List
IEFSJINP	DSECT	SJF Initialization Parm List
IEFSJJDP	DSECT	SJF Find JDVT Parm List
IEFSJKEY	DSECT	SJF Key Constants
IEFSJPFX	DSECT	NJE Prefix Mapping
IEFSJPUP	DSECT	SJF Put SWB Parm List
IEFSJRC	DSECT	SJF Reason Codes
IEFSJREP	DSECT	SJF Retrieve Parm List
IEFSJRUP	DSECT	SJF Update Parm List
IEFSJVEP	DSECT	SJF Verify Parm List
IEFSJWRP	DSECT	SJF Write SWB Parm List
IEFSSAG	DSECT	Allocation SUBSYS DD requests—part of IEFJSSOB
IEFSSAL	DSECT	Allocation SYSOUT fields—of IEFJSSOB
IEFSSARB	DSECT	Subsystem Allocation Request Block
IEFSSCA	DSECT	Common Allocation/JES3 exit—part of IEFJSSOB
IEFSSCF	DSECT	Failing SVC 34 Command—part of IEFJSSOB
IEFSSCI	DSECT	SUBSYS keyword cvtr exit—part of IEFJSSOB

Member	Type	Description
IEFSSCU	DSECT	Common Unallocation JES3 Exit—part of IEFJSSOB
IEFSSDA	DSECT	Functional Extension (OPEN/CLOSE)—part of IEFJSSOB
IEFSSDD	DSECT	Change DDNAME function JES3 exit—part of IEFJSSOB
IEFSSDM	DSECT	Delete Operator Message Extension—part of IEFJSSOB
IEFSSDR	DSECT	JES3 Dynamic Device Reconfiguration—part of IEFJSSOB
IEFSSDY	DSECT	JES3 Dynamic Allocation—part of IEFJSSOB
IEFSSJS	DSECT	Job Select Function—part of IEFJSSOB
IEFSSJT	DSECT	Job Deletion Function—part of IEFJSSOB
IEFSSMS	DSECT	Mass Storage Msg Task JES3 Exit—part of IEFJSSOB
IEFSSNQ	DSECT	Dynamic Allocation change ENQ use attribute—part of IEFJSSOB
IEFSSRQ	DSECT	Re-enqueue a job—part of IEFJSSOB
IEFSSRR	DSECT	Request/Return Job ID—part of IEFJSSOB
IEFSSSA	DSECT	SMS Services SSOB Extension—part of IEFJSSOB
IEFSSSI	DSECT	Step Init Notification—part of IEFJSSOB
IEFSSSO	DSECT	Process Sysout Data Sets—part of IEFJSSOB
IEFSSUS	DSECT	Remote Destination Validity check—part of IEFJSSOB
IEFSSVR	DSECT	Volume DEQ JES3 Exit—part of IEFJSSOB
IEFSWB	DSECT	Scheduler Work Block—JCL intermediate text form
IEFTCT	DSECT	SMF Timing Control Table
IEFTXTFT	DSECT	JCL Text Format
IEFVKEYS	DSECT	Converter/Interpreter Keys
IEFZB4DB	DSECT	Allocation verb codes/text unit keys
IEFZB431	DSECT	Volume mount and verify request block
IEFZB432	DSECT	Allocation Global work area (IEFATECB)
IEFZB502	DSECT	SWA Block prefix
IEFZB610	DSECT	Program Properties Table mapping macro
IEFZB611	DSECT	Virtual Address Table—automatic restart
IEFZB902	DSECT	Data Set Enqueue Table
IEZATTCH	DSECT	ATTACH macro parm list
IEZATTCX	DSECT	ATTACHS macro parm list
IEZBITS	Macro	Define BIT2 EQU X'20', etc.
IEZCTGCV	DSECT	Catalog Control Volume List

Member	Type	Description
IEZCTGVL	DSECT	VSAM Catalog Volume List and Extension
IEZDEB	DSECT	Data Extent Block
IEZEACOD	DSECT	System Addr Spc Init Wait/Post Event Codes
IEZEATTR	DSECT	System Addr Spc Init Attribute List
IEZIOB	DSECT	Input/Output Block
IEZMTPRM	DSECT	IEETRACE Parm List Mapping Macro
IEZPIPL	DSECT	Parser Parm List (IEEMB882)
IEZPRULE	DSECT	Positional Parser Rules List (IEEMB882)
IEZVG100	DSECT	Subsystem Console Svc Rtn Parm List
IEZVX100	DSECT	Comm Task User Exit Rtn Parm List
IEZWPL	DSECT	WTO/WTOR/MLWTO/WTP Parm List
IFGACB	DSECT	ACB
IFGACBVS	DSECT	VSAM ACB Extension
IFGACB35	DSECT	3540 ACB extension
IFGEXLST	DSECT	Exit List (VSAM/VTAM)
IFGEXLVS	DSECT	VSAM Exit List Extension
IFGRPL	DSECT	VSAM/VTAM/JES RPL
IFGRPLVS	DSECT	VSAM RPL Extension
IFGRPLVT	DSECT	VTAM RPL Extension
IGBDCSIE	DSECT	DASD Calc Svcs Installation Exit Parm List
IGDACERO	DSECT	Executor Read Only Variables (SMS?)
IGDACERW	DSECT	Executor Read/Write Variables Returned (SMS?)
IGDACSPM	DSECT	Parm List For ACS Installation Exit
IGDACT	DSECT	Access token Definition for Configuration
IGDBCD	DSECT	Base Config Info Mapping
IGDCAT	DSECT	SMS Caching Atribute Token
IGDCATSL	DSECT	JES3 Locate Data Set Info Map
IGDCSF	DSECT	SMS Caching Attribute Selection Facility Parm List
IGDCSR	DSECT	SMS Config Services Return Code Equates
IGDDCD	DSECT	SMS Data class Construct definition
IGDENT	DSECT	Maps external branch entry points in SMS
IGDENVPL	DSECT	SMS Event Notification Facility Parm list
IGDFCN	DSECT	Function codes for calling Configuration Servs
IGDIDONS	DSECT	Map Non-SMS catalog volumes
IGDMCD	DSECT	Management Class Definition
IGDMCSMG	DSECT	Format of Returned Message
IGDRSN	DSECT	Device Control Facility Reason Codes
IGDSCD	DSECT	SMS Storage Class Construct Definition

Member	Type	Description
IGDSCHRL	DSECT	SMS Scheduling Servs Required Resource List
IGDSGD	DSECT	Storage Group definition mapping
IGDTYP	DSECT	Equated configuration element types
IGDVLD	DSECT	Volume Definition Mapping
IGGBISAM	DSECT	ISAM data area—no comments
IGGBISAV	DSECT	ISAM Save area
IGGCPOPS	DSECT	ISAM Equates—internal macro for IGGBISAM
IGGCP1	Macro	ISAM CCW definition
IGGCP10A	Macro	ISAM CCW definition
IGGCP10B	Macro	ISAM CCW definition
IGGCP11A	Macro	ISAM CCW Definition
IGGCP11B	Macro	ISAM CCW Definition
IGGCP12A	Macro	ISAM CCW Definition
IGGCP12B	Macro	ISAM CCW Definition
IGGCP12C	Macro	ISAM CCW Definition
IGGCP123	Macro	ISAM CCW Definition
IGGCP13A	Macro	ISAM CCW Definition
IGGCP13B	Macro	ISAM CCW Definition
IGGCP13C	Macro	ISAM CCW Definition
IGGCP14	Macro	ISAM CCW Definition
IGGCP15	Macro	ISAM CCW Definition
IGGCP16	Macro	ISAM CCW Definition
IGGCP17	Macro	ISAM CCW Definition
IGGCP2	Macro	ISAM CCW Definition
IGGCP22	Macro	ISAM CCW Definition
IGGCP23	Macro	ISAM CCW Definition
IGGCP24	Macro	ISAM CCW Definition
IGGCP25	Macro	ISAM CCW Definition
IGGCP26	Macro	ISAM CCW Definition
IGGCP4	Macro	ISAM CCW Definition
IGGCP47	Macro	ISAM CCW Definition
IGGCP5	Macro	ISAM CCW Definition
IGGCP6	Macro	ISAM CCW Definition
IGGCP7	Macro	ISAM CCW Definition
IGGCP8	Macro	ISAM CCW Definition
IGGCP9A	Macro	ISAM CCW Definition
IGGCP9B	Macro	ISAM CCW Definition
IGGCP9C	Macro	ISAM CCW Definition
IGGDACRE	DSECT	DADSM Create Branch Entry Parm List
IGGDAREN	DSECT	DADSM Rename Branch Entry Parm List

Member	Type	Description
IGGDASCR	DSECT	DADSM Scratch Branch Entry Parm List
IGGDAVLL	DSECT	DADSM Scratch/Rename Volume List Mapping
IGGDCBFA	DSECT	ISAM DCB Field Area
IGGDEBD	DSECT	Appendage Vector Table for DEB
IGGIOBD	DSECT	ISAM IOB layout
IGGLDCP	Macro	Creates ISAM Load Mode CCWs
IGGLOAD	DSECT	ISAM work area
IGGPDC	DSECT	Printer Device Char Table mapping macro
IGGSCAN	DSECT	ISAM work area
IGGUCS5	Source	4245 image table
IGGUCS6	Source	4248 image table
IGGUCSIT	DSECT	UCS image table entry (also macro)
IGGWKNCP	Macro	ISAM
IHAABEPL	DSECT	Predump exit parameter list (IEAVTABD)
IHAAE	DSECT	Allocated Element—Task/job step LSQA space
IHAAQAT	DSECT	Address Queue Anchor Table—SQA/LSQA VSM
IHAASTE	DSECT	Address Space Second Table—Cross-memory
IHAASVT	DSECT	Address Space Vector Table—Supervisor
IHAASXB	DSECT	Address Space Extension Block
IHACBLS	DSECT/Macro	Define/generate lengths of control blocks
IHACDE	DSECT	Contents Directory Entry—describes programs
IHACMS	DSECT	Map CMS lock entry
IHACPAB	DSECT	Cell Pool Anchor Block
IHACSD	DSECT	Common System Data—multiprocessor management
IHACTM	DSECT	Various Communications Task DSECTs
IHADATOF	DSECT	Table of DAT-off linkages
IHADDR	DSECT	DDR (Swap) common data area
IHADECB	DSECT	Data Event Control Block
IHADFE	DSECT	Double Free Element—SQA/LSQA free space
IHADFVT	DSECT	Data Facilities Vector Table
IHADOMC	DSECT	Delete-Operator-Message CB
IHADQE	DSECT	Descriptor Queue Element allocated pages
IHADVCT	DSECT	Device Characteristics Table—DASD type info

Member	Type	Description
IHAEVNT	DSECT	Event table (EVENTS macro)
IHAFBQE	DSECT	Free Block Queue Element—describes CSA/PVT /etc 4K free areas
IHAFETWK	DSECT	Fetch Work Area
IHAFQE	DSECT	Free Queue Element—CSA/PVT free areas 4K
IHAGDA	DSECT	Global Data Area—VSM SQA/CSA info
IHAGSDA	DSECT	Global System Duplex Area—copies CVT/ASVT fields
IHAGWT	DSECT	Get Region Work Area—V=R/Restart processing
IHAHCLOG	DSECT	Hardcopy Log Format
IHAIHSA	DSECT	Interrupt Handler Save Area
IHAIRB	DSECT	Interruption Response Block—used with TSCH
IHALCCA	DSECT	Logical Configuration Communication Area
IHALDA	DSECT	Local Data Area—Address space VSM information
IHALLE	DSECT	Load List Element—contents supervision
IHALLP1	DSECT	Library Lookaside Fetch Installation Exit Parmlist
IHALLP2	DSECT	Library Lookaside Staging Installation Exit Parms
IHALPDE	DSECT	Link Pack Directory Entry—contents supervision
IHALRB	DSECT	LOGREC Buffer Record—Machine Check Handler
IHAMBCB	DSECT	Main SVRB Pool Control Block
IHAMPL	DSECT	MVS Assist Parameter List
IHAMSF	DSECT	Maint & Service Supp Fac Data Block— Console Proc
IHANSSA	DSECT	Normal Stack Save Area—FRRs with SETFRR EUT=YES
IHAORB	DSECT	Operation Request Block—Used with SSCH
IHAORE	DSECT	Operator Reply Element—Comm Task
IHAOUSB	DSECT	Resources Manager Swappable Control Block—SRM
IHAOUXB	DSECT	Resources Manager User Extension Block— SRM
IHAPCCA	DSECT	Physical Configuration Communication Area
IHAPDS	DSECT	PDS Directory entry for load modules
IHAPRD	DSECT	Dump Header mapping for SVC Dump

Member	Type	Description
IHAPSW	DSECT	Program Status Word
IHAPVT	DSECT	RSM Page Vector Table
IHAQVOD	DSECT	Queue Verification Output Data Area (data spaces)
IHAQVPL	DSECT	Queue Verification Parameter List
IHARD	DSECT	Region Descriptor—VSM
IHARGR	DSECT	Region Request Element—V=R
IHARVT	DSECT	Machine Check Handler Vector Table
IHASCA	DSECT	SPIE/ESPIE Control Area
IHASCCB	DSECT	Service Call Control Block (maint. console)
IHASCHIB	DSECT	Subchannel Information Block
IHASCVT	DSECT	Secondary CVT
IHASDEPL	DSECT	SDUMP POST Exit Parm List
IHASDMPX	DSECT	SDUMP Parm List
IHASDRSB	DSECT	Summary Dump Real Storage Control Block
IHASDUMP	DSECT	SDUMP Parm List
IHASETSU	Macro	Invokes IHASUxx macros to set up bit string
IHASMWK	DSECT	Summary Dump Work Area
IHASNAP	DSECT	SNAP Parm List
IHASNAPX	DSECT	SNAPX Parm List
IHASPP	DSECT	SETPRT Parm List
IHASPQA	DSECT	Subpool Queue Element (Anchor)—VSM
IHASPQE	DSECT	Subpool Queue Element—VSM
IHASPT	DSECT	Subpool Table (CSA)—VSM
IHASQAT	DSECT	Size Queue Anchor Table (SQA/LSQA)—VSM
IHASSAT	DSECT	Subsystem Affinity Table
IHASTCB	DSECT	Secondary TCB
IHASTKH	DSECT	PCLINK Stack Pool Head
IHASUBIT	DSECT	SU Bit String
IHASU1 - IHASU100	Macros	Used with above
IHATRVT	DSECT	System Trace Vector Table
IHAUDA	DSECT	DCB Usage Description Area—DFP
IHAVSSA	DSECT	Vector Status Save Area
IHAWPRB	DSECT	Wait/Post Request Block
IHAWQE	DSECT	WTO Queue Element
IHAWSAVT	DSECT	Work/Save Area Vector Table (Interrupts)
IHAXSB	DSECT	Extended Status Block—Dispatcher
IHAXTLST	DSECT	Extent List (Contents Management)
IHBRELNO	Macro	Generates CVTRELNO (C' 3.8')
IKJRB	DSECT	Request Block

Member	Type	Description
IKJTAXE	DSECT	Terminal Attention Exit Element
ILRASMHD	DSECT	Auxiliary Storage Management Header
IMGLIB	Macro	SYS1.IMAGELIB access—SVC 105
INTSECT	Macro	Intersect with Dispatcher
INTSECT7	Macro	Internal macro for INTSECT
IOHALT	Macro	I/O halt request—SVC 33
IOPIDENT	Macro	I/O prevention ID
IOSDCCW	DSECT	Channel Command Word
IOSDDSE	DSECT	Device Service Exit
IOSDHIDT	DSECT	Maps Hot I/O Detection Table
IOSDNAME	Macro	Validate a name as legal module name A–Z, 0–9, etc.
IOSDNPPL	DSECT	New (31-bit) Purge Parameter List—SVC 16
IOSDUCBC	DSECT	UCB Common Extension Fields Mapping macro
IOSGEN	Macro	IOS internal functions (UCB bit setting, etc.)
IOSINTRP	Macro	Simulates an I/O interrupt
IOSLEVEL	Macro	Obtain UCB status
IRAOUCB	DSECT	SRM User Control Block
IRAPMP	Macro	Equates for HOOK Macro
IRRPRIPL	DSECT	RACINIT SVC Parameter List
ISGPEL	DSECT	GRS Parameter Element List (ENQ, etc.)
ISGRNLE	DSECT	GRS Resource Name List Entry
ISPPMP	Macro	Equates for HOOK Macro
LSPACE	Macro	DADSM Disk Space Information
MMCALL	Macro	Invoke Media Manager I/O
MODID	Macro	Generate Module/Date/PTF Eyecatcher
OBTAIN	Macro	Obtain DSCB—SVC 27
PREVNTIO	Macro	I/O Prevention
PROTPSA	Macro	Enable/Disable Low Address Protection
PUTIX	Macro	Write VSAM Index record
QMNGRIO	Macro	JES Queue Manager Interface
REALLOC	Macro	Disk space allocation—SVC 32
RECORD	Macro	RTM Recording interface
RSMCOUNT	Macro	Interface to DIV Frame counter service
SGIFF0BT	Macro	Generate 2250 buffer information (MVT)
SGIKJ0EB	Macro	Generate Default TSO Edit data set characteristics
SGIKJ0E2	Macro	Generate table of TSO Edit suffix values
SJFACC	Macro	Scheduler JCL Facility interface—see comments

Member	Type	Description
SJFREQ	Macro	Scheduler JCL Facility request—see comments
STARTIO	Macro	I/O Supervisor direct interface—see comments
TERMRPL	Macro	Terminate RPL, release resources
TESTPROT	Macro	Generates TPROT instruction
TSEVENT	Macro	Generate SYSEVENT—SVC 95
WAITR	Macro	Alternate name for WAIT macro
WINDOW	Macro	Mask off various external interrupts
XCTLTABL	Macro	O/C/EOV Module address table for IECRES, IECDSECS
XXIEF0PT	Macro	Generate IEFSDPPT Program Properties Table

Annotated MVS SYSUDUMP

The purpose of this appendix is to show how some of the control blocks discussed in the text appear in a typical MVS dump. I chose a SYSUDUMP for this due to the excessive size of other dump types, but the control block explanations in this appendix will be equally useful when examining other dump types, e.g., SVC dumps. The formatting (through IPCS), however, will be different. Additionally, SYSUDUMPs will be the most commonly encountered dumps for most of you.

I developed three assembly language programs in order to create some typical control block situations: APP3PGM1, APP3PGM2, and APP3PGM3. These programs do no useful work; their sole purpose is to create control blocks that can then be explained in this appendix. The specifics of each of these programs will be explained before its listing.

Following the listing of these three programs will be the SYSUDUMP listing. I'll discuss each formatted control block in the dump, making cross-references back to the appropriate chapter in the text. I'll also discuss selected control blocks that aren't formatted within the body of the dump listing. Finally, I'll annotate the trace table so you can relate the trace entries back to actions in the program that caused the entry.

Due to size restrictions, I've edited out a number of dump sections. These include parts of IBM modules, a large quantity of nonessential trace entries, and parts of some formatted control blocks. Notes within the dump listing will indicate where this has occurred.

A number of control blocks will also appear in this appendix that don't appear in most SYSUDUMPs. One reason for this is to show some control blocks that exist in LSQA. Where appropriate, I've included figures to help explain the control block relationships buried within the hexadecimal dump.

The first program of the three created for this appendix is APP3PGM1. This program does several things to create control blocks. Table C.1 shows the program action and the control block it creates.

Note that BAKR and LPSW are instructions rather than macros, but they serve to generate information in the dump. APP3PGM1 also includes some additional processing that doesn't produce control blocks—specifically BLDL, POINT, and READ macros using the BPAM access method. The function of these is to read some data into the area acquired with the STORAGE macro; to simplify coding, the data used is the source for program APP3PGM1 itself. Note also that page breaks in the programs are indicated by a solid line starting at the left margin and extending for approximately an inch. The program listing follows.

TABLE C.1 Macros and Related Control Blocks

Action	Control block
BAKR	Linkage stack entry
ESTAE	SCB
LOAD	LPDE
IDENTIFY	Minor CDE
ATTACH	TCB
OPEN	DEB, IOB
STORAGE	DQE, FBQE, FQE, etc.
LPSW	RTM2WA, SDWA

```
APP3PGM1 MVS CONTROL BLOCKS APPENDIX 3 PROGRAM 1                                    ASM H V 02 12.55 04/10/94      PAGE   1
LOC    OBJECT CODE    ADDR1 ADDR2  STMT   SOURCE STATEMENT

                                     2 *        THIS PROGRAM'S FUNCTION IS TO USE SOME MVS SERVICES THAT
                                     3 *        WILL CREATE SOME ASSOCIATED CONTROL BLOCKS, THEN ABEND TO
                                     4 *        PRODUCE A SAMPLE DUMP. IT DOES NOTHING PRODUCTIVE.
                                     5 *
                                     6 *
000000                               7 APP3PGM1 CSECT
                                     8 APP3PGM1 AMODE 24                 24-BIT MODE FOR PUT
                                     9 APP3PGM1 RMODE 24
000000 B240 00E0                    10          BAKR  R14,0              ESA LINKAGE
000004 18CF                         11          LR    R12,R15            COPY PROGRAM ADDRESS
              00000                 12          USING APP3PGM1,R12       ESTABLISH ADDRESSABILITY
000006 41D0 C4E4    004E4           13          LA    R13,ASAVE          GET FORMAT-1 SAVE AREA ADDRESS
00000A 50C0 C42C    0042C           15          ST    R12,STAESAVE       SAVE BASE REG FOR ESTAE EXIT
                                    17 *        ISSUE AN ESTAE MACRO TO ALLOW YOU TO HANDLE YOUR OWN
                                    18 *        ABNORMAL TERMINATIONS (ABENDS).
                                    19          ESTAE STAEEXIT,CT,PURGE=QUIESCE,ASYNCH=NO
                                    20+*         MACDATE 07/01/81
00000E 0700                         21+         CNOP  0,4                ESTAB. FULL WD. BOUND. ALIGN.    01-ESTAE
000010 4510 C02C    0002C           22+         BAL   1,*+28             LIST ADDR IN REG1 SKIP LIST     01-ESTAE
              00014                 23+IHB0001  EQU   *                                                  01-ESTAE
000014 10                           24+         DC    AL1(16)            FLAGS FOR TCB, PURGE,          X01-ESTAE
                                      +                                  ASYNCH AND CANCEL      @D1C
000015 000000                       25+         DC    AL3(0)             FIELD NO LONGER USED @G860P38   01-ESTAE
000018 00000000                     26+         DC    A(0)               SPACE FOR PARM LIST ADDR        01-ESTAE
00001C 00000000                     27+         DC    A(0)               SPACE FOR TCB ADDR              01-ESTAE
000020 00                           28+         DC    AL1(0)             FLAGS FOR TERM AND RECORD       01-ESTAE
000021 01                           29+         DC    AL1(1)             THIRD FLAG BYTE      @G860P1C   01-ESTAE
000022 0000                         30+         DC    AL2(0)             RESERVED             @G860P1C   01-ESTAE
000024 00000000                     31+         DC    A(0)               SPACE FOR TOKEN      @G81CP2F   01-ESTAE
000028 0000022C                     32+         DC    AL4(STAEEXIT)      FOUR BYTE EXIT ADDR  @G860P1C   01-ESTAE
00002C 4100 0100    00100           33+         LA    0,256(0,0)         CREATE & PARMLST EQ 0 @ZMD0006  01-ESTAE
000030 4110 1000    00000           34+         LA    1,0(0,1)           MAKE REG1 POS. XCTL=NO          01-ESTAE
000034 0A3C                         35+         SVC   60                 ISSUE STAE SVC                  01-ESTAE
000036 127F                         36          LTR   R7,R15             TEST THE RETURN CODE
000038 4780 C08A    0008A           37          BZ    STAEDONE           IF ZERO, GO TO NORMAL PROGRAM
                                    39 *        PRINT AN ERROR MESSAGE AND END EXECUTION IF ERROR IN ESTAE
00003C 4E70 C3D8    003D8           40          CVD   R7,DOUBLEWD
000040 960F C3DF    003DF           41          OI    DOUBLEWD+7,X'0F'
```

```
000044 F347 C055 C3D8 00055 003D8   42  STAEWTO  UNPK  STAEWTO+9(5),DOUBLEWD
                                     43           WTO   '******* WAS RETURN CODE FROM ESTAE - ENDING'
00004A 0700                          44+          CNOP  0,4                                                01-WTO
00004C 4510 C080            00080    45+STAEWTO   BAL   1,IHB0004A       BRANCH AROUND MESSAGE   @YA17152  01-WTO
000050 002F                          46+          DC    AL2(47)          TEXT LENGTH                       01-WTO
000052 0000                          47+          DC    B'0000000000000000'  MCSFLAGS                      01-WTO
000054 5C5C5C5C5C5C5C40              48+          DC    C'******* WAS RETURN CODE FROM ESTAE - ENDING'    X01-WTO
00005C E6C1E240D9C5E3E4               +                                  MESSAGE TEXT            @L6C
000080                               49+IHB0004A  DS    0H
000080 0A23                          50+          SVC   35               ISSUE SVC 35                      01-WTO
000082 4070 C548            00548    51           STH   R7,RETCODE                               @L6A      01-WTO
000086 47F0 C216            00216    52           B     ENDEXEC2         END EXECUTION
```

```
APP3PGM1 MVS CONTROL BLOCKS APPENDIX 3 PROGRAM 1                        ASM H V 02 12.55 04/10/94   PAGE   2
 LOC  OBJECT CODE    ADDR1 ADDR2   STMT  SOURCE STATEMENT
0008A                                55  STAEDONE EQU   *
                                     57 * LOAD A PROGRAM TO CREATE CONTENTS SUPERVISOR CONTROL BLOCKS
                                     58           LOAD  EP=APP3PGM2      LOAD A PROGRAM
00008A 0700                          59+          CNOP  0,4                                                01-LOAD
00008C 4100 C094            00094    60+          LA    0,*+8            LOAD PARAMETER INTO REGISTER ZERO  @YA29363 01-LOAD
000090 47F0 C09C            0009C    61+          B     *+12             BRANCH AROUND CONSTANT(S)          01-LOAD
000094 C1D7D7F3D7C7D4F2              62+          DC    CL8'APP3PGM2'    ENTRY POINT NAME                   01-LOAD
00009C 1B11                          63+          SR    1,1              SHOW NO DCB PRESENT                01-LOAD
00009E 0A08                          64+          SVC   8                                                  01-LOAD
                                     66  IDENTIFY EP=BRUINS,             IDENTIFY AN ENTRY POINT            X
                                                  ENTRY=URSA               AND ITS LOCATION
0000A0 4500 C0AC            000AC    67+          BAL   0,*+12           LOAD EP SYMBOL ADDR                01-IDENT
0000A4 C2D9E4C9D5E24040              68+          DC    CL8'BRUINS'      EP SYMBOL                          01-IDENT
0000AC 4110 C126            00126    69+          LA    1,URSA           LOAD PARAMETER REG 1               02-IHBIN
0000B0 0A29                          70+          SVC   41               ISSUE IDENTIFY SVC                 01-IDENT
                                     72 * CREATE A SEPARATE (DAUGHTER) TCB
                                     73  ATTACH   EP=APP3PGM3,           ATTACH ANOTHER PROGRAM             X
                                                  PARAM=(XECB),VL=1,       ONE PARAMETER PASSED             X
                                                  ECB=TASKECB,             POSTED BY MVS WHEN TCB ENDS      X
                                                  SHSPV=33                 SHARE SUBPOOL 33
                                     74+* /* MACDATE 11/11/91                                      @L2C*/
                                     75+* /*
0000B2 0700                          76+          CNOP  0,4                                                02-IHBOP
```

```
0000B4 4110 C0BC            77+        LA    1,IHB0011        LIST ADDRESS                    @L1C     02-IHBOP
0000B8 47F0 C0C0            78+        B     IHB0011A         BYPASS LIST                     @ZMC3742 02-IHBOP
0000BC             000BC    79+IHB0011 EQU   *                                                         02-IHBOP
0000BC 80000530             80+        DC    A(XECB+X'80000000')                              @860P40  02-IHBOP
                   000C0    81+IHB0011A EQU  *                                                         02-IHBOP
0000C0 41F0 C0C8   000C8    82+        LA    15,IHB0008       SET UP LIST ADDRESS             @860PXB  01-ATTAC
0000C4 47F0 F048   00048    83+        B     72(,15)          BRANCH AROUND LIST              @860PXB  01-ATTAC
0000C8             000C8    84+IHB0008 DS    0F               SUP. PARAM. LIST                @860PXB  01-ATTAC
0000C8 000000E4             85+        DC    A(*+28)          ADDRESS OF SYMB NAME            @860PXB  01-ATTAC
0000CC 00000000             86+        DC    A(0)             DCB ADDRESS                     @860PXB  01-ATTAC
0000D0 80000534             87+        DC    A(X'80000000'+TASKECB)                           X01-ATTAC
                            +                                 ECB ADDRESS, NEW FORMAT         @860PXB
0000D4 00000000             88+        DC    A(0)             GSPV VALUE OR GSPL ADDRESS      @860PXB  01-ATTAC
0000D8 00000021             89+        DC    A(33)            SHSPV VALUE                     @860PXB  01-ATTAC
0000DC 00000000             90+        DC    A(0)             EXIT ROUTINE ADDRESS            @860PXB  01-ATTAC
0000E0 0000                 91+        DC    AL2(0)           DPMOD VALUE                     @860PXB  01-ATTAC
0000E2 00                   92+        DC    AL1(0)           LPMOD VALUE                     @860PXB  01-ATTAC
0000E3 00                   93+        DC    AL1(0)           STATUS BYTE                     @860PXB  01-ATTAC
0000E4 C1D7D7F3D7C7D4F3     94+        DC    CL8'APP3PGM3'    EP SYMBOL                       @860PXB  01-ATTAC
0000EC 00000000             95+        DC    A(0)             ADDRESS OF JSCB                 @860PXB  01-ATTAC
0000F0 00000000             96+        DC    A(0)             NO STAI/ESTAI PARM LIST ADDR    @860PXB  01-ATTAC
0000F4 00000000             97+        DC    A(0)             NO EXIT ADDRESS                 @860PXB  01-ATTAC
0000F8 00000000             98+        DC    A(0)             TASKLIB DCB ADDRESS             @860PXB  01-ATTAC
0000FC 00                   99+        DC    AL1(0)           FLAG BYTE                       @860PXB  01-ATTAC
0000FD 00                  100+        DC    AL1(0)           TASK ID                         @860PXB  01-ATTAC
0000FE 0048               101+        DC    AL2(72)          PARM LIST LENGTH                @860PXB  01-ATTAC
000100 00000000           102+        DC    A(0)             NSHSPV VALUE OR NSHSPL ADDR     @860PXB  01-ATTAC
000104 00                 103+        DC    AL1(0)           FLAG BYTE                       @860PXB  01-ATTAC
000105 01                 104+        DC    AL1(1)           SET UP FORMAT NUMBER            @860PXB  01-ATTAC
```

```
APP3PGM1 MVS CONTROL BLOCKS APPENDIX 3 PROGRAM 1                     ASM H V 02 12.55 04/10/94    PAGE  3
  LOC   OBJECT CODE    ADDR1 ADDR2  STMT  SOURCE STATEMENT
000106 0000000000000000        105+        DC    XL10'00'         RESERVED BYTES AT END           @860PXB  01-ATTAC
000110 0A2A                    106+        SVC   42               ISSUE ATTACH SVC                @860PXB  01-ATTAC
                               108 *     ENQ ON SOME IMAGINARY NAME TO CREATE GRS CONTROL BLOCKS
                               109        ENQ   (FOO,BAR,E,3,SYSTEM)  ENQ ON FOO-BAR
                               110+*     MACRO-DATE = 93/01/04
000112 0700                    111+        CNOP  0,4                                                        01-ENQ
```

```
000114 4510 C124          112+        BAL   1,IHB0013              BRANCH AROUND AND ADDRESS LIST   01-ENQ
000118 C0                 113+        DC    AL1(192)               LISTEND BYTE          X02113     01-ENQ
000119 03                 114+        DC    AL1(3)                 RNAME LENGTH                     01-ENQ
00011A 40                 115+        DC    BL1'01000000'                       OPTIONS            01-ENQ
00011B 00                 116+        DC    AL1(0)                 RETURN CODE FIELD                01-ENQ
00011C 0000054A           117+        DC    A(FOO)                 QNAME ADDRESS                    01-ENQ
000120 00000552           118+        DC    A(BAR)                 RNAME ADDRESS                    01-ENQ
000124                    119+IHB0013 DS    0H                     OBJECT OF THE BAL                01-ENQ
000124 0A38               120+        SVC   56                                                      01-ENQ
                          122+      * PERFORM A VECTOR OPERATION TO FORCE CPU AFFINITY
             00126        123  URSA   EQU   *
                          124       *
000126 A640 0000          126       * VTVM  ,                       TEST VECTOR MASK REGISTER
                          127       * OPEN THE OUTPUT PRINT FILE
                                      OPEN  (SYSPRINT,OUTPUT)
00012A 0700               128+        CNOP  0,4                     ALIGN LIST TO FULLWORD   @L2A    01-OPEN
00012C 4510 C134 00134    129+        BAL   1,*+8                   LOAD REG1 W/LIST ADDR.   @L2A    01-OPEN
000130 8F                 130+        DC    AL1(143)                OPTION BYTE                      01-OPEN
000131 00068C             131+        DC    AL3(SYSPRINT)           DCB ADDRESS                      01-OPEN
000134 0A13               132+        SVC   19                      ISSUE OPEN SVC                   01-OPEN
000136 4110 C68C 0068C    133         LA    R1,SYSPRINT             GET ADDRESS OF DCB
                          134         USING IHADCB,R1               ESTABLISH ADDRESSABILITY
00013A 9110 1030 00030    135         TM    DCBOFLGS,X'10'          TEST FOR SUCCESSFUL OPEN
00013E 47E0 C218 00218    136         BNO   BADOPEN                 OPEN FAILED - END JOB
                          138       * OPEN THE PARTITIONED DATA SET DCB
                                      OPEN  (PDS,INPUT)
000142 0700               139+        CNOP  0,4                     ALIGN LIST TO FULLWORD   @L2A    01-OPEN
000144 4510 C14C 0014C    140+        BAL   1,*+8                   LOAD REG1 W/LIST ADDR.   @L2A    01-OPEN
000148 80                 141+        DC    AL1(128)                OPTION BYTE                      01-OPEN
000149 000634             142+        DC    AL3(PDS)                DCB ADDRESS                      01-OPEN
00014C 0A13               143+        SVC   19                      ISSUE OPEN SVC                   01-OPEN
00014E 4110 C634 00634    144+        LA    R1,PDS                  GET ADDRESS OF DCB
000152 48B0 103E 0003E    145         LH    R11,DCBBLKSI            GET BLOCK SIZE
000156 9110 1030 00030    146         TM    DCBOFLGS,X'10'          TEST FOR SUCCESSFUL OPEN
00015A 4710 C178 00178    147         BO    GO                      OKAY - CONTINUE
                          148         DROP  R1                      END DCB DSECT ADDRESSABILITY
                          149       * ERROR IN OPEN OF P.D.S. - ISSUE ERROR MESSAGE AND END
                          151         PUT   SYSPRINT,OPENLINE
00015E 4110 C68C 0068C    152+        LA    1,SYSPRINT              LOAD PARAMETER REG 1   02-IHBIN
000162 4100 C556 00556    153+        LA    0,OPENLINE              LOAD PARAMETER REG 0   02-IHBIN
000166 1FFF               154+        SLR   15,15                   CLEAR REGISTER         @L1A     01-PUT
```

```
000168 BFF7 1031          00031    156+    ICM   15,7,49(1)         LOAD PUT ROUTINE ADDR    @L1C 01-PUT
00016C 05EF                        157+    BALR  14,15              LINK TO PUT ROUTINE           01-PUT
00016E D201 C548 C6F0 00548 006F0  158     MVC   RETCODE,=H'16'     SET BAD RETURN CODE
000174 47F0 C216           00216   159     B     ENDEXEC2           GO END EXECUTION
```

APP3PGM1 MVS CONTROL BLOCKS APPENDIX 3 PROGRAM 1   ASM H V 02 12.55 04/10/94   PAGE 4
LOC   OBJECT CODE   ADDR1 ADDR2 STMT   SOURCE STATEMENT

```
                                   160     PRINT ON,GEN
                                   162 *   DO SOME I/O PROCESSING
                           00178   163 GO  EQU  *
                                   165 *   GET A STORAGE AREA TO USE AS A BUFFER, SINCE WE
                                   166 *   DON'T KNOW THE BLOCK SIZE OF THE P.D.S. BEFOREHAND
                                   167     STORAGE  OBTAIN,SP=22,LENGTH=(11),BNDRY=PAGE,LOC=BELOW
000178                             168+    CNOP  0,4
000178 47F0 C180           00180   169+    B     IHB0018B          .BRANCH AROUND DATA
00017C 00                 170+-IHB0018F DC   BL1'00000000'         .FLAGS                   @D4C  01-STORA
00017D 00                          171+    DC    AL1(0*16)         .KEY                           01-STORA
00017E 16                          172+    DC    AL1(22)           .SUBPOOL                       01-STORA
00017F 16                          173+    DC    BL1'00010110'     .FLAGS                         01-STORA
000180                    174+-IHB0018B DS   0F                    .STORAGE LENGTH                01-STORA
000180 180B                        175+    LR    0,11              .CONTROL INFORMATION           01-STORA
000182 58F0 C17C           0017C   176+    L     15,IHB0018F       .CVT ADDRESS                   01-STORA
000186 5880 0010           00010   177+    L     14,16(0,0)        .ADDR SYST LINKAGE TABLE       01-STORA
00018A 58EE 0304           00304   178+    L     14,772(14,0)      .OBTAIN LX/EX FOR OBTAIN       01-STORA
00018E 58EE 00A0           000A0   179+    L     14,160(14,0)      .PC TO STORAGE RTN             01-STORA
000192 B218 E000 00000             180+    PC    0(14)                                            01-STORA
000196 18A1                        181+    LR    R10,R1            SAVE ADDRESS IN REG 10         01-STORA
```

APP3PGM1 MVS CONTROL BLOCKS APPENDIX 3 PROGRAM 1   ASM H V 02 12.55 04/10/94   PAGE 5
LOC   OBJECT CODE   ADDR1 ADDR2 STMT   SOURCE STATEMENT

```
                                   183 *   ISSUE BLDL MACRO TO LOCATE THE MEMBER WE WANT
                                   184     BLDL  PDS,MEMLIST
000198 4110 C634           00634   185+    LA    1,PDS             LOAD PARAMETER REG 1     02-IHBIN
00019C 4100 C538           00538   186+    LA    0,MEMLIST         LOAD PARAMETER REG 0     02-IHBIN
0001A0 4111 0000           00000   187+    LA    1,0(1)            CLEAR HIGH ORDER BYTE ZA00734 01-BLDL
0001A4 1FFF                        188+    SLR   15,15             FOR NO OPTION            @L0A 01-BLDL
```

```
APP3PGM1 MVS CONTROL BLOCKS APPENDIX 3 PROGRAM 1                          ASM H V 02 12.55 04/10/94   PAGE   6
   LOC    OBJECT CODE    ADDR1 ADDR2  STMT   SOURCE STATEMENT

0001A6 0A12                          189+       SVC   18                          LINK TO BLDL ROUTINE          01-BLDL
0001A8 12FF                          190        LTR   R15,R15                      TEST FOR GOOD BLDL
0001AA 40F0 C548       00548         191        STH   R15,RETCODE                  SAVE RETURN CODE FOR LATER
0001AE 4770 C208       00208         192        BNZ   ENDEXEC                      NOT ZERO - GIVE UP
                                     194  *      ISSUE BLDL MACRO TO LOCATE THE MEMBER WE WANT
                                     195        POINT PDS,TTR                      POSITION TO THAT MEMBER
0001B2 4110 C634       00634         196+       LA    1,PDS                        LOAD PARAMETER REG 1          02-IHBIN
0001B6 4100 C544       00544         197+       LA    0,TTR                        LOAD PARAMETER REG 0          02-IHBIN
0001BA 1FFF                          198+       SLR   15,15                        CLEAR REGISTER                01-POINT
0001BC BFF7 1055       00055         199+       ICM   15,7,85(1)                   LOAD POINT RTN ADDR    @L1A   01-POINT
0001C0 45EF 0004       00004         200+       BAL   14,4(15,0)                   LINK TO POINT ROUTINE  @L1C   01-POINT
                                     202  *      ISSUE READ MACRO TO READ IN THE FIRST BLOCK
                                     203        READ  DECB1,SF,PDS,(10),(11)       READ A BLOCK OF DATA
0001C4                               204+       CNOP  0,4
0001C4 4510 C1DC       001DC         205+       BAL   1,*+24                       LOAD DECB ADDRESS             02-IHBRD
0001C8 00000000                      206+DECB1  DC    F'0'                         EVENT CONTROL BLOCK           02-IHBRD
0001CC 00                            207+       DC    X'00'                        TYPE FIELD                    02-IHBRD
0001CD 80                            208+       DC    X'80'                        TYPE FIELD                    02-IHBRD
0001CE 0000                          209+       DC    AL2(0)                       LENGTH                        02-IHBRD
0001D0 00000634                      210+       DC    A(PDS)                       DCB ADDRESS                   02-IHBRD
0001D4 00000000                      211+       DC    A(0)                         AREA ADDRESS                  02-IHBRD
0001D8 00000000                      212+       DC    A(0)                         RECORD POINTER WORD           02-IHBRD
0001DC 50A1 000C       0000C         213+       ST    10,12(1,0)                   STORE AREA ADDRESS            02-IHBRD
0001E0 40B1 0006       00006         214+       STH   11,6(1,0)                    STORE LENGTH                  02-IHBRD
0001E4 58F0 1008       00008         215+       L     15,8(,1)                     LOAD DCB ADDR                 02-IHBRD
0001E8 BFF7 F031       00031         216+       ICM   15,B'0111',49(15)            LOAD RDWR ROUTINE ADDR @01M   02-IHBRD
0001EC 05EF                          217+       BALR  14,15                        LINK TO RDWR ROUTINE   @01M   02-IHBRD
0001EE D703 C1C8 C1C8  001C8 001C8   218        XC    DECB1,DECB1                                         @L1C   02-IHBRD
                                     219        CHECK DECB1
0001F4 4110 C1C8       001C8         220+       LA    1,DECB1                      LOAD PARAMETER REG 1          02-IHBIN
0001F8 58E0 1008       00008         221+       L     14,8(0,1)                    PICK UP DCB ADDR              01-CHECK
0001FC 1BFF                          222+       SR    15,15                                                      01-CHECK
0001FE BFF7 E035       00035         223+       ICM   15,B'0111',53(14)            LOAD CHECK ROUTINE ADDR @01A  01-CHECK
000202 05EF                          224+       BALR  14,15                        LINK TO CHECK ROUTINE   @01C  01-CHECK
                                     226  *      NOW LET'S FORCE AN ABEND.
000204 8200 0000       00000         227        LPSW  0                            SUPERVISOR-STATE INSTRUCTION
```

```
                     229  *            END EXECUTION
00208                230  ENDEXEC   EQU  *
00208 4510 C214 00208 231           CLOSE (PDS,,SYSPRINT)    CLOSE FILES
                     232+           CNOP 0,4                 ALIGN LIST TO FULLWORD    01-CLOSE
00020C 00            233+           BAL  1,*+12              LOAD REG1 W/LIST ADDR. @L2A 01-CLOSE
00020D 80            234+           DC   AL1(0)              OPTION BYTE               01-CLOSE
                     235+           DC   AL3(PDS)            DCB ADDRESS               01-CLOSE
00211 00068C         236+           DC   AL1(128)            OPTION BYTE               01-CLOSE
                     237+           DC   AL3(SYSPRINT)       DCB ADDRESS               01-CLOSE
00214 0A14           238+           SVC  20                  ISSUE CLOSE SVC           01-CLOSE
00216           00214 239  ENDEXEC2 EQU  *
                     240           PR   ,                    RETURN TO MVS
00216 0101      00216 242  BADOPEN  EQU  *
00218           00218 243           PUT  SYSPRINT,OPENLINE   DISPLAY ERROR MESSAGE
00218 4110 C68C 0068C 244+          LA   1,SYSPRINT          LOAD PARAMETER REG 1      02-IHBIN
0021C 4100 C556 00556 245+          LA   0,OPENLINE          LOAD PARAMETER REG 0      02-IHBIN
00220 1FFF            246+          SLR  15,15               CLEAR REGISTER      @L1A  01-PUT
00222 BFF7 1031 00031 247+          ICM  15,7,49(1)          LOAD PUT ROUTINE ADDR @L1C 01-PUT
00226 05EF            248+          BALR 14,15               LINK TO PUT ROUTINE       01-PUT
00228 47F0 C216 00216 249           B    ENDEXEC2            END EXECUTION
```

```
APP3PGM1 MVS CONTROL BLOCKS APPENDIX 3 PROGRAM 1                    ASM H V 02 12.55 04/10/94  PAGE  7
  LOC    OBJECT CODE  ADDR1 ADDR2  STMT  SOURCE STATEMENT
                            0022C  251  STAEEXIT EQU  *
                                   252           PUSH USING
                                   253           USING *,R15           TEMP ADDRESSABILITY
0022C 90EC D00C       0000C 254           STM  14,R12,12(R13)  SAVE REGISTERS
00230 4120 F1B8       003E4 255           LA   R2,STAEREGS     CHAIN SAVE AREAS
00234 502D 0008       00008 256           ST   R2,8(R13)
00238 50D2 0004       00004 257           ST   R13,4(R2)
0023C 18D2                  258           LR   R13,R2
0023E 1821                  259           LR   R2,R1
00240 58C0 F200       00200 260           L    R12,STAESAVE    SAVE SDWA POINTER
                            261           DROP R15             GET OLD BASE REGISTERS
                            262           POP  USING           END TEMPORARY
                            263           USING SDWA,R2        ADDRESSABILITY
00244 4110 C42C       0042C 264           LA   R1,STAESAVE     POINT TO PROGRAM ADDRESS
00248 45E0 C4BC       004BC 265           BAL  R14,HEXCONV     FORMAT PROGRAM
```

```
00024C D207 C463 C4CA  00463 004CA  266      MVC   ABENDBEG,EBCDICEQ        ADDRESS
000252 4110 2005        00005       267      LA    R1,SDWACMPC              POINT TO COMPLETION CODES (SYS/USER)
000256 45E0 C4BC        004BC       268      BAL   R14,HEXCONV              FORMAT SYSTEM
00025A D202 C447 C44A  00447 0044A  269      MVC   ABENDCD(3),EBCDICEQ      COMPLETION
000260 9261 C44A        0044A       270      MVI   ABENDCD+3,C'/'           CODE
000264 BF17 2005        00005       271      ICM   R1,7,SDWACMPC            GET COMPLETION CODES (SYS/USER)
000268 8910 0014        00014       272      SLL   R1,20                    SHIFT OUT SYSTEM ABEND CODE
00026C 8810 0014        00014       273      SRL   R1,20                    SHIFT USER CODE BACK
000270 4E10 C3D8        003D8       274      CVD   R1,DOUBLEWD              CONVERT TO DECIMAL
000274 960F C3DF        003DF       275      OI    DOUBLEWD+7,X'0F'         SET SIGN
000278 F337 C44B C3D8  0044B 003D8  276      UNPK  ABENDCD+4(4),DOUBLEWD    DOUBLEWD UNPACK INTO MESSAGE
                                    277      PUT   SYSPRINT,ABENDLN
00027E 4110 C68C        0068C       278+     LA    1,SYSPRINT               LOAD PARAMETER REG 1       02-IHBIN
000282 4100 C434        00434       279+     LA    0,ABENDLN                LOAD PARAMETER REG 0       02-IHBIN
000286 1FFF                         280+     SLR   15,15                    CLEAR REGISTER      @L1A   01-PUT
000288 BFF7 1031        00031       281+     ICM   15,7,49(1)               LOAD PUT ROUTINE ADDR @L1C 01-PUT
00028C 05EF                         282+     BALR  14,15                    LINK TO PUT ROUTINE        01-PUT
00028E 9260 C434        00434       283      MVI   ABENDLN,C' '             RESET CARRIAGE CONTROL
000292 D201 C548 C6F2  00548 006F2  284      MVC   RETCODE,=H'8'            INDICATE ABEND OCCURRED
000298 9620 2144        00144       285      OI    SDWASDA0,SDWALSQA        REQUEST DUMP OF LSQA
00029C 58DD 0004        00004       286      L     R13,4(R13)               GET OLD SAVE AREA ADDRESS
0002A0 1812                         287      LR    R1,R2
0002A2 5830 C3E0        003E0       288      L     R3,RETRYRTN              GET ADDRESS OF RETRY ROUTINE
0002A6 4140 C3C0        003C0       289      LA    R4,OPT                   GET ADDRESS OF DUMP OPTIONS
                                    290      SETRP RETADDR=(3),RETREGS=YES,REGS=(14,12),                       X
                                    291+           FRESDWA=NO,RC=4,DUMP=YES,DUMPOPT=(4),
0002AA 0700                         292+     NOPR  SDWANOPR       IF THIS STATEMENT CAUSES ASSEMBLER ERROR  @G38AP2F  01-SETRP
                                    293+*                        IT IMPLIES THAT SETRP AND THE SDWA ARE
                                    294+*                        BEING USED INCOMPATIBLY
0002AC                              295+     ORG   *-2            OVERLAY THE PREVIOUS INSTRUCTION          @G38AP2F  01-SETRP
0002AA 9204 10FC        002AA       296+     MVI   SDWARCDE-SDWA(1),4  . INITIALIZE RC FIELD                          01-SETRP
0002AE 18F3                         297+     LR    15,3                 ACCESS RETRY ADDRESS                          01-SETRP
0002B0 50F0 10F0        000F0       298+     ST    15,SDWARTYA-SDWA(1)  . INITIALIZE RETRY ADDRESS FIELD              01-SETRP
0002B4 9680 1004        00004       299+     OI    SDWACMPF-SDWA(1),SDWAREQ   TURN ON DUMP INDICATOR                  01-SETRP
0002B8 41F0 4000        00000       300+     LA    15,0(,4)           . ACCESS PTR TO DUMP PARAMETERS @L2C           01-SETRP
0002BC 9640 1141        00141       301+     OI    SDWADPFS-SDWA(1),SDWADLST  TURN ON DUMP OPTION INDICATOR           01-SETRP
0002C0 D203 1144 F004  00144 00141  302+     MVC   SDWADDAT-SDWA(4,1),4(15)   ACCESS SDATA AND PDATA FIELDS           01-SETRP
0002C6 9620 1141        00141       303+     OI    SDWADPFS-SDWA(1),SDWAENSN  INDICATE ENHANCED DUMP                  01-SETRP
                                                                                                           @G382P2F
0002CA 9604 1142        00142       304+     OI    SDWADPF2-SDWA(1),SDWALVL2  INDICATE HBB2102 VERSION                01-SETRP
```

```
APP3PGM1 MVS CONTROL BLOCKS APPENDIX 3 PROGRAM 1                              ASM H V 02 12.55 04/10/94   PAGE   8
   LOC  OBJECT CODE   ADDR1  ADDR2  STMT   SOURCE STATEMENT

                                    305+*                   OF SNAP PARMLIST                              @G860P1C
0002CE 9102 F001      00001         306+      TM   1(15),X'02'         TEST FOR STORAGE LIST               01-SETRP
0002D2 4710 C2E0             002E0  307+      BO   M0032               BRANCH IF STORAGE LIST SPECIFIED    01-SETRP
0002D6 1BEE                         308+      SR   14,14 .             ZERO REGISTER FOR COMPARE           01-SETRP
0002D8 55E0 F010            00010   309+      CL   14,16(,15) .        FURTHER TEST FOR STORAGE LIST       01-SETRP
0002DC 4780 C352            00352   310+      BE   Q0032               BRANCH IF NO STORAGE LIST  @G860P1C 01-SETRP
0002E0                              311+M0032 EQU  *                                                      01-SETRP
0002E0 58E0 1170            00170   312+      L    14,SDWAXPAD-SDWA(0,1) ADDRESS OF EXTENSION PTRS @G382P2F 01-SETRP
0002E4 58E0 E000            00000   313+      L    14,SDWADSRP-SDWAPTRS(0,14) ADDR OF DUMP STORAGE RANGES  01-SETRP
                                    314+*                   EXTENSION                          @G382P2F
0002E8 12EE                         315+      LTR  14,14               TEST IF EXTENSION EXISTS  @G382P2F 01-SETRP
0002EA 4780 C352            00352   316+      BZ   Q0032               BRANCH IF NO DUMP STORAGE RANGES    01-SETRP
                                    317+*                   EXTENSION                          @G860P1C
0002EE 9602 1141            00141   318+      OI   SDWADFPS-SDWA(1),SDWASLST  TURN ON STORAGE LIST @G382P2F 01-SETRP
                                    319+*                   FLAG                               @G382P2F
0002F2 9680 1142            00142   320+      OI   SDWADPF2-SDWA(1),SDWADVS3  INDICATE RANGES ARE IN       01-SETRP
                                    321+*                   SDWADSR                            @G382P2F
0002F6 1FEE                         322+      SLR  14,14               ZERO LENGTH REG           @G382P2F 01-SETRP
0002F8 9180 F002            00002   323+      TM   2(15),X'80'         TEST MAX NUMBER OF RANGES @G382P2F 01-SETRP
0002FC 58F0 F010            00010   324+      L    15,16(,15) .        ACCESS POINTER TO STORAGE LIST      01-SETRP
000300 4710 C30C            0030C   325+      BO   K0032               BRANCH IF 30 RANGES ALLOWED @G382P2F 01-SETRP
000304 4100 0020            00020   326+      LA   0,32                INIT MAX LENGTH TO 4      @G382P2F 01-SETRP
000308 47F0 C310            00310   327+      B    L0032                                         @G382P2F 01-SETRP
00030C                              328+K0032 EQU  *                                            @G382P2F
00030C 4100 00F0            000F0   329+      LA   0,240               INIT MAX LENGTH TO 30     @G382P2F 01-SETRP
000310                              330+L0032 EQU  *                                            @G382P2F
000310                              331+N0032 EQU  *                                            @G382P2F
                                    332+*                   TOP OF LOOP WHICH CALCULATES       @G382P2F
                                                            MVC LENGTH
000310 41E0 E008            00008   333+      LA   14,8(,14)           INCREMENT LENGTH REG BY 8 @G382P2F 01-SETRP
000314 9180 F004            00008   334+      TM   4(15),X'80'         TEST IF END OF LIST       @G382P2F 01-SETRP
000318 41F0 F008            00326   335+      LA   15,8(,15)           POINT TO NEXT RANGE       @G382P2F 01-SETRP
00031C 4710 C326                    336+      BO   O0032               BRANCH IF END OF LIST     @G382P2F 01-SETRP
000320 19E0                         337+      CR   14,0                TEST IF MAX LENGTH REACHED @G382P2F 01-SETRP
000322 4740 C310            00310   338+      BL   N0032               BRANCH IF NOT REACHED     @G382P2F 01-SETRP
000326                      00326   339+O0032 EQU  *                   EXIT OF LOOP WHICH CALC MVC         01-SETRP
                                                            LENGTH
                                    340+*                   POINT TO BEGINNING OF STORAGE      @G382P2F
                                                            LIST
000326 1BFE                         341+      SR   15,14                                         @G382P2F
                                    342+*
```

```
000328 06E0                343+         BCTR  14,0                    ADJUST LENGTH FOR EXECUTE FORM    @G382P2F  01-SETRP
                           344+*                                      OF MVC                           @G382P2F
00032A 1801                345+         LR    0,1                     SAVE SDWA ADDRESS                @G382P2F  01-SETRP
00032C 5810 1170    00170  346+         L     1,SDWAXPAD-SDWA(0,1)    ADDRESS OF EXTENSION PTRS        @G382P2F  01-SETRP
000330 5810 1000    00000  347+         L     1,SDWADSRP-SDWAPTRS(0,1) ADDRESS OF DUMP STORAGE RANGE   @G382P2F  01-SETRP
                           348+*                                      EXTENSION                        @G382P2F
000334 44E0 C34A    0034A  349+         EX    14,P0032                EXECUTE MVC INSTRUCTION           @G382P2F  01-SETRP
000338 41F0 0003    00003  350+         LA    15,3                    LOAD 3 INTO REG 15               @G382P2F  01-SETRP
00033C 1BEF                351+         SR    14,15                   CALC LENGTH TO LAST ADDR         @G382P2F  01-SETRP
00033E 1A1E                352+         AR    1,14                    CALC ADDR OF LAST ADDR MOVED INTO @G382P2F 01-SETRP
                           353+*                                      THE SDWA                         @G382P2F
000340 9680 1000    00000  354+         OI    0(1),X'80'              ENSURE LAST RANGE IS IND         @G382P2F  01-SETRP
000344 1810                355+         LR    1,0                     RESTORE REG 1 WITH SDWA          @G382P2F  01-SETRP
                           356+*                                      ADDRESS                          @G382P2F
000346 47F0 C350    00350  357+         B     E0032                                                    @G382P2F  01-SETRP
00034A              0034A  358+P0032    EQU   *                                                        @G382P2F  01-SETRP
00034A D200 1000 F000 00000 00000 359+  MVC   0(0,1),0(15)            MOVE DUMP STORAGE RANGES INTO    @G382P2F  01-SETRP
```

```
APP3PGM1 MVS CONTROL BLOCKS APPENDIX 3 PROGRAM 1                                         PAGE    9
  LOC  OBJECT CODE    ADDR1 ADDR2  STMT  SOURCE STATEMENT                 ASM H V 02 12.55 04/10/94
                           360+*                                      SDWA EXTENSION                   @G382P2F
000350              00350  361+E0032    EQU   *                                                        @G860P1C  01-SETRP
000350 18F4                362+         LR    15,4                    ACCESS PTR TO DUMP PARMS         @G860P1C  01-SETRP
000352              00352  363+Q0032    EQU   *                                                        @G860P1C  01-SETRP
000352 9102 F002    00002  364+         TM    2(15),X'02'             TEST FOR SUBPOOL LIST            @G860P1C  01-SETRP
000356 4780 C3B4    003B4  365+         BZ    U0032                   BRANCH IF NO SUBPOOL             @ZMC3083  01-SETRP
                           366+*                                      LIST SPECIFIED                   @ZMC3083
00035A 1BEE                367+         SR    14,14                   ZERO REGISTER FOR COMPARE        @G860P1C  01-SETRP
00035C 55E0 F018    00018  368+         CL    14,24(0,15)             FURTHER TEST FOR SUBPOOL LIST    @ZMC2078  01-SETRP
                           369+*                                                                       @ZMC2078
000360 4780 C3B4    003B4  370+         BE    U0032                   BRANCH IF NO SUBPOOL LIST        @G860P1C  01-SETRP
000364              00364  371+V0032    EQU   *                                                        @G860P1C  01-SETRP
000364 58E0 1170    00170  372+         L     14,SDWAXPAD-SDWA(0,1)   ADDR OF EXTENSION PTRS           @G860P1C  01-SETRP
000368 58E0 E00C    0000C  373+         L     14,SDWAXSPL-SDWAPTRS(0,14) ADDR OF SUBPOOL LIST          @G860P1C  01-SETRP
                           374+*                                      EXTENSION                        @G860P1C
00036C 12EE                375+         LTR   14,14                   TEST IF EXTENSION EXISTS         @G860P1C  01-SETRP
00036E 4780 C3B4    003B4  376+         BZ    U0032                   BRANCH IF NO SUBPOOL LIST        @G860P1C  01-SETRP
                           377+*                                      EXTENSION                        @G860P1C
```

```
LOC      OBJECT CODE       ADDR1  ADDR2   STMT              SOURCE STATEMENT

000372   9602 1142         00142          378+          OI   SDWADPF2-SDWA(1),SDWASUBL   TURN ON SUBPOOL LIST       @G860P1C  01-SETRP
                                                                                         FLAG
000376   58F0 F018         00018          379+*         L    15,24(0,15)                 ACCESS POINTER TO SUBPOOL  @ZMC2078  X01-SETRP
                                                        380+ +                           LIST
00037A   48E0 F000         00000          381+          LH   14,0,(15)                   PICK UP NUMBER OF SUBPOOLS @G860P1C  01-SETRP
00037E   12EE                             382+          LTR  14,14                       TEST FOR ZERO             @G860P1C  01-SETRP
000380   47D0 C3B4         003B4          383+          BNP  U0032                       BRANCH IF NO SUBPOOLS     @ZMC3083  01-SETRP
000384   4100 0007         00007          384+          LA   0,SDWASPMX(0,0)             GET MAX NUMBER SUBPOOLS   @G860P1C  01-SETRP
000388   19E0                             385+          CR   14,0                        TEST FOR MAX SUBPOOLS     @G860P1C  01-SETRP
00038A   47D0 C390         00390          386+          BNH  S0032                       BRANCH IF EQUAL OR LESS   @G860P1C  01-SETRP
00038E   18E0                             387+          LR   14,0                        MOVE ONLY MAX SUBPOOL IDS @G860P1C  01-SETRP
000390                     00390          388+S0032     EQU  *                                                     @G860P1C  01-SETRP
000390   1801                             389+          LR   0,1                         SAVE SDWA ADDRESS         @G860P1C  01-SETRP
000392   5810 1170         00170          390+          L    1,SDWAXPAD-SDWA(0,1)        ADDR OF EXTENSION POINTERS @G860P1C 01-SETRP
000396   5810 100C         0000C          391+*         L    1,SDWAXSPL-SDWAPTRS(0,1)    ADDR OF SUBPOOL LIST      @G860P1C  01-SETRP
                                                        392+ +                           EXTENSION
00039A   40E0 1000         00000          393+*         STH  14,SDWASPLN-SDWANRC2(0,1)   STORE NUMBER OF SUBPOOLS  @G860P1C  01-SETRP
                                                        394+ +
00039E   89E0 0001         00001          395+*         SLL  14,1                        DOUBLE NUMBER TO GET LENGTH @G860P1C 01-SETRP
                                                        396+ +                           OF MOVE
0003A2   06E0                             397+*         BCTR 14,0                        ADJUST LENGTH FOR EXECUTE FORM @G860P1C 01-SETRP
                                                        398+ +                           OF MVC
0003A4   44E0 C3AE         003AE          399+*         EX   14,T0032                    MOVE THE SUBPOOL IDS      @G860P1C  01-SETRP
0003A8   1810                             400+          LR   1,0                         RESTORE REG1 WITH SDWA ADDRESS @G860P1C 01-SETRP
                                                        401+
0003AA   47F0 C3B4         003B4          402+*         B    U0032                                                 @G860P1C  01-SETRP
                                                        403+          EQU  *                                       @G860P1C  01-SETRP
0003AE   D200 1002 F002  00002 F002 00002 404+T0032     MVC  SDWASPLS-SDWANRC2(0,1),2(15) MOVE SUBPOOL IDS INTO    @G860P1C  01-SETRP
                                                        405+*                            SDWA EXTENSION
                                                        406+*         EQU  *                                       @G860P1C  01-SETRP
0003B4   9608 10FD         000FD          407+U0032     OI   SDWAACF2-SDWA(1),SDWAUPRG   TURN ON RETREGS INDICATOR @G860P1C  01-SETRP
0003B8   98EC D00C         0000C          408+          LM   14,12,12(13)                RESTORE THE REGISTERS               01-SETRP
0003BC   07FE                             409+          BR   14                          RETURN                              02-RETUR
                                                        410+          DROP R2                                                02-RETUR
                                                        411           SNAP SDATA=(CB,LSQA,TRT,Q,DM,IO,PCDATA),     GENERATE DUMP PARM LIST  X
                                                        412 OPT            PDATA=(ALL),MF=L
```

```
APP3PGM1 MVS CONTROL BLOCKS APPENDIX 3 PROGRAM 1                                    ASM H V 02 12.55 04/10/94
  LOC  OBJECT CODE      ADDR1 ADDR2  STMT   SOURCE STATEMENT                                           PAGE  10

                                      413+* /* MACDATE Y-1 860219 LAST UPDATED 11/01/85 HBB3310 */
0003C0                                414+OPT      DS    0F                                                  01-SNAP
0003C0 00                             415+         DC    AL1(0)            ID NUMBER                         01-SNAP
0003C1 70                             416+         DC    AL1(112)          OPTION FLAGS             Y02705   01-SNAP
0003C2 80                             417+         DC    AL1(128)          OPTIONS FLAG 2           @G860P1Y 01-SNAP
0003C3 00                             418+         DC    AL1(0)            RESERVED                 @G382P12 01-SNAP
0003C4 2F                             419+         DC    AL1(47)           SDATA FLAGS ONE          Y02705   01-SNAP
0003C5 A0                             420+         DC    AL1(160)          SDATA FLAGS TWO          G33SPHW  01-SNAP
0003C6 BF                             421+         DC    AL1(191)          PDATA FLAGS              Y02705   01-SNAP
0003C7 00                             422+         DC    AL1(0)            RESERVED                 Y02705   01-SNAP
0003C8 00000000                       423+         DC    A(0)              DCB ADDRESS                       01-SNAP
0003CC 00000000                       424+         DC    A(0)              TCB ADDRESS                       01-SNAP
0003D0 00000000                       425+         DC    A(0)              ADDRESS OF SNAP-SHOT LIST         01-SNAP
0003D4 00000000                       426+         DC    A(0)              ADDRESS OF HEADER LIST   G33SPHW  01-SNAP
                                      427 *              DATA AREAS
0003D8 0000000000000000               428 DOUBLEWD DC    D'0'
0003E0 00000208                       429 RETRYRTN DC    A(ENDEXEC)        ADDRESS OF RETRY FOR ESTAE EXIT
0003E4 0000000000000000               431 STAEREGS DC    18F'0'            SEPARATE SAVE AREA FOR EXIT
00042C 0000000000000000               432 STAESAVE DC    2F'0'             SAVE REGS 14-2
000434                                434 ABENDLN  DS    0CL133
000434 F15C5C5CC1C2C5D5               435          DC    C'1***ABEND OCCURRED:'
000447                                436 ABENDCD  DS    CL8
00044F 4040D7D9D6C7D9C1               437          DC    C' PROGRAM BEGINS AT:'
000463 4040404040404040               438 ABENDBEG DC    CL8' ',CL48' '
00049B 4040404040404040               439          DC    CL(ABENDLN+133-*)' '    FILLER
0004BA 00                             441          CNOP  0,4                      ALIGN FOR NEXT ROUTINE
                                      442 * ROUTINE TO CONVERT FROM HEX TO DISPLAYABLE EBCDIC
0004BC                          004BC 443 HEXCONV  EQU   *
0004BC F384 C4CA 1000     004CA 00000 444          UNPK  EBCDICEQ(9),0(5,R1)      UNPACK TO GET FXFXFXFX
0004C2 DC07 C4CA C3E3     004CA 003E3 445          TR    EBCDICEQ(8),HEXTAB-240   TRANSLATE TO EBCDIC
0004C8 07FE                           446          BR    R14                      RETURN TO CALLER
0004CA 4040404040404040               447 EBCDICEQ DC    CL8' ',C' '
0004D3 F0F1F2F3F4F5F6F7               448 HEXTAB   DC    C'0123456789ABCDEF'
0004E3 00                             449
0004E4                                451 *              DATA AREAS
0004E4 00000000C6F1E2C1               452 ASAVE    DC    F'0',C'F1SA',16F'0'
```

```
00052C 00000000           453 SAVER14   DC   F'+0'                     USED TO SAVE REGISTER 14
000530 00000000           454 XECB      DC   F'0'                      SUBTASK'S COMMUNICATION ECB
000534 00000000           455 TASKECB   DC   F'0'                      SUBTASK'S TERMINATION ECB
000538 0001000CC1D7D7F3   456 MEMLIST   DC   H'1',H'12',CL8'APP3PGM1'  NAME OF MEMBER
000544 00000000           457 TTR       DC   XL4'00'                   TTR PUT HERE
000548 0000               458 RETCODE   DC   H'0'
00054A C6D6D6404040404040 460 FOO       DC   CL8'FOO'
000552 01C2C1D9           461 BAR       DC   X'01',C'BAR'
000556 60606060606060     463 OPENLINE  DC   CL133'-------------> OPEN ERROR '
                          465           PRINT ON,NOGEN
```

```
APP3PGM1 MVS CONTROL BLOCKS APPENDIX 3 PROGRAM 1          ASM H V 02 12.55 04/10/94     PAGE   11
  LOC  OBJECT CODE   ADDR1 ADDR2 STMT  SOURCE STATEMENT
                          466 SNAPDCB1 DCB  DDNAME=DUMPDD,MACRF=(W),DEVD=DA,DSORG=PS,                X
                                            RECFM=VBA,LRECL=125,BLKSIZE=1632
                          507 *             DATA CONTROL BLOCK FOR P.D.S.
                          508 PDS      DCB  DDNAME=PDS,        DIRECT ACCESS                         X
                                            DEVD=DA,          PARTITIONED ORGANIZATION              X
                                            DSORG=PO,                                              X
                                            MACRF=(R),        BSAM ACCESS METHOD                   X
                                            EODAD=ENDEXEC
                          549 *             DATA CONTROL BLOCK FOR PRINT OUTPUT FILE
                          550 SYSPRINT DCB  DDNAME=SYSPRINT,DEVD=DA,DSORG=PS,MACRF=(PM),RECFM=FBA,  X
                                            LRECL=121,BLKSIZE=0
```

```
APP3PGM1 MVS CONTROL BLOCKS APPENDIX 3 PROGRAM 1          ASM H V 02 12.55 04/10/94     PAGE   12
  LOC  OBJECT CODE   ADDR1 ADDR2 STMT  SOURCE STATEMENT
                          592 *
                          593 *             REGISTER EQUATES
00000                     594 R0       EQU  0
00001                     595 R1       EQU  1
00002                     596 R2       EQU  2
00003                     597 R3       EQU  3
00004                     598 R4       EQU  4
00005                     599 R5       EQU  5
00006                     600 R6       EQU  6
```

```
00007    601 R7     EQU   7
00008    602 R8     EQU   8
00009    603 R9     EQU   9
0000A    604 R10    EQU   10
0000B    605 R11    EQU   11
0000C    606 R12    EQU   12
0000D    607 R13    EQU   13
0000E    608 R14    EQU   14
0000F    609 R15    EQU   15

         611        PRINT NOGEN
         612 *      DEFINE DCB DSECT MACRO
         613        DCBD  DSORG=(PS),DEVD=(DA)
        1174 *      DEFINE SYSTEM DIAGNOSTIC WORK AREA
        1175 IHASDWA DSECT=YES
        2921        END   APP3PGM1
000000
0006F0 0010  2922              =H'16'
0006F2 0008  2923              =H'8'
```

```
APP3PGM1              DIAGNOSTIC CROSS REFERENCE AND ASSEMBLER SUMMARY          ASM H V 02 12.55 04/10/94    PAGE   13

    NO STATEMENTS FLAGGED IN THIS ASSEMBLY
    OVERRIDING PARAMETERS -  NOXREF,NODECK,OBJECT,NOTERM,NOESD,NORLD
    OPTIONS FOR THIS ASSEMBLY
    NODECK, OBJECT, LIST, NOXREF, NORENT, NOTEST, NOBATCH, ALIGN, NOESD, NORLD, NOTERM, NODBCS,
    LINECOUNT(55), FLAG(0), SYSPARM()
    NO OVERRIDING DD NAMES
        227 CARDS FROM SYSIN    16274 CARDS FROM SYSLIB
        522 LINES OUTPUT           37 CARDS OUTPUT
```

The next program in the series is APP3PGM2. This program is really just a data area, used to illustrate the control blocks associated with a loaded program. It contains an EBCDIC character string to aid in locating it in the dump.

```
APP3PGM2 MVS CONTROL BLOCKS APPENDIX 3 PROGRAM 2                                    ASM H V 02 12.55 04/10/94    PAGE   1
    LOC    OBJECT CODE      ADDR1 ADDR2    STMT   SOURCE STATEMENT
 000000                                       2 APP3PGM2 CSECT
                                              3 APP3PGM2 AMODE 31
                                              4 APP3PGM2 RMODE ANY
                                              6 *          THIS CSECT JUST CONTAINS DATA.  IT REPRESENTS HOW A LOADED
                                              7 *          PROGRAM LOOKS IN CONTENTS SUPERVISOR CONTROL BLOCKS.
 000000 D4E5E240C3D6D5E3                      9          DC   C'MVS CONTROL BLOCKS APPENDIX 3 PROGRAM 2. '
 000029 E3C8C9E240D9C5D7                     10          DC   C'THIS REPRESENTS A LOAD MODULE CONTAINING ONLY DATA.'
 000000                                      11          END  APP3PGM2
```

```
APP3PGM2                        DIAGNOSTIC CROSS REFERENCE AND ASSEMBLER SUMMARY                ASM H V 02 12.55 04/10/94    PAGE   2

    NO STATEMENTS FLAGGED IN THIS ASSEMBLY
 OVERRIDING PARAMETERS-  NOXREF,NODECK,OBJECT,NOTERM,NOESD,NORLD
 OPTIONS FOR THIS ASSEMBLY
 NODECK, OBJECT, LIST, NOXREF, NORENT, NOTEST, NOBATCH, ALIGN, NOESD, NORLD, NOTERM, NODBCS,
 LINECOUNT(55), FLAG(0), SYSPARM()
 NO OVERRIDING DD NAMES
    11 CARDS FROM SYSIN        0 CARDS FROM SYSLIB
    22 LINES OUTPUT            4 CARDS OUTPUT
```

The final program in the series is APP3PGM3. This program is invoked as a subtask via an ATTACH macro. It does nothing but wait for one second, then end. It's included to show a subtask relationship, along with an additional TCB and STCB.

```
APP3PGM3 MVS CONTROL BLOCKS APPENDIX 3 PROGRAM 3                                    ASM H V 02 12.55 04/10/94    PAGE   1
    LOC    OBJECT CODE      ADDR1 ADDR2    STMT   SOURCE STATEMENT
 000000                                       2 APP3PGM3 CSECT
                                              3 APP3PGM3 AMODE 31
                                              4 APP3PGM3 RMODE ANY
                                              6 *          THIS CSECT IS ATTACHED BY PROGRAM 1.  IT REPRESENTS A PROGRAM
                                              7 *          RUNNING AS A SUBTASK.  IT WILL WAIT FOR ONE MINUTE, THEN ENDS.
 000000 B240 00E0                             9          BAKR R14,0          ESA LINKAGE
 000004 18CF                                 10          LR   R12,R15        GET BASE ADDRESS
```

```
000006 41D0 C020      11         USING APP3PGM3,R12          ESTABLISH ADDRESSABILITY
000020                12         LA    R13,PGM3SAVE          GET SAVE AREA ADDRESS
                      14         STIMER WAIT,BINTVL=ONEMIN   WAIT ONE MINUTE
                      15+*       MACDATE = 08/19/88                            @L1C
00000A 4110 C068      16+        LA    1,ONEMIN              LOAD ADDR TIME VALUE   01-STIME
00000E 1BFF           17+        SR    15,15                 INDICATE NO EXIT       01-STIME
000010 4100 0091      18+        LA    0,145(0,0)            LOAD FLAG BYTE         01-STIME
000014 8900 0018      19+        SLL   0,24(0)               SHIFT TO HI-ORDER BYTE 01-STIME
000018 0A2F           20+        SVC   47                    ISSUE STIMER SVC       01-STIME
00001A 1BFF           22         SR    R15,R15               CLEAR REGISTER 15
00001C 0101           23         PR    ,                     RETURN
00001E 0000
000020 00000000C6F1E2C1  24  PGM3SAVE DC F'0',C'F1SA',16F'0' FORMAT-1 SAVE AREA
000068 00001770       25  ONEMIN   DC F'6000'                60.00 SECONDS
                      27 *        REGISTER EQUATES
                      28 *
00000                 29  R0      EQU 0
00001                 30  R1      EQU 1
00002                 31  R2      EQU 2
00003                 32  R3      EQU 3
00004                 33  R4      EQU 4
00005                 34  R5      EQU 5
00006                 35  R6      EQU 6
00007                 36  R7      EQU 7
00008                 37  R8      EQU 8
00009                 38  R9      EQU 9
0000A                 39  R10     EQU 10
0000B                 40  R11     EQU 11
0000C                 41  R12     EQU 12
0000D                 42  R13     EQU 13
0000E                 43  R14     EQU 14
0000F                 44  R15     EQU 15
                      46         END   APP3PGM3
```

000000

APP3PGM3   DIAGNOSTIC CROSS REFERENCE AND ASSEMBLER SUMMARY

NO STATEMENTS FLAGGED IN THIS ASSEMBLY
OVERRIDING PARAMETERS- NOXREF,NODECK,OBJECT,NOTERM,NOESD,NORLD

ASM H V 02 12.55 04/10/94   PAGE   2

```
OPTIONS FOR THIS ASSEMBLY
 NODECK, OBJECT, LIST, NOXREF, NORENT, NOTEST, NOBATCH, ALIGN, NOESD, NORLD, NOTERM, NODBCS,
 LINECOUNT(55), FLAG(0), SYSPARM()
NO OVERRIDING DD NAMES
    40 CARDS FROM SYSIN        381 CARDS FROM SYSLIB
    54 LINES OUTPUT              4 CARDS OUTPUT
```

At this point, we'll begin looking at the dump produced by running the preceding programs. The JCL used to execute this is:

```
//EXA7JHMX  JOB   -----
//APP3      EXEC  PGM=APP3PGM1,PARM='THE PARMS'
//STEPLIB   DD    DSNAME=EXA7JHM.PDS.LOAD,DISP=SHR
//SYSPRINT  DD    SYSOUT=*
//SYSUDUMP  DD    DSNAME=EXA7JHM.LISTING4,DISP=SHR
//PDS       DD    DSNAME=EXA7JHM.PDS.ASM,DISP=SHR
//
```

The job was executed on a Sunday afternoon at the UCLA Office of Academic Computing (OAC) data center. This was a period of low system activity, resulting in a voluminous trace table, which I edited to reduce its size. On the day the job was executed, OAC operated a five-gigabyte IBM ES/9000, model 900, with six Vector Facility features, under the MVS/ESA operating system, version 4.3. The first lines of the dump were:

```
JOB EXA7JHMX          STEP APP3         TIME 125832    DATE 94100   ID = 000    CPUID = A62112999021   PAGE 00000001
COMPLETION CODE       SYSTEM = 0C2      REASON CODE = 00000002
```

The 0C2 ABEND was intentionally forced in APP3PGM1. The REASON CODE will list the return code in register 15 where appropriate, e.g., 213-04.

```
 PSW AT ENTRY TO ABEND   078D1000   00006B10   ILC  04   INTC  0002
PSW LOAD MODULE
 NAME=APP3PGM1
```

Dump formatting attempts to identify the program in which the ABEND occurred.

```
ASCB: 00F7F080
+0000 ASCB..... ASCB      FWDP..... 00F88E80   BWDP..... 00F17580   CMSF..... 00000000   SVRB..... 009FF978
+0014 SYNC..... 0006B0B0  IOSP..... 00000000   TNEW..... 009DF348   CPUS..... 00000001   ASID..... 0321
+0026 R026..... 0000      LL5...... 00         HLHI..... 01         DPHI..... 00         DP....... 71
+002C TRQP..... 80F7C701  LDA...... 7FF16EB0   RSMF..... 00         R035..... 0000       TRQI..... 43
+0038 CSCB..... 00B92080  TSB...... 00000000   EJST..... 00000000   R035..... 10284580
+0048 EWST..... A91BE664  93639684   JSTL..... 00000014   ECB...... 809FFD78   UBET..... A91BE1EA
+005C TLCH..... 00000000  DUMP..... 009FF158   AFFN..... FFFF       RCTF..... 00         FLG1..... 00
+0068 TMCH..... 00000000  ASXB..... 009FE038   SWCT..... 932E       DSP1..... 00         FLG2..... 00
+0074 RSV...... 0000      SRBS..... 0000       LLSQ..... 00000000   RCTP..... 009FE240   LOCK..... 00000000
+0084 LSQH..... 00000000  QECB..... 00000000   MECB..... 40000000   OUCB..... 01D2DBF8   OUXB..... 017F2C28
+0098 FMCT..... 0000      LEVL..... 03         FL2A..... 80         XMPQ..... 00000000   IQEA..... 00000000
+00A4 RTMC..... 00000000  MCC...... 00000000   JBNI..... 00FAFCOC   JBNS..... 00FAE7CC   SRQ1..... 00
+00B5 SRQ2..... 00        SRQ3..... 00         SRQ4..... 00         VGTT..... 00000000   PCTT..... 00000000
+00C0 SSRB..... 0000      SMCT..... 00         SRBM..... 00         SWTL..... 0000035A
+00C8 SRBT..... 00000000  002D8380   LSMQ..... 00000000   LSPL..... 00000000   TCBS..... 00000001
+00DC TCBL..... 00000000  WPRB..... 009FEA40   NDP...... 71        TNDP..... 81         NTSG..... 03
+00E7 IODP..... 70        LOCI..... 00000000   CMLH..... 00000000   CMLC..... 00000000   SSO1..... 000000
+00F7 SSO4..... 00        ASTE..... 01FE9840   LTOV..... 7FFE2000   ATOV..... 7FFE3CA8   ETC...... 0000
+0106 ETCN..... 0000      LXR...... 0000       AXR...... 0000       STKH..... 009FEA50   GQEL..... 00000000
+0114 LQEL..... 09E5BF30  GSYN..... 00000000   XTCB..... 009DF348   CS1...... 00         R121..... 000000
+0124 GXL...... 0209A020  EATT..... 00000000   167F8700   INTS..... A91BE664   37B4D680
+0138 LL1...... 00000000  LL2...... 00         LL3...... 00         LL4...... 00         RCMS..... 00000000
+0140 IOSC..... 00000010  PKML..... 0000       XCNT..... 01F4       NSQA..... 00000000   ASM...... 01D351A8
+0150 ASSB..... 01D2DB80  TCME..... 00000000   GQIR..... 00000000   R15C..... 00000000   00000000
+0168 CREQ..... 00000000  RSME..... 01D2DB98   AVM1..... 00         AVM2..... 00         AGEN..... 0000
+0174 ARC...... 00000000  RSMA..... 01D2DA88   DCTI..... 00000143
```

I'll examine several of the ASCB fields, or more precisely the control blocks to which they point. Chapter 3 discusses the ASCB. The ASID field (second line, right side) shows the address space ID (ASN) to be 0321. The AFFN field (seventh line, middle) value of FFFF indicates that you can run on any processor in the system. The EATT field (sixth line from the end, middle) shows the amount of CPU time expended so far; the value is in timer unit format and the value is .092152 CPU seconds at the time the dump was formatted. I'll be referring to several control blocks whose addresses are in the ASCB, including the LDA, DUMP TCB, ASXB, RCT, OUCB, OUXB, and XTCB (job step TCB).

```
ASSB: 01D2DD80
 +0000  ASSB..... ASSB      VAFN..... 0BAD2D80   EVST..... 00000000   00000000           XMCC..... 0000
 +0010  VFAT..... 00000000  VSC...... 00000001   XMF1..... 00         XMF2..... 00       DEXP..... 7FFFBF00
 +001C  CBTP..... 00000C84  XMSE..... 00000000   NVSC..... 00000000   ASRR..... 00000000  BALV..... 020A6000
 +0030  STKN..... 15485F00  RMA...... 09DFF368   BPSA..... 00000000   CSCT..... 00000000  PALV..... 00000001
 +0044  BALD..... 00000000  ANEC..... 00000000   TSQN..... 0000057F   VCNT..... 00000001  IIPT..... 00000000
 +0058  ASEI..... 00324F80  FLG1..... 00         HST...... 00000000   00000000           DFAS..... 00F7F080
 +006C  FLG0..... 00        ASRB..... 01D35080   SDOV..... 00000000   MCSO..... 00000000  ASCB..... 00000000
 +0080  ASRF..... 01D2D900  SCH...... 00000000   FLG2..... 00         FLG3..... 00       LASB..... 00000000
 +0088           00000000   CRQA..... 00000000   SSD...... 00000000   R094..... 00000000  FSRB..... 00000000
 +009C  CREQ..... 00000001  ECT1..... 00000001   FSC...... 00000000   JSAB..... 01CB2318  TPIN..... 00000000
 +00B0  SPIN..... 00000000  NTTP..... 00000000   ROB8..... 00000005   SDAS..... 7FFE9C98  DFP...... 00000000
 +00C4  ROD8..... 00000000  VAB...... 021220B0   ECT2..... 00000000   MT#...... 00000000  XSBA..... 7FFFEF60
 +00D8  ROEC..... 00000000  R104..... 00000000   OECB..... 00000000   OASB..... 00000000          00000000
 +00EC  R100..... 00000000                        LMAB..... 00000000   ROF8..... 00000000  ROSU..... 00000000
 +0100  R104..... 00000000                        R108..... 00000000   TPMA..... 00000000

JOB EXA7JHMX    STEP APP3        TIME 125832   DATE 94100   ID = 000         PAGE 00000002
 +0114  TPMT..... 00000000
```

The ASSB was discussed in chapter 3. Fields of interest include the STKN (fourth line), which shows the STOKEN for the address space. See chapter 9 for a discussion of the STOKEN. The VAFN shows the number of tasks in the address space using the Vector Feature (first line), which APP3PGM1 does.

```
*** ADDRESS SPACE SWITCH EVENT MASK OFF  (ASTESSEM = 0) ***
```

This print line appears based on the setting of control register 1 bit 0. If it's on, a program exception will occur if a space-switching Program Call instruction is issued. Most users can ignore this.

```
ALE: 7F7439C8
 +0000  OPTB1..... 80        SN....... 00      EAX....... 0000      R004..... 00000000   ASTE..... 00000000
 +000C  ASTSN..... 00000000
```

```
ALE: 7F7439D8
 +0000  OPTB1..... 80        SN....... 00        EAX...... 0000      R004..... 00000000    ASTE..... 00000000
 +000C  ASTSN.... 001B8003

ALE: 7F7439E8
 +0000  OPTB1..... 00        SN....... FF        EAX...... 0001      R004..... 00000000    ASTE..... 260D7200
 +000C  ASTSN.... 00000000

ASTE: 020A6200
 +0000  ATO...... 00000000   AX....... 0000      ATL...... 0000      STD...... 015C513F    LTD...... 00000000
 +0010  PALD..... 00000000   SQN...... 00000000  R018..... 00000000  PROG..... 80000400    R020..... 00000000
 +0024           00000000             00000000            00000000            00000000
```

The Access List Elements (ALEs) and Address Space Second Table Entries (ASTEs) are formatted at this point in the dump. There's one entry for every potential address space to which your address space can make an access register connection and an ASTE for every active connection, oversimplifying somewhat. The remaining 29 ALEs in this dump aren't shown.

```
JOB EXA7JHMX          STEP APP3          TIME 125832    DATE 94100    ID = 000                    PAGE 00000007

TCB: 009DF348
 +0000  RBP...... 009FF7B0   PIE...... 00000000  DEB...... 00000000  TIO...... 009DE08C    CMP...... 940C2000
 +0014  TRN...... 00000000   MSS...... 7F72D958  PKF...... 80        FLGS..... 01000000              00
 +0022  LMP...... FF         DSP...... FF        LLS...... 009DF0A8  JLB...... 009FD060    JPQ...... 009DF0E8
GENERAL PURPOSE REGISTER VALUES
  0-3   00000158  7F748368  00000000  00000158
  4-7   00000158  009DD36C  00000158  04C51C40
  8-11  00000070  009D06D2  009D0732  84BC2008
 12-15  84624000  009CE920  009DF348  00000000
 +0070  FSA...... 00005F98   TCB...... 009DF128  TME...... 00000000  JSTCB.... 009DF348    NTC...... 00000000
 +0084  OTC...... 009F9028   LTC...... 009DF128  IQE...... 00000000  ECB...... 009FF084    TSFLG.... 20
 +0095  STPCT.... 00         TSLP..... 00        TSDP..... 00        RD....... 7FF16EE4    AE....... 7F72D370
 +00A0  STAB..... 009FF510   TCT...... 809DF510  USER..... 00000000  NDSP..... 00000000    MDIDS.... 00000000
 +00B4  JSCB..... 009F91CC   SSAT..... 00FD6E48  IOBRC.... 00000000  EXCPD.... 00000000    EXT1..... 00000000
 +00C8  BITS..... 00000000   DAR...... 00000000  RSV37.... 00        SYSCT.... 00          STMCT.... 00
 +00D0  EXT2..... 009DF4A0   AECB..... 00000000  XSB...... 7FFFCA78  BACK..... 009F9028    RTWA..... 7F752090
 +00E4  NSSP..... 00000000   XLAS..... 00000000  ABCUR.... 00        FJMCT.... 00          TID...... 00
```

```
+00EF  RSV..... 00        XSCT.... 80000042  FOE..... 7F7433FC  SWA..... 7F751058  STAWA... 00000000
+0100  TCBID... TCB       RTM12... 00000000  ESTAE... 00000000  UKYSP... 7F751310  SEQNO... 0005
+0112  AFFN.... FFFF      FBYT1... 08        FBYT2... 04        FBYT3... 80        RSV..... 00
+0118  RPT..... 00000000  VAT..... 00000000  SWASA... 00000000  SVCA2... 00000000  ERD..... 7FF16EF4
+012C  EAE..... 7F72D400  ARC..... 1C3D2680  GRES.... 00000000  STCB.... 7FFFC160
+013C  TTIME... 00000000                     R144.... 0005FE0   000000             LEVEL.... 03
+014C  BDT..... 00000000  NDAXP... 00000000  SENV.... 00000000
```

```
EXT2: 009DF4A0
+0000  GTF..... 00000000  RSV..... 00        RCMP.... 000000    EVENT... 000000    RTMCT... 0000001D
+0010  TQE..... 00000000  CAUF.... 00000000  PERCP... 00000000  PERCT... 80000000  00000000
```

This is the TCB for the APP3PGM1 task. The TCB contains a wealth of information, but I'll mention only a few items here. The RBP field (first line) contains the address of the current Request Block. In this case, it points to the SVRB for the SNAP macro used by ABEND SVC 51 (hexadecimal 33). The DEB field (first line, middle) points to the chain of Data Extent Blocks, which are formatted later in the dump. The TIO field (first line, right side) points to the Task I/O Table, which will also be formatted later. The CMP field (first line, right side) contains the ABEND code and dump options for this ABEND. Note the 0C2 system ABEND code in the middle of the field. The EXT2 is the OS/VS1-OS/VS2 common extension. The TCB is discussed in chapter 3.

```
STCB: 7FFFC160
+0000  STCB.... STCB      RACP.... 00000000  DIVF.... 00000000  DIVL.... 7FFFC168  AFNS.... FFFF
+0012  RSV..... 0000      VSSA.... 7F73EC0   VAFN.... 7F73EC0   FLG1.... 20        SRSN.... 0002
+001C  VFRB.... 00000000  ALOV.... 7FFFBF00  ALD..... 15485F00  DUCV.... 7FFFBDC0  DUCR.... 15485DC0
+0030  AR0..... 00F7F080  AR1..... 00000000  AR2..... 00000000  AR3..... 00000000  AR4..... 00000000
+0044  AR5..... 00000000  AR6..... 00000000  AR7..... 00000000  AR8..... 00000000  AR9..... 00000000
+0058  AR10.... 00000000  AR11.... 00000000  AR12.... 00000000  AR13.... 00000000  AR14.... 00000000
+006C  AR15.... 00000000  LSSD.... 7FFFBD90  LSDP.... 7F7550B0  RMEF.... 7F7550B0  RMEL.... 00000000
+0080  ESTK.... 7F755008  FLG2.... 00        FLG3.... 00        NSTP.... 0000      TLSD.... 7FFFBD90
+008C  TLSP.... 7F755008  TTKN.... 0000C84   00000001           009DF348           ALOC.... 00000000
+00A4  ASRB.... 00000000  VTME.... 00000000  JSAB.... 00000000  MEMC.... 00000000  XCFF.... 00
+00B5  R0B5.... 000000    DFTS.... 00000000  ARCT.... 0000      DRCT.... 0000
+00C8  NTTP.... 00000000  ROCC.... 00000000  00000000           00000000           DFP..... 00000000
+00D8  OTCB.... 00000000  CDXH.... 7F743CB8  SJST.... 00000000  ATAD.... 80E34FC4  ROE8.... 00000000
+00EC  SEQN.... 00000130
```

The STCB is an extension to the TCB that resides above the 16MB line. The VSSA field points to the Vector Status Save Area for those using that feature. The DUCV field contains the virtual address of the Dispatchable Unit Control Table (see chapter 9). Fields AR0 through AR15 hold the access register contents at the time of the last interruption. The LSDP field points to the current Linkage Stack Entry Descriptor. (The linkage stack will be formatted later in the dump, and is described in chapter 9.) The TLSP points the first linkage stack entry descriptor. The TTKN field is the TCBTOKEN; see chapter 9. The ARCT field is a count of the number of active REFPAT macros; see chapter 3. The STCB itself is described in chapter 3.

```
ALE: 7FFFBF00
     +0000   OPTB1.... 80        SN...... 00       EAX...... 0000    R004..... 00000000  ASTE..... 00000000
     +000C   ASTSN.... 00000000

ALE: 7FFFBF10
     +0000   OPTB1.... 80        SN...... 00       EAX...... 0000    R004..... 00000000  ASTE..... 00000000
     +000C   ASTSN.... 00001000

ALE: 7FFFBF20
     +0000   OPTB1.... 00        SN...... 00       EAX...... FFFF    R004..... 00000000  ASTE..... 258DA840
     +000C   ASTSN.... 00000001

ASTE: 01FE9840
     +0000   ATO...... 01F4BCA8  AX...... 0000     ATL...... 0030    STD...... 046F307F  LTD...... 811B2002
     +0010   PALD..... 260D7003  SQN..... 00000001 R018..... 00000000 PROG..... 00F7F080  R020..... 00000000
     +0024            00000000          00000000          00000000          00000000
```

These ALEs and ASTEs are associated with the TCB rather than the address space. The DSPSERV macro with the CREATE option (SCOPE=LOCAL) will generate valid ALEs at this point in the dump. See chapter 9 for an overview of the ALE and ASTE. The remaining five ALEs aren't shown.

```
LSSD: 7FFFBD90
     LSSD..... LSSD     VERS..... 01      FLG1..... 80      NEXT..... 00000000  NLSG..... 0001
     RLSS..... 0001     RSLO..... 7F759000 RSHI..... 7F759000 LSSP..... 7FFFBDB0
```

The LSSD is the starting point for locating linkage stack entries. It's pointed to by the STCB LSSD field. The LSSP field points to the LSSG control block, which is formatted in the following. I'm not aware of any mapping macros for these control blocks.

```
LSSG: 7FFFBDB0
      NLSS..... 0004      AFLG..... 00      NSLO..... 7F755000  NSHI..... 7F758000
```

The previous NSLO field points to the beginning of the linkage stack itself.

```
LINKAGE STACK ENTRY  00  LSED: 7F755008
LSEH: 7F755000
      BSEA..... 00000000  TYPE..... 81
      HEADER ENTRY
      RFS...... 0FE0      NES...... 00A8
```

The linkage stack is then formatted, entry by entry. There might be multiple header entries, depending on the size of the used linkage stack. The RFS and NES fields occur for each entry; RFS is the remaining free size, and NES is the next-entry size field.

```
LINKAGE STACK ENTRY  01  LSED: 7F7550B0
LSE: 7F755010
      GENERAL PURPOSE REGISTER VALUES
      00-03.... FD000012  00005FE8  00000040  009F1954
      04-07.... 009F1930  009F9028  009D1FF8  FD000000
      08-11.... 009FF060  809DF510  00000000  009F9028
      12-15.... 00E349F2  00005F98  80FD5118  00006908
      ACCESS REGISTER VALUES
      00-03.... 00000000  00000000  00000000  00000000
      04-07.... 00000000  00000000  00000000  00000000
      08-11.... 00000000  00000000  00000000  00000000
      12-15.... 00000000  00000000  00000000  00000000
      PKM...... 00C0      SASN..... 0321      EAX...... 0000      PASN..... 0321      PSW...... 078D0000  80FD5118
      TARG..... 0006690C  MSTA..... 00000000
```

```
TYPE..... 84
BAKR STATE ENTRY
RFS...... 0F38        NES...... 0000
```

This linkage stack entry is for the BAKR instruction at the beginning of APP3PGM1. It contains the register contents the program got from MVS.

```
PRB: 009DF2C0

-0020  XSB...... 7FFFED80  FLAGS2... 00        RTPSW1... 078D1000  00006B10  RTPSW2... 00040002
-000C  RSV...... 009D9000  FLAGS1... 02000005  WLIC..... 00040002
+0000  RSV...... 00000000           SZSTAB... 00110082  CDE...... 009FF010
+0010  OPSW..... 078D1000  00006B10  SQE...... 009F1954  LINK..... 009DF348
+0020  GPR0-3... FD000012  00000040  FD000000
+0030  GPR4-7... 009F1930  009D1FF8  009F9028
+0040  GPR8-11.. 009FF060  809DF510  00000000
+0050  GPR12-15. 00E349F2  80E34FB4  009FF090
+0060  RSV...... C1D7D7F3  D7C7D4F1
```

The previous Program Request Block is for APP3PGM1 (note the contents of the RSV field). This contains a PSW associated with the 0C2 ABEND. Note, however, that the registers at entry to ABEND are stored in the next RB, which is an SVRB. The WLIC field shows the interruption code in the right-hand halfword (0002). See chapter 3 for coverage of PRBs and SVRBs.

```
XSB: 7FFFED80

+0000  XSB...... XSB       LINK..... 00000000  KM....... 00C0       SASID.... 0321  AX....... 0000
+000E  PASID.... 0321      XLIDR.... 00000000  XLAS..... 00000000   TKN...... 0000  ASD...... 0000
+001C  SEL...... 00000000  SRSN..... 00000000  EAXW..... 00000000   ALOV..... 7FFFBF00  ALD...... 15485F00

ACCESS REGISTER VALUES
0-3    00000000  00000000  00000000  00000000
4-7    00000000  00000000  00000000  00000000
8-11   00000000  00000000  00000000  00000000
12-15  00000000  00000000  00000000  00000000

+0070  FLAG2.... 80        R071..... 000000  LSCP..... 7F7550B0  SXSB..... 7FFFEE00  R07C..... 00000000
```

The Extended Status Block saves information relating to program status at the time of a cross-memory transfer of control. The LSCP (Linkage Stack Check Point) shows the next entry address in the linkage stack. Each XSB is associated with the preceding RB. See chapter 9.

```
SVRB: 009FF6B8
-0020  XSB......  7FFFC9D8  FLAGS2...  00        RTPSW1.....  00000000  00000000            RTPSW2...  00000000
-000C             00000000  FLAGS1...  22000000  WLIC......   00020033
+0000  RSV......  00000000             00000000  SZSTAB...    001ED022  CDE......  00000000
+0010  OPSW.....  070C1000             84C61318  Q........    009F1954  LINK.....  009DF2C0
+0020  GPR0-3...  00006E4C             00006AD0  00000040     009D1FF8
+0030  GPR4-7...  009F1930             009F9028  00000000     00009000
+0040  GPR8-11..  009FF060             809DF510  00002260
+0050  GPR12-15.  00006908             00006DEC  00D60548
+0060  EXSAVE...  00006E4C             00006AD0  009DF348     00FF6F00  0211ACC0  7F752090
+0084             FF000F70  40000101   940C2000  SCBB.....    00000000  839FF6B8  2400DB00
+00A4  SXPTR....  009FF778             00000000  FEPARM...    00000000  00000000  00000000
+00C0  SCBX.....  00000000             00000000  009FF6B8
```

This SVRB is for the ABEND macro itself. For this particular example, there's not too much of interest. Note the WLIC field shows an interruption code of 0033, which is for the SNAP macro invoked to produce the dump.

```
XSB: 7FFFC9D8
+0000  XSB......  XSB       LINK.....  00000000  KM........  0000      SASID....  0321      AX........  0000
+000E  PASID....  0321      XLIDR....  00000000  XLAS......  00000000  TKN......  0000      ASD......  0000
+001C  SEL......  00000000  SRSN.....  00000002  EAXW......  00000000  ALOV.....  00000000  ALD......  00000000
ACCESS REGISTER VALUES
 0-3   00F7F080  00000000  00000000  00000000
 4-7   00000000  00000000  00000000  00000000
 8-11  00000000  00000000  00000000  00000000
12-15  00000000  00000000  860A9DC0  00010321
+0070  FLAG2....  80        R071......  000000   LSCP......  7F7550B0   SXSB.....  7FFFCA58   R07C.....  00000000
```

This is the XSB for the ABEND SVRB.

```
SVRB: 009FF7B0
      -0020  XSB.....  7FFFCA78  FLAGS2..  00        RTPSW1..  00000000
      -000C            00000000  FLAGS1..  02000000  WLIC....  00020078            RTPSW2...  00000000
      +0000  RSV.....  00000000            00000000  SZSTAB..  001ED022  CDE.....  00000000
      +0010  OPSW....  070C1000  80BF50AE            Q.......  4080E610  LINK....  009FF6B8
      +0020  GPR0-3..  00000948  7F752190  04C6205E  7F752090
      +0030  GPR4-7..  7F73E928  04C6105F  84C60060  009DAEC0
      +0040  GPR8-11.  00FC8BB8  000C2000  009DAE68  04C61330
      +0050  GPR12-15  7F73E3F8  7F73E3F8            00000000
      +0060  EXSAVE..  00000000  009D0228  00000000  00000000  SCBB....  00000000  00000000  00000000  839FF7B0
      +0084            00000000  00000000  00000000  00000000            16000000  00000000  2400DB00
      +00A4  SXPTR...  009FF870  FEPARM..  00000000  00000000  00000000
      +00C0  SCBX....  00000000  00000000  009CF180
```

This is the SVRB for the SNAP macro.

```
XSB: 7FFFCA78
      +0000  XSB.....  XSB        LINK....  00000000  KM......  0000      SASID...  0321
      +000E  PASID...  0321       XLIDR...  00000000  XLAS....  00000000  TKN.....  0000      AX......  0000
      +001C  SEL.....  00000000   SRSN....  00000000  EAXW....  00000000  ALOV....  00000000  ASD.....  0000
      ACCESS REGISTER VALUES                                                                  ALD.....  00000000
      0-3    00F7F080  00000000  00000000  00000000
      4-7    00000000  00000000  00000000  00000000
      8-11   00000000  00000000  860A9DC0  00010321
      12-15  00000000  00000000  R071....  000000   LSCP....  7F7550B0  SXSB....  7FFFCAF8  R07C....  00000000
      +0070  FLAG2...  80
```

This is the XSB for the SNAP macro SVRB.

```
LLE
      009DF0A8  CHN.....  009DF0B8  CDPT....  00BDC348  COUNT...  0002  SYSCT...  0002
      009DF0B8  CHN.....  009DF0C8  CDPT....  00BDD310  COUNT...  0002  SYSCT...  0002
```

```
009DF0C8  CHN......  009DF008  CDPT.....  00BE3058  COUNT....  0002  SYSCT....  0002
009DF008  CHN......  009FE028  CDPT.....  00BD70A0  COUNT....  0001  SYSCT....  0001
009FE028  CHN......  00000000  CDPT.....  009FD000  COUNT....  0001  SYSCT....  0000
```

The Load List Elements (LLEs) show the modules that have been brought into storage via the LOAD macro instruction. The first four entries are for IBM access method routines, such as IGG019BB. These are loaded into storage as a result of the OPEN macro for a DCB, and are usually placed into the Link Pack Area. The last entry in the list is for program APP3PGM1, which was loaded into storage by APP3PGM2. See Fig. C.1 for a description of the LLE chain in this dump.

```
CDE
009FF010  NAME.....  APP3PGM1  ENTPT....  00006908  CHAIN....  009FE008  RRBP.....  009DF2C0  XLMJP....  009FF000
          USE......  0001      SP........ FB
          USED. JOB PACK AREA.
          CDE EXTENSION EXISTS.
009FD000  NAME.....  APP3PGM2  ENTPT....  89E00FA0  CHAIN....  009FF010  RRBP.....  00000000  XLMJP....  009FE130
          USE......  0001      SP........ FB
          JOB PACK AREA.
          CDE EXTENSION EXISTS.
```

Contents Directory Entries (CDEs) exist for all programs in the region's private area (or in LPA), should the program be placed there by the installation). However, not all CDEs are formatted when a SYSUDUMP is printed. CDEs for other tasks in the address space and for entry points created by the IDENTIFY macro don't appear here, unless some program in the task requests them.

```
XTLST
009FF000  LNTH.....  00000010  NRFAC....  00000001  MSBLA....  800006F8  MSBAD....  00006908
009FE130  LNTH.....  00000010  NRFAC....  00000001  MSBLA....  80000060  MSBAD....  09E00FA0
```

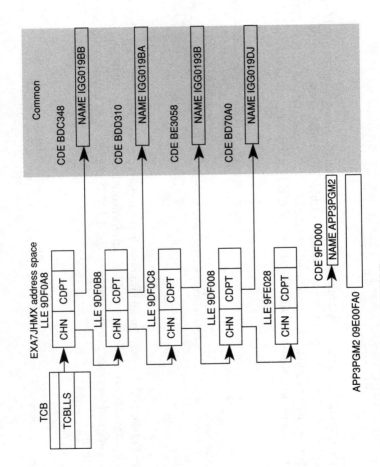

Figure C.1 The LLE chain in the SYSUDUMP.

The Extent List (XTLST) defines where a program is and how much storage it occupies. The CDE field XLMJP relates the XTLST to a particular CDE. Note, as with the CDEs, not all XTLSTs are formatted in a SYSUDUMP. See Fig. C.2 for the relationship between the CDEs and XTLSTs in this dump.

```
TIOT: 009D2000
      JOB...... EXA7JHMX  STEP..... APP3

               LN-STA     DDNAME    TTR-STC    STB-UCB
      +0018    14010100   STEPLIB   9ED23000   80F24D90
      +002C    14010102   SYSPRINT  9ECB8000   80000000
      +0040    14010100   SYSUDUMP  9ECA0000   80F24D90
      +0054    14010100   PDS       9EC88000   80F24D90
```

The Task I/O Table (TIOT) stores information about the device allocations associated with a particular DD name. The first three fields in the TIOT are the job name, step name, and procedure step name (which didn't apply to the job that created this dump). Following that, a number of variable-length entries appear, one per DD statement.

```
                              **VIRTUAL STORAGE MAP**

SUBPOOL 000  KEY 08   SHARED BY TCB 009F9028
   ADDRESS 00005000  LENGTH 00001000
      FREE AREA 00005000  LENGTH 00000548
      FREE AREA 00005CE0  LENGTH 00000048
   ADDRESS 00007000  LENGTH 00001000
      FREE AREA 00007000  LENGTH 000009A0
   ADDRESS 00008000  LENGTH 00001000


JOB EXA7JHMX        STEP APP3           TIME 125832    DATE 94100    ID = 000                          PAGE 00000011

      FREE AREA 00008000  LENGTH 00000F78

SUBPOOL 022  KEY 08   OWNED BY TCB 009DF348
   ADDRESS 00009000  LENGTH 00003000
      FREE AREA 0000B260  LENGTH 00000DA0
```

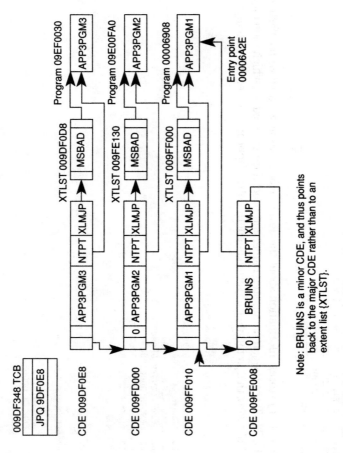

Figure C.2 Relationship between CDEs and XTLSTs.

```
SUBPOOL 230  KEY 00  OWNED BY TCB 009DF348
  ADDRESS 009DC000  LENGTH 00001000
    FREE AREA 009DC000  LENGTH 000009D0
  ADDRESS 7F749000  LENGTH 00001000
    FREE AREA 7F749000  LENGTH 00000D88
    FREE AREA 7F749E18  LENGTH 000001A0

SUBPOOL 230  KEY 05  OWNED BY TCB 009DF348
  ADDRESS 009DB000  LENGTH 00001000
    FREE AREA 009DB000  LENGTH 00000140
    FREE AREA 009DB198  LENGTH 000003C0
    FREE AREA 009DB638  LENGTH 000009C8
  ADDRESS 009DE000  LENGTH 00001000
    FREE AREA 009DE000  LENGTH 00000068
    FREE AREA 009DE148  LENGTH 00000D08
    FREE AREA 009DEF08  LENGTH 000000F8

SUBPOOL 230  KEY 08  OWNED BY TCB 009DF348
  ADDRESS 009DA000  LENGTH 00001000
    FREE AREA 009DA000  LENGTH 00000E68

SUBPOOL 237  KEY 01  SHARED BY TCB 009F9028
  ADDRESS 009D1000  LENGTH 00009000
    FREE AREA 009D1000  LENGTH 00000FC8
  ADDRESS 009E1000  LENGTH 00002000
    FREE AREA 009E1000  LENGTH 00000300
  ADDRESS 009EC000  LENGTH 00001000
    FREE AREA 009EC000  LENGTH 00000270
  ADDRESS 009ED000  LENGTH 00001000
    FREE AREA 009ED000  LENGTH 000000B0

SUBPOOL 251  KEY 08  OWNED BY TCB 009DF348
  ADDRESS 00006000  LENGTH 00001000
    FREE AREA 00006000  LENGTH 00000908
  ADDRESS 09E00000  LENGTH 00001000
    FREE AREA 09E00000  LENGTH 00000F30
```

This VIRTUAL STORAGE MAP is essentially the output of the VSMLIST macro. Thus, the actual VSM control blocks that specifically define storage usage aren't formatted, although the same information is presented. A complete definition of all the VSM control blocks involved in this address space would be too large to present in detail. However, see Fig. C.3 for the VSM control blocks related to subpool 22; you should be able to follow the equivalent control blocks for other subpools through the dump if you want. Subpool 22 is used because of the following instruction:

```
STORAGE  OBTAIN,SP=22,LENGTH=(11),BNDRY=PAGE,LOC=BELOW
```

in APP3PGM1.

```
SSAT: 00FD6E48
     +0000  SSAT......  SSAT      LNK......  00000000  CT.......  00000000  HIDX......  00000000  ENTS.....  00000000
     +0014             00000000  00000000  00000000  00000000  00000000  00000000  00000000  00000000
     +0038             C1E2C3C2  00FB5480  00000000  00000000  009E9028  000268DE
```

The Sub System Affinity Table (SSAT) is used when more than one subsystem (e.g., JES2 or JES3) is running in a system, or if there are multiple copies of the job entry subsystem. This isn't used for typical jobs, and it's the system-wide null SSAT uses for most cases.

TCB SUMMARY

TCB ADDRESS	COMPLETION CODE	TCB PKF	PRIMARY DISP FLAGS	TCB LMP	TCB DSP	SECONDARY DISP FLAGS	RTM2 WA ADDRESS	TCB FBYT
---	---	---	---	---	---	---	---	---
009FE240	00000000	00	00008004 00	FF	FF	00000000	00000000	0000
009FF158	00000000	00	00008004 00	FF	FF	00000000	00000000	0004
009FDE88	00000000	00	00008004 00	FF	FF	00000000	00000000	0004
009F9028	00000000	80	00000000 00	FF	FF	00000000	00000000	0004
009DF348	940C2000	80	01000000 00	FF	FF	00000000	7F752090	0804
009DF128	00000000	80	00000004 00	FF	FF	00000000	00000000	0000

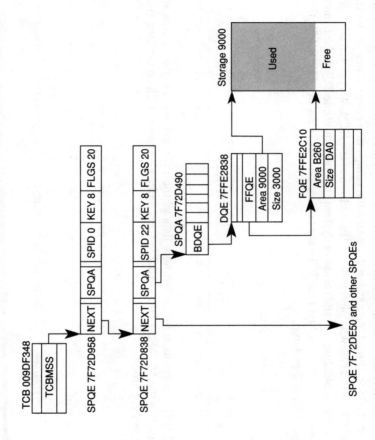

Figure C.3 VSM control blocks for subpool 22.

While the TCB that suffered the ABEND is formatted toward the start of the dump, this TCB summary lists salient information about all the tasks in the address space. Note that the completion code column shows the 0C2 ABEND for the APP3PGM1 task, and that the RTM2WA column shows the address of the RTM2WA printed later in this dump. These two columns are useful when debugging an application or system that uses multiple TCBs; the summary will show if other tasks have failed as well. Note that the first four TCBs are normal system TCBs. See Fig. C.4 for the layout of the TCBs in the address space involved in this dump.

```
**PC INFORMATION**

                  AUTH                      EXEC                   EXEC                          ASTE
PC       KEY   EXEC  ENTRY      EXEC  LATENT    KEY   ETE    ENTRY         REAL      ARR
NUMBER   MASK  ASID  ADDRESS    STATE PARMS     MASK  OPTION KEY   EAX     ADDRESS   ADDRESS    OPTIONS
------   ----  ----  -------    ----- ------    ----  ------ ----  ---     -------   -------    -------
000000   FF00  0002  89E02C40   S     00000000 00000000  8000  00    00    0000    26088080  00000000   00000000
```

The Program Call (PC) information formatted here lists all the PC numbers available to this address space. All MVS base entries are defined in the *MVS/ESA Diagnosis: System Reference* manual. The remaining entries in this table won't be shown in the interests of brevity.

```
***** LOCAL QUEUE CONTROL BLOCK PRINT *****
-------------------------------------------

MAJOR NAME-FOO

  MINOR NAME-01C2C1                                                                         *
          STATUS-EXCLUSIVE/OWN        SCOPE-SYSTEM    ASID-0321   *.BA    TCB-009DF348    SVRB-009FF6B8
```

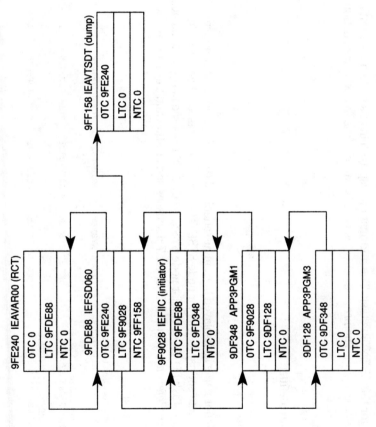

Figure C.4 TCB structure in the SYSDUMP.

The Local Queue Control Block Print (and the Global Queue Control Block Print that follows) display the currently ENQ'd resources for the ABENDing task. The information displayed in this section is essentially what's available through a GQSCAN macro instruction. The previous entry is here because of the following instruction in APP3PGM1:

```
ENQ    (FOO,BAR,E,3,SYSTEM)
```

FOO and BAR are defined as:

```
FOO    DC    CL8'FOO   '
BAR    DC    X'01',C'BAR'
```

Note that the minor name is displayed both in hexadecimal (01C2C1) and character form (.BA). The remaining entries that follow are for data set names (major node SYSDSN), dump data sets and hence the dump process itself (major node SYSIEA01), and the Task I/O Table (major node SYSZTIOT). MVS resource major node names are listed in the *MVS/ESA Diagnosis: System Reference* manual. Chapter 7 discusses serialization and the data involved in this section.

```
MAJOR NAME-SYSDSN

  MINOR NAME-EXA7JHM.LISTING4
        STATUS-EXCLUSIVE/OWN        SCOPE-SYSTEM    ASID-0321    TCB-009F9028    ECB-009FF078

  MINOR NAME-EXA7JHM.PDS.ASM
        STATUS-SHARE/OWN            SCOPE-SYSTEM    ASID-0321    TCB-009F9028    ECB-009FF078

  MINOR NAME-EXA7JHM.PDS.LOAD
        STATUS-SHARE/OWN            SCOPE-SYSTEM    ASID-0321    TCB-009F9028    ECB-009FF078

MAJOR NAME-SYSIEA01

  MINOR NAME-IEA
        STATUS-EXCLUSIVE/OWN        SCOPE-STEP      ASID-0321    TCB-009DF348    SVRB-009FF7B0
```

```
MAJOR NAME-SYSZTIOT

   MINOR NAME-0321009D9FE0
        STATUS-SHARE/OWN        SCOPE-SYSTEM   ASID-0321  *......*  TCB-009DF348   SVRB-009FF7B0

                     ***** GLOBAL QUEUE CONTROL BLOCK PRINT *****

NO GLOBAL RESOURCES EXIST
```

The following section displays the control blocks associated with open data sets. Comments are interspersed throughout the section, rather than in one block.

```
-DEB-------------------------------------------------AT LOCATION 009DE08C
-----
-24  DEBAVT   00FEB898 80DB11A8  DEBPCIA  00FEB898  DEBCEA   80DAE000  DEBXCEA  00DAE006
-10  PREFIX   00000005 2D000716  EXTNSION 109DE0F0  LENGTH   A8000000  11  AMTYPE  20  TBLOF  0003
+0   TCBADR   039DF348 NEXTDEB   109DEE74 IRBADR    FF000000 PATB      0F001100
+10  USRPG    01000000 RRQ       00000818 DCBADR    8F9DAE68 APPADR    049DE068
+20  18F24D90 00000818 00050845  00000000 000B02AA
+30  00010001 00000000 00000000  0000007D
+40  F3C2C2C1 C2C20000 00000000  00000000
+50  00000000 00000000 00000000  00000000
+60  00000000
```

This Data Extent Block (DEB) is for the SYSUDUMP data set; while the DD name isn't printed, it can be inferred from the DCB that follows it. Refer to chapter 8 for information regarding these control blocks.

```
-DCB-  (BSAM)                              AT LOCATION 009DAE68
-----
+10  002E9180 00000001 00000001 00004000 000055A8 02000001 54000000 00400020 009DE08C
+30  92C88D38 00D60548 0A000001 00000660 30013030 00005518 01DB36F0 00DB36F0
+50  0000007D 00000001
```

The Data Control Block (DCB) follows the DEB with which it's associated in the dump. Offset X'0028' contains the TIOT offset for the DCB's DD name. In this case, it's X'0040'. A review of the TIOT, which was printed earlier in the dump, will show that offset +0040 is associated with the DD name SYSUDUMP. You can also locate the blocksize (DCB offset X'003E–X'0660' in this case).

```
-IOB-    (SAM, BPAM-NORMAL SCHEDULING)    AT LOCATION   00005620
-----

-8    41005618 7F000000
+0    FLAG  0200  SENS  0000      ECBPT  00005548  CSW  00005650  0C000000
+10   START 00005648 DCBPT 009DAE68 RESTR 00000000 VARIABLE 00000000
```

The Input/Output Block (IOB) associated with the DCB is printed next. Depending on the access method and I/O options in use, you might see several IOBs for the same DCB.

```
-DEB-------------------------------AT LOCATION  009DEE74
-----

-24   DEBAVT    00FEE898 80DB11A8 DEBPCIA  00FEE898 DEBCEA   80DAE000 DEBXCEA 00DAE006
-10   PREFIX    00000005 2D00007C EXTNSION 009DB140 LENGTH   17       AMTYPE  20        TBLOF  0002
+0    TCBADR    039DF348 NEXTDEB  009DB560 IRBADR   68000000 PATB     00001100
+10   USRPG     05000000 RRQ      FF000000 DCBADR   8F006F3C APPADR   049DEE50
+20   58F24D90  000000C4 00100001
+30   58F24D90  0000043F 00000001
+40   58F24D90  0000053A 00070001
+50   58F24D90  0000046B 00050001
+60   58F24D90  0000046C 00040001
+70   F3C2C2C1  C2C20000 00000000
+80   00000000  00000000 00000000
+90   00000000
```

This DEB is for the DD name PDS. It represents a library. The library has gone into multiple one-track extents and each extent is displayed here as a 16-byte section, beginning at the line with the offset of +20. (If you want to, consult the

IEZDEB mapping starting with field DEBDVMOD. The beginning and ending track address are in DEBSTRCC, DEB-STRHH, DEBENDCC, and DEBENDHH.) In the previous example, the first extent begins at cylinder X'00C4', track X'0001' and ends at cylinder X'00C4', track X'0001'. The other fields are similarly formatted. The field beginning at offset +70 is DEBSUBAD and isn't part of the DASD extent information. The DEBNMEXT field, one byte long, will indicate how many extents are present. This field is shown as the first two digits of the USRPG field at offset +10.

```
-DCB-     (BPAM)                    AT LOCATION 00006F3C
-----
1JOB EXA7JHMX         STEP APP3         TIME 125832   DATE 94100   ID = 000                    PAGE 00000028

+10    002EBB60 00000001 00000200 00005D28 02006B10 90000000 00542400 009DEE74
+30    12C88D38 00D60548 0A000001 00002260 30013030 00005D98 01DB36F0 00DB36F0
+50    00000050 00DB4258
```

The TIOT offset is X'0054' for this DCB and the block size is X'2260' (decimal 8800). The LRECL for the file can be found at offset +52 (X'0050' or decimal 80), although these fields aren't always present for all access methods.

```
-IOB-     (SAM, BPAM-NORMAL SCHEDULING)     AT LOCATION 00005DA0
-----

-8     21005D98 7F000000
+0     FLAG    0200    SENS    0000      ECBPT   80006AD0 CSW     00005DD0 0C000000
+10    START   00005DC8 DCBPT           00006F3C RESTR   00000000 VARIABLE 00000000
```

This is the IOB for the preceding DCB. The prefix beginning at –8 is unique to BSAM. The CSW shows ending status of X'0C00'—you'd expect to see different contents for an I/O error ABEND such as 001.

```
-DEB--------------------------------AT LOCATION 009DB560
-----

-8     EXTNSION 009DB5E0 LENGTH  11      AMTYPE  81       TBLOF   0001
+0     TCBADR   009DF348 NEXTDEB 00000000 IRBADR 089F7548 PATB    0F000900
```

```
+10  USRPG     00000000  RRQ       00006F94  DCBADR   8F005E00  APPADR    00B38D80
+20  00F25420  E2E2C9C2  00240000  D1C5E2F2
+30  00000000  00000000  00000000  00000000
+40  00000000  00000000  E2E2D6C2  001C0010
+50  009DB584  00000000  009DB5C4  00000000
+60  00000000  001C0000  009DC0C4  00000000
+70  009DB560  009F7548  00000000  00000000
```

The format of this DEB doesn't follow that of normal DEBs shown up to this point. The message that follows indicates that this DEB was created for an Access Control Block (ACB) rather than for a DCB. This indicates that VSAM, VTAM, or JES2 is being used. In this case, it's JES2 because there are no ACBs in APP3PGM1 program.

```
*** FOR THIS DEB THERE IS NO DCB, THE CONTROL BLOCK POINTED TO BY THE DEB IS AN ACB ***

FOR DEB AT LOCATION 009DE08C
----------------------------------------
```

The following section dumps the Unit Control Blocks (UCBs) allocated to the DCBs dumped up to this point.

```
UCB-     (DIRECT ACCESS TYPE)              AT LOCATION  00F24D90
----

UCBPRFIX: 00F24D60
-0030  RSTEM....  00         MIHKY....  04        MIHTI....  00         HOTIO....  40     IOQF.....  00000000
-0028  IOQL.....  00000000   SIDA.....  0001      SCHNO....  014C       PMCW1....  289C   MBI......  006B
-001C  LPM......  F0         RSV......  00        LPUM.....  80         PIM......  F0     CHPID....  34C4B444
-0014  LEVEL....  FFFFFFFF   LEVEL....  01        IOSF1....  08         IOTKY....  00     MIHFG....  00
-000C  LVMSK....  00000001   LOCK.....  00000000  IOQ......  00FBAA00

UCBOB: 00F24D90
+0000  JBNR.....  00         FL5......  8A        ID.......  FF         STAT.....  8C     CHAN.....  02CA
+0006  FL1......  00         FLB......  00        NXUCB....  00F24E38   WGT......  00     NAME.....  2CA
+0010  TBYT1....  30         TBYT2....  10        DVCLS....  20         UNTYP....  0E     FLC......  00
+0015  EXTP.....  F24D40     VTOC.....  4D760100  VOLI.....  DATA8B     STAB.....  04     DMCT.....  07
+0024  SQC......  00         FL4......  00        USER.....  0011
```

```
UCBCMXT: 00F24D40
 +0000  ETI......00        STI......00        FL6......09        ATI......40        SNSCT.....20
 +0005  FLP1.....A2        STLI.....00        FL7......00        IEXT.....01FF9AC8  CHPRM....00
 +000D  SATI.....00        ASID.....0321      RSV......00        WTOID....000000    DDT......00FD17C8
 +0018  CLEXT....00F24DB8  DCTOF....0000      RSV......0000

DEVICE IS INSTALLATION-STATIC
```

Note the volume in the VOLI field (offset +1C). I'll leave further analysis of the UCB to you, as an exercise. UCBs are discussed in chapter 8.

```
FOR DEB AT LOCATION 009DEE74
-------------------------------

-UCB-     (DIRECT ACCESS TYPE)                AT LOCATION  00F24D90
-----

UCBPRFIX: 00F24D60
 -0030  RSTEM....00        MIHKY....04        MIHTI....00        HOTIO....40        IOQF.....00000000
 -0028  IOQL.....00000000  SIDA.....0001      SCHNO....014C      PMCW1....289C      MBI......006B
 -001C  LPM......F0        RSV......00        LPUM.....80        PIM......F0        CHPID....34C4B444
 -0014  FFFFFFFF           LEVEL....01        IOSF1....08        IOTKY....00        MIHFG....00
 -000C  LVMSK....00000001  LOCK.....00000000  IOQ......00FBA900

UCBOB: 00F24D90
 +0000  JBNR.....00        FL5......8A        ID.......FF        STAT.....8C        CHAN.....02CA
 +0006  FL1......00        FLB......00        NXUCB....00F24E38  WGT......00        NAME.....2CA
 +0010  TBYT1....30        TBYT2....10        DVCLS....20        UNTYP....0E        FLC......00
 +0015  EXTP.....F24D40    VTOC.....4D760100  VOLI.....DATA8B    STAB.....04        DMCT.....07
 +0024  SQC......00        FL4......00        USER.....0011

UCBCMXT: 00F24D40
 +0000  ETI......00        STI......00        FL6......09        ATI......40        SNSCT.....20
 +0005  FLP1.....A2        STLI.....00        FL7......00        IEXT.....01FF9AC8  CHPRM....00
 +000D  SATI.....00        ASID.....0321      RSV......00        WTOID....000000    DDT......00FD17C8
 +0018  CLEXT....00F24DB8  DCTOF....0000      RSV......0000
```

This concludes the data management control blocks formatted in the dump. The Recovery/Termination Manager control blocks follow. The Recovery/Termination Manager second level Work Area (RTM2WA) and STAE Control Block (SCB) are covered in chapter 10.

```
DEVICE IS INSTALLATION-STATIC

FOR DEB AT LOCATION 009DB560
----------

*** FOR THIS DEB, THERE ARE NO UCBS ***

RTM2WA: 7F752090

+0000  ID....... RTM2      ADDR...... 7F752090  SPID..... FF        LGTH..... 000F70    CVT...... 00FD50C8
+0010  TCBC..... 009DF348  VRBC...... 009FF6B8  ASC...... 00F7F080  CCF...... 84        CC....... 0C2000
+0020  SFWA..... 00000000  00000000   00000000  TCBT..... 009DF348  VRBT..... 009FF6B8
+0038  CT....... 00FC8BB8

       GPRS AT TIME OF ERROR
0-3    00006E4C  00006AD0  00000040  009F1954
4-7    009F1930  009F9028  009D1FF8  00000000
8-11   009FF060  809DF510  00009000  00002260
12-15  00006908  00006DEC  50006B0C  00D60548

+007C  PSW1..... 078D1000  NXT1..... 00006B10  RSV...... 00        ILC1..... 04        RSV...... 00
+0087  ICD1..... 02        TRAN..... 009D9000  ABNM..... APP3PGM1  ABEP..... 00006908  SCKB..... 00000000
+009C  SCKE..... 00000000  MCHI..... 0000      CPID..... 0000      RSR1..... 00        RSR2..... 00
+00A6  RSV...... 0000      RFSA..... 00000000  TIME..... 00000000  00000000            FLGS..... 40040001
+00B8  FMID..... 0000      IOFS..... 20        RSV...... 80        RSV...... 00000000  RBST..... 009DF2C0
+00C4  LSRT..... 7F7550B0  SCBC..... 009FF540  SCBN..... 009FF540  SCBO..... 00000000  FLAG..... 00
+00D5  FLG2..... 00        RCT2..... 00        RSV...... 00        RBPR..... 009DF2C0  COMP..... 00000000
+00E0  RTYA..... 00006B10  RYRB..... 009DF2C0  PARQ..... 04000000  CTL1..... FF850002  90006B10
+00F4  CTL2..... FF850002  90006B10            DPLA..... 7F752190  SNPL..... 006C0500  2FB0BE00
+010C            009DF348  SPSL..... 7F752630  HLST..... 00000000  SPSP..... 7F752720  SALE..... 009DAE68
+0120            00000000  00000000            STKN..... 00000000  00000000            DD....... E2E8E2E4
+0138            C4E4D4D7  SNCC..... 00000000  DTCB..... 009DF348  ECBA..... 7F7521E4  7F7521EC
+0150            7F7521F0  ECBS..... 00000000  00000000            00000000            RSV...... 00000000
+0168            00000000  PREV..... 00000000  PRWA..... 7F752090  SFSA..... 00000000  7F73E3F8
+0180            84C54A96  84C60060  7F755008  7F752090  04C54C57  04C54AEC  009FF6B8  84C53C58
+01A4            009DF348  7F752090  00000000  7F7523F8  7F7523F8  7F752DB0  PKEY..... 00
```

```
+01BD  CCTL..... 0C00      TCTL..... 00        MCTL..... 00        ABID..... 00        ABND..... 00
+01C3  RCTL..... 18        COMF..... 40000000  ABDP..... 80        ASIR..... 40        FLXI..... 00
+01CB  FLX2..... 00        SCTC..... 00080000  SCTR..... 00000000  SCTX..... 00000000  RSV...... 0000
+01DA  TMER..... 0000      TRF1..... 0808      TRF2..... 00        TRF3..... 00        TRRA..... 00000000
+01E4  SKRA..... 04C54AEC  STRA..... 00000000  CTRA..... 04C5341E  RECT..... 0000      WARG..... 07
+01F3  RBRG..... 00        RREG..... 00000008  00000000            009DF2C0            009DF540
+0210  00005660            04C586CE            04C53C58            7F752090            009DF2C0
+0234  00000000            00000000            84C5339A            00000001            84C588E8
+0258  CREG..... 009DF348  009FF6B8            009FF718            00F7F080            04C5301F
+027C  TRSA..... 02000000  009F93E4            84C5830C            00005660            7F7523F8
+02A0  009DF2C0            009FF540            00005660            84C566D0            009DF2C0

       SPKM..... 00C0      SYNL..... 000A      SSAN..... 0321      SEAX..... 0000      SPAN..... 0321
                           RSV...... 00000000  SDW1..... 00005660  SUBP..... FA        SIZE..... 000680
       XDES..... 00000000  ALET..... 00000000  STRR..... 00000000  SEQ#..... 0429      CPUI..... 0000
       ERTM..... 000720B3  ERAS..... 0321      RSV...... 0000      TRSN..... 7F752918  RSV...... 00000000
       SNPH..... 0000      CTR...... 0000      RSV...... 00000040  TEAR..... 06        MFLG..... 00
       RYRS..... 00006E4C  TECB..... 40404040  LSET..... 7F7550B0  COMU..... 009F1930  LSCT..... 7F7550B0
       LSBT..... 809DF510  SDW2..... 7F752938  ANCH..... 7F752090  SCBP..... 7F752730  FAIN..... 05EF8200
       CRC...... 00000002  RSV...... 00000000  MCIC..... 00000000  00006908            SABC..... 940C2000
       RSV...... 00000000  OCRC..... 00000002  ASCB..... 00F7F080  ASST..... 046F307F
                                               009F1954            009D1FF8
                                               009F9028            0D60548
                                               50006DEC

       ACCESS REGISTERS AT TIME OF ERROR
0-3    00F7F080   00000000   00000000   00000000
4-7    00000000   00000000   00000000   00000000
8-11   00000000   00000000   00000000   860A9DC0
12-15  00000000   00000000   860A9DC0   00010321

       ACCESS REGISTERS FOR RETRY
0-3    00F7F080   00000000   00000000   00000000
4-7    00000000   00000000   00000000   00000000
8-11   00000000   00000000   00000000   860A9DC0
12-15  00000000   00000000   860A9DC0   00010321

       CONTROL REGISTERS AT TIME OF ERROR
0-3    5FB3EE40   046F307F   15485DC0   00C00321
4-7    00000321   258DA840   FE000000   046F307F
8-11   00000000   00000000   00000000   00000000
12-15  0378415B   046F307F   DF8A60AC   7F7550B0
```

The presence of the control registers in the RTM2WA allows for some insight into how the control registers are set for a given version of MVS. Control register 0 has bit 14 on since APP3PGM1 issued a vector instruction; otherwise, the contents of the previous are unremarkable.

```
+045C  DUCT.....  00000000  00000000  00000000  15485F00  00000000  00000000  00000000  00000000
+0480             00000000  00000000  00000000  00000000  00000000  00000000  RMNP.....  009F93B8
+04A0  RSV......  7F7550B0  RSV......  00000000            00000000  00000000  00000000  00000000
+04BC  RSV......  00000000            7FFFBF00  15485F00  00000000  00000000  00000000  00000000
+04D8             00000000  00000000  00000000  00000000  00000000  00000000  00000000
+04FC  RSV......  00000000  RSV......  00000000  00000000  00000000  00000000  00000000
+0518             00000000  00000000  00000000  00000000  00000000  00000000
+053C             00000000  00000000  RME......  00000000  RETY.....  00000000
+0554  ARP1.....  7F7525F4  ARP2.....  7F7525F8  ARP3.....  7F752600  ARP4.....  7F752620  ARPC.....  00000000
+0568  ARID.....  00000000  LVL......  7F752090  ARET.....  00000000            00000000  00000000
+0584             00000000  00000000            ARAD.....  00000000  ARRO.....  00000000  CSCB.....  00000000
+059C  LSO......  00000000
```

The following is often the most valuable part of a SYSUDUMP. The RTM2WA Summary provides an overview of error information.

```
                              RTM2WA SUMMARY
                              --------------
+001C  COMPLETION CODE                              840C2000
+008C  ABENDING PROGRAM NAME/SVRB ADDRESS  APP3PGM1 00006908
+0094  ABENDING PROGRAM ADDR                        00006908

       GPRS AT TIME OF ERROR
       0-3    00006E4C  00006AD0  00000040  009F1954
       4-7    009F1930  009F9028  009D1FF8  00000000
       8-11   009FF060  809DF510  00009000  00002260
       12-15  00006908  00006DEC  50006B0C  00D60548

+007C  EC PSW AT TIME OF ERROR  078D1000  00006B10  00040002  009D9000
+00DC  SDWACOMP                 00000000
```

For an 0C4 ABEND, certain additional checks could be useful when reviewing the previous two lines of the RTM2WA. The interruption code for the program check is stored in the second half of the third fullword of the EC PSW line; the value is 0002 in this example. For 0C4 ABENDs, this field might contain X'0010' or X'0011' (segment-translation and page-translation exceptions). If these values are found, the next fullword (which contains 009D9000 in this example) will be the address the program was trying to reference when the error occurred—in other words, the bad address. In this case, this value will be the address of the last normal page fault.

```
+00E8   RETURN CODE FROM RECOVERY ROUTINE-04
        RETRY
+00E0   RETRY ADDRESS RETURNED FROM RECOVERY EXIT 00006B10
+00E4   RB ADDRESS FOR RETRY                       009DF2C0
```

The previous section is present because APP3PGM1 included an ESTAE exit. The exit issues a return code 4, which indicates that it wants to attempt to retry, and the retry routine is at location X'00006B10'.

```
+000C   CVT ADDRESS                     00FD50C8
+0038   RTCT ADDRESS                    00FC8BB8
+00C8   SCB ADDRESS                     009FF540
+0354   SDWA ADDRESS                    00005660
+0014   SVRB ADDRESS                    009FF6B8
+016C   PREVIOUS RTM2WA FOR THE TASK    00000000
+0170   PREVIOUS RTM2WA FOR RECURSION   00000000
```

There are various addresses of control blocks whose value varies from problem to problem. The SCB address is for the ESTAE exit last issued at the time of the ABEND. Since the ABEND and the SNAP macro both need to recover from problems during their processing, both of these will issue ESTAEs, so the SCB relationship can get confusing if the starting point isn't known. Note that, if the two lines beginning with PREVIOUS RTM2WA don't have zero values, your program might have encountered more than one error. It's usually simplest to find the RTM2WA for the first problem and correct that.

```
+00B8  ASID OF ERROR IF CROSS MEMORY ABTERM    0000
+036C  ERROR ASID                              0321

                RTM2WA BIT FLAG SUMMARY
                -----------------------
        RETRY REQUESTED BY EXIT
        PROGRAM CHECK
        ENABLED RB IN CONTROL AT TIME OF ERROR
        ERRORID INFORMATION AVAILABLE
```

The following two sections show the storage to be dumped if the ESTAE exit routine sets up selected areas to dump. These will be zero in the majority of cases.

```
STGRNG: 7F752630

                DUMP STORAGE RANGES
                -------------------
+0000  00000000 00000000 00000000 00000000 00000000 00000000 00000000 00000000
+0030  00000000 00000000 00000000 00000000 00000000 00000000 00000000 00000000
+0060  00000000 00000000 00000000 00000000 00000000 00000000 00000000 00000000
+0090  00000000 00000000 00000000 00000000 00000000 00000000 00000000 00000000
+00C0  00000000 00000000 00000000 00000000 00000000 00000000 00000000 00000000
```

DXSTGRNG: 7F752760

```
                 DUMP DATA SPACE STORAGE RANGES

+0000  00000000 00000000 00000000 00000000 00000000 00000000 00000000 00000000
+0030  00000000 00000000 00000000 00000000 00000000 00000000 00000000 00000000
+0060  00000000 00000000 00000000 00000000 00000000 00000000 00000000 00000000
+0090  00000000 00000000 00000000 00000000 00000000 00000000 00000000 00000000
+00C0  00000000 00000000 00000000 00000000 00000000 00000000 00000000 00000000
```

STGRNG: 009F93B8

The following area is the Resource Manager Parameter List, used by resource management exits created by the RESMGR macro. Refer to chapter 10 for a discussion of RESMGR.

```
                           RMPL AREA
+0000  RMLN.... 000000C8 RMP1.... 009F93C4 RMP2.... 00000000
+000C  RMPL.... 84000321 00F7F080 009DF348 00000000 009F93E4 00000000          PARM.... 00000000 00000000
+002C  RMWS.... FF030100 009F93F0 009F93F8 E2E8E2C9 C5C1F0F1 C9C5C100 00000000 00000000 00000000
+0058           00000000 00000000 00000000 00000000
+006C  RMSA.... 7F73E928 7F73E3F8 00000000 84C61412 84C63000 009DB000 009DAEC4 04C6205E 4080E610 009DAEC4 04C6105F
+0098           84C60060 7F752090 04C6105E 00FD50C8 00FC8BB8 7F73E928 7F73E3F8 RSV..... 00       FIOB.... FFFFFFF
+00B8  EXCL.... 00000000 00000000          DCBA.... 00000000 RSV..... 00000000

                   ESA BIT FLAG SUMMARY (RTM1 RELATED INFORMATION) FROM SVRB AT 009FF6B8
          --------------------------------------------------------------------------------
+88   RTM2 ENTERED VIA RTM1
+8A   RTM1 ENTERED FOR PROGRAM CHECK
+8B   SYSTEM STATE: TASK MODE

      SDWA GPRS AT TIME OF ERROR
      --------------------------
      GPR0-3...  00006E4C  00006AD0  00000040  009F1954
      GPR4-7...  009F1930  009F9028  009D1FF8  00000000
      GPR8-11..  009FF060  809DF510  00009000  00002260
      GPR12-15.  00006908  00006DEC  5006B0C   00D60548

      SDWA ARS  AT TIME OF ERROR
      --------------------------
```

```
AR0-3.....  00F7F080  00000000  00000000  00000000
AR4-7.....  00000000  00000000  00000000  00000000
AR8-11....  00000000  00000000  00000000  00000000
AR12-15...  00000000  00000000  860A9DC0  00010321
```

At this point, the SCBs are dumped. The following SCB is for the exit in APP3PGM1.

```
SCB: 009FF540
  +0000  CHAIN....  00000000  EXIT.....  00006B34  FLGS1.....  10  PARMA.....  000000  FLGS2.....  00
  +000D  OWNRA....  9DF2C0    FLGS3.....  08        PKEY......  80  ID........  DB      PCFLG.....  00
  +0014  XPTR......  809FF558
SCBX: 809FF558
  +0000  KMSK.....  00C0      SASN......  0000      EAX.......  0000  PASN......  0000  TOKN......  00000000
  +000C  PARM......  00000000  ALET......  00000000  LSEA......  7F7550B0

                  SCB BIT FLAG SUMMARY
                  -------------------

  +8   ESTAE INDICATOR ON
       QUIESCE I/O
```

The SCBs which follow were added during ABEND and dump processing.

```
SCB: 009FF4B0
  +0000  CHAIN....  009FF540  EXIT.....  04C61A06  FLGS1.....  16  PARMA.....  000000  FLGS2.....  83
  +000D  OWNRA....  9FF6B8    FLGS3.....  61        PKEY......  00  ID........  DB      PCFLG.....  00
  +0014  XPTR......  809FF4C8
SCBX: 809FF4C8
  +0000  KMSK.....  0000      SASN......  0000      EAX.......  0000  PASN......  0000  TOKN......  00000000
  +000C  PARM......  7F73E928  ALET......  00000000  LSEA......  7F7550B0

                  SCB BIT FLAG SUMMARY
                  -------------------

  +8   ALLOW ASYNCHRONOUS INTERRUPTS
       BYPASS I/O INTERVENTION
```

```
+C   ESTAE INDICATOR ON
     USER IN KEY 0-7
     USER IN SUPERVISOR STATE

SCB:  009FF510
      +0000  CHAIN..... 009FF4B0  EXIT..... 04BDB4B6  FLGS1..... 16    PARMA..... 000000  FLGS2..... 83
      +000D  OWNRA..... 9FF7B0    FLGS3..... 41       PKEY...... 00    ID........ DB      PCFLG..... 00
      +0014  XPTR...... 809FF528

SCBX: 809FF528
      +0000  KMSK...... 0000      SASN...... 0000     EAX....... 0000  PASN...... 0000    TOKN...... 00000000
      +000C  PARM...... 009D036C  ALET...... 00000000 LSEA...... 7F7550B0

                       SCB BIT FLAG SUMMARY
                       -------------------

+8   ALLOW ASYNCHRONOUS INTERRUPTS
     BYPASS I/O INTERVENTION
     ESTAE INDICATOR ON
+C   USER IN KEY 0-7
     USER IN SUPERVISOR STATE

SCB:  009FF480
      +0000  CHAIN..... 009FF510  EXIT..... 0497A490  FLGS1..... 16    PARMA..... 000000  FLGS2..... 83
      +000D  OWNRA..... 9FF7B0    FLGS3..... 03       PKEY...... 00    ID........ DB      PCFLG..... 00
      +0014  XPTR...... 809FF498

SCBX: 809FF498
      +0000  KMSK...... 0000      SASN...... 0000     EAX....... 0000  PASN...... 0000    TOKN...... 00000000
      +000C  PARM...... 009CF8E0  ALET...... 00000000 LSEA...... 7F7550B0

                       SCB BIT FLAG SUMMARY
                       -------------------

+8   ALLOW ASYNCHRONOUS INTERRUPTS
     BYPASS I/O INTERVENTION
     ESTAE INDICATOR ON
+C   USER IN KEY 0-7
     USER IN SUPERVISOR STATE
```

SNAP attempts to print a Save Area Trace at this point. However, since APP3PGM1 uses ESA linkage, the register content information is stored in the Linkage Stack Entries, which are printed after the TCB, STCB, and associated ALEs.

```
SAVE AREA TRACE
PROCEEDING FORWARD FROM TCBFSAB
INTERRUPT AT 00006B10
PROCEEDING BACK VIA REG 13

NAME=APP3PGM1
WAS ENTERED VIA CALL
SA  00006DEC WD1 00000000  HSA C6F1E2C1  LSA 00000000  RET 00006E4C  EPA 00006F3C  R0 50006B0C
             R1  00D60548  R2  00006E4C  R3  00006AD0  R4  00000040  R5  009F1954  R6  009F1930
             R7  009F9028  R8  009D1FF8  R9  00000000  R10 009FF060  R11 809DF510  R12 00009000
```

You can determine if a program is using ESA linkage by examining the formatted HSA field in the save area dump output. (HSA means high save area, and is the address of the previous save area in normal S/370 linkage.) Programs using ESA linkage must put the constant FMT1 in this field, since there is no prior save area. X'C6F1E2C1' is FMT1 in hexadecimal. The registers in this save area will often be those associated with the last subroutine call or I/O instruction.

The next part of the dump isn't present for typical SYSUDUMPs, and was added specifically for this appendix. The Local System Queue Area (LSQA) is normally not dumped in its entirety for a SYSUDUMP. The ESTAE exit modified the dump parameters to allow it to be produced here. The purpose in doing this was to dump some control blocks that would otherwise not be accessable.

```
ALLOCATED LSQA
009CF000 00000000 00000000 00000000 00000000    00000000 00000000 00000000 00000000    *................................*
         LINES 009CF020-009CF8C0  SAME AS ABOVE
009CF8E0 8497946E 84979472 84979476 00000000    00000000 00000000 00000000 00000000    *dpm>dpm.dpm.....................*
009CF900 00000000 849799E2 84979A84 009D06D2    0497A6C0 009CFA2C 00000000 00000000    *....dprSdp.d...K.pw(.............*
009CF920 00000000 00000000 00000000 00000000    00000000 940C2000 00000000 00000000    *................m...............*
009CF940 00000000 00000000 00000000 00000000    40404040 40404040 40404040 40404040    *................................*
009CF960 40404040 40404040 40404040 40404040    40404040 40404040 40404040 40404040    *................................*
```

```
           LINES 009CF980-009CF9A0  SAME AS ABOVE
009CF9C0 40404040 00000000 40404040 00000000   009DD3C8 009CEF98 8497A44E 80BF6000  *............LH..qdpu+..-.*
009CF9E0 00000000 009CF90C 009FF480 009CF8E0   009CFB40 009CF9CC 00000001 009D06D2  *.........9...4..8\....9....K*
009CFA00 00000000 0497A6C0 0497A490 84979310   0497A30F 16000000 009CFBE0 00000000  *....pw{..dpl.pt....8\....*
009CFA20 00010000 00000000 0497A490 00000003   E2C3C240 40404040 00000000 00000000  *.........pu...SCB.......*
009CFA40 00000000 009FF480 00000000 00000000   00000000 00000000 00000000 00000000  *....4........5........*
009CFA60 00000000 00000000 00000000 00000000   009FF540 00000000 00000000 00000000  *.........5........*
009CFA80 00000000 00000000 00000000 00000000   00000000 00000000 00000000 00000000  *................*
009CFAA0 000002F8 009CF8E0 000006E0 009CF9CC   00000000 0497A458 84979310 009D06F2  *...8.8\....9....pu.dpl...2*
009CFAC0 00000000 009CF8E0 84979310 009CF9CC   7F7485B0 009D06D2 04BE6C5E 009CFBD8  *..8\....9."..e...K.%;..Q*
009CFAE0 00000000 0497A30F 0497A30F 009CF9CC   009D06EE 00000000 00000000 0497A458  *...dpl.pt..9.......pu.*
009CFB00 009FF480 009CFB40 84979310 009CF9CC   00000001 009D06D2 00000000 0497A6C0  *..4..8\....9....K...pw{*
009CFB20 00000000 84979310 0497A30F 009CF9CC   84979A84 00000000 00000000 00000000  *....9.dpl.pt..9.dp.d....*
009CFB40 00000000 00006B34 009FF480 009FF510   009FF1B0 00000000 00000000 00000000  *.......4..5..4...5*

JOB EXA7JHMX     STEP APP3     TIME 125832   DATE 94100   ID = 000           PAGE 00000035

           LINES 009CFB80-009CFBA0  SAME AS ABOVE
009CFB60 00000000 00000000 00000000 00000000   00000000 00000000 00000000 00000000  *................*
009CFBC0 84994BF8 84994A42 84994A46 84994C3A   84994C42 84995056 84978448 84978544  *dr.8dr\.dr\.dr<.<dr&.dpd.dpe.*
009CFBE0 8497855A 849782CE 84978376 00000000   00000000 009D06D2 049788A4 009CFC58  *dpe!dpb.dpc....K.phu.*
009CFC00 009FF6B8 00000010 00005660 009FF718   00000000 00005660 0005ADC 0005ADC  *..6.....-.7...!.!.*
009CFC20 84994A4C 80CB7ED0 009D03B1 009D06D2   009CFCF8 009D06D2 01000000 40404040  *dr<.=}.....K...8.{..K....*
009CFC40 00000004 00000000 089F7548 00000000   84994872 009DB580 01000000 40404040  *........Jq..}.....dr.....*
009CFC60 40404040 009DD198 000059D0 00000040   000059D0 00000000 00000008B 04404040  *...Jq..}.....dr........*
009CFC80 00000000 40404040 40404040 851B11E6   40404040 40404040 40404040 40404040  *.........e..W........*
009CFCA0 40404040 40404040 40404040 40404040   40404040 40404040 40404040 009CFE3D  *............e..W....*
009CFCC0 40404040 40404040 009FF743 00B374F0   00000019 4EF8C240 40401000 089F7548  *.....7...0...0...+8B....*
009CFCE0 40404040 009FF743 00B374F0 00F24D90   00F24D90 00000000 00000000 00000000  *.2(..2(..2(.2(..*
009CFD00 00F24D90 00F24D90 00F24D90 00000000   00F24D90 00000000 00000000 00000000  *.2(..2(..2(.2(..*
009CFD20 00000000 009FF743 00000000 00000000   00058FF8 00005AA8 009CFC60 01305E18  *.....8.!y....*
009CFD40 7FFE5B30 8106E90E 8106F300 00000000   009CFC98 009CFC60 009CFC60 01305E18  *".$.a.Z.a.3......q..-.;*
009CFD60 8106E85A 009FFA98 7F7749B04 00000044   8106EB50 7F749B00 009FFD60 8106E33A  *a.Y!..q".....a.&"..)-a.T.*
009CFD80 007AC1D7 D7F3D7C7 D4F10001 162C0001   1B000000 00E5E7F3 F3404040 40000000  *.:APP3PGM1.....VX33*
009CFDA0 88000101 0000C1D7 D7F3D7C7 D4F20001   1E2C0001 23000000 000003F2 00006000  *h....APP3PGM2....2...*
009CFDC0 60000000 0000C1D7 D7F3D7C7 D4F30001   D4F30001 252C0001 2A000000 000003F2  *-..h....APP3PGM3.....2*
009CFDE0 70000000 70000000 88120001 88120001   FFFFFFFF FFFF0000 00000000 00000000  *....h............*
009CFE00 00000000 00000000 00000000 00000000   00000000 00000000 00000000 00000000  *................*
```

```
009CFE20  00000000 00000000 00000000 00000000  00000000 00000000 00000000 FD000000  *................*
009CFE40  00009D06 D2000000 00000000 00000000  00000000 00000000 00000000 00000000  *....K...........*
009CFE60  0000B374 F0000000 00000000 00000000  00000000 00000000 00000000 00000000  *....0...........*
009CFE80  F0F361F2 F561F9F3 D1C4E9F1 F1F1F040  E4E8F9F2 F1F4F440 00000000 01080100  *03/25/93JDZ1110 UY92144 .....*
009CFEA0  639CFEE0 40000010 239CFEFD 40000001  639CFEE0 40000010 479CFEF0 40000010  *.\.....\.......*
009CFEC0  929CFE98 40000008 699CFF20 40000008  089CFEC0 00000000 069CFD80 00000100  *k.q.....{......*
009CFEE0  00C00000 00000080 00000000 00000000  00000000 009D0003 009D0003 00000000  *................*
009CFF00  319CFF53 40000005 089CFEB0 00000000  639CFEE0 40000010 479CFEF0 40000010  *...0.......\....*
009CFF20  C2D3E2D8 C5E7E3C9 04000000 7F000000  03000000 7F9CFF2C 009CFEE0 0C000000  *BLSQEXTI......"..\..*
009CFF40  009CFEB0 009FD060 00000000 00000000  9D000300 00000000 00000000 00000000  *........)-......*
009CFF60  00000000 00000000 00000000 00000000  00000000 00000000 00000000 00000000  *................*
009CFF80  00000000 00000000 00000000 00000000  40000000 009CFD80 00000000 000000F8  *............8.*
009CFFA0  7FFE5BC8 00020000 009CFFAC D3D3D7D7  01000010 009E023C 04BDA84C 009D0228  *."$H......LLPP.*
009CFFC0  7FFFC118 009DD3C8 84BDA848 009DF348  810A5430 04BDA84C 009D0228 009D0228  *."..A...LHd.y.a...y<*
009CFFE0  009D0FBF 04BDB4FE 009DF348 84BD9500  04BDA4FF 00FC8BB8 009D06D2 009D06D2  *...3.d.n..u..K...K*
009D0000  009DF348 009CFFC0 84BDA4CA 00000000  00000000 00000000 00000000 00000000  *3...(d.u*
009D0020  00000000 00000000 00000000 00000000  00000000 00000000 00000000 00000000  *................*
        LINES 009D0040-009D0080   SAME AS ABOVE
009D00A0  00000000 00000000 00000000 00000000  00000000 84BDA4FA 00000000 00000000  *............d.u.*
009D00C0  00000000 00000000 00000000 00000000  009D0198 00000000 00000000 00000000  *........q......*
009D00E0  009DF348 009FF7B0 009DAE68 00000000  009CFFC0 7F7484C0 7F7484C0 00000000  *3...3..7....{".d{".d{*
009D0100  00000000 009D0590 00000000 00000000  00000000 009DF348 00000000 00000000  *...........3....*
009D0120  00000000 FFFFFFFC 00000000 00000000  00000000 7F749FB8 00000000 003C0000  *...........".....*
009D0140  009DF348 00000000 00000000 00000000  04BDB4FE 009D0FBF 08000000 08000000  *3.......*
009D0160  0000003D 00000000 009D06D2 009D0F32  00000000 006C0500 2FB0BE00 2FB0BE00  *.K........&*
009D0180  009D06D2 009DAE68 009DF348 7F752630  00000088 00000660 00000000 00000000  *.K...3."....h..*
009D01A0  009DAE68 009DF348 7F752760 00000000  7F752720 00000088 00000000 00000000  *.......h..-*
009D01C0  00000000 7F752760 00000000 00000000  00000000 00000660 00000000 00000000  *..-*
009D01E0  00000000 00000000 00000000 00000000  00000000 00000000 00000000 00000000  *................*
        LINE 009D0200   SAME AS ABOVE
009D0220  00000000 009DF348 009DF348 009DF348  009FF7B0 00680500 2FB0BE00 009DAE68  *.....3...3...7.*
009D0240  009DF348 7F752630 7F752720 7F752720  00000000 00000000 00000000 00000000  *.3.."..d{..q*
009D0260  7F752760 00000000 003B0008 77F7484C0  009D0198 00005548 009DF32 00005560  *."..-...d{...q.*
009D0280  00000000 009DAE68 009DAE68 00000000  00368100 009DF32 00000000 00000023  *......d..a.*
009D02A0  000079A0 00007D8C 00008000 00000000  00000000 00000000 00000000 04BE1060  *....'........-*
```

```
JOB EXA7JHMX        STEP APP3        TIME 125832    DATE 94100    ID = 000                    PAGE 00000036

009D02C0  00000000 00000000 0000034C 01830028  A0000000 00000000 00000000 80DF0BC2  *..........%......<.c........B*
009D02E0  C9C7C3F0 F9F0F5C1 E4E2C5D9 61D7D740  00000000 00000000 00000000 00000000  *IGC0905AUSER/PP.............*
009D0300  00000000 00000000 009D06D2 009D0300  04BE189A 009D041A F0F0F9C4 C6F9C3F4  *...........K...........00000000*
009D0320  3C600000 009D0320 009D0000 00001000  00001000 009D0320 00000070 00007838  *%-..........................*
009D0340  20FD0000 00000000 00000000 00079A0   00000660 009DD210 00000070 009D0354  *....................-.K......*
009D0360  C1C4F6F1 C9C7C3F0 F0F0F5C1 84BD9500  04BDA4FF 009CFFC0 009D0228 C9C5C1E5  *............d.n...u...(....IEAV*
009D0380  00000000 00000063 065D4040 007D0000  F061F9F2 40C8C2C2 F4F4F3F0 04BE6D86  *AD51IGC0005A06/10/92 HBB4430.._f*
009D03A0  00000000 40404040 F0F4F040 C6F0C6F4  40F0F0F9 C4F0F3C1 F040F0F0 F0F0F0F0  *.....) .'..*
009D03C0  40404040 40404040 C6F0F4F0 C6F0C6F4  C6F0F4F0 40C3F6C6 F0C3F6C6 F4404040  *...........*
          LINES 009D03E0-009D0440  SAME AS ABOVE
009D0460  40404040 40404040 40404040 40404040  40404040 40404040 40404040 40000000  *...........*
009D0480  D1D6C240 C5E7C1F7 D1C8D4E7 40404040  40404040 40E2E3C5 D740C1D7 D7F34040  *JOB EXA7JHMX    STEP APP3*
009D04A0  40404040 40404040 40404040 D4C540F1  F2F5F8F3 F2404040 C4C1E3C5 40F9F4F1  *TIME 125832    DATE 941*
009D04C0  F0F04040 4040C9C4 407E40F0 F0F00000  00000000 7F745000 00001000 00000000  *00    ID = 000*
009D04E0  00000000 00000000 00006908 7F671000  84BE67BE 009D0410 00F7F080 00000000  *.......&.*
009D0500  00000000 00000000 00006FF8 009DD3C8  009DD470 009DD410 009D0470 00000000  *....8....d....M..70..*
009D0520  00000000 009DD2C8 C9C5C1E5 C1C4F7F1  F0F0F5C1 F1F061F0 00F7F080 40C8C2C2  *...8.......LH..M....*
009D0540  F4F4F1F0 00000000 00000000 C9C7C3F0  F0F0F5C1 F1F061F0 00000000 7F749FB8  *.KHIEAVAD71IGC0005A10/07/89 HBB*
009D0560  8112ADE0 00F99460 00000000 00000000  009DF348 009D0622 009D05A4 9ECA0000  **4410.........u...*
009D0580  00B08000 00000000 00000000 04000000  40404040 40E2E3C5 D740C1D7 9ECA0000  *a..\.9m....3......u...*
009D05A0  00000000 019D05C8 009D0622 9ECA001C  5DDF0784 00D9C100 009DD470 009D0590  *.....&....d.RA...M....*
009D05C0  00000000 009D0590 04BDB4FE 00F24D90  00000000 00D9C100 009DD470 009D0590  *.....H....&..d.RA...M.*
009D05E0  00000000 00000000 00000000 00000000  00000001 C4C1E3C1 F8C24040 00000000  *.....2(....*
009D0600  00000000 00000000 E2E3C9D5 40404040  C7F44040 40404040 40404040 40404040  *.....*
009D0620  9FE0C5E7 C1F7D1C8 D44BD3C9 E2E3C9D5  40404040 4040804D AA160000 00000000  *\.EXA7JHM.LISTING4*
009D0640  40404040 40404040 40404040 40404040  00005E00 64000000 00800002 00000000  *..(......*
009D0660  0000BB60 00005400 0660007D 40404040  40404040 40000009E C4C1E3C1 F8C24040  *...-..'......*
009D0680  40404040 40005400 40404040 00000660  40400009E C3300000 0050000B 03B180CB  *.......DATA8B*
009D06A0  B8800000 40404040 0E3A80E4 51000000  0100009D F3480321 FD20009D 03B180CB  *....C..&..*
009D06C0  7ED000FD 50C800DF 0E3A80E4 51000000  0360009D 06FA00FD 06E0009C FC60009C  *....3.....*
009D06E0  ECB4009F F48C009D 0F3A0000 00000000  000080BF 60000000 00380019 3CE00000  *=}..&H...U......*
009D0700  800000DF 0E580000 0024009D 07320000  00007F73 E08009C3 00000000 00000000  *..4........*
009D0720  00000000 00000000 00000000 00000000  00000000 00000000 00000000 00000000  *......"..\..C.\....*
009D0740  00000000 00000000 00000000 00008510  1EF080BF 500080BF 50780000 00000000  *.....*
          LINE 009D0760  SAME AS ABOVE
009D0780  00000000 F2F3F4F5 F6F7F8F9 C1C2C3C4  C5C6F0F1 F2F3F4F5 F6F7F8F9 C1C2C3C4  *.........e..0..&......*
009D07A0  0000F0F1 F2F3F4F5 F6F7F8F9 C1C2C3C4  C5C6F0F1 F2F3F4F5 F6F7F8F9 C1C2C3C4  *..0123456789ABCDEF0123456789ABCD*
009D07C0  C5C6F0F1 F2F3F4F5 F6F7F8F9 C1C2C3C4  C5C6F0F1 F2F3F4F5 F6F7F8F9 C1C2C3C4  *EF0123456789ABCDEF0123456789ABCD*
```

```
        LINES 009D07E0-009D0880    SAME AS ABOVE
009D08A0 C5C60000 00000000 00000000 00000000 00000000 00000000    *EF..............*
009D08C0 00000000 00000000 00000000 00000000 00000000 00000000    *................*
        LINES 009D08E0-009D0980    SAME AS ABOVE
009D09A0 00000000 00000000 00008462 40010000 13A00000 400084C5    *.........d. .dE.*
009D09C0 00000000 00000000 00000000 00000000 A3580000 00008540C   *........e<t.....*
009D09E0 00000000 00000000 00008471 B0000000 00000000 00000000    *.......d........*
009D0A00 00000000 00000000 00000000 00000000 00000000 00000000    *................*
        LINES 009D0A20-009D0A40    SAME AS ABOVE
009D0A60 00000000 00000000 000000DF 07220000 00000000 00000000    *................*
009D0A80 00000000 00000000 00000000 00000000 00000000 00000000    *................*
        LINES 009D0AA0-009D0C60    SAME AS ABOVE
009D0C80 00004040 40404040 40400000 00000000 00000000 00000000    *................*
009D0CA0 00000000 00000000 00000000 00000000 00000000 00000000    *................*
        LINES 009D0CC0-009D0F00    SAME AS ABOVE
009D0F20 00000000 00000000 00000000 00000000 0000009D F0580000    *...............0*
009D0F40 00000000 00000000 0000790A 14000000 00000000 00000000    *................*
009D0F60 00000000 00000000 00000000 00000000 00000000 16000000    *................*
```

```
JOB EXA7JHMX        STEP APP3        TIME 125832    DATE 94100    ID = 000                    PAGE 00000037

009D0F80 7FFF5B30 009D036C 00000000 40010000 04BDB4B6 00000000    *...%...&.....%...*
009D0FA0 D006C108 04BDBF94 009D061C 05109C98 00000000 00000000    *)..A....m.....q..*
009D0FC0 00000000 40000000 00000000 00000000 00000000 00000000    *.... ...........*
009D0FE0 00000000 00000000 00000000 00000000 00000000 00000000    *................*
009D0D00 00111011 10000000 88030101 00000000 00000000 00000000    *................*
        LINES 009D0D020-009D0D040    SAME AS ABOVE
009D0D060 7FFF5B30 8106E90E 8106F300 00000001 00FD5000 01305E18   *..$.a.Z.a.3....K.........&..;.*
009D0D080 8106E85A 009FFA98 7FFF5B30 8106E90E 00000288 009DD2E0   *a.Y!..q".$.a.Z.a.3...h..K\..*
009D0D0A0 00FD5000 01305E18 8106E834 009FFA98 00000044 8106E702   *.&..;.a.Y...q"...a.X."..*
009D0D0C0 00FD8564 8106E33A C9C5C1E5 E3D9C6F4 012C005D 18000000   *..e.a.T.IEAVTRF4.).-...BT*
009D0D0E0 00111011 10000000 88030101 00000000 7FFFEF60 00000000   *.............h...*
009D0D100 00000000 00000000 00000000 00020003 00000000 00110002   *...............-.*
009D0D120 00000000 00000000 00000000 009DD274 009DD1F8 00BE34B8   *........K..J8.....*
009D0D140 070C2000 80FD511A 00000000 009FF7B0 009DD228 00DF0E97   *...K..J8.....p*
009D0D160 04BDB4FE 00000006 00000000 80DF0942 00000000 80DF0A2A   *...K...B...*
009D0D180 009DD1E0 009DD198 7FFFEF60 00000000 00DF0CC2 80DF511A   *.J\..Jq".-...*
009D0D1A0 00000005 00020003 00000000 00110002 14000000 078D0000   *................*
009D0D1C0 00000000 009FF7B0 009DD280 00005548 000079A4 00008000   *......7..K.....u..*
```

```
009DD1E0  04BE189A 009D0228 009DD470 00000000   FFFFFFE0 80DF074E 40DF033A 00005560  *.........M....\....-*
009DD200  009D02C0 00DF05D7 00000000 00000000   F8F9F2F7 009DD280 00005560 80DF0874  *...(..P......8927.K.....*
009DD220  00DF0318 009DD280 009D0228 009D0228   80DF0876 00000000 00000070 04BE189A  *...........K....+....*
009DD240  80DF085A 00000020 FFFFFFE0            80DF074E 009DD258 00000000 00000000  *...|.......\..+.K......*
009DD260  C9C5C1E5 C1C4F7F1 C9C7C3F0 F0F0F5C1   F1F061F0 F761F8F9 40C8C2C2 F4F4F1F0  *IEAVAD71IGC0005A10/07/89 HBB410*
009DD280  00005560 7F7472B0 00000000 84BE1440   04BE0F76 00000000 009D0228 FFFFFFE0  *...-"....d...8........K..*
009DD2A0  00000000 00000000 0000006B C1C4F0C1   009DD280 00000020 00000000 FFFFFFE0  *...........K..K....\.*
009DD2C0  009DD338 84BE11E2 C9C5C1E5            C9C7C3F0 F0F0F5C1 F9F3F1F4 F0404040  *...d..S.IEAVAD0AIGC0005A93140 *
009DD2E0  E4E8F9F4 F5F3F140 009DD308            00010001 00010001 F9F3F1F4 F0404040  *UY94531..lh.L....*
009DD300  80001110 0000CEF0 009F9398            C9C5C1E5 E3D9C6F4 0000CEF0 009DD2F8  *...0..lq..IEAVTRF4...0.K8*
009DD320  000110FC 312A0000 009DF0A8            00010001 00000000 00000010 00000001  *...0y.L....*
009DD340  80001SD8 09E03A28 009DF0E8            C9D6E2E5 C6D4E3E4 89E03A28 009DD338  *...0y.....IOSVFMTU..L.*
009DD360  000110FC 31220000 00000000            80001E50 09E011B0 00000010 00000001  *...Q.....0Y.....KY...8*
009DD380  00000000 40000000 00000000 80800040   0000D4E5 E2D9C5E2 E2E8E2F1 4BD4C9C7  *...........&.\..KY..MIG*
009DD3A0  D3C9C240 40404040 40404040 40404040   40404040 40404040 40404040 40404040  *LIB*
009DD3C0  40404040 00000000 009CFFC0            7F7472B0 84BE6D7C 84BE1958 84BE6C4C  *.........("...d_.@d...d.&.<*
009DD3E0  009DD228 00000022 04BDB4FE            00000007 7F748640 04BDA4FF 009DF348  *.........f..u...3.*
009DD400  7F751310 84BE67BE 009DD413            0000000B 7F748640 7F748640 00C9C5C1  *..".d...M.d....f.IEA*
009DD420  E5C1C4F0 F1C9C7C3 C1F9F3F1            F4F04040 40E4E8F9 F4F5F3F1 40000000  *VAD01IGC0005A93140  UY94531*
009DD440  009D0F32 F0F0F0F5 F0F0F3F4            009DF348 04000000 04BE72AF 80000000  *...K...00000034..3.....*
009DD460  04BE7190 00000000 F5F3F140            007D0000 40404040 40404040 40404040  *.........531 '..*
009DD480  40404040 40404040 40404040            40404040 40404040 40404040 40404040  *                 *
            LINES 009DD4A0-009DD4C0  SAME AS ABOVE
009DD4E0  40404040 40404040                    40404040 40404040 40404040 40000000  *                  *
009DD500  00000000 00000000 00000000 00000000   00000000 00000000 00000000 00000000  *                  *
009DD520  00000000 00000000 00000000 00000000   00000000 00270000 00000000 00000000  *                  *
009DD540  00000000 00000000 7FFE4020 00000000   00000000 00000000 00000000 00000000  *                  *
009DD560  00000000 0002002F 00000000 00000000   00110082 009DF0E8 078D0000 89E00F4A  *......".......b..0Y....i\.*
009DD580  00000000 009DF128 00000020 000069C4   00000040 009F1954 009F1930 009F9028  *........D.....*
009DD5A0  009D1FF8 000069D0 009FF060 809DF510   00000000 009F9028 00006908 00005F48  *....1....0--5.........*
009DD5C0  80FD5118 00000000 C1D7D7F3 D7C7D4F3   C1C3C6F2 D7D3D840 FF000A30 00000000  *..8....0-.5.....}APP3PGM3ACF2PLQ*
009DD5E0  00010040 00080000 009DD600 00000028   009DD718 009DE000 009DF7B8 00000000  *......O....P..\..7...*
009DD600  C1D7D7F3 E2E3C5D7 D3C9C240 D3C9C240   E2E3C5D7 4BD6B705 009DF020 009DF348  *APP3PGM1STEPLIB z.W.O...}...3.*
009DD620  00FF010  002C1004 C1D7D7F3 D7C7D4F2   E2E3C5D7 D3C9C240 A91BE664 518C6383  *.0....APP3PGM2STEPLIB z.W...c*
009DD640  009DF348 009DF020 00FD0000 002C7004   C1D7D7F3 D7C7D4F3 E2E3C5D7 D3C9C240  *.}...3....}....APP3PGM3STEPLIB*
009DD660  A91BE664 55C8EA02 009DF020 009DF348   009DF0E8 002C7004 C9D6E2E5 C6D4E3E8  *z.W.H..}...3...0Y...IOSVFMTY*
009DD680  D3C9D5D2 D3C9C240 A91BE667 C1639B85   009DD388 009DF348 C9D6E2E5 012E6090  *LINKLIB z.W.A..e..Lh..3..lh..-*
009DD6A0  C9D6E2E5 C6D4E3E4 D3C9D5D2 D3C9D5D2   A91BE667 CB316885 009DD388 009DF348  *IOSVFMTULINKLIB z.W...e..Lh..3.*
```

```
JOB EXA7JHMX           STEP APP3          TIME 125832    DATE 94100    ID = 000                      PAGE 00000038

009DD6C0  009DD348 012C6090 C9D6E2E5 C6D4E3E8   D3C9D5D2 D3C9C240 A91BE667 DD19C485   *..L...-.IOSVFMTYLINKLIB z.W...De*
009DD6E0  009DD388 009DF348 009DD368 012E6090   C9C5C1E5 E3D9D7F2 D3C9D5D2 D3C9C240   *..Lh..3...L...-.IEAVTRP2LINKLIB *
009DD700  A91BE667 FEC43481 009DD388 009DF348   009F9398 012E6090 C9C5C1E5 E3D9C6F4   *z.W..D.a.Lh..3...lq..-.IEAVTRF4*
009DD720  D3C9D5D2 D3C9C240 A91BE668 2A005683   009DD388 009DF348 009DD308 012C4090   *LINKLIB z.W...c..Lh..3...L... .*
009DD740  00000000 00000000 00000000 00000000   00000000 00000000 00000000 00000000   *................................*
         LINES 009DD760-009DDFE0  SAME AS ABOVE
```

Several control blocks appear in the next 4K of storage, including the following:

- 9DF008 LLE for program at C65950 (IGG019DJ, loaded for OPEN of SYSPRINT DD)
- 9DF0A8 LLE for program at D60548 (IGG019BB, loaded for OPEN of PDS DD)
- 9DF0B8 LLE for program at C88D38 (IGG019BA, loaded for OPEN of PDS DD)
- 9DF0C8 LLE for program at DAFA60 (within IGG0193B, loaded for OPEN of PDS DD)
- 9DF0D8 XTLST for APP3PGM8
- 9DF0E8 CDE for APP3PGM3
- 9DF128 TCB for APP3PGM3
- 9DF348 TCB for APP3PGM1
- 9DF510 TCT for APP3PGM1 TCB

The LLEs (Load List Elements) are normally identified by the CDE to which they point. However, since these are for common modules in the LPA, the CDEs aren't in the LSQA, and hence don't appear in this dump. The LLEs are formatted following the PRBs and SVRBs, but they aren't identified there. The method to associate these LLEs with specific program names is to locate the point at which they're loaded in the trace table. The appropriate LOAD macro entries (SVC 8) are discussed in the trace table section of the dump.

```
009DF000  00000000 00000000 00000000 009FE028   00110001 0000004C C4C5C2E3 00000000   *............<DEBT....*
009DF020  00000038 009DF038 009DF018 000000FF   009DF018 009DF018 00180010 009DB560   *...\....0...0...0....-.*
009DF040  009DEE74 009DE08C 00000000 00000000   7FFFEF60 00000000 80E45100 00000064   *.&.....dE.....&....d......*
009DF060  80BF5000 84C513A0 0000001F 0000018C   80BF5078 0000001F 84624000 000006CD   *.-.....$e.0....=)....e<t..n*
009DF080  80BF6000 85101EF0 0000005B 00000022   80CB7ED0 00000026 854CA358 00000195   *d........0..C...)...0H.L.*
009DF0A0  8471B000 009DF0B8 00000466 00BDC348   00220002 00005D28 009DF0C8 00BDD310   *.......E..0.............*
009DF0C0  00020002 009DC590 009DF008 00BE3058   00020002 00000010 00000010 00000001   *........................*
009DF0E0  80000070 09E00F30 009FD000 009DD568   C1D7D7F3 D7C7D4F3 89E00F30 009DF0D8   *.......}.N.APP3PGM3i\...0Q*
009DF100  000110FB 0B200000 00000000 00000000   00000000 00000000 00000000 00000000   *........................*
009DF120  00000000 00000000 00000000 009FF8A8   00000000 009D2000 00000000 00000000   *.................8y......*
009DF140  7F746550 80000000 8400FFFF 8400FFFF   009FD060 00000000 00000080 01C41BC4   *.&....d.......)-.....D.D*
009DF160  81263BAC 009DF502 009DF128 009DF8A8   80110000 00F7F080 80000000 01262B58   *a.....5..1..8y....70........*
009DF180  01263B58 00FD85A8 00000000 00000000   81263C88 80FE6EC4 00005F48 00000000   *aD.y..3....ey....a..h..>D.^*
009DF1A0  81C41BA8 009DF348 00000000 009DF348   00000000 00000000 00006E3C 009F91CC   *"1>U......9..5..........j.*
009DF1C0  7FF16EE4 00000000 009FF938 809DF510   7FF16EF4 00000000 00000000 20000000   *".>.......3..............2.*
009DF1E0  00FD6E48 009DF348 00000000 00000000   00000000 00000000 009DF280 00000000   *".....3.....................*
009DF200  7FFFCB18 00000000 00000000 00000000   00000000 00000000 00000040 00000000   *"........................*
009DF220  7F7512B0 00000000 E3C3C240 00000000   7FFE2E20 00000000 006FFFFF 00008000   *"......TCB........."1>4....*
009DF240  00000000 00000000 00000000 00000000   00000000 00000000 00000000 00000000   *"........................*
009DF260  7F743BC8 00000000 01078500 00005F90   00000003 00000000 00000000 00000000   *"...........H....e..^....*
009DF280  00000000 00000000 00000000 00000001   00000000 00000000 00000000 00000000   *"........................*
009DF2A0  7FFFED80 00000000 078D1000 00006B10   00040002 00000000 02000000 00040002   *"...................3..*
009DF2C0  00000000 00000000 00110082 009FF010   00000000 009D9000 00000000 009DF348   *"..................Y......*
009DF2E0  FD000012 00005FE8 00000040 009F1954   078D1000 00006B10 009F9028 009D1FF8   *".......b..0.......8.*
009DF300  009FF060 809DF510 00000000 009F9028   0E3492F2 00005F98 80E34FB4 009DF090   *".0-...5......T.2.^q.T!..0.*
009DF320  C1D7D7F3 D7C7D4F1 00000000 00000000   00000000 009D2000 940C2000 00000000   *APP3PGM1.......7....\...m....*
009DF340  00000000 00000000 00000000 009FF7B0   009DE08C 009DD308 00000000 009DD358   *"...R...........KY..)-.L...*
009DF360  7F72D958 80010000 00000FFF 009DD2E8   009DF060 009DD308 00000000 009DD358   *"......\...+.K...K....^q..1.*
009DF380  009D0228 80DF0876 00000000 00000065   04BE189A 80DF087C 00000020 00000000   *"......\...+.K...K....^q..1.*
009DF3A0  FFFFFFE0 80DF074E 009DD258 009DD280   009D0354 00005F98 009DF128 00000000   *"1>U".L...5...5.....0d......*
009DF3C0  00000000 009DF348 00000000 009F9028   009DF128 00000000 009FF084 20000000   *".>................4.....*
009DF3E0  7FF16EE4 7F72D3B8 009FF510 809DF510   00000000 00000000 009DF4A0 009F91CC   *"............."..........*
009DF400  00FD6E48 00FD6E48 00000000 00000000   00000002 00000000 009DF4A0 00000000   *"........................*
009DF420  7FFFCA78 009F9028 7F752090 00000000   00000000 80000000 80000041 7F7438FC   *"......TCB........."1>4....*
009DF440  7F751058 00000000 E3C3C240 00000000   7FF16EF4 7F746280 0005FFFF 08048000   *"......TCB........."1>4....*
009DF460  00000000 00000000 7FFE3E00 00000000   7FF16EF4 00000000 00000002 00000000   *"..A--...M.5...^\...........*
009DF480  7FFFC160 00000000 D4B7F500 00005FE0   00000003 00000000 00000000 00000000   *"..A--...M.5...^\...........*
009DF4A0  00000000 00000000 00000000 00000026   00000000 80000000 00000000 00000000   *........................*
009DF4C0  C5E7C1F7 D1C8D4E7 004746F6 0094100F   D6C1C3F1 64000000 00000000 01F802C6   *EXA7JHMX....6.m..OAC1......8.F*
009DF4E0  00000000 009DF4C0 004746FF 0094100F   00000000 0000F800 00000000 02000000   *.....4{...m....8.....*
```

```
009DF500 00005148 00005185 00000000                   *..........e....d......6...m.*
009DF520 FF000200 009DF4E4 009DF4C0                   *.....4U..4{.................*
009DF540 00000000 0047471E 00474724                   *...........................*
009DF560 00000000 00000000 00000000                   *...........................*
009DF580 00000000 00000000 7F77B600                   *..........................."*
009DF5A0 7F77C400 7F77C000 00000000                   *"..D......................."*
009DF5C0 009DF710 01C3B018 00000000                   *.7....C...................j..*
009DF5E0 E3C3E340 40404040 80000000                   *TCT.....................APP3 *
009DF600 00000000 00000000 0047471D                   *...........................*
009DF620 0094100F 7F776000 00FF1000                   *.m.."-.-...............&...*

                                                        PAGE 00000039

JOB EXA7JHMX      STEP APP3        TIME 125832   DATE 94100   ID = 000

009DF640 00000000 00000000 00000000 00000000          *...........................*
          LINE 009DF660 SAME AS ABOVE
009DF680 00000000 D1C5E2F2 7FFFC298 7F77C600          *....JES2".Bq".F..*
009DF6A0 7F77C800 A91B E664 37C7D180 00010000          *."."."...z.W.GJ..*
009DF6C0 00000000 00000000 00000000 00000000          *...........................*
009DF6E0 00038000 00005000 009FB000 76200000 00000400 *....&...........*
009DF700 00000000 00000000 00F15948 40DAF810          *..........1...8..*
009DF720 00000000 009DF348 00F24D90 009DE08C          *....3.....IQ....1..*
009DF740 00F24D90 00F15A2C 00DAE00E C1C3E4C3 C2C3D6D4 *.2(.1!.....\.7.2(..\.ACUCBCOM*
009DF760 FF0008A8 009E1A74 00000000 00000000          *...y...........\.ACUCBCOM*
009DF780 00000000 00000000 00000000 00000000          *...........................*
009DF7A0 00000000 00000000 C1C3E4C3 C2404040 02000047 *..............ACUCB........*
009DF7C0 C5E7C1F7 D1C8D440 009DFB58 00000000          *.m..EXA7JHM.................*
009DF7E0 471A0094 100FD6C1 C3F1C5E7 471A0094 100F4040 *....m.OAC1EXA7JHMX....m....*
009DF800 4040D1D6 C2F0F8F3 D4F1C1D7 D7F34040 4040C4E2 D7D3F0C6 *..JOB0839IAPP3PGM1APP3  DSPL0F*
009DF820 C4C20000 40404040 F9F1C1D7 D7F3D7C7 FFFFFFFF 02000000 *DB.........  .............*
009DF840 00000000 00000000 D1C8D44B D7C4E24B D3D6C1C4 *.........EXA7JHM.PDS.LOAD*
009DF860 40404040 40404040 40404040 C4C1E3C1          *............DATA*
009DF880 F8C24040 C5E7C1F7 D1C8D44B D7C4E24B C4C1E3C1 40404040 *8B  EXA7JHM.PDS.LOAD     DATA*
009DF8A0 40404040 C4C1E3C1 F8C24040 C9D5C9E3 40404040 *....DATA8B  INIT     *
009DF8C0 40404040 40404040 40404040 40404040          *...........................*
009DF8E0 40404040 40404040 40404040 40404040          *...........................*
009DF900 00000000 00000000 00000000 00000000          *...........................*
009DF920 00000000 00000000 00000000 00000000          *...........................*
     LINES 009DF940-009DFA40  SAME AS ABOVE
```

```
009DFA60  00000000 00000000 40404040 40404040  40404040 40404040 40404040 40404040  *................                *
009DFA80  40404040 40404040 40404040 40404040  40404040 E2E8E2F1 4BD3C9D5 D2D3C9C2  *                    SYS1.LINKLIB*
009DFAA0  40404040 40404040 40404040 40404040  40404040 40404040 40404040 40404040  *                                *
009DFAC0  40404040 40404040 C9D5C9E3 40404040  40404040 40404040 40404040 40404040  *        INIT                    *
009DFAE0  00000000 009F9028 00000000 00000000  000003A0 00000000 00000000 009DD5D0  *..............................N}*
009DFB00  00000000 009FD020 00000000 00000000  00000000 00000000 00000000 00000000  *....)...........................*
009DFB20  00000000 00000000 00000000 00000000  00000000 C5E7C1F7 D1C8D440 00000000  *....................EXA7JHM ....*
009DFB40  00000000 00000000 00000000 40D4E4D9  D7C8E840 40404040 F5F4F0F2 F3404040  *............ MURPHY     54023   *
009DFB60  0001103C D1D6E2C5 D7C840C8 40D4E4D9  A8F726E2 DBDB8505 D6C1C3C3 D4C4F0F1  *....JOSEPH H MURy7.S..e.OACCMD01*
009DFB80  40404040 A91BE324 3F690405 00000000  0045F257 00000239 C5E7C1F7 D1C8D440  *    z.T..........2....EXA7JHM   *
009DFBA0  0000000C 00000000 40404040 0094100F  0000000C C5E7C1F7 D1C8D440 00000000  *............m.......EXA7JHM ....*
009DFBC0  00000000 C5E7C1F7 D1C8D440 40404040  00000037 16627123 E4E2C5D9 C5404040  *....EXA7JHM ..........m...2.....*
009DFBE0  40404040 40404040 40404040 40404040  40404040 40404040 40404040 40404040  *                                *
009DFC00  40404040 5BC4C5C6 40404040 40404040  40404040 E4E2C5D9 C5404040 00000000  *    $DEF           USERE .......*
009DFC20  40404040 C5E7C1F7 D1C8D400 40404040  40404040 40404040 0000000F 00000000  *    EXA7JHM.                .....*
009DFC40  C5E7C1F7 D1C8D440 C5E7C1F7 D1C8D440  40404040 40404040 40404040 40404040  *EXA7JHM EXA7JHM                 *
009DFC60  00000000 00000000 00000000 00000000  40404040 40404040 40404040 C5404040  *........................    E   *
009DFC80  00000000 BF3AC4F5 4CA3F9D4 00000000  00000000 E4E2C5D9 C5404040 C54040C1  *....D5<t9M..........USERE E  A  *
009DFCA0  D9400000 00299CBC 0000C15C F2404040  C8D44040 8C000000 0094152C 00000FA0  *R .......A*2   HM .....m........*
009DFCC0  00000000 00000CE4 40404040 00000000  00000000 00000000 00000000 0000000C  * U ............................*
009DFCE0  00000000 00000000 00000000 00000000  00000000 00000000 00000000 00000000  *................................*
009DFD00  40404040 00000000 00000000 00000000  00000000 00000000 00000000 0000000C  *                ................*
009DFD20  00000000 00000000 00000000 00000000  00000000 00000000 00000000 00000000  *................................*
009DFD40  00000000 00000000 C4E2D7D3 F0C6C4C2  00000000 00000000 00000000 00000000  *........DSPL0FDB................*
009DFD60  00000000 00000000 00000000 00000000  00000000 00000000 00000000 00000000  *................................*
009DFD80  0000000C 00000000 00000000 00000000  00000000 00000000 00000000 00000000  *................................*
009DFDA0  00000000 00000000 C4E2D7D3 F0C6F8F8  0023AEF1 40404040 00000000 00000000  *........DSPL0F88...1            *
009DFDC0  00000000 00000000 00000000 00000000  00000000 00000000 00000000 00000000  *................................*
        LINES 009DFDE0-009DFF20  SAME AS ABOVE
009DFF40  40404040 40404040 00000000 00000000  00000000 C5E7C1F7 D1C8D440 00000000  *                   EXA7JHM      *
009DFF60  40404040 40404040 00000000 00000000  00000000 00000000 00000000 00000000  *                                *
009DFF80  00000000 00000000 00000000 00000000  00000000 00000000 00000000 00000000  *................................*
        LINES 009DFFA0-009DFFE0  SAME AS ABOVE
```

JOB EXA7JHMX   STEP APP3   TIME 125832   DATE 94100   ID = 000   PAGE 00000040

The next 4K segment of LSQA contains the following control blocks:

- 9F9028 TCB for IEFIIC (The initiator)
- 9F91CC Job Step Control Block (JSCB)
- 9F91D0 Accessor Environment Element (ACEE)

I haven't discussed the last two control blocks in the text. The JSCB contains pointers to a number of other control blocks, notably the Job Control Table (JCT). Its mapping macro is IEZJSCB. The ACEE is an RACF interface control block, and its mapping macro is IHAACEE. ACEE contains a number of other fields of interest, such as ACEEUSER, the user ID associated with the address space. I'll leave it up to you to research this control block.

```
009F9000  809F9004 00000000 00000000 00000000   00000000 00000000 00000000 00000000   *................*
009F9020  00000000 00000000 009FD1B8 00000000   009E023C 009E4000 00000000 00000000   *..........J.....*
009F9040  7F72DEB0 80000000 0400FFFF 00000000   00000000 00000000 00000001 FF600F88   *"............-.h*
009F9060  009F1B30 7FFE59B0 009F1930 80B9A7BC   009F0718 009F1B30 00000000 809DF510   *"....x...0-....5.*
009F9080  009F0718 009F0718 00E35820 009FDE88   80E352BE 809FD1B8 00000000 009DF348   *.0d....T....T..3.*
009F90A0  00000000 009F9028 00000000 009FDE88   009DF348 00000000 009FFFAC 00000000   *........h.3.....*
009F90C0  7FF16EE4 7F751958 009FF570 809DF510   7FFFC250 00000000 00000000 009FD01C   *1>U"..5...5."B&..).*
009F90E0  00FD6E48 00000000 00000000 00000000   00000000 00000000 009F9180 00000000   *.>......j.......*
009F9100  7FFFEE20 009FDE88 00000000 00000000   00000000 00000041 00000000 00000000   *"....h..........*
009F9120  7FFE2730 00000000 E3C3C240 00000000   7FFE2790 0004FFFF 00048000 00000000   *"......TCB......*
009F9140  7FFFC2E8 00000017 7FFE3E00 00005FF0   7FF16EF4 7F751340 00000000 00000000   *"BY..."1>4"......*
009F9160  00000000 00000000 46693CC0 00003D23   00000003 00000000 00000000 00000000   *.......(.^0....j)*
009F9180  00000000 00000000 00000000 00000000   009F91C0 009F9028 01C3B018 009F1930   *..........jD.j(...C*
009F91A0  009F91BC 009F91B4 009F91B8 009F91C4   C1C3C5C5 FF0000B8 02000000 009DF7B8   *.j.j.j.jD..ACEE.....*
009F91C0  009EDF00 D1D6C2F0 F8F3F9F1 55555555   C1C3C5C5 FF0000B8 02000000 009DF7B8   *..JOB08391..ACEE*
009F91E0  00000000 009FDF38 00000000 00010000   00000000 00000000 03210000 00000000   *.....0.....x....0.*
009F9200  00000000 00010000 00010000 00B9A780   00EDEF00 00000000 00000000 00000000   *................*
009F9220  00000000 00000000 00000000 42000000   00000000 009EDFB0 00000000 00000000   *................*
009F9240  00000000 00000000 009F0F00 009F9FE0   00000000 009EDD70 009D1FE0 00000000   *..........\...../*
009F9260  00000000 000400ED 009F91CC 00000000   00000000 C1D7D7F3 D7C7D4F1 00000000   *.....j.......APP3PGM1...*
009F9280  00FAFBF4 00000000 C4C5C2E3 00000000   00000038 009F9368 009F9348 00000000   *....4....DEBT......l.*
009F92A0  009F9348 009F9348 00180008 009E023C   00010001 C6D4E3E8 009DD348 00000000   *...l..l...l..l.....*
009F92C0  009F9390 00BDA318 009DD328 009F9398   000110FC 31220000 000000C8 009F93C4   *..l..t..L..lq....FMTY.L....*
009F93A0  C9C5C1E5 E3D9D7F2 89E011B0 89DD7F2    00110001 ........ ........ ........   *IEAVTRP2i\...L......H..1D*
```

```
009F93C0  00000000 84000321 00F7F080 009DF348   00000000 009F93E4 00000000 00000000   *..d...70...3.....1U.......*
009F93E0  00000000 FF030100 009F93F0 009F93F8   E2E8E2C9 C5C1F0F1 C9C5C100 00000000   *........10..18SYSIEA01IEA.....*
009F9400  00000000 00000000 00000000 00000000   84C61412 84C63000 009DB000 009DAEC4   *..........Z."T8..dF..dF.....D*
009F9420  00000000 7F73E928 7F73E3F8 00000000   84C60060 7F752090 04C6105E 00FD50C8   *.F.;.W...D.F.^dF.-"...F.;.&H*
009F9440  04C6205E 4080E610 009DAEC4 04C6105F   84C60060 00000000 00000050 00000000   *.Z."T8..D.F.^dF.-"....*
009F9460  00FC8BB8 7F73E3F8 7F73E3F8 00FFFFFF   0000002C 00000000 00000040 00000070   *.....&.....*
009F9480  FF0000B0 00000060 00000018 00000030   00F24D90 01004800 00000004 00000000   *......-.....2(....*
009F94A0  00000054 00000090 00000000 00000000   00F24D90 01000000 00000000 00000000   *...E........2(....*
009F94C0  000000C5 00000000 00000000 00000000   00F24D90 01000660 000000AD 00000000   *...E........2(..-....*
009F94E0  00000000 00000000 00000000 00000000   00F24D90 01002260 00000002 00000000   *..1.........2(..-....*
009F9500  00000B93 00000000 00000000 00000000   E2E2C1E3 009F9580 0000000F 0000001F   *..........SSAT.n.".....*
009F9520  0000001D 00000000 00000000 00000000   7FFD3000 00000000 00000000 00000000   *............"...*
009F9540  00000000 00000000 00000000 00000000   00000000 00000000 00000000 00000000   *...............*
009F9560  00000000 00000000 0000001F 00000000   00000000 00000000 00000000 00000000   *...............*
009F9580  E2E2C1E3 00000000 00000000 0000001F   00000000 00000000 00000000 00000000   *SSAT...........*
009F95A0  00000000 00000000 00000000 00000000   00000000 00000000 00000000 00000000   *...............*
009F95C0  00000000 00020000 00000000 00000028   C1C3C6F2 D7D3D840 FF000A30 00000000   *...........ACF2PLQ .......*
009F95E0  00010040 00020000 009F9600 00000028   009F9628 009FA000 009D7D98 00000000   *..........o...o....Nq..*
009F9600  C1C3C6D9 D1C5E2F2 D3C9D5D2 D3C9C240   A91B9A80 90BAEC01 009FD2E0 009FDE88   *ACFRJES2LINKLIB z...K\..h*
009F9620  009FFFE0 012C0090 C1C3C6E4 D1C5E2F2   D3C9D5D2 D3C9C240 A91B9A91 ECDEBA84   *........ACFUJES2LINKLIB z..j..d*
009F9640  009FD2E0 009FDE88 009FF010 012C0090   00000000 00000000 00000000 00000000   *.K\..h..0..............*
009F9660  00000000 00000000 00000000 00000000   00000000 00000000 00000000 00000000   *...............*

          LINES 009F9680-009F9FE0   SAME AS ABOVE
```

The next 4K segment of LSQA contains the following control blocks:

- 9FD000 CDE for APP3PGM2
- 9FDE88 TCB for IEFSD060

```
009FD000  009FF010 00000000 C1D7D7F3 D7C7D4F2   89E00FA0 009FE130 000110FB 03200000   *.O.....APP3PGM2i\........*
009FD020  009DD388 40004040 0000C4C1 E3C1F8C2   C5E7C1F7 D1C8D44B D7C4E24B D3D6C1C4   *.Lh .....DATA8BEXA7JHM.PDS.LOAD*
009FD040  40404040 40404040 40404040 40404040   40404040 40404040 40404040 40404040   *................*
009FD060  00000000 00000000 00000000 00F1D076   002E0000 00000001 00000200 00000001   *..........1)....*
009FD080  02000001 C0000000 018D0008 009E023C   1200D008 D1C5E2F2 009FE240 009FDE00   *...}....}.....}.JES2.K...*
009FD0A0  009FD1B8 009FFD78 009FF8A8 009FD0B0   009FD0B4 009FD0B8 009FD0BC 009FD0C0   *..J...}..8y..}..}..}{*
009FD0C0  009FDCC4 009FD0D4 009FD0D0 009FDE88   009FD0B4 009FD0DC 009FD0D0 00000000   *.}D..}H..}}..}M....*
009FD0E0  00000000 00000000 00000000 00000000   00000000 009F9368 00000000 00000000   *..........h...l....*
```

```
009FD100  00000000 01000000 00000000 00000000   009FB940 00000000 00000000 00B92080   *................*
009FD120  009F6EF0 00000000 03210000 00000000   00000000 00000000 00000000 42000000   *.>0.....?......\*
009FD140  009F6FB0 00000000 009E3FE0 00000000   00000000 000000EC 009FD3FC 009EBFE0   *...........L...\*
009FD160  00000000 00000000 009E3FE0 00000000   00000000 000000EC 009F91CC 00000000   *...........X...j*
009FD180  00000000 C9C5C6C9 C9C34040 00000000   00FAE7B4 7FFFEE20 00000000 00000080   *IEFIIC..........*
009FD1A0  00000000 00000000 00000000 00000000   42800002 00020001 FD000000 00000000   *..............^8*
009FD1C0  00110083 00BD93F0 070C1000 80E35958   00000000 019F9028 FD000008 00005FF8   *.c.10...T.....^8*
009FD1E0  00000040 009FB86C 009FB848 00005FA8   009E3FF8 FD000000 009FFF88 809F92E8   *.&...h..8...h.kY*
009FD200  00000040 009FDE88 00E349F2 00005FA8   80E34FB4 009FFFB8 C9C5C6C9 C9C34040   *.h.T.2..y.T!...IEFIIC*
009FD220  7FFFEC40 00000080 00000000 00000000   80E34FB4 42800000 42800001 00000000   *"...............*
009FD240  00000000 00000000 00110003 00BD5C00   070C1000 80E35958 00000000 019FD480   *...*....T....M.*
009FD260  00000028 009FCB94 809FF030 809FF0D8   00000002 00B92080 00000028 0000000C   *.......0Q....0&*
009FD280  009FFD08 009FF030 009FCAA8 00E3F02C   00E3FCE4 009FCB98 00000028 009FCBB0   *.m....0Q..y.T0.T.U..q*
009FD2A0  C9C5C6E2 C4F0F6F0 C4C5C2E3 00180004   00000038 009FD2C8 000000FF 009FD2A8   *IEFSD060DEBT....KH...Ky*
009FD2C0  009FD2A8 009FD2A8 808000C0 0000D4E5   E2E8E2F1 4BC6D6D6 D3C9D5D2 40404040   *Ky..Ky....(.MVSYS9SYS1.FOOLINK*
009FD2E0  00000000 00000000 40404040 40404040   40404040 40404040 40404040 40404040   *................*
009FD300  40404040 40404040 40404040 40404040   40404040 40404040 40404040 00000000   *................*
009FD320  00000000 00000000 00000000 00000000   00000000 009FDE88 00000000 009FD2C8   *.............h....KH*
009FD340  00000000 00000000 00000000 00000000   00000000 00000000 00000000 009FBFD8   *.............Q...*
009FD360  00000000 00B92080 00000000 00000000   03210000 00000000 00000000 00000000   *................*
009FD380  40000000 00000000 00000000 00000000   009F4FE0 00000000 00000000 000000ED   *................*
009FD3A0  009FD3FC 009F5FE0 00000000 009FBE58   00000000 00000000 00FAE7B4 00000000   *.}....L.....x...*
009FD3C0  009FD01C 00000000 00000000 009FD3FC   00000000 00000000 00FAE7B4 00000000   *.}....L.....x...*
009FD3E0  E2E2D6C2 001C0000 009FD3FC 00000000   00000000 00000000 00000000 E2E2C9C2   *SSOB..L.....SSIB*
009FD400  00240002 D1C5E2F2 E2E3C3F0 F6F7F4F2   00000000 00000000 00000000 09BE6B50   *...JES2STC06742...&*
009FD420  E2E2D6C2 001C000F 009FD43C 00000000   009FCB18 00000000 00000000 E2E2C9C2   *SSOB..M.....SSIB*
009FD440  00240002 D1C5E2F2 D1C5E2F2 40404040   00000000 00000000 00000000 00020006   *...JES2JES2*
009FD460  7FFFEB00 00000000 00000000 00000000   00000000 02000000 00000000 009FDE88   *"...............*
009FD480  00000000 00000000 00110082 00BD9FA8   070C1000 80E3F706 00000000 00F7F080   *........b..y...h*
009FD4A0  00000000 00F7F080 00000000 009FE524   00000000 8494808C 84948026 00F7F080   *.......70....T7..*
009FD4C0  00000000 00000000 00000000 00000000   00000017 00000000 04948AA0 009FE4D0   *....V...dm..dm..70.*
009FD4E0  C9C5C5D7 D9E6C9F2 50018051 55555555   B7BDB786 83B31515 55555555 55555555   *IEEPRWI2&......fc...*
009FD500  55555555 55555555 55555555 55555555   55555555 55555555 C1C3E4C3 C2C3D6D4   *...........ACUCBCOM*
009FD520  55555555 55555555 9C809CB6 15151515   55555555 55555555 C1C3E4C3 C2C3D6D4   *.y..........ACUCB*
009FD540  FF0008A8 00000000 00000000 009FAA74   00000000 00000000 00000000 00000000   *...........*
009FD560  00000000 00000000 00000000 00000000   00000000 00000000 00000000 00000000   *................*
009FD580  00000000 00000000 00000000 40404040   C1C3E4C3 C2404040 C2404040 40404040   *...........ACUCB*
009FD5A0  31890094 100FD6C1 C9D5C9E3 C9E34040   009FDD38 009FD938 31890094 02000028   *.i.m.OAC1INIT...R...*
009FD5C0  31890094 100FD6C1 C3F1C9D5 C9E34040   4040C9C5 40400028 100F4040 40404040   *.i.m.OAC1INIT...i.m.*
009FD5E0  4040E2E3 C3F0F6F7 F4F2C9C5 C6C9C9C3   4040C9C5 C6C9C9C3 C6D7D9D6 C3400000   *STC06742IEFIIC IEFPROC*
```

```
009FD600  00000000 00000000 00000000 FFFFFFFF   00000000 00000000 40404040 40404040   00000000 00000000   *................*  *................*
009FD620  00000000 00000000 00000000 00000000   00000000 00000000 00000000 00000000   00000000 00000000   *................*  *................*
          LINE 009FD640   SAME AS ABOVE
009FD660  00000000 E2E8E2F1 4BD3C9D5 4BD3C9C2   D2D3C9C2 40404040 40404040 40404040   40404040 40404040   *....SYS1.LINKLIB*  *................*
009FD680  40404040 40404040 40404040 C9D5C9E3   40404040 40404040 40404040 40404040   40404040 C9D5C9E3   *        INIT    *  *................*
009FD6A0  40404040 40404040 40404040 40404040   40404040 40404040 40404040 40404040   40404040 40404040   *                *  *................*
009FD6C0  40404040 40404040 40404040 40404040   40404040 40404040 40404040 40404040   40404040 40404040   *                *  *................*
009FD6E0  00000000 00000000 00000000 00000000   00000000 00000000 00000000 00000000   00000000 00000000   *................*  *................*
009FD700  00000000 00000000 00000000 00000000   00000000 00000000 00000000 00000000   00000000 00000000   *................*  *................*
```

JOB EXA7JHMX   STEP APP3   TIME 125832   DATE 94100   ID = 000   PAGE 00000042

```
          LINES 009FD720-009FD820   SAME AS ABOVE
009FD840  00000000 40404040 40404040 40404040   40404040 40404040 E2E8E2F1 4BD3C9D5   D2D3C9C2 40404040   *....        SYS1.LINKLIB*
009FD860  40404040 40404040 40404040 40404040   40404040 E2E8E2F1 4BD3C9D5 D2D3C9C2   40404040 40404040   *        SYS1.LINKLIB*
009FD880  40404040 40404040 40404040 C9D5C9E3   40404040 40404040 40404040 40404040   00000000 00000000   *        INIT    *
009FD8A0  00000000 40404040 C9D5C9E3 40404040   00000000 00000000 00000000 00000000   00000000 00000000   *....INIT........*
009FD8C0  00000000 00000000 00000000 00000000   00000000 00000000 009F95D0 00000000   00000000 00000000   *..............n}*
009FD8E0  009FDE88 00000000 000003A0 00000000   00000000 00000000 00000000 00000000   00000000 00000000   *.K\..h..........*
009FD900  00000000 00000000 00000000 00000000   00000000 00000000 00000000 00000000   00000000 00000000   *................*
009FD920  00000000 00000000 00000000 00000000   C9D5C9E3 C9D5C9E3 40404040 40404040   00000000 00000000   *........INIT....*  *....INIT........*
009FD940  00004100 C9D5C9E3 C9C1E3D6 D9404040   E7F5F7F4 F2F44040 E7F5F7F4 F2F44040   00000000 00000000   *....INITIATOR   *  *....INIT........*
                                                                                                          *X57424*
009FD960  40404040 A91B9A80 87D12F04 40404040   40404040 40404040 40404040 40404040   00000000 00000000   *z..gJ...........*
009FD980  0000000C 40404040 00000000 0094100F   0000000C 00000000 00000000 00000000   00000000 00000000   *................*
009FD9A0  00000000 C9D5C9E3 40404040 40404040   0001F9E6 40404040 40404040 40404040   00000000 00000000   *....INIT  .m...i..9W*
009FD9C0  40404040 40404040 40404040 40404040   40404040 40404040 40404040 40404040   00000000 00000000   *                *
009FD9E0  40404040 40404040 40404040 00000000   00200103 E2E8E240 E2E8E240 00000000   00000000 0000000C   *............SYS SYS*
009FDA00  40404040 40404040 40404040 40404040   40404040 40404040 40404040 40404040   00000000 40404000   *            ....SYS*
009FDA20  C9D5C9E3 40404040 40404040 40404040   40404040 40404040 40404040 40404040   00000000 00000000   *INIT        *
009FDA40  40404040 40404040 40404040 40404040   E2E8E240 E2E8E240 40404040 40404040   00000000 00000000   *....        SYS*
009FDA60  40404040 40404040 00000000 40404040   00000000 00000000 00000000 0000000C   00000000 00000000   *....            SYS*
009FDA80  40404000 00000000 00000000 F9F9F0F4   00000000 00000000 00000000 00000000   00000000 00000000   *.        9904....*
009FDAA0  00000000 00000000 00000000 00000000   00000000 00000000 00000000 00000000   00000000 0000000C   *................*
009FDAC0  40404040 40404040 40404040 00000000   00000000 00000000 00000000 00000000   00000000 00000000   *................*
009FDAE0  00000000 00000000 00000000 0000000C   00000000 00000000 00000000 00000000   00000000 00000000   *................*
009FDB00  00000000 00000000 00000000 00000000   00000000 00000000 00000000 00000000   00000000 00000000   *................*
009FDB20  00000000 00000000 00000000 00000000   00000000 00000000 00000000 00000000   00000000 00000000   *................*
          LINES 009FDB40-009FDB60   SAME AS ABOVE
```

```
009FDB80  00000000 00000000 00000000 00000000   00000000 40404040 40404040 00000000  *................*
009FDBA0  00000000 00000000 00000000 00000000   00000000 00000000 C9D5C9E3 40404040  *............INIT    *
          LINES 009FDBC0-009FDD00  SAME AS ABOVE
009FDD20  00000000 40404040 40404040 40404040   00000000 00000000 00000000 40404040  *................*
009FDD40  40404040 40404040 40404040 40404040   00000000 00000000 00000000 00000000  *................*
009FDD60  00000000 00000000 00000000 00000000   00000000 00000000 00000000 00000000  *................*
          LINES 009FDD80-009FDDC0  SAME AS ABOVE
009FDDE0  7FFFECE0 00000000 00000000 00000000   00000000 00000000 46800001 00020078  *".\.............*
009FDE00  00000000 00000000 00110082 00BD4030   070C2000 84BF533E 00000000 019FF158  *......b...d....1.*
009FDE20  00000000 00000000 00000000 00F7F0D4   00000000 84948026 84948026 00F7F080  *......70M..dm..dm..70.*
009FDE40  00000000 00000000 00000000 00000000   00000017 00000000 04948AA8 009FE4D0  *...........m.y..U)*
009FDE60  C9C5C1E5 E3E2C4E3 00000000 009FD240   00000000 00000000 00000000 40000000  *IEAVTSDT...K......*
009FDE80  00000000 00000000 009FD240 00000000   00000000 009F5000 00000000 40000000  *...........&....*
009FDEA0  00000080 0400FFFF 00000000 00000000   00000000 00000001 FF600060 FF600060  *1.{.........K...-.-*
009FDEC0  7FFE5A70 009FBA48 80B920BC 009FC438   009FFF88 009FBA48 809F92E8 809F92E8  *...".!....h.....kY*
009FDEE0  009FFFAC 009FC438 0E35820 009FE240    80E352BE 809FD240 009F9028 009FC438   *....D.T...D.T...K...*
009FDF00  00000000 009FDE88 009FF158 009FF5A0   009F9028 00000000 009FE524 009FD264  *....h..l..S.....V.*
009FDF20  7FF16EE4 7FFE24A8 009FF5A0 00000000   7FFFC500 00000000 00000000 009FDFE0  *1>U".y.5.....E.....K.*
009FDF40  009F9530 00000000 00000000 00000000   00000000 00000000 00000000 00000044  *.n...........\..>*
009FDF60  7FFFEC40 009FF158 00000000 E3C3C240   00000000 00000000 7FFE20B8 0003FFFF  *...1............*
009FDF80  7FFE24D8 00000000 E3C3C240 00000000   7FFE20B8 7FFE26E8 00000000 00048000  *..Q...TCB......"*
009FDFA0  00000000 00000000 7FFFE3E0 00000000   7FF16EF4 7FFE26E8 00000000 00000000  *...".....1>4".Y.*
009FDFC0  7FFFC728 00000000 0BEEA96F 00000000   00000003 00000000 00000000 00000000  *..G.....z?.........*
009FDFE0  00000000 00000000 00000000 0000001F   00000000 00000000 00000000 00000000  *................*
```

The next 4K segment of LSQA contains the following control blocks:

- 9FE008 CDE for BRUINS (a minor CDE)
- 9FE028 LLE for APP3PGM2
- 9FE038 ASXB
- 9FE130 XTLST for APP3PGM2
- 9FE168 ACEE for initiator
- 9FE240 TCB for the Region Control Task

```
009FE000  FF000038 00000018 00000000 009DF2C0  C2D9E4C9 D5E24040 00006A2E 009FF010  *........2(BRUINS  ........0.*
009FE020  000050FB 37000000 00000000 009FD000  C1E2E7C2 009FE598 00010000 009FE240  *...&......).....ASXB..S.*
009FE040  009DF128 00060000 00000000 00000000  00F24D90 0FCCA2C0 009FE598 00FEE114  *..1........R...2(....Vq..*
009FE060  F49DC9E0 009DE08C 8F9DAE68 00FED9EA  00FEE876 00000100 0FCCAA00 00FEE05C  *4.I\.\......R....2(....*
009FE080  00F7F080 0FCCC900 000C0C80 009FFD5C  809FDE00 00000000 7FFFD218 00000000  *.70..I....\*.Y...S....-.*
009FE0A0  8100F962 00000000 009FEA68 00000000  809FDE00 809FDE8B 009FE3D8 009FE240  *a.9........U....K....TQ..S.*
009FE0C0  00000000 00000000 00000000 00000000  00000000 C5E7C1F7 D1C8D400 00000000  *..........EXA7JHM.*
009FE0E0  009F91D0 7FFFCE38 0000077D 00000000  00000000 00000060 80000060 09E00FA0  *..j).....,.....)-.....)-....*
009FE100  009F91D0 00000000 00000001 00000000  00000010 00000001 80000060 09E00FA0  *..j)..........-.\.*
009FE120  00000000 00000000 809FD060 809FDE00  00000000 80000060 09E00FA0 009FCB2C  *......)-.....-.\..^U..*
009FE140  00280070 009FF030 00B6E000 009FFE04  009FFDB8 009FD3E0 00005FE4 009FCB2C  *....0..\....0Q..L\..^U..*
009FE160  00000000 00BAB1E8 C1C3C5C5 00000000  00000000 00000000 00000000 00000000  *....YACEE.............*
009FE220  00000000 009FFD78 00000000 00B6E000  00000000 00000000 00000000 00000080  *....................*
009FE240  00000000 0400FFFF 00000000 00F7F080  FF601AE4 009FE480 0FD50C8  009FE51C  *..........\.......-..U..U...&H*
009FE260  00000000 009FE240 84948BE6 00F7F080  849480B0 0109B458 7FF16F04 009FE240  *.S....dm...70....dm....V.*
009FE280  84948B90 009FE480 84948BE6 809FFD78  009FF158 00000000 7FF16F04 7FF16748  *dm...U.dm.W....1...S....*
009FE2A0  00000000 009FDE88 00000000 00000000  00000000 00000000 00FD6E48 00000000  *.....h..........."!?."!..*
009FE2C0  009FE660 00000000 00000000 00000000  009FFE04 00000000 7FFFEBA0 00000000  *...6-.............>...*
009FE2E0  00000000 00000000 00000000 00000000  009FE398 00000044 00000000 00000000  *..............Tq......".*
009FE300  00000000 00000000 00000000 00000000  00000000 00000000 00000000 00000000  *..............................*
009FE320  E3C3C240 00000000 00000000 7FF16718  00100000 00080000 00000000 00000000  *TCB......."1........L...*
009FE340  00000000 00000000 7FF16F14 7FF16778  00000000 7FFFD318 00000000 00000000  *....."1?."1..........*
009FE360  00000000 00000000 00000000 00000000  00000000 00000000 00000000 00000000  *..........................*
009FE380  008F4280 00000003 00000000 00000000  00000000 7FFFE9C0 00000000 00000000  *................z{.......*
009FE3A0  00000000 00000000 00000000 00000000  C9C7C5F0 F0F0F1C5 00000000 00000000  *...........................*
009FE3C0  00198000 80FF0FC9 070C0000 89D3B5D8  009FFD78 00000001 FF601AE4 00000000  *.........I..iL.Q.......-U*
009FE3E0  009FE480 00FD50C8 009FE240 809FFD78  84948026 00F7F080 849480B0 00000000  *.U..&H..S...dm...70....dm...*
009FE400  0109B458 84948B90 009FE480 00FF1314  84948BE6 809FFD78 00FCB92C 00000000  *.....V.dm...U.dm.W........*
009FE420  00000000 00000000 0000015C 00000000  40000000 89D3B188 120000000 00000000  *................iL.h......*
009FE440  10000321 00000000 00000000 84948BE6  0109B458 00000000 009FDE88 009FFE038  *.............*......*
009FE460  00FD50C8 009FE240 009FFD78 84948026  84948026 00000000 849480B0 00F7FDE88  *..........dm.W.....h..\.*
009FE480  84948B90 009FFF158 009FE480 00000000  C0050000 0109BD2A 009FDE88 00F7F080  *....&H..S...dm...70....dm...*
009FE4A0  00FD50C8 009FE240 009FE480 00FE1BF8  00F7F080 FFFF8F40 80000000 009FE524  *.....dm...1..hf.......70.*
009FE4E0  0109B458 FFFFFF7F 009FE4D0 00000000  8109B910 010C4170 80000000 00000000  *.U..&H..S...8...70....*
009FE500  80F7F0D4 80FD5118 00000000 00000000  00FFFFFF 00000000 00000000 00000000  *.70M........."..U}a.....V.*
009FE520  00000000 00000000 00000000 00000000  00000000 40900000 00000000 00000000  *.70M................*
009FE540  00000000 00000000 00000000 00000000  00000000 00000000 00000000 00000000  *....................*
009FE560  00000000 00000000 00000000 00000000  00000000 00000000 00000000 00000000  *....................*
009FE580  00000000 00000000 00000000 00000000  00000000 00000000 00000000 01770000  *....................*
```

```
009FE5A0  009DF348  009DF348  00000000  00000000  00000000  7FF151E4  070C2000  81260324  *.3...3.....a.............*
009FE5C0  00000000  00000000  00000000  00000002  7FF151E4  009DF348  00000000  00050321  *...........1.U..3...*
009FE5E0  00000000  20FD0000  03210000  0128DBF0  0128DBF0  00FF9700  00000070  009DD210  *....K....0.p..q.*
009FE600  00FF7F080 7FF15110  00000000  00000000  7FFFEA60  8128EB7A  81260300  *.."1.a..a....."..-.*
009FE620  00F7F080  00000000  00000000  00000000  00000000  00000000  00000000  00000000  *.70.............*
009FE640  00000000  00000000  00000000  00000000  00000088  009DD188  00000C00  00000304  *...............*
009FE660  7F7550B0  00000C58  810AFB3A  00000304  00000000  00000000  00000C00  0000FF01  *".&....a......h..Jh.*
009FE680  00010100  00400020  00000000  00000000  00000088  00000000  00000000  00000000  *...............*
009FE6A0  00000000  00000023  00000000  00000000  01010000  00000000  00000000  00000000  *...............*
009FE6C0  00000000  00000000  00000000  940C2000  00000002  00000000  00000000  01D5C980  *...............m.*
009FE6E0  00000000  00000000  00000000  00000000  00000000  00000000  00000000  00000000  *...............NI.*
009FE700  01D5C988  00C00321  0000321  0000321  00000000  0C00321  00C00321  00000321  *.NIh.{.....(..*
009FE720  00000000  7F7550B0  00000321  00000321  01F60008  8128BE3C  00000000B  *.&.....6..a.*
009FE740  7FF15000  00000000  00000321  00000000  00FEF908  00000000  0000000B  *"1&......9*
009FE760  FF9DF348  00FCC900  50000303  00000000  009FE05C  00000000  00000000  *.3....I.&..a.\.\/*.*
009FE780  00000000  81112439  00000001  01DA3000  00000000  00000000  00000000  *.3......a.*
009FE7A0
```

```
009FE7C0  00000000  00000000  00000002  00000000  00000000  81112439  00000001  *................a....*
009FE7E0  01DFA000  00000000  00000000  00000000  00000000  00000000  00000000  *...............*
009FE800  00000000  00000000  00000000  00000000  00000000  00000000  00000000  *...............*
        LINES 009FE820-009FEA20   SAME AS ABOVE
009FEA40  009FDDAC  009FD098  01000000  00040000  00000000  00000000  *.).)q....STKH...*
009FEA60  FFFB7A72  009FFE50  009FEAD0  009FEB38  7FFD408  009FEBC8  009FEC18  *..:...&.).)...."..M...H.*
009FEA80  009FEC68  009FECB8  009FED38  009FEE48  7FFEEC0  009FEEF30  009FEF78  *..."..M..{.....*
009FEAA0  7FFFD5F0  009FFE798  7FFFE7C0  7FFFEBC0  7FFDB38  7FFFDB98  8109B7E6  *"..NO".O..,"..0"...q".q*
009FEAC0  7FFFE398  7FFFE798  7FFFE7C0  009FEA68  81123084  8109028  *"..Tq".Xq".X{".Y{..7.a.d...a..W*
009FEAE0  00FDC2AE  0000000D  80000000  009FE480  009FE240  00000000  80000000  *..B..........U..S*
009FEB00  00F7F080  00000C60  009FED38  0109B458  009FE038  00000000  00F1E2C1  *.70...-...\........1SA*
009FEB20  00000000  00F1E2C1  009DF348  00000000  00000000  04BDA4FF  00F1E2C1  *.......1SA.3.....&H..1SA*
009FEB40  00FD50C8  009DF348  00000000  00FD50C8  04BDED87  00FD50C8  *..1SA.3.....&H..u....g...&H*
009FEB60  009D0228  84BDDD88  7F7482E0  84BDE9DA  00000000  00000000  *...d..h".b\.b\d.Z*
009FEB80  00000000  00000000  00000000  00000000  00000000  00000000  *...............*
        LINE 009FEBA0   SAME AS ABOVE
009FEBC0  009DF128  012527A0  00000000  07000000  0013E000  009DF128  04C5301F  *.3......\........1..E..*
009FEBE0  009DF348  00000C60  012527A0  8125293C  00000000  009DF128  01252DB6  *.3......a.*
```

```
009FEC00  009DF128 009F9424 81252A18 00000000   00000000 00000000 80011832 478A0036   *.1....m.a.........*
009FEC20  7FFFC190 00FD50C8 009DDD68 009FF6B8   80FF7918 00FF7080 00000000 80FF049C   *"..A...&H..}..6...70.*
009FEC40  7FFFC9D8 7FFFC160 00000040 00000000   00FF6F00 00000000 009DD068 00000C60   *"..IQ".A-...?....*
009FEC60  00000000 012527A0 00F7F080 009FECB8   009DB360 00000000 009DD068 009FECB8   *.........<Q..-...).-*
009FEC80  81252C60 00FE3D68 80000000 00000000   009FEC68 00000000 00000C58 009FECB8   *........70....&H...*
009FECA0  7FFFD638 810AFB00 810629F0 009DD1A8   00000000 34FFC190 00000000 00005560   *a........70....A...*
009FECC0  7FFFD638 009DD1A8 00F7F080 009FECB8   009FED14 7FFFC9D8 009DD288 009DF348   *".O.a..a.O..Jy.."..IQ..K..3..*
009FECE0  00000038 009C4064 00FF7768 00000000   01D2DD80 010B04CF 020A6000 00000000   *".Jya.4).70...K...-*
009FED00  20000321 00F7F080 009DF348 009DD1A8   00000000 009FED20 7FFFBD90 000F0000   *........K..."..*
009FED20  00000000 00FD50C8 8F9DAE68 00005618   00000082 00000001 80005618 00FCEE40   *.IQ..&H....b.....*
009FED40  009DC9D8 00000000 009DF348 00FC9548   00000000 00000000 00000000 00055A8   *.......3..Jy.....y*
009FED60  00000000 00000000 00000000 00000000   00000000 00000000 00000000 00000000   *.......3..n......*
009FED80  00000000 00000000 00000000 00000000   00000000 00000000 00000000 00000000   *................*
          LINE 009FEDA0  SAME AS ABOVE
009FEDC0  00000000 00000000 00000000 00000000   00000000 809DD1A8 00000000 00000000   *.............Jy......*
009FEDE0  00000000 80DAF6B8 00FF188A 00000001   009FEE20 009DC9D8 00FD50C8 8F9DAE68   *......6.........IQ..&H.*
009FEE00  00005618 00000082 00F7F080 00FF2889   00005548 7F000000 009FED38 009DF348   *....b.70...i...".....3.*
009FEE20  80DAF6B8 00005548 7F000000 00000000   00000000 81263C88 00FFAF48 80000001   *.6..."............3..*
009FEE40  00000000 00000001 00000001 00005548   00000000 01C41BC4 00F7F080 00FD50C8   *...............a.h.....*
009FEE60  009FEE90 A91BE664 CFE8E302 009FEE90   01C41BC4 01C41BC4 00F7F080 00FD50C8   *.z.W.YT....D.D.D.70...&H*
009FEE80  00FFB074 01263B58 00FD85A8 00000000   81263C88 80000001 00000000 00000000   *........ey...a.h.D.D..*
009FEEA0  00000000 00000000 00000000 00000000   00000000 00000000 00000000 00000000   *................*
          LINES 009FEEC0-009FEEE0  SAME AS ABOVE
009FEF00  00000000 00000000 009FF480 00031E37   7FFFC908 00062949 80000000 00000000   *..........4....."I..*
009FEF20  00000000 00000000 009FEF60  SAME AS ABOVE
          LINES 009FEF40-009FEF60  SAME AS ABOVE
009FEF80  00000001 009DCAB0 F49DC9E0 00F7F080   8F9DAE68 00FED9EA 00FCEEC0 00F24D90   *......4.I\.70....R....{.2(.*
009FEFA0  00F19B2C 00FEED80 00000C60 00F19400   0000C80 009FEF78 00FEEE8C 811FD518   *.1......-.1m....a.N.*
009FEFC0  00000000 009FF8C8 7FFFCB48 00FD50C8   00FD6000 7FFFD4B0 8115BDA4 00F7F080   *......8H".-."M.a..u.70.*
009FEFE0  009FF7B0 0115CDA4 00010007 00000007   0115DDA4 009FF8C8 8115D238 00FE9142   *.7...u....u..8Ha.K..j.*
```

The next 4K segment of LSQA contains the following control blocks:

- 9FF000 XTLST for APP3PGM1
- 9FF010 CDE for APP3PGM1
- 9FF158 TCB for Dump Task

Additionally, several SVRBs will be found in this 4K segment.

```
009FF000  00000010 00000001 800006F8 00006908  009FE008 009DF2C0 C1D7D7F3 D7C7D4F1  *............8......\...2{APP3PGM1*
009FF020  00006908 009FF000 000110FB 0B200000  00000000 00000000 00B92080 00000000  *...........0........0.....2.....*
009FF040  009FF048 00F7F080 00100000 00000000  C080C9C5 C5D9C7D5 E2E8B2C4 E2D54040  *...0.70....(.IEERGNSYSDSN       *
009FF060  009DF348 00000000 009FF090 009F1930  009F9028 009D1FF8 809FF084 80B9A7BC  *.3....0....8.......0d..x.*
009FF080  CA690000 809FD1B8 000000C2 C1D7D7F3  D7C7D4F1 009F91CC 009FD3E0 00B92080  *.....J.....BAPP3PGM1.j...L\...*
009FF0A0  009FD060 00000048 000000EC 02010000  001C0444 009FF030 0000EC00 00000000  *.}-..........1.....0......*
009FF0C0  009FF0F0 00000000 00000000 809FF10C  009FF030 00000000 00000000 00000000  *.00..........1.....0......*
009FF0E0  00000000 00000000 00000000 00280000  D9E6C9F2 00000000 009FDE00 00000000  *................RWI2......*
009FF100  00000000 00000000 00000000 00000000  00000080 0400FFFF 00000000 00000000  *........................*
009FF120  00000000 00000000 00000000 00000000  7FFFC598 7FFE9CB0 00000008 00000000  *.............Eq.........*
009FF140  00000000 00B6E000 00000000 00000000  00000100 04BF7060 00000000 009FE240  *......................*
009FF160  00000000 0B6E0000 00000000 00000000  009FF158 00000000 009FE240 00000000  *......................*
009FF180  00000000 00000001 80000000 09FFE0B4  7FF16F04 00000000 00000000 00000000  *.............\.......1 " Eq"...*
009FF1A0  04BF6061 0203D650 7FFFC598 84BF5062  00FD6E48 00000000 00000000 00000000  *-./.O&" Eqd.&......-.-.*
009FF1C0  84BF528A 00000000 00000000 00000000  7FFF8CE0 009FE240 00000000 00000000  *d..........h....1....S*
009FF1E0  00000000 00000000 00F7F0D4 00000000  00000000 00000000 E3C3C240 00000000  *..........70M......"!?.....6....*
009FF200  00000000 00000000 00000000 009FFE04  00000000 00000000 00B44000 00000000  *................>...>..*
009FF220  00000000 00000000 00000000 009FF2B0  7FFC818  00000000 00B44000 00000000  *............2......\..S....*
009FF240  00000000 00000000 00000044 00000000  00000000 84AB1D30 3A000000 839FF7B0  *....................TCB*
009FF260  00000000 7FF167D8 0002FFFF 00048000  00000019 009BA128 00000000 7F734008  *"!1.Q..............c.7.*
009FF280  7FF16F14 7FF167A8 00000000 00000000  6100DB00 809FF318 00C00321 00000321  *"!?."1.y.......H.......*
009FF2A0  00000003 00000000 00000000 00000000  009FF3F0 0124ED2C 16000000 839FF7B0  *...........2Y.{..........*
009FF2C0  00000000 00000000 00000000 00000000  00000000 809FF378 FFFFF321 00000321  *.2}......c.8y/...3.{......"..*
009FF2E0  2310DB00 809FF2E8 0CC00000 00000000  4300DB00 809FF330 84F6C9B0 809E0208  *.........".....30......c.7.*
009FF300  809FF2D0 0DDCB9BA 16000000 839FF8A8  009FF330 00000000 96000000 809E0208  *.......3......{........3........*
009FF320  00000000 809C1224 00000000 7F734008  009FF378 009E1ECF8 00000321 00000321  *.....4.i?k......c.7......3.......*
009FF340  2100DB00 809FF348 0CC00000 00000000  6300DB00 809FF3D8 00C00321 00000321  *......".q......c.7....3.d6I.o....*
009FF360  009FF420 896F92B8 1E000000 839FF7B0  009FF3C0 0539463C 1E000000 839FF7B0  *..........3y.{......8........*
009FF380  00000026 7F745998 00000000 7F755158  0000001B 009BBDF4 00000000 7F734008  *.3..B......c.7.....3Q....c.7.*
009FF3A0  0080DB00 809FF3A8 0CC00000 00000000  6300DB00 809FF438 FFFFF000 00000000  *...".W<....".....3{.....c.7.*
009FF3C0  009FF300 09C20E00 1A000000 00000000  896F92B8 1E000000 839FF7B0 839FF7B0  *......4..{.......4........."..*
009FF3E0  0000001C 7FFDE64C 00000000 839FF7B0  00000024 7F745998 00000000 7F755158  *.3.d......c.k....4........*
009FF400  6300DB00 809FF408 0CC00000 00000000  6300DB00 809FF498 00000000 00000000  *.......y......4.i?k....c.7.*
009FF420  009FF390 84717858 10000000 839F9220  04C61A06 16000000 839FF6B8           *......4.........".q.....*
009FF440  00000000 809DA804 00000000 7F786200                                       *.....c.7....4q......*
009FF460  4200DB00 809FF468 FFFFF321 00000321                                       *.4&......".&...5 .F....c.6.*
009FF480  009FF450 0112B8DE 10000000 839FF7B0
009FF4A0  00000000 00000000 00000000 7F747228
```

```
009FF4C0 6100DB00 809FF4C8 00000000 00000000   00000000 7F73E928 00000000 7F7550B0  */....4H.........."Z....&.*
009FF4E0 009FF360 896F92B8 1E000000 839FF7B0   4300DB00 809FF4F8 FFFF0321 00000000  *.3-i?k.....c.7........&.*
009FF500 00000025 7F745998 00000000 00000000   009FF4B0 04BDB4B6 16000000 839FF7B0  *......q......4...48....c.7.*
009FF520 4100DB00 809FF528 00000000 009FDF2C0  009D036C 00C00000 00000000 7F7550B0  *......q.....5.{.....&.*
009FF540 00000000 00006B34 10000000 00000000   809FF558 00C00000 00000000 00000000  *......5........&...*.&.*
009FF560 00000000 2000DB00 80400000 00000000   00E2CDB0 1E000000 00000000 839FD1B8  *.......2{.....&....S..c.J.*
009FF580 00000000 809FF588 80400000 00000000   009F0D44 00000000 00000000 7F7860B0  *.......5h....&.....c.J.-.*
009FF5A0 00000014 009FCA64 1E000000 839FD240   2100DB00 809FF5B8 80400000 00000000  *.....5}.S......5....C.M.*
009FF5C0 00000000 00E2CDB0 1E000000 7FFEC008   009FF600 00DAAA90 16000000 00000000  *......5h...c.K...5....5....*
009FF5E0 2300DB00 809FF5E8 80400321 00000000   00000000 009FCB2C 16000000 C39FD480  *......5Y...{..6.....C.M.*
009FF600 00000000 0DDDFB68 16000000 C39FD480   2100DB00 809FF618 80400321 00000000  *.......C.M....&.....{.(.*
009FF620 00000000 009FCC58 00000000 01262740   00000000 04BF5058 16000000 839FDE00  *.........6......&...C..*
009FF640 6100DB00 809FF648 80400000 00000000   00000000 2100DB00 16000000 839FDE00  */....6....6....Eq.....*
009FF660 00000000 0494801E 16000000 839FFD78   2100DB00 809FF678 80400000 00000000  *......m....6......C..*
009FF680 00000000 009FE480 00000000 01262740   E2E5D9C2 009FF788 7FFFC9D8 00000000  *......U....SVRB.7h.IQ..*
009FF6A0 00000000 00000000 070C1000 84C61318   22000000 00020033 00000000 00006AD0  *....}......dF....2{..><...)*
009FF6C0 001ED022 00000000 00000000 00000000   00000000 00DF2C0 00006E4C 80DF510   *.........dF....8..0--5.*
009FF6E0 00000040 00000000 009F1954 009F9028   009D1FF8 00000000 00006E4C 00006AD0  *.......8...&.,.O...><..)*
009FF700 00009000 00002260 00006908 00006DEC   50006B0C 00D60548 7F752090 00006AD0  *....-...3..6.70..?..{"..*
009FF720 00000000 009DF348 009FF6B8 00F7F080   00FF6F00 0211ACC0 839FF6B8 FF000F70  *......m......c.6....7.*
009FF740 40000101 940C2000 00000000 00000000   00000000 839FF6B8 2400DB00 009FF778  *......6.SVRB..9."....*
009FF760 00000000 00000000 00000000 00000000   7FFFCA78 00000000 00000000 00000000  *.......&.....6....."..}.*
009FF780 00000000 009FF6B8 E2E5D9C2 009FF978   00000000 00000000 001ED022 00000000  *.......&..dF.-".....F.;.W.*
009FF7A0 00000000 00000000 02000000 00020005   00000948 7F752190 04C6205E 4080E610  *".Z..F.^dF.-".......{*
009FF7C0 070C2000 80DF0850 00000000 009FF6B8   00FC8BB8 000C2000 009DAEC0                                          *
009FF7E0 7F73E928 04C6105F 84C60060 7F752090                                                                       *
```

```
009FF800 7F73E3F8 7F73E3F8 04C61330 00000000   00000000 009D0228 00000000 00000000  *".T8".T8.F.........*
009FF820 00000000 00000000 16000000 839FF7B0   00000000 009FF870 00000000 00000000  *...........c.7.....*
009FF840 00000000 00000000 00000000 00000000   2400DB00 809FF870 00000000 009CF180  *.....c.7...8......1.*
009FF860 00000000 00000000 00000000 00000080   00000000 00000000 00000000 00000000  *...........8.......*
009FF880 E2E5D9C2 46800004 7FFFCB18 00000000   00000000 009FF978 00000000 009CF180  *SVRB..9."........1.*
009FF8A0 00000000 019DD568 91000000 09E00F98   001EC022 00000000 070C0000 81263C88  *.....N.j..q....a.h*
009FF8C0 00000000 00000000 00000000 09E00F98   00000040 00000000 009F1930 009F9028  *.....{.......q...*
009FF8E0 009D1FF8 00000000 009FF060 809DF510   00000000 009F9028 89E00F30 09E00F50  *...8...0-.5..i\.\&*
009FF900 00FD5118 00000000 A91BE664 CFE8E302   A91BE69D 8E46E302 80000000 09E00F98  *.z.W.YT.z.W..T....\.q*
```

```
009FF920  00FF6F00  00009102  00000000  01C41BA8   00000000  00000000  00000000  01263EF2  *.........?..j.....D.y.........2*
009FF940  839FF8A8  16000000  4400DB00  009FF968   00000000  00000000  E2E5D9C2  00000000  *....c.8y......9............*
009FF960  00000000  00000000  00000000  00000000   009FF8A8  E2E5D9C2  00000000  009FFA70  *.............8ySVRB.....*
009FF980  7FFFCBB8  00000000  00000000  04000000   070C0000  00000000  00000000  009DD1A8  *."....................*
009FF9A0  00000000  00000000  00000000  00000000   00000000  00000000  04BE189A  009DD1A8  *.............(.........Jy*
009FF9C0  009DD280  00005548  009DAE68  000079A0   04DF033A  40DF033A  00008000  009D0228  *.K............u........*
009FF9E0  009DD470  FFFFFFE0  80DF074E  000079A0   40DF033A  00005560  00FD5118  00DF05D7  *.M.....\..+........P*
009FFA00  00000000  00000400  00000000  00000000   00000000  00000000  00000000  00000000  *......-................*
009FFA20  00000000  00000000  00000000  839FF9A0   00000000  16000000  00000000  839FF9A0  *..............c.9.*
009FFA40  6400DB00  00000000  00000000  009FFA60   00000000  00000000  7FFFCC58  00000000  *.....................*
009FFA60  00000000  00000000  00000000  009FFA00   E2E5D9C2  7FFFCC58  00000000  00000080  *.........SVRB....."...*
009FFA80  00000000  00000000  00000000  00000000   00020078  00000005  00000000  00000000  *..........................*
009FFAA0  001EC022  070C0000  8106F118  009FF9A0   009FF9A0  7F749B00  7F749B00  009FD060  *.{......a.l.......9...)-*
009FFAC0  00000008  7F73E072  7F744EF0  00000001   00000001  00000001  00000002  7F7450C0  *.."..\.....,+0.......&({*
009FFAE0  7F749B00  7F7450AE  84EBE59A  7F7498A0   00000007  00000007  00A00000  009CFD38  *."..&.d.v.".q.........)-a.T*
009FFB00  00FF6F00  009E023C  009E023C  00000000   009FD060  7F749B00  8106B33A  009CFFB58  *.?.......)-a.T...c..q........*
009FFB20  00000000  00000001  009FF510  00000000   839FFA98  15000000  2400DB00  009FFB58  *......5.........c..q........*
009FFB40  00000000  00000000  00000000  00000000   00000000  00000000  00000000  00000000  *...................*
009FFB60  00000000  009FFA98  E2E5D9C2  009FFC60   7FFFCCF8  00000000  00000000  00000000  *....qSVRB..-.8.......*
009FFB80  00000000  00000000  00000000  009FFA98   00000084  00000000  001EC022  04BD0008  *...............{.*
009FFBA0  070C0000  00000000  00000000  0000003D   00008448  00008448  04BBD011  84BBD012  *........q..d..d..)..\.d.).*
009FFBC0  00000218  00008448  84BBD2B4  00000000   00000008  00000008  04BBD011  84BBD012  *....d......d.K.*
009FFBE0  00019000  00019000  00000000  00000000   00000000  00000000  00000000  00000000  *........*
009FFC00  00000000  00000000  00000000  009FFB90   009DB00  00000000  00000000  00000000  *.......*
009FFC20  00000000  00000000  009FFC88  00000000   00000DB00  00000000  00000000  00000000  *.....h........*
009FFC40  00000000  00000000  00000000  00000000   00000000  00000000  7FFFFBA0  7FFFEBA0  *................"..."...*
009FFC60  E2E5D9C2  00000000  7FFFCD98  00000000   001EC022  001EC022  070C0000  00CC13A0  *SVRB..".q......{..(...*
009FFC80  00000000  00000000  00000000  00000084   00000000  00000000  00000400  000078A0  *..............d....{.*
009FFCA0  00000000  00000000  009FFB90  009DFB58   009DFB58  00000000  053C1A50  00CC13A0  *...............d...).*
009FFCC0  00CC1188  009DF7B8  00F83048  00000000   000CEF8  0000DE18  000DDE18  000078A0  *.h....7.8...8.....&.*
009FFCE0  00FD50C8  070C1000  8109B490  00000000   00000000  019FE240  053C1A50  00000000  *.&H..............S..*
009FFD00  00000000  00000000  00000000  00000000   00000DB00  00000000  00000000  00000000  *.......*
009FFD20  00000000  009FFC88  0000DB00  00000000   00000000  00000000  7FFFEBA0  00000080  *.....h........"..*
009FFD40  00000000  00000000  00000000  00000000   00000000  00000000  00000000  00000080  *.................*
009FFD60  00000000  00000000  00000000  00000000   52800003  52800003  00020001  00000000  *.........*
009FFD80  00110083  00BD89C8  070C1000  8109B490   00000000  019FE240  00000000  00000000  *...iH...a...S...*
009FFDA0  00000000  00000000  00000000  00000000   00000000  00000000  00000000  00000000  *.....*
009FFDC0  00000000  00000000  00000000  00000000   00000000  00000000  C9C5C1E5  C1D9F0F0  *.............IEAVAR00*
009FFDE0  E2E3D2D7  009FEA50  009DEF44  00000321   00000321  009DEF84  812B6FA6  80008902  *STKP.&......da.?w.i.*
009FFE00  00000C60  00010200  00CC0321  0206E060   0206E060  8000892E  E2E3D2D7  009FEA50  *.-...(...\-.i.STKP...&*
```

```
009FFE20  00010321 009FFDE0 00000321 009DEF00   80CBAE4C 00000000 7F73D800 009DEF58   *.....\.........<....."..Q.....*
009FFE40  00160000 FFC00321 01D84680 860A9DC0   E2E3D2D7 009FFEA5 00000000 009FFE88   *........(...Q..f..{STKP.&.....h*
009FFE60  00000321 7F7472B0 84BE1C12 00000321   7F745000 7F745000 00030300 00000321   *........d.....&."&............*
009FFE80  017F1440 810A0DB2 E2E3D2D7 009FFEA5   00010321 009FFE18 00000321 009DC8D0   *..." a...STKP.&............H)*
009FFEA0  80CBAE4C 00000000 7F73B800 009DC928   00160000 FF800321 01D84680 860A9DC0   *...<....."......I.....Q..f..{*
009FFEC0  00000000 00000000 00000000 00000000   00000000 00000000 00000000 00000000   *..............................*
          LINE 009FFEE0  SAME AS ABOVE
```

```
JOB EXA7JHMX        STEP APP3          TIME 125832    DATE 94100    ID = 000                          PAGE 00000047

009FFF00  00000000 00B92080 0B70F28 00000000    03210000 00000000 00000000 00000000   *..............................*
009FFF20  00000000 40000000 00000000 00000000    00000000 00000000 00000000 00000000   *.. ...........................*
009FFF40  009FD3FC 00B6EFE0 00000000 00B70DA8    00000000 00000000 00FAE7B4 00000000   *..L...........y..........X....*
009FFF60  009FFE04 00000000 00000000 00F9028     00000000 00000000 00FB8848 009E3FF8   *.........................h..8*
009FFF80  00000080 00000000 009F9028 00000000    009FFB8 009FDE88 009FFDF4 00009E3FF8  *...............................*
009FFFA0  009FFFAC 80B920BC FCCB0000 809FD240    00000000 009FDE88 009FFDF4 00000000   *......................h..8.M..*
009FFFC0  809FFFAC 00000000 00000000 00000000    000000C2 C9C5C6C9 C9C34040 009FD01C   *.........K.....BIEFIIC...).*
009FFFE0  00000000 00000000 00000000 00000048    000000ED 10010000 00000000 00000000   *..............................*
```

This continues the LSQA dump with the Extended LSQA area (31-bit addressable). The following control blocks are contained in the next 4K of LSQA:

- 7F72D958 SPQE for subpool 0, key 8
- 7F72D838 SPQE for subpool 22, key 8
- 7F72D490 SPQA for subpool 22

```
7F72D000  E5E2D4D7 7F751000 00001000 00000004   7F72C0D8 00000F28 7F751D78 7F751D78   *VSMP".............."..(Q....."..*
7F72D020  7F751D78 00007000 7F746238 7F751088   7F745000 00001000 FD751088 00000000   *.."...........h".&....."...h.....*
7F72D040  7F72D7F0 7F72D8E0 7FF164A8 7F72D430   7F433000 000008F0 7F72D538 7F72D538   *.."P0.Q\"1.y".M...0".N."..*
7F72D060  7F751E08 7F751E08 009DC000 00001000   7F746790 7FFE2268 00000000 009D9000   *.."P0.Q\"1.y".M.."0".N.*N.*
7F72D080  7F72D9A0 00001000 7FFE2DD8 00000000   7F7430F8 000001B8 FD9BC000 00000000   *.."..(..."...Q....8....(..&.*
7F72D0A0  7F72DFB8 7F7518E0 00001000 7F746000   7FFE2958 00001000 7FFE2EF8 00001000   *.."R...".Q....8...-..."..8....*
7F72D0C0  7FFE2EF8 7FFE2EF8 00001000 7F72D190   7F751DC0 7F7517C0 7F72D190 7F72D430   *.."8".8".."{("{".J"."..J..*
7F72D0E0  009BC000 00001000 7F72D928 7F72D430   7F72DBE0 009D8000 00001000            *.(...R."M."..\"..*
```

```
7F72D100  7FFE2F28 7F72D1A8 7F7518C8 7F72D1A8   00105000 00005000 7F751610 7F72D6A0   *"..."..H".Jy".Jy".&..&.."..."...O.*
7F72D120  7F72D118 7F72D120 0A108000 00001000   7F72DA78 7F751248 7F72D130 7F72D130   *".J.".J."."."."."."."."..J.".J.*
7F72D140  7F74F000 00001000 7F751248 7F751248   7F72D148 7F754000 00001000            *".O..".".".".".".)..JQ*
7F72D160  7F751838 00000000 7F746208 009DD040   004E8080 00000000 009E0118 000000D0   *"..".".".).).).)*
7F72D180  7F751418 009FE000 00000000 00000000   7F72D0D0 00000000 7F77D000 00001000   *".}.".".".)..)).)..)*
7F72D1A0  FE72D0D0 00003000 7F751F10 7FFE2428   7F72D1A8 00001000 7F72D1A8 7F746370   *"..".&".Q".".W...Q".Jy".Jy".*
7F72D1C0  7F751850 7F751C10 7F751C10 009C1190   00E60020 00001000 7F72D1F8 7F72D1F8   *".&".Q".".W...Q".J.".J.*
7F72D1E0  7F746430 009F9380 00000008            7F72D1F0 7F72D1F0 7F72D1F8            *".1..1.".JO".JO".J8".J8*
7F72D200  7F72D200 7F746928 00000000            009DB2A8 00000080 7F751010 7F751FE8   *"."..y..".mq.".Y*
7F72D220  009DA000 00000E68 7F72D628 7F72D628   00003000 7F751010 7F72D250            *".".".".O..O..O.".Y*
7F72D240  7F72D238 7F72D628 0A0C4000 00002000   7F72D628 00003000 7F72D250 7F72D250   *".K".K".".".&".K&".K&*
7F72D260  7FFCD000 00001000 7FFE2560 7FFE2560   7FFE2400 7FFE2B98 7F77B000 00020000   *".}.".".-.-.q".q".".O.*
7F72D280  7F751C88 7F72DB50 7F72D280 7F72D280   7FFE2B98 00001000 00000000 7F72D610   *".&".K..K..K.".\.".i>4..(..\&.*
7F72D2A0  009F9288 000000C0 FD9FD000 00000000   0A0DE000 00001000 7590C000 09E05000   *".h".&".K".K.".i>4..(..\&.*
7F72D2C0  09E01000 00001000 7F72D370 7F751148   7FF16EF4 7FF16430 009DD000 00000280   *"kh..{..}....1..)..L."*
7F72D2E0  7FFE2268 7FFE2EB0 7FFE2EB0 7FFE2EB0   7F7513A0 00001000 7F751E38 7F746140   *".".".".1..).).).L.*
7F72D300  7F72DB08 7F72DB08 7F72D268 7F72DB08   009D9000 7F72D478 7F72D318 7F72D318   *".O..M..M..M.".L.*
7F72D320  7F7468E0 7F72DE38 00008000 00000F78   7F751C70 7F751C70 7F751C70 00001000   *".M..M..M.".L.*
7F72D340  7F746730 7F751418 7F746970 009DF348   7F751C70 00000000 7F746A30 7FFE2010   *"..".".".".3.".".".*
7F72D360  7F72D358 7F72D358 0A193000 00004000   00FB8020 7F72D2C8 7FFE1630 7FFE1618   *".L.".L.".&".".KH".1.*
7F72D380  009DD378 00000010 7F751550 7F72DFA0   7F751358 00000AC8 FD74B000 00001000   *".L.".&".L.".L..T8..H.*
7F72D3A0  7F751B38 7F7511C0 7F72D3A0 7F72D3A0   7F73E3F8 00001000 7F72D078 00000000   *".K.".).).".L..*
7F72D3C0  009DD280 00000068 FDE1D000 00002000   0A114000 00000218 7FFE2868 7F751CB8   *".K.".).)..LY.LY.-.*
7F72D3E0  7F751CB8 00000000 7F72DB80 7F751BE0   009E0000 7F72D3E8 0A0F6000 00001000   *".".".\"."1".1.A.".*
7F72D400  7FFE2D60 7F751430 7F716490 7F716478   7FFFC108 00000010 7F72D040 7F751A18   *".-"1".A.".Q".NH".}.N8*
7F72D420  009CFFC0 00001040 FD73B000 00003000   7F72D5C8 7F72D040 7F72D5F8            *".R."..".{.Oh".Q".)..NH".}.N8*
7F72D440  7F748000 000004C0 7F72D688 7F72D808   7F73E080 00000378 FDE01000 00001000   *".R."..".".".L".L.*
7F72D460  7F72D970 7F746268 7F7467D8 009C1770   00018020 00000000 7F72D310 7F72D310   *".R."..(...".L".L.*
7F72D480  7FFE2F10 0000C000 0000C000 00002000   7F72DB68 7FFE2838 7F72D498 7F72D498   *".".Mq".Mq*
7F72D4A0  7F72D4A0 7F72D4A0 7F72D4A0 00001000   009E0BF8 00E68020 00001000            *".M..M.".M{.MH".M}.M}.8.W...0*
7F72D4C0  7FFE2E68 7F72D4C0 7F72D4C8 7F72D4C8   7F72D4D0 7F72D238 7F746568 7F751CB8   *".".M{.MH".M}.M}.8.W...0*
7F72D4E0  7F751BB0 009DC000 00001000            7F751A90 7F72D4D0 7F72D4F0 7F72D4F0   *".&".".K.".M0".M0*
7F72D500  0A0D5000 00002000 00000000 00000548   00E68020 7F72D530 7F72D058 7F72D058   *".".&".".W..N.Q".Q.*
7F72D520  7F751EB0 00001000 7F72D2D8 009C1190   7FFE2238 7F7517D8 7F7517D8 00040000   *".{.MH".MH".Q".").)".1.Q*
7F72D540  7F72D540 7F72D540 7F72D880 7F72D880   7FFE2340 7F72D238 7F72D4F0            *".&".".\".K\".).)".1.Q*
7F72D560  00000010 7F751D00 7F751D00 7F7512F8   7F7466B8 7F747000 7F7516D0 7FF164D8   *".".".K\./.K\./..OY".N0*
7F72D580  7FFFBD30 00000410 7F746100 00001000   00000000 00000003 7FFE2EC8 00001000   *".8".8".".".".N..N.*
7F72D5A0  7F72DBE0 00000000 7F748000 00001000   7F7464C0 7F746100 7F72D6E8 7F72D5F0   *".".".H".Q".*
7F72D5C0  00510000 00006000 7F72D430 7F7512C8   7FFE2EF8 7F72D30 7F72D5B0 7F72D5B0    *".-".M.".H".Q".").*
7F72D5E0  7F72DE08 7F72D5E0 7F72D5F0 7F72D5E8   7F7512C8 7F7514D8 7F747000 000002B0   *".N\".NY".NY".N0".\".1y*
                                                 7F72D5F0 7F72D5F0 7F7512E0 7FF164A8
```

```
JOB EXA7JHMX        STEP APP3        TIME 125832    DATE 94100    ID = 000        PAGE 00000048

7F72D600  7F72D430  7F73A000  00000378  7F72D298  7FF165E0  009FF060  00000078   *.M."...........Kq"1.\.0-....*
7F72D620  FD776000  00001000  7F7460A0  7F72D220  009DA000  09DA0000  00001000   *........-...K.."K...........*
7F72D640  7F7460B8  7F72D7D8  7F72D640  0A104000  00001000  7F72D130  00000080   *-...."P.-....... ......J.-..*
7F72D660  7FFE2B80  7FFE2B80  00003000  009DEF08  000000F8  FFE2E2B0  7F72DBF8   *...............8"....8*
7F72D680  00001000  7FFE26B8  7F72D448  7484C000  00000B40  FD9CC000  00002000   *.....d{..........M.d(....*
7F72D6A0  7F72D118  7F72D9E8  0A107000  7F72D6A0  0A107000  7F72D160  7F751A78   *.J..J-RY".O...J-."*
7F72D6C0  009DB360  00E50020  00001000  7F7517C0  7F751868  7F72D6D8  7F72D6D8   *.....V..........{.O)"OQ".OQ*
7F72D6E0  7F72D6E0  7F751868  7F751868  7F751868  00001000  7F72D6D8            *.O\".O).....{.O)"*
7F72D700  7F7515B0  7F72D700  0A0EF000  00001000  7F72D088  7F746268            *.....&..."P."P.0...}h"*
7F72D720  7FF16448  7F751958  009C5000  00000000  7F751F70  7F751F70            *1.......&......P.P.)h"*
7F72D740  7F751F70  00001000  7F72D750  7F72D770  7F72D758  7F72D758            *P...."P."P.."P."*
7F72D760  7F751040  7F72D760  7F72D768  7F72D768  7FFE2B80  7F751CB8            *.P-"..\.."P."P."*
7F72D780  7F7512E0  7F7512E0  009D9000  7F72D5E0  7F751118  7F746178  009C1770   *.........N\.../.-.*
7F72D7A0  00E51020  00009000  7469D000  00000000  7F743620  FE751688  7F7516B8   *.V.......y...Q&".h.*
7F72D7C0  7F72DA08  7F72D7D8  7F72D850  7F72F000  00001000  7F72D640  7F751B88   *...PQ".."H."Q&".O..*
7F72D7E0  7F7439C0  0A103000  7F72D448  7F7512C8  00000200  009CE000            *...M...H.....1-*
7F72D800  00000008  7F72D448  7F746238  7F7439C8  00000200  FD9CE000  00000000   *.h.h.}...M..H...*
7F72D820  7FFE2990  7F746868  7F72DF88  009ED000  00001000  7F72D7C0  7F72D7C0   *.P(...)"P(".P(*
7F72D840  7F72D490  009DF348  00168020  00002000  7F72D7C0  00001000  7F72D7C0   *.M..3...{..."Nq".R.*
7F72D860  00001000  7F72D598  7F72D910  7F751BB0  009BB000  00001000  7F72D058   *.P(.."Nq".R."*
7F72D880  7F72D548  7F72D2E0  7F746838  7F749000  00001000  7F72D210  7F72D058   *.N."N.\.........}.*
7F72D8A0  7F7464D8  00018000  00007000  7FFE2B80  7F72DBB0  7F72DBB0            *.Q".Q...........}.*
7F72D8C0  7F72D2B80  7F7465B0  7F72D8C8  7F72D8C8  09F0E000  00002000            *..."Q".QH".QH.0\..*
7F72D8E0  7F72D040  7F751430  7FFE2B80  00000080  7F73E000  7FFE2388  7F746958   *.R-"..../0".h"*
7F72D900  7F72D8F8  0A050000  7F72D8F8  7FFE2E50  7F72D910  7F72D918  7F72D918   *&."R."R."R."R.*
7F72D920  7F72D920  7F72D070  7F72D920  7F743620  0000002D  FE74F000  00001000   *.R.R."..}.0....*
7F72D940  7F72D8B0  7FF51D60  7FFE2AD8  0A1BF000  00004000  7F72D838  00000000   *.Q.."..-..)..Q.*
7F72D960  7F751268  009F9028  00008080  7F72DA18  7F72D970  7F72D978  7F72D978   *.R."R."R."R.*
7F72D980  7F72D980  7F72D980  7F751748  7F751FB8  009DF180  00EC1080  00000000   *.R.R....1..*
7F72D9A0  7FFE2A48  00001000  7FFE2A48  7FFE2A48  7F72D9B0  7FFE2FA0  00000000   *."R.R."R.*
7F72D9C0  7F746028  004E8080  00001000  7F751070  00000000  009C3000  00005000   *.-.1.+....Q.*
7F72D9E0  FD749000  00003000  7F72D6A0  7F72D9E8  7F72D9E8  0A106000  00001000   *..."RY".RY....*
7F72DA00  7FFE2FA0  7FFE2B20  00001000  7F72DA00  00008000  7F751790  7F7514F0  00001000   *."......0-..*
7F72DA20  7F72D970  009C1770  00008020  7F72DA48  7F72DD60  7F72DA30  7F72DA00   *.R...........Y*
7F72DA40  0A0A8000  00001000  7F746958  7F72DA48  7F72DA48  0A04C000  7F7513B8   *........{-...(..H*
7F72DA60  7F751A90  7F72DDC0  7F72DA60  7F752000  0AOD9000  00001000  7F7513B8  7F72DEC8   *.........-..(.H*
7F72DA80  00000000  7F752000  7F72DE68  00000000  7FF16EE4  009DC000  00195000   *.R..1>U...&.*
7F72DAA0  00001000  7F72DD00  00001000  7F746328  7F72D9A0  00000000  7F72D4D8  00001000   *.R.....(."MQ*
```

```
7F72DAC0  7FFE2CB8  7F72D730  7F72DAC0  7F72DAC0   0A0FC000  00001000  7F72DC70  7F72DCA0   *...*.P."..(...(..."...*
7F72DAE0  7F72DAD8  7F72DAD8  0A16B000  00002000   7F746610  7F72DAF8  7F72DAF8  7F72DCA0   *...Q.".Q..".K8..".0".".8*
7F72DB00  7F72DB00  7F72DB00  7F72DB08  00001000   7F72D2F8  7F72D2F8  7F72DAF8  00001000   *..."..".."..K8...".K8..K8..*
7F72DB20  7F72DB20  7F72DB20  7F72DB28  00001000   7F72D2F8  7F72DB30  7FFE2D18  7F72DB38   *..."..".".\."...K....*
7F72DB40  7F7510A0  009C1190  00E57020  00000000   7F72D280  7F72DB70  7FFE2D18  000001B8   *....V...".....K..*
7F72DB60  FD0DD000  00001000  00000050  7F72D4A8   7F72D280  7F72DB70  7F743A10  000001B8   *....}....My...*
7F72DB80  7F751C28  7F72D3E8  7F72DB80  7F72DB80   0A0F7000  00001000  00007000  000009A0   *..}..Ly...*
7F72DBA0  7F746268  7F746268  7F746268  00001000   7F72D0E8  7F72D940  7F72D8B0  7F72D8B0   *...)Y".R..Q.".Q.*
7F72DBC0  0A1C3000  0000B000  7F72D988  7F751358   7F462C8   7FF164D8  7FFFBAB0  00000010   *...."..Rh"...H"1.Q*
7F72DBE0  7F746928  7F746928  7F72DD78  7FF16430   009DB570  00000020  009DE148  00000D08   *...."...."..1......*
7F72DC00  7F72D670  7F751EC8  7FFE2B80  00001000   7F751490  7F72DC10  7F72DC10  00000D08   *...O..H"...."..*
7F72DC20  0A0AD000  00001000  7F746880  00001000   7F746880  7F746880  7F746880  00001000   *...)...."..*
7F72DC40  7F746A48  00000000  009C3000  00005000   FD702000  00003000  7F751FA0  7F7519A0   *..."...&...."..*
7F72DC60  004E8000  004E8000  7FF165E0  00000270   7F751SE0  7F72DAD8  7F746868  00003000   *...+.+..1.\."..Q*
7F72DCA0  7F72DAD8  0A16D000  009EC000  00000270   7F746868  7F746868  7F746868  7F746148   *..."..h"./*
7F72DCC0  7F72DCB8  7F72DCB8  0052E000  0000C000   0A16A000  00001000  7FFE2710  009F9028   *.."...\.(..."..h".*
7F72DCE0  00E55020  00003000  7FFE2D48  FD745000   7F73D378  0000C88   FD745000  00001000   *.V&....h"...L..h.&*
```

```
JOB EXA7JHMX        STEP APP3        TIME 125832   DATE 94100   ID = 000              PAGE 00000049

7F72DD00  7F72DD48  7F746A30  7F751B80   00001000  7F746A30  00001000  7F7464F0  00008000   *...Q."..."...0.*
7F72DD20  7F7464F0  7F7464F0  00003000   7F7465F8  7FFE2B50  7F72DB50  7F72DD30  7F72DD30   *...0.".0."..&".8".*
7F72DD40  0A0DC000  7FFE2F88  00001000   7FFE2F88  7FFE2F88  7FFE2F88  7F72DD30  00000A30   *....(..h...h..h.*
7F72DD60  009DF058  7F751CA0  7F72DD60   0A0A4000  00004000  7F746058  7F7468B0  7F72DB8   *...&..-.".L.*
7F72DD80  00000050  FD744000  00002000   7F72DF70  7F746058  7F72D290  7F72DD90  7F72DD90   *...0.&..-.".L.*
7F72DDA0  0A17F000  7F72DA60  7F72DDC0   7F751CB8  7F751CB8  7F72E000  00011000  7F72DD90   *...0...."..\.*
7F72DDC0  7F72DDC0  7F72DDC0  00001000   00001000  0A0DA000  7F72DBC8  7F72D3E0  7F72D3E0   *...0.."..(.....QH".L\*
7F72DDE0  00E57020  09F0D000  00001000   7FFE2CB8  7F7463B8  7F751BC8  009DB360  009DB360   *...8"..(..{.QH".L\*
7F72DE00  00E57020  7F751AD8  00001000   009C1770  00E50020  7F751BC8  7F72DE00  7F72DE00   *...Q".Q0)..N\..V*
7F72DE20  7F751580  7F72D910  7F7462B0   00028000  0A1CC000  00E50020  7F72D320  7F7468E0   *...R."..(....L."..*
7F72DE40  7FFE2F58  09E03000  00002000   00000000  7F72D340  7F72D1F0  009DF348  009DF348   *...(...\..L.\.*
7F72DE60  002180A0  00000000  7F751388   00001000  7F72D68   09C5000   00003000  00003000   *..h".h..&..*
7F72DE80  009DFB00  7F751530  7F751F58   7F730000  00001000  7F72DE68  009C5000  009F9028   *..h".h..-Y.*
7F72DEA0  7F746400  7F746400  7F72DEA8   00000000  00000000  7F72D7D0  7F751268  009F9028   *...y...y..P0*
7F72DEC0  000080A0  00000000  00000160   7FFE2B80  7F751DD8  7FFE2B80  00001000  00001000   *...y.-"..Q"..*
7F72DEE0  7F746298  7F72DEE8  7F72DEE8   7F751700  7F72DEF0  7F72DEC8  7F746148  7F72D5B0   *...q".".Y"..Q"./".N.*
7F72DF00  7F72DEF8  00516000  0000C000   7F72D850  7F72DEF8  7F72DEF8  7F7519A0  7F7519A0   *...8...(..Q&.K8"..*
```

```
7F72DF20  00B90000 00001000 7F7469E8 7FFE2F40  7F72DF28 7F72DF28 0A18D000 00002000  *..........Y".....)..*
7F72DF40  7F7468C8 7F72DD90 7F72DF40 7F72DF40  0A181000 00002000 7F746478 7F7515E0  *".H"......."..."..\*
7F72DF60  7F72DF58 7F72DF58 0A173000 000000B0  7F7465C8 7F746940 7F72DF78 7F72D778  *"....."....."..H".P..P.*
7F72DF80  0A042000 00006000 009ED000 00000000  7F72D820 7F72D820 7F72D820 00001000  *......-..}...Q.."Q..Q.*
7F72DFA0  7F72D388 7FFE26B8 7F74A000 00002000  FD00C000 00002000 7F72DFD0 00000000  **.Lh"......".Q.."Q..*
7F72DFC0  00000000 00000000 00000000 00000000  7F72DFE8 00000000 00000000 00000000  *..........".".).*
7F72DFE0  00000000 00000000 7FF169B8 00000000  00000000 00000000 00000000           *.........".1.....Y..*
```

The 7F73EEC0 Vector Status Save Area (VSSA) control block is contained within the next 4K segment of LSQA.

```
7F73E000  E7E2C240 00000000 009DD178 09D2D178  00000000 00000000 00000007 00000000  *XSB .....J.KJ....*
7F73E020  00000000 00000000 00000000 00000000  E2E2C1E3 01000000 00000000 00000000  *........SSAT....*
7F73E040  00F7F080 00000000 00000000 00000000  00000008 C2D3E2D8 C5E7E3C9 00010321  *.70............BLSQEXTI...e.f.*
7F73E060  00000000 00000000 00000000 00000000  00000000 40000000 00000000 85198648  *..........dq.......e.f.*
7F73E080  00000374 40000000 00000000 8498FB00  00000000 00000000 00000000 00000000  *...........d.........*
7F73E0A0  00000000 40000000 00000000 84BD3B70  00000000 00000000 00000000 00000000  *...........do........*
7F73E0C0  00000000 00000000 00000000 8496BD00  00000000 00000000 00000000 00000000  *...........f.........*
7F73E0E0  00000000 40000000 00000000 860A0B68  00000000 00000000 00000000 00000000  *.....................*
7F73E100  00000000 00000000 00000000 00000000  00000000 00000000 00000000 00000000  *.....................*
          LINE 7F73E120  SAME AS ABOVE
7F73E140  00000000 40000000 00000000 845B4488  00000000 00000000 00000000 00000000  *............d$.h.......*
7F73E160  00000000 00000000 00000000 00000000  00000000 00000000 00000000 00000000  *.....................*
          LINE 7F73E180  SAME AS ABOVE
7F73E1A0  00000000 40000000 00000000 00000000  84950268 00000000 00000000 85301938  *.................dn...e..*
7F73E1C0  00000000 40000000 00000000 85301AED  00000000 00000000 00000000 00000000  *............e........e.*
7F73E1E0  00000000 00000000 00000000 00000000  00000000 40000000 00000000 84717B88  *............d........d..*
7F73E200  00000000 40000000 00000000 8471779D  00000000 00000000 00000000 00000000  *............d.........*
7F73E220  00000000 00000000 00000000 00000000  00000000 40000000 00000000 00000000  *.....d......d?h......*
7F73E240  849D2578 40000000 00000000 846F88A0  00000000 00000000 00000000 00000000  *d......................*
7F73E260  00000000 00000000 00000000 00000000  00000000 40000000 00000000 8608E3B8  *...................f.T...*
7F73E280  00000000 00000000 00000000 00000000  00000000 40000000 00000000 860C1D00  *.................f...*
7F73E2A0  00000000 00000000 00000000 89E011B0  00000000 40000000 00000000 00000000  *........i\.........f..*
7F73E2C0  8000CEF0 00000000 00000000 00000000  00000000 40000000 00000000 86083B48  *.....0.........f...*
7F73E2E0  00000000 40000000 00000000 854D4770  00000000 00000000 00000000 84BC2008  *............e(......d..*
7F73E300  00000000 00000000 00000000 00000000  00000000 40000000 00000000 00000000  *.................f.....*
7F73E320  00000000 40000000 00000000 00000000  86182968 00000000 00000000 00000000  *..............f........*
7F73E340  00000000 00000000 00000000 00000000  89E03A28 00000000 00000000 00000000  *...............i\......*
7F73E360  00000000 00000000 00000000 00000000  00000000 00000000 00000000 00000000  *.....................*
          LINES 7F73E380-7F73E3A0  SAME AS ABOVE
```

```
7F73E3C0  00000000 00000000 00000000 00000000  40000000 00000000 00000000 84FB33E0  *................d..\*
7F73E3E0  00000000 40000000 00000000 849B7B40  00000000 00000000 00000000 7F752204  *....@........d.="*
7F73E400  00000000 00000000 00000000 00000000  00000000 00000000 00000000 00000000  *................"*

JOB EXA7JHMX        STEP APP3       TIME 125832     DATE 94100     ID = 000              PAGE 00000050

      LINE 7F73E420  SAME AS ABOVE
7F73E440  00000000 84C60DE0 00000000 00000000  00000000 00000000 00000000 00000000  *...dF.\.........*
7F73E460  00000000 00000000 00000000 00000000  00000000 00000000 00000000 00000000  *................*
      LINES 7F73E480-7F73E4C0  SAME AS ABOVE
7F73E4E0  00000000 00000000 00000000 009DAE68  009DAE68 00000000 00000000 00000000  *................*
7F73E500  009DAF50 00000000 00000000 00000000  00000000 00000000 00000000 00000000  *.&..............*
7F73E520  00000000 7F73E6BC 00000000 009DF348  009D2028 00000000 00000198 00000000  *...W......3.....*
7F73E540  00000000 00000000 00000000 00000000  00000000 00000000 00000000 00000000  *................*
      LINES 7F73E560-7F73E680  SAME AS ABOVE
7F73E6A0  00000000 00000000 00000000 00000000  00000000 00000000 00000000 E2E8D4D7  *............SYMP*
7F73E6C0  7F74B000 7F74A000 7F752090 00000000  00000000 0321009D 9FE00000 00000000  *...."..(........*
7F73E6E0  00000000 00000000 00000000 00000000  00000000 00000000 00000000 00000000  *................*
7F73E700  00000000 00000000 00000000 009DAE68  00000000 00000000 00000000 00000000  *.............q..*
7F73E720  00000000 00000000 00000000 00000000  00000000 00000000 00000000 00000000  *................*
      LINES 7F73E740-7F73E900  SAME AS ABOVE
7F73E920  00000000 00000000 84C60060 04C6105F  04C6205E 7F73E3F8 7F752090 7F73E3F8  *...dF..-.F._.F.^.F.;"T8".."T8*
7F73E940  04C61330 00000000 00000000 00000000  00000000 00000000 00000000 00000000  *.F..............*
7F73E960  00000000 00000000 00000000 00000000  00000000 C9C5C1E5 E3C1C2C4 E0100020  *........IGC0101CIEAVTABD\...*
7F73E980  00000000 16000000 00000000 C9C7C3F0  F1F0F1C3 00000000 00000000 00000000  *...........Z..-..F.*
7F73E9A0  00000000 00000000 7F73E928 00000000  60010000 04C61A06 00000000 00000000  *.........F......*
7F73E9C0  00000000 00000000 00000000 00000000  00000000 00000000 00000000 00000000  *................*
      LINES 7F73E9E0-7F73EBE0  SAME AS ABOVE
7F73EC00  00000000 00000000 00000000 00000000  C006C100 04C62984 7F73E6F4 00000000  *.....{.A..F.d"W4....*
7F73EC20  00000000 00000000 00000000 00000000  00000000 00000000 00000000 00000000  *................*
      LINES 7F73EC40-7F73ECA0  SAME AS ABOVE
7F73ECC0  00000000 00000000 00000000 00000000  00000000 40000000 00000000 00000000  *"-..............*
7F73ECE0  00000000 00000000 00000000 00000000  00000000 00000000 00000000 00000000  *................*
      LINES 7F73ED00-7F73EE40  SAME AS ABOVE
7F73EE60  00000000 00000000 00280000 00010000  04C62A3A 04C62A3A 7F73EC60 00000000  *.........F...F.".-....*
7F73EE80  00000028 38000000 08000000  02000000  22000000 00000000 00000000 00000000  *.F...F.".....*
7F73EEA0  00000000 00000000 00000000 04C62C48  04C62A42 00000000 0000F7A  00000000  *.......F..N......*
7F73EEC0  E5E2E2C1 7F73F000 00000F7A B23C9000  00000000 0C4BD580 0000F7A B23C9000  *VSSA".0......N.....*
```

```
7F73EEE0  00000000 00000000 00000000 00000000  00000000 01000004 00000000 00000000  *................................*
7F73EF00  00000000 00000000 00000000 00000000  00000000 00000000 00000000 00000000  *................................*
          LINES 7F73EF20-7F73EFE0  SAME AS ABOVE
7F73F000  00000000 00000000 00000000 00000000  00000000 00000000 00000000 00000000  *................................*
          LINES 7F73F020-7F73FFE0  SAME AS ABOVE
7F740000  00000000 00000000 00000000 00000000  00000000 00000000 00000000 00000000  *................................*
          LINES 7F740020-7F740FE0  SAME AS ABOVE
7F741000  00000000 00000000 00000000 00000000  00000000 00000000 00000000 00000000  *................................*
          LINES 7F741020-7F741FE0  SAME AS ABOVE
7F742000  00000000 00000000 00000000 00000000  00000000 00000000 00000000 00000000  *................................*
          LINES 7F742020-7F742FE0  SAME AS ABOVE
7F743000  C3C4E7D3 7F743310 00000000 009C4F84  09E01EFD 09E01F51 00000000 00000000  *CDXL"............!d.\..\.........*
7F743020  00000000 00000000 00000000 00000000  00000000 02000007 02000000 50000C16  *...................&.....&..*
7F743040  00E3E6C1 04C104C2 00000000 7F000000  009C4F24 00F7F080 00000006 00000006  *.TWA.A.B...."..!.70...........*
7F743060  009DB068 00000002 009FE000 7F48FA8   00000000 009FECB8 7FF15198 8128FDD2  *.............y....."l.qa.K*
7F743080  81291214 FF000000 7F7512E0 009C1770  000000E6 7FF15000 09E01F51 009C1770  *a...."\..y...W"l&.l&...*
7F7430A0  00F7F080 009C1770 8128FAD2 7F743070  09E01EFD 09E01F51 09090001 7F743188  *.70...\..a.K"..\..\...h*
7F7430C0  00A7575  00040200 00000000 00000000  00000000 00000000 09E01D3B 09E01E0F  *................................*
7F7430E0  09120001 7F743268 000B5151 000C0200  00000000 00000000 00000000 00000000  *.................................*
7F743100  00000000 00000000 00000000 00030000  09120840 2D360440 3F480440 00000000  *................................*
7F743120  00000000 00000000 00000000 00000000  00000000 00000000 00000000 00000000  *................................*
          LINES 7F743140-7F743180  SAME AS ABOVE
7F7431A0  00000000 00000000 00000000 009F93E4  000000C8 009F93C4 00000000 84000321  *.........H.1D...d...*
7F7431C0  00F7F080 009DF348 00000000 009F93E4  00000000 00000000 00000000 FF030100  *.70..3....1U...*
```

JOB EXA7JHMX   STEP APP3   TIME 125832   DATE 94100   ID = 000   PAGE 00000051

```
7F7431E0  009F93F0 009F93F8 E2E8E2C9 C5C1F0F1  C9C5C100 00000000 00000000 00000000  *..10..18SYSIEA01IEA.............*
7F743200  00000000 00000000 00000000 00000000  00000000 009DAEC4 04C6205E 7F73E928  *.............D.F.^.Z.*
7F743220  7F73E3F8 00000000 84C61412 84C63000  009DB000 009DAEC4 04C6205E 4080E610  *.T8...dF..dF....D.F.^. W.*
7F743240  009DAEC4 04C6105F 84C60060 7F752090  04C6105E 00FD50C8 00FC8BB8 7F73E928  *.D.F..dF.-".F.&H...Z.*
7F743260  7F73E3F8 00FFFFFF 7F7438EC 00000000  00000000 00000000 89E011B0 09E01C64  *.T8....i\..Z.*
7F743280  121C0001 003D2626 00AA0200 00000000  121C0440 4E580440 626C0440 4E580440  *.".....i\..+..*
7F7432A0  00000000 00000000 00C0000  00000000  00000000 4E580440 626C0440 4E580440  *..+.%+.*
7F7432C0  626C0440 00000000 00000000 00000000  00000000 00000000 00000000 00000000  *%....%+.*
7F7432E0  00000000 00000000 01000000 00000000  00000000 00000000 00000000 00000000  *.................................*
7F743300  00000000 00000000 00000000 3F000318  00E3E6C1 04110482 00000000 7F000000  *......TWA..b..."*
7F743320  00000000 00000000 00000000 00000002  009DD308 00000001 00FD8564 00000000  *.L....e..*
```

```
7F743340  00000000 00F503D0 00000000 00000001   0000DFFF 00000000 00001110 0000CEF0   *......5.).............0*
7F743360  00000000 009C90A8 00000002 00FD50C8   00000000 00000000 00005000 009C9000   *.......y.......&H......*
7F743380  0000DFFF 0000C000 00000001 00000098   009C90B0 8107076E 8107076E 00018000   *.......(.....q.....a..>..*
7F7433A0  0000DFFF 00011110 00000000 00F503D0   00000000 00000001 00000001 00000001   *.....(....5.).#..\*a...*
7F7433C0  00000000 00000000 00000000 00000000   00FF7B08 009FE05C 810704BA 00000010   *a..a....3.a....a.8a..8..*
7F7433E0  81070AB6 81070568 009DF348 8106FA10   01070A10 8108EBF8 8108FBF8 00000010   *...."..u.....9..9........*
7F743400  00000000 00000000 00FE0540 00FC1968   00000000 00000000 00FB7FED 00000000   *...M..3.......9..Y......*
7F743420  00000000 7F7438A4 00000000 009FF9A0   009FF9A0 009CA020 009CA000 00000000   *...(...2........Y.....*
7F743440  00FC19D4 009DF348 00000000 00000000   0000DFFF 00001110 0000CEF0 00000000   *....a..;.....).....&.F.DB*
7F743460  0000C000 00000000 00F25420 00000000   00000000 10000000 7F7432E8 00000000   *........a.......q........*
7F743480  40010000 00000000 8108FF5E 00000000   005D1801 009C9000 00005000 C6FDC4C2   *.....a..;.....).....&.F.DB*
7F7434A0  FFFF0000 00000000 8108EFB2 00000000   00BF3098 00000000 00000000 00000000   *........a.......q........*
7F7434C0  00000000 00000000 00000000 00000000   00000000 00000000 00000000 00000000   *.....................*

LINES 7F7434E0-7F7435C0  SAME AS ABOVE

7F7435E0  00000000 00000000 00000000 009DD2F8   00FD50C8 009C93CC 8107057E 8107057E   *.......K8..&H......l.a..=*
7F743600  810C0AE0 00000094 7F743680 0000DFFF   00000000 00FD50C8 7F7432E8 7F7432E8   *a..\..m".........&H"..Y*
7F743620  009C9000 8106FA10 01070A10 00000001   00000007 00FC1968 00000000 00000000   *..a......a..........70.*
7F743640  00000000 00000000 00000000 860A9DC0   00010321 00F7F080 00000000 00000000   *.......f..(....70.....*
7F743660  00000000 00000000 00000000 00000000   00000000 00000000 00000000 00000000   *........&H"..Y.....*
7F743680  00000000 7F743680 00000000 009C9000   00FD50C8 7F7432E8 7F7432E8 009C9000   *.......a...."..Y...*
7F7436A0  8106FA10 01070A10 00000000 0000DFFF   00FC1900 7F7435F0 81070764 8108FC00   *a...a..B....".d.h".&..9.9.*
7F7436C0  8108FBB4 811FC210 00000000 00000007   84BA7088 7F7450A0 009FF9A0 009FF9A0   *a..a.B.."...Y..8....&Hd..h".Y*
7F7436E0  7F744E38 00FD8564 7F7432E8 7F745128   000000FC 00FD50C8 84BA7088 7F7432E8   *d..+..e."..Y...&Hd..h".Y*
7F743700  84BA7332 80CD9000 00006908 FF622CF8   50006B0C 00D60548 40404040 7F755008   *...&..O....."..&.*
7F743720  7F7550B0 00000000 00006DEC 7F752938   00000000 7F752090 7F752730 7F7550B0   *"..&.."..-.&.."..&.*
7F743740  00000000 00000000 00000000 00000000   05EF8200 00004510 C2140000 00F7F080   *....b...B...70.*
7F743760  046F307F 940C2000 00000002 5FB3EE40   046F307F 15485DC0 00C00321 00000321   *.?."m......?.")(.(...*
7F743780  258DA840 FE000000 046F307F 00000000   00000000 00000000 00000000 0378415B   *..y......?."....$*
7F7437A0  046F307F DF8A60AC 7F7550B0 00000000   00000000 00000000 00000000 15485F00   *.?..-.&......^*
7F7437C0  DF8A60AC 00000000 00000000 00000000   7FFFBF00 15485F00 00000000 00000000   *..?.."..l.&..*
7F7437E0  00000000 00000000 00000000 009F93B8   7F7550B0 00000000 00000000 00000000   *.........l.&..*
7F743800  00000000 00000000 00000000 00000000   00000000 00000000 00000000 00000000   *.....^*
7F743820  00000000 00000000 00000000 00000000   00000000 00000000 00000000 00000000   *....................*

LINE 7F743840  SAME AS ABOVE

7F743860  00000000 00000000 00000000 00000000   00000000 00000000 00F503D0 009DD308   *...........5.}..L..*
7F743880  00000000 00C08000 00000000 00000000   00000000 009FF9A0 00FD8564 00FD8564   *.......(.....)....9..e..*
7F7438A0  00000000 C9C5C1E5 E3D9C6F4 005D1201   012C005D 18000000 0000C2E3 00111011   *...IEAVTRF4.)......BT.*
7F7438C0  10000000 88030101 00000000 00000000   00000000 00000000 D7D6D6D3 00000000   *...h...........FOE POOL..*
7F7438E0  00000000 00000000 00000000 00000000   C6D6C540 D7D6D6D3 000000CC 00000000   *....................*
7F743900  00000000 00000002 7F743914 009B7000   00000000 7F743920 00000000 00000000   *....(...........*
```

```
7F743920 7F74392C 00000000 00000000 7F743938    00000000 00000000 7F743944 00000000   *"........."*
7F743940 00000000 7F743950 00000000 00000000    7F74395C 00000000 00000000 7F743968   *."..&...."*
7F743960 00000000 00000000 7F743974 00000000    00000000 7F743980 00000000 00000000   *."..."..."*
7F743980 7F74398C 00000000 00000000 7F743998    00000000 00000000 7F7439A4 00000000   *"........."*
7F7439A0 00000000 7F7439B0 00000000 00000000    00000000 00000000 00000000 00000000   *....q.....u..*
```

JOB EXA7JHMX   STEP APP3   TIME 125832   DATE 94100   ID = 000   PAGE 00000052

The following is an undocumented control block, to the best of my knowledge. The ASPC contains the Access List Entries (ALEs) related to the ASCB; these were formatted following the ASCB at the beginning of the dump.

```
7F7439C0 C1E2D7C3 00000016 80000000 00000000    00000000 00000000 80000000 00000000   *ASPC........*
7F7439E0 00000000 001B8003 00FF0001 00000000    260D7200 00000000 00FF0001 00000000   *............*
7F743A00 260D7280 00000000 00FF0001 00000000    260D7300 00000000 00FF0001 00000000   *............*
7F743A20 260D7380 00000000 00FF0001 00000000    260D7400 00000000 00FF0001 00000000   *............*
7F743A40 260D7480 00000000 00FF0001 00000000    260D7500 00000000 00FF0001 00000000   *............*
7F743A60 260D7580 00000000 00FF0001 00000000    260D7600 00000000 00FF0001 00000000   *............*
7F743A80 260D7680 00000000 00FF0001 00000000    260D7700 00000000 00FF0001 00000000   *............*
7F743AA0 260D7780 00000000 00FF0001 00000000    260D7800 00000000 00FF0001 00000000   *............*
7F743AC0 260D7880 00000000 00FF0001 00000000    260D7900 00000000 00FF0001 00000000   *............*
7F743AE0 260D7980 00000000 00FF0001 00000000    260D7A00 00000000 00FF0001 00000000   *........#...*
7F743B00 260D7A80 00000000 00FF0001 00000000    260D7B00 00000000 00FF0001 00000000   *...#........*
7F743B20 260D7B80 00000000 00FF0001 00000000    260D7C00 00000000 00FF0001 00000000   *........@...*
7F743B40 260D7C80 00000000 00FF0001 00000000    260D7D00 00000000 00FF0001 00000000   *...@........*
7F743B60 260D7D80 00000000 001C0000 80000000    00000000 001D0000 80000000 00000000   *........=...*
7F743B80 00000000 001E0000 80000000 00000000    001F0000 80000000 00000000 00000000   *............*
7F743BA0 00000000 00000000 E2E3C3C2 00000000    7F743BD0 7F743BD0 00000000 00000000   *....STCB....*
7F743BC0 00000001 7FFFBF00 7FFFBF00 00000000    7F743BD0 15485D40 00000000 00000000   *........")"..*
7F743BE0 00000000 0000057E 7FFFBFD0 00000000    00000000 7FFFFBD10 00000000 7F74C0B0   *....^ ".)..*
7F743C00 00000001 00000000 7F74C008 00000000    7FFFFBD10 00000C84 00000001           *..{.."..{..d.*
7F743C20 00000000 00000000 00000000 00000000    00000000 00000000 00000000 00000000   *............*
7F743C40 0000057E 0000057E 00000000 00000000    00000000 00000000 00000000 00000000   *.=.1...........*
7F743C60 0000057E 009DF128 00000000 00000000    00000006 C3C4E7C8 00000000             *....1....CDXHT 01*
7F743C80 00000000 00000000 00000000 00000000    00000000 E340F0F1 00000000
7F743CA0 00000000 00000000 00000000 0006A18
7F743CC0 00000067 00000057 00000000 00000000
```

```
7F743CE0  00000000 00000000 00000000 00000000   7FFE4B34 7FFE4B34 00000000 00000000   *..................*
7F743D00  00000000 00000000 00000000 00000000   00000000 00000000 00000000 00000000   *..................*
      LINES 7F743D20-7F743DE0  SAME AS ABOVE
7F743E00  00000000 00000000 7FFE4AF4 7FFE4AF4   00000000 00000000 00000000 00000000   *..... \4".\4......*
7F743E20  00000000 00000000 00000000 00000000   00000000 00000000 00000000 00000000   *..................*
      LINES 7F743E40-7F743E80  SAME AS ABOVE
7F743EA0  00000000 00000000 00000000 00000000   7FFE4A34 7FFE4A34 00000000 00000000   *........".\.\.....*
7F743EC0  00000000 00000000 00000000 00000000   00000000 00000000 00000000 00000000   *..................*
      LINES 7F743EE0-7F743F40  SAME AS ABOVE
7F743F60  00000000 7FFE49F4 7FFE49B4 7FFE49B4   7FFE4A74 00000000 00000000 00000000   *...."."."."......*
7F743F80  7FFE49F4 7FFE49B4 00000000 00000000   00000000 00000000 00000000 00000000   *."."..............*
7F743FA0  00000000 7FFE4AB4 00000000 00000000   00000000 00000000 00000000 00000000   *."........&.......*
7F743FC0  00000000 7FFE4AB4 00000000 00000000   00000000 00000000 00000000 00000000   *."........&.......*
7F743FE0  00000000 00000000 00000000 00001000   02004000 00000000 00000000 00000000   *...............0..*
7F745000  00000000 7F745050 7F745050 00001000   7FF16EB0 00000000 00000000 00000000   *..&&..U...........*
7F745020  00000000 7F745134 7F745FE0 7F745050   00000004 0008CD00 00000000 00000001   *"1.."..^.\".&&"1>.*
7F745040  00FF0000 05000000 7FF15348 0240FF00   00000005 0008CD00 00005000 7F753000   *.&....P...........*
7F745060  7FFE5000 00002000 0008D700 00000000   00000005 07FEC000 00005000 0008E100   *".&..&.".-..&.{.0.*
7F745080  00001000 00755000 00005000 7F786000   0008FF00 0000000F 0000000F 009CF000   *...............0..*
7F7450A0  00000000 00000001 7FFFB000 00001000   00000001 009F9000 00011000 009FD000   *................}.*
7F7450C0  00002000 009DD000 00001000 009DF000   00000000 009D9000 00011000 0074A000   *...}.......0......*
7F7450E0  00003000 7F72D000 00001000 7F73E000   00006000 7F745000 00004000 7FFE2000   *...}...&-....b&...*
7F745100  00002000 7F751000 00002000 7F776000   00001000 7FFA7000 00825000 00000000   *."...&..".........*
7F745120  00001000 7FFE4000 00001000 7FFFC000   00003000 00000000 00000000 00000000   *."..{.............*
7F745140  00000000 00000000 00000000 00000000   00000000 00000000 00000000 00000000   *..................*
      LINES 7F745160-7F745FE0  SAME AS ABOVE
7F746000  E5E2D4D7 7F72D000 00001000 00001000   00000FB0 7F751778 7F751778 7F751778   *VSMP".}...........*
7F746020  7F751778 00005000 7FFE2670 00001000   009DF348 00E65020 00000000 00000000   *.&."............3.*
7F746040  00000000 00000000 7FFE2028 009DF180   004E8080 7F72DD90 7F746988 7F746988   *".Q..-..1.+.."..h*
7F746060  FD72E000 7F746058 0A17D000 00002000   7FF16EE4 00000000 00000000 00195000   *."-."..}..-}"1>U..*
7F746080  7F72D580 00002000 7F72DDD8 7F746428   7F746088 09ECD000 00040000            *".N......Q".-"h..*
```

JOB EXA7JHMX   STEP APP3   TIME 125832   DATE 94100   ID = 000

```
7F7460A0  7F72D628 7F72D628 7F7460A8 7F7460A8   7F7460B0 7F7460B0 7F72D9E8 7F72D640   *".O..O..-y"-y"-..-..RY".O *
7F7460C0  7F7460B8 0A105000 00001000 7FF16448   7FFE2C88 00000000 7F7523B8 00000608   *.-.-.&...".h...".h*
7F7460E0  FD72E000 00003000 7F751BB0 7FF16448   7FF16448 7F7511F0 009BC000 00000000   *".Q...-..1.+-".."..&.*
7F746100  7F72D580 7F72DC28 7F746100 7F746100   009C5000 00003000 7FFE2A90 7F746850   *".N......./../.&....&*
```

PAGE 00000053

```
7F746120  7F746118  7F746140  7F7466E8  7F746130  7F746138  7F746138    *."/./............"Y"./././.*
7F746140  7F746140  7F746148  7F746148  7F746148  00522000  0000C000    *"./././........."8"./.,/./.*
7F746160  7F751A78  7F751010  09E01000  7F72DB98  7F746178  7F746178    *.../.{."......\.../.*
7F746180  7F746180  7F746188  7F7463C8  7F7461A8  7F746568  7F746568    *"./.,/./..$..\....P./.*
7F7461A0  7F74B000  7F746760  7F7461A8  0A185000  00002000  00002000    *"/././.../h","/h"..H"/.*
7F7461C0  7FF166D0  7F751418  009FF058  7F7510A0  00000000  00000000    *"....-.H"./y".H"./.y.&.*
7F7461E0  7FFE2D90  009C1190  7F72DBE0  7F7510A0  00000000  00000000    *"1.}........0....".*
7F746200  7F73D000  00000378  7F746688  7F746688  7F7512C8  00000000    *......W../Y".Q"/.h".h".H*
7F746220  7FFE2DF0  7FF16EE4  009C1000  009C1000  00009000  00002000    *.."..}>U">U>U.\..*
7F746240  7F7472B0  7F7460A0  009DF180  00018080  7F72D808  7F72D028    *".....1>U">1>U.\..*
7F746260  004E6000  FD9CE000  00000000  00000000  7F72D808  7F746250    *.0..-..1...".Q".).*
7F746280  7F7465E0  00006000  00000000  00000000  00007000  00001000    *.+-......".&."..&..&.*
7F7462A0  7F72DEE0  7F751268  7F751628  7F751208  7FFE2910  00001000    *"...t...h..{......*
7F7462C0  7F72DBC0  7F73A378  7F72DB98  7F72DB98  7FFBB00  00001000      *".......0.V..."...."..*
7F7462E0  7F749000  00000C88  FDE1C000  00001000  7F72DE20  7F72DE20    *"......."..H".../(..*
7F746300  7F746898  009BACF0  7FFE29D0  7FF164D8  7FFE2910  00000010    *".......{."1.Q".*
7F746320  7F746320  00001000  7F72DBC8  7F72D880  7F72DD80  00000908    *"....".(.Q..Q.".".*
7F746340  7F751BE0  00000B58  7F746898  7F746310  7F746318  7F746318    *"..y......"y"./.*
7F746360  009C3000  7F746898  7F746340  7F746328  0A0F3000  00001000    *".....y".".y".*
7F746380  009F9000  7F746328  7F746340  0A0F4000  0A0F3000  00000000    *.........y".*
7F7463A0  7F751D18  00005000  FD731000  7F746430  7FF166D0  7F7461C0    *.......&...........*
7F7463C0  7F7463C0  00000008  7F72D9B8  009C3000  00E05020  00001000    *.........JQ".*
7F7463E0  09E00000  00001000  00003000  7F732000  7F732000  00001000    *"...R...1.}"/.{"..*
7F746400  7F72DE98  7F7463C8  7F746980  7F746980  7F72D6B8  7F7463B8    *"....&..."...."..*
7F746420  7FF16448  7F7518E0  7F72DB98  7F751358  7F751298  7F751298    *".{."."..H"."H"...*
7F746440  009DF050  00000E00  7F510B8  7F510B8  7F7510B8  7F7463F8       *".q".q"...q".q"...*
7F746460  7F7515F8  009BB000  00013000  00001000  7FFE2640  7FF16448     *"..q"....1.8"*
7F746480  FFFE2940  7F746670  7F746370  7F751358  7F751358  7F72D1D8    *"1."...q".1."JQ"*
7F7464A0  7F744478  0A175000  7F746448  7F746448  0A0BB000  00002000    *.0&........q"..*
7F7464C0  FD9BC000  00005008  0A111000  0A111000  00001000  7FFE28B0    *.0&."....".*
7F7464E0  00005CE0  00000048  00000000  00000000  7F743008  000001B8    *"."....."...."..0*
7F746500  7F72DB98  7F7518B0  7FFE2FA0  009BACF0  00002000  00003000    *"......&."...0.Q"*
7F746520  0A058000  7F7517D8  7F7517D8  7F746940  7F72D898  00007000    *"..."..*.&"..Q"..0..Qq"*
7F746540  7F751D60  7F72DB98  7F72DB98  7F746940  7F72DD18  00002000    *".".."...Qq".Qg"".8*
7F746560  00008000  7F751B20  7F746508  7F746508  0A0AA000  00002000    *"........."..0..*
7F746580  7F751BF8  7F751D60  7F746F0  7F746F0  7F746808  009F9028       *"......"...0..."*
7F7465A0  7F7465A0  7F746548  7F746190  7F746190  7F751268  00001000    *".8".8"."..q".q"..*
7F7465C0  7F7465C8  00003000  7F72D040  7F72D040  7F746190  7F746598    *".8".y"."."."."y".&*
7F7465E0  7FFE2D48  7F746280  7F7465B0  7F7465B0  0A060000  0A04A000    *"...H".0".".}..8"*
7F746600  7F7465F8  0A0DB000  7F751C10  7F72D058  7F72DD30  7F72DAF0    *".8".8"..}.}..0..*
```

```
7F746620  00E61020 00007000 7FFE2D90 00001000   7F751D00 009C1190 00E61020 00001000   *.W.............W........*
7F746640  7FFE2CD0 7F7512F8 00000000 7F747000   7F7519D0 00001000 7F72D700 7F7466D0   *."..)".8......).....P."..)*
7F746660  7F746658 0A0EA000 0ADEA000 00001000   7F751460 7F746448 7F746670 7F746670   *..........."...).-......"..*
7F746680  0A0BD000 00001000 7F7461F0 7F7512E0   7F7512E0 7F7461F0 7F73C000 00000378   *...)...-"..\"./0".(...*
7F7466A0  7F7469B8 7F751220 7F751D30 009C1770   7F751820 00001000 7F751400 7F7517F0   *."..../0".\"./0"...&...0.*
7F7466C0  7F72D550 009DB360 00E65020 00001000   7F746658 7F7468F8 7F7466D0 7F7466D0   *.......N&.....W&......8".)"}*
7F7466E0  0A0B9000 00001000 7F751520 7F7466E8   7F746130 009BAE88 00E57020 7F7466F8   *."..N&...-.W&....Y"./..}"*
7F746700  7FFE2B08 7F751340 7FFFC160 000000F0   FD7511F0 00001000 7FFE2BC8 7F751B08   *."....-..Y"./..h.V.."..8*
7F746720  7F746718 7F746718 0A056000 00000000   00000000 00000000 7F72D310 009DF348   *."..."...A-..0...0....H"..*
7F746740  00FC0020 00003000 7F746760 00000000   7F746028 009DF180 004E8080 00000000   *..."........"..."..L..3*
7F746760  7FFE2688 7F7461A8 7F746760 7F746760   0A187000 00002000 7F751F88 7F72D478   *.."......O)....-...1..+*
7F746780  00000000 7F72E000 7F72DDA8 00006000   7F751AF0 7FF16EE4 00000000 00195000   *.."..h".../y"....y.-."..h".M.*


JOB EXA7JHMX        STEP APP3            TIME 125832    DATE 94100    ID = 000                          PAGE 00000054

7F7467A0  7F72DD78 00001000 7F751CE8 7F751C58   7F7467A8 7F7467A8 0A163000 00001000   *."........Y"...y".Y......*
7F7467C0  7F746400 7F72D028 009A9000 00014000   00015000 00001000 7F72D460 7F7467D8   *.".......).\".Y.......M-".Q*
7F7467E0  7F7467E0 7F7467E0 7F7467E8 7F7467E8   00000000 00000000 7F72D1F0 009DF348   *."..\".\".Y".Y........J0.3.*
7F746800  00218080 00000000 7F72D760 7F72D350   7F746538 009E0BF8 00E65020 00001000   *."..........P-".L&.....8.W&.*
7F746820  7F751BC8 7F751DA8 7F7517F0 009DB360   00E60020 00001000 7F749E18 000001A0   *."..H".y".0.-.W........&".Q*
7F746840  7F72D880 7F751AC0 7F72D880 00001000   7F746118 7F751610 7F746850 7F746850   *."..Q".{.Q...-."......&.&*
7F746860  0A10A000 00001000 7F72D820 7F751940   7F72DC88 7F72DC88 009EC000 00001000   *."..."...Q".h".h..&."..&*
7F746880  7F72D658 7F7467F0 7F72DC28 7F72DC28   009C7000 00001000 7F746970 7F746970   *."..h".h".(".(..O.*.".p"*
7F7468A0  7F72D028 FD72D028 00006000 00001000   7F751A18 7F72DD78 009DD3C8 000000A8   *."..)..).8.-./y"..H".H.y*
7F7468C0  FD72D028 00001000 7F7461A8 7F72DF40   7F7468C8 7F7468C8 0A183000 00002000   *.")...-."..L".8.\.8.\.*
7F7468E0  7F72DE38 7F72D320 7FFE2BF8 7FFE2BF8   09E01000 00002000 7F746580 7F751880   *."..8.).8.\.8.\.......&..*
7F746900  7F7468F8 7F7468F8 0A0E8000 00001000   7F746070 00000000 009C3000 00005000   *."..8".8"....q"...&...Q*
7F746920  FD749000 00003000 7F751E68 7FFE2898   7FF16448 7F746550 009DB328 00000CD8   *."..".....h.V.."...q".Q8*
7F746940  7F751760 7FF16568 7F751520 009BAE88   00E50020 00000000 7F72D8F8 7F72DA48   *."..-"...-.W&...."..Q".q"*
7F746960  7F746958 0A04E000 00002000 7FFE2D00   7F746898 7F746898 7F746978 7F746978   *.".}"....\.&".&".q".q"*
7F746980  7F746D30 7F7463D0 7F746058 7FFE2D00   7F746988 7F746988 0A17B000 00002000   *."..}".h".m...m...Y"*
7F7469A0  7F72DB68 00000000 009F9460 00000010   FD9F94B0 00000010 7F7513E8 7F7513E8   *."..,"....m-.h.{."...h..(*
7F7469C0  7F751760 7F7469C0 7F7469C8 7F7469C8   7F72DA90 7FFE2688 00000000 009D9000   *."..-."..{".Y.q"..LH..y*
7F7469E0  7F7510E8 00001000 7FFE2010 7F72DF28   7F72DA90 7F7469E8 0A18F000 00002000   *."..Y..../y"..8.-..H..H.y*
7F746A00  7F72DC40 7F7513D0 7FFE2C70 7FFE2C70   009C3000 00000000 7F7513D0 00000000   *."..(".H..%".%..O..H*
7F746A20  009DC000 7F7513D0 7F751B80 7F751B80   7F72DD00 7F72DC28 7F751B80 7F751B80   *.".L".H".8.8.."..).8.8*
7F746A40  7F746A78 00000000 7F746A60 7FF16EE4   00000000 00195000 7F746A30 00000000   *.".".-...&.-."....&.*
7F746A60  00000000 00000000 00000000 00000000   00000000 00000000 7F746A90 00000000   *.".................*
```

```
7F746A80  00000000 00000000  7F746AA8  00000000 00000000 00000000 00000000  *................*
7F746AA0  00000000 00000000  ........  00000000 00000000 00000000 00000000  *.....".y........*
7F746AC0  00000000 00000000  7F746AC0  00000000 00000000 00000000 00000000  *.Q..."(....".....*
7F746AE0  00000000 00000000  7F746AD8  00000000 00000000 00000000 00000000  *."...."..... .0..*
7F746B00  00000000 00000000  7F746B08  00000000 00000000 00000000 00000000  *................*
7F746B20  00000000 00000000  7F746B20  00000000 00000000 00000000 00000000  *."..."....".....*
7F746B38  00000000 00000000                                                 *................*
7F746B40  00000000 00000000  7F746B68  00000000 00000000 00000000 00000000  *.."...."...,.&..*
7F746B60  00000000 00000000  7F746B80  00000000 00000000 00000000 00000000  *................*
7F746B80  00000000 00000000            00000000 00000000 00000000 00000000  *................*
7F746B98  00000000 00000000                                                 *."...."....".....*
7F746BA0  00000000 00000000  7F746BC8  00000000 00000000 00000000 00000000  *.,q....H..."....*
7F746BC0  00000000 00000000            00000000 00000000 00000000 00000000  *................*
7F746BE0  00000000 00000000                                                 *."...,.\...".....*
7F746BF8  00000000 00000000                                                 *................*
7F746C00  00000000 00000000  7F746C10  00000000 00000000 00000000 00000000  *.,8..."....".....*
7F746C20  00000000 00000000  7F746C28  00000000 00000000 00000000 00000000  *..%...%...%.....*
7F746C40  00000000 00000000            00000000 00000000 00000000 00000000  *................*
7F746C58  00000000 00000000                                                 *..%....%...&....*
7F746C60  00000000 00000000  7F746C70  00000000 00000000 00000000 00000000  *..%h..."....".....*
7F746C80  00000000 00000000  7F746C88  00000000 00000000 00000000 00000000  *................*
7F746CA0  00000000 00000000  7F746CB8  00000000 00000000 00000000 00000000  *..%....%....%)..*
7F746CB8  00000000 00000000                                                 *................*
7F746CC0  00000000 00000000  7F746CE8  00000000 00000000 00000000 00000000  *..&Y...."....".....*
7F746CE0  00000000 00000000            00000000 00000000 00000000 00000000  *................*
7F746D00  00000000 00000000  7F746D30  00000000 00000000 00000000 00000000  *................*
7F746D18  00000000 00000000                                                 *................*
7F746D20  00000000 00000000  7F746D48  00000000 00000000 00000000 00000000  *..|...._..."....*
7F746D40  00000000 00000000            00000000 00000000 00000000 00000000  *................*
7F746D60  00000000 00000000  7F746D90  00000000 00000000 00000000 00000000  *..|...._..."....*
7F746D78  00000000 00000000                                                 *................*
7F746D80  00000000 00000000  7F746DA8  00000000 00000000 00000000 00000000  *................*
7F746DA0  00000000 00000000            00000000 00000000 00000000 00000000  *..|....y..."....*
7F746DC0  00000000 00000000  7F746DE8  00000000 00000000 00000000 00000000  *.._{..."{..."....*
7F746DD8  00000000 00000000                                                 *................*
7F746DE0  00000000 00000000  7F746E08  00000000 00000000 00000000 00000000  *.._..."_..."..0..*
7F746E00  00000000 00000000            00000000 00000000 00000000 00000000  *................*
7F746E20  00000000 00000000  7F746E50  00000000 00000000 00000000 00000000  *.>....">....">&..*
7F746E38  00000000 00000000                                                 *................*
7F746E40  00000000 00000000  7F746E68  00000000 00000000 00000000 00000000  *.>....">...".....*
7F746E60  00000000 00000000            00000000 00000000 00000000 00000000  *................*
7F746E80  00000000 00000000  7F746EB0  00000000 00000000 00000000 00000000  *.>q...".>.....">..*
7F746E98  00000000 00000000                                                 *................*

JOB EXA7JHMX        STEP APP3         TIME 125832   DATE 94100   ID = 000        PAGE 00000055

7F746EA0  00000000 00000000 00000000  7F746EC8  00000000 00000000 00000000  *......">\..">H....*
7F746EC0  00000000 00000000 7F746EE0  00000000 00000000                      *......">\........*
```

```
7F746EE0  7F746EF8  00000000  00000000  00000000  00000000  7F746F10  00000000   *...>8....*
7F746F00  00000000  00000000  00000000  7F746F28  00000000  00000000  00000000   *.........*
7F746F20  00000000  00000000  7F746F40  00000000  00000000  00000000  00000000   *.........*
7F746F40  00000000  7F746F58  00000000  00000000  00000000  7F746F70  00000000   *.........*
7F746F60  00000000  00000000  00000000  7F746F88  00000000  00000000  00000000   *.........*
7F746F80  00000000  00000000  7F746FA0  00000000  00000000  00000000  00000000   *.........*
7F746FA0  00000000  7F746FB8  00000000  00000000  00000000  7F746FD0  00000000   *.........*
7F746FC0  00000000  00000000  00000000  7F746FE8  00000000  00000000  00000000   *.........*
7F746FE0  00000000  00000000  7F72D0A0  00000000  00000000  00000000  00000000   *.........*
7F747000  00000000  00000000  00000000  00000000  00000000  00000000  00000000   *.........*
          LINES 7F747020-7F7470C0  SAME AS ABOVE
7F7470E0  00000000  00000000  00000000  8112AF4C  0000C00  00F7F080   0000000    *.......a.<...70.*
7F747100  01D31060  0000003C  00000C60  00FD50C8  7F7472B0  00FE4380  00000048    *.L-..'-.&H..Y.9m-*
7F747120  00000001  8112ADE0  0112BDDF  7F747210  04BE21D0  7F747300  0112BE15    *..a.\..)'.--*
7F747140  0112BEEE  7F747160  8112AF4C  7F747168  0112BE15  7F747168  0112BE15    *.L-."8.-a.<*
7F747160  01D31060  7F7472F8  000001FC  00000000  00000000  10000000  7F747228    *.........*
7F747180  00000000  60010000  0112B8DE  00000000  00000000  00000000  00000000    *.........*
7F7471A0  00000000  00000000  00000000  00000000  00000000  00000000  00000000    *.........*
          LINES 7F7471C0-7F7471E0  SAME AS ABOVE
7F747200  00000000  00000000  00000000  00000001  00000000  00000000  7F747210    *.........a...*
7F747220  0000133C  00000C60  7F7470E8  0112BDDF  8112ADE0  0112BDDF  7F747210    *...Y.9m-a.\.-*
7F747240  7F7470E8  00000000  00000000  00000000  00000000  00000000  00000000    *.Y.........*
7F747260  00000000  00000000  00000000  00000000  00000101  0112AF88  00000000    *.........h*
7F747280  00000000  00000000  00000000  009DD3C8  009DD280  84BE20C0  0112AF88    *.9m-....LH.K.d.(*
7F7472A0  00F99460  7F747226  009D228   009DF348  00001000  84BE1958  84BE20C0    *d..(".....3....d.*
7F7472C0  84BE11C0  7F747000  009D0228  009DDC8   04BE21D0  7F747300  84BE1D00    *.d...(".&...d.)"*
7F7472E0  0F381000  7F747378  7F751310  7F7472B0  7F747378  00001000  7F747300    *.d..&....d..d.>*
7F747300  009D0584  00000000  7F74513C  84BE1AAC  84BE1D50  00001010  84BE1F6E    *d..d..sd....d.&.*
7F747320  84BE1AB0  84BE1AA2  7F745000  00000000  E5C1C4C9  00001000  00000004    *.d.........IEAVADINIGC0005A921*
7F747340  84BE1AB0  08440012  00000000  E5C1C4C9  D5C9C7C3  F0F0F0F5  C1F9F2F1    *.d..sd....&..IEAVADINIGC0005A921*
7F747360  F2F74040  00C9C5C1  7FFE6000  7F744378  F0F0F0F5  C1F9F2F1  00000000    *27   HBB4430  ..-.-....*
7F747380  009CF000  009D0000  009DD000  009FE000  009FF000  009DF000  00001000    *.0...)..\.0....0.*
7F7473A0  009F9000  009FD000  7F73E000  009DD000  009FE000  009FF000  00001000    *..)..\.0....0.*
7F7473C0  7F72D000  00001000  7F73F000  7F73E000  7F73F000  00740000  00001000    *."..)..\.0...&..*
7F7473E0  7F741000  00001000  7F742000  7F743000  7F745000  7F74A000  00001000    *."...-....&..*
7F747400  7F746000  00001000  7F747000  7F748000  7F752000  7F776000  00001000    *."........*
7F747420  7F74B000  00001000  7F751000  7F751000  7F752000  7F7AA000  00001000    *."...:.....*
7F747440  7F7A7000  00001000  7F7A8000  7F7A9000  7F7A9000  7F7AA000  00001000    *."...:.).....*
7F747460  7F7AB000  00001000  7F7AC000  7F7AC000  7F7AD000  7F7AE000  00001000    *."...)..:.\..*
7F747480  7F7AF000  00001000  7F7B0000  7F7B0000  7F7B1000  7F7B2000  00001000    *."::0....#..#.*
```

```
7F7474A0  7F7B3000 00001000 7F7B4000 00001000 7F7B5000 00001000 7F7B6000 00001000  *"#......"# ....."#&....."#-....*
7F7474C0  7F7B7000 00001000 7F7B8000 00001000 7F7B9000 00001000 7F7BA000 00001000  *"#......"#......"#......"#....*
7F7474E0  7F7BB000 00001000 7F7BC000 00001000 7F7BD000 00001000 7F7BE000 00001000  *"#......"#{....."#}....."#\....*
7F747500  7F7BF000 00001000 7F7C0000 00001000 7F7C1000 00001000 7F7C2000 00001000  *"#0....."@......"@......"@....*
7F747520  7F7C3000 00001000 7F7C4000 00001000 7F7C5000 00001000 7F7C6000 00001000  *"@......"@ ....."@&....."@-....*
7F747540  7F7C7000 00001000 7F7C8000 00001000 7F7C9000 00001000 7F7CA000 00001000  *"@......"@......"@......"@....*
7F747560  7F7CB000 00001000 7F7CC000 00001000 7F7CD000 00001000 7F7CE000 00001000  *"@......"@{....."@}....."@\....*
7F747580  7F7CF000 00001000 7F7D0000 00001000 7F7D1000 00001000 7F7D2000 00001000  *"@0....."'......"'......"'....*
7F7475A0  7F7D3000 00001000 7F7D4000 00001000 7F7D5000 00001000 7F7D6000 00001000  *"'......"' ....."'&....."'-....*
7F7475C0  7F7D7000 00001000 7F7D8000 00001000 7F7D9000 00001000 7F7DA000 00001000  *"'......"'......"'......"'....*
7F7475E0  7F7DB000 00001000 7F7DC000 00001000 7F7DD000 00001000 7F7DE000 00001000  *"'......"'{....."'}....."'\....*
7F747600  7F7DF000 00001000 7F7E0000 00001000 7F7E1000 00001000 7F7E2000 00001000  *"'0....."=......"=......"=....*
7F747620  7F7E3000 00001000 7F7E4000 00001000 7F7E5000 00001000 7F7E6000 00001000  *"=......"= ....."=&....."=-....*
7F747640  7F7E7000 00001000 7F7E8000 00001000 7F7E9000 00001000 7F7EA000 00001000  *"=......"=......"=......"=....*

JOB EXA7JHMX      STEP APP3        TIME 125832    DATE 94100     ID = 000       PAGE 00000056

7F747660  7F7EB000 00001000 7F7EC000 00001000 7F7ED000 00001000 7F7EE000 00001000  *"=......"={....."=}....."=\....*
7F747680  7F7EF000 00001000 7F7F0000 00001000 7F7F1000 00001000 7F7F2000 00001000  *"=0....."".....""....."".....*
7F7476A0  7F7F3000 00001000 7F7F4000 00001000 7F7F5000 00001000 7F7F6000 00001000  *""......"" .....""&....""-....*
7F7476C0  7F7F7000 00001000 7F7F8000 00001000 7F7F9000 00001000 7F7FA000 00001000  *""......""......""......""....*
7F7476E0  7F7FB000 00001000 7F7FC000 00001000 7F7FD000 00001000 7F7FE000 00001000  *""......""{.....""}.....""\....*
7F747700  7F7FF000 00001000 7F800000 00001000 7F801000 00001000 7F802000 00001000  *""0.....".......".......".....*
7F747720  7F803000 00001000 7F804000 00001000 7F805000 00001000 7F806000 00001000  *".......". .....".&.....".-....*
7F747740  7F807000 00001000 7F808000 00001000 7F809000 00001000 7F80A000 00001000  *".......".......".......".....*
7F747760  7F80B000 00001000 7F80C000 00001000 7F80D000 00001000 7F80E000 00001000  *".......".{.....".}.....".\....*
7F747780  7F80F000 00001000 7F810000 00001000 7F811000 00001000 7F812000 00001000  *".0....."a......"a......"a....*
7F7477A0  7F813000 00001000 7F814000 00001000 7F815000 00001000 7F816000 00001000  *"a......"a ....."a&....."a-....*
7F7477C0  7F817000 00001000 7F818000 00001000 7F819000 00001000 7F81A000 00001000  *"a......"a......"a......"a....*
7F7477E0  7F81B000 00001000 7F81C000 00001000 7F81D000 00001000 7F81E000 00001000  *"a......"a{....."a}....."a\....*
7F747800  7F81F000 00001000 7F820000 00001000 7F821000 00001000 7F822000 00001000  *"a0....."b......"b......"b....*
7F747820  7F823000 00001000 7F824000 00001000 7F825000 00001000 7F826000 00001000  *"b......"b ....."b&....."b-....*
7F747840  7F827000 00001000 7F828000 00001000 7F829000 00001000 7F82A000 00001000  *"b......"b......"b......"b....*
7F747860  7F82B000 00001000 7F82C000 00001000 7F82D000 00001000 7F82E000 00001000  *"b......"b{....."b}....."b\....*
7F747880  7F82F000 00001000 7F830000 00001000 7F831000 00001000 7F832000 00001000  *"b0....."c......"c......"c....*
7F7478A0  7F833000 00001000 7F834000 00001000 7F835000 00001000 7F836000 00001000  *"c......"c ....."c&....."c-....*
7F7478C0  7F837000 00001000 7F838000 00001000 7F839000 00001000 7F83A000 00001000  *"c......"c......"c......"c....*
7F7478E0  7F83B000 00001000 7F83C000 00001000 7F83D000 00001000 7F83E000 00001000  *"c......"c{....."c}....."c\....*
```

Address			Address		Address		Address		ASCII
7F747900	7F83F000	00001000	7F840000	00001000	7F841000	00001000	7F842000	00001000	`*"c0....."d....."d....."d-....*`
7F747920	7F843000	00001000	7F844000	00001000	7F845000	00001000	7F846000	00001000	`*"d....."d....."dk....."d-....*`
7F747940	7F847000	00001000	7F848000	00001000	7F849000	00001000	7F84A000	00001000	`*"d....."d....."d)....."d-....*`
7F747960	7F84B000	00001000	7F84C000	00001000	7F84D000	00001000	7F84E000	00001000	`*"d....."d(....."d\....."d\....*`
7F747980	7F84F000	00001000	7F850000	00001000	7F851000	00001000	7F852000	00001000	`*"d0....."d)....."e(....."e-....*`
7F7479A0	7F853000	00001000	7F854000	00001000	7F855000	00001000	7F856000	00001000	`*"e....."e....."e&....."e-....*`
7F7479C0	7F857000	00001000	7F858000	00001000	7F859000	00001000	7F85A000	00001000	`*"e....."e....."e)....."e-....*`
7F7479E0	7F85B000	00001000	7F85C000	00001000	7F85D000	00001000	7F85E000	00001000	`*"e....."e(....."e)....."e\....*`
7F747A00	7F85F000	00001000	7F860000	00001000	7F861000	00001000	7F862000	00001000	`*"e0....."f....."f)....."f-....*`
7F747A20	7F863000	00001000	7F864000	00001000	7F865000	00001000	7F866000	00001000	`*"f....."f....."f&....."f-....*`
7F747A40	7F867000	00001000	7F868000	00001000	7F869000	00001000	7F86A000	00001000	`*"f....."f....."f)....."f-....*`
7F747A60	7F86B000	00001000	7F86C000	00001000	7F86D000	00001000	7F86E000	00001000	`*"f....."f(....."f)....."f\....*`
7F747A80	7F86F000	00001000	7F870000	00001000	7F871000	00001000	7F872000	00001000	`*"f0....."g....."g&....."g-....*`
7F747AA0	7F873000	00001000	7F874000	00001000	7F875000	00001000	7F876000	00001000	`*"g....."g....."g&....."g-....*`
7F747AC0	7F877000	00001000	7F878000	00001000	7F879000	00001000	7F87A000	00001000	`*"g....."g....."g)....."g-....*`
7F747AE0	7F87B000	00001000	7F87C000	00001000	7F87D000	00001000	7F87E000	00001000	`*"g....."g(....."g)....."g\....*`
7F747B00	7F87F000	00001000	7F880000	00001000	7F881000	00001000	7F882000	00001000	`*"g0....."h....."h&....."h-....*`
7F747B20	7F883000	00001000	7F884000	00001000	7F885000	00001000	7F886000	00001000	`*"h....."h....."h&....."h-....*`
7F747B40	7F887000	00001000	7F888000	00001000	7F889000	00001000	7F88A000	00001000	`*"h....."h....."h)....."h-....*`
7F747B60	7F88B000	00001000	7F88C000	00001000	7F88D000	00001000	7F88E000	00001000	`*"h....."h(....."h)....."h\....*`
7F747B80	7F88F000	00001000	7F890000	00001000	7F891000	00001000	7F892000	00001000	`*"h0....."i....."i&....."i-....*`
7F747BA0	7F893000	00001000	7F894000	00001000	7F895000	00001000	7F896000	00001000	`*"i....."i....."i&....."i-....*`
7F747BC0	7F897000	00001000	7F898000	00001000	7F899000	00001000	7F89A000	00001000	`*"i....."i....."i)....."i-....*`
7F747BE0	7F89B000	00001000	7F89C000	00001000	7F89D000	00001000	7F89E000	00001000	`*"i....."i(....."i)....."i\....*`
7F747C00	7F89F000	00001000	7F8A0000	00001000	7F8A1000	00001000	7F8A2000	00001000	`*"i0....."..........*`
7F747C20	7F8A3000	00001000	7F8A4000	00001000	7F8A5000	00001000	7F8A6000	00001000	`*".........&....*`
7F747C40	7F8A7000	00001000	7F8A8000	00001000	7F8A9000	00001000	7F8AA000	00001000	`*".....(.....)....*`
7F747C60	7F8AB000	00001000	7F8AC000	00001000	7F8AD000	00001000	7F8AE000	00001000	`*".....(.....).....\....*`
7F747C80	7F8AF000	00001000	7F8B0000	00001000	7F8B1000	00001000	7F8B2000	00001000	`*".0..........*`
7F747CA0	7F8B3000	00001000	7F8B4000	00001000	7F8B5000	00001000	7F8B6000	00001000	`*".........&....*`
7F747CC0	7F8B7000	00001000	7F8B8000	00001000	7F8B9000	00001000	7F8BA000	00001000	`*".....(.....)....*`
7F747CE0	7F8BB000	00001000	7F8BC000	00001000	7F8BD000	00001000	7F8BE000	00001000	`*".....(.....).....\....*`
7F747D00	7F8BF000	00001000	7F8C0000	00001000	7F8C1000	00001000	7F8C2000	00001000	`*".0..........*`
7F747D20	7F8C3000	00001000	7F8C4000	00001000	7F8C5000	00001000	7F8C6000	00001000	`*".........&....*`
7F747D40	7F8C7000	00001000	7F8C8000	00001000	7F8C9000	00001000	7F8CA000	00001000	`*".....(.........*`

```
JOB EXA7JHMX        STEP APP3        TIME 125832      DATE 94100      ID = 000                    PAGE 00000057

7F747D60  00001000 7F8CB000 7F8CC000 00001000  7F8CD000 00001000 7F8CE000 00001000   *...."...".{....".}....".\....*
7F747D80  00001000 7F8CF000 7F8D0000 00001000  7F8D1000 00001000 7F8D2000 00001000   *....".0.".....".....".....*
7F747DA0  00001000 7F8D3000 7F8D4000 00001000  7F8D5000 00001000 7F8D6000 00001000   *...."...".....".&....".-....*
7F747DC0  00001000 7F8D7000 7F8D8000 00001000  7F8D9000 00001000 7F8DA000 00001000   *...."...".....".....".....*
7F747DE0  00001000 7F8DB000 7F8DC000 00001000  7F8DD000 00001000 7F8DE000 00001000   *...."...".{....".}....".\....*
7F747E00  00001000 7F8DF000 7F8E0000 00001000  7F8E1000 00001000 7F8E2000 00001000   *....".0.".....".....".....*
7F747E20  00001000 7F8E3000 7F8E4000 00001000  7F8E5000 00001000 7F8E6000 00001000   *...."...".....".&....".-....*
7F747E40  00001000 7F8E7000 7F8E8000 00001000  7F8E9000 00001000 7F8EA000 00001000   *...."...".....".....".....*
7F747E60  00001000 7F8EB000 7F8EC000 00001000  7F8ED000 00001000 7F8EE000 00001000   *...."...".{....".}....".\....*
7F747E80  00001000 7F8EF000 7F8F0000 00001000  7F8F1000 00001000 7F8F2000 00001000   *....".0.".....".....".....*
7F747EA0  00001000 7F8F3000 7F8F4000 00001000  7F8F5000 00001000 7F8F6000 00001000   *...."...".....".&....".-....*
7F747EC0  00001000 7F8F7000 7F8F8000 00001000  7F8F9000 00001000 7F8FA000 00001000   *...."...".....".....".....*
7F747EE0  00001000 7F8FB000 7F8FC000 00001000  7F8FD000 00001000 7F8FE000 00001000   *...."...".{....".}....".\....*
7F747F00  00001000 7F8FF000 7F900000 00001000  7F901000 00001000 7F902000 00001000   *....".0.".....".....".....*
7F747F20  00001000 7F903000 7F904000 00001000  7F905000 00001000 7F906000 00001000   *...."...".....".&....".-....*
7F747F40  00001000 7F907000 7F908000 00001000  7F909000 00001000 7F90A000 00001000   *...."...".....".....".....*
7F747F60  00001000 7F90B000 7F90C000 00001000  7F90D000 00001000 7F90E000 00001000   *...."...".j....".j....".j....*
7F747F80  00001000 7F90F000 7F910000 00001000  7F911000 00001000 7F912000 00001000   *....".0.".....".....".....*
7F747FA0  00001000 7F913000 7F914000 00001000  7F915000 00001000 7F916000 00001000   *...."...".j&...".j....".j....*
7F747FC0  00001000 7F917000 7F918000 00001000  7F919000 00001000 7F91A000 00001000   *...."...".j....".j....".j....*
7F747FE0  00001000 7F91B000 7F91C000 00001000  7F91D000 00001000 7F91E000 00001000   *...."...".j....".j....".j....*
7F748000  00000000 00000000 00000000 00000000  00000000 00000000 00000000 00000000   *................................*

LINES 7F748020-7F748080 SAME AS ABOVE

7F7480A0  02020001 7F74843D 00026767 00070200  850245B0 05024634 00070200 00000000   *....e.....".d.*
7F7480C0  00000000 00000000 00000000 00000000  00000000 00000000 02020340 0A0A0240   *................................*
7F7480E0  20200580 27270840 3B3B0240 41410020  10100240 16160440 47470020 43430140   *................................*
7F748100  53530440 5D5D0440 00000000 00000000  49490140 4D4D0240 47470020 00000000   *....((....)).....*
7F748120  00000000 00000000 00000000 00000000  00000000 00000000 00000000 00000000   *................................*

LINES 7F748140-7F748160 SAME AS ABOVE

7F748180  01F4BA04 011B28C4 01F4B000 01F4B0CB  011B2543 011B2E42 80000000 011B2300   *.4.....D.4...4.....*
7F7481A0  02396480 0187D102 02396202 011B2B84  011B2781 80000000 023963C0 80000000   *...gJ....d..a...{....*
7F7481C0  80000000 8187D040 8187D040 80000000  011B2480 011B23C0 2595E01F 0285B01F   *...ag}....{.n}...e.*
7F748200  0357401F 034C601F 02396840 02396541  02396D81 02396A45 0187D040 02396901   *...>A...._a...g}....*
7F748220  80000000 80000000 80000000 80000000  070C1640 80000000 80000000 80000000   *..<--....)).....*
7F748240  80000000 80000000 80000000 80000000  80000000 80000000 80000000 80000000   *................................*
7F748260  009D06D2 7F748325 009CEF70 8515D45E  80CB7ED0 7F748325 009D06D2 7F748325   *...LH...e.M;..=}".c...K".c.*
7F748280  7F748240 8515D022 8515D310 8515D1E4  8515D1F6 8515D200 8515D2EA 8515D518   *".b.e.}.e.L.e.JUe.J6e.K.e.K.e.N.*
```

```
7F7482A0  7F7470A8  009D040F  8515DD28  8515DC98  7F74708C  7F7482CC  009D03C6  *".y.....e.O.e...e.q".."..b....F*
7F7482C0  7F7470A8  009D040F  009D03C6  00000000  009D06D2  009DF348  7F748325  *".y.....F....K....3.".c..*
7F7482E0  00000014  009DD3C8  00000000  84BDE82A  84BE0C48  009D0228  009D0228  *............LH...d.Y.d.......*
7F748300  00006DEC  04BDEEA1  00FD50C8  04BDA4FF  04BDED87  00006E1C  00FC8BB8  *.d_.h".b\d.\...&H..u...g..>..*
7F748320  84BDDD88  7F7482E0  84BDE0DC  04BDEEA1  84BDE94   00000000  7F749FDC  *d.m.............d..m.......*
7F748340  7F748384  00000000  00000000  00000000  009DF2C0  00F7P080  00000028  *.......................3..2{.70.*
7F748360  7F7483E0  00000000  00000000  00000000  009FF6B8  00006F3C  00000000  *..c..............6..?.*
7F748380  00006E4C  7F749FB8  84BDE10A  84BDE280  00000000  0000FFFF  00110080  *..>........d..d.S.........*
7F7483A0  00000000  009D057C  00000000  00000000  00000000  0000FFFF  00020C9   *..><"....".d..d.S..*
7F7483C0  C5C1E5C1  C4C9D5C7  C7C3F0F0  F0F5C1F9  F2F1F2F7  40404040  F3F04000  *EAVADINIGC0005A92127  HBB4430 .*
7F7483E0  00000000  00000000  00000000  00000000  00000000  00C00000  00000000  *............................*
7F748400  00000000  00000000  7F748418  054104F0  009D057C  00000000  00000000  *.............d..0...@........*
7F748420  00000000  009PF2C0  00000000  E6C1E240  C5D5E3C5  D9C5C440  E5C9C140  *......d...2{...WAS ENTERED VIA CALL*
7F748460  40404040  40404040  40404040  40404040  40404040  40404040  40404040  *                            *
        LINES 7F748480-7F7484A0  SAME AS ABOVE
7F7484C0  C1D9C5C1  E240D9C5  D3C1E3C5  C440E3D6  40E0C3C2  40C1E37A  40F0F0F9  C4C6F3F4  *AREAS RELATED TO TCB AT: 009DF34*
7F7484E0  F8614B4B  4B4B4040  F0F0F0F0  F0F0F0F1  C5D5D861  C4C5D840  C3D6D5E3  D9D6D340  *8/....  000000001ENQ/DEQ CONTROL *

JOB EXA7JHMX          STEP APP3          TIME 125832   DATE 94100   ID = 000          PAGE 00000058

7F748500  C2D3D6C3  D2E24B4B  4B4B4B4B  4B4B4B4B  4B4B4040  F0F0F0F0  F0F0F2F6  *BLOCKS...............  00000026*
7F748520  C4C1E3C1  40D4C1D5  C1C7C5D4  C5D5E340  C3D6D5E3  D9D6D3C6  D2E24B4B  *DATA MANAGEMENT CONTROL BLOCKS..*
7F748540  4B4B4B4B  4B4B4040  F0F0F0F0  F0F0F2F7  C9D6E240  C3D6D5E3  D9D6D3C3  *.....  000000027IOS CONTROL BLOC*
7F748560  D2E24B4B  4B4B4B4B  4B4B4B4B  4B4B4040  F0F0F0F0  F0F0F2F8  *KS............  00000028*
7F748580  D9E3D440  C3D6D5E3  D9D6D340  F0F0F0F0  4B4B4B4B  E3C1C3D2  E2406140  *RTM CONTROL BLOCKS.....  /*
7F7485A0  4B4B4B4B  F0F0F0F0  F0F0F2F9  C1C1E34B  D5D240E2  E3C1C3D2  E2406140  *........0000029PCLINK STACKS / *
7F7485C0  E2C1E5C5  40C1D9C5  C1E24B4B  4B4B4B4B  C5D440E2  F0F0F0F0  F0F0F3F4  *SAVE AREAS.......  00000034*
7F7485E0  C9D5E2E3  C1D3D3C1  E3C9D6D5  61E2E4C2  E2E82E3  4B4B4B4B  4B4B4B4B  *INSTALLATION/SUBSYSTEM AREA....*
7F748600  4B4B4B4B  4B4B4040  F0F0F0F0  F0F0F3F4  D3E2D8C1  4B4B4B4B  4B4B4B4B  *.....  00000034LSQA...........*
7F748620  4B4B4B4B  4B4B4B4B  4B4B4040  F0F0F0F0  F0F0F3F4  4B4B4B4B  4B4B4B4B  *........  00000034........*
7F748640  40404040  40404040  40404040  40404040  40404040  40404040  40404040  *                            *
        LINES 7F748660-7F7486F0  SAME AS ABOVE
7F74A000  000C2000  078D1000  00006B10  D7C7D4F1  00006908  00000208  05EF8200  *...............,APP3PGM1.....b.*
7F74A020  00004510  C2140000  00006E4C  00000040  009F1954  009F1930  009F9028  *....B......)...B....><..}....*
7F74A040  009D1FF8  009FF060  809DF510  00009000  00002260  00006908  00006DEC  *.........0--.5........0--.5-..*
7F74A060  50006B0C  00D60548  00F7F080  00000000  00002260  00006908  00000000  *&.,.O.........70.............*
7F74A080  00000000  00000000  00000000  00000000  00000000  00000000  00000000  *............................*
```

```
7F74A0A0  00000000 860A9DC0 00010321 5FB3EE40  046F307F 15485DC0 0C000321 00000321  *...f.{....^. .?..)(.{......*
7F74A0C0  258DA840 FE000000 046F307F 00000000  00000000 00000000 00000000 0378415B  *..y.......?.".........$*
7F74A0E0  046F307F DF8A60AC 7F7550B0 00000000  00000000 00000000 00000000 00000000  *.?..-".&...............*
7F74A100  00000000 00000000 00000000 00000000  00000000 00000000 00000000 00000000  *........................*
          LINES 7F74A120-7F74AFE0  SAME AS ABOVE
7F74B000  004A8040 C9C5C1F9 F9F5C940 E2E8D4D7  E3D6D440 C4E4D4D7 40D6E4E3 D7E4E340  *.\. IEA995I SYMPTOM DUMP OUTPUT *
7F74B020  40404040 40404040 40404040 40404040  40404040 40404040 40404040 40404040  *                                *
7F74B040  40404040 40404040 40400000 00202000  000C004A 2000E2E8 E2E3C5D4 40C3D6D4  *........\..SYSTEM COM*
7F74B060  D7D3C5E3 C9D6D540 C3D6C4C5 7EF0C3F2  4040D9C5 C1E2D6D5 40C3D6C4 C57EF0F0  *PLETION CODE=0C2  REASON CODE=00*
7F74B080  F0F0F0F0 F0F24040 40404040 40404040  40404040 40404040 40404040 004A2000  *000002            .\..*
7F74B0A0  40E3C9D4 C57EF1F2 4BF5F84B F3F24040  E2C5D87E F0F1F0F6 F54040C3 D7E47EF0  * TIME=12.58.32  SEQ=01065  CPU=0*
7F74B0C0  F0F0F040 40C1E2C9 C47EF0F3 F2F14040  40404040 40404040 40404040 40404040  *000 ASID=0321*
7F74B0E0  40004A20 40D7E2E6 40C1E340 E3C9D4C5  40D6C640 C5D9D9D6 D9404040 40404040  * .\. PSW AT TIME OF ERROR *
7F74B100  4BF0F7F8 C4F1F0F0 F04040F0 F0F0F0F6  C2F1F040 C9D3C340 F440C9D5 E3404040  *.078D1000  00006B10 ILC 4 INT*
7F74B120  C340F0F2 40404040 40404000 4A200040  C1C3E3C9 E5C540D3 D6404040 40404040  *C 02       .\.. ACTIVE LO*
7F74B140  C1C440D4 D6C4E4D3 C5404040 40404040  40C1C4C4 D9C5E2E2 7EF0F0F0 F0404040  *AD MODULE        ADDRESS=0000*
7F74B160  F6F9F0F8 40D6C6C6 E2C5E37E F0F0F0F0  F0F2F0F8 4040004A 20004040 40404040  *6908 OFFSET=00000208  .\..*
7F74B180  40D5C1D4 C57EC1D7 D7F3D7C7 D4F14040  40404040 40404040 40404040 40404040  * NAME=APP3PGM1*
7F74B1A0  40404040 40404040 40404040 40404040  40404040 40404040 40404040 40404040  *                           *
7F74B1C0  40004A20 00404040 C4C1E3C1 40C1E340  D7E2E640 40F0F0F0 F0F6C2F0 C1404040  * .\..   DATA AT PSW  00006B0A*
7F74B1E0  6040F0F5 C5C6F8F2 F0F040F0 F0F0F0F4  F5F1F040 C3F2F1F4 F0F0F0F0 40404040  *- 05EF8200 00004510 C2140000 *
7F74B200  40404040 40404040 004A2000 4040C7D7  D94040F0 60F34040 F0404040 40404040  *        .\..  GPR  0-3  0*
7F74B220  F0F0F0F6 C5F4C340 40F0F0F0 F6C1C4F0  4040F0F0 F0F0F0F0 F4F040F0 F0F94040  *0006E4C  0006AD0  00000040 009*
7F74B240  C6F1F9F5 F4404040 40404040 40404040  40404040 004A2000 40C74040 40404040  *F1954               .\.. G*
7F74B260  D7D940F4 60F740F0 F0F9C6F1 F9F3F040  F0F0F9C6 F9F0F2F8 40F0F0F9 40404040  *PR 4-7 009F1930 009F9028 009*
7F74B280  C4F1C6C6 F84040F0 F0F0F0F0 F0F0F040  40404040 40404040 40404040 40404040  *D1FF8  00000000*
7F74B2A0  40004A20 404040C7 D7D940F8 60F1F140  F0F0F9C6 C6F0F6F0 4040F8F0 F9404040  * .\.   GPR 8-11 009FF060  809*
7F74B2C0  C4C6F5F1 F04040F0 F0F0F0F9 F0F0F040  40F0F0F0 F0F2F2F6 F0404040 40404040  *DF510  00009000  00002260*
7F74B2E0  40404040 40404040 40404040 4040004A  200040C7 D7D940F1 F260F1F5 40F0F0F0  *              .\.. GPR 12-15 000*
7F74B300  F0F6F9F0 F840F0F0 F0F0F6C4 C5C340F5  F0F0F0F6 C2F0C340 F0F0C4F6 F0404040  *06908 00006DEC 50006B0C 00D60*
7F74B320  F5F4F840 40404040 40404040 40404040  40404040 40C5D5C4 40D64040 40404040  *548                 END O*
7F74B340  C640E2E8 D4D7E3D6 D440C4E4 D4D74040  40404040 40404040 40404040 40404040  *F SYMPTOM DUMP*
7F74B360  40404040 40404040 40404040 40404040  40404040 40404040 40404040 40404040  *                           *
7F74B380  40004A20 0040C1D9 40F460F7 40E7E7E7  E7E7E7E7 E740E7E7 E7E7E7E7 E7404040  * .\.. AR 4-7 XXXXXXXX XXXXXXX*
7F74B3A0  E7E7E740 E7E7E7E7 E7E7E7E7 4040E7E7  E7E7E7E7 E7E740E7 E7E7E7E7 E7E74040  *XXX XXXXXXXX  XXXXXXXX XXXXXXX*
7F74B3C0  40404040 40004A20 0040C1D9 40F860F1  F140E7E7 E7E7E7E7 E7404040 40404040  *     .\.. AR 8-11 XXXXXXX*
7F74B3E0  E7E7E740 E7E7E7E7 E7E7E7E7 4040E7E7  E7E7E7E7 E7E740E7 E7E7E7E7 E7E74040  *XXX XXXXXXXX  XXXXXXXX XXXXXXX*
7F74B400  E7404040 40404040 40404000 4A200040  C1D940F1 40404040 40404040 40404040  *X          .\.. AR 1*
7F74B420  F260F1F5 40E7E7E7 E7E7E7E7 E740E7E7  E7E7E7E7 E7E740E7 E7E7E7E7 E7E74040  *2-15 XXXXXXXX XXXXXXXX XXXXXXX*
```

```
JOB EXA7JHMX      STEP APP3        TIME 125832    DATE 94100    ID = 000              PAGE 00000059

7F74B440  E74040E7 E7E7E740 E7E7E740 40404040  40404040 40404040 40404040 4040004A  *X  XXXXXXXX              .\*
7F74B460  300040C5 D5C440D6 C640E2E8 D4D7E3D6  D44DC4E4 D4D70000 00000000 00000000  *.  . END OF SYMPTOM DUMP   *
7F74B480  40404040 40404040 40404040 00000000  40404040 40404040 40404040 40404040  *                           *
7F74B4A0  40404040 00000000 00000000 00000000  00000000 00000000 00000000 00000000  *                           *
7F74B4C0  00000000 00000000 00000000 00000000  00000000 00000000 00000000 00000000  *                           *
          LINES 7F74B4E0-7F74BFE0  SAME AS ABOVE

7F751000  E5E2D4D7 7FFE2000 00000000 7FFE2000  7F72D4F0 7FFE2BC8 7563A000 0A0D7000  *VSMP"..........MO".H.....*
7F751020  7FFE2C58 00001000 7FF16FD8 7FFF16568  7FF16568 7FF16550 7FF753000 00000FD0  *"....."1?Q"1..1.&.....)*
7F751040  7FFE2D4C0 7FFE2868 7F72D760 009E0BF8  00E61020 00000000 00000000 00000000  *"M{..."-..8.W..........*
7F751060  009F9028 00ED1080 00000000 00000000  7F746A00 7FF16EE4 00000000 00195000  *".h......"..."1>U....&..*
7F751080  7F72DF28 7F72D028 7F72DCE8 00000000  00000C88 00000000 FD747000 00000000  *"...."....").."Y".......*
7F7510A0  7F72DB38 7F7510A0 7F7510A8 7F7510A8  7F7510B0 7F7510B0 7F7463E8 7F72D770  *"...."....."...h."....Y"*
7F7510B8  7F7510B8 7F749000 00001000 00001000  7FFE27D8 7F7516E8 009F9028 7F72DB38  *"....."........."Q".Y..*
7F7510E0  00E65020 00002000 7FFE2A30 7FFE2368  7F7510E8 7F7510E8 7F77E000 00001000  *.W&.....".".h"....Y".Y".*
7F751100  00000010 7F72D778 7F746A30 7F72DD00  7F746A30 00001000 7FFE2DA8 7FF169B0  *....."...."....."..Y"\..*
7F751118  7F751D18 7F731000 00001000 00000000  7F7511D8 7F7511A30 7F751130 7F751130  *".......".....".Q".y"1..*
7F751140  0A0B6000 00001000 7F72D2C8 7FF16448  7FF16448 009C4000 7FFE2AF0 7FFE2E80  *"........".-..".1.KH.O..*
7F751160  7F751E20 7FF16448 7F751958 7F751958  7F751328 00000000 00001000 009BACF0  *".......".1.....".....O.*
7F751178  7F751178 7FF16448 0A0E1000 00000300  7F751940 7F751940 00002000 7F751130  *".............."1......1*
7F7511A0  00008020 00001000 009E1000 00001000  0A113000 00001000 7F751A00 7F751448  *"................P....O.*
7F7511C0  7F7515F8 7F7511C0 0A0B7000 00001000  7FF16790 7F751448 7FFE16790 7F751448  *"L..8"..{.."...{"........*
7F7511E0  7F7511D8 7F751D8 0A0B7000 00001000  7FF16790 7F751448 7FFF16790 7F751448  *"..Q.Q..".1.........1...*
7F751200  7FFFBE00 00000110 7F746250 7F751FA0  7F751208 7F751208 004E0000 00006000  *".......{.."..&....&....*
7F751220  7F746640 7F7512F8 00000000 7F747000  7F746490 7F751238 7F751238 7F751238  *".8......"....8..-+.-...*
7F751240  7F751240 7F751240 7F72D148 7F72D148  7FF16670 00000870 7F751328 7F751328  *"...."...J.J."1.........*
7F751260  7F751328 00003000 7F7517D8 7F746268  7F751C70 7F751C70 7F751278 7F751278  *"........"...Q".......*
7F751280  7FFE2538 7FFE2D48 7FFE2D48 009FE240  00E58020 00002000 09E00000 00000F30  *"..."...."...S .V.......*
7F7512A0  7F7463D0 7F7463D0 7F7463D0 7F72D7F0  00000000 00000000 7FFE2988 009F9028  *"....."..."...}......h..*
7F7512C0  00ED1080 00000000 7F72DCC8 7F72D7F0  7F7461F0 7F72D5C8 7F72DCC8 00000378  *"........"..NH".PO./O"NH*
7F7512E0  7F746688 7F72D5F8 7F746688 00000000  7F73B000 00000378 7F744000 00000378  *"..h".N8".N8".h".....&..*
7F751300  7F743CB8 00000348 FEFEE49A8 00000000  7F7514C0 7FF16568 7FF16568 009DF348  *"..."..{"....."..Y...{"..3.*
7F751320  00E50020 00000000 7F751250 7F751250  7F751328 7F751328 00017000 00020000  *".V....."..{.&..P."1......*
7F751340  7F746700 00000000 7F73EEC0 00004140  FD754000 00001000 7F746430 7F72D370  *".....")....{"..&..P."L..*
7F751360  7F72D178 7F746430 009DF000 00000000  7F72D208 7F751460 7F751370 7F751370  *""....."......"J.".O..."*
7F751380  0A0BF000 00002000 7F751568 00000000  7F7523B8 00000608 FD706000 00003000  *".O..."......."#....-."*
7F7513A0  7FF16EF4 00000000 0000C000 00000000  7F72E000 00000005 FD751808 00000080  *""1>4..K..{.\/..&.."....*
7F7513C0  7F72DC28 7F746430 7F72D4C28 00001000  7F751688 7F751580 7F746A18 7F746A18  *"...."...."..h."....".."*
7F7513E0  0A1F8000 0000B000 7F7467C0 7F72DCC8  7F7469B8 009C1770 00000820 00001000  *"......."..")....{"..}H"*
```

```
7F751400  7F751928 7F751400 7F751408  7F751410 7F751410 7F7461C0 7F72D178   *..."..."..."/{".J.*
7F751420  7F7461C0 7F72D178 00000090  7F72D400 7FFE2928 7F7514D8 7F72D8E0   *.."...."..M...Q".*
7F751440  7FFFC000 00000090 7F7511F0  7FFF16F0 7FFFBD80 7FFFBFB0 00000010   *....0"......Q".Q"\*
7F751460  7F751370 7F751460 7F751460  0A0BE000 00001000 7F72DC10 7F746400   *.."...-.\...R".*
7F751480  7F751DC0 009C1770 00E61020  7FFE2CA0 7F72DC10 7F751490 7F751490   *....W.....R".*
7F7514A0  0A0AE000 00002000 7F751A30  7FFE28F8 7F7514A8 0A0B3000 00001000   *..........Y".*
7F7514C0  7F751598 7F751430 7F7512C8  00B57020 7FFE2928 7F72D430 7F72D430   *.q".H"..q.3..V...M.*
7F7514E0  7F72D5C8 7F751430 7F746598  00B57020 00000FB0 7F746838 7F746838   *.NH".....8...h...&.*
7F751500  7F746838 7F752000 00000090  7F751F28 00000FB0 00008020 00005000   *..."....8....&...*
7F751520  7F751520 7FFE28F8 7F751528  7FF16970 009BAE88 7F751530 7FFE2CA0   *."....&...1......*
7F751540  7F751538 00001000 7F751528  7F751530 7F751530 7F7514A8 7F743BC8   *."....."...."..y"*
7F751560  FD751448 0A0B1000 00002000  7F72D388 7F72D388 7F743BC8 000000F0   *...."..."..8..H".0*
7F751580  7F746A18 00003000 7FF16448  7FFE2C70 7FFE2C70 009C3000 00000000   *..."..........R)"*
7F7515A0  7F72D538 7F72DE20 7F72DE20  0A1F4000 00004000 7F746028 7FFE2710   *.N..3..W....."....*
7F7515C0  0A0F0000 009DF348 00E60020  7F72DAA8 7F72D700 7F7515B0 7F7515B0   *......MQ".0".H"..*
7F7515E0  7F72DF58 00001000 7F72D4D8  7F751CC8 7F7515C8 0A0E6000 7F746460   *."..."..\"..H"..*
7F751600  7F7515F8 7F7515E0 7FFE2AF0  0A171000 00002000 7F72D118 7F751610   *."...."..&"..(".-*
7F751620  0A109000 00001000 7F746250  7F746850 7F751628 7F751628 004EC000   *.8..8.......l..&..*
```

JOB EXA7JHMX   STEP APP3   TIME 125832   DATE 94100   ID = 000   PAGE 00000060

```
7F751640  7F7519E8 7F7510B0 7FFE2670  7F747000 00001000 009D1000 00000FC8   *..Y...........H*
7F751660  7F751E50 7F751E50 00001000  7FFE28E0 7F72D490 7F7518E0 009E0BF8   *.Y..&.&...\.M..\.8*
7F751680  00B57020 00000010 7F751E80  7F751E80 7F751E80 7F751E80 00001000   *.....\.M..\.M..8*
7F7516A0  7FFE2EE0 7F751650 7F746490  7F748000 00001000 7F72D7D8 7FFE2F70   *.V.\.&......PQ".*
7F7516C0  7F7516B8 7F7516B8 00001000  7F72D550 7FFE2340 7F7467C0 7FFF164D8   *..........N&".*
7F7516E0  7FFFBD80 00000010 7F751CB8  7F7516F0 7F7516F0 7F7516F8 7F7516F8   *.......{.."1.Q*
7F751700  7FFFBD80 000006F0 7F751A18  7F72D058 000C0C00 7F7516B8 7F751BD8   *.......0...8.8*
7F751720  7FFE2F70 7F72D058 00001000  7FFE2C58 7FFE2F28 7F746550 7F72DD48   *.N...0...).(..&.*
7F751740  009CD520 00000000 00000000  009E0518 00000010 FD9E0518 7FFE2BB0   *.N....&.*
7F751760  7FF16970 7FF16970 7F746028  004E8080 00000000 00000000 7F751FD0   *.1...N..}*
7F751780  7F751780 7F751780 009DF180  7F746508 7F72DA30 7F751790 7F751790   *......1.h".h*
7F7517A0  0A0A9000 00001000 7F751EF8  7F751EF8 7F7517B0 7F751790 7F7517B8   *.........8.y*
7F7517C0  7F746010 00001000 7F72D6D0  00008020 7F7517D0 7F746268 7F751268   *.....O).&*
7F7517E0  7F72D508 7F7464C0 00005000  00008020 7F7517F0 7F7517F8 7F7517F8   *.N..(.}..&.8.8*
7F751800  7F751800 7F751800 00001000  7F746820 000000F0 FD00B000 00002000   *......N.{.)..8*
7F751820  7F746418 7F72D340 009F9028  7FFE4AD8 00000000 00000000 00000000   *...L..Q*
7F751840  7F746040 009F9028 00008080  7FFE29A0 7F751850 7F751858 7F751858   *...&.Q.&*
```

```
JOB EXA7JHMX      STEP APP3      TIME 125832   DATE 94100   ID = 000                        PAGE 00000061

7F751D40  7F751D40 7FFE2CE8 7FFE2520 7F746520  7F7523B8 00000608 FD732000 00003000  *................Y...*
7F751D60  7FFE2AD8 7FFE2C58 7F711000 0001C000  0A197000 00028000 7FFE22C0 7FFE22C0  *...."..".....Q"..{".(*
7F751D80  7F72D010 7F711000 0001C000 7F751CE8  00000000 00000000 7F7460A0 009DF180  *".}.."...(.."..{".-.1.*
7F751DA0  00018000 00000000 7F751880 7F751B50  7F751DA8 7F751DA8 0A165000 00001000  *".}..".."....."..Y".Y.-&.*
7F751DC0  7F751B50 00001000 7F751FD0 00001000  009DB638 000009C8 009DB000 00000140  *"..&...".&".&",.}....*
7F751DE0  7FFE2898 7F751FD0 00000000 000009D0  7F72D058 7F72D058 7F751FD0 7FFE2898  *"..q".)".}...}..H"..q*
7F751E00  7F751FD0 00000000 009DC000 00001000  FD9BC000 00005000 7FFE2FD0 00003000  *".}..."......}.}..}.&..}..*
7F751E20  00000000 009DC000 009DC000 000001B8  7F751940 7FFE2990 7F751658 7F751658  *"..}....".....8...(..&..}..*
7F751E40  7F751E38 7F7430F8 7F730000 00001000  7F72D5C8 7F751DF0 7FFE2FB8 00001000  *".......".h"..h...."..*
7F751E60  009D1000 00000000 7FFE2628 000000B8  009D8000 00001000 7F72D730 7F751C28  *"Py"...h"..h....NH".0"..*
7F751E80  7F72D7A8 7FFE2628 7F751688 7F751688  7FFE2958 7F751EB0 7F751EB8 7F751EB8  *"..q".q.........P.."..*
7F751EA0  7F751E98 0A0F9000 009DE000 00000068  7F72D8F8 7FFE2BB0 7FFE2BB0 00002000  *"./.."...(..\...".8"..*
7F751EC0  7F751EC0 009DE000 7F72D820 009C1770  00E57020 00001000 7FFE2E98 7FF16568  *"....".....V....V..."..q"1..*
7F751EE0  7F746178 7F7513A0 7F72D0B8 00000000  7FFE2B50 7F72D1A8 7F751F10 7F751F10  *"..y....V...".&".Jy"..*
7F751F00  7F7517A8 009C1190 00E50020 7F511F0   7F751958 7F746268 009C1018 00000158  *".0.."..)."..0"....."..*
7F751F20  7F77F000 00001000 7F72D0B8 7F72DB38  009BC000 00001000 7F72D80  00000000  *".J.."..Y"..".."..."..*
7F751F40  7F72D190 7F7463E8 FD9B5000 00005000  7F72DAC0 7F751800 7F72D730 7F72D730  *"....".&..&"..(".."..P.."P..*
7F751F60  7F743B38 000001B8 FD9B5000 7F746778  7F751F88 7F751F88 004CD000 00006000  *"......"...."...h".h.<}..-.*
7F751F80  7F74B000 00000000 7FFE2A00 7F751FA0  004DA000 00006000 00000000 7F72D418  *".......".....(...".M.*
7F751FA0  7F751208 7FFE2A00 7F751FA0 7F751FA0  7FFE2BB0 7F751778 7F751DD8 7F751DF0  *".1..q.......".....Q"..0*
7F751FC0  009DF108 00000198 FD754000 00001000  7F751FE8 7F751FE8 0A0C2000 00002000  *".....".."..."..K.-".Y"..*
7F751FE0  009DB000 00000000 7F72D238 7F751A60  00000000 00000000 009F9398 09D2D178  *".....".."...Y"..Y...*
7F752000  00000000 00000000 00000000 00000000  00000000 00000000 00000000 00000000  *".....".."..."..lq.KJ.*
7F752020  00000000 00000000 00000000 00000000  00000000 00000000 00000000 00000000  *.................*
7F752040  00000000 01000000 00000000 00000000  00000000 00000000 00000000 00000000  *.................*
7F752060  00000000 00000000 00000000 00000000  00000000 00000000 00000000 00000000  *.................*
7F752080  00000008 C2D3E2D8 C5E7E3C9 00000000  D9E3D4F2 7F752090 FF000F70 00FD50C8  *........BLSQEXTI....RTM2"....&H*
7F7520A0  009DF348 00F7F080 00F7F080 840C2000  00000000 00000000 00000000 00000000  *...3..6..70.d.........*
7F7520C0  009DF348 00FC8BB8 00FC8BB8 00006E4C  00006AD0 00000040 009F1954 009F1930  *...3..6....><...}..*
7F7520E0  009F9028 009D1FF8 00000000 009FF060  809DF510 00009000 00002260 00006908  *........8...0--5.......*
7F752100  00006DEC 50006B0C 00D60548 078D1000  00006B10 00040002 009D9000 C1D7D7F3  *.&.,.O.........APP3*
7F752120  D7C7D4F1 00000000 00000000 00000000  00000000 00000000 00000000 00000000  *PGM1................*
7F752140  00000000 40040001 00002080 00000000  009DF2C0 7F7550B0 009FF540 009FF540  *..............."..2{.&..5..5.*
7F752160  00000000 00000000 009DF2C0 00000000  009DF2C0 009DF2C0 04000000 FF850002  *..............2{....2{....e..*
7F752180  90006B10 FF850002 90006B10 7F752190  06C00500 2FB0BE00 009DAE68 009DF348  *......&..........3..*
7F7521A0  00000000 00000000 7F752630 00000000  00000000 00000000 00000000 7F752760  *".......".........SYSUDUMP...*
7F7521C0  00000000 E2E8E2E4 C4E4D4D7 00000000  009DF348 7F7521E4 7F7521E8 7F7521EC  *".0................."..Y"..*
7F7521E0  7F7521F0 00000000 00000000 00000000  00000000 00000000 00000000 00000000  *.0...............*
```

```
7F752200  00000000 00000000 00000000 7F73E3F8   84C54A96 84C60060 7F755008 7F752090   *....T8dE\odF.-".&."...*
7F752220  04C54AEC 04C54C57 009DF348 009FF6B8   84C53C58 009DF348 7F752090 7F752938   *.E\.E<..3..6.dE..3.."..*
7F752240  00000000 7F7523F8 7F752DB0 00C0000    00000018 40000000 80400000 00080000   *......8".......E\......*
7F752260  00000000 00000008 00005660 08080000   00000000 04C54AEC 00000000 04C5341E   *..............E\....E..*
7F752280  00000700 00000000 04C586CE 84C566D0   7F752090 009DF2C0 009FF540 009DF2C0   *........Ef.dEf."..2...5..2.*
7F7522A0  00005660 04C586CE 04C576CF 84C566D0   009DF2C0 00000000 7F75230C 84C582FE   *..-.Ef.Ef.dEf..2....."...dEb.*
7F7522C0  84C588E8 00000000 00000000 00000000   84C5339A 84C53C58 00000001 7F752404   *dEhY.......dE..dE........*
7F7522E0  7FFFC160 04C5301F 009DF348 009FF6B8   84C52020 009FF718 7F752090 00F7F080   *."..A-.E....3..6.dE....7."..70.*
7F752300  00000008 00005660 00000000 7F752090   009F93E4 7F752090 84C5830C 84C59468   *.........8..."..1U"..dEc.dEm.*
7F752320  00000000 00005660 00000000 009DF2C0   009DF2C0 009FF540 009DF2C0 00005660   *.......2..2..5..2..-.*
7F752340  04C586CE 04C576CF 84C566D0 00000000   00F7F080 00F7F080 00000000 00000000   *.Ef.Ef.dEf....70...70.....*
7F752360  00000000 00000000 00000000 860A9DC0   00000000 00000000 00000000 00000000   *.............f.........*
7F752380  00000000 00000000 00000000 00000000   00010321 00F7F080 00000000 00000000   *..............f.......*
7F7523A0  00000000 00000000 00000000 860A9DC0   00010321 00A00C0 03210000 03210007    *.............f.........*
7F7523C0  00000000 00000000 00000000 00000000   00010321 00A00C0 04290000 03210007    *...................*
7F7523E0  00000000 00005660 00005660 FA000680   00000000 03210000 00006E4C 00006AD0   *....................><..)*
7F752400  20B30000 7F752918 00000000 00000000   00000000 06000000 06000000 009FF060   *...........8......0-.*
7F752420  00000040 009F1954 009F1930 009F9028   009D1FF8 00000000 009FF060 809DF510   *...........8....0-..5.*
```

JOB EXA7JHMX   STEP APP3   TIME 125832   DATE 94100   ID = 000   PAGE 00000062

```
7F752440  00009000 00002260 00006908 00006DEC   50006B0C 00D60548 40404040 7F755008   *..........._.&....O...&.*
7F752460  7F7550B0 00000000 00000000 7F752938   00000002 7F752730 7F752730 7F7550B0   *.&.............".".&.*
7F752480  00000000 00000000 00000000 00000000   05EF8200 00004510 C2140000 00F7F080   *..........b...B...70.*
7F7524A0  046F307F 940C2000 00000002 5FB3EE40   046F307F 15485DC0 00C00321 00000321   *.?..m....?.).(..$.*
7F7524C0  25DA840 FE000000 046F307F 7F7550B0     00000000 00000000 0378415B 15485F00   *.y....?..&....^.*
7F7524E0  046F307F DF8A60AC 7F7550B0 00000000   00000000 00000000 15485F00 00000000   *.?.-.&.......*
7F752500  00000000 00000000 00000000 009F93B8   7F7550B0 00000000 00000000 00000000   *.......l.&.*
7F752520  00000000 00000000 00000000 00000000   00000000 00000000 7FFFBF00 15485F00   *............"...^.*
7F752540  00000000 00000000 00000000 00000000   00000000 7FFFBF00 00000000 00000000   *.........".*
7F752560  00000000 00000000 00000000 00000000   00000000 00000000 00000000 00000000   *.........*
      LINES 7F752580-7F7525C0  SAME AS ABOVE
7F7525E0  00000000 7F7525F4 7F7525F8 7F7525C0   7F752620 00000000 00000000 7F752090   *....4".8"...*
7F752600  00000000 00000000 00000000 00000000   00000000 00000000 00000000 00000000   *.........*
      LINES 7F752620-7F7528E0  SAME AS ABOVE
```

There are a number of data areas related to the SNAP process itself that are involved with producing the dump. One of these follows, starting at address 7F752938—the Trace Snap Parameter List (TRSN), discussed in chapter 11.

```
7F752900 00000000 00000000 00000000 00000000  00000000 00000000 E3D9E2D5 01000000  *................TRSN....*
7F752920 00010004 7F671000 000A2000 00000000  00000000 00000000 00000000 840C2000  *...."............d..*
7F752940 FF850002 90006B10 FF850002 90006B10  00006E4C 00006AD0 00000040 009F1954  *.e...,..e...,..>< ...)..*
7F752960 009F1930 009F9028 009D1FF8 00000000  009FF060 809DF510 D7C7D4F1 00002260  *........8.....0-..5..*
7F752980 00006908 00006DEC 50006B0C 00D60548  C1D7D7F3 D7C7D4F1 00006908 00000000  *..._&.,.O.APP3PGM1..*
7F7529A0 009FF060 809DF510 00009000 00040002  078D1000 00006B10 00040002 009D9000  *.0-..5........,......*
7F7529C0 0000E84C 00006AD0 00000040 009F1954  009F1930 009F9028 009D1FF8 009FF000  *..Y<..,..... ...)..8..0.*
7F7529E0 00006680 00009000 00000000 00000000  00006908 00006DEC 50006B0C 00D60548  *.............&.,.O.*
7F752A00 00006908 00006DEC 50006B0C 00006B10  00000680 00009000 009D1FF8 00000548  *...&.,..,........8...*
7F752A20 40040001 00002000 00006B10 7F752AC8  04080000 00000000 03210000 00000000  * ......,....H........*
7F752A40 00000000 00000000 00000000 00000000  00000000 04080000 03210000 2FA0BF00  *....................*
7F752A60 00000000 00000000 00000000 00000000  7F752A78 00600400 00000000 00000000  *.......".H..........*
7F752A80 00000000 00000000 00000000 00000000  00000000 00000000 00000000 00000000  *....................*
7F752AA0 FFFF0005 7F752DB0 00C00321 00000000  00000321 00000000 00000000 00000000  *....."......(.......*
7F752AC0 00000000 00FF0000 00000000 00000000  00000000 00000000 00000000 00000000  *....................*
7F752AE0 00000000 00000000 00000000 00000000  00000000 00000000 00000000 00000000  *....................*
      LINES 7F752B00-7F752BA0  SAME AS ABOVE
7F752BC0 00000000 000000E2 C4E6C140           00000000 00000000 00000000 00000000  *.......SDWA .......*
7F752BE0 00000000 00000000 00000000 00000000  00000000 00000000 00000002 00000000  *....................*
7F752C00 00000000 00000000 00000000 00000000  00000000 00000000 00000000 00006B34  *...................,.*
7F752C20 00000000 00000000 00000000 00000000  00000000 00000000 00000000 00000000  *....................*
7F752C40 00000000 00000000 00000321 00000002  00004510 C2140000 00F7F080 046F307F  *......3..b..B..70.?."*
7F752C60 940C2000 00000002 5FB3EE40 046F307F  00004510 00C00321 00000321 258DA840  *m..^.?.).(..$.?."*
7F752C80 FE000000 046F307F 046F307F 00000000  15485DC0 00C00321 0378415B 046F307F  *...?."?."...y....$.?."*
7F752CA0 DF8A60AC 046F307F 00000000 00000000  00000000 00000000 00000000 00000000  *..-..?."..............*
7F752CC0 00000000 00F7F080 00000000 00000000  00000000 00000000 00000000 00000000  *.....70.............*
7F752CE0 860A9DC0 00010321 00000000 00000000  00000000 00000000 00000000 00000000  *f..{................*
7F752D00 00000000 00000000 00000000 00000000  00000000 00000000 00000000 00000000  *....................*
7F752D20 860A9DC0 00010321 00000000 00000000  00000000 00000000 15485F00 00000000  *f..{.............^...*
7F752D40 00000000 00000000 00000000 06000000  00000000 00000000 00000000 00000000  *....................*
7F752D60 00000000 00000000 00000000 00000000  7F7550B0 7F7550B0 00000000 00000000  *.........."&..."&...*
7F752D80 00000000 00000000 00000000 00000000  7F752DC8 7F752BD0 7F752D80 7F752EB8  *..........."..H".."*
7F752DA0 00000000 7F752D90 7F752EC8 00000000  00000000 00000000 00000000 00000000  *..."..."..H.........*
7F752DC0 00000000 00000000 00000000 00000000  00000000 00000000 00000000 00000000  *....................*
7F752DE0 00000000 00000000 00000000 00000000  00000000 00000000 00000000 00000000  *....................*
      LINES 7F752E00-7F752FA0  SAME AS ABOVE
```

```
7F752FC0  00006CEC 80FD5118 00006B34 00000008   00005660 00000000 00000000 00000000   *..%......,............-.........*
7F752FE0  00000000 00000000 00000000 00000000   00000000 00000000 00000000 00000000   *................................*
7F776000  C5E3C3E3 C9D6E301 00000000 009E13B8   80000000 009E1370 00000008 80000000   *ETCTIOT.........................*
7F776020  009E1328 00000010 80000000 00000007   00000018 80000000 009E1400 00000020   *................................*
7F776040  00000006 00000000 00000000 00000000   00000000 00000000 00000008 00000000   *................................*
7F776060  00000000 00000009 00000000 0000000B   0000000A 00000000 00000000 0000000B   *................................*


JOB EXA7JHMX        STEP APP3        TIME 125832        DATE 94100        ID = 000        PAGE 00000063


7F776080  00000000 00000000 00000000 00000000   0000000D 0000000C 00000000 00000000   *................................*
7F7760A0  0000000E 00000000 00000000 00000000   00000000 00000000 00000010 0000000F   *................................*
7F7760C0  00000011 00000000 00000014 00000000   00000012 00000013 00000000 00000000   *................................*
7F7760E0  00000000 00000000 00000000 00000017   00000015 00000000 00000018 00000000   *................................*
7F776100  00000016 00000019 00000000 00000000   0000001A 00000000 00000000 00000000   *................................*
7F776120  00000000 00000000 00000000 00000000   0000001D 00000000 00000000 0000001B   *................................*
7F776140  00000000 0000001C 00000000 0000001F   00000000 00000000 00000000 00000000   *................................*
7F776160  0000001E 00000000 00000000 00000000   00000022 00000021 00000000 00000000   *................................*
7F776180  00000000 00000000 00000000 00000000   00000025 00000024 00000000 00000023   *................................*
7F7761A0  00000020 00000000 00000000 00000000   00000000 00000000 00000000 00000000   *................................*
7F7761C0  00000026 00000000 00000029 00000027   0000002A 00000000 00000000 00000000   *................................*
7F7761E0  00000000 00000000 00000000 0000002C   00000000 00000000 0000002B 00000000   *................................*
7F776200  00000028 0000002F 00000000 00000000   0000002D 00000000 00000000 00000000   *................................*
7F776220  0000002E 00000000 00000000 0000002F   00000032 00000000 00000000 00000033   *................................*
7F776240  00000031 00000000 00000034 00000000   00000035 00000000 00000000 00000000   *................................*
7F776260  00000000 00000000 00000000 00000000   00000000 00000000 00000000 00000037   *................................*
7F776280  00000036 00000000 00000000 00000037   00000000 00000000 00000038 00000000   *................................*
7F7762A0  00000039 00000000 00000000 00000000   0000003A 00000000 00000000 0000003B   *................................*
7F7762C0  00000000 0000003C 00000000 00000000   0000003D 00000000 00000000 00000000   *................................*
7F7762E0  0000003E 0000003E 00000000 00000000   00000000 00000000 00000040 0000003F   *................................*
7F776300  00000000 00000000 00000000 00000000   00000042 00000000 00000000 00000043   *................................*
7F776320  00000041 00000000 00000044 00000000   00000045 00000000 00000000 00000000   *................................*
7F776340  00000000 00000000 00000000 00000047   0000004A 00000000 00000048 00000000   *...........................<...(*
7F776360  00000046 00000049 00000000 0000004C   0000004D 00000000 00000000 0000004B   *...(...+...&....................*
7F776380  00000000 00000000 00000000 0000004F   00000000 00000000 00000000 00000000   *................................*
7F7763A0  0000004E 00000000 00000000 00000000   00000000 00000000 00000000 00000053   *...............................&*
7F7763C0  00000051 00000000 00000054 00000050   00000000 00000000 00000000 0000004B   *..............\.................*
7F7763E0  00000000 00000000 00000000 0000004F   00000000 00000000 00000000 00000000   *................................*
7F776400  00000056 00000057 00000000 00000000   00000055 00000000 00000000 00000000   *................................*
```

```
7F776420   00000000 00000000 00000000 00000000 0000005A 00000000 00000000 0000005B  *...................!..........$*
7F776440   00000000 00000000 0000005C 00000000 00000000 0000005D 00000000 00000000  *...........*...........)........*
7F776460   0000005E 00000000 00000000 0000005F 00000000 00000000 00000060 00000000  *...;...........¬...........-....*
7F776480   00000000 00000061 00000000 00000000 00000062 00000000 00000000 00000063  *......./........................*
7F7764A0   00000000 00000000 00000064 00000000 00000000 00000065 00000000 00000000  *................................*
7F7764C0   00000066 00000000 00000000 00000067 00000000 00000000 00000068 00000000  *................................*
7F7764E0   00000000 00000069 00000000 00000000 0000006A 00000000 00000000 0000006B  *...............................,*
7F776500   00000000 00000000 0000006C 00000000 00000000 0000006D 00000000 00000000  *...........%..........._........*
7F776520   0000006E 00000000 00000000 0000006F 00000000 00000000 00000070 00000000  *...>...........?................*
7F776540   00000000 00000071 00000000 00000000 00000072 00000000 00000000 00000073  *................................*
7F776560   00000000 00000000 00000074 00000000 00000000 00000075 00000000 00000000  *................................*
7F776580   00000076 00000000 00000000 00000077 00000000 00000000 00000078 00000000  *................................*
7F7765A0   00000000 00000079 00000000 00000000 0000007A 00000000 00000000 0000007B  *...................:..........#*
7F7765C0   00000000 00000000 0000007C 00000000 00000000 0000007D 00000000 00000000  *...........@...........'........*
7F7765E0   0000007E 00000000 00000000 0000007F 00000000 00000000 00000080 00000000  *...=..........."................*
7F776600   00000000 00000081 00000000 00000000 00000082 00000000 00000000 00000083  *.......a...........b...........c*
7F776620   00000000 00000000 00000084 00000000 00000000 00000085 00000000 00000000  *...........d...........e........*
7F776640   00000086 00000000 00000000 00000087 00000000 00000000 00000088 00000000  *...f...........g...........h....*
7F776660   00000000 00000089 00000000 00000000 0000008A 00000000 00000000 0000008B  *.......i........................*
7F776680   00000000 00000000 0000008C 00000000 00000000 0000008D 00000000 00000000  *................................*
7F7766A0   0000008E 00000000 00000000 0000008F 00000000 00000000 00000090 00000000  *................................*
7F7766C0   00000000 00000091 00000000 00000000 00000092 00000000 00000000 00000093  *.......j...........k...........l*
7F7766E0   00000000 00000000 00000094 00000000 00000000 00000095 00000000 00000000  *...........m...........n........*
7F776700   00000096 00000000 00000000 00000097 00000000 00000000 00000098 00000000  *...o...........p...........q....*
7F776720   00000000 00000099 00000000 00000000 0000009A 00000000 00000000 0000009B  *.......r........................*
7F776740   00000000 00000000 0000009C 00000000 00000000 0000009D 00000000 00000000  *................................*
7F776760   0000009E 00000000 00000000 0000009F 00000000 00000000 000000A0 00000000  *................................*
```

```
JOB EXA7JHMX        STEP APP3        TIME 125832    DATE 94100    ID = 000          PAGE 00000064

7F776780   00000000 000000A1 00000000 00000000 000000A2 00000000 00000000 000000A3  *...................s..........t*
7F7767A0   00000000 00000000 000000A4 00000000 00000000 000000A5 00000000 00000000  *...........u...........v........*
7F7767C0   000000A6 00000000 00000000 000000A7 00000000 00000000 000000A8 00000000  *...w...........x...........y....*
7F7767E0   00000000 000000A9 00000000 00000000 000000AA 00000000 00000000 000000AB  *.......z........................*
7F776800   00000000 00000000 000000AC 00000000 00000000 000000AD 00000000 00000000  *................................*
7F776820   000000AE 00000000 00000000 000000AF 00000000 00000000 000000B0 00000000  *................................*
7F776840   00000000 000000B1 00000000 00000000 000000B2 00000000 00000000 000000B3  *................................*
7F776860   00000000 00000000 000000B4 00000000 00000000 000000B5 00000000 00000000  *................................*
```

```
7F776880  00000000 00000000 00000000 00000000  000000B4 000000B5 000000B6 000000B7  *........*
7F7768A0  00000000 00000000 00000000 00000000  000000B8 000000B9 000000BA 000000BB  *........*
7F7768C0  00000000 00000000 00000000 00000000  000000BC 000000BD 000000BE 000000BF  *........*
7F7768E0  00000000 00000000 00000000 00000000  000000C0 000000C1 000000C2 000000C3  *....{ABC*
7F776900  00000000 00000000 00000000 00000000  000000C4 000000C5 000000C6 000000C7  *....DEFG*
7F776920  00000000 00000000 00000000 00000000  000000C8 000000C9 000000CA 000000CB  *....HI..*
7F776940  00000000 00000000 00000000 00000000  000000CC 000000CD 000000CE 000000CF  *........*
7F776960  00000000 00000000 00000000 00000000  000000D0 000000D1 000000D2 000000D3  *....}JKL*
7F776980  00000000 00000000 00000000 00000000  000000D4 000000D5 000000D6 000000D7  *....MNOP*
7F7769A0  00000000 00000000 00000000 00000000  000000D8 000000D9 000000DA 000000DB  *....QR..*
7F7769C0  00000000 00000000 00000000 00000000  000000DC 000000DD 000000DE 000000DF  *........*
7F7769E0  00000000 00000000 00000000 00000000  000000E0 000000E1 000000E2 000000E3  *....\.ST*
7F776A00  00000000 00000000 00000000 00000000  000000E4 000000E5 000000E6 000000E7  *....UVWX*
7F776A20  00000000 00000000 00000000 00000000  000000E8 000000E9 000000EA 000000EB  *....YZ..*
7F776A40  00000000 00000000 00000000 00000000  000000EC 000000ED 000000EE 000000EF  *........*
7F776A60  00000000 00000000 00000000 00000000  000000F0 000000F1 000000F2 000000F3  *....0123*
7F776A80  00000000 00000000 00000000 00000000  000000F4 000000F5 000000F6 000000F7  *....4567*
7F776AA0  00000000 00000000 00000000 00000000  000000F8 000000F9 000000FA 000000FB  *....89..*
7F776AC0  00000000 00000000 00000000 00000000  000000FC 000000FD 000000FE 000000FF  *........*
7F776AE0  00000000 00000000 00000000 00000000  00000100 00000101 00000102 00000103  *........*
7F776B00  00000000 00000000 00000000 00000000  00000104 00000105 00000106 00000107  *........*
7F776B20  00000000 00000000 00000000 00000000  00000108 00000109 0000010A 0000010B  *........*
7F776B40  00000000 00000000 00000000 00000000  0000010C 0000010D 0000010E 0000010F  *........*
7F776B60  00000000 00000000 00000000 00000000  00000110 00000111 00000112 00000113  *........*
7F776B80  00000000 00000000 00000000 00000000  00000114 00000115 00000116 00000117  *........*
7F776BA0  00000000 00000000 00000000 00000000  00000118 00000119 0000011A 0000011B  *........*
7F776BC0  00000000 00000000 00000000 00000000  0000011C 0000011D 0000011E 0000011F  *........*
7F776BE0  00000000 00000000 00000000 00000000  00000000 00000000 00000000 00000000  *........*
7F776C00  00000000 00000000 00000000 00000000  00000000 00000000 00000000 00000000  *........*
7F776C20  00000000 00000000 00000000 00000000  00000000 00000000 00000000 00000000  *........*
7F776C40  00000000 00000000 00000000 00000000  00000000 00000000 00000000 00000000  *........*
7F776C60  00000000 00000000 00000000 00000000  00000000 00000000 00000000 00000000  *........*
7F776C80  00000000 00000000 00000000 00000000  00000000 00000000 00000000 00000000  *........*
7F776CA0  00000000 00000000 00000000 00000000  00000000 00000000 00000000 00000000  *........*
7F776CC0  00000000 00000000 00000000 00000000  00000000 00000000 00000000 00000000  *........*
7F776CE0  00000000 00000000 00000000 00000000  00000000 00000000 00000000 00000000  *........*
7F776D00  00000000 00000000 00000000 00000000  00000000 00000000 00000000 00000000  *........*
7F776D20  00000000 00000000 00000000 00000000  00000000 00000000 00000000 00000000  *........*
7F776D40  00000000 00000000 00000000 00000000  00000000 00000000 00000000 00000000  *........*
7F776D60  00000000 00000000 00000000 00000000  00000000 00000000 00000000 00000000  *........*
```

```
7F776D80  00000000  00000121  00000000  00000122  00000000  00000123   *................*
7F776DA0  00000000  00000124  00000000  00000125  00000000  00000000   *................*
7F776DC0  00000000  00000126  00000000  00000000  00000128  00000000   *................*
7F776DE0  00000000  00000129  00000000  00000000  00000000  0000012B   *................*
7F776E00  00000000  00000000  00000000  00000000  00000000  00000000   *................*
7F776E20  0000012E  0000012C  0000012D  00000000  00000000  0000012B   *................*
7F776E40  00000000  00000000  00000000  00000130  00000000  00000133   *................*
7F776E60  00000000  00000134  00000000  00000135  00000000  00000000   *................*


JOB EXA7JHMX          STEP APP3          TIME 125832     DATE 94100     ID = 000          PAGE 00000065


7F776E80  00000136  00000137  00000000  00000000  00000138  00000000   *................*
7F776EA0  00000000  00000139  00000000  0000013A  00000000  0000013B   *................*
7F776EC0  00000000  0000013C  00000000  0000013D  00000000  00000000   *................*
7F776EE0  0000013E  0000013F  00000000  00000000  00000000  00000000   *................*
7F776F00  00000000  00000000  00000000  00000000  00000000  00000000   *................*
7F776F20  00000000  00000141  00000000  00000142  00000000  00000143   *................*
7F776F40  00000000  00000144  00000000  00000145  00000000  00000000   *................*
7F776F60  00000000  00000146  00000000  00000147  00000000  00000148   *................*
7F776F80  00000000  00000149  00000000  0000014A  00000000  0000014B   *................*
7F776FA0  0000014E  0000014C  0000014D  00000000  00000000  00000000   *................*
7F776FC0  00000000  00000151  00000000  00000152  00000000  00000153   *..+.....<.|.-.(.*
7F776FE0  00000000  00000154  00000000  00000000  00000000  00000000   *................*
7F7A7000  1D7AB011  0F8BF011  03399011  1F59011   00000410  00000400   *.........).5....*
7F7A7020  00000400  00000400  00000400  00000400  00000400  00000400   *................*
          LINES 7F7A7040-7F7A73E0  SAME AS ABOVE
7F7A7400  88000000  00000000  00000000  00000000  00000000  00000000   *h...............*
7F7A7420  00000000  00000000  00000000  00000000  00000000  00000000   *................*
          LINES 7F7A7440-7F7A7FE0  SAME AS ABOVE
7FF00000  00000410  00000410  00000410  00000410  00000410  00000410   *................*
          LINE 7FF00020 SAME AS ABOVE
7FF00040  00000410  071AE411  00000411  00000411  17382411  05AE4411   *.....U..........*
7FF00060  064D1411  122CB411  00000411  00000411  1932C411  19932C411  *.(..............*
7FF00080  1D631411  00000411  00000411  00000411  00000411  00000411   *................*
7FF000A0  00000411  223A7011  223A7011  00000410  00000410  00000411   *.D..............*
7FF000C0  00000410  00000410  00000410  00000410  00000410  00000410   *................*
7FF000E0  0D198011  025BD011  0E178011  0D698011  0CE30011  0CE30011   *...$.g....t.....*
7FF00100  2158F011  1A169011  1F83A011  22A33011  10883011  0F381011   *.0...9...c...h..*
```

```
7FF00120  166BC011 1EF22011 0001B011 0000E011  0DB33011 0EF4B011 222E5011 00000411  *..,.{.2........\....*
7FF00140  00000411 1570A011 222F7011 11D0D411  00000411 00000411 00000411 0F767011  *.........}M..4.....*
7FF00160  00000411 01A5D011 14AA5011 00000411  00000411 00000411 00000411 0883C411  *......v}..&......cD.*
7FF00180  157A7011 1153E011 00000411 00000411  186D7011 118D5411 10595411 00000411  *.........\.........*
7FF001A0  1E712011 00000411 00000411 00000411  00000411 21D6B011 00000411 14B7F011  *..........O......O.*
7FF001C0  00000411 00000411 02024011 00000411  00000411 062E9011 00000411 222A5011  *..............O.*
7FF001E0  09DAB411 0F241011 02024011 00000411  1B2D3011 16360011 0EE19011 00000411  *............&..&.*
7FF00200  09248011 09FC1011 02C36011 00000411  01505011 1B67B011 1C5E7011 00000411  *........C-.&&..*
7FF00220  00000411 00000411 0C26A011 00000411  146EE011 00000411 00000411 00000411  *.......&.....;..*
7FF00240  21E24011 05EDE011 1C1D9011 00000411  11B8B011 04A81011 1DF74011 04554011  *.S....>\....y..7.*
7FF00260  20D7A011 12BF4011 00000411 00000411  00000411 00000411 1274C011 00000411  *.P.......\.{..*
7FF00280  00000411 00000411 00000411 00000411  00000411 00000411 00000411 12E02020  *..............*
7FF002A0  0002E420 0B984420 10FFD420 0AE24420  00000400 00000400 00000400 12E02020  *..U..d..M..S.*
7FF002C0  00000400 00000400 00000400 00000400  00000400 00000400 00000400 00000400  *..............*
LINES 7FF002E0-7FF003E0  SAME AS ABOVE
7FF00400  00000000 00000000 00000000 00000000  00000000 00000000 00000000 00000000  *................*
LINES 7FF00420-7FF004A0  SAME AS ABOVE
7FF004C0  00000000 00000000 00000000 00000000  03F8EFE8 00000000 00000000 00000000  *.....8.Y....&...*
7FF004E0  00000000 00000000 50000000 00000000  50000000 00000000 50000000 00000000  *....&...&.......*
7FF00500  00000000 50000000 00000000 00000000  00000000 50000000 00000000 00000000  *....&...&.......*
7FF00520  50000000 00000000 00000000 50000000  00000000 00000000 50000000 00000000  *&.....&.........*
7FF00540  00000000 50000000 00000000 00000000  50000000 00000000 00000000 00000000  *....&...&.......*
7FF00560  00000000 00000000 50000000 00000000  50000000 50000030 00000000 00000000  *....&....m@y...&..*
7FF00580  50000000 00000000 00000000 00000000  00000000 00000000 03E37CE8 00000000  *&.......&...&..*
7FF005A0  00000000 50000000 00000000 00000000  50000000 03A71D48 00000000 00000000  *....&...&..x...&..*
7FF005C0  00000000 00000000 50000000 00000000  50000000 00000000 00000000 00000000  *....&...&.......*
7FF005E0  50000000 00000000 00000000 00000000  00000000 00000000 00000000 00000000  *&.....&.........*
7FF00600  00000000 50000000 00000000 00000000  50000000 00000000 00000000 00000000  *....&...&.......*
7FF00620  00000000 00000000 00000000 00000000  00000000 00000000 00000000 00000000  *................*

JOB EXA7JHMX       STEP APP3       TIME 125832    DATE 94100    ID = 000       PAGE 00000066

LINES 7FF00640-7FF00760  SAME AS ABOVE
7FF00780  00000000 00000000 00000000 00000000  08000100 00000000 00000000 08000100  *................*
7FF007A0  00000000 00000000 00000000 08000100  00000000 08000100 00000000 00000000  *................*
7FF007C0  08000100 00000100 00000000 00000000  00000000 00000000 00000000 00000000  *................*
7FF007E0  00000000 08000130 038610A8 00000000  88000000 00000000 00000000 08000100  *.....f.y..h......*
7FF00800  00000000 00000000 08000100 00000000  00000000 00000000 00000000 00000000  *................*
```

```
7FF00820  08000100 00000000 00000000 00000000   00000000 10000000 00000000 03FAEF68  *................*
7FF00840  00000000 10000000 00000000 00000000   10000000 00000000 00000000 10000000  *................*
7FF00860  00000000 00000000 00000000 10000000   00000000 10000000 00000000 00000000  *................*
7FF00880  10000000 00000000 10000000 00000000   10000000 00000000 00000000 10000000  *................*
7FF008A0  00000000 00000000 00000000 00000000   10000000 03893568 00000000 10000000  *................*
7FF008C0  00000000 00000000 10000000 00000000   10000000 10000000 00000000 00000000  *................*
7FF008E0  10000000 03AD7688 00000000 10000000   10000000 00000000 00000000 10000000  *..........i.....*
7FF00900  00000000 00000000 00000000 00000000   00000000 00000000 00000000 00000000  *.....h..........*
7FF00920  03A0BCC8 00000000 00000000 00000000   00000000 00000000 00000000 00000000  *...H............*
7FF00940  10000000 10000000 00000000 00000000   10000000 00000000 00000000 10000000  *........f.h.....*
7FF00960  00000000 10000000 00000000 00000000   00000000 00000000 10000000 10000000  *................*
7FF00980  10000000 00000000 00000000 00000000   00000000 03860288 00000000 10000000  *................*
7FF009A0  00000000 04237368 04237348 00000000   00000000 00000000 00000000 04022D08  *..........3.h...*
7FF009C0  00000000 00000000 00000000 18000000   58000000 00000000 58000000 58000000  *....D.\.........*
7FF009E0  00000000 00000000 00000000 00000000   03F3BB88 10000000 00000000 00000000  *.......my.......*
7FF00A00  00000000 18000000 18000000 00000000   10000000 042394A8 00000000 10000000  *................*
7FF00A20  18000000 00000000 00000000 03DEC408   10000000 042394A8 00000000 00000000  *......y.........*
7FF00A40  04363008 00000000 18000000 08000100   00000000 08000100 00000000 00000000  *................*
7FF00A60  08000100 00000000 00000000 04154A28   00000000 08000100 00000000 00000000  *................*
7FF00A80  00000000 00000000 00000000 03AB01A8   00000000 00000100 00000000 00000000  *................*
7FF00AA0  00000000 00000000 00000000 00000000   00000000 00000000 00000000 00000000  *................*
               LINES 7FF00AC0-7FF00B00  SAME AS ABOVE
7FF00B20  0340C1E8 00000000 00000000 00000000   00000000 00000000 00000000 00000000  *..AY............*
7FF00B40  00000000 00000000 00000000 00000000   00000000 00000000 00000000 00000000  *................*
7FF00B60  00000000 041EE1E8 00000000 00000000   00000000 00000000 00000000 00000000  *.......Y........*
7FF00B80  00000000 00000000 00000000 00000000   00000000 00000000 00000000 00000000  *................*
               LINES 7FF00BA0-7FF00FE0  SAME AS ABOVE
7FF08000  0B263000 00000400 00000400 00000400   00000400 00000400 00000400 1D143400  *.?......?...m..4*
7FF08020  08EFB001 046F3001 046F4001 1BF65001   1C972400 11B34400 0F769400 1DB6F400  *.6&.p......m..4.*
7FF08040  1E777400 00000400 00000400 00000400   1946E000 02E28001 03D25001 00015001  *.\.S.K&...&.....*
7FF08060  16D69001 03C07011 00000400 00000400   00000400 00000400 00000400 00000400  *.O.(............*
7FF08080  00000000 00000000 00000400 00000400   00000400 00000400 00000400 00000400  *................*
               LINES 7FF080A0-7FF08100  SAME AS ABOVE
7FF08120  00000000 00000400 00000400 00000400   0C40B400 00000400 00000400 00000400  *................*
7FF08140  00000000 00000400 00000400 00000400   00000400 00000400 00000400 00000400  *................*
               LINES 7FF08160-7FF08300  SAME AS ABOVE
7FF08320  14071011 00000400 18AAE011 08000400   14071011 0C048011 0512A411 0593A411  *......u.lu.*
7FF08340  05DC5411 05F06411 04A64411 18AAF011   04BAB411 05C8D411 05173411 026FE411  *.O..w..\....HM..?U*
7FF08360  054BA411 048D9411 04255411 03CF3411   039B6411 040CBA11 13ED8011 10D3B011  *.u..m..-..L..*
7FF08380  02A0A411 02807411 1E9F6011 053CF011   12738011 0ABDC011 18501011 03C76411  *.u.....O...(.&..G.*
```

```
7FF083A0 00000411 02082411 00000411 00000411  02790411 00000411 00000411 00000411  *................*
7FF083C0 00000411 00000411 00000411 00000411  0E9EC011 0516F011 2119A011 00000400  *..........&.{...*
7FF083E0 00000411 00000411 00000411 15485011  0E9EC011 0516F011 2119A011 00000400  *...........&.{.0.*
7FF08400 00000000 00000000 00000000 00000000  00000000 00000000 00000000 00000000  *................*
         LINES 7FF08420-7FF08440   SAME AS ABOVE
7FF08460 08000000 00000000 00000000 08000000  00000000 08000000 00000000 00000000  *................*
7FF08480 00000000 18000000 00000000 00000000  00000000 00000000 00000000 00000000  *................*
7FF084A0 00000000 00000000 00000000 00000000  00000000 00000000 00000000 00000000  *................*
         LINES 7FF084C0-7FF08D60   SAME AS ABOVE
7FF08D80 00000000 00000000 00000000 00000000  18000000 00000000 00000000 10000000  *................*


JOB EXA7JHMX      STEP APP3         TIME 125832    DATE 94100    ID = 000          PAGE 00000067

7FF08DA0 00000000 00000000 00000030 04237588  00000000 00000000 04237568 00000000  *................*
7FF08DC0 00000030 04237548 00000000 00000000  04237528 00000000 58000030 042375A8  *......h..........y.*
7FF08DE0 00000000 00000000 03F96FA8 00000000  18000000 04237608 18000000 58000030  *.........9?y....*
7FF08E00 04237628 00000000 18000030 04237648  00000000 58000030 04237668 00000030  *................*
7FF08E20 18000000 04237688 18000000 10000030  042376A8 00000000 10000030 042376C8  *......y.......H.*
7FF08E40 00000000 18000000 04237728 00000000  10000030 04237748 00000000 10000030  *................*
7FF08E60 042375C8 00000000 10000000 03DECE88  00000000 10000000 039ED3C8 00000000  *..H.......LH....*
7FF08E80 10000030 04237408 00000000 10000030  04237788 00000000 00000000 00000000  *..h.........h...*
7FF08EA0 00000000 10000000 0388A408 00000000  00000000 00000000 00000000 00000100  *......hu........*
7FF08EC0 0347FE88 00000100 0413F348 00000000  04237768 00000000 00000000 00000000  *..h......3......*
7FF08EE0 08000000 00000000 00000000 08000030  042374A8 08000100 00000000 08000100  *.............y..*
7FF08F00 08000000 00000000 00000000 00000000  08000100 08000100 00000000 08000100  *................*
7FF08F20 08000100 00000000 00000000 08000100  08000100 00000000 00000000 08000000  *................*
7FF08F40 08000100 00000000 00000000 00000000  00000000 08000100 00000000 08000100  *................*
7FF08F60 00000000 08000100 00000000 00000000  08000100 00000000 08000100 00000000  *................*
7FF08F80 00000000 00000000 08000100 00000000  00000000 08000100 00000000 08000100  *................*
7FF08FA0 08000100 00000000 00000000 00000000  00000000 08000100 00000000 08000100  *................*
7FF08FC0 00000000 00000000 00000000 00000000  00000000 00000000 00000000 00000000  *................*
7FF08FE0 00000000 00000000 0000002F 0000002F  0000002F 0000002F 0000002F 0000002F  *................*
7FF09000 1BF6500F 0000002F 2603D01F 2603D01F  2603E01F 2603F01F 258D101F 25DA301F  *.6&...}...\...0.*
7FF09020 0000002F 1946E00F 2525501F 25DA501F  2553E01F 2563F01F 2574001F 2582C01F  *......&..}.\.&..b{.*
7FF09040 25DA401F 25DA501F 25DA601F 25DA701F  2553E01F 2563F01F 2536501F 25A4301F  *.}.}.}.}.&.-..u.*
7FF09060 2536401F 25362D01F 25363101F 25363101F 2536401F 2536601F 25A4301F 25A4301F  *.q...l..l..k0.k!.k}.*
7FF09080 2598301F 258B201F 2593101F 2593101F  2592F01F 2592D01F 2592C01F 2592C01F  *...l...l..l-.l&.l.*
7FF090A0 2592B01F 2593901F 2593801F 2593701F  2593601F 2593501F 2593401F 2593301F  *.k.l..l..l..l.l..l.*
```

```
7FF090C0 2593201F 2593D01F 2593F01F 2593E01F 2593D01F 2593C01F  *.l...m..m...m..l0..1\..1)..1{.*
7FF090E0 2593801F 2594A01F 2594701F 2594601F 2594501F 2594401F  *.l...m..m...m..m..m-.m&..m.*
7FF09100 2594301F 2595001F 2594F01F 2594C01F 2594801F 2594101F  *.m..n...m0..m\.m}.m{...m.*
7FF09120 2604201F 2604301F 2604401F 2604601F 2604701F 2604101F  *............&..........*
7FF09140 2604A01F 2604B01F 2604C01F 2604D01F 2604E01F 2604901F  *..........{..).\..0...*
7FF09160 2605201F 2605301F 2605401F 2605501F 2605601F 2605101F  *.....{...).\..0.....*
7FF09180 2605A01F 260C801F 260C501F 258D801F 2605701F 2605901F  *.....&......&........*
7FF091A0 260C801F 260CC01F 260CE01F 260D401F 260D401F 2606701F  *.......0..............*
7FF091C0 2608A01F 25A2001F 260CE01F 25A1401F 260AD01F 260B701F  *.....{.........(......*
7FF091E0 260D001F 260BE01F 2531801F 260D601F 25A2901F 260EA01F  *....s...(..\...)......*
7FF09200 2607201F 260B801F 2530F01F 2531801F 2530601F 260C001F  *...s....-...0......*
7FF09220 260BF01F 2608301F 2532801F 260B601F 260FA01F 2532E01F  *.......0......}...).*
7FF09240 260C401F 260B101F 260E301F 2607701F 260B901F 260C201F  *......(.......).&.*
7FF09260 260A801F 260A701F 2609101F 260DB01F 2531001F 2609A01F  *.....-...(....-..*
7FF09280 2607901F 25A1801F 25A1801F 2606D01F 2606201F 260A201F  *..........\..-.*
7FF09280 0000002F 0000002F 0000002F 260E401F 25A1C01F 12E0200F 260A201F  *...........*
         LINES 7FF092A0-7FF09FE0  SAME AS ABOVE
7FF0A000 0000002F 0000002F 0000002F 0000002F 0000002F 0000002F
         LINES 7FF0A020-7FF0AFA0  SAME AS ABOVE
7FF0AFC0 0000002F 0000002F 0000002F 0000002F 0000002F 0000002F
7FF0AFE0 0000002F 00000001 0000002F 0000002F 0000002F 0000002F  *..............*
7FF0B000 00000001 00000400 00000400 12670001 0000002F 0B26300F  *..............*
7FF0B020 0FEDA011 00B61005 00D9E005 00B84001 00D34001 08EFB00F  *.......R\.\....*
7FF0B040 00000400 00000400 0DDE005 00512001 00000400 00B27005  *.......Y....*
7FF0B060 00000400 00000400 00000400 00000400 00000400 00000400  *............*
7FF0B080 00000410 00000410 00000410 00000410 00000410 00000410  *............*
7FF0B0A0 00000400 00000400 00000400 00000400 00000400 00000400  *............*
         LINES 7FF0B0C0-7FF0B3E0  SAME AS ABOVE
7FF0B400 00000000 00000000 00000000 00000000 00000000 00000000  *............*
7FF0B420 00000000 00000000 00000000 00000000 00000000 00000000  *............*
7FF0B440 00000000 88000000 88000000 88000000 88000000 00000000  *..h.....h....h.*
7FF0B460 88000000 00000000 00000000 00000000 00000000 00000000  *.h.........h....h.*

JOB EXA7JHMX          STEP APP3          TIME 125832   DATE 94100   ID = 000          PAGE 00000068

7FF0B480 00000000 88000000 00000000 00000000 00000000 00000000  *...h....*
7FF0B4A0 00000000 00000000 00000400 00000000 00000000 00000000  *....*
         LINES 7FF0B4C0-7FF0BFE0  SAME AS ABOVE
7FF14000 00000400 00000400 00000400 00000400 00000000 00000400  *....*
         LINES 7FF14020-7FF14200  SAME AS ABOVE
```

```
7FF14220  00000410 00000410 00000410 00000410 00000410 00000410 00000410 00000410  *....................*
7FF14240  00000400 00000400 00000400 00000400 00000400 00000400 00000400 00000400  *....................*
7FF14260  00000400 00000400 00000400 00000400 00000400 00000400 00000400 00000400  *....................*
7FF14280  00000410 00000410 00000410 00000410 00000410 00000410 00000410 00000410  *....................*
7FF142A0  00000410 00000400 00000400 00000410 00000400 00000400 00000400 00000400  *....................*
7FF142C0  00000400 00000400 00000400 00000400 00000400 00000400 00000400 00000400  *....................*
7FF142E0  00000400 00000400 00000400 00000400 00000400 00000400 00000400 00000400  *....................*
7FF14300  00000410 00000410 00000410 00000410 00000410 00000400 00000400 00000410  *....................*
7FF14320  00000410 00000410 00000410 00000410 00000410 00000410 00000400 00000410  *....................*
7FF14340  00006011 15A20011 119EF011 00000411 00000411 00000411 15A20011 1B79B011  *.......s...0........*
7FF14360  00000411 1B512011 21BED001 0017F005 0035F005 58DD011 1341A001 01448011    *.......).0..0..)....*
7FF14380  029A3001 1F403011 0FC30011 04DE6411 1D0B6011 00000411 00000411 00000411   *.....C......-.......*
7FF143A0  00000411 00000411 00000411 04FEB411 015C9011 0548C011 00CD3005 00C2E005   *.........*...(...B\.*
7FF143C0  23D7B001 1F759011 0D4C4C411 035E3411 03B2A411 0217B411 05987411 06D2005   *.P......D.;..u...q..|*
7FF143E0  08CF405 21810011 004CA405 030D9411 0386F401 01050011 02B73011 0F550011    *.4.a..<u..m..f4.....*
7FF14400  00000000 00000000 00000000 00000000 00000000 00000000 00000000 00000000   *....................*

          LINES 7FF14420-7FF14DA0  SAME AS ABOVE

7FF14DC0  00000000 00000000 00000000 00000000 10000000 00000000 10000000 00000000   *....................*
7FF14DE0  00000000 10000000 00000000 00000000 00000000 10000000 00000000 10000000   *....................*
7FF14E00  00000000 00000000 10000000 00000000 10000000 00000000 00000000 00000000   *....................*
7FF14E20  10000000 00000000 00000000 10000000 80000000 00000000 00000000 00000000   *....................*
7FF14E40  00000000 50000000 00000000 00000000 00000000 00000000 00000000 00000000   *....................*
7FF14E60  00000000 00000000 50000000 00000000 00000000 00000000 00000000 00000000   *.&..................*
7FF14E80  50000000 00000000 00000000 00000000 10000000 00000000 10000000 00000000   *.&..&...............*
7FF14EA0  10000000 04237508 04237508 00000000 03F0AAE8 10000000 03F0AAE8 10000000   *........O.Y.........*
7FF14EC0  00000000 10000000 00000000 00000000 10000000 00000000 00000000 00000000   *.......O.Y..........*
7FF14EE0  10000000 00000000 00000000 10000000 00000000 10000000 00000000 10000000   *....................*
7FF14F00  00000000 10000000 042374E8 042374E8 00000000 00000000 00000000 10000000   *.......Y............*
7FF14F20  10000000 00000000 10000000 00000000 039069A8 10000000 039069A8 03E8D9A8   *.......Y....y..YRy..*
7FF14F40  00000000 03DE7EE8 00000000 00000000 035654A8 10000000 10000030 10000030   *....=Y....y...y.....*
7FF14F60  10000030 042377A8 042377A8 10000000 04237468 10000030 04237468 10000030   *.....y...Y.....8<y..*
7FF14F80  04237448 00000000 10000000 042375E8 00000000 03F84CA8 00000000 00000000   *.....Y...Y..........*
7FF14FA0  10000030 03C9BB68 10000030 00000000 00000000 10000000 10000030 035B6D68   *......I...y...$_....*
7FF14FC0  00000000 10000000 042374C8 042374C8 042374C8 00000000 00000000 00000000   *.......h...H........*
7FF14FE0  50000000 7FF15110 00000020 009EFEB4 7F7472B0 00FF6F00 7FF15000 7FF15000   *"1&.................*
7FF15000  E5E2E6D2 009D0358 00FD50C8 009DF348 009FF7B0 8128DC0A 00F7F080 03E8D9A8   *VSWK"1....A..&H.3..7.a..?...."1&.*
7FF15040  80FF049C 04237448 7FFFC160 00000043 01FEB170 7FF16BB0 009DF348 06050000   *....A-........70....*
7FF15060  05400C00 7FF15298 7FF15008 00000000 009DD210 0203BE00 D00000FD 7FF15008    *"1q....3............*
7FF15080  00000000 00000000 00000000 00000070 00000000 00000000 D00000FD 00080008   *....K....}.....1&...*
```

```
7FF150A0  00FD0001 00000000 00000000 00000000  00000000 7FF16F58 7FF16EB4 00000000  *.........................."1?."1>...*
7FF150C0  00000000 00000000 00000000 7FF17C04  7FF72DC8 00000000 00000000 7FF183C6  *.........................."1cF"1@..KH..*
7FF150E0  00000000 20FD0000 00000000 00000000  80DF0850 00000000 00000000 00000000  *..............................&......*
7FF15100  00000000 00000000 00000002 7FF151E4  7FF45050 7FF15000 7FF15080 8128EA82  *.......................&&&"1.qa..b*
7FF15120  8129231C 00000000 00000002 0128DBF0  0128EBEF 01322688 7FF15348 000000FD  *a........."1.U....."1&....*
7FF15140  01322688 0128EBEF 0128DBF0 7FF15FB8  7FF15B0B 009D0358 0200FF00 810AFB3A  *.h.......0"1....K.....-a..*
7FF15160  0128FA5E 7FF15FB8 7FF15B0B 810A13C0  8111BEA0 00000020 009DD188 810AFB3A  *.;"1."1&.a.(a....-a..*
7FF15180  000FFF01 00000088 009DD188 03210000  00F7F080 010A0C98 010A1C97 7FF15110  *...h..Jh...70..q..p"1.*
7FF151A0  7FF15240 81292958 009D0354 00000088  00000C60 009DD188 00000000 7FF15000  *"1.a.....h...h.--Jh---"1&.*
7FF151C0  7FF15080 01FEB170 1FEB170 7FF15094   012922F0 7FF15198 00000C60 00000030  *"1&."1&.m..0"1.q.--..*
7FF151E0  000001F9 00000000 20FD0000 00000070  009DD210 03210000 000002F8 7FF15148  *.....9..........K......8"1..*
```

```
7FF15200  7FF1FFFF FFFF8000 00000000 00000000  00000000 00000000 00F7F080 7FF745000  *"1...........70...*
7FF15220  00000819 00010321 8127FC66 00000000  00200E6 04000000 00000088 00000020    *.^.........W.......&.*
7FF15240  009DC60 7FF15158 7FF152A0 01FEB170   00000088 8127C17C 7FF16BB0 7FF16EB4    *...-"1.q"1.a..a.A@..h"1>."1>.*
7FF15260  000FF01 7FF15000 7FF15080 01FEB170   00000088 009DD188 0127FA40 00000088    *.-"1.q"1.a...a.A@...h*
7FF15280  009DF3E4 00000030 000001F9 7FF15198  7FF15310 8104C81A 8127BF24 7FF15110    *.3U....."1&...Jh....."1..*
7FF152A0  7FF15340 81292958 8127FA6C 00000002  00000000 00000C60 00000005 7FF15000    *."1.a....9"1.q"1.a.H.a..."1.*
7FF152C0  7FF15080 000000FD 01322688 009DD20F  012922F0 7FF15298 000001ED 00000030    *"1&..a...%......0"1.q....."1&.*
7FF152E0  7FF700000 7FF73A000 00F70004 00038000  009DD188 7FF72DC8 000007F6 80000000  *."1&....h....0"1.q.*
7FF15300  00000001 7FF73A000 00F70004 00038000  8127C0D2 7FF72DC8 7FF15358 000007F7  *.6....K..Jh.6..7..*
7FF15320  009DD000 7FF15080 7FF15080 8127FB34  8127C17C 00000002 7FF72DC8 009DD210    *..}....7...a.{K"1...h.K..*
7FF15340  7FF15310 7FF15298 00000188 8127FB34  0000007F 009DD210 0127FA40 009DD210    *"1."1&."1&..KH"1&.KH"KH"1...8*
7FF15360  7FF18314 7FF15000 7FF15080 7FF183C6  8127C17C 00000006 0127FA40 7FFE2BE0    *"1..q..ha..a.A@....\*
7FF15380  009DF3E4 00000030 00000000 009DD280  00000002 8104C81A 8127BF24 00000070    *.3U....."1.....K......K..*
7FF153A0  009DD280 8127C21A 7FF153E8 00000002  0127C150 7FF16430 7FF153A0 7FF15000    *..K.a.B.."1.Y.....a.H.a.*
7FF153C0  7FF15080 7FF72DC8 00000548 009DD280  7FF72DC8 00000280 7FF72DC8 009DD210    *"1&..K.."1&..KH".K..A&"1&.*
7FF153E0  009DF6DC 00000000 00220000 009FE037  7FF153A0 00000001 00000280 009DD280    *.6...-.\".N.h....*
7FF15400  009CF000 00F70080 00000000 00000000  8127C0D2 00000002 009DD280 0127BEF8    *.70..0..7.-.a.{K"1...K.*
7FF15420  009DD000 7FF72DC8 00000210 7FF15080  7FF72DC8 7FF72DC8 7FF16430 0127BEF8    *.K.."1&."1&.KH".KH"1&.8*
7FF15440  7FF15410 00000210 7FF183C6 7FF15080  011FC000 02041D78 01C1B6D0 009DDFFFF    *"1&."1&.KH".KH"1&.8*
7FF15460  009DF000 02041EC8 00000018 7FF15080  7FF00000 00000001 7FF10001 009DFFFF    *."1cF.{....A.}.*
7FF15480  00FB8088 7FF15000 7FF15080 80000000  00000001 7FF746000 81270080 7FF154E0    *.0"..H........"1..*
7FF154A0  00000002 00FC56A0 00FC5000 00FC5000  7FF15000 7FF15080 81270080 01FF35A4    *.h"1&."1&..-a..."1.\*
7FF154C0  01FF2D4C 0127BEF8 7FF17BF8 00000460  00000460 80000000 01FFB35A4 017B0110   *.&..&."1&."1&.u..u*
7FF154E0  00F7F080 00000000 7FF72D000 7FF746FFF  7FF74600 00000000 00000000 7FF72D000  *.70.......?.-.*
7FF15500  00000000 00000000 00000200 00000000  00000000 00000000 00000000 00000000    *..................*
```

```
7FF15520  00000000 00000000 00000000 00000000  00000000 7F72DFFF 7F72D000 00000000  *................")......*
7FF15540  00000000 00000000 00000000 00000000  00000004 00000000 00000000 00000000  *........................*
7FF15560  00000000 00000000 00000000 00000000  00000000 00000000 00000000 00000000  *........................*
          LINES 7FF15580-7FF15FE0  SAME AS ABOVE
7FF16000  00000000 00000000 00000000 00000000  00000000 00000000 00000000 00000000  *........................*
          LINES 7FF16020-7FF163C0  SAME AS ABOVE
7FF163E0  00000000 00000000 00000000 00000000  E5E2D4D7 00000000 000009F8 00000001  *............VSMP.....8...*
7FF16400  00000000 7FF16EBC 7F72D1D8 00000000  00000000 7FF16430 7F72D2C8 7FF16400  *....1>".JQ......1.."1.KH"*
7FF16420  7FF16418 7FF16D6D 00000000 7F751148  7FF16448 7F72D2C8 7F72D370 00000000  *.L."1.}.....1>"1.KH"L.*
7FF16440  00000000 7FF16ED4 7F72D7F0 00000000  00000000 7FF16490 7FF16460 7FF16460  *..."1>M".P0......1.y"1.-*
7FF16460  7FF16478 7F72D400 7F72D400 00000000  7FFE2928 7F72D400 7FF16478 7FF16490  *.M.".P0...."1.y"1..".M.*
7FF16480  7F72D400 00000000 00000000 7FF16490  00000000 7F72D040 00000000 00000000  *.......N8"1.......}.*
7FF164A0  00000000 7FF164D8 7FF16FF0 00000000  00000000 7FF164F0 7FF164C0 7FF164C0  *.1.Q"120"1.Q......"1.0"1.(*
7FF164C0  7FF164D8 7FF16FF0 7FF164D8 00000000  7FF16508 7FF164D8 7FFE2340 7FFE2340  *."....1.{....."1..1.Q".*
7FF164E0  7FF751448 7FF16FF0 00000000 00000000  7FF16508 7FF164D8 7FFE2340 7FFE2340  *.....1.h"1.0...."1.h.*
7FF16500  00000000 00000000 7FF16688 00000000  7FF16688 00000000 7FF16688 00000000  *..."1.?Q"1......"1..1.&"1.*
7FF16520  7FF16538 7FF16FD8 7FF16538 00000000  7FF16520 7FF16550 7FF16520 7FF16538  *.1.&"1......"1.&....*
7FF16540  7FF16550 00000000 00000000 7FF16550  7FF16538 7FF751028 7F751028 7FF16538  *.......1.....1..."1.*
7FF16560  00000000 00000000 7F751028 7FF16550  00000000 00000000 7F751028 7FF16580  *.1.q"1?{1.q......"1.q.*
7FF16580  7FF16598 7FF16FC0 7FF16580 00000000  7FF165B0 7FF16598 7FF168C8 7FF16598  *."1.H"1.......1.H"1.q"1.H"1.q*
7FF165A0  7FF165B0 7FF16580 00000000 00000000  7FF165C8 7FF16598 7FF168C8 7FF168C8  *..."....1.H"1......1.H.*
7FF165C0  00000000 00000000 7FF168C8 7FF165B0  7FF16598 7FF168C8 00000000 00000000  *.O."...}-....O...."1?.1?.*
7FF165E0  7F72D610 009FD060 00000038  FD72D610 00022000 7FF16F04 7FF16F04  *.....".../..."...R..h*
7FF16600  00004000 00001000 00000000 0000FC8  7FF74613D 00000000 7F72D9A0 009BAE88  *.W.."1....H".".".*
7FF16620  00E60020 7FF16620 7FFE25F8 7FFE26A0  7FFE2490 7FFE2490 7FFE2490 00000000  *."1..1.8"...."....\.*
7FF16640  7FFE25B0 7FFE25F8 004F8000 000C000  7FFCE000 00004000 7FFE2D30 7F751628  *.."1..1.!.....".{."...&.*
7FF16660  7FF16658 7FF16658 7FFE2340 00000000  7F7519A0 00000730 7F751250 7F751328  *."....1....".."....&".*
7FF16680  00001000 7FFE2340 7FF16508  7FFE2340 00000010 7FFFB000 00000B90  *.1?0"1.0"1.....".....1.Y"*
7FF166A0  7FF16FF0 7FF164F0 7FF16790  7FFFBFC0 00000000 00000000 7FF16EE8  *.(...1.&..."1>.//{"1..*
7FF166C0  009FFEC0 000000C0 FDFF5000  7FF16EBC 7F7461C0 7FF16418 7F746370  *.....1..1......1.q.*
7FF166E0  00000008 7FF166B8 7FF16748  009FF138 FD9FE128 00000000  *.....1..1......1.q.*
```

```
7FF16700  00000000 7FF16778 7FFFC818 000000F0  FD000000 00000000 7FFE2328 7FF16568  *....1..H....0....."1.."1.*
7FF16720  7FF16730 009FE240 00E50020 00000000  7FF16730 7FF16730 7FF16738 7FF16738  *.1..S .V...."1..1..1..1.*
7FF16740  7FF16740 7FF16740 7FF166E8 00000000  009FDE68 00000198 FDFF0000 00001000  *.1..1."1.Y....q.........*
7FF16760  7F72D100 7F7465C8 7FFE2BC8 7FFE2BC8  0A0C6000 000F000 7FF16700 00000000  *."J."H".H"....0."1.....*
```

```
7FF16780  7FFFC728 000000F0 FD000000 00000000  7FF166A0 7FF511F0 7FF511F0   *.G....0.........."1.."...0"1.."...0*
7FF167A0  7FFFBE80 00000010 00000000 00000000  7FFFC598 00000190 FDFEB000 00001000   *."............."..Eq.*
7FF167C0  00000000 00000000 7FFE26D0 009FDE88  000000A0 00000000 00000000 00001000   *..........}...h....*
7FF167E0  7FF167F0 009FF158 00E50020 00000000  7FF167F0 7FF167F8 7FFE9000 00003000   *"1.0..1..V...."1.0"1.0"1.8"1.8*
7FF16800  7FF16838 7FF16808 7FF16808 7FF16838  7FF16820 7FF16808 7FF16808 00000000   *"1.."1..1.."1.."1.."1..*
7FF16820  7FFE9000 000003A0 7FF16850 7FFE7000  7FF16808 00000000 00000FC8 00000000   *"1.&"1.&".........."1.."1..*
7FF16840  7FF16850 7FF16838 7FFE2028 00002000  7FF7000 00000FC8 00000000 00000000   *"1......."1...h.W.*
7FF16860  7FF16838 00000000 7FFE2028 7FF16888  7FF16880 00E50020 009FDE88 00000000   *"1.q"1.q"1.h"1.h"..8"..1."1..*
7FF16880  7FF16898 7FF16898 7FF16888 7FF16888  7FFE25F8 7FF25B0 00E60020 00001000   *"1..".....{...(...-1.q"1.q*
7FF168A0  7FF168B0 00000000 009FC000 00001000  009FC000 7FF16880 7FF16898 00000000   *"1.q.."1?("1.H"1.H"1..&..*
7FF168C0  7FF16898 7FF168B0 009FC000 7FF16C0  7FF165C8 7FF165B0 7FFE5000 000009B0   *"1..".......h.V..*
7FF168E0  7FF16868 00001000 7FF16FC0 009FDE88  7FF165C8 00001020 00E51020 00000000   *"1.8"1.8.\...)*..0...Q"*
7FF16900  7FF168F8 7FF168F8 7FF16E20A0 009EE000  00E51020 00001000 7FFE2310 7FFE2118   *"1..".)*.).*1..*
7FF16920  7FFE2118 00000000 009EE000 7FFE26D0  7FFDF000 00000000 00000000 7FFE2208   *"1.."1..".."1.."1..*
7FF16940  7FF16940 7FF16940 7FF16948 7FF16948  7FF16940 009F9028 00E51020 00001000   *"..<...".........."1.h"1.h*
7FF16960  7FF16960 00000348 FEFE1000 00000000  7FFE2820 00000000 7FF16978 7FF16978   *"1.."1..".)*..).*..")*1.)*..*1.}..*
7FF16980  7FF16980 7FF16980 7F751DD0 00000000  7FF16970 7FF16988 7F747000 00001000   *".)*..".........."1.Y..*
7FF169A0  00003000 7FFE29D0 7FFE29D0 7FFE29D0  7FF16988 7FF16988 7FFE29D0 00000000   *"1.0.........."1..*
7FF169C0  00000000 00000000 00000000 00000000  7FFE29E8 00000010 7FF169D0 00000000   *".........."1..*
7FF169E0  00000000 00000000 00000000 00000000  7FF169E8 00000000 00000000 00000000   *"1......".........."1..*
7FF16A00  00000000 7FF16A18 00000000 00000000  00000000 00000000 7FF16A30 00000000   *"1.-.......")*..*
7FF16A20  00000000 00000000 00000000 00000000  7FF16A48 00000000 00000000 00000000   *"1..".........."1.*
7FF16A40  00000000 7FF16A78 00000000 7FF16A60  00000000 00000000 7FF16A90 00000000   *".........."1.y........"1..*
7FF16A60  00000000 00000000 00000000 7FF16A60  00000000 00000000 00000000 00000000   *"1.Q.."1.{.........."1.0*
7FF16A80  00000000 00000000 00000000 00000000  7FF16AA8 00000000 00000000 00000000   *"1.............."1..*
7FF16AA0  00000000 00000000 00000000 7FF16AC0  00000000 00000000 7FF16AF0 00000000   *".........."1.&..*
7FF16AC0  7FF16AD8 00000000 00000000 00000000  7FF16B08 00000000 00000000 00000000   *".........."1,..*
7FF16AE0  00000000 00000000 00000000 00000000  00000000 00000000 00000000 00000000   *".........."1,&..*
7FF16B00  00000000 7FF16B20 00000000 7FF16B20  7FF16B08 00000000 00000000 00000000   *"1.............."1..*
7FF16B20  7FF16B38 00000000 00000000 00000000  7FF16B68 00000000 00000000 00000000   *"1.q........"1,\..*
7FF16B40  00000000 00000000 00000000 7FF16B80  7FF16B68 00000000 00000000 00000000   *"1,8........"1,H..*
7FF16B60  00000000 00000000 00000000 00000000  7FF16B50 00000000 00000000 00000000   *".........."1.H..*
7FF16B80  00000000 7FF16B98 00000000 7FF16B80  7FF16BB0 00000000 00000000 00000000   *".........."1..*
7FF16BA0  00000000 00000000 00000000 7FF16BE0  7FF16BC8 00000000 00000000 00000000   *".........."1..*
7FF16BC0  7FF16BF0 00000000 00000000 00000000  7FF16BB0 00000000 00000000 00000000   *".........."1..*
7FF16BE0  00000000 00000000 00000000 7FF16BE0  00000000 00000000 00000000 00000000   *"1%...........18..*
7FF16C00  00000000 7FF16C40 00800000 7FF16C28  00000000 7FF16C10 00000000 00000000   *".........18h..*
7FF16C20  7FF16C40 00000000 00000000 00000000  7FF16C28 00000000 00000000 00000000   *".........."18..*
7FF16C40  00000000 7FF16C58 00000000 00000000  7FF16C88 00000000 7FF16C70 00000000   *"18..*
7FF16C60  00000000 00000000 00000000 00000000  00000000 00000000 00000000 00000000   *"18h..*
7FF16C80  00000000 7FF16CA0 00000000 00000000  00000000 00000000 00000000 00000000   *
```

```
7FF16CA0 7FF16CB8 00000000 00000000 00000000 00000000 7FF16CD0 00000000   *"1%..............."1}....*
7FF16CC0 00000000 00000000 00000000 00000000 7FF16CE8 00000000 00000000   *.................."18Y....*
7FF16CE0 00000000 00000000 7FF16D00 00000000 00000000 00000000 00000000   *..."1_..........."1_....*
7FF16D00 00000000 00000000 00000000 00000000 00000000 7FF16D30 00000000   *.................."1_....*
7FF16D20 00000000 00000000 7FF16D48 00000000 00000000 00000000 00000000   *..."1_..........."1_....*
7FF16D40 00000000 7FF16D60 00000000 00000000 00000000 00000000 00000000   *..."1_..........."1_....*
7FF16D60 7FF16D78 00000000 00000000 00000000 00000000 7FF16D90 00000000   *..."1_..........."1_....*
7FF16D80 00000000 00000000 00000000 00000000 7FF16DA8 00000000 00000000   *..."1_y........."1_y....*
7FF16DA0 00000000 00000000 7FF16DC0 00000000 00000000 00000000 00000000   *......"1_{......."1_....*
7FF16DC0 00000000 00000000 00000000 00000000 00000000 7FF16580 00000000   *..............SQAT.."1....*
7FF16DE0 00000000 00000000 E2D8C1E3 00000000 00000018 00000008 00000010   *..........SQAT..........*
```

```
7FF16E00 7FF16598 00000018 7FF165B0 00000000 E2D8C1E3 00000003 00000018 00000008   *"1.q....."1.....SQAT....*
7FF16E20 7FF16520 00000010 7FF16538 00000018 7FF16550 00000000 E2D8C1E3 00000003   *"1....."1....."1.&....SQAT....*
7FF16E40 00000018 00000008 7FF164C0 00000010 7FF164D8 00000018 7FF164F0 00000000   *"1.{....."1.Q....."1.0....*
7FF16E60 E2D8C1E3 00000003 00000018 00000008 7FF16460 00000010 7FF16478 00000018   *SQAT.........."1.-....."1....*
7FF16E80 7FF16490 E2D8C1E3 00000003 00000018 00000008 00000010 00000010 7FF16400   *"1....SQAT.........."1....*
7FF16EA0 7FF16418 00000018 7FF16430 00000000 D3C4C140 7FF16E88 7FF17C00 7FF16400   *"1.......nnn1.....LDA "1>h"1@."1*
```

The Local Data Area (LDA) contains storage management information for the address space. It begins at address 7FF16EB0. Note that there are Size Queue Anchor Tables beginning above at 7FF16DE8. Several related Address Queue Anchor Tables (AQATs) follow the LDA, beginning at location 7FF18010. The LDA and SQAT were discussed in chapter 4.

```
7FF16EC0 7FF166D0 7FF16400 7FF16448 7FF16E60 7FF17C00 7FF16460 7FFE2D60 7FF16460   *"1.}"1."1.."1>-"1@."1.-"1.-*
7FF16EE0 7FF164A8 7FF746208 7FF746208 00005000 009FB000 7FF72D2B0 7FF7513A0 09E00000   *"1.y"."....&.....K."....\.-*
7FF16F00 76200000 7FF165F8 7FF165F8 00001000 00004000 7FF16F14 7FF16F14 00000000   *........."1.8"1.8......"1?."1?......*
7FF16F20 00000000 7FF16F24 7FF16F24 00000000 00000000 7FF19608 7FF746000 000001EE   *........."1?."1?........."1?."1?....*
7FF16F40 00000000 0000E000 09E05000 7FFFC090 00000000 00000000 80000000 00100000   *.......\./&....."1o.-........*
7FF16F60 7FFE2BE0 00F7F080 00220000 00220000 00000000 00000000 00000000 00031000   *"..\"1&.70."{.-......b&.....-*
7FF16F80 00220000 00220000 008E2000 00220000 7F7A7000 00825000 00009000 7FF16DE8   *.....................b&.......*
7FF16FA0 00005000 008E2000 00220000 00220000 00220000 00200000 00200000 7FF17000   *.....&......................"1_Y"1..*
```

```
7FF16FC0  7FF16580 7FF168C8 7FF16580 7FF165C8   7FF16E10 7FF17400 7FF16520 7FF751028   *"1.."1.H"1..>."1...."1.."*
7FF16FE0  7FF16520 7FF16568 7FF16E38 7FF17800   7FF164C0 7FF166A0 7FF164C0 7FF16508   *"1.."1.."1>."1.."1.{"1.(1.*
7FF17000  00000000 00000000 00000000 00000000   00000000 00000000 00000000 00000000   *........................*
  LINES 7FF17020-7FF173C0  SAME AS ABOVE
7FF173E0  00000000 00000000 00000000 00000000   00000000 00000000 00000000 7FF18C20   *...................."1..*
7FF17400  00000000 00000000 00000000 00000000   00000000 00000000 00000000 00000000   *........................*
  LINES 7FF17420-7FF177C0  SAME AS ABOVE
7FF177E0  00000000 00000000 00000000 00000000   00000000 7FF19304 7FF1891C            *........"11."1i*
7FF17800  00000000 00000000 00000000 00000000   00000000 00000000 00000000 00000000   *........................*
  LINES 7FF17820-7FF17BC0  SAME AS ABOVE
7FF17BE0  00000000 00000000 00000000 00000000   00000000 00000000 00000000 7FF18618   *...................."1f.*
7FF17C00  00000000 7FF18314 00000000 00000000   00000000 00000000 00000000 00000000   *.............."1c.*
7FF17C20  00000000 00000000 00000000 00000000   00000000 00000000 00000000 00000000   *........................*
  LINES 7FF17C40-7FF17FC0  SAME AS ABOVE
7FF17FE0  00000000 00000000 00000000 00000000   00000000 00000000 7FF19000 7FF18010   *AQST.........AQAT..."1.."1.*
7FF18000  C1D8E2E3 00000000 00000000 00034000   C1D8C1E3 00000000 00000000 00000000   *........................*
7FF18020  00000000 00000000 00000000 00000000   00000000 00000000 00000000 00000000   *.............AQAT......*
  LINES 7FF18040-7FF182E0  SAME AS ABOVE
7FF18300  00000000 00000000 7FFE2928 28007F75   1430000E C1D8C1E3 00000000 00000000   *"..........".KH......AQAT*
7FF18320  00000000 00000000 00000000 00000000   00000000 00000000 00000000 00000000   *........................*
  LINES 7FF18340-7FF183A0  SAME AS ABOVE
7FF183C0  7F751148 00017F72 D2C88005 00000000   00007F74 63700047 00000000 00000000   *............"1.h..AQAT*
7FF183E0  00000000 00000000 00000000 00000000   00000000 00000000 00000000 00000000   *........................*
  LINES 7FF18400-7FF185E0  SAME AS ABOVE
7FF18600  00000000 00000000 00000000 00000000   00000000 00000000 C1D8C1E3 00000000   *.......................*
7FF18620  00000000 00000000 00000000 00000000   00000000 00000000 00000000 00000000   *........................*
  LINES 7FF18640-7FF188E0  SAME AS ABOVE
7FF18900  00000000 00000000 00000000 00000000   00007FF1 66880010 C1D8C1E3            *..................."1.h..AQAT*
7FF18920  00000000 00000000 00000000 00000000   00000000 00000000 00000000 00000000   *........................*
  LINES 7FF18940-7FF18BE0  SAME AS ABOVE
7FF18C00  00000000 C1D8C1E3 00000000 00000000   00000000 000F0000 0000FFE0 00000000   *AQAT.........\*
7FF18C20  C1D8C1E3 00000000 00000000 00000000   00000000 00000000 00000000 00000000   *AQAT.........*
7FF18C40  00000000 00000000 00000000 00000000   00000000 00000000 00000000 00000000   *........................*
  LINES 7FF18C60-7FF18EE0  SAME AS ABOVE
7FF18F00  00000000 00000000 00000000 00000000   00000000 00000000 7FF168C8 06000000   *..........."1.H....*
7FF18F20  00000000 00000000 00000000 00000000   00000000 00000000 00000000 00000000   *........................*
  LINES 7FF18F40-7FF18FE0  SAME AS ABOVE
7FF19000  C1D8C1E3 00000000 00000000 00000000   00000000 00000000 00000000 00000000   *AQAT.........*
7FF19020  00000000 00000000 00000000 00000000   00000000 00000000 00000000 00000000   *........................*
  LINES 7FF19040-7FF19280  SAME AS ABOVE
```

```
7FF192A0 00000000 00000000 00000000 00000000   00000000 00047F72 D5F8003F 7F72D040   *.............."N8..")*
7FF192C0 FFB07F75 14D86000 00000000 00000000   00000200 00000000 00000000 00000000   *..."...Q.............*


JOB EXA7JHMX        STEP APP3        TIME 125832    DATE 94100   ID = 000                    PAGE 00000072


7FF19300 00000000 C1D8C1E3 00000000 00000000   00000000 00000000 00000000 00000000   *....AQAT.............*
7FF19320 00000000 00000000 00000000 00000000   00000000 00000000 00000000 00000000   *....................*
       LINES 7FF19340-7FF195A0  SAME AS ABOVE
7FF195C0 00000000 000F7F75 102897C0 00000000   00000000 00000000 00000000 03E00000   *......"...p{.........*
7FF195E0 00000000 00000000 00000000 00000000   00000000 00000000 00000000 00000000   *...............\.....*
7FF19600 00000000 00000000 C1D8C1E3 00000000   00000000 00000000 00000000 00000000   *........AQAT.........*
7FF19620 00000000 00000000 00000000 00000000   00000000 00000000 00000000 00000000   *....................*
       LINES 7FF19640-7FF19FE0  SAME AS ABOVE


7FFE2000 E5E2D4D7 7FF163F0 00001000 00000002   7F72D358 7F7469E8 7FFE2010 7FFE2010   *VSMP"1.0....."L."..Y".*
7FFE2020 0A191000 00002000 7FFE2298 009FE140   00E61020 00E61020 00E61020 00000000   *.........q......h.W..*
7FFE2040 7FFE20D0 7FFE2130 009FE140 00000028   FDE00000 00002000 7FFE2100 7FFE2100   *...........\.".......*
7FFE2060 7FFEAA8  7FFE2060 00001000 7FFE2088   7FFE2238 7FFE2310 7FFE2070 7FFE2070   *...-...".y"..........*
7FFE2080 009F8000 7FFE2088 7FFE2088 7FFE20A8   7FFE2090 7FFE2090 7FFE2098 7FFE2098   *...".h".h"...........*
7FFE20A0 7FFE20A0 7FFE20A8 00E50020 7FFE20A8   7FFE22C8 7FFE22C8 7FF168E0 7FF16628   *...h".y".y".H".H"1.\"1*
7FFE20C0 7FFE2088 009FDE88 00E50020 01001000   7FFE2040 7FFE2040 009FF030 00002028   *..h..h.V...........0.*
7FFE20E0 FDFE20B8 00000000 00000000 7FFE2058   7FFE2238 009FE240 00E61020 00020000   *.........S..W.......*
7FFE2100 7FFE2058 009FA000 009FA000 00002000   00010000 7FFE24C0 009FD320 7FFE2400   *.."..........8..8....*
7FFE2120 7FF16910 00002000 7FF16910 00002000   7FFE24C0 7FFE2178 7FFE2280 000000C0   *1.".\......"..{..L..{*
7FFE2140 FD005000 00002000 009FE000 00000848   7FFE2250 7FFE2178 00003000 7FFE21D8   *.&.....".............*
7FFE2160 009FB000 00000848 7FFE23A0 009FB000   00000000 7FFE16628 7FFE2148 009FDE88   *.)"...".....&.."Q.*
7FFE2180 7FFE2160 7FFE23A0 009FB000 7FFE22E0   7FFE16628 7FFE21C0 7FFE3000 00001000   *..-.".............h*
7FFE21A0 00ED1020 7FFE2068 7FFE21A8 7FFE22E0   7FFE21A8 00011000 00001000 7FFE2250   *.......1......"....1.*
7FFE21C0 7FFE3000 00000E00 00002000 7FFE21A8   7FFE21C0 00001000 00001000 7FFE2178   *...".y".\".{..{......*
7FFE21E0 7FFE21F0 009F4000 00022000 009F4000   009F4000 00000FC8 7FFE21D8 7FFE21D8   *..0...0...y".y...&.*
7FFE2200 7FFE21D8 00000300 7FF16958 7FFE26E8   7FFC500 00000048 FD9FD198 00000000   *.0".0".Q".....H".Q".Q*
7FFE2220 009F2000 7FFE2240 7FFE2250 7FFE2250   7FFE2250 7FFE2150 7FF168F8 7FFE2070   *.Q.....1...Y".E....Jq.*
7FFE2240 7FFE2240 00002000 7FFE2850 7FFE21D8   7FFE21D8 7FFE2150 7FFE2220 7FFE2220   *.&.".&..&...&...1.8".*
7FFE2260 009F2000 00002000 746100 7FF72DCF8    7FF72D538 7FF72D538 7FF72370 00003000   *.&.".&...Q"..&"......*
7FFE2280 7FFE2158 7FFE2280 7FFE2280 7FFE2280    7FFE0000 00002000 7FFE22B0 7FFE22B8   *.............8".N..N.*
7FFE22A0 7FFE22B0 009FDE88 00000000 00000000    7FFE22B0 7FFE22B0 7FFDB000 00001000   *..h.W&..............*
7FFE22C0 7F751D78 7F751D78 00E65020 7FFE20B0    7FFE2370 7FFE2370 009FA000 00000000   *.y".y".\".\"........*
7FFE22E0 7FFE21A8 7FFE2AA8 7FFE22E0 7FFE22E0    00020000 009FA000 00000000 00000A78   *..y".y"...\".\"..{...*
```

```
7FFE2300  7FFE2100  7FFE2100  7FFE23B8  7FFE23B8  00000020   *.....".....".1.8".....*
7FFE2320  009F7000  7FFE23D0  7FF168F8  009FE240  00000000   *....".....)....".....*
7FFE2340  7FF51448  7FF16688  7FFFBC00  00E51020  00002000   *"1.h"1.h"1.0"..S .V.*
7FFE2360  7FFE2360  7F7510E8  7FFFDB00  00000110  00002000   *"...-.."1.".Y".H".H*
7FFE2380  7FFE22C8  009FBB58  7FFE2388  0A052000  00002000   *"...H...".....Y".-.h.*
7FFE23A0  009FBB58  00000180  7FFE2178  00001000  00000548   *"...Q8".h.*
7FFE23C0  7FFE2310  7FFE2310  7FFE23E8  009F7000  009FE240   *".....".....h.-.h.*
7FFE23E0  00E55020  00003000  7FFE23E8  7FFD8000  00001000   *"V&..".K&".....Y".*
7FFE2400  7FFE2118  7FFE2400  7FFD9000  00002000  7FFE2418   *".....".K&".Y".Y".*
7FFE2420  7FFE2420  7F72D250  7FFE2428  7FFE2460  7FFE2430   *".....Jy".....Y"-..*
7FFE2440  7FFD7000  7F72D1A8  7FFE2448  7FFD6000  00001000   *".....".....Y".*
7FFE2460  7FFE2430  7FFE2478  7FFE2460  00001000  7FF751A48  *".....".....&..-..*
7FFE2480  7FFE2478  7FFE2568  7FFE2448  7FFE24F8  7FF16628   *".....".....".8"1..*
7FFE24A0  009E3000  00009000  009F9008  00000198  00000068   *".....q..BH.*
7FFE24C0  7FFE2130  7FFE25E0  FD000000  00000000  FDFFC2C8   *".0...h...q.*
7FFE24E0  7FFE24F0  009FDE88  00EC10A0  00000000  7FFE2190   *"...h..8"..0".0".*
7FFE2500  7FFE2500  7FFE2500  009F6000  7FFE2520  009F6000   *"-...".....".&".."..*
7FFE2520  009F6000  000000B0  7FFE2520  7FFE2508  7FFE2508   *".&.S .W..&"...Y.*
7FFE2540  7FFE2550  009FE240  00E60020  7FFE2550  7FFE2558   *".K..K...q"..q..*
7FFE2560  7F72D268  7F72D268  7FFE2460  7FFE2568  7FFE2558   *"...".q".q".....*
7FFE2580  7FFE2508  7FFE2490  7FFE2580  7FFD2000  00010000   *".....".q"1..".1..*
7FFE25A0  7FFE2580  7FFE2580  00F16890  009F1000  00000930   *".....".1..H".H*
7FFE25C0  7FFD3000  00001000  7FFE25B0  7FFE25B0  00000000   *".....".....".....*
```

```
JOB EXA7JHMX          STEP APP3          TIME 125832    DATE 94100    ID = 000
```

```
7FFE25E0  7FFE24C0  7FFE2658  009F9530  000000A0   FD000000  00000000  7FF16640  7FF16890  *...{....n....".1. "1..*
7FFE2600  7FFE2610  7F78B000  0001C000            0000000F  00000F28  7FFE25F8  7FFE25F8  *"...{...Q..".8"..8.*
7FFE2620  7FFE25F8  00000000  7F7516D0  7FFE2C70   7F743BC8  000000F0  FD7516D0  00001000  *"...8...(.}"....H..0..*
7FFE2640  7FFE2A18  00000000  7FFE4070  000001B8   FD9B6000  00005000  7F7464C0  7FFE25E0  *".8....}".0..).*
7FFE2660  009FFF88  00000078  FDFCD000  00003000   00000000  7F7464C0  7FFE2688  009DF348  *".h...}..(.\".-.y*
7FFE2680  00B68020  00003000  7FFE2F40  7F746760   7FFE2688  00001000  0A189000  00002000  *".h...}..h".h....3.*
7FFE26A0  7FFD1338  00000CC8  7FFE1640  7FFE1640   7FF16640  00001000  7F72DFA0  7F72D688  *".W....}".h.".h..*
7FFE26C0  7FFFC118  00000048  FD72D688  00001000   7FFE26D0  7FFE26D0  7F72D688  7FFE26D8  *"..A.".}...h...Oh*
7FFE26E0  7FFE26E0  7FFE26E0  7FFE2208  00000000   7FFC2E8  00000F0  FD000000  00000000   *".....}".}..Q"..Q.*
7FFE2700  7FFE2760  7FFE2708  7FFE2708   7FFE2AC0  000000F0  7FFE2AC0  7FFE27C0  00001000  *"....BY..0..Q*
7FFE2720  7FFE2700  009F9028  00E60020  00000000   7FFE2970  00000000  00000000  009FDE88  *"...{..{...{....0..h*
7FFE2740  00EC1080  00000000  7FFE27E8  7FFE27E8   7FFE2748  7FFE2748  7F784000  00002000  *"....W...Y".Y".h*
```

```
7FFE2760  7FFE2700 7FFE2778 7FFE2778   009F0000 00001000 009F0000 00000718   *"...."...."...."....*
7FFE2780  7FFE2760 7FFE2760 00000000   7FF16928 00000000 7FFE27A8 009F9028   *..-."....."..-.."1...*
7FFE27A0  00E50020 00000000 00000000   7FFE27B0 7FFE27B0 7FFE27B8 7FFE27A8   *.V..."...."..y".y"..*
7FFE27C0  7FF510D0 00000000 009F9028   00E61020 00001000 7FFE27F0 7FFE27F0   *".}..."...Q...W...0.0*
7FFE27E0  7FFE27E0 7FFE27E0 009F0000   7FFE27D8 7FFE27D8 7FFE2808 7FFE2808   *"...."..\/."..."..Q".Q"..*
7FFE2800  009EF000 00001000 00000A78   7FFE27F0 7FFE27F0 7FFE2808 7FFE2818   *.0...."...."..0".0"..0"..*
```

The DQE for subpool 22 is at location 7FFE2838. The DQE was discussed in chapter 4.

```
7FFE2820  7FF16950 7FFE2880 7FFE2880   7F783000 00001000 7F72D490 7F72D490   *"1.&"1.&".....M."M.*
7FFE2840  7FFE2C10 00009000 00003000   7F72D250 7FFE2248 7FFE2850 7FFE2850   *...."........K&".&".*
7FFE2860  7F781000 00001000 009E02F8   7F751CB8 7F72D3D0 7F751CB8 00001000   *......8.......L}-".*
7FFE2880  7F783000 00000CB0 7FFE2820   7FFE2820 00000000 009DB198 000003C0   *..........."...q..(*
7FFE28A0  7F751DF0 7F751DD8 7F751FD0   7FFE2D00 7F746478 7FFE28B0 7FFE28B0   *.0."Q".)..."....q..q*
7FFE28C0  0A177000 00002000 7F751CA0   7FFE28C8 7FFE28C8 0A087000 00003000   *.0..Q".}....H.....*
7FFE28E0  7F751C40 7FFE28E8 7FFE28E8   7FFE28F0 7F751988 7FFE16970 00001000   *..\."Y"..Y".0."H".*
7FFE2900  7FFE28F8 7FFE28F8 00016000   7F746388 7FFE2910 7FFE2918 7FFE2918   *...."8".Y"..Y".h"h"1.*
7FFE2920  7FFE2920 7FFE2920 7F751430   7FFE2D60 7FF16490 7FFE4000 00000020   *...."8.-....h"....*
7FFE2940  7F746460 7FFE2B68 7FFE2940   0A110000 00000000 7FFE2DAF0 00001000   *...."...Q"..Q"-1.*
7FFE2960  7F751EB0 009C1190 00E65020   00000000 00000000 7FFE2988 009F9028   *......W&"....".0...*
7FFE2980  00ED10A0 00000000 7FFE2988   7F751E50 7F72D820 7FFE2998 7FFE2998   *.........h".h".&"Q.".h.*
7FFE29A0  7F7517A8 00000000 7F751850   00E57020 00000000 7FFE2E38 00001000   *......h".&".V.....q".q*
7FFE29C0  7FFE2E38 7FFE2E38 7FFE2E38   7F751478 7FFE2A00 7FF169A0 7FF169A0   *...y.....&..V....1.*
7FFE29E0  7F736000 00003000 00000000   7FFE4660 FEFE2A00 7FFE2998 7F751C10   *......0.0"..01.*
7FFE2A00  7F72DC58 7F751F88 7FFE2A00   004D3000 00006000 7FFE2998 7FFE2A30   *.......-.-....h".-..h.*
7FFE2A20  7FFE2640 7FFE2640 009BA000   7F751A48 7FFE2A30 7F72F000 00001000   *.......-.."h"h"...(..*
7FFE2A40  7F780000 00001000 7FF16610   7F72D9A0 7F72D9A0 00003000 00001000   *.......-...".Y"..Y"..*
7FFE2A60  7F77A338 7FFE2AC0 7FFE2AC0   7FFE2AC0 00003000 7F775DD8 00000F28   *......."1...."R".R.0.*
7FFE2A80  7FFE2AA8 7FFE2AA8 00003000   7F751970 7F746118 7FFE2A90 7FFE2A90   *.....t...H".(.(..&Q.*
7FFE2AA0  0A10C000 00001000 7FFE2068   7FFE2A78 7FFE2A78 7FFE2A78 0001C000   *...".y".y"..y"/.(.(..*
7FFE2AC0  7FFE2710 7FFE2710 7FFE2A60   7F777000 00004000 7F72D940 00004000   *......(..."\."/../.(.*
7FFE2AE0  7F72D940 7F72D940 00001000   7F72D78 7F751400 7FFE2AF0 7FFE2AF0   *...."..."-."-.-....R.*
7FFE2B00  009C3000 00005000 7FFE29E8   7FFC250 00000048 FDFE2A18 00001000   *...R".R".R...-.".0"..0.*
7FFE2B20  7F72D748 00000760 7F72DA00   7F72DA00 00001000 7FFE2EC8 7FFE28F0   *....&".Y"."B&...0"..0*
7FFE2B40  7FFE2C40 7FFE2C40 00001000   7F751F10 7FFE2B50 7FFE2B50 7FFE2B50   *...P.......".&".H".0*
7FFE2B60  7F782000 00001000 7FFE2940   7FFE2568 7FFE2B68 0A10F000 00001000   *...".0..."...&".&".&*
7FFE2B80  7F72DEC8 7F751DD8 7F751DD8   009D0000 00001000 7F77B000 00000600   *..."H".0".Q"....0....*
7FFE2BA0  7F72D268 7F72D268 00000000   7F751778 7F751FD0 7F751EC8 7F72D670   *..."K".K".K....}.".H".O.*
```

```
7FFE2BC0  009DE000  00001000  7FFE28C8  7F7465B0    75687000  0A08A000  7FF16760  00003000   *......."H........"1.-....*
7FFE2BE0  7FFE2B80  00000000  09DD0210  00000070    FD72D1D8  00001000  09E01000  000001B0   *".........K......JQ...\........*
```

The Free Queue Element (FQE) for the free space within subpool 22 starts at location 7FFE2838. This FQE is related to the used storage described by the subpool 22 DQE at the previous 7FFE2C10.

```
7FFE2C00  7F7468E0  7F7468E0  7F7468E0  00001000    0000B260  00000DA0  7FFE2838  7FFE2838   *......\./\.........."......"...*
7FFE2C20  7FFE2838  00003000  7F746448  7F751A00    7FFE2C28  0A0BA000  7FFE2838  00001000   *"......."1......-...."...*
7FFE2C40  7FFE2B38  00001000  7FFE2B38  7FFE2B38    7FFE2B38  00001000  7F746520  7FF16760   *"...."..."."......."1.-*
7FFE2C60  7F751010  0A116000  00024000  7F751010    7F72DB20  00000E00  7FF16988  7FF16988   *......-...@.......".h."1.h*
7FFE2C80  7FF16988  00000000  7FFE2CA0  7F7468E0    7F746550  009C3000  7FFE2F70  7F72DAC0   *"1.h.......\...."1..."...*
7FFE2CA0  7F751538  7F751490  7FFE2CA0  7FFE2CA0    0A0B0000  00001000  7FFE2F70  7F72DAC0   *......."."......"....*
7FFE2CC0  7FFE2CB8  7FFE2CB8  0A0FD000  00001000    7F751F40  7F72D028  00000000  009C0000   *".".."...}......"......*
```

JOB EXA7JHMX   STEP APP3   TIME 125832 DATE 94100 ID = 000   PAGE 00000074

```
7FFE2CE0  7F7519D0  00003000  7F746910  7FF16448    7FF16448  7F746550  009C3000  00000000   *.}......."1....."1.&...*
7FFE2D00  7F746988  7FFE28B0  7FFE2D00  7FFE2D00    0A179000  00002000  7F751B98  7FFE2D18   *.h."...."....."..q."..*
7FFE2D20  7FFE2D20  7FFE2D28  7FFE2D28  7FFE2D28    7F72D5B0  7FF16658  7FFE2D30  7FFE2D30   *"...."...."..N."1...."..*
7FFE2D40  00504000  0000C000  7F72DCE8  7F7465E0    7F73C378  00000C88  FD9C8000  00000000   *.. @......Y.\.....C..h....*
7FFE2D60  7FF16ED4  7F72D400  7F72D8E0  7FFE2928    7FFFC4C8  00000038  7F7515C8  7F751178   *"1>M".M..Q\....DH......H....*
7FFE2D80  7FFE2D78  0A0E2000  00001000  7FFE2DA0    7FFE2D90  7FFE2D90  7FFE2D98  7FFE2D98   *"../.../Q".q".q*
7FFE2DA0  7FFE2DA0  7FFE2DA0  7FFE2DA8  7FFE2DA8    7FFE2DC0  7FFE2DC0  00001000  7FFE2DC0   *"..".."...."..*
7FFE2DC0  7F7462C8  7FF169A0  00002000  7FFE2DA8    009B5000  00002000  7FFE2C40  7F72D4C0   *.H."1......."..{.."..M".*
7FFE2DE0  7F72D088  7F72D088  009C4000  00001000    7F72D718  7FFE2D18  7F72D340  009F9028   *.h.h.. @.......".L...*
7FFE2E00  00008080  00000000  7F746490  7F746268    7FF16448  7F751958  009C4000  7F72D2A0   *...........h.."1...@..*
7FFE2E20  00000000  7FFE2E20  7F751898  009DF128    00E60020  7FFE2E30  7F72D9A0  7F7517B8   *..".....q.1.W...R.*
7FFE2E40  7FFE29B8  7FFE29B8  7F730000  00001000    7FF16988  00001000  7F72D910  009C1770   *".."......"1.h....R..*
7FFE2E60  00E60020  00001000  7F7510B8  7FF16EF4    7F72D4C0  009E0BF8  00E60020  00001000   *.W.......1>4.M(..8.W...*
7FFE2E80  7F751178  7F751C88  7FFE2E80  7FFE2E80    0A0E0000  00011000  7F751BD0  00000000   *....h."."....*
7FFE2EA0  7F746028  009DF180  004E8080  00000000    7F72D2E0  00000000  009DB100  00000000   *......N...K\.*
7FFE2EC0  FE72D2E0  00003000  7F72D568  7F7518F0    7FFE2670  00000000  7F747000  00001000   *....1.+...."...*
7FFE2EE0  7F751220  7F751E30  00011000  00000000    0000C000  00000EF0  7FFE2E08  7F72D058   *.K......N..0".*
7FFE2F00  7F72D0B8  00011000  00000000  7F751730    7FFE2480  07F72D478  7FFE2E08  7F72D478   *".".}.......{.."..*
7FFE2F20  7F72D478  00003000  7FFE2F40  7F751730    7FF16448  7F746550  009CD000  00000A28   *.&"1.&.}...*
7FFE2F40  7F72DF28  7FFE2688  7FFE2F40  7FFE2F40    0A18B000  00002000  09E03000  00000A28   *.."h.."......\.*
```

```
7FFE2F60  7F72DE38  7F72DE38  7F72DE38  00003000   7F751718  7F751718  00001000  7F751718   *"........."*
7FFE2F80  7F751718  00001000  7F751100  7FFE2BF8   7F72DD48  000C4000  7F72DD48  00C4000    *".......8."*
7FFE2FA0  7F7464A8  7FFE2FA0  7FFE2FA8  7FFE2FA8   7FFE2FB0  7FFE2FB0  7FFE2FB0  7F746220   *" .y"..y"*
7FFE2FC0  7F746028  009DF180  004E8080  00000000   00000E00  00000E00  00000E00  7F751E38   *"-.1.+..\"*
7FFE2FE0  7F751E38  00011000  7F72DA48  7F751B68   7FFE2FE8  0A04A000  7FFE2FE8  00002000   *"...\.Y".Y"*
7FFE4000  00000940  20A20000  00000000  00000000   00000000  09CF8E0   00000000  7F7550B0   *"...s....&."*
7FFE4020  E7E2C240  00000000  00C00321  00000321   00000000  00000000  00000000  00000000   *"XSB...{..."*
7FFE4040  00000000  00000000  00000000  00000000   00000000  00000000  00000000  00000000   *"........."*
LINE 7FFE4060  SAME AS ABOVE
7FFE4080  00000000  00000000  00000000  00000000   00000000  7F74C0B0  7FFE40A0  00000000   *"........."*
7FFE40A0  E2E7E2C2  80000000  00000004  00000000   00000000  00000000  00000000  00000000   *"SXSB......"*
7FFE40C0  E7E2C240  7FFE4160  00000060  09E00FA0   00000000  09E00FFF  00000001  00FD50C8   *"XSB "-.-.\.&H"*
7FFE40E0  00000000  00005000  009CC000  09E00FFF   09E00FFF  09E00FFF  00000000  00000098   *"........q."*
7FFE4100  00000000  009CC068  8107076E  00018000   00000000  00000060  00000000  009E023C   *"........."*
7FFE4120  00000000  00000000  00000000  00000000   7FFE4140  00000000  7FFE4140  00000000   *"........."*
7FFE4140  E2E7E2C2  80000000  00000000  00000000   00000000  00000000  00000000  00000000   *"SXSB......"*
7FFE4160  E7E2C240  7FFE4200  8108FBF8  00000010   00FE0540  00000000  00FC1968  00000000   *"XSB "..a..8...."*
7FFE4180  E7E2C240  00000000  00000000  00000000   7FFE4614  00000000  009FF6B8  00000000   *"XSB "..a..8..6."*
7FFE41A0  009FF6B8  00000000  00000000  00000000   00FC19D4  09DF348   00000000  00000000   *"..6...M.3"*
7FFE41C0  09E00FFF  00000000  09E00FA0  00000000   09E00000  00000000  7FFE41E0  00000000   *".\..-.\..\."*
7FFE41E0  E2E7E2C2  80000000  00005000  C6FDC4C1   FFFF0000  00000000  00000000  00000000   *"SXSB....&.F.DA."*
7FFE4200  E7E2C240  00000000  00000000  00000000   00000000  00000000  00000000  00000000   *"XSB "......"*
7FFE4220  00000000  00000000  00000000  00000000   00000000  00000000  00000000  00000000   *"........."*
LINE 7FFE4240  SAME AS ABOVE
7FFE4260  00000000  00000000  00000000  00000000   00000000  00000000  7FFE4280  00000000   *"........."*
7FFE4280  E2E7E2C2  80000000  00000000  00000000   00000000  00000000  00000000  00000000   *"SXSB......"*
7FFE42A0  E7E2C240  7FFE4340  00000000  00000000   00F7F080  00000000  00000000  00000000   *"XSB "......"*
7FFE42C0  00000000  00000000  00000000  00000000   00000000  00000000  00000000  00000000   *"........."*
LINE 7FFE42E0  SAME AS ABOVE
7FFE4300  00000000  00000000  00000000  000000FD   00000000  00000000  7FFE4320  00000040   *"........."*
7FFE4320  E2E7E2C2  80000000  00000000  00000000   00F7F080  00000000  00000000  00000000   *"SXSB......"*
7FFE4340  E7E2C240  00006DEC  80FD5118  00000000   078D0000  00000000  00000000  0C000321   *"XSB "..\.-...70"*
7FFE4360  00000000  00000000  00000000  00000000   81258D00  0000A2E   00000000  00000000   *"........."*
7FFE4380  00000000  00005000  860A9DC0  00000000   00007000  00000000  7FFE43C0  00000000   *"....f.{....(."*
7FFE43A0  00003321  00000000  00000000  00000000   00000000  00000000  00000000  00000000   *".....a.i)"....(."*
7FFE43C0  E2E7E2C2  80000000  00000000  00000000   00000000  00000000  00000000  00000000   *"SXSB......"*
```

```
JOB EXA7JHMX     STEP APP3        TIME 125832    DATE 94100    ID = 000                        PAGE 00000075

7FFE43E0  E7E2C240 7FFE4480 7FFE4310 81257E54   00000000 7FFE43F0 09E00FFF 009CC000   *XSB  ".."..a.=....."..0.\...{.*
7FFE4400  00000000 00FD50C8 7FFE4058 009CC000   8106FA10 01070A10 8111FC21 8108FC00   *.....&H"..(.a.....*
7FFE4420  00FC1900 84BA7088 7FFE4360 81070764   8108FBB4 8111FC21 00000000 009FF6B8   *....-a..a..a.B....*
7FFE4440  84BA7088 7F500A0  009FF6B8 009FF6B8   7FFE45F4 009FD060 7FFE4460 FF603000   *d..h"...6..6.".4..)-"..--.*
7FFE4460  E2E7E2C2 80000000 7FFE4520 00000000   00000000 00000000 00000000 00000000   *SXSB  "...."....*
7FFE4480  E7E2C240 7FFE4240 00000000 00000000   7FFE4500 00000000 00000000 00000000   *XSB  "...."....*
7FFE44A0  00000000 00000000 00000000 00000000   00000000 00000000 00000000 00000000   *.....*
          LINE 7FFE44C0  SAME AS ABOVE
7FFE44E0  00000000 E2E7E2C2 80000000 00000000   00000000 00000000 7FFE4500 00000000   *.....*
7FFE4500  E2E7E2C2 80000000 E7E2C240 00000000   00000000 00000000 00000000 00000000   *SXSB.....*
7FFE4520  E7E2C240 7FFE45C0 00000000 00000000   7FFE45A0 00000000 00000000 00000000   *XSB  "{....*
7FFE4540  00000000 00000000 00000000 00000000   00000000 00000000 00000000 00000000   *.....*
          LINE 7FFE4560  SAME AS ABOVE
7FFE4580  00000000 E2E7E2C2 80000000 00000000   00000000 00000000 7FFE45A0 00000000   *.....*
7FFE45A0  E2E7E2C2 80000000 E7E2C240 00000000   00000000 00000000 00000000 00000000   *SXSB.....*
7FFE45C0  E7E2C240 00000000 00000000 009E023C   00000000 00000000 00000000 00280000   *XSB.....*
7FFE45E0  00000000 00000000 00000000 009FD000   00000000 00000000 00000000 38000000   *.....*
7FFE4600  00110000 02000000 00000000 7FFE43F0   04000000 00000000 00000028 38000000   *.....).....*
7FFE4620  08000000 00000000 00000000 00000000   00000000 00000000 00000000 00000000   *.....0.....*
7FFE4640  E2E7E2C2 80000000 00000000 00000000   00000000 00000000 7FFE4640 00000000   *SXSB.....*
7FFE4660  C3C4E7C8 E340F0F1 00000067 00000000   00000000 00000000 00000000 00000000   *CDXHT 01.....*
7FFE4680  00000000 00000000 00000000 00000052   00000000 00000000 00000000 00000000   *.....*
          LINES 7FFE46A0-7FFE4980  SAME AS ABOVE
7FFE49A0  00000000 00000000 00000000 C3C4E7D3   7FFE4B34 7F7743F8 7F7743F8 C3C4E7F1   *......CDXL...."...".h"..hCDX1*
7FFE49C0  7FFE49EC 00080321 80000000 000011F0   00000002 00000002 00000000 00011600   *"........0.....*
7FFE49E0  E2E3C5D7 D3C9C240 000011F0 C1D7D7F3   D7C7D4F1 7F7743F8 7F7743F8 C3C4E7F1   *STEPLIB ..0APP3PGM1".."...CDX1*
7FFE4A00  7FFE4A2C 00080321 80000000 000011F1   00000000 00000002 00000000 00011E00   *" \..).....*
7FFE4A20  E2E3C5D7 D3C9C240 000011F1 C1D7D7F3   D7C7D4F2 7F743EB8 7F743EB8 C3C4E7F1   *STEPLIB ..1APP3PGM2"..."...CDX1*
7FFE4A40  7FFE4A6C 00080321 80000000 000011F2   00000000 00000002 00000000 00011600   *" \%....).....*
7FFE4A60  E2E3C5D7 D3C9C240 000011F2 C2D9E4C9   D5E24040 7F743F78 7F743F78 C3C4E7F1   *STEPLIB ..2BRUINS "..."...CDX1*
7FFE4A80  7FFE4AAC 00080321 80000000 000011F5   00000000 00000002 00000000 00012500   *" \...0Y.....*
7FFE4AA0  E2E3C5D7 D3C9C240 000011F5 C1D7D7F3   D7C7D4F3 7F743FC0 7F743FC0 C3C4E7F1   *STEPLIB ..5APP3PGM3".{"..{CDX1*
7FFE4AC0  7FFE4AEC 00080321 80000000 000011F7   00000010 00000010 00010000 00620301   *" \......L.....*
7FFE4AE0  60D3D5D2 D3E2E360 000011F7 C9D6E2E5   C6D4E3E4 7F743E08 7F743E08 C3C4E7F1   *-LNKLST- ..7IOSVFMTU"..."...CDX1*
7FFE4B00  7FFE4B2C 00080321 80000000 000011F9   00000000 00000002 00010000 00332001   *" \......lq.....*
7FFE4B20  60D3D5D2 D3E2E360 000011F9 C9C5C1E5   E3D9D7F2 7F743CF0 7F743CF0 C3C4E7F1   *-LNKLST- ..9IEAVTRP2".0"..0CDX1*
7FFE4B40  7FFE4B6C 00080321 80000000 000011FA   00000000 00000002 00010000 005D1201   *" \ %....0.....*
7FFE4B60  60D3D5D2 D3E2E360 000011FA C9C5C1E5   E3D9C6F4 009F9028 00000000 7F72D340   *-LNKLST-....IEAVTRF4.....,.L*
```

```
7FFE4B80  00FD50C8  810A3A10  7FFE4AF0  7F758F80  00000000  01C81080  00000000  7FFE4B60  *..&Ha..."\0".....H......"...-.*
7FFE4BA0  81281B92  8122F620  810A013C  810A0144  7FFE4B60  00000000  810A0318  7FFE4C1C  *a..ka.6.a..a...-...a..."<.<*
7FFE4BC0  009F9040  7FFE4C28  7FFE4C20  009F9040  7FFE4C28  7FFE4C20  00000008  7FFE4AF0  *...<."<..<..."<...."..\0*
7FFE4BE0  00F7F080  7FF16EB0  7FFE4AF0  00E34B42  7FFFBDC0  03A2FDC0  00F7F080  00000001  *.70."1>..\0.T..".{.s.{.70....*
7FFE4C00  7F754FP0  00000C80  009DF348  009F9028  00000003  009DF360  7F72D958  7F72D958  *".!0....3....3....3-".R.*
7FFE4C20  009F9040  00000000  7F72DEB0  009DF348  00000C80  00000C78  810A0962  810A0962  *.........3.......a..*
7FFE4C40  00000C80  010A005E  00F7F080  00FD50C8  8109FF78  7FFE4B60  00000004  009FF718  *....";.70..&Ha..."...7.*
7FFE4C60  7FFE4B60  8109FFCE  00000000  00000000  00000000  00000000  00000000  00000000  *"..-a..".......*
7FFE4C80  16000000  7FFE4B84  00000000  00000000  00000000  010A0F4  C3C4E7C8  E340F0F1  *....."..d.....".4CDXHT 01*
7FFE4CA0  00000067  00000000  00010000  00000000  00000000  00000000  00000000  00000000  *....."...........*
7FFE4CC0  00000052  00000000  00000000  00000000  00000000  00000000  00000000  00000000  *...............*
7FFE4CE0  00000000  00000000  00000000  00000000  00000000  00000000  00000000  00000000  *...............*
      LINES 7FFE4D00-7FFE4FE0  SAME AS ABOVE
7FFE5000  00000000  00000000  00000000  00000000  00000000  00000000  00000000  00000000  *...............*
      LINES 7FFE5020-7FFE5980  SAME AS ABOVE
7FFE59A0  00000000  00000000  00000000  00000000  00000000  40404040  C5E7C1F7  D1C8D4E7  *..............JES2     EXA7JHMX*
7FFE59C0  C5E7C1F7  D1C8D440  C6404040  40404040  00000069  07C5E7C1  F7D1C8D4  00000000  *EXA7JHM F.....EXA7JHM...*
7FFE59E0  00000000  00000000  40404040  40404040  00000000  00000000  00000000  00000000  *...............*


JOB EXA7JHMX        STEP APP3        TIME 125832    DATE 94100    ID = 000              PAGE 00000076

7FFE5A60  00000000  00000000  A91BE663  D68A7C84  D1C52EF2  40404040  C9D5C9E3  40404040  *......z.W.O.@dJES2     INIT          *
7FFE5A80  40404040  40404040  D0404040  40404040  000003CB  00000000  00000000  00000000  *.           }..*
7FFE5AA0  00000000  00000000  00000000  00000000  00000000  00000000  00000000  00000000  *...............*
      LINES 7FFE5AC0-7FFE5B00  SAME AS ABOVE
7FFE5B20  00000000  00000000  A91B9A8E  18706601  00000000  009CFD38  00000000  00000000  *......z.....*
7FFE5B40  40404040  40404040  00000000  00000000  00000000  00000000  009CF98  00000000  *.............*
7FFE5B60  00000000  00000000  00000000  00000008  00000000  00000000  009CF98  009DF348  *........q.....3.*
7FFE5B80  009CFF98  01305E18  00000000  0000000F8  7FFE5BC8  009CF38  D3D3D7D7  01000010  *.....8".."$.LLPP..3.*
7FFE5BA0  00000000  009DADC0  00000000  00000000  8D020000  7FFE5BB8  D3D3D7D7  01000010  *.....;..$H..."$.LLPP...*
7FFE5BC0  009DEE74  00000000  00000000  00000000  00F24D90  009D0003  00000000  00000000  *.......2(...*
7FFE5BE0  00000000  00000000  00000000  00000000  00000000  00000000  00000000  00000000  *...............*
7FFE5C00  00500050  009FECB8  7FFFD688  8117F1E6  8114C986  00DF0E97  C2D3E2D8  C5E7E3C9  *.&.&...."Oha.1Wa.If..pBLSQEXTI*
7FFE5C20  00000000  00DF0E97  009F9A0  8117F078  80DF0CC2  009DD260  00DF0E97  009FFA60  *....p..9.a.0..B.K.....-*
7FFE5C40  7FFFD638  009DD1E0  83000001  00000000  02D00320  00000320  7FFE5F20  8114CA00  *".O..J\c..}..".O..^..a..*
7FFE5C60  8111D330  00DF0E97  7FFFD774  C5E7E3C9  009FFA00  009FFA28  009F9A0  7FFFD688  *a.L..p".P.EXTI.......9."Oh*
7FFE5C80  009FFA24  8114C658  0114D657  7FFFD638  7FFFD790  009FFA24  7FFFD638  009FFA2C  *...a.F..O...-".O..P....*
```

```
7FFE5CA0  8114CD16 00000000 0000000C 009DD378  009FF7B0 0000FF03 009DF348 009FF9A0  *a........L..7......3...9.*
7FFE5CC0  7FFFD680 00F7F080 8114C658 0114D657  009DF348 009DD378 00FD50C8 7FFFD638  *".O..70.a.F..O...L...&H".O.*
7FFE5CE0  009FFA28 009FFA24 009FFA28 8114C9E4  8114C986 00DF0E97 7FFFD774 C5E7E3C9  *...a.IUa.If..p".P.EXTI*
7FFE5D00  009FFA00 009FFA28 7FFFD688 009FFA24  8114C658 0114D657 009FFA60 009FFA60  *.....9..Oh...a.F..O...-*
7FFE5D20  7FFFD638 7FFFD790 009FFA00 009FFA28  7FFFD790 009FFA28 009FFA28 009FFA00  *"..O..P......P......*
7FFE5D40  009FFA28 009FFA24 7FFFD790 7FFE49B4  7FFFD790 009FFA28 009FFA28 009FFA00  *....P.....P......*
7FFE5D60  00000222 09E01C78 7FFE49B4 009FF000  009DD308 009DD348 00000000 009DD348  *....\.......O..L..L...L.*
7FFE5D80  009FF9A0 00001388 00000002 00000000  009DD308 00000000 00040004 00000270  *.9.h........O.....*
7FFE5DA0  00000321 00600000 00000000 00000000  00520052 00000000 00000321 00000270  *...-........*
7FFE5DC0  00000000 00000000 00000000 C9D6E2E5  C6D4E3E8 C9D2D1C5 C2C3E8F2 C2C3E8F2  *.........IOSV...IOSVFMTYIKJEBCY2*
7FFE5DE0  C2D3E2D8 C5E7E3C9 C2D3E2D8 C5E7E3C9  00000000 00000000 00000000 00000000  *BLSQEXTIBLSQEXTI*
7FFE5E00  00000000 00000000 0114E188 7FFFD890  00000000 C9D6E2E5 60D3D5D2 C6D4E3E8  *.......h".Q..L...IOSVFMTY*
7FFE5E20  89E01C78 009F9398 000010FC 31220000  00110000 003A2901 60D3D5D2 D3E2E360  *i\...lq......-LNKLST-*
7FFE5E40  000010FC 31220000 00000000 00000000  00000000 00000000 00000000 E2E5D740  *...............IEWLSVP *
7FFE5E60  00000074 01000000 00000000 00000000  009DD348 00000000 00000000 00000000  *...........L....*
7FFE5E80  00000000 00000000 00000000 00000000  7FFFD848 7FFFD868 00000000 00000000  *........."..Q.."..Q...*
7FFE5EA0  00000000 00000000 00000000 00000000  00000000 00000000 00000000 00000000  *................*
          LINES 7FFE5EC0-7FFE5EE0  SAME AS ABOVE
7FFE5F00  00000000 00000000 00000000 00000000  00000000 00000000 00A003B8 7FFFD680  *..............".O.*
7FFE5F20  07B00AD0 7FFE5C50 7F745030 8111E118  04BA6DC8 00DF0E97 7FFE62E8 7F73E008  *....*&".&.a....H..p".Y".\.*
7FFE5F40  0209A020 0111FF58 7FFE5F20 00000000  00FD50C8 0111E359 0111F358 00FD34F4  *......9."...&H..T..3..4*
7FFE5F60  8111D35A 00FD3528 8111D8DA 00000000  00000020 009DD308 7F744F18 7F744F18  *a.L!.......a.Q....T..3..L.!.!.*
7FFE5F80  009FF9A0 7FFE5F20 00000036 0111E359  0111F358 7F73E008 7F744F18 00FD8564  *.9."......L.!.!..e.*
7FFE5FA0  8111E122 00000000 0111E359 7FFE62E8  7F73E008 009DD308 8111D35A 009FF9A0  *a....9.."..Y..\..T..3..L.a.L!..9.*
7FFE5FC0  7FFE5F20 00FD50C8 0111F358 7F73E008  0209A020 0209A020 00FD3528 8111D630  *".9..&H..3..\........a.O.*
7FFE5FE0  7FFE61B8 00000000 009DD178 7F73E008  8111D35A 009FD060 00FD50C8 7FFE5F20  *"..^..&H..T..J".a.L!..}..&H.".*
7FFE6000  7FFE6044 7FFE6048 7F743CF0 00000028  09D2D178 7FFE6308 7FFE620E 7FFFC1F8  *"../..T..3..0..KJ."..^.."..-A8*
7FFE6020  00BE34B8 00BE34B8 7F743E3C 00000000  00000348 00000012 009C31E8 7FFFC1F1  *................Y....*
7FFE6040  00000000 00000000 0000C548 40404040  00000000 00000000 00000005 00000000  *.....E.....*
7FFE6060  00000000 0000CBF0 40404040 40404040  00F9028 009F9028 C9D2D1C5 C6C5F1F1  *......0.....J..IKJEFF11*
7FFE6080  40404040 40404040 40404040 40404040  00F503D0 009E023C 009DF348 40404040  *..........3..*
7FFE60A0  40404040 40404040 40404040 40404040  D1C5C6C5 F1F1D740 C9C5E6D3 E2E5D740  *.....5.).IKJEFF11P IEWLSVP *
          LINES 7FFE60C0-7FFE6160  SAME AS ABOVE
7FFE6180  40404040 40404040 40404040 40404040  40404040 00000000 00000000 00000000  *................*
7FFE61A0  00000000 00000000 00000000 00000000  009DD178 00000000 00000000 00000000  *.......J........*
7FFE61C0  00000000 00000000 00000000 00000000  00F503D0 00000000 009E023C 00000000  *..........J.....*
7FFE61E0  00000000 00000000 00000000 0107C9D2  D1C5C6C5 F1F1D740 C9C5E6D3 E2E5D740  *......IKJEFF11P IEWLSVP *
7FFE6200  00000000 00000000 00000000 00000000  7FFE6200 00000000 00000000 00000000  *.......*
7FFE6220  00000074 01000000 00000000 00000000  00000000 00000000 00000000 00000000  *.......*
```

```
JOB EXA7JHMX        STEP APP3        TIME 125832     DATE 94100      ID = 000             PAGE 00000077

7FFE6240  00000000 00000000 00000000 00000000   C6C5F1F1 C9C5C1E5 E3D9C6F4 009FF9A0   *................IKJEFE11IEAVTRF4..9.*
          LINE 7FFE6260   SAME AS ABOVE
7FFE6280  00000000 00F503D0 7FFE6310 C2D3E2D8   C5E7E3C9 0000CEF0 00000000 00000000   *.5.}.;."..../....0...*
7FFE62A0  00000000 C2D3E2D8 7FFE6310 C5E7E3C9   C5E7E3C9 00000000 00000000 00000000   *..BLSQEXTIBLSQEXTI...*
7FFE62C0  00000000 0111FF54 7FFE6210 0111FF58   C9C7E6E2 00000000 00000000 01000000   *..............IGWS..*
7FFE62E0  00000000 00000000 00000000 C9C7E6E2   D4C4C540 0000006B 00000000 01000000   *..........IGWSMDE IGWSMDE....*
7FFE6300  00400000 00005D12 0101002C 00350036   00000001 00000000 0008C9C5           *.....)..........IE*
7FFE6320  00000000 C1E5E3D9 0103C2E3 88030000   00001110 00000000 00000000           *AVTRF4...BTh........*
7FFE6340  00000000 C1E5E3D9 0017005D 18000000   00000100 00000000 01000000           *AVTRF4...)......*
7FFE6360  00000000 00000000 00000000 00000000   00001110 00000000 00000000           *....................*
7FFE6380  00000000 00000000 00000000 00000000   00000000 00000000 00000000           *....................*
          LINES 7FFE63A0-7FFE63C0   SAME AS ABOVE
7FFE63E0  00000000 00000000 00000000 00000000   FB280000 00000000 FC681211 00000000   *....................*
7FFE6400  00000000 00000000 00000000 00000000   00000000 00000000 00000000 00000000   *....................*
7FFE6420  00000000 00000000 00000000 00000000   C9D2D1C5 C2C3E8F2 C9C5C1E5 00000000   *............IKJEBCY2IEAV*
7FFE6440  E3D9C6F4 00F503D0 00010000 00000000   E3D9C6F4 00000000 00000000 00000000   *TRF4.5.}............*
7FFE6460  00000000 00000000 00000000 00000000   00000000 00000000 00000000 00000000   *....................*
          LINES 7FFE6480-7FFE64A0   SAME AS ABOVE
7FFE64C0  00000000 00000000 00000000 00000000   00000000 00000000 7FFE6678 00000000   *....................*
7FFE64E0  7FFE6680 00000000 00000000 00000000   00000000 00000000 00000000 00000000   *.".................*
7FFE6500  00000000 00000000 00000000 00000000   00000000 00000000 00000000 00000000   *....................*
          LINES 7FFE6520-7FFE6640   SAME AS ABOVE
7FFE6660  00000000 00000004 00000028 00020000   00000004 0111FFE2 7FFE6480 00000000   *...........S".*
7FFE6680  00000004 00000028 02000000 7FFE643C   0111FFEA 00000000 00000000 7FFE63FC   *....................*
7FFE66A0  00000000 00000028 D7D9D6C7 D9C1D440   01120070 00000000 7FFE5B30 81120F36   *...PROGRAM "^....8..."*
7FFE66C0  810C0AE0 000000B4 00000022 7FFE6AF8   00A00B70 7F744F18 7F744F4E 81120080   *a...&H.."..;..j..j".*
7FFE66E0  00FD50C8 0112107F 01305E18 00256868   00000001 7FFE6AD0 009DF4A0 009DF180   *a..+a..L...a.......4.*
7FFE6700  009DD308 00000000 8114D816 00256868   00000020 7FFE6A90 009F9490 009DF180   *..L...a.Q.......m..1.*
7FFE6720  7FFE6044 009FF6B8 7FFE66D0 7FFE6040   00000020 0114D657 00000008 00000278   *.-..6..}"-...O......*
7FFE6740  7FFE6044 7FFE6AA4 7FFE6040 8114CB5A   00000022 8114CAFA 00000020 7FFE66D0   *."..u".-..a..!a....})*
7FFE6760  000069C8 00005250 7FFE61B8           7FFE6018 7FFE629C 009FF9A0 00000000   *...H.....&"./..".....9..*
7FFE6780  27FAEA03 1A000000 7FFE6AA4           60010000 00000022 01120F4C 00000000   *.z.W.........u...-..<*
7FFE67A0  A91BE668 7FFE6040 7FFE6048           7FFE620E 00000000 00000000 00000000   *.."--"-"...*
7FFE67C0  00000000 00000000 00000000           00000000 00000000 00000000 00000000   *....................*
7FFE67E0  00000000 00000000 00000000           00000000 00000000 00000000 000069C8   *.................H*
          LINE 7FFE6800   SAME AS ABOVE
7FFE6820  00000000 00120000 00000000           00000000 00000000 00000000 000069C8   *...\....z.W...dc....*
7FFE6840  009FE010 00001778 A91BE668           2A048483 00000000
```

```
7FFE6860 C9D2D1C5 C6C5F1F1 C9D2D1C5 C6C5F1F1   00000000 00000000 00000000 00000000   *IKJEFE11IKJEFE11................*
7FFE6880 00000000 00000000 00000000 00000000   00000000 00000000 00000000 00000000   *................................*
         LINES 7FFE68A0-7FFE6A40   SAME AS ABOVE
7FFE6A60 00000000 00000000 00000000 00000000   00000000 00000000 00000000 00004400   *................................*
7FFE6A80 00000000 00004400 00000000 00000000   80000000 00000288 00000270 00005250   *.........................h......*
7FFE6AA0 A91B9A0D 00000899 81120080 0112107F   00000000 7FFE66D0 00000270 E3D9C6F4   *z........ra............&.&*
7FFE6AC0 00000000 7FFE6B40 00030000 7FFE6AD0   D3D3D7D3 02000028 C9C5C1E5 E3D9C6F4   *.......,....)LLPL...IEAVTRF4*
7FFE6AE0 00000000 C9C5C1E5 E3D9C6F4 00000000   02099A80 0000CEF0 D3D3D7E2 02000048   *....IEAVTRF4...PGMF.....0LLPS...*
7FFE6B00 C9C5C1E5 005D1201 7FFE6A90   00F503D0 00000000 00000000 00000000   *IEAVTRF4.).."...5.}.............*
7FFE6B20 021096F4 A91B9A07 00F25420 06390000   A91BE668 27FAEA03 C9C5C1E5 E3D9C6F4   *...o4z..z..2....z.W...IEAVTRF4*
7FFE6B40 005D1201 00000018 D0000000 00000002   00000000 00005250 C9C5C1E5 00000270   *.)...........}...........&......*
7FFE6B80 C9C5C1E5 E2E5D740 C9C5E6D3 E2E5D740   00000074 01000000 00000000 00000000   *IEWLSVP IEWLSVP.................*
7FFE6BC0 000001FC 7FFE62B0 00000000 00000000   00000000 00000000 00000000 00000000   *.....L."./......................*
7FFE6BE0 009DD308 7FFE61DC 00000000 00000000   00000000 00000000 00000000 00000000   *..L."...........................*
7FFE6C00 00000000   SAME AS ABOVE
         LINE 7FFE6C20 SAME AS ABOVE

JOB EXA7JHMX        STEP APP3        TIME 125832   DATE 94100   ID = 000                PAGE 00000078

7FFE6C40 00000000 00000000 011218B8 7FFE6BA0   011218B8 7FFE6BA8 00000000 00000288   *............."...."....y......h*
7FFE6C60 09E34050 00000001 00008000 00110001   0000001C 7FFE6B6C 00000000 00000000   *.T &......."..%........*
7FFE6C80 00000000 00000000 00000000 00000000   7FFE66D0 00FD50C8 7FFE6C90 811205D6   *.........}.&.&H".&.a.O*
7FFE6CA0 00000000 00000000 00000000 00000000   00000000 00000000 00000000 00000000   *................................*
         LINES 7FFE6CC0-7FFE6FE0   SAME AS ABOVE
7FFFC000 7FFFC208 7FFFC4F8 7FFFC00C 7FFE4AF0   40E3D8C5 009F1998 009F9398 09D2D178   *.B.".D8".(.".\0 TQE..q..lq.KJ.*
7FFFC020 00000000 00000007 00000007 7FF080   00000000 00000010 0000FC01 0000FC01   *.................a...."...(..*
7FFFC040 009F9028 01FE4B84 7FFFC028 00FD50C8   009F9028 81281900 7FFFC028 00000000   *..d.&H.70..a.."..(.(*
7FFFC060 7FFE4B84 00000000 81281B92 8122F620   D7D7C440 00000000 09E11300 7FFFC0C8   *".d".(.a.ka.6..d....(*
7FFFC080 00000008 C2D3E2D8 C5E7E3C9 009FECB8   00001300 00001D00 00001D00 7FFFC3D8   *....BLSQEXTI......PPD...(H..*
7FFFC0A0 00000066 00ED0030 009F9028 00000048   00001D00 00001D00 00F7F080 7FFFC3D8   *.................70..CQ*
7FFFC0C0 00000000 E2D7C440 00000000 00000000   00000000 00000000 00000000 00000000   *....SPD.........................*
7FFFC0E0 00000000 00000000 00000010 00000001   80000060 09E00FA0 000000C9 00E60164   *...................I.W.*
7FFFC100 00000000 00000000 00000000 00000048   FF752190 FF752190 0000FD00 00DF348   *..............(d./od.n........3.*
7FFFC120 009CFFC0 84BD6196 84BD9500 00FD50C8   84BD6020 0000000C 7FFFCA00 04BD801E   *....70.&Hd.-..."*
7FFFC160 E2E3C3C2 00000000 7FFFC168 00000000   FFFF0000 7F73EEC0 02200007 00000000   *STCB....".A."..A.....(.........*
```

```
7FFFC180  7FFFBF00 15485F00 7FFFBDC0 15485DC0 00F7F080 00000000 00000000 00000000  *"......^...(..)(.70.*
7FFFC1A0  00000000 00000000 00000000 00000000 00000000 00000000 7F7550B0 00000000  *....................*
7FFFC1C0  00000000 7F755008 00000000 00000000 7FFFBD90 00000C84 0000057D 009DF348  *"...........".&....3.*
7FFFC1E0  7F755008 7FFFBD90 7FFFBD90 7F755008 00000001 00000000 00000000 7F743CB8  *"...".&......d.......*
7FFFC200  00000000 00000000 00000000 00000000 00000000 00000000 00000000 00000000  *.....................*
7FFFC220  00000000 00000000 00000000 00000000 00000000 00000000 00000000 00000000  *.....................*
7FFFC240  00000000 80E34FC4 80E34FC4 00000A2E D6C1C3E3 E2D2E5E3 00000044 00FD0000  *....T!D..T!D....OACTSKVT....*
7FFFC260  00000000 7F777000 00000000 00000000 00000000 00000000 8109FFCE 00000000  *..."................a....*
7FFFC280  00000000 00000000 00000000 00000000 00000000 00000000 E3C3E3D6 FF000050  *......TCTO...&.*
7FFFC2A0  00000000 00000000 00000000 00000000 00000000 00000000 00000000 00000000  *.....................*

LINE 7FFFC2C0  SAME AS ABOVE

7FFFC2E0  00000000 00000000 E2E3C3C2 00000000 7FFFC2F0 7FFFC2F0 00000000 00000000  *......STCB....."B0".B0....*
7FFFC300  00000D4B 7FFFBF00 7FFFBF00 15485F00 15485BC0 00F7F080 00000000 00000000  *...."......<.".(..$(.70.*
7FFFC320  00000000 00000000 00000000 00000000 860A9DC0 00000000 7FFFBB90 7F7860B0  *.............f..(......*
7FFFC340  00000000 00000000 7F786008 00000000 7FFFBB90 7F786008 00000C84 00000001  *....".....".....-...*
7FFFC360  00000000 00000000 7F786008 00000000 00000000 00000000 00000000 00000000  *....."....-....d*
7FFFC380  00000000 00000003 009F9028 00000000 00000000 00000000 00000000 00000000  *.....................*
7FFFC3A0  00000000 00000000 00000000 00000000 00000000 00019C9E D7D7C440 7FFDE000  *...........T!D......PPD."\.*
7FFFC3C0  00000000 00000000 7FFE4660 80E34FC4 009FE240 00000188 00001000 00001000  *"..D....W.@..S...h...*
7FFFC3E0  7FFFC410 0000000A 0000000A 00E6017C E2D7C440 00000000 00000000 00000000  *.70.".D&.....SPD...*
7FFFC400  00F7F080 7FFFC450 00000000 00000000 00000000 00000000 00000000 00000066  *.........PPD..."Dh..*
7FFFC420  00000000 00000000 00000000 00000000 D7D7C440 009F2300 7FFFC488 00000000  *...........h......70.*
7FFFC440  00000000 00000066 009FDE88 00000048 00001D00 00001D00 00F7F080 00000000  *......SPD.........*
7FFFC460  00000066 00ED0030 E2D7C440 00000000 00000000 00000000 00000000 00000000  *.....................*
7FFFC480  00000000 00000000 00000000 00000000 00000040 00000000 008AFF8C 02CA0000  *............2.q.....*
7FFFC4A0  00000000 00000000 00000004 00F24B98 4D760100 C4C1E3C1 F8C20407 00000011  *..2+..2CA...2((..DATA8B..*
7FFFC4C0  00000000 3010200E 00F24D40 00F24D40 00000000 7FFCE000 00000000 00000000  *.OACTSKVT........".\....*
7FFFC4E0  00F2C3C1 00000044 00FD0000 00FD0000 00000000 00000000 00000000 00000000  *....a.P.&......fc...ofma..*
7FFFC500  D6C1C3E3 E2D2E5E3 00000000 00000000 B7BDB786 83B31515 B1968694 81B0B715  *.msd.a.......j.bfvljp*
7FFFC520  00000000 00000000 00000000 00000000 55555555 55555555 91B78286 A5939197  *.msd.a.....O&....*
7FFFC540  00000000 8127D762 50018052 55565555 55555555 55555555 0203D650 00000000  *......"..E........*
7FFFC560  90B294A2 849D8115 55555555 55555555 55555555 55555555 00000000 00000000  *.....................*
7FFFC580  55555555 55555555 90B294A2 849D8115 00000000 00000000 00000000 00000000  *.....................*
7FFFC5A0  00000000 7FFFC5B0 00000000 00000000 00000000 00000000 00000000 00000000  *.....................*
7FFFC5C0  00000000 00000000 00000000 00000000 00000000 00000000 00000000 00000000  *.....................*

LINES 7FFFC5E0-7FFFC680  SAME AS ABOVE

7FFFC6A0  00000000 00000000 00000000 00000000 00000000 00000000 00000000 00FD50C8  *...................&H*
7FFFC6C0  8109FF78 7FFFC5D0 8109FFCE 009FF718 8109FFCE 00000000 00000000 00000000  *a..."..E}....7.".E}a....*
7FFFC6E0  00000000 00000000 00000000 00000000 00000000 00000000 00000000 00000000  *.....................*
```

```
JOB EXA7JHMX        STEP APP3            TIME 125832   DATE 94100   ID = 000                    PAGE 00000079

7FFFC700 00000000 00000000 810A013C 00000000   00000000 00000000 00000000 00000000   *................a...*
7FFFC720 009FE338 7FFFC788 E2E3C3C2 00000000   7FFFC730 00000000 7FFFC290 00000000   *..T."..GhSTCB.."..G.."G.*
7FFFC740 00000006 00000000 7FFFBF00 15485F00   7FFFBE40 15485E40 7FFFC730 00000001   *........."...^...;..B.*
7FFFC760 0101001B 00000000 00000000 00000000   00000000 00000000 00000000 00000000   *....................*
7FFFC780 00000000 00000000 00000000 7FFEC008   00000000 7FFFBE10 7FFFBE10 7FFEC008   *..."..{..."..."{.*
7FFFC7A0 00000002 009FDE88 00000000 00000000   7FFEC008 00000C84 00000000 00000001   *....h..........d...*
7FFFC7C0 00000000 00000000 00000000 00000000   00000000 00000000 00000000 00000000   *....................*
7FFFC7E0 00000000 00000000 00000000 00000000   00000000 00000000 00000000 00000000   *....................*
7FFFC800 00000000 00000000 7FFE4CB8 8494839C   000000AA E2E3C3C2 00000000 00000000   *.......dmc.....STCB.*
7FFFC820 7FFFC820 7FFFC820 00000000 00000000   00000000 7FFFBF00 7FFFBF00 15485F00   *."..<....dmc...*
7FFFC840 7FFFBEC0 15485EC0 00000000 00000000   15485F00 00000000 00000000 00000000   *."..H.."H.....^.*
7FFFC860 00000000 00000000 00000000 00000000   00000000 00000000 00000000 00000000   *."..{..;{.*
7FFFC880 00000000 00000000 01262758 01262740   01262740 00000000 01262740 00000000   *....................*
7FFFC8A0 7FFFBB90 7FFF1008 00000C84 00000001   009FF158 00000000 00000000 00000000   *...........d....1*
7FFFC8C0 00000000 00000000 00000000 00000000   00000000 00000000 00000000 00000000   *....................*
7FFFC8E0 00000000 00000000 00000000 00000000   00000000 00000000 00000000 00000000   *....................*
7FFFC900 00000000 00000000 00000003 00000000   8494835C 00000000 00000000 00000000   *.............dmc**
7FFFC920 00000000 00000000 00000000 00000000   00000000 00000000 00000000 00000000   *....................*
             LINES 7FFFC940-7FFFC9A0  SAME AS ABOVE
7FFFC9C0 7F748000 00000321 00000000 00000000   C5E2E3C1 E6D6D9D2 E7E2C240 00000000   *"...Aq.......ESTAWORKXSB .*
7FFFC9E0 00000321 00000000 00000000 00000000   00000000 00000000 00000002 00000000   *....................*
7FFFCA00 00000000 00000000 00F7F080 00000000   00000000 00000000 00000000 00000000   *..........70....*
7FFFCA20 00000000 00000000 00000000 00000000   00000000 00000000 00000000 00000000   *....................*
7FFFCA40 860A9DC0 00010321 80000000 00000000   7FFFCA58 00000000 E2E7E2C2 80000000   *f..{.....&.".....SXSB.*
7FFFCA60 00000073 00000000 00000000 00000000   00000000 00000000 E7E2C240 00000000   *.........&.".....XSB .*
7FFFCA80 00000321 00000000 00000000 00000000   00000000 00000000 00000000 00000000   *....................*
7FFFCAA0 00000000 00000000 00F7F080 00000000   00000000 00000000 00000000 00000000   *..........70....*
7FFFCAC0 00000000 00000000 00000000 00000000   00000000 00000000 00000000 00000000   *....................*
7FFFCAE0 860A9DC0 00010321 80000000 00000000   7FFFCAF8 00000000 E2E7E2C2 80000000   *f..{...."..&."..8..SXSB.*
7FFFCB00 000000CE 00000000 00000000 00000000   00000000 00000000 E7E2C240 00000000   *.........&.".....XSB .*
7FFFCB20 00C00321 00000000 00000000 00000000   00000000 00000000 00000000 00000000   *...{............*
7FFFCB40 00000000 00000000 00F7F080 00000000   00000000 00000000 00000000 00000000   *..........70....*
             LINE 7FFFCB60  SAME AS ABOVE
7FFFCB80 00000000 00000000 80000000 7F7550B0   7FFFCB98 00000000 E2E7E2C2 80000000   *......"..&."..q..SXSB.*
7FFFCBA0 00000005 00000000 00000000 00000000   00000000 00000000 E7E2C240 00000000   *.........&.".....XSB .*
7FFFCBC0 84000321 00000000 00000000 00000000   00000000 00000000 00000007 00000000   *d.................*
7FFFCBE0 00000000 00000000 00F7F080 00000000   00000000 00000000 00000000 00000000   *..........70....*
7FFFCC00 00000000 00000000 00000000 00000000   00000000 00000000 00000000 00000000   *....................*
```

```
7FFFCC20  00000000  00000000  00000000  7F755158  00000000  00000000  E2E7E2C2  80000000  *................SXSB....*
7FFFCC40  00000A36  00000000  00000000  00000000  00000000  00000000  E7E2C240  00000000  *"..............XSB .....*
7FFFCC60  84000321  00000321  00000000  00000000  00000000  00000000  00000000  00000000  *d..............70.......*
7FFFCC80  00000000  00000000  00F7F080  00000000  00000000  00000000  00000000  00000000  *.................70.....*
7FFFCCA0  00000000  00000000  00000000  80000000  00000000  00000000  E2E7E2C2  80000000  *..............."...SXSB.*
7FFFCCC0  00000000  00000000  00000000  7F755158  00000000  00000000  E7E2C240  80000000  *...........Q....XSB ....*
7FFFCCE0  00000895  00000000  00000000  00000000  00000000  00000000  E7E2C240  00000000  *.n............XSB ......*
7FFFCD00  00000000  00000000  00000000  00000000  00000000  00000000  00000000  00000000  *........................*
          LINES 7FFFCD20-7FFFCD40  SAME AS ABOVE
7FFFCD60  00000000  00000000  00000000  00000000  00000000  00000000  E2E7E2C2  80000000  *..............."...SXSB.*
7FFFCD80  00000000  00000000  00000000  00000000  00000000  00000000  E7E2C240  00000000  *..............XSB ......*
7FFFCDA0  00000000  00000000  00000000  00000000  00000000  00000000  00000000  00000000  *........................*
          LINES 7FFFCDC0-7FFFCDE0  SAME AS ABOVE
7FFFCE00  00000000  00000000  00000000  00000000  00000000  00000000  E2E7E2C2  80000000  *..............."...SXSB.*
7FFFCE20  00000000  00000000  00000000  00000000  00000000  00000000  D5E2E2C1  00000000  *...............\.\.NSSA.*
7FFFCE40  00000C58  00000311  00000000  00000070  09E00AE0  00000000  00000000  00010100  *..............\.\.......*
7FFFCE60  04000020  0026B030  00000000  00000000  00000000  00000000  00000001  00000000  *........................*
7FFFCE80  00000023  00000000  00000000  00000000  00000000  00000000  00000000  00000000  *........................*
```

```
JOB EXA7JHMX        STEP APP3        TIME 125832    DATE 94100    ID = 000                        PAGE 00000080
```

```
7FFFCEA0  00000000  00000000  00000000  01010000  00000000  00000000  00000000  00000000  *........................*
7FFFCEC0  00000000  00000000  94C2000   00000002  00000000  00000000  00000000  00000000  *.......m................*
7FFFCEE0  00000000  00000321  00000000  00000000  00000000  01D5C980  01D5C988  *.........NI..NIh.*
7FFFCF00  00C00321  00000002  00010002  80000000  00000002  00010002  0000008A  00000070  *...{..."...a....a.......*
7FFFCF20  7F755200  00010002  00000000  7F755200  81322E69  0000008A  00000008B  *."....."...a...."1&..a..*
7FFFCF40  09E00AE0  00000003  00000000  1000890C  8128BE3D  0000000B  7FF15000  *.\.\....i.a..."1&.*
7FFFCF60  00000000  00000000  00000000  00000000  810296A0  00800001  *..a...a.o.......*
7FFFCF80  4C000000  81112439  00000001  01DDE400  00000000  810296A0  00000000  *<...a....U.......*
7FFFCFA0  00000000  00000000  00000000  00000000  00000000  00000000  00000000  00000000  *........................*
          LINES 7FFFCFC0-7FFFCFE0  SAME AS ABOVE
7FFFD000  00000000  00000000  00000000  00000000  00000000  00000000  00000000  00000000  *........................*
          LINES 7FFFD020-7FFFD1E0  SAME AS ABOVE
7FFFD200  00000000  00000000  00000000  00000000  00000000  D6E4E2C2  00000000  *..........OUSB..*
7FFFD220  00000000  00000321  00000000  00000027  00000000  00000000  00000000  *........................*
7FFFD240  00000000  00000000  00000000  00000000  00000000  00000000  00000000  00000000  *........................*
7FFFD260  00000000  00000000  00000000  00000000  00000000  00000000  00000000  00000000  *........................*
7FFFD280  00000000  00000000  00000000  00000000  00000000  00000000  0000002B  00000233  *........................*
```

```
7FFFD2A0  00000000 00000000 00000000 00000000  00000000 00000000 00000000 013107B1  *.........................k......*
7FFFD2C0  00000000 92FB0000 00000000 00000000  00000000 00000000 00000000 00000000  *................................*
7FFFD2E0  00000000 00000000 00000000 00000000  00000000 00000000 00000000 00000000  *................................*
7FFFD300  00000000 00000000 7FFFD320 00000000  00000000 00000000 E2E3C3C2 00000000  *..................STCB..........*
7FFFD320  00000000 00000000 7FFFD320 7FFFD320  15485F80 00000000 7FFFBF00 15485F00  *..."...."L..L...................*
7FFFD340  00000000 7FFFBF80 15485F80 00000000  7FFFBF80 00000000 7FFFBF00 00000000  *....^...........................*
7FFFD360  00000000 00000000 00000000 00000000  00000000 00000000 00000000 00000000  *................................*
7FFFD380  00000000 00000000 01262758 01262740  00000000 00000000 01262740 00000000  *................................*
7FFFD3A0  00000000 7FFFBFD0 7FFF6008 00000C84  00000000 00000000 01262740 00000000  *.............d..................*
7FFFD3C0  00000000 00000000 00000000 00000001  00000000 009FE240 00000000 00000000  *)"..........S...................*
  LINE 7FFFD3E0  SAME AS ABOVE
7FFFD400  00000000 000003B2 00000000 00000000  00000000 00000000 00000000 00000000  *................................*
7FFFD420  00000000 00000000 00000000 00000000  00000000 00000000 00000000 00000000  *................................*
  LINE 7FFFD440  SAME AS ABOVE
7FFFD460  00000000 00000000 00000000 00F7F080  00000003 00000000 7FFFCBE8 00FD50C8  *.............70....Y..&H*
7FFFD480  009DF348 009FF9A0 7FFFD470 00F7F080  80FF049C 009FFA60 7FFFC160            *..3..9.".M.70..."..A-*
7FFFD4A0  7F747210 009FF9C0 00FF6F00 00000000  00F7F080 00000000 009DF348 00000C60  *.."...9(..?..70...3..*
7FFFD4C0  009FF9C0 00000000 00000000 8115C6E0  00000000 8115C6D6 8115D952 8115C6D2  *..9(...a.F\...a.FOa.R.a.FK*
7FFFD4E0  8115BFC0 00000000 00000000 00000000  00000000 40000000 00000000 00800000  *a..{............................*
7FFFD500  00000000 00000000 10000000 00000000  00000003 00000000 00000000 00000000  *................................*
7FFFD520  00000000 00000000 00000000 00000000  00000000 00000000 00000000 00000000  *................................*
  LINES 7FFFD540-7FFFD600  SAME AS ABOVE
7FFFD620  00000000 00000000 00000000 00000088  00000000 00000000 00600060 009FECB8  *"..O.a.mdp...h.....Jy"..-..7.*
7FFFD640  7FFFD680 8117FA94 84977458 00000088  00000000 009D01A8 7FFFEF60 009FF7B0  *.9.a.7.&H.J..&H.70."O."*
7FFFD660  009FF9A0 8117F770 00FD50C8 009DD168  00FD50C8 00F7F080 7FFFD638 7FFFCA78  *.C....Ha..D...a..Ha..|."P%.7.*
7FFFD680  83000001 00000000 00000000 8114CBC8  8114CB5E 009D02E0 7FFFD76C 00FF7B0   *.L...9.".O....a.F..O...3.*
7FFFD6A0  009DD378 009FFA00 009FF9A0 7FFFD680  009FFA28 8114C658 0114D657 009DF348  *.L...7...3...9.".O.70.*
7FFFD6C0  009FFA24 009FFA2C 009FFA28 009FFF03  009FFA2C 8114CD16 8114CD16 00F7F080  *a.F..O...3...L..&H".O.*
7FFFD6E0  0000000C 009DF378 009FFF7B0 0000FF03  009DF348 009FF9A0 009FFA28 00F7F080  *.........a.*
7FFFD700  8114C658 0114D657 009DF348 009DD378  00FD50C8 7FFFD680 009FFA28 009FFA28  *a.F..O...3...L..&H".O.*
7FFFD720  009FFA24 8114C7CE 8114C658 009D02E0  7FFFD774 009FF7B0 7FFFD790 7FFFD790  *..a.G.a.F...\".P..7.*
7FFFD740  009FF9A0 7FFFD688 009FFA00 8114C658  0114D657 009FFA60 7FFFD638 009FFA28  *.9.".Oh...a.F..O...-..O.*
7FFFD760  009FFA00 009FFA24 009FFA24 009FFA00  009FFA24 009FFA2C 009FFA2C 009FFA24  *................................*
7FFFD780  009FFA28 000000FC 009FF000 009DD348  00000000 00000004 09E01C78 09E01C78  *"..P..........*
7FFFD7A0  7FFE49B4 009FF000 009DD178 009DD348  009DD348 009FF9A0 00001388 00001388  *".....0..J..L...9....h*
7FFFD7C0  00000000 00000000 00000000 00000000  00040004 00000270 00000321 00070000  *................................*
7FFFD7E0  00000000 00000000 00520052 00000000  00000321 00000000 00000321 00070000  *................................*
7FFFD800  C9D6E2E5 80000000 C9D6C8E8 C6D4E3E8  C9D2D1C5 C2C3E8F2 C9C7C3F0 F9F0F5C1  *IOSV....IOSVPMTYIKJEBCY2IGC0905A*
7FFFD820  C9C7C3F0 F9F0F5C1 00000000 00000000  00000000 00000000 00000000 00000000  *IGC0905A........................*
```

```
JOB EXA7JHMX      STEP APP3      TIME 125832   DATE 94100   ID = 000              PAGE 00000081

7FFFD840  0114E188 7FFFD890 009DD348 00000000 C9D6E2E5 C6D4E3E8 89E01C78 009F9398  *..h".Q..L.....IOSVFMTYi\....lq*
7FFFD860  000010FC 31220000 00010000 003A2901 60D3D5D2 D3E2E3D8 000010FC 31220000  *........-LNKLST-..........*
7FFFD880  00000000 00000000 00000000 00000000 C9C5E6D3 E2E5D740 01000000 00000000  *..........IEWLSVP .........*
7FFFD8A0  00000000 00000000 00000000 7FFFD848 7FFFD868 00000000 00000000 00000000  *............"Q."Q.........*
7FFFD8C0  00000000 00000000 00000000 00000000 00000000 00000000 00000000 00000000  *..........................*
7FFFD8E0  00000000 00000000 00000000 7FFFD868 00000000 00000000 00000000 00000000  *............"Q............*
   LINES 7FFFD900-7FFFD920  SAME AS ABOVE
7FFFD940  00000000 00000000 00000000 00000000 00A003B8 7FFFD680 00A003C0 7FFFD688  *................"O.....{".Oh*
7FFFD960  00000000 00000000 00000000 00000000 00000000 00000000 8117FEE6 8117FD08  *..........................*
7FFFD980  00000000 00000000 00000000 8117FE56 8117FEE6 00FD8564 009FFA00 009FF9A0  *...........a...a...a..a...*
7FFFD9A0  8117FE56 009FFA00 8117FD08 009D02E0 00FD8564 00FD8564 009FFA28 009FF9A0  *a...a....\.."P..7.e..e..9.*
7FFFD9C0  00FFF7B0 8117FD08 8117FD08 7FFFD638 00FD50C8 009FFA28 C9D2D1C5 C9D2D1C5  *.R..a...O..&H".O...IKJE*
7FFFD9E0  02C3EBF2 C9C7C3F0 F9F0F5C1 C9C7C3F0 F9F0F5C1 00000000 00000000 00000000  *.CY2IGC0905AIGC0905A......*
7FFFDA00  00000000 00000000 00000000 00000000 00000000 00000000 00000000 00000000  *..........................*
   LINES 7FFFDA20-7FFFDA80  SAME AS ABOVE
7FFFDAA0  00000000 00000000 C3E2E5C2 7FFE5C00 00000000 00000000 00000000 00000000  *.........CSVB".*.....$....*
7FFFDAC0  00000000 00000000 00000000 00000000 00000000 00000000 00000000 00000000  *..........................*
7FFFDAE0  00000000 00000000 00000000 00000000 00000000 00000000 84BD45BC 00000000  *.............d............*
7FFFDB00  010F36C8 009DA250 7FFFBD00 00FD6000 00F9390 00000000 009DF348 84BD4000  *..H..s&"....l..3..1.d.....*
7FFFDB20  00F7F080 009FE038 04BD5000 7F743CB8 009FEA68 009FF718 009DF128 0012AAEF  *.70..\..&."....7.....\....*
7FFFDB40  00000043 00000000 00000001 A12007F0 01142FA1 00FA7600 00F7F080 01141FA2  *.....0.....70.............*
7FFFDB60  00FD6000 00000001 81145206 7FFFDB38 81142444 7FFFDB38 00000000 00FA7600  *.a........70..s...........*
7FFFDB80  81145406 00000000 03210300 00000000 00000000 00000000 00000000 00000000  *.a.......a................*
7FFFDBA0  00000000 00000000 00000000 00000000 00000000 00000000 00000000 00000000  *..........................*
   LINES 7FFFDBC0-7FFFDFE0  SAME AS ABOVE
7FFFE000  00000000 00000000 00000000 00000000 00000000 00000000 00000000 00000000  *..........................*
   LINES 7FFFE020-7FFFE8A0  SAME AS ABOVE
7FFFE8C0  00000088 009DD1A8 7FFFE8C0 009DD1A8 009DF348 8117F770 00F7F080 0000FF12  *...h".Y{..Jy....3...9.a.7.70.*
7FFFE8E0  009DD168 00FD50C8 009FFA60 7FFFD638 00000020 8117F9AA 81302048 7FFFD638  *.J..&H..-".O....O.a.9.a..*
7FFFE900  00F7F080 00000000 00000000 00000000 00000000 00000000 00000000 00000000  *.70.......................*
7FFFE920  00000000 00000000 00000000 00000000 00000000 00000000 00000000 00000000  *..........................*
   LINES 7FFFE940-7FFFE9A0  SAME AS ABOVE
7FFFE9C0  E7E2C240 7FFFEA60 80400321 00000321 00000000 00000000 00000000 00000000  *XSB "..-..................*
7FFFE9E0  E2E7E2C2 00000000 00000000 00000000 00000000 00000000 00000000 00000000  *SXSB......................*
   LINE 7FFFEA00  SAME AS ABOVE
7FFFEA20  00000000 E2E7E2C2 00000000 00000000 80000000 01262740 7FFFEA40 00000000  *.....SXSB........."........*
7FFFEA40  E2E7E2C2 00000002 00000000 00000000 00000000 00000000 00000000 00000000  *XSB "....."...............*
7FFFEA60  E7E2C240 7FFFEB00 00000321 00000321 00000000 00000000 00000000 00000000  *XSB "..-..................*
```

```
7FFFEA80 00000000 00000000 00000000 00000000   00000000 00000000 00000000 00000000  *................*
         LINE 7FFFEAA0  SAME AS ABOVE
7FFFEAC0 00000000 00000000 00000000 00000000   00000000 00000000 00000000 7FFFEAE0  *................*
7FFFEAE0 E2E7E2C2 00000000 00000000 80400321   00000000 00000000 00000000 00000000  *SXSB......  .\..*
7FFFEB00 E7E2C240 00000003 00000000 00000321   00000000 00000000 00000000 00000000  *XSB.............*
7FFFEB20 00000003 00000000 00000000 00000000   00000000 00000000 00000000 00000000  *................*
7FFFEB40 00000000 00000000 00000000 00000000   00000000 00000000 00000000 00000000  *................*
7FFFEB60 00000000 00000000 00000000 0000001E   80000000 00000000 7FFEC008 7FFFEB80  *................*
7FFFEB80 E2E7E2C2 00000000 00000000 00000321   00000000 00000000 00000000 00000000  *SXSB....".{.....*
7FFFEBA0 E7E2C240 00000000 80400321 00000321   00000000 00000000 00000000 00000000  *XSB.......".....*
7FFFEBC0 00000000 00000000 00000000 7FFFBF00   00000000 00000000 00000000 00000000  *................*
7FFFEBE0 00000000 00000000 00000000 0D75F00    80000000 01262740 7FFFEC20 00000000  *.........P^.....*
7FFFEC00 00000000 00000000 00000003 00000000   00000000 00000000 00000000 00000000  *................*
7FFFEC20 E2E7E2C2 00000000 80400321 00000321   00000000 00000000 00000000 00000000  *SXSB............*
7FFFEC40 E7E2C240 00000003 00000000 00000000   00000000 00000000 0101001B 00000000  *XSB.............*
7FFFEC60 00000000 00000000 00000000 00000000   00000000 00000000 00000000 00000000  *................*
7FFFEC80 00000000 00000000 80400321 00000000   80000000 00000000 7FFEC008 7FFFECC0  *................*
7FFFECA0 00000000 00000000 00000000 00000000   00000000 00000000 00000000 00000000  *.{.{............*

JOB EXA7JHMX       STEP APP3       TIME 125832    DATE 94100    ID = 000          PAGE 00000082

7FFFECC0 E2E7E2C2 00000000 00000065 00000000   80000000 00000000 01262740 7FFFFD60  *SXSB............*
7FFFECE0 E7E2C240 00000000 80400321 00000321   00000000 00000000 00000000 00000000  *XSB.......-.....*
7FFFED00 00000000 00000000 00000000 00000000   00000000 00000000 00000000 00000000  *................*
         LINE 7FFFED20  SAME AS ABOVE
7FFFED40 00000000 00000000 00000000 00000000   80000000 00000000 01262740 7FFFFD60  *................*
7FFFED60 E2E7E2C2 00000000 00000001 00000321   00000000 00000000 00000000 00000000  *SXSB....".......*
7FFFED80 E7E2C240 00000000 0C000321 00000321   00000000 00000000 00000000 00000000  *XSB.{...........*
7FFFEDA0 00000000 00000000 7FFFBF00 15485F00   00000000 00000000 00000000 00000000  *..........^.....*
7FFFEDC0 00000000 00000000 00000000 00000000   00000000 00000000 00000000 00000000  *................*
7FFFEDE0 00000000 7F7550B0 00000000 00000004   80000000 00000000 7FFFEE00 00000000  *................*
7FFFEE00 E2E7E2C2 00000000 00000000 00000321   80000000 00000001 00000000 00000000  *SXSB....&.......*
7FFFEE20 E7E2C240 00000000 80400321 00000321   00000000 00000000 00000000 00000000  *XSB.............*
7FFFEE40 0000CEA  00000000 00000000 00000000   00000000 00000000 00000000 00000000  *................*
7FFFEE60 00000000 00000000 00000000 00000000   7F786DB0 00000000 00000000 00000000  *........-.......*
7FFFEE80 00000000 00000000 00000000 00000000   00000000 00000000 00000000 00000000  *................*
7FFFEEA0 E2E7E2C2 00000000 00000001 00000000   00000000 00000000 7FFFEEA0 00000000  *SXSB".{.........*
7FFFEEC0 E7E2C240 7FFE40C0 0CC00321 00000321   00000000 00000000 00000000 00000000  *XSB.............*
```

```
7FFFEEE0  00000001  00000000  00000000  00000000  00000000  00000000  *................*
7FFFEEF0  00000000  00000000  00000000  00000000  00000000  00000000  *................*
7FFFEF20  00000000  E2E7E2C2  80000000  7F74C008  7FFFEF40  00000000  *....SXSB...(."..*
7FFFEF40  E2E7E2C2  00000000  7FFFEEC0  00000000  00000000  00000000  *SXSB...(........*
7FFFEF60  E7E2C240  7FFFEEC0  00C00321  00000321  00000000  00000000  *XSB "..(.{.."...*
7FFFEF80  00000000  00000000  00F7F080  00000000  00000000  00000000  *.......70.......*
7FFFEFA0  00000000  00000000  00000000  00000000  00000000  00000000  *................*
7FFFEFC0  00000000  00000000  80000000  7F7550B0  7FFFEFE0  00000000  *.......&."..\...*
7FFFEFE0  E2E7E2C2  00000000  00000A51  00000000  00000000  00000000  *SXSB............*
```

The following subpools aren't part of LSQA, but they contain some control blocks that are related. Subpool 230 is obtained from the high end of the private area. DEBs are among the control blocks found in this subpool.

```
SP 230   KEY   00

009DC9C0  02000000  7F0055A8  009DCC48  0C000000  E6000318  00000000  41000000  E2C1D4C2  *W..........SAMB*
009DC9E0  00000008  19000608  1D0079A0  8000065D  009DCC20  009DAE68  0800065D  00000000  *...."..y........)*
009DCA00  000000B8  00FCDE80  009DCC58  009DCC40  08190006  009DCC6C  009DCAB0  7F000000  *.......)..)....*
009DCA20  01010200  00000000  00000000  00000000  00000000  00000000  00000000  00000000  *..........&.....*
009DCA40  00000000  00000000  00000000  00000000  00000000  00000000  00000000  00000000  *................*
009DCA60  82000218  00080000  04000000  00000000  00000001  00000C80  0067D000  00000002  *................*
009DCA80  00000000  00000048  00000000  00000000  00000001  00000C80  0067D000  00000000  *b..........).*
009DCAA0  00000000  00000000  00000000  00000000  00007000  80008000  00000000  00000000  *................*
009DCAC0  00000000  00000000  00000000  00000000  00000000  00000000  00000000  00000000  *................*
   LINES 009DCAE0-009DCB20  SAME AS ABOVE
009DCB40  00000000  00000000  00000000  00000000  80DB13B6  80DAE0BA  90DAE8CA  80DAEA10  *..........\...Y.*
009DCB60  A0DAF16E  A0DAF6E4  00000000  00000000  A0DAF16E  A0DAF6E4  00DAE0CA  00000001  *.1>..6U....\...*
009DCB80  00000001  009DC9D8  00005618  8F9DAE68  00005618  00000082  00005618  80005618  *..IQ........b...*
009DCBA0  000055A8  7F000000  00DAF00D  00DAE00E  00F15748  A0DAF16E  80DAE018  00000000  *.y"..0..\..1>.\..*
009DCBC0  00000000  009DCBCC  03800001            08190006  08190006  08480665  00000000  *................*
009DCBE0  00000000  00000000  00000000  00000000  00000000  00000000  009DCC30            *................*
009DCC00  009DCC50  009DCC68  009DCCE8  00000000  009DCC50  60000001  31000000  009DCC30  *.&.....Y...x..*
009DCC20  4735FBCC  40000010  0835FC30  40000001  2335FAA7  60000008  1D35FC68  60000005  *x-..Y...x-..-.*
009DCC40  4735FBCC  2235FAA7  20000001  00000000  1D35FC50  C0000008  1D35FC68  4400065D  *x-..&(....).*
009DCC60  00000000  00000000  00B279A0  00000000  08190006  0900065D  00000000  00000000  *.x.............*
009DCC80  00000000  00000000  00000000  00000000  00000000  00000000  00000000  00000000  *................*
   LINES 009DCCA0-009DCCC0  SAME AS ABOVE
```

```
009DCCE0 00000000 00000000 E6000318 00000000   29000000 E2C1D4C2 02000000 7F005D28   *......W.......SAMB.....").*
009DCD00 009DCF68 0C000000 009DCF38 00006F3C   00000000 00000000 04000004 6C000408   *.........?.........%..*
009DCD20 06009000 A0002260 009DCF60 00000000   00000000 00000000 000000B8 00FCD6C0   *.......-........O.(*
009DCD40 009DCF78 009DCF60 009DCF94 009DCDC8   00000000 7F000000 01010300 00000000   *.....-..m..H..."..*
009DCD60 00000000 00000000 00000000 00000000   00000000 00000000 00000000 00000000   *................*
         LINES 009DCE00-009DCE40  SAME AS ABOVE

JOB EXA7JHMX       STEP APP3        TIME 125832    DATE 94100    ID = 000        PAGE 00000083

009DCD80 00000000 00000000 00000000 00000000   00000000 82000218 00080000            *.................b...*
009DCDA0 04000000 00000000 00000000 00000C80   0067D000 00000000 00000000 00226051   *..............}....-.*
009DCDC0 00000000 00000000 00009000 8000C000   00000000 00000000 00000000 00000000   *......(....*
009DCDE0 00000000 00000000 00000000 00000000   00000000 00000000 00000000 00000000   *....*
         LINES 009DCE00-009DCE40  SAME AS ABOVE
009DCE60 00000000 00000000 80DB13B6 80DAE0BA   90DAE8CA 80DAEA10 A0DAF16E A0DAF6E4   *..........Y.....1>...6U*
009DCE80 00000000 8F006F3C 00005D98 00000082   00DAE0CA 00000001 009DCCF0            *.....)q.?..)q..b....0*
009DCEA0 00005D98 8F006F3C 00005D98 00000082   80DAE018 00005D28 7F000000            *)q..?..)q..b...)q..."*
009DCEC0 00DAF00D 00DAE00E 00F15C48 A0DAF16E   06002260 00000000 00000000            *.0.\..1*.1>.\.....*
009DCEE0 009DCEE4 86800001 046C0004 046C0004   06002260 00000000 00000000            *.Uf..%..%.....*
009DCF00 00000000 00000000 00000000 00000000   009DCF48 009DCF68 009DCF80            *.....&.%.....*
009DCF20 00000000 00000000 00000000 2335FDBF   31000000 60000005 4735FEE4 40000010   *.........).....U....*
009DCF40 0835FF48 40000001 0835FDBF 60000000   0635FF80 64002260 9235FF70 40000008   *.....).....-.k....*
009DCF60 2235FDBF 20000001 046C0004 07002260   046C0004 08002260 00000000 00000000   *.).......%..%..-..*
009DCF80 00B61000 00B61800 00D9E000 00D9E800   00DDE000 00000000 00000000            *......R\.RY.\....*
009DCFA0 00000000 00000000 00000000 00000000   00000000 00000000 00000000 00000000   *....*
         LINES 009DCFC0-009DCFE0  SAME AS ABOVE

7F749B40 00000000 00000000 00000000 7F749B94   0000001C 7F749BB0 C1C2D4C5 00000000   *........ABME....*
7F749B60 00000028 00000000 00000000 00000000   00000000 0000000C 7F749BBC            *...."..."...*
7F749B80 00006908 00000000 00000000 000100FB   009DF2C0 C1D7D7F3 D7C7D4F1            *...m...2{APP3PGM1*
7F749BA0 00000002 00000000 00000000 00080321   000006F8 00006908 00080321            *....8........*
7F749BC0 D7C7D4F1 40404040 00000058 C1D7D7F3   D3C9C240 000011F0 00000058 C1D7D7F3   *PGM1    STEPLIB...0...APP3*
7F749BE0 D7C7D4F1 40404040 00000058 C1D7D7F3                                         *PGM1*

7F749D80 00000000 00000000 C1C2D4C5 00000000   00000000 00000000 7F749DC4            *....ABME......D*
7F749DA0 0000001C 7F749DE0 0000000C 7F749DEC   00000028 00000000 00000000 7F749DC4   *...."...."........D*
7F749DC0 00000000 009DF2C0 C1D7D7F3 D7C7D4F1   00006908 00000000 000100FB 0B000000   *...2{APP3PGM1.....*
7F749DE0 00000001 000006F8 00006908 00080321   00000002 00000000 00100FB 00011600    *...8...........*
7F749E00 D3C9C240 40404040 D7C7D4F1 40404040   D7C7D4F1 40404040 E2E3C5D7 E2E3C5D7   *LIB ...0...APP3PGM1...STEP*
```

```
7F749FA0                                      C1C2D4C9 00000000   *ABMI....*
7F749FC0   00000000 7F749D88 009DF348 00000000   00000000 00000000 7F749B58   *...".h..3.........."...*
7F749FE0   009DF2C0 00000000 E6000000 054104F0   05109C98 00000000 00000000   *.2(...W....0...q.....*

SP 230   KEY  05

009DB140   00540000 009E1400 20003FE2 00000000                                *...............0*
009DB160   0047472A 00C0000 00000000 00000000                                 *................*
009DB180   00000000 00000000 00000000 00000000                                *................*

009DB540                              009DB5E0 11810001                        *...............*
009DB560   009DF348 089F7548 0F000900   00000000 00006F94 8F005E00 00B38D80   *.3............?m../....*
009DB580   00F25420 00240000 D1C5E2F2   00000000 00000000 009DB5C4 00000000   *.2..SSIB..JES2.........D...*
009DB5A0   E2E2D6C2 001C0010             009DB584 00000000 009DB5C4 00000000   *.....SSOB..d....(D..-...*
009DB5C0   00000000 001C0000 009DC0C4   009DB560 009F7548 00000000 00000000   *...........\.-...*
009DB5E0   00540000 009E1328 00011BE0   009DB560 00080000 00000000 00000000   *...........\...*
009DB600   00474729 00000000 00000000   00000000 00000000 00000000 00000000   *................*
009DB620   00000000 00000000 00000000   00000000 00000000 00000000 00000000   *................*

009DE060                              00FEE898 80DB11A8   00FEE898 00DAE006 00000005   *Yq..y..Yq..\...*
009DE080   2D000716 009DE0F0 11200003 039DF348   109DE074 A8000000 0F001100 01000000   *-......0......3...y...*
009DE0A0   FF000000 8F9DAE68 049DE068 18F24D90   00000818 00050845 000B02AA 00010001   *......\..2(....'3BBABB....*
009DE0C0   00000000 00000000 0000007D F3C2C2C1   C2C20000 00000000 20002BE0 00000000   *..........\.-.*
009DE0E0   00000000 00000000 00000000 00000000   00540000 009E13B8 20002BE0 00000000   *...........IQ......*
009DE100   40000020 00000000 00000000 009DC9D8   00474737 00000000 402C0000 00000000   *...............*

JOB EXA7JHMX        STEP APP3           TIME 125832     DATE 94100    ID = 000              PAGE 00000084

009DE120   00000000 00000000 00000000 00000000   00000000 00000000 00000000 00000000   *................*
009DE140   00000000 00000000

009DEE40                                        00FEE898 80DB11A8 00FEE898 80DAE000   *..Yq..y..Yq..\..*
009DEE60   00DAE006 00000005 2D000070C 009DB140   17200002 039DF348 009DB560 68000000   *.......\...3...-.D*
009DEE80   00011100 05000000 FF000000 8F006F3C   049DEE50 58F24D90 000000C4 00100C4   *...........?..&.2(...D..D*
009DEEA0   00010001 58F24D90 0000043F 0000043F   00000001 58F24D90 0000053A 0007053A   *...2(.....2(...D...*
009DEEC0   00070001 58F24D90 0000046B 0005046B   00050001 58F24D90 0000046C 0007046C   *...2(...8..%...*
009DEEE0   00040001 F3C2C2C1 C2C20000 00000000   00050001 F3C2C2C1 C2C20000 00000000   *....3BBABB........*
009DEF00   00000000 00000000                     00000000 00000000 00000000 00000000   *...*
```

```
SP 230   KEY  08

009DAE60  00000100 00000000  08190006 0FF1D076 002E3DC0 00000001  *..........1)...(.....*
009DAE80  00004000 000055A8  02000001 54000000  0400020 009DE08C 92C88D38 00D60548  *....y.......\.kH..O..*
009DAEA0  0A000001 00006660  30013030 00005618  01DB36F0 0000007D 00000001  *.....-......0..0..,..*
009DAEC0  8F9DAE68 009DF348  009DAF50 009DAED8  9ECA0000 00B08000 00000000 00000000  *.....3..&..Q.........*
009DAEE0  04000000 00000000  00000000 00000000  00000000 00000000 019DAEFC 009DAF50  *...............&.*
009DAF00  9ECA001C 40D591EE  009DC100 00000048  009DAEC4 04C6205E 40805E10 009DAEC4  *....Nj.RA......D.F.; .W..D.*
009DAF20  04C6105F 00000000  00000000 00000000  00000000 00000000 00000000 00000000  *.F.^.................*
009DAF40  00000000 00000000  40404040 40404040  C5E7C1F7 D1C8D44B D3C9E2E3 C9D5C7F4  *........    EXA7JHM.LISTING4*
009DAF60  40404040 40404040  40404040 40404040  40404040 00000200 00000000 40404040  *                ....    *
009DAF80  40404040 804DAA16  00000000 00000000  00000200 00000000 00000000 00000000  *.....(...............*
009DAFA0  5E006400 00000080  00000000 00000000  00000000 00000000 00000000 00000000  *;...................*
009DAFC0  00000000 0001C4C1  E3C1F8C2 40404040  40404040 40404040 40404040 40404040  *......DATA8B    *
009DAFE0  40404040 009EC330  00000000 00000000  00000000 00000000 00000000 00000100  *....C................*
```

The registers are now printed. These were also printed in the RTM2WA Summary much earlier in the dump, which is usually an easier place to find them unless you need the floating-point or vector register values.

```
REGISTERS AT ENTRY TO ABEND

FLOATING POINT REGISTER VALUES
  0-6  00000000 00000000   00000000 00000000   00000000 00000000   00000000 00000000

GPR VALUES
  0-3   00006E4C  00006AD0  00000040  009F1954
  4-7   009F1930  009F9028  009D1FF8  00000000
  8-11  009FF060  809DF510  00009000  00002260
  12-15 00006908  00006DEC  50006B0C  00D60548

ACCESS REGISTER VALUES
  0-3   00F7F080  00000000  00000000  00000000
  4-7   00000000  00000000  00000000  00000000
  8-11  00000000  00000000  00000000  860A9DC0
  12-15 00000000  00000000  00000000  00010321

VECTOR STATUS SAVE AREA DATA
```

The VSSA is present only if a program uses the Vector Facility. Since program APP3PGM1 does, a VSSA was created by MVS to save the status for any future use.

```
VSSA: 7F73EEC0

            VSSA..... VSSA        RPTR...... 7F73F000   EVST...... 00000F7A   B23C9000   VNUT...... 00000000
+0000       VSSA..... 0C4BD580    VAC....... 00000F7A   B23C9000   R020...... 00000000   00000000
+0014                 00000000                          SCSZ...... 0100       PSUM...... 0004
+002C                 00          VSRF...... 00          VCT....... 0000       VIX....... 0000   VIU....... 00
+003F       VCH...... 00          VMR....... 00000000    00000000   00000000   00000000   00000000
+005C                 00000000    00000000    00000000   00000000   00000000
+0080                 00000000    00000000    00000000   00000000   00000000
+00A4                 00000000    00000000    00000000   00000000   00000000
+00C8                 00000000    00000000    00000000   00000000   00000000

JOB EXA7JHMX       STEP APP3       TIME 125832       DATE 94100       ID = 000                   PAGE 00000085

+00EC       00000000    00000000    00000000   00000000   00000000   00000000   00000000
+0110       00000000    00000000    00000000   00000000   00000000   00000000   00000000
+0134       00000000    00000000    00000000
```

VECTOR REGISTERS (LISTED VERTICALLY FROM ELEMENT 000 TO ELEMENT 255)

The vector register sets are now printed. Vector registers come in sets of some power of 2, which varies depending on the underlying CPU and other factors. Each set of registers comprises 16 registers, which are treated like general-purpose registers for vector operations only. The processor on which this sample was run had 256 sets of 16 vector registers, or 4096 registers altogether.

```
       --00--   --01--   --02--   --03--   --04--   --05--   --06--   --07--

000    00000000 00000000 00000000 00000000 00000000 00000000 00000000 00000000
```

Since you didn't do anything with the Vector Feature to alter the register contents, all 256 sets of vector registers will be zero. These won't be shown in the interests of brevity.

```
255 00000000 00000000 00000000 00000000 00000000 00000000 00000000 00000000

    --08--  --09--  --10--  --11--  --12--  --13--  --14--  --15--
000 00000000 00000000 00000000 00000000 00000000 00000000 00000000 00000000
```

The vector registers are printed 0 through 7, then 8 through 15. In the interests of brevity, the additional 256 lines of zeroes will also be omitted.

```
255 00000000 00000000 00000000 00000000 00000000 00000000 00000000 00000000
```

The storage allocated to the task is now dumped. Note that some of this storage is in use by the other TCBs in the address space (Region Control Task, Initiator, etc.).

```
00005900                   00000000 00000000  00000000 00000000 00000000 00000000   *................*
00005920 00000000 00000002 00000002 00006B34  00000000 00000002 00000000 00000000   *................*
00005940 00000000 00000000 00000000 00000321  00000000 00000000 00000000 00000000   *................*
00005960 00000000 00000000 00000000 00000321  009DF348 05EF8200 0004510 C2140000     *........3..b...B.*
00005980 00F7F080 046F307F 940C2000 00000002  5FB3EE40 046F307F 15485DC0 00C00321    *.70.?.m...?.)(.(.*
000059A0 00000321 258DA840 FE000000 046F307F  00000000 00000000 00000000 00000000   *....y....?.......*
000059C0 0378415B 046F307F DF8A60AC 7F7550B0  00F7F080 00000000 00000000 00000000   *$.?.".-.&.70.....*
000059E0 00000000 00000000 00000000 860A9DC0  00F7F080 00000000 00000000 00000000   *........f.(..70..*
00005A00 00000000 00000000 00000000 00010321  00000000 00000000 00000000 00000000   *................*
00005A20 00000000 00000000 00000000 00000000  00000000 00000000 00000000 00000000   *................*
00005A40 00000000 00000000 00000000 860A9DC0  00010321 00000000 00000000 00000000   *........f.(.....*
```

```
JOB EXA7JHMX       STEP APP3        TIME 125832    DATE 94100    ID = 000                              PAGE 00000095

00005A60 15485F00 00000000 00000000 00000000  00000000 00000000 00000000 7F7550B0  *<...............*
00005A80 00000000 00000000 00000000 00000000  06000000 00000000 00000000 00000000  *..............&.*
00005AA0 00000000 00000000 00000000 00000000  00000000 00000000 00000000 00000000  *................*
00005AC0 00000000 00000000 00000000 00000000  00000000 00000000 00005AF0 000058F8  *...........!0..8*
00005AE0 00005AA8 00005BE0 00005AB8 00005BF0  00000000 00000000 00005AF0 00000000  *..!y..$..!..$0..*
00005B00 00000000 00000000 00000000 00000000  00000000 00000000 00000000 00000000  *................*
      LINES 00005B20-00005CC0  SAME AS ABOVE
00005CE0 00000000 00006CEC 80FD5118 00000000  00006B34 00000008 00005660 00000000  *....%.........-.*
00005D00 00000000 00000000 00000000 00000000  00000000 00000000 00000000 00000000  *................*
00005D20 00000000 7F000000 009DCCF8 00000000  80005D98 80005D98 00000000 00000000  *...."..8.)q..)q.*
00005D40 00000000 00000000 00000000 00000000  00000000 00000000 00000000 00000000  *................*
      LINE 00005D60  SAME AS ABOVE
00005D80 00000000 0C000000 00000000 00000000  00000000 21005D98 7F000000 00000000  *.............)q"*
00005DA0 02000000 80006AD0 00005DD0 A0002260  00005DC8 00006F3C 00000000 00000000  *....}..)..-..}.H.?*
00005DC0 04000004 6C000406 06009000 A0002260  00000000 00000000 00000000 00006F94  *...%..........?m*
00005DE0 7F000000 00005DE0 00B33D80 52000000  00000000 00000000 00000000 00000000  *"..)....\..U.....*
00005E00 A000004C 00000000 00B33D80 52000000  92000000 00005D2C 00000000 00790079  *..<......\m.....*
00005E20 00000000 00000000 022C0041 009DB560  00000000 00005D2C 00006CEC 00000000  *....-k...).....*
00005E40 00000000 00000000 00000000 C9C7C7F0  F1F9C1C8 00005EA0 0006F94 00000000  *....IGG019AH..%.*
00005E60 50C65E82 00000001 00005EA0 00005EA0  00005EA0 00005DE0 0006F94 00006D3C  *&F;b....;..;..).?m.._.*
00005E80 00006D3C 0000000C 00000000 00005E00  00000078 00C6595C 00006908 00000000  *....;..;..)\..?m.._.*
00005EA0 0000014C 00000000 40000000 00000200  00000078 00006D3C 00005E00 00000000  *F.*...........*
00005EC0 00006D3D 00000000 20002000 00005EFC  00000079 00000000 000212E0 00000000  *.<............*
00005EE0 06000001 00000000 00005DE0 00000000  00000078 00000000 00008F80 00000000  *._..;..)\.....*
00005F00 00000000 00000000 00000000 00005E00  00000000 00000000 04000000 00000000  *._..;..)\.....\*
00005F20 00000000 00000000 00000000 00000000  08000000 00000000 00000000 00000000  *..............;.*
00005F40 00000000 00000000 00000000 00000000  00000000 00000000 00000000 00000000  *................*
      LINES 00005F60-00005FC0  SAME AS ABOVE
```

The parameter information for the program (PARM=) begins in the following. Register 1 on entry to APP3PGM1 contained X'00005FE8', which points to the parameter address list. This begins at location 00005FEE with the halfword length (X'000A', or decimal 10) of the PARM= information. The actual value (THE PARMS) then follows. The register 1 value can be found in the PRB for APP3PGM1 or the first linkage stack entry, both of which were formatted earlier in the dump.

```
00005FE0  00000000 00000000 00000000 80005FEE  0000000A  E3C8C540 D7C1D9D4 E2400000 00000000  00000000  *.............^......THE PARMS .....*
00006000  00000000 00000000 00000000 000068E0  SAME AS ABOVE                                             *.................................*
          LINES 00006020-000068E0  SAME AS ABOVE
```

Program APP3PGM1 begins in the following at location 00006908. It will also be formatted later in the dump.

```
00006900  00000000 00000000 B24000E0 18CF41D0   C4E450C0 C42C0700 4510C02C 10000000  *......\....)DU&{D.....{....*
00006920  00000000 00000000 00010000 00000000   00006B34 41000100 41101000 0A3C127F  *...+.CQo.C.3.{.CQ..{....."*
00006940  4780C08A 4E70C3D8 960FC3DF F347C055   C3D80700 4510C080 002F0000 5C5C5C5C  *...(.+CQo.C.3.{.CQ..{....*****
00006960  5C5C5C40 E6C1E240 D9C5E3E4 D9D540C3   D6C4C540 C6D9D6D4 40C5E3E3 C1C54060  *** WAS RETURN CODE FROM ESTAE -*
00006980  40C5D5C4 C9D5C700 0A234070 C54847F0   C2160700 4100C094 47F0C09C C1D7D7F3  * ENDING...E..0B.....{m.0{.APP3*
000069A0  D7C7D4F2 1B110A08 4500C0AC C2D9E4C9   D5E24040 4110C126 0A290700 4110C0BC  *PGM2....{.BRUINS  .A.....{..*
000069C0  47F0C0C0 80006E38 41F0C0C8 47F0F048   000069EC 00000000 80006E3C 00000000  *.0{{.>..0{H.00.......>....*
000069E0  00000021 00000000 00000000 C1D7F7F3   D7C7D4F3 00000000 00000000 00000000  *.......APP3PGM3..............*
00006A00  00000000 00000048 00000000 00010000   00000700 4510C134 0A2A0700 4510C124  *.........................A..*
00006A20  C0034000 0006E52 0006E5A 0A38A640      00000700 4510C134 8F006F94 0A134110  *{{...>..>!..w........A..?m..*
00006A40  C68C9110 103047E0 C2180700 4510C14C   80006F3C 0A134110 C63448B0 103E9110  *F.j...\B...A<..?....F...j.*
00006A60  10304710 C1784110 C68C4100 C5561FFF   BFF71031 05EFD201 C548C6F0 47F0C216  *.A...F..E...7...K.E.F0.0B.*
00006A80  47F0C180 00001616 180B58F0 C17C58E0   001058EE 030458EE 00A0B218 E00018A1  *.0A......0A@.\...*
00006AA0  4110C634 4100C538 41110000 1FFF0A12   12FF40F0 C5484770 C2084110 C6344100  *..F..E..........0E..B..F...*
00006AC0  C5441FFF 50A1000C 40B10006 58F01008   7F000000 00802260 0006F3C 00009000   *E...7......A."....?...A.*
00006B00  58E01008 1BFFBFF7 1FFFBFF7 103105EF   BFF7F031 05EFD703 C1C8C1C8 4110C1C8  *..).&...0...70..P.AHAH..AH*
00006B20  4110C68C 4100C556 1FFFBFF7 103105EF   47F0C216 90ECD00C 4120F1B8 502D0008  *.\...7\..b....B..?..?m..*
00006B40  50D20004 18D21821 58C0F200 4110C42C   45E0C4BC D207C463 C4CA4110 20054550  *..F..E..7....0B..}..1.&...*
00006B60  C4BCD202 C447C4CA 9261C44A BF172005   89100014 88100014 4E10C3D8 960FC3DF  *&K..K..{2..D.\D.K.D....\*
00006B80  F337C44B C3D84110 C68C4100 C4341FFF   BFF71031 05EF9260 C434D201 C548C6F2  *D.K.D.D.k/D\..i..h...+.CQo.C.*
00006BA0  96202144 58DD0004 18125830 C3E04140   C3C09204 10FC18F3 11429102 C2E01BEE  *3.D.CQ..F..D...7..k-D.K.E.F2*
00006BC0  41F04000 96401141 D2031144 F0049620   11419604 11429102 C3529602 11421FEE  *o.........C\.C{k...3&0.0o..*
00006BE0  55E0F010 4780C352 58E01170 58E0E000   12EE4780 C3529602 11419680 11421FEE  *.0.o..K...o..j.0..B\..*
00006C00  9180F002 58F0F010 4710C30C 41000020   47F0C310 410000F0 41E0E008 9180F004  *.\0..C.\..\\..C.o..o...*
```

```
JOB EXA70JHMX     STEP APP3     TIME 125832     DATE 94100     ID = 000     PAGE 00000096

00006C20  41F0F008 4710C326 19E04740 C3101BFE  C3101BFE  06E01801 58101170 58101000 44E0C34A  *.00...C..\..C......\C\*
00006C40  41F00003 1BEF1A1E 96801000 181047F0  C350D200  1000F000 18F49102 F0024780           *.0......o.....0C&K...0..4j.0...*
```

```
00006C60  C3B41BEE 55E0F018 4780C3B4 58E01170  58E0E00C 12EE4780 C3B49602 114258F0  *C...\0...C..\...\\....C.o....0*
00006C80  F01848E0 F00012EE 47D0C3B4 41000007  19E047D0 C39018E0 18015810 11705810  *0..\0...)C..\.....)C..\......*
00006CA0  100C40E0 100089E0 000106E0 44E0C3AE  181047F0 C3B4D200 1002F002 960810FD  *...i.\..\.C...0C.K..0.o...*
00006CC0  98ECD00C 07FE0000 00708000 2FA0BF00  00000000 00000000 00000000 00000000  *q.}...........*
00006CE0  00000000 0000000F 00006B10 00000000  0005CE00 50006B96 00C65968 00000000  *.........*\....&.,.o.F.*
00006D00  00006D3C 00006D3C 00005660 00000000  00000000 00000000 00000000 00000000  *.-.-.......*
00006D20  00000000 00000000 00000000 00000000  00006908 00000000 605C5C5C C7D9C1D4  *......--.****.PROGRAM*
00006D40  C1C2C5D5 C440D6C3 C3E4D9D9 C5C47AF0  C3F261F0 F0F0F040 40D7D9D6 C7D9C1D4  *ABEND OCCURRED:0C2/0000 PROGRAM*
00006D60  40C2C5C7 C9D5E240 C1E37AF0 F0F0F6F6  F9F0F840 40404040 40404040 40404040  * BEGINS AT:00006908        *
00006D80  40404040 40404040 40404040 40404040  40404040 40404040 40404040 40404040  *                          *
          LINE 00006DA0  SAME AS ABOVE
00006DC0  40000700 F384C4CA 1000DC07 C4CAC3E3  07FEF0C3 F2F0F0F0 C6C658F0 F1F2F3F4  * ...3dD....D.CT..0C2000FF.01234*
00006DE0  F5F6F7F8 F9C1C2C3 C4C5C600 00006E4C  C6F1E2C1 00000000 00006E3C 00006F3C  *56789ABCDEF....F1SA.....><..?.*
00006E00  50006B0C 00D60548 00006E4C 00000040  D6404040 009F1954 009F1930 009F9028  *&..O...>...)......*
00006E20  009D1FF8 00009FF060 809DF510 00040700  00000200 00000000 C1D96060 C1D96060  *..8...0-.5........*
00006E40  0001000C C1D7D7F3 D7C7D4F1 00040700  0008C6D6 D6404040 404001C2 C1D96060  *....APP3PGM1.....FOO  .BAR-*
00006E60  60606060 60606060 6E40D6D7 C5D540C5  C5D540C5 D9D9D6D9 40404040 40404040  *---------> OPEN ERROR        *
00006E80  40404040 40404040 40404040 40404040  40404040 40404040 40404040 40404040  *                          *
          LINES 00006EA0-00006EC0  SAME AS ABOVE
00006EE0  40404040 00000000 00000000 00000000  00000000 00000000 00000001 00000000  *                          *
00006F00  00000001 00000001 54000000 C4E4D4D7  C4C44040 02000020 00000001 00000001  *.........DUMPDD   *
00006F20  00000660 00000000 00000000 00000001  00000001 0000007D 00000001 00000001  *..-.....'........*
00006F40  00040000 046C0004 07F1D076 02EBB60  00000001 0A000001 00005D28 02006B10  *...%..1}..-..)......*
00006F60  90000000 00542400 009DEE74 12C88D38  00D60548 00002260 30013030 00000000  *...8....H.O..*
00006F80  00005D98 01DB36F0 00DB36F0 00000050  00DB4258 00000000 00000000 00000000  *..)q...0...0..&...*
00006FA0  00000000 00000000 01008F78 00794000  00005F30 02000001 94000000 002C0050  *.......0...&....m....&*
00006FC0  009DB560 92C65968 00000000 00000001  08090079 00000000 00005DE0 00008FF9  *....-kF......)\..9*
00006FE0  00008FF9 00000000 00000001 00000000  00000000 00100008 00000000 00000000  *..9.........*
00007000  00000000 00000000 00000000 00000000  00000000 00000000 00000000 00000000  *                          *
          LINES 00007020-00007980  SAME AS ABOVE
```

This storage is in use by SNAP processing to print the dump. It should be ignored, in almost all cases.

```
000079A0  065D0000 40F0F6F0 40F0F6C6F0 F0F6C5F8  F040F4F0 F4F0F4F4 F0F4F0F4 F0F6C5F8  *.)../...  00006E80 40404040 40404*
000079C0  F0F0F040 F4F0F0F6C6F0 C6F0C6F0 40C6F0C6  F6C3F5C6 F8404040 40C6F0C6 F0C6C4C6  *000 40F0F0F0 F0F6C5F8   F040F4F*
000079E0  F040C6F4 C6F0C6F4 C6F0C6F4 F0C6C6F4  F0C6F4F0 C6F0C6F4 4040405C F0F4F0F4  *0 F4F0F4F4 F4F0F4F4 F0F4F040 40404*
00007A00  4B5D4B4B 40F0F0F0 F4F0F0F4 F0F4F0F4  F0F4F0F4 40404040 00006E80 F0F4F0F4  *.)...  00006E80 40404040 40404*
00007A20  5C007D00 0040F0F0 F0F0F7F9 C3F040C6  F0C6F4C6 C6F0C6F0 C3F6C6F0 F4F0C6F0  **.'.  000079C0 F0F0F0F040 F4F0C6F0*
```

```
00007A40  40C3F6C6 F0C3F6C6 F040F4F0 C3F6C6F0   C3F64040 4040C6F6 C3F3C6F5 C3F640C6   * C6F0C6F0 40C6F0C6      F6C3F5C6 F*
00007A60  F8F4F0F4 F4F0C3F6 F9C5F040 C6F0F4F0   40C6F0C3 F6C6F4C3 F6404040 5CF0F0F0   *8404040 40C6F0F4 F0C6F4C6      *000*
00007A80  40F4F0C6 000040F0 F0F0F0F7 C25C0040   C6F84040 4040C6F0 F4F0C6F4 C65C007D   * 40F0F0F0 F0F6C5F8      F040F4F*.'*
00007AA0  000040F0 F0F0F0F7 F9C5F040 C6F0F4F0   C3F6C6F6 4040C3F6 C6F04040 F440C3F6   *.. 000079E0 F040C6F4 C6F0C6F4 C6*
00007AC0  C6F0F4F0 40C3F6C6 F4C3F6C6 F0C3F6C6   4040F0C6 F0C3F6C6 F440F4F0 C3F6C6F0   *F040C6 F4C6F0F4      F0C6F440 C6F0*
00007AE0  C3F6C6F4 40C3F6C6 F0F0F4F0 F4F0F4F0   F5C34040 405CF040 405CC340 F440C6F0   *C6F4 F0C6F0C6F4 4040405C   *0 F4F0*
00007B00  F0F0F0F0 F0F7C1F0 F0F04040 4040F4F0   C6F44040 405CC5C0 7D000040 F0C6F0C6   *F4F0 F4F040F4 F0F4F0F4      ** .'.*
00007B20  F0F0F0F0 F7C1F0F0 F040F4C2 F5C34040   C240F4C2 F7C4F4C2 F4C240F4 F0C6F0C6   *00007A00 4B5D4B4B 4B7D4B4B 40F0F*
00007B40  F0C6F040 F0C6F0F0 C6F040C6 F040C6F0   C6F0F440 40405C4B 5D4B4B40 F0C6F0C6   *0F0 F0F6C5F8      F040F4F0 F4F0F4F*
00007B60  F040C6F4 C6F0F0F0 C6F0F040 F0C6F0F0   40405C4B 5D4B4B40 7D4B4B40 F0C6F4C6   *0 F4F040F4 F0F4F0F4      *.).'...*
00007B80  F0F0F0F0 F0F6C5F8 F0404040 40F4F0F4   F4F0F45C 007D0000 007D0000 40F0F0F0   *00006B80 40404040 40404**..'.. 000*
00007BA0  F0F0F7C1 F2F040F5 C3F0F0F7 C4F0F040   F6C6F040 C6F4C6F0 C6F0C6F9 C6F7C6F9   *07A20 5C007D00 0040F0F0 F0F0F7F9*
00007BC0  40C3F3C6 F0F4F5C3 F6C6F040 C6F4C6F0   F6C6F0C3 F640C6F0 C6F0C6F0 C6F040C3   * C3F040C6      F0C6F0C6 F0F4F040 C*
00007BE0  F6C6F4C3 F6C6F0C3 F640C6F0 C6F4C6F0   4040405C 40C3F3C6 F6404040 F0F0F7C2   *6F4C6F0 F4F040C3     * C3F040C6  *
00007C00  40C6F0C3 F6C6F040 C6F4C6F0 F640C3F6   F0C6F0F0 0040F0F0 F0F0F7C2 F040C6F4   * F0C6F0C6 F0F4F040 C*.'.. 00007B*
00007C20  C5F040C6 F6C6F4C3 F6C6F0C3 F640C3F6   40C3F6C6 F4C3F6C6 F3C3F640 40405C40   *E0 F6C6F4C3 F6C6F040 C6F4C6F0 F4*
00007C40  C6F0C3F3 C6F34040 40C6F4C3 F6404040   C6F0F4F0 405C4003 F3C6F040 F4F0F4C3   *F0C3F3 4040405C 40C3F3C6 F0F4*
00007C60  C6F0C3F3 40C6F6F4 40C6F6F4 F0F4F0F4   C6F3C6F6 C3F6C6F4 4040F0C6 F0C6F0C3   *F0C3 F6404040     *6F4C6F0 F4F040C*
00007C80  F3404040 5C40C3F3 C6F64040           000040F0 F0F0F7C0                      *3 * C3F040C6   *.'.. 00007C00 *


JOB EXA7JHMX        STEP APP3        TIME 125832    DATE 94100    ID = 000            PAGE 00000097

00007CA0  F4F0C3F6 C6F0C3F3 40C6F6C3 F6C6F0C3   F340C6F6 F4F0C3F6 C6F040C3 F6C6F4C3   *40C6F0C3 F6C6F0C3 F640C6F0 C6F4C*
00007CC0  F6C6F040 404040C6 F4C6F0F4 F0C3F340   F5C3F0F0 F7C4F0F0 40F0F0F4 F6C6F0C6   *6F0   F4F040C3 5C007D00 0040F0F*
00007CE0  F040C6F0 C6F0C6F7 C3F24040 405C40C6   F0C3F6C6 F0C3F6C6 40C6F4C6 C6F0F4F0   *0 F0F0F7C2 * F0C6F0C6 F0F4F040*
00007D00  40C35C4B 7D4B4B40 F0F0F0F0 F7C25C00   7D000040 F0F0F0F0 F7C3F2F0 40C3F5F6   * C*.'.. 00007B*.'.  00007C20 C5F*
00007D20  F0F4F0C3 F640C6C6 C3F3C6F6 C3F640C6   F4C3F3C6 F3F4F040 C3F6C6F6 40C3F3C6   * *040C6 F6C3F5C6 F4C3F340 C6F6C3F6*
00007D40  40404040 40405CC5 F040C6F6 C3F6C6F6   F3C6F6C6 F640C3F6 C3F3C6F6 C3F640C6   *         *E0 F6C6F4C3 F6C6F040 C*
00007D60  F0F4F0C3 F6C6F440 40405C45 F040C6F0   40F0F0F0 F0F0F7C3 F4F040C3 F6C6F040   *040C6F4 *E0 F6C6F4C3 F6C6F040 *
00007D80  C3F6C6F6 40C6F6C6 F0F0F7C3 F4F0F4F0   F040C3F6 C6F4C6F6 C6F3C6F6 C6F040F4   *C6F4F0 *F3 C6F34040 404040F4F0*
00007DA0  C6F340C3 F6C6F3F4 40404040 C6F340C3   C3F6C6F4 C6F0C6F4 C6F0C6F3 C6F040F4   *C6F4C6 *.  00007C40 C6F0C3*
00007DC0  40C3F6C6 F4C3F3C6 F440F040 405C40C6   C6F6C6F0 C3F6F4C6 C6F3C6F6 40404040   *C6F4C6F0 F0C6F4C6 F0C3F6F4 F040*
00007DE0  F4F0F4F0 C6F040C6 F0404040 C3F6F3F4   F0F4F0F4 F0F4F0F4 F4F0C3F6 C6F3F4F0   *4040 *F3 C6F34040 4040F4F0 F4F*
00007E00  C6F0C6F4 C6F040C6 F4C6F3C6 F6404040   F0F4F0F4 F4F0C6F4 C6F3C6F6 F6C3F640   *0F4F0  *.'.  00007DC0 40C3F6C6*
00007E20  C6F4C3F3 C6F6C6F4 F0C3F6F3 C6F6C3F6   C6F6C3F6 C3F6C6F4 F4F0F4F0 40C3F3F3   *F4C3F6C6 F040F4F0 C3F6C6F4 C3*
00007E40  C6F6C6F4 40C6F6F4 C3F6C6F4 C6F0C3F3   C6F6F0C3 F6C6F440 40404040           *F640C6 F0C3F*
00008000  00000000 00000000 00000000 00000000   00000000 00000000 00000000 00000000   *................*

LINES 00008020-00008F40   SAME AS ABOVE
```

The following is the buffer area obtained for use by the READ macro in APP3PGM1 when reading the member from the PDS. This address is determined by examining the contents of register 11 in the RTM2WA summary; it could also have been determined by looking at the trace table.

```
00008F60  00000000 00000000 00000000 00000000  00000000 00000000 00008F80 00010080  *................*
00008F80  00000000 00000000 00000000 00000000  00000000 00000000 00008FE0 00000000  *................*
LINES 00008FA0-00008FE0  SAME AS ABOVE

00009000  C1D7D7F3 D7C7D4F1 40E3C9E3 D3C5407D  D4E5E240 C3D6D5E3 D9D6D340 C2D3D6C3  *APP3PGM1 TITLE 'MVS CONTROL BLOC*
00009020  D2E240C1 D7D7C5D5 C4C9E740 F340D7D9  D6C7D9C1 D440F17D 40404040 40404040  *KS APPENDIX 3 PROGRAM 1'        *
00009040  40404040 40404040 40404040 40404040  5C404040 40404040 40404040 40404040  *                *               *
00009060  40404040 40404040 40404040 40404040  40404040 40404040 40404040 40404040  *                                *
LINE 00009080  SAME AS ABOVE
000090A0  5C404040 40E3C8C9 E240D7D9 D6C7D9C1  D47DE240 C6E4D5C3 E3C9D6D5 40404040  **        THIS PROGRAM'S FUNCTION*
000090C0  40C9E240 E3D640E4 E2C540E2 D6D4C540  D4E5E240 E2C5D9E5 C9C3C5E2 40E6C8C9  * IS TO USE SOME MVS SERVICES WHI*
000090E0  C3C84040 40404040 40404040 40404040  5C404040 40404040 40E6C9D3 D340C3D9  *CH              *        WILL CR*
00009100  C5C1E3C5 40E2D6D4 C540C1E2 E2D6C3C9  C1E3C5C4 40C3D6D5 E3D9D6D3 40C2D3D6  *EATE SOME ASSOCIATED CONTROL BLO*
00009120  C3D2E26B 40E3C8C5 D540C1C2 C5D5C440  E3D64040 40404040 40404040 40404040  *CKS, THEN ABEND TO              *
00009140  5C404040 40D7D9D6 C4E4C3C5 40C1E240  E2C1D4D7 D3C540C4 E4D4D74B 40404040  **        PRODUCE A SAMPLE DUMP. *
00009160  40C9E340 C4D6C5E2 40D5D6E3 C8C9D5C7  40D7D9D6 C4E4C3E3 C9E5C54B 40404040  * IT DOES NOTHING PRODUCTIVE.    *
00009180  40404040 40404040 40404040 40404040  40404040 40404040 40404040 40404040  *                                *
000091A0  40404040 40404040 40404040 40404040  40404040 40404040 40404040 40404040  *                                *
LINE 000091C0  SAME AS ABOVE
000091E0  C1D7D7F3 D7C7D4F1 40C3E2C5 C3E34040  40404040 40404040 40404040 40404040  *APP3PGM1 CSECT                  *
00009200  40404040 40404040 40404040 40404040  40404040 40404040 40404040 40404040  *                                *
00009220  40404040 40404040 40404040 40404040  40C1D7D7 F3D7C7D4 F140C1D4 D6C4C540  *                 APP3PGM1 AMODE *
00009240  F2F44040 40404040 40404040 40404040  40404040 F2F460C2 C9E340D4 40404040  *24                      24-BIT M*
00009260  D6C4C540 C6D6D940 D7E4E340 40404040  40404040 40404040 40404040 40404040  *ODE FOR PUT                     *
00009280  C1D7D7F3 D7C7D4F1 40D9D4D6 C4C54040  F2F44040 40404040 40404040 40404040  *APP3PGM1 RMODE 24               *
000092A0  40404040 40404040 40404040 40404040  40404040 40404040 40404040 40404040  *                                *
000092C0  40404040 40404040 40404040 40404040  40404040 40404040 C2C1D2D9 40404040  *                          BAKR  *
000092E0  D9F1F46B F0404040 40404040 40404040  40404040 C5E2C140 D3C9D5D2 40404040  *R14,0                ESA LINK   *
00009300  C1C7C540 40404040 40404040 40404040  40404040 40404040 40404040 40404040  *AGE                             *
00009320  40404040 40404040 40D3D940 40D7D9D6  C7D9C1D4 40C1C4C4 D9C5E2E2 40404040  *          LR    R12,R15         *
00009340  40404040 40404040 C3D6D7E8 40D7D9D6  C7D9C1D4 40C1C4C4 D9C5E2E2 40404040  *          COPY PROGRAM ADDRESS  *
00009360  40404040 40404040 40404040 40D7D9D6  D9F1F540 40404040 40404040 40404040  *                          USING *
00009380  C1D7D7F3 D7C7D4F1 6BD9F1F2 40404040  D9F1F26B D9F1F540 40E4E2C9 D5C74040  *APP3PGM1,R12             ESTABLIS*
```

```
000093A0  C840C1C4 C4D9C5E2 E2C1C2C9 D3C9E3E8   40404040 40404040 C1E2C1E5 C5404040   *H ADDRESSABILITY        *
000093C0  40404040 40D3C140 C7C5E340 C6D6D9D4   D9F1F36B C1E2C1E5 C5404040 C5C140C1   *     LA   R13,ASAVE      *
000093E0  C1C36BD9 E2E2C1C2 C7C5E340 C6D6D9D4   C1E3F16B C540E2C1 E5C54040 40C6D6D9   *          GET FORMAT-1 SAVE AREA A*
00009400  C4C4D9C5 E2E24040 E2E2C1C2 40404040   C1E3F16B C540E2C1 E5C54040 C3C3140C1   *DDRESS                  SPACE 1 *
00009420  40404040 40404040 40404040 40404040   40404040 40404040 40E2D7C1 C3C5C140   *                                *

        LINE 00009440  SAME AS ABOVE

00009460  40404040 40E2E340 F1F26BE2 E3C1C5E2   C1E5C540 40404040 C1E5C5C1 40404040   *     ST   R12,STAESAVE          *
00009480  40404040 E2C1E5C5 C540D9C5 C7404040   C740C6D6 D940C5E2 E3C1C5E8 E3C1C5C2   *          SAVE BASE REG FOR ESTAE *
```

JOB EXA7JHMX   STEP APP3   TIME 125832   DATE 94100   ID = 000   PAGE 00000098

```
000094A0  C5E7C9E3 40404040 40404040 40404040   40404040 40404040 40E2D7C1 C3C5C6F1   *EXIT                    SPACE 1 *
000094C0  40404040 40404040 40404040 40404040   40404040 40404040 40404040 40404040   *                                *

        LINE 000094E0  SAME AS ABOVE

00009500  5C404040 40C9E2E2 E4C540C1 D540C5E2   D540C5E2 E3C1C540 D4C1C3D9 D640E3D6   *     ISSUE AN ESTAE MACRO TO*
00009520  40C1D3D3 D6E640E4 E240E3D6 40C8C1D5   C4D3C540 D6E6D540 D6E6D540 40404040   *     ALLOW US TO HANDLE OUR OWN  *
00009540  5C404040 40404040 40404040 5CE2A404D   5C404040 40C1C2D5 D6D9D4C1 40404040   *          *          ABNORMA*
00009560  D340E3C5 D9D4C9D5 C1E3C9D6 D5E240404D   C1C2C5D5 C4E25D4B 40404040 40404040   *L TERMINATIONS (ABENDS).        *
00009580  40404040 40404040 40404040 40404040   40404040 40404040 40404040 40404040   *                                *
000095A0  E3C1C5C5 40C5E2E3 C1C5C5E2 C1C540E2   E3C1C5C5 E7C9E36B C3E36BD7 E4D9C7C5   *          ESTAE STAEEXIT,CT,PURGE*
000095E0  7ED8E4C9 C5E2C3C5 6BC1E2E8 D5C3C87E   D5D64040 40404040 C3E36BD7 E4D9C7C5   *=QUIESCE,ASYNCH=NO              *
00009600  F76BD9F1 F5404040 40404040 40404040   40404040 40D3E3D9 40404040 40404040   *                        LTR   R*
00009620  C4C54040 40404040 40404040 40404040   E2E340E3 C8C540D9 C5E3E4D9 D540C3D6   *7,R15              TEST THE RETURN CO*
00009640  40404040 40404040 40C2E940 40C2E940   D6D5C540 40404040 40404040 4040C9C6   *DE                          IF*
00009660  40E9C5D9 D66BC7D6 40E3D640 D5D6D9D4   D7D9D6C7 D9C1D440 40E2D7C1 40404040   *     BZ   STAEDONE         ZERO, GO TO NORMAL PROGRAM  *
00009680  40404040 40404040 40404040 40404040   40404040 40404040 40E2D7C1 C3C5C6F1   *                        SPACE 1 *
000096A0  40404040 40404040 40404040 40404040   40404040 40404040 40404040 40404040   *                                *

        LINE 000096C0  SAME AS ABOVE

000096E0  5C404040 40404040 40D7D9C9 D5E340C1   D540C5D9 D9D6D940 D4C5E2E2 C1C7C540   *          PRINT AN ERROR MESSAGE *
00009700  C1D5C440 C5D5C440 C5E7C5C3 E4E3C9D6   D540C9C6 40C5D9D9 D6D940C9 D540C5E2   *AND END EXECUTION IF ERROR IN ES*
00009720  E3C1C540 40404040 40404040 40404040   40404040 40404040 40C3E5C4 404040D9   *TAE                       CVD   R*
00009740  F76BC4D6 E4C2D3C5 E6C44040 40404040   40404040 40404040 40404040 40404040   *7,DOUBLEWD                      *
00009760  40404040 40404040 40404040 40404040   40404040 40404040 40404040 40404040   *                                *
00009780  40404040 40404040 40D6C940 40404040C4   D6E4C2D3 C5E6C44E F76BE77D F0C67D40   *          OI   DOUBLEWD+7,X'0F' *
000097A0  40404040 40404040 40404040 40404040   40404040 40404040 40E4D5D7 D24040E2   *                                *
000097C0  40404040 40404040 40404040 40404040   40404040 40E4D5D7 D24040E2 D24040E2   *                        UNPK  S*
000097E0  E3C1C5E6 E3D64EF9 4DF55D6B C4D6E4C2   D3C5E6C4 40404040 40404040 40404040   *TAEWTO+9(5),DOUBLEWD            *
```

```
00009800  40404040 40404040 40404040 40404040 5C5C5C5C 5C5C5C40 E6C1E240 D9C5E3E4  *STAEWTO WTO '******** WAS RETU*
00009820  E2E3C1C5 E6E3D640 40E6E3D6 40404040 5C5C5C40 40C5D5C4 C9D5C77D 40404040  *RN CODE FROM ESTAE - ENDING'     STH   R*
00009840  D9D540C3 D6C4C540 C6D9D6D4 40C5E2E3 C1C54060 40C5D5C4 C9D5C77D 40404040
00009860  40404040 40404040 40404040 40E2E3C8 40404040 40E2E3C8 40404040 40E2E3C8  *7,RETCODE
00009880  F76BD9C5 E3C3D6C4 C5404040 40404040 40404040 40404040 40404040 40404040
000098A0  40404040 40404040 40C24040 404040C5 40404040 40404040 40404040 404040C5
000098C0  D5C4C5E7 C5C3F240 40404040 40404040 D5C4C5E7 C5C3F240 40404040 40404040  *               B        ENDEXEC2
000098E0  E3C9D6D5 40404040 40E2D7C1 C3C540F1 E3C9D6D5 40404040 40E2D7C1 C3C540F1  *               END EXECUTION        SPACE 1*
00009900  40404040 40E2D7C1 C3C540F1 40404040 40404040 40E2D7C1 C3C540F1 40404040
00009920  40404040 40404040 40404040 40404040 40404040 40404040 40404040 40404040
LINE 00009940  SAME AS ABOVE
00009960  5C404040 40D6D7C5 D540C6C9 D540C6C9 D3C5E240 40404040 40404040 40404040  **               OPEN FILES
00009980  40404040 40404040 40404040 40404040 40404040 40404040 40404040 40404040
000099A0  40404040 40404040 40404040 40404040 E2E3C1C5 C4D6D5C5 40C5D8E4 4040405C  *               STAEDONE EQU      **
000099C0  40404040 40404040 40404040 40404040 40404040 40404040 40404040 40404040
LINE 000099E0  SAME AS ABOVE
00009A00  40404040 40E2D7C1 C3C540F1 40404040 40404040 40404040 40404040 40404040  *               SPACE 1
00009A20  40404040 40404040 40404040 40404040 40404040 40404040 40404040 40404040
00009A40  5C404040 40404040 40404040 40404040 5C404040 40D3D6C1 C440C140 40404040  *              *     LOAD A *
00009A60  D7D9D6C7 D9C1D440 E3D640C3 D9C5C1E3 C540C3D6 D5E3C5D5 E3E24DE4 E4D7C5D9  *PROGRAM TO CREATE CONTENTS SUPER*
00009A80  E5C9E2D6 D940C3D6 D5E3D9D6 D340C2D3 D6C3D2E2 40404040 40404040 40404040  *VISOR CONTROL BLOCKS
00009AA0  40404040 40404040 D6C1C440 C140D7D9 D77EC1D7 D7F3D7C7 D4F24040 40404040  *               LOAD EP=APP3PGM2
00009AC0  40404040 40404040 D6C1C440 C140D7D9 D6C7D9C1 D4404040 40404040 40404040  *               LOAD A PROGRAM       SPACE 1*
00009AE0  40404040 40404040 40E2D7C1 C3C540F1 40E2D7C1 C3C540F1 40404040 40404040
00009B00  40404040 40404040 40404040 40404040 40404040 40404040 40404040 40404040
LINE 00009B20  SAME AS ABOVE
00009B40  40C9C4C5 D5E3C9C6 E84040C5 D77EC2D9 E84BC9C5 D5E3C9C6 6B404040 40404040  *               IDENTIFY EP=BRUINS,
00009B60  40404040 404040C9 C4C5D5E3 C9C6E840 C1D540C5 5E3D9E8 40D7D6C9 D5E34040  *               IDENTIFY AN ENTRY POINT *
00009B80  40404040 404040E7 40404040 40404040 40404040 40404040 40404040 404040C5  *               X                       E*
```

JOB EXA7JHMX   STEP APP3   TIME 125832   DATE 94100   ID = 000   PAGE 00000099

```
00009BA0  D5E3D9E8 7EE4D9E2 C1404040 40404040 40404040 40C1D5C4 40C9E3E2 40404040  *NTRY=URSA                           AND ITS*
00009BC0  40D3D6C3 C1E3C9D6 D5404040 40404040 40404040 40404040 40404040 40404040  * LOCATION
00009BE0  40404040 40E2D7C1 C3C540F1 40404040 40404040 40404040 40404040 40404040  *               SPACE 1
00009C00  40404040 40404040 40404040 40404040 40404040 40C3D9C5 C1E3C540 40404040  *              *     CREATE *
00009C20  40404040 C140E2C5 D7C1D9C1 E3C5404D C4C1E4C7 C8E3C5D9 5D40E3C3 C2404040  *A SEPARATE (DAUGHTER) TCB
00009C40  C140E2C5 D7C1D9C1 E3C5404D C4C1E4C7 40404040 40404040 40404040 40404040
00009C60  40404040 40404040 40404040 40404040 40404040 40404040 40404040 40404040
```

```
00009C80  40404040 40404040 40C1E3E3 C1C3C840  C5D77EC1 D7D7F3D7 C7D4F36B 40404040  *  ATTACH EP=APP3PGM3,       *
00009CA0  40404040 40C1E3E3 E3C1C3C8 40C1D5D6  E3C8C5D9 40D7D9D6 C7D9C1D4 40404040  *  ATTACH ANOTHER PROGRAM   P*
00009CC0  40404040 404040E7 40404040 40404040  6B404040 4040D6D5 C540D7C1 D9C1D4C5  *   X             ONE PARAME*
00009CE0  C1D9C1D4 7E4DE7C5 C3C25D6B E5D37EF1  6B404040 404040E7 40404040 40404040  *ARAM=(XECB),VL=1,     X    *
00009D00  E3C5D940 D7C1E2E2 C5C44040 40404040  C5C3C27E E3C1E2D2 C5C3C26B 40404040  *TER PASSED      ECB=TASKECB,*
00009D20  40404040 4040D7D6 E2E3C5C4 40C2E840  D4E5E240 E6C8C5D5 40E3C3C2 40C5D5C4  *      POSTED BY MVS WHEN TCB END*
00009D40  E2404040 40404040 E7404040 40404040  40404040 40404040 40404040 404040E2  *S        X                     S*
00009D60  C8E2D7E5 7EF3F340 40404040 40404040  40404040 4040E2C8 C1D9C540 E2E4C2D7  *HSPV=33            SHARE SUBP*
00009D80  D6D6D340 F3F34040 40404040 40404040  40404040 40404040 40404040 40404040  *OOL 33                      *
00009DA0  40404040 40404040 40404040 E2D7C1C3  C540F140 40404040 40404040 40404040  *            SPACE 1         *
00009DC0  40404040 40404040 40404040 40404040  40404040 40404040 40404040 40404040  *                            *
00009DE0  40404040 40404040 40404040 40404040  40404040 40404040 40404040 40404040  *                            *
00009E00  40404040 40404040 40404040 40404040  40404040 C5D5D840 D6D54040 40404040  *                 ENQ ON     *
00009E20  E2D6D4C5 40C9D4C1 C7C9D5C1 D9E840D5  C1D4C540 E3D640C3 D9C5C1E3 C540C7D9  *SOME IMAGINARY NAME TO CREATE GR*
00009E40  D6E4D740 40404040 C3D6D5E3 D9D6D340  C2D3D6C3 D2E24040 40404040 40404040  *S CONTROL BLOCKS            *
00009E60  40404040 4040C5D5 D8404040 4040404D  C6D6D66B C2C1D96B C56BF36B E2E8E2E3  *      ENQ   (FOO,BAR,E,3,SYST*
00009E80  C5D45D40 40404040 C5D5D840 D6D540C6  D6D66060 C2C1D940 40404040 40404040  *EM)    ENQ ON FOO-BAR       *
00009EA0  40404040 40404040 40404040 40404040  40404040 E2D7C1C3 C540F140 40404040  *                   SPACE 1  *
00009EC0  40404040 40404040 40404040 40404040  40404040 40404040 40404040 40404040  *                            *
     LINE 00009EE0  SAME AS ABOVE
00009F00  40404040 40404040 D7C5D9C6 D6D9D440  C140E5C5 C3E3D6D9 40D6D7C5 D9C1E3C9  *      PERFORM A VECTOR OPERAT*
00009F20  D6D540E3 D640C6D6 D9C3C540 C3D7E440  C1C6C6C9 D5C9E3E8 40404040 40404040  *ION TO FORCE CPU AFFINITY   *
00009F40  40404040 4040E4D9 E2C14040 40404040  C5D8E440 40404040 5C5C4040 40404040  *      URSA      EQU   **     *
00009F60  40404040 40404040 40404040 40404040  40404040 40404040 40404040 40404040  *                            *
     LINE 00009F80  SAME AS ABOVE
00009FA0  40404040 40404040 E5E3E5D4 40404040  40406B40 40404040 40404040 40404040  *      VTVM ,                *
00009FC0  40404040 4040E3C5 E2E340E5 C5C3E3D6  D940D4C1 E2D240D9 C5C7C9E2 E3C5D940  *      TEST VECTOR MASK REGISTER*
00009FE0  40404040 40404040 40404040 40404040  40404040 E2D7C1C3 C540F140 40404040  *                   SPACE 1  *
0009D0FE0 00000000 00000000 00000000 00000000  00000000 00000004 00000000 00007FE0  *................*
0009D1000 00000000 00000000 00000000 00000000  00000000  SAME AS ABOVE
     LINES 009D1020-009D1FC0  SAME AS ABOVE
0009D1FE0 009D206C 00007F74 00000000 009D1FC8  *.&.".........H.........."\*
```

The Task I/O Table follows. This was formatted earlier in the dump.

```
009D2000  C5E7C1F7 D1C8D4E7 C1D7D7F3 40404040  40404040 40404040 14010100 E2E3C5D7  *EXA7JHMXAPP3        ....STEP*
009D2020  D3C9C240 9ED23000 80F24D90 14010102  E2E8E2D7 D9C9D5E3 9ECB8000 80000000  *LIB K..2(....SYSPRINT.......*
009D2040  14010100 E2E8E2E4 C4E4D4D7 9ECA0000  80F24D90 14010100 D7C4E240 40404040  *....SYSUDUMP....2(.....PDS  *
```

```
009D2060  9EC88000 80F24D90 00000000 14010100 E2E3C5D7 D3C9C240 9ED23000 80F24D90  *.H...2(........STEPLIB .K...2(.*
009D2080  14010102 E2E8E2D7 D9C9D5E3 9EC88000 80000000 14010100 E2E8E2E4 C4E4D4D7  *....SYSPRINT.H......SYSUDUMP*
009D20A0  9ECA0000 80F24D90 14010100 D7C4E240 40404040 9EC88000 80F24D90 00000000  *......2(....PDS     .H...2(....*
009D20C0  00000000 00000000 00000000 00000000 00000000 00000000 00000000 00000000  *................................*
          LINES 009D20E0-009D2FC0  SAME AS ABOVE
009D2FE0  00000000 00000000 00000000 00000000 00000000 00000000 00000000 00000000  *................................*

009DE500  00000000 00000948 00000000 00000000 00000000 009DE528 009DE508 00000000  *................................*
009DE520  009DE508 009DE508 009DE528 40E1E970 009DE1F0 40E1E970 810C0AE0 00000094  *........V.&...W..V.*
009DE540  009DE528 00000050 00E010D2 00E01E000 00E019EE 00480000 009DE5CC 00000000  *.V...V...<..S....0 .Z.a..\..m*
009DE560  00000000 00E013F6 009DE5A4 009DE5D4 009DE5F4 009DE5F8 00000000 00000000  *.V...&.\K..\......V.*
009DE580  00000000 009DE5EC 009DE528 01000000 00000000 00000000 00000000 00000000  *...\.6...0.V..Vu.VM.V4.V8*
009DE5A0  00C0C000 C9C6C7F0 F1F9F8D5 00000000 00000000 0000C379 00040004 00000000  *......V...............*
009DE5C0  00C0C000 00000000 13308000 E0000000 0C0C379 00040004 00000000 00000000  *...IFG0198N...........V..C...*
009DE5E0  00000000 009DE1F0 8F9DE1F0 8F000000 F0E2E000 00000000 00000000 00000000  *........0S\.......0...0.....*
```

JOB EXA7JHMX   STEP APP3   TIME 125832   DATE 94100   ID = 000   PAGE 00000100

```
009DE600  009DAEC0 00000000 00000000 00000000 00000000 00000000 00000000 00000000  *...(............................*
009DE620  00000000 00000000 00000000 00000000 00000000 00000000 00000000 00000000  *................................*
          LINES 009DE640-009DEE20  SAME AS ABOVE
009DEE40  00000000 00000000 00000000 00000000 00FEE898 80DB11A8 00FEE898 80DAE000  *...(.........Yq..y.Yq..\.*
009DEE60  00DAE006 2D00070C 00000005 17200002 039DF348 009DB560 68000000 00000000  *.\...........3....-...*
009DEE80  00011100 05000000 FF000000 8F006F3C 049DEE50 58F24D90 000000C4 001100C4  *.......?..&.2(...D..D*
009DEEA0  00010001 58F24D90 0000043F 00000001 58F24D90 0000053A 0007053A 00000000  *...2(....?...2(...D..D*
009DEEC0  00070001 58F24D90 0000046B 00050001 58F24D90 0000046C 0004046C 00000000  *...2(.....2(....%..%*
009DEEE0  00040001 F3C2C2C1 C2C20000 00040001 00000000 00000000 00000000 00000000  *.3BBABB..............%.*
009DEF00  00000000 00000000 C3E5C3D7 000000F8 009DEF28 500000E6 009DB6B8 00000000  *........CVCP....8..&..W...*
009DEF20  00000000 009DB090 00000100 00000000 009DEF28 00000004 009DB448 00000000  *................................*
009DEF40  00000000 00000000 80E0A6C6 80E21936 009D2054 009DB0B0 009DB2C0 00000000  *........wF.S....{.....*
009DEF60  00000000 00000000 00000000 009DEFA8 009DB240 00E0A04A 009DB2C0 00000000  *................................*
009DEF80  00E21898 009DB754 009DB7A4 009D2054 00F24D90 009DEF28 009DEFA8 00000000  *.S.q...u......y...(*
009DEFA0  009DEF60 80E21A7E C3E5D7D3 80000400 00F24D90 009DB0B0 009DEFE8 00000000  *..S.=CVPL......2(...Y*
009DEFC0  00000000 00000000 00400100 00000000 00000000 009DB0B0 00000000 00000000  *................................*
009DEFE0  00000000 00000000 015400E6 40008C05 2D00071A 009DB0B0 00000000 00000000  *...............W.........*
```

Some addresses are duplicated from the LSQA section of the dump. These are deleted through location 9DFFFE0 for brevity.

```
009E0000  00000000 00000000 00000000 00000000   00000000 00000000 00000000 00000000   *................................*
          LINES 009E0020-009E00E0  SAME AS ABOVE
009E0100  00000000 00000000 00000000 C3E5C9D6   E6500118 C9D5C9E3 00000000 009E0120   *.........CVIOW&..INIT...*
009E0120  00000000 0000052A E2E6C1D4 00000000   01000000 009E00F0 00FEE948 00FEE948   *.2(....SWAM....}...&.W...*
009E0140  00F24D90 00000000 00000000 000000D0   000000B0 009E0168 500000E6 009E06B8   *................0..Z.*
009E0160  009E0380 009E06B8 009E0240 9ED2301C   00000000 009E0180 00E2186C 00E21853   *........K .K.......S.*
009E0180  80E2167E 84A29358 009E0168 7FFE3E08   00000000 80E2186C 80E21DD6 009E0178   *.....".....S.=dsl..S.%...*
009E01A0  009E0484 00E21578 009E023C 00E1E000   00000000 80E21DD6 009E0168 40404040   *..d.S........}......S.O...*
009E01C0  00E21853 F8C20000 00000000 009E06B8   00000000 40404040 40404040 40404040   *.S..............*
009E01E0  C4C1E3C1 F8C20000 00FEE898 00FEE898   00000000 00000000 00FEE898 00FEE898   *DATA8B..............*
009E0200  00FEE898 00000000 00000000 00000000   00000000 00000000 00FEE898 00FEE898   *...........Yq..Yq*
009E0220  00000000 68000000 00001100 2A000D20   009E02A0 11020001 009F9028 009F9028   *..Yq.Yq.Yq.........Yq..Yq*
009E0240  68000000 0000009D 0003009D FF000000   0F9FD060 049E0218 58F24D90 58F24D90   *.......&2(....)-...2(.*
009E0260  0000009D 0003009D 00030001 50F24D90   0000046F 0000046F 000E000F 00000000   *.....&2(....?.?.?....*
009E0280  C4C3C240 00000080 009E03A0 0200D008   00000000 00000000 00000000 00000000   *........\....}...*
009E02A0  00540000 009E1370 200007E0 00000000   00000000 00000000 00000000 00000000   *.........\....}...}.*
009E02C0  00474723 00000000 00000000 00000000   00000000 00000000 00000000 00000000   *..................*
009E02E0  00000088 009E0318 500000E6 009E0380   009E06B8 E2E6C1D4 9ED2301C 9ED2301C   *............SWAM.*
009E0300  000000B0 009E0330 00E21851 009E0318   00000000 009ED240 7FFE3E08 7FFE3E08   *.h..&.W.......K .K.*
009E0320  84A29358 00000000 80E216D6 009E02F8   00E21578 000000E6 00E1E000 00E1E000   *.......S........."..*
009E0340  80E1E57E 00000000 00000080 00E21851   009E06B8 009E06B8 009E06B8 009E06B8   *.S.=dsl........8.S....W.\.*
009E0360  C4C3C240 00000000 00000000 500000E6   009E06B8 009E0400 009E0400 00000001   *.V=....S.O...S........*
009E0380  02000001 0018D008 002E0000 00000001   00000200 00000001 00000000 00000000   *DCB.......&.W....*
009E03A0  C0000000 00000000 000002B8 1200D008   00000000 00000000 00000000 00000000   *.........1}...}..*
009E03C0  D6D7E6C1 00000000 009E0420 500000E6   009E06B8 009E06B8 009E06B8 009E06B8   *.....(..}....}.}.*
009E03E0  F1C4C1E3 C1F8C200 015E005E 00000002   000C9C2 D4D6E2E5 E2F24040 4040405E   *.................*
009E0400  00640000 C0000200 C0004800 00828000   00010001 2B4E0000 4040405E 01010000   *OPWA.......&..W.....*
009E0420  9D000300 01046F00 0046F00 0E000000    00000000 00000000 01010000 00000000   *1DATA8B..;.;...IBMOSVS2 .;*
009E0440  C5E7C1F7 D1C8D44B D7C4E24B D3D6C1C4   40404040 40404040 40404040 40404040   *.......+....b.....*
009E0460  40404040 40404040 40404040 40404040   804D8320 00000000 00020000 00020000   *.....a.?.?........*
009E0480  40404040 00000200 C0004800 5E005E00   00000048 00000000 00000000 00000000   *.......EXA7JHM.PDS.LOAD*
009E04A0  40404040 40404040 40404040 40404040   40404040 804D8320 00020000 00020000   *..............(c........*
009E04C0  00000000 00000200 C0004800 5E005E00   00000048 00000000 00000000 00000000   *............;.;..*
009E04E0  40404040 40404040 40404040 40404040   0001C4C1 E3C1F8C2 E3C1F8C2 00000000   *.........(.........DATA8B*
009E0500  40404040 40404040 40404040 40404040
009F0920
009F0940  009F1B30 009F1930 009F0A64 00000000   00FD5B90 009EDF00 009EC580 009F1930   *...........$......E..*
009F0960  009EDF58 009EDCO0 009F0BDC 009F1A6C   00000000 00E2F647 009F08A0 80E2E648   *............S6....SW.*
009F0980  00000000 00000000 00000000 809F0EE4   00000000 00000000 009F1930 00000000   *.......%.........*
009F09A0  00000000 00000000 00000000 00000000   00000000 00000000 00000000 00000000   *......u..U........*
```

```
          LINES 009F09C0-009F09E0   SAME AS ABOVE
009F0A00  00000000 00000000 80CBA850 00006128 009F0A54 00160100 84715ECC   *................hd.;..y&../.......*
009F0A20  80E2E8C2 00000008 00F7F1B0 009EDF00 009EC580 009F1B30 009F1930   *.SYB......71.......E...........*

JOB EXA7JHMX    STEP APP3    TIME 125832    DATE 94100    ID = 000    PAGE 00000103

009F0A40  009F1930 009F0A64 00000000 00000000 00E2F647 009F08A0 80E2E648 009F08A0   *......S6.....SW.....*
009F0A60  00000010 00000000 0000FFFF 00000000 00000000 80000000 00000000 00000000   *...................*
009F0A80  80000000 00000000 00000000 00000000 00000000 00000000 00000000 00000000   *...................*
009F0AA0  00000000 9ED83001 000000B0 00000000 00000000 009ED830 00100000           *..........Q.Q......*
009F0AC0  00000000 00000000 00000000 009F0BF0 00000000 00060F00 00160100 00100000   *...................*
009F0AE0  00000000 00000000 00010321 847159A4 7FFFC9F0 009F0AF0 0000E612 00000000   *....0d..u..-0......W.*
009F0B00  009F9028 009F0A00 00010321 847159A4 7FFFC9F0 009F0AF0 00F7F080 00000000   *...70." IO...0..-0.70.*
009F0B20  04715818 009F0A00 847159E2 04715EA6 00000000 009F0AF0 00000000 00000000   *.....d..S..;w......*
009F0B40  00000000 00000000 00000000 00000000 00000000 00000000 00000000 00000000   *...................*
          LINES 009F0B60-009F0BA0   SAME AS ABOVE
009F0BC0  00000000 00000000 00000000 009FF068 00000003 009F1B30 009F0BE0           *.....0...0q.......\*
009F0BE0  00005C00 0000002F 00000003 00000025 0000000F 00000000 D7D7E2C3 00140080   *.*.........PPSC....*
009F0C00  009EDDEC 009F0A62 00000000 00000000 00AA0400 00000280 009F1930 009EFED4   *..................M*
009F0C20  00000000 009EFE68 00000000 009EE3C0 00000400 00000000 0000C5E7 C1F7D1C8   *.......T(.....EXA7JH*
009F0C40  00000000 00000000 00000000 00000000 D4400000 00005001 00005000 C1F7D1C8   *M......&....ofma.*
009F0C60  D4400000 94A2849D 81155555 80525556 5555B7BD 1515B196 869481B0           *.M..msd.a......j.bfvl*
009F0C80  B71590B2 94A2849D 81155555 55555555 55555555 55555555 8286A593           *.....msd.a......j.bfvl*
009F0CA0  91975555 55555555 55555902 94A2849D 81155555 555591B7 00000000           *jp........msd.a.....*
009F0CC0  7F783800 009F0D88 009F08A0 80B2CAEE 80E2E648 00000000 009F0E9D           *".....h...S..SW....*
009F0CE0  009F0EE4 00000000 009F1930 009F1B30 00000001 000000C0 00000250           *.U.....h.......{..&*
009F0D00  009F0CC0 80E2C880 009F0E9D 00000000 00000000 009F1930 80CBAE4C           *................(*
009F0D20  00000000 00000000 00000000 10000000 00000000 00000000 00000000           *(.SH..............<*
009F0D40  009F1930 009FF060 00000000 00000000 009F0D44 00000000 20010000           *...............5...*
009F0D60  00000000 00000000 1E000000 009DF510 009F0CC0 80E2C29A 009F0D88           *.......0-....5.....*
009F0D80  00000001 0E2CDB0 00000000 C6F1E2C1 009F0CC0 80E2C880 0321002A            *...S....F1SA..{.SB..SH.*
009F0DA0  009F0E14 009F9028 009FD01C 009F0E9D 00B92080 009F0E9D 009FD01C           *.....&H..h.S{..}..}.*
009F0DC0  00000000 00FD50C8 009F0D88 80E2C000 80005FFE 80E2C1D0 0321002A           *.....J...9.....}.*
009F0DE0  009F0E14 00000004 809F0ED1 00F90148 009F0E9D 009F0E9D 009FD01C           *.....d..h.S{..d....*
009F0E00  00000001 009F0E84 009F0D88 80E2C000 009F0E84 00000057 00000041           *...................*
009F0E20  00000000 00000000 00000000 00000000 00000000 00000000 00000000           *...................*
          LINES 009F0E40-009F0E60   SAME AS ABOVE
009F0E80  00000000 80000000 00000000 00000000 00000000 00000000 009F0F0E           *..................*
```

```
009F0EA0  E4000000 00009F0E B5000000 00000000   00809F0E D1001C00 080000ED 00000000  *U..................J.........*
009F0EC0  00000000 00000000 00000000 00000000   00001000 00000000 00000000 00000000  *..............................*
009F0EE0  00000000 E2E2D6C2 001C0000 009F0F00   00000000 E63C0000 00000000 00000000  *.....SSOB.....................*
009F0F00  E2E2C9C2 00240002 D1C5E2F2 D1D6C2F0   F8F3F9F1 00000000 00000000 00000000  *SSIB....JES2JOB08391..........*
009F0F20  099C5E80 00144000 00BAB2D8 00010000   00000000 D1C5E2F2 2D0740F4 00000000  *..;....Q........JES2.. 4.....*
009F0F40  00000000 80800080 0000000C 00B00100   E2E2E5C9 00000030 00300000 E2D740F4  *................SSVI........SP 4*
009F0F60  4BF34BF0 C8D1C5F4 F4F3F040 D1C5E2F2   40404040 407D6BD1 C5E26DD4 06D6D6D1  *.3.0HJE4430 JES2    .',JES_M...J*
009F0F80  C5E26DD5 D6C4C57E 7DE4C3D3 C1D4E5E2   406BD1C5 E26DD4C5 D4C2C5D9 D5C1D4C5  *ES_NODE='UCLAMVS ,JES_MEMBERNAM*
009F0FA0  C57E7DD6 C1C3F17D 6BC4E8D5 C1D4C9C3   7DE4E37E 7DE8C5E2 7D6BC9D5 D3C56DE2  *E='OAC1',DYNAMIC_OUTPUT='YES',IN*
009F0FC0  C9E3C9C1 E3D6D96D D9C5E2E3 C1D9E37E   7DE8C5E2 7D6BD4E4 D3E3C9D7 D3C56DE2  *ITIATOR_RESTART='YES',MULTIPLE_S*
009F0FE0  E3C3E3E2 D67E7DE8 C5E27D00 00000000   00000000 00000000 00000000 00000000  *TCTSO='YES',..................*
009F1000  00000000 00000000 00000000 00000000   00000000 00000000 00000000 00000000  *..............................*
          LINES 009F1020-009F1900  SAME AS ABOVE
009F1920  00000000 009EDF00 9EDD7000 D1C5E2F2   00B9A780 68000000 009F9028 00000000  *.................x.....JES2...*
009F1940  009EDF00 009EDD80 9EDD7000 00000000   68000000 009F1930 009D2000 00000000  *.........................JES2.*
009F1960  009F1930 009F1930 00000000 00000000   00000000 00000000 00000000 00000000  *.........................}....*
009F1980  009F1980 00000000 00007FD0 00000000   009FD060 00000000 809FE000 00000000  *..........."..........}-....*
009F19A0  009F0718 80E352BE 00E35820 0321000A   009FD060 00E35840 7FFE59B0 009F1930  *......T.T....-.0-.Q..*
009F19C0  009F1B30 FFFFFFFF 009EDDB0 009DF060   809DF510 00F7F080 009DF348 00E349F2  *.............0-.5.70..3.T.2*
009F19E0  009ED840 9ED83001 000000B0 00000000   00000000 009EDB30 00100000 009F19E0  *..Q..Q..................\*
009F1A00  009F19FC 00E35818 EDE00000 009F1A10   009EDE40 9EDE3000 000000B0 00000000  *.........Q..T.............*
009F1A20  00000000 00000000 ED000000 00000000   02000000 00000025 00000000 00000000  *................\..........*
009F1A40  00000000 00000000 119F19E0 00000000   00000000 00000000 009EDC00 009F91D0  *..........................*
009F1A60  00000000 00000000 00000000 009F1B30   00F7F080 00000000 00000000 00000000  *.................70.........*
          LINES 009F1A80-... 
```

JOB EXA7JHMX   STEP APP3   TIME 125832   DATE 94100   ID = 000   PAGE 00000104

```
009F1A80  00000000 810A3A10 00000000 00000000   009F0E9D 08008000 009F91CC 00000004  *....a.............j....*
009F1AA0  00000000 009F0D44 009F0EE4 9EDEF000   08008000 009EDE40 7FFE59B0 00000000  *.........U..."..*
009F1AC0  00000000 00000000 009D9FE0 9EDEF000   00180000 009D1FE0 00000000 00000000  *.........\....*
009F1AE0  00000000 00000000 167F8700 00000000   009EDDC0 00000000 00000000 00000000  *......."g....*
009F1B00  00000000 00000000 C5D5C4D6 C6D3C3E3   009EDDC0 00000000 00000000 00FC23B0  *........ENDOFLCT....*
009F1B20  00000000 00000080 C5D5C4D6 C000F0C0   C9D5C9E3 D7D5E3 80BF00C0 00FC23B0  *........ENDOFLCTINITPNT.{.*
009F1B40  E0000EEC 80000080 C5D5C4D6 EE3FC000   C9D5C9E3 D7D5E3 80BF00C0 00E0009F  *.{.(.(..W.\.*
009F1B60  EFFE8000 0000B87F E0000000 0017FFE1   FFE08000 00000000 E0E0009F 00000000  *.......".\..\\\..*
009F1B80  80000000 00001A   809F1B80 C1C3E340   9F1B8001 00000000 00000000 00000000  *............ACT.*
009F1BA0  00000000 00000000 010000B0 C1C3E340   00000000 00000000 00000000 00000000  *............ACT...*
          LINES 009F1BC0-009F1C20  SAME AS ABOVE
```

```
009F1C40  00000019  009F1C40  0C0000B0  E2C3E3E7                                            *..............SCTX.*
009F1C60  00000000  00000000  00000000  00000000                                            *...................*
   LINES 009F1C80-009F1CE0  SAME AS ABOVE
009F1D00  00000018  809F1D00  0C0000B0  E2C3E3E7                                            *..............SCTX.*
009F1D20  00000000  00000000  00000000  00000000                                            *...................*
   LINE 009F1D40  SAME AS ABOVE
009F1D60  00000000  00000000  00000000  0083D600                                            *..............cO.*
009F1D80  00000000  00000000  00000000  00000000                                            *...................*
   LINE 009F1DA0  SAME AS ABOVE
009F1DC0  00000017  009F1DC0  010000B0  C1C3E340                                            *......{...ACT .*
009F1DE0  00000000  00000000  00000000  00000000                                            *...................*
   LINES 009F1E00-009F1E60  SAME AS ABOVE
009F1E80  00000016  009F1E80  000000B0  00000000                                            *...................*
009F1EA0  00000000  00000000  00000000  00000000                                            *...................*
   LINES 009F1EC0-009F1F20  SAME AS ABOVE
009F1F40  00000015  009F1F40  030000B0  E2C9D6E3                                            *........SIOT .*
009F1F60  00000000  00000000  00000000  00000000                                            *...................*
   LINES 009F1F80-009F1FE0  SAME AS ABOVE
009F2000  00000000  00000000  00000000  00000000                                            *...................*
   LINES 009F2020-009F22E0  SAME AS ABOVE
009F2300  C3D7D6D6  D340C3C5  D3D34D07  D6D6D340  40404040  40404040  00000001  009F2328   *CPOOL CELL POOL ..*
009F2320  7FFFC450  00000000  009F2370  00000000  00480000  009F5018  009FBC18              *".D&.........&.*
009F2340  00000000  00000000  00009180  00000000  009FDE88  D1C5E2F2  09BE0824              *...j...h...JES2*
009F2360  00000000  00000000  009FBC28  00000000  009F23B8  00000000  00000000              *...................*
009F2380  00000000  00000000  00000000  00000000  00000000  00000000  00000000              *...................*
009F23A0  00000000  00000000  00000000  00000000  00000000  009F2400  00000000              *...................*
009F23C0  00000000  00000000  00000000  00000000  00000000  00000000  00000000              *...................*
   LINE 009F23E0  SAME AS ABOVE
009F2400  009F2448  00000000  00000000  00000000  00000000  00000000  00000000              *...................*
009F2420  00000000  00000000  009F2370  00000000  00000000  00000000  00000000              *...................*
009F2440  00000000  00000000  009F2490  00000000  00000000  00000000  00000000              *...................*
009F2460  00000000  00000000  009FBC28  00000000  00000000  00000000  00000000              *...................*
009F2480  00000000  00000000  00000000  00000000  009F24D8  00000000  00000000              *...........Q.*
009F24A0  00000000  00000000  00000000  00000000  00000000  00000000  00000000              *...................*
009F24C0  00000000  00000000  009F2490  00000000  00000000  009F2520  00000000              *...................*
009F24E0  00000000  00000000  00000000  00000000  00000000  00000000  00000000              *...................*
   LINE 009F2500  SAME AS ABOVE
009F2520  009F2568  00000000  00000000  00000000  00000000  00000000  00000000              *...................*
009F2540  00000000  00000000  009F25B0  00000000  00000000  00000000  00000000              *...................*
009F2560  00000000  00000000  009F25B0  00000000  00000000  00000000  00000000              *...................*
```

```
            LINE 009F2620  SAME AS ABOVE
009F2580 00000000 00000000 00000000 00000000    00000000 00000000 00000000 00000000    *................................*
009F25A0 00000000 00000000 00000000 00000000    009F25F8 00000000 00000000 00000000    *...............8................*
009F25C0 00000000 00000000 00000000 00000000    00000000 00000000 009F2640 00000000    *................................*
009F25E0 00000000 00000000 00000000 00000000    00000000 00000000 00000000 00000000    *................................*
009F2600 00000000 00000000 00000000 00000000    00000000 00000000 00000000 00000000    *................................*

JOB EXA7JHMX        STEP APP3         TIME 125832      DATE 94100    ID = 000                PAGE 00000105

            LINE 009F2620  SAME AS ABOVE
009F2640 009F2688 00000000 00000000 00000000    00000000 00000000 00000000 00000000    *.h..............................*
009F2660 00000000 00000000 009F26D0 00000000    00000000 00000000 00000000 00000000    *...........)....................*
009F2680 00000000 00000000 00000000 00000000    00000000 00000000 00000000 00000000    *................................*
009F26A0 00000000 00000000 00000000 00000000    00000000 00000000 00000000 00000000    *................................*
009F26C0 00000000 00000000 00000000 00000000    009F2718 00000000 00000000 00000000    *................................*
009F26E0 00000000 00000000 00000000 00000000    00000000 00000000 00000000 00000000    *............-...................*
009F2700 00000000 00000000 00000000 00000000    00000000 00000000 009F2760 00000000    *................................*
009F2720 00000000 00000000 00000000 00000000    00000000 00000000 00000000 00000000    *................................*
            LINE 009F2740  SAME AS ABOVE
009F2760 009F27A8 00000000 00000000 00000000    00000000 00000000 00000000 00000000    *.y..............................*
009F2780 00000000 00000000 00000000 00000000    00000000 00000000 00000000 00000000    *................................*
009F27A0 00000000 00000000 009F27F0 00000000    00000000 00000000 00000000 00000000    *...........0....................*
009F27C0 00000000 00000000 00000000 00000000    00000000 00000000 00000000 00000000    *................................*
009F27E0 00000000 00000000 00000000 00000000    009F2838 00000000 00000000 00000000    *................................*
009F2800 00000000 00000000 00000000 00000000    00000000 00000000 00000000 00000000    *................................*
009F2820 00000000 00000000 00000000 00000000    00000000 00000000 009F2880 00000000    *................................*
009F2840 00000000 00000000 00000000 00000000    00000000 00000000 00000000 00000000    *................................*
            LINE 009F2860  SAME AS ABOVE
009F2880 009F28C8 00000000 00000000 00000000    00000000 00000000 00000000 00000000    *.H..............................*
009F28A0 00000000 00000000 00000000 00000000    00000000 00000000 00000000 00000000    *................................*
009F28C0 00000000 00000000 009F2910 00000000    00000000 00000000 00000000 00000000    *................................*
009F28E0 00000000 00000000 00000000 00000000    00000000 00000000 00000000 00000000    *................................*
009F2900 00000000 00000000 00000000 00000000    009F2958 00000000 00000000 00000000    *................................*
009F2920 00000000 00000000 00000000 00000000    00000000 00000000 00000000 00000000    *................................*
009F2940 00000000 00000000 00000000 00000000    00000000 00000000 00000000 00000000    *................................*
009F8020 00000000 00000000 00000000 00000000    00000000 00000000 00000000 00000000    *................................*
009F8040 00000000 00000000 00000000 00000000    A91B9AA3 00000000 00000000 0204FC03    *...........z..t.................*
009F8060 00000000 00000000 D1C3E340 09B00000    FFFFFFFF FFFFFFFF FFFFFFFF 0204FC03    *.........JCT....................*
009F8080 00000000 00000000 0204FB06 00000000    00000000 00000000 00000000 FFFFFFFF    *................................*
```

```
009F80A0  FFFFFFFF FFFFFFFF FFFFFFFF FFFFFFFF   FFFFFFFF 00000064 00000064 00000000   *................*
009F80C0  00000000 00000000 00000000 00000000   00000000 00000000 00000000 00000000   *................*
          LINE 009F80E0  SAME AS ABOVE
009F8100  40400000 03211700 54600000 30040000   E2E3C3F0 F6F7F4F2 C9D5C9E3 40404040   *......-....STC06742INIT *
009F8120  40404040 40404040 40404040 40404040   40404040 E8D08080 00000000 00010000   *           Y)......*
009F8140  E2E3C3C9 D5D9C4D9 00015180 3B9AC618   3B9AC618 000F423F E2E3C440 00010000   *STCINRDR..9904....F....STD.*
009F8160  40404040 00010000 000F423F 7FFFFD78   40404040 40404040 40404040 00010000   *.........."......*
009F8180  40404040 40404040 D7D9D6C3 F0F04040   00000000 00000000 40404040 40404040   *........PROC00 ......*
009F81A0  00000000 00000000 00000000 00000000   0004C9D5 C9E34040 00000000 40404040   *..........INIT ......*
009F81C0  404009B0 00000000 50018051 B7BDB786   83B31515 B1968694 81B0B715 808C918C   *&.....fc...ofma.*
009F81E0  9C809CB6 15151515 55555555 55555555   55555555 B7B6969C 808C918C 0094100F   *.....o..j.*
009F8200  55555555 55555555 9C809CB6 15151515   55555555 55555555 B7B6969C 0028384F   *.......!.m.*
009F8220  0028385A 0094100F 00283898 00283717   00000000 00000242 00000009 00000000   *..!.m...q.m.*
009F8240  00000000 00000000 00000000 00000242   00000000 D6C1C3F1 D6C1C3F1 D6C1C3F1   *..........OAC1OAC1OAC1*
009F8260  00000000 00000000 00000009 00000000   00000000 00000000 00000000 00000000   *................*
009F8280  00000000 00010000 00000000 00000000   E2E3C3F0 F6F7F4F2 00000000 00000000   *....STC06742....*
009F82A0  E4C3D3C1 D4E5E240 C9D5C9E3 40404040   E4C3D3C1 D4E5E240 00000000 00000000   *UCLAMVS INIT    UCLAMVS*
009F82C0  00000000 3BAA0857 00000000 00000000   00000000 00000000 00000000 00000000   *................*
009F82E0  E4C3D3C1 D4E5E240 40404040 40404040   E4C3D3C1 D4E5E240 40404040 40404040   *UCLAMVS    UCLAMVS    *
          LINE 009F8300  SAME AS ABOVE
009F8320  0F000000 00000000 00000000 00000000   00000000 00000000 00000000 00000000   *................*
009F8340  00000000 00000000 00000000 00000000   00000000 00000000 00000000 00000000   *................*
          LINES 009F8360-009F83A0  SAME AS ABOVE
009F83C0  C9D5C9E3 40404040 00283717 0094100F   D6C1C3F1 64000000 00000000 01F802D0   *INIT    ...m..OAC1.....8.)*
009F83E0  00000000 002837A9 00000000 0094100F   00000000 0000F800 FFFFFFFF FFFFFFFF   *.....z.m.....8..*
009F8400  FFFFFFFF FFFFFFFF FFFFFFFF FFFFFFFF   FFFFFFFF 0000E658 00000000 00000000   *..........W.....*
```

```
JOB EXA7JHMX        STEP APP3          TIME 125832    DATE 94100    ID = 000              PAGE 00000106

009F8420  00000000 A91B9A91 C4690485 40404040   0204FB04 0204FB05 D0080000 00000000   *...z..jD..e......).....*
009F8440  A91B9A91 C4690485 40404040 40404040   A91B9A8E 18706601 40404040 40404040   *z..jD..e......z.....*
009F8460  40404040 40404040 40404040 40404040   40404040 40404040 40404040 40404040   *                    *
009F8480  00000000 00000000 00000000 00000000   00000000 00000000 00000000 00000000   *................*
009F84A0  00000000 00000000 00000000 00000000   D6C1C3D1 04000000 00000000 00000000   *............OACJ....*
009F84C0  00000000 00000000 00000000 00000000   00000000 00000000 00000000 00000000   *................*
          LINES 009F84E0-009F8500  SAME AS ABOVE
009F8520  00000000 64000000 00000000 00000000   00000000 00000000 00000000 00000000   *................*
009F8540  00000000 00000000 00000000 00000000   00000000 00000000 00000000 00000000   *................*
```

```
                 LINES 009F8560-009F8580  SAME AS ABOVE
009F85A0 00000000 00000000 00000000 00000000   C9D5C9E3 40404040 00004100 C9D5C9E3   *................INIT........INIT*
009F85C0 C9C1E3D6 D9404040 40404040 40404040   E7F5F7F4 F2F44040 40404040 A91B9A8F   *IATOR        X57424       z...*
009F85E0 6F013F01 00000000 00000000 0000000C   40404040 40404040 0000000C 40404040   *?...............            *
009F8600 40404040 40404040 0000000C 00000000   00000000 00000000 00000000 C9D5C9E3   *........................INIT*
009F8620 40404040 0094100F 002837A3 0001FA02   40404040 40404040 40404040 40404040   *.....m...t......            *
009F8640 40404040 40404040 40404040 40404040   40404040 40404040 40404040 40404040   *                            *
009F8660 40404040 00000000 00000000 00200103   E2E8E240 40404040 40404040 40404040   *..............SYS           *
009F8680 40404040 00000000 00000000 00000000   0000000C 00000000 C9D5C9E3 40404040   *..................INIT      *
009F86A0 40404040 40404040 40404040 40404040   40404040 40404040 40404040 40404040   *                            *
009F86C0 40404040 40404040 40404040 00000000   00000000 00000000 00000000 00000000   *                            *
009F86E0 00000000 40404040 F9F9F0F4 00000000   E2E8E240 40404040 40404000 00000000   *....    9904....SYS         *
009F8700 00000000 00000000 00000000 00000000   0000000C 00000000 00000000 00000000   *                            *
009F8720 00000000 00000000 00000000 00000000   00000000 0000000C 40404040 40404040   *                            *
009F8740 00000000 00000000 00000000 00000000   00000000 40404040 00000000 00000000   *                            *
009F8760 00000000 00000000 00000000 00000000   00000000 00000000 00000000 00000000   *                            *
009F8780 00000000 0000000C 00000000 00000000   E2E3C3C9 D5D9C4D9 00000000 00000000   *............STCINRDR.       *
009F87A0 00000000 00000000 00000000 00000000   00000000 00000000 00000000 00000000   *                            *
009F87C0 00000000 00000000 00000000 00000000   00000000 00000000 00000000 00000000   *                            *
                 LINE 009F87E0  SAME AS ABOVE
009F8800 00000000 00000000 00000000 40404040   40404040 00000000 00000000 00000000   *                            *
009F8820 00000000 00000000 00000000 00000000   00000000 00000000 00000000 00000000   *                            *
                 LINES 009F8840-009F8FE0  SAME AS ABOVE
```

The 4K segment of storage beginning at location 9F9000 is duplicated from the LSQA section of the dump and isn't shown for brevity.

```
009FA000 00000000 00000000 00000000 00000000   00000000 00000000 00000000 00000000   *............................*
009FA020 00000000 00000000 00000000            00000000 00000000                     *......................*
```

The 12K of storage beginning at 9FD000 is duplicated from the LSQA section of the dump, and isn't shown for brevity.

```
00D5F540                   B00C47D0 3A3A5040   B00C47F0 3A3A5820 C0085420 3F025500   *........&...0....).&...0...{*
00D5F560 200847D0 3A3A5840 B0241840 5F402008   50002008 5A40B024 5040B024 594B8010   *.........&..!.&.....).&....&*
00D5F580 47D0339A 5040B010 5B40B028 5940B00C   47D03A3A 5040B00C 47F03A3A D5027061   *.).&..^.).&.).&...0..N./.*
00D5F5A0 70014770 00049102 340458FD 340458FD   34049180 700F4710 34045800 70601F01   *.....j.....j.0.....-..,.*
```

```
00D5F5C0 58E0B004 1BE050E0 B0045010 70605410 3F025010 70009500 70604770 33FA58E0  *\...\&\..&....n.-....\*
00D5F5E0 C13C1BE0 50E0C13C 56003EB6 58F03E92 05EF4120 70181266 47B0355A 41207074  *A..\&\A.....0.k......!*
00D5F600 9110705C 4770355A 58F07068 58107070 12114770 352C1BE0 41100008 1E1A1910  *.j..*!.0.........j .*.*
00D5F620 47D03442 41000FFF 1E015400 3EC218F0 50F07070 12334720 35029140 705C4770  *.}....B.0&0.........*
00D5F640 35029180 C07C4710 34649640 705C47F0 3502950F C07F47B0 34820700 47F03476  *.j.{@...o *.0.n.{"..b..0.*
00D5F660 00000476 58F03472 1B110A78 47F034FA 58F0C25C D203F050 C26D0203 F07CC258  *.......0B*K.0&B-K.0@B-*
00D5F680 4110F054 50D0F004 18DF41E0 000450D0 10245000 10201BFF 50F0102C 9640102C  *...&}0..\.&.&0..o.*
00D5F6A0 41E01020 41F01024 41001028 90E01000 41E0102C 41F01030 41001034 90E0100C  *./..0...\...0....0*
00D5F6C0 41E01038 41F0103C 90EF1018 58F0D050 05EFBFFF 10384780 34F24110 0FAC0A0D  *.\..0....0)&....2...*
00D5F6E0 58101030 58D0D004 9608C07C 47F03518 59003ED2 4740350E 58003ED6 56003EBA  *....}).o.{@.0....K...0.*
```

```
JOB EXA7JHMX        STEP APP3        TIME 125832   DATE 94100   ID = 000

00D5F700 58F03E8E 05EF58F0 B03841FF 000150F0 B03858F0 70705010 70705010 70741B00  *.0.......&0..0..&..*
00D5F720 50001000 5000100C 50F01004 50F0B044 50F0B040 5BF03E9A 50F01008 41001008  *&...&...&0..$0..&0.*
00D5F740 50007078 9610705C 180A5846 3EA21266 4720358E 05F01892 58220004 12224780  *&..o..*...s....0.k..*
00D5F760 35C85882 00001980 074F1948 07DF1848 181218A9 194047B0 35C807FF 05F01892  *.H.b...!....z...H...0.k*
00D5F780 58220004 12224780 35C85882 00001980 074F1848 181218A9 05F01892 58220004  *.H.b...!....z.0.k....*
00D5F7A0 12224780 35C85882 00001948 07BF1848 181218A9 07FF5946 3EA24780 36641266  *....H.b....z..s....o.*
00D5F7C0 47203650 4780364A 589D0004 D5079050 3ECA4780 364A950F C07F4740 364A5900  *..&..\.).N.&...n.{".*
00D5F7E0 70F84740 364A1890 89900014 18E91A90 12994720 364A1891 1A941889 89900014  *.8..\.i..h...r..\.j.m.ii*
00D5F800 88900014 12994780 364A1B89 18E91A90 19944720 364450E0 80005010 80045080  *h...r..\.i.Z..m..&\.&.&.*
00D5F820 A0041B49 4770365A D2038004 100447F0 39DA5846 3EA207FF 1B404770 365AD203  *........!K...0....s....!K.*
00D5F840 A0041004 47F039DA 47039DA D2038004 39DA1840 12664780 39444740 36945900  *...0....d....0....m..*
00D5F860 70644780 398C4720 36845800 706447F0 398C18F0 41000FFF 1E0F5400 3EC247F0  *.&...0...8........B..*
00D5F880 39C85800 706C4110 00081E14 191047D0 36AE4100 0FFF1E01 54003EC2 18201233  *.H...%....}....B.0*
00D5F8A0 47203802 9140705C 47703802 950DC07F 474036CE 9140C21C 4710376A 950FC07F  *...j..*..n.{"..j B...n.{"*
00D5F8C0 47B036EA 47F036DE 00000476 58F036DA 1B110A78 47F03762 58F0C25C D203F050  *..0.......0....0B*K.0&*
00D5F8E0 C26D0203 F07CC258 4110F054 50D0F004 18DF41E0 000450D0 10245000 10201BFF  *B-K.0@B...&}0..\.&..*
00D5F900 50F0102C 9640102C 41E01020 41F01024 41001028 41E0102C 41F01030 41001030  *&0..o....\....0*
00D5F920 41001034 90E0100C 41E0103C 41F0103C 90EF1018 58F0D050 05EFBFFF 10384780  *....\.....0)&....*
00D5F940 375A4110 0FAC0A0D 58101030 58D0D004 9608C07C 950FC07F 47B03786           *.!......))..o.{@.0.n.{".f.*
00D5F960 47F0377A 00000474 58F03776 1B110A78 4F037F4 58F0C25C D203F050 C26D0203    *.0.*....0...0B*K.0&B-K.*
00D5F980 F07CC258 4110F054 50D0F004 18DF41E0 000450E0 10245000 10201BFF 50F0102C  *0@B...&}0..\.&..&0.*
00D5F9A0 9640102C 41E01020 41F01024 41001028 90E01000 41E0102C 41F01030 41001034  *o.....\.....&0*
00D5F9C0 90E0100C 41E01038 41F0103C 90EF1018 58F0D050 05EFBFFF 10385810 103058D0  *....\...0)&....K....)*
00D5F9E0 D00412FF 477038CE 9608C07C 47F038DA 59003ED2 4740380E 58003ED6 950DC07F  *........o.{@.0..K...On.{"*
00D5FA00 4740381E 9140C21C 4710382C 56003EBA 58F03E8E 05EF4F0 38DA950F C07F47B0   *....j B....0...0.n.{".*
```

```
00D5FA20  385641E0 70E44110 70E85000 10009230   100850E1 00049204 10090A04 581070E4  *...\.U..Y&..k..&..k.....U*
00D5FA40  047F03C8 58FC25C0 D203F050 C260D203   F07CC258 4110F054 50D0F004 18DF41E0  *.O.H.OB*K.O&B-K.O@B..O.&JO..\*
00D5FA60  000450E0 10245000 10201BFF 50F0102C   9640102C 9680102C 41E01020 41F01024  *.&\..&...&0..o..\..O..*
00D5FA80  41001028 90E01000 41E0102C 41F01030   41001034 90E0100C 41E01038 41F0103C  *......\..\.o.....\..o.*
00D5FAA0  90EF1018 58F0D050 05EFBFFF 10385810   103058D0 D00412FF 478038DA 58D0D004  *.....0)&...}}...}}.*
00D5FAC0  1B001B11 47F039F0 58F0B038 41FF0001   50F0B038 58F0B044 1AF250F0 B04459F0  *.....0.O.O.O..&0...2&0..0*
00D5FAE0  B04047F0 38FC50F0 B04041A0 707418FA   58AF0000 191A4740 390050A1 0000501F  *.).&...&0......&.....&.*
00D5FB00  00005020 10045B20 3E9A5020 10081804   18424110 10084120 707418A2 582A0004  *.&..$..&..s.......*
00D5FB20  19124740 392C5021 0004501A 000447F0   35DA9500 70604770 398C5810 70601F10  *...&..&..0.n.-....*
00D5FB40  58FD0004 591F004C 4740398C 50107060   95007060 477039DA 58E07060 5FEF004C  *...&..<...&.-n.-..\.-^.<*
00D5FB60  50E0B028 58FC6024 1BFE59F0 B00C47F0   39DA50F0 B00C47F0 39DA1820 59003ED2  *&\...0....).&0...0.....K*
00D5FB80  4740399A 58003ED6 56003EB6 58F03E8E   05EF58E0 B01441EE 000150E0 B0145800  *......0....0.....&\..\.*
00D5FBA0  B0241E04 5000B010 5900B010 47D039C6   5000B010 5B00B028 5900B00C 47D039D6  *......&......).0*
00D5FBC0  5000B00C 18041842 12664720 39FE58DD   00044740 39EC5410 3F025A1D 00145050  *&......).}.q.}.....FE&..$.*
00D5FBE0  700858E0 D00C982B D01C07FE 54103F02   D2031000 C008D203 10047060 4320C008  *&....(..(..\..q.}....{.*
00D5FC00  5010C008 1E145010 70600620 4220C008   42207060 5810C008 1E011821 54203F02  *&..;..o...&&..j.}..)..-*
00D5FC20  50002008 5E103E96 54103F02 50507008   9108D044 47E03A5E 18215810 D00C5810  *&..}.}.}}..\}.q.}.}}..{.*
00D5FC40  D018983B D0205BD0 D00407FE 58E0D00C   982BD01C 58D0D004 07FE5810 C0085800  *&.......K.(..K.......q.*
00D5FC60  70601F01 54103F02 D203C008 1000D203   70601004 41207018 12664780 3A984120  *...0....{(....*
00D5FC80  707447F0 3AAE5410 3F0241C0 C000191C   47403C04 59107000 47B03C04 41101000  *.1.0.k.......8.......*
00D5FCA0  18F11AF0 18925822 00041222 47803AF8   19214740 3ADE192F 47703AB6 5A020000  *K.....0...b!b...8!..&.*
00D5FCC0  D2039004 20041829 47F03AB6 18825A82   00001918 47703AF8 5A020000 50020000  *&...0...-&..-&....&....)*
00D5FCE0  181247F0 3B2C1266 47403B20 58807060   54803F02 19184770 3B205880 B0281A80  *&..*.$.........j..*
00D5FD00  5080B028 5E007060 50007060 07FE5001   00005021 00045019 00041266 07BE9180  *!.....;...=K....K.O...*
00D5FD20  705C078E 5B103E9A 59107070 078E41A0   707418FA 58AF0000 19A1074E 47203B44  *&\...\..&\...8n.("...O.o*
00D5FD40  5A003E9A 590A0004 077ED203 9004100C   D203F000 A000182E 58E0B03C 41EE0001  *.O.&)O...O.6.OB*K.O&B.K.O.B.\*
00D5FD60  50E0B03C 58E0B042 1BEE50E0 B0441233   47203BF8 950FC07F 47B03BA0 47F03B96  *.O.&)O...&O\.&\..\...O.&*
00D5FD80  00000403 00000000 0A7847F0 3BF658F0   C25CD203 F050C264 D203F07F C25841E0  *......\...\.....O)&..*
00D5FDA0  F05450D0 F00418DF 41F00004 50F0E01C   5000E018 5010E024 181E41E0 101841F0  *0.&)0...&0\.&\..\...0.&*
00D5FDC0  101C4100 102090E0 100041E0 102441F0   10284100 102C90E0 100C58F0 D5505EF0  *......\...\.....0)&.*
00D5FDE0  58D0D004 07F25600 3EBA58F0 3E9205EF   07F2182E 58B0B018 41EE0001 50E0B018  *.}}.2....0.k..2...&\..*
```

```
JOB EXA7JHMX          STEP APP3          TIME 125832     DATE 94100     ID = 000                 PAGE 00000113
```

```
00D5FE00  58E0B024 12664770 3C221FE0 47F03C2E   58F01008 54F03F02 1BF11BEF 50E0B024  *\......\.0...0...1.&\..*
00D5FE20  56003EB6 58F03E92 05EF07F2 950FC07F   47B03C50 4510C4A4 0A0A47F0 3CD658F0  *...O.k..2n.(".&..\..0.O.0*
00D5FE40  C25C50E0 F04BD203 F050C260 D203F07C   C2584110 F05450D0 F00418DF BE081027  *B*&\0.K.O&B-K.O@B..O.&}0.*
00D5FE60  1BFF50F0 1020BE07 10211BFF 50F0102C   9640102C 9680102C 41E01020 41F01024  *.&O.......\..O..&O...0..*
```

```
00D5FE80  41001028 90E01000 41E0102C 41F01030  41001034 90E0100C 41E01038 41F0103C  *.........\..\...0..*
00D5FEA0  90EF1018 58F0D050 05EFBFFF 10384780  3CCA4110 0FAC0A0D 58101030 58E0D048  *.....0)&......\.}.*
00D5FEC0  58D0D004 C264D203 C07F47B0 3CE60A0A  47F03D46 58F0C25C 50E0F048 D203F050  *.).}.n.(".W...0B*&\0.K.0&*
00D5FEE0  C264D203 F074C258 41E0F054 50D0F004  18DFBE08 E01F1BFF 50F0E018 BE07E019  *B.K.O.B.\0.&)0...&0\..\.*
00D5FF00  5010E024 181E41E0 101C4100 101C4100  102090E0 100041E0 100041F0 10284100  *&.\...0....(..0.....*
00D5FF20  102C90E0 100C58F0 D005005F 58E0D048  58D0D004 07FE9104 C0014710 31A84100  *...0)&..\.}..J..J..y.*
00D5FF40  005058F0 3E8E05EF 92881000 92001001  50D10004 18D14110 3E8A950F C07F47B0  *.&.0..kh.k..&J..J..n.{".*
00D5FF60  3D900700 45F03D8A 00D5FF70 00000000  C9C2D4C2 D7C5D9C1 0A0647F0 3E684100  *.0..N...IBMBPERA..0...*
00D5FF80  3EFA58F0 C25CD203 F050C268 D203F07C  C2585010 F04C4110 F05450D0 F00418DF  *..0B*K.0&B.K.0@B.&.<..0.&)0..*
00D5FFA0  50001020 41E00008 58E01024 1BFF50F0  102C41E0 102041F0 10244100 102890E0  *&..\..&\..&0..&*
00D5FFC0  100041E0 102C41F0 10304100 103490E0  100C41E0 102041F0 103C90EF 101858F0  *...\..\..0.......0.*
00D5FFE0  D05005EF 58001030 5810D04C 58DD004   41003EFA 18DF5000 41E01024 00D5FE2C  *)&..;<.}}.0....0B*K.0&*
00D60000  C26CD203 F074C258 5010F04C 4110F054  50D0F004 18DF5000 41E01024 41001028  *B&K.0.B.&.<..0.&)0..&..&\.*
00D60020  101C1BFF 50F01024 41E01018 41F0101C  90E0100C 41E01024 41F01028 D7C1C640  *&0...\..0.&...0..&.*
00D60040  4100102C 90E0100C 90E0100C 05EF5810  41001024 41E01028 41000050 00000000  *..\..0)&...}<.)}.....&*
00D60060  58F03E92 05EF4110 0FBC4100 00808900  0018161O 0A0D0008 8000001C 00D5FE2C  *.0.k....i....N..*
00D60080  00D5FEC6 00000010 00000008 7FFFFFFF  7FFFFFFF FFFFFFF8 00FFFFF8 FFFFFFF8  *.N.F...."..".8..8..8*
00D600A0  00000007 01000000 04000000 00000000  FFFFF000 FFFFFFFC C9C2D4C2 D7C1C640  *...........IBMBPAF*
00D600C0  01000000 00FFFFF8 00000000 00000000  00000000 00000000 00000000 00000000  *.......8.........*
00D600E0  00000000 00000000 C9C2D4C2 D7C5D9C1  00000000 00000000 00000000 00000000  *...........IBMBPERA.....*
00D60100  00000000 00000000 01000000 00000000  00FFFFFF 01000000 00000000 00000000  *...................*
00D60120  00000000 00000000 47F0F044 5810300C  58C02030 47F0C032 20C9C7C7 F0F1F9C4  *.........0....0(..(..IGG019D*
00D60140  C1F0F861 F1F461F9 F2C8C4D7 F4F4F1F0  40D5D6D5 C5404040 40009610 3000184E  *A08/14/92HDP4410 NONE .o...j+*
00D60160  9120203C 4710C246 47F0C0C4 90EC D00C  58201008 5850202C 18CF5830 20449120  *.j...B..0{D..}..&....j..*
00D60180  203D4710 C1905830 30009300 30044780  C07241F0 000C47F0 C24C5030 20444160  *.....A..l....{..0..0B<&...-*
00D601A0  30085060 10105010 300C9523 30484770  C0A6943F 30949180 20344710 C09A943F  *.&.-.&...A{o.m.0A{o..j...*
00D601C0  30749120 203C4710 C24647F0 C0C4943F  307C9180 20344710 C0B6943F 3064D202  *.j..B..0{Dm..@j...{.m...K.*
00D601E0  3061100D 9120203C 4710C246 95233048  4770C0D2 D2023069 100D9140 203D4710  */..j...B.n...{KK....j....*
00D60200  C268D207 30282005 D5032008 C4184780  C2464380 200C4180 80014280 200CD204  *B.K...N..D..B........K.*
00D60220  30302008 58703018 41103010 58F0200C  50F01000 92101004 48F02012 40F01006  *.0..&0...k..0..0.0..*
00D60240  58F03034 50F01008 58F00010 58F0F0E8  45E0F00C 12FF4780 C13A5070 301847F0  *.0..&0..0..OOY.\0...A.&..0*
00D60260  C3464000 201243F0 301841FF 000142F0  30184110 301058F0 001058F0 F0E845E0  *C.........0....0...OOY..*
00D60280  F0C5070  30185810 300C9110 10054780  C1821B66 43602010 12664780 C1825890  *0.&..j....Ab..-.Ab...*
00D602A0  100C4286 900092FF 900012FF 4770C190  4160C24A 47F0C384 9640203D 95233048  *.f..k...A..-.B).0Cdo.n..*
00D602C0  4770C1B0 96403074 91802034 96403064  93093094 47F0C1C0 96403064 91802034  *.A.o..j..\A{o.m.0A{o..j..*
00D602E0  4780C1C0 9640307C D2033038 2008D204  30402008 4560C384 4710C24C 96403094  *.A{o..@K...k..-Cd...&..*
00D60300  89700004 1A75D503 2008702A 41F00004  4770C24C 9120203C 4710C24C 41F00008  *i..N....0...B<j..B<.0.*
00D60320  47F0C24C 9620203C 06804280 20059680  30005870 30189201 30344110 301058F0  *.0B<o........k....0.*
00D60340  200C50F0 100458F0 10458F0 303450F0   100858F0 001058F0 F0E845E0 F00C5070  *.&0..k...0..&0...0..OOY.\0.&.*
00D60360  30185810 300C4600 C24A47F0 C1D09680  30001BFF 91103000 47E0C25A 94EF3000  *..\.0Aj0...j...\B!m..*
```

```
00D60380  07F458E0 D00C980C D0149601 D00F07FE  9740203D 5860200C 1BBBBF87 50219180  *...4.\).q.).o.}....&.j.*
00D603A0  B0004780 C29A1BAA 1B9958B0 C3DCBF93  60021DA9 89B00010 169B5090 301047F0  *...B...r.C.1-..zi...&....0*
00D603C0  C2B8D203 30106000 1B77BF77 B0155860  70189120 60014780 C2B8D201 30106012  *.B.K...-.....j...B.K...-.*
00D603E0  5860200C D2033014 20081B77 43702005  89700004 1A754130 30004180 30035890  *...K......i....j...B.K...*
00D60400  30149102 60094780 C3084A90 C3DA9102  60094710 C3564090 8014D501 80148010  *.j..C.\.C.j....C...N...*
00D60420  4740C370 88900010 D2018014 C3D80680  06801983 47A0C2E2 43802005 41808001  *.C.h..K...CQ...C..BS..*
00D60440  42802005 D5002005 50104780 C1FC4170  7010D205 20067024 9202000C 58803048  *..N..&..A....K...k....*
00D60460  92008001 D2012012 600447F0 C0DA96C0  202C4112 00004100 00CD1111 0A374290  *.k..K....0(.o(...0C.N...*
00D60480  80148890 00D8D500 80148010 4740C370  92008014 47F0C308 D5033014 702A4720  *..h..N.....C.K...0C.N..*
00D604A0  C310D203 20083014 47F0C330 1B119523  30484770 C3924110 00109120 203D47E0  *.C.K....0C...n...Ck...j.\*
00D604C0  C3BA4111 30689180 20344780 C3B64110  30809523 30484770 C3B64110 1185010   *.C......j....C....n...C...&.*
00D604E0  30184110 30080A00 9120203D 4710C24C  91803000 07E6947F 30094EF  30007F4   *.......j....B<j...Wm"..m....4*
```

JOB EXA7JHMX   STEP APP3   TIME 125832   DATE 94100   ID = 000   PAGE 00000114

```
00D60500  00000001 0000FFFF 00000000 00000000  00000000 00000000 00000000 00000000  *........................*
00D60520  00000000 00000000 00000000 00000000  00000000 00000000 00000000 00000000  *........................*
00D60540  FFFFFFFF 00000000 90E8D014 415F0000  0B5047F0 503020C9 C7C7F0F1 F9C2C2F0  *.........Y}.^...&.0&.IGG019BB0*
00D60560  F661F1F6 61F9F3D1 C4E9F1F1 F1F040E4  E8F9F5F4 F8F24000 58210008 58310010  *6/16/93JDZ1110 UY95482 ...*
00D60580  18414144 00009108 203C4710 526C9120  20114780 52509101 201F47E0 50A01F66  *....j......8j...&j...\&..*
00D605A0  BF67202D 41700010 1B675860 6008BF6F  60401266 47805AA0 4170507E 41805250  *........?-...&.&=-.&*
00D605C0  56705520 0B879180 605C47E0 508CAF03  0C4C0B08 9140605C 47E0509A AF03C04D  *...gj.-*.\&..<.j.-*.\&..(*
00D605E0  0B08AF03 0C4E0B08 1F66BF67 202D9102  201A47E0 50D69104 603047E0 50C69103  *..-.+...\&..0..j...\&Oj...0.j*
00D60600  603047E0 50CEAF03 0C5047F0 50F69103  0C4F47F0 5102AF03 0C5347F0 5102AF03  *..-.\&..&.0../.\&6j.-..\&.....0.*
00D60620  201A47E0 50CEAF03 603047E0 50F69103  603047E0 5102AF03 0C5347F0 51029140  *...j.-.\..\&6j-..\&.....0.*
00D60640  0C5247F0 5102AF03 0C549101 201F47E0  52061F66 BF67202D 41700010 1B675860  *......0...\...<.......*
00D60660  60089180 603D47E0 52065860 604C4170  51305670 55200B07 58706070 BF8F7014  *.......j........3.0.U.?..6....*
00D60680  478051FC 91404000 471051FC 18F34BF0  54E4BF6F 701019F6 47805160 BF676001  *......+.0.....i....i....0.0*
00D606A0  4680514E 47F051FC 181241E0 51724100  00018900 001F16E0 0B1E58F0 001058F0  *0H.00y.00..04...i.......\i.*
00D606C0  F0C858F0 F0A858F0 F03C58F0 F4144100  00018900 001F1401 41E051A0 16E08910  *..h....i\......0.P...*
00D606E0  00018810 00010B0E 41E00003 89E00008  41000010 1A0EB218 F000D703 70147014  *.........7.....0h0..7...*
00D60700  12FF4780 51FC4170 000C19F7 477051DC  4170001E 18F088F0 0018119F7 477051DC  *............Y..Y..qY)...2...*
00D60720  410000EF 12554740 51584170 51E80B07  98E8D014 41105F2 0B014112 00001800  *........7...n.--.&j*
00D60740  11110A37 41705250 12550747 0B075860  201C9500 60154780 52509140 40004710  *...&j.-..&j...&K.--.K..*
00D60760  52509180 600C4780 52509140 40004710  5250D203 60086010 D202600D 20459200  *-.k.--...0..4....k.*
00D60780  60159200 60C5810  600447F0 5248F400  BF185246 1B000A72 917F4000 47105374  *..&......0.&..j".*
00D607A0  47405350 18144100 00014110 10000A01  47F05250 AF03C055 917F4000 471054DE  *.n............&}..}...%.*
00D607C0  95424000 478052B6 1F33BF37 204550D0  307841D0 30744100 306C0700 1B110A08  *.n............&}..}...%.*
```

```
00D607E0  18F04110 30C09601 30BE0DEF 4100306C  0A0958D0 307894FE 30BE47F0 54DE1B00  *.0....(o......%....).m....0...*
00D60800  18124111 00000A37 94DF2030 91082030  471054DE 41000048 451052D4 0A0A501D  *......m..j.........M.&..*
00D60820  000850D1 000418D1 1FFFBFF7 20311814  1B44BF47 10119500 100C4780 53084180  *.&J.J..7......n.........*
00D60840  530A4170 53045670 55200B87 0DEF0B08  0DEF1244 477052E0 181D58DD 00044100  *......g........\....*
00D60860  00484110 10000A0A 98E1D014 18411FFF  BFF7202D D502F021 55244770 50301FFF  *.......q.}....7..N.0....&..*
00D60880  BFF72035 18140D04 0A3712FF 47F05030  471052C0 47F05046 18121803 4B0054E4  *.7....0&.j........0&....U*
00D608A0  9001D040 41110000 0A3712FF 47805344  0DEF9801 D0404111 00000A37 91C04005  *.)......j.....q.).....j{*
00D608C0  478054DE 91082034 478054AC 5870400C  4860203E 91C02024 4710547C 9104203D  *......-..j...@j.*
00D608E0  471053A0 4B63000E 91404005 478053AE  1B764177 00011817 18060A67 91202024  *......j...j........j.*
00D60900  478054DE 91402050 4780545A 4D805436  48670000 1A674177 00044D80 53F21A7F  *.......j.&..!(.........j.*
00D60920  197647B0 54DE9110 202447E0 54DE955F  70004780 54DE47F0 53D29108 202247E0  *....j...n^......0.Kj..\*
00D60940  5436D707 30083008 F223300D 70014FF3  000806F0 40F30008 D2037001 30089403  *...P...2...!3..0 3.K...m.*
00D60960  70001BFF 43F70000 43FF54E6 42F70003  48F30008 41FF0001 92007000 07F89801  *.......7...W.7..3....k..8q.*
00D60980  3008D707 3008D707 F223300D 70004FF3  000840D3 70003008 90013008 90013A78  *...P...2...!3. 3.K......*
00D609A0  07F84060 20529104 203D47E0 546E9110  20244710 54DE1A67 1B888380 20511A78  *.8.-..j...\..>j........*
00D609C0  47F053D2 9104203D 4780548E D2012052  203E47F0 53A01B88 43802042 1A834B80  *.0.Kj......K....0..h....c...*
00D609E0  54E44888 478054C6 000E4080 20521868  47F053A0 91C02024 47E054DE 9104203D  *.U.h...c.....0..j{..\..j...*
00D60A00  478054C6 D2012052 203D47F0 54DE1B88  43802042 1A834B80 54E44888 00064B83  *......FK....0...h.....U.h...c*
00D60A20  000E4080 205298E8 D01407FE 00080001  03024040 40404040 40404040 40404040  *......qY)......*
00D60A40  40404040 40404040 40404040 40404040  40404040 40404040 40404040 40404040  *..........*
00D60A60  40404040 07000700 80000000 00000000  47F0F00C 001847F0 F0060342 90ECD00C  *...........00....00...}..*
00D60A80  05C04AF0 F00407FF 47F0C02C 20C9C7C7  F0F1F9C1 C8F0F861 F2F761F9 F2D1C4E9  *...{\00....0{..IGG019AH08/27/92JDZ*
00D60AA0  F1F1F1F0 40D5D6D5 C5404040 40001831  5840304C 5880401C 58703054 91848020  *1110 NONE......<....jd..*
00D60AC0  47E0C05C 58E08000 BFAFE02C 4770C058  D5028039 C45B4780 C18C47F0 C066D502  *..\(.*.\....}..(.N..D$..A..0{.N.*
00D60AE0  8039C45B 4780C18C 189D58D0 40784100  00484510 C0740A0A 910140BE 47E0C094  *..D$..A...}........j....\(m*
00D60B00  D20F100C D00CD21B 101CD024 D20F1038  903847F0 C09AD23B 100CD00C 50901004  *K...}.K...}.K...0{.K..}.&...*
00D60B20  50109008 50D01008 18915010 D01858E0  C46250E0 41509610 8039D101 803D47E0  *&...&}...j&.}..\D.&\.&o...j*
00D60B40  C0E04100 400858E0 30345FE0 303050E0  401412EE 4720C106 1FEE50E0 401447F0  *{(....\..^\.&\....A...&\...0*
00D60B60  C106D200 50BC7001 950040BC 4770C0F2  920740BC 18071FEE BFE37002 50E04014  *A.K.......{2k....T..&\.*
00D60B80  41E04008 50E07010 18181F22 432040BC  4122C4DC BF182000 91848020 47E0C132  *.\.&\...n....D....jd...\A.*
00D60BA0  58E08000 58E0E02C 12E84780 C13218FE  47F0C138 1FFFBFF7 8039902D D01C982C  *.\...\\......A....0A...7..}.q.*
00D60BC0  901C0DEF 581C0DEF 902C101C 982CD01C  58909004 910140BE 47E0C170 D20FD00C  *....\\.......q.j.....\A.K.}.*
00D60BE0  100CD21B D024101C D20F9038 103847F0  C176D23B D00C100C 18D94100 00484110  *.K.}...K......0A.K.}....R....*
```

```
JOB EXA7JHMX        STEP APP3        TIME 125832    DATE 94100    ID = 000                    PAGE 0000115

00D60C00  10000A0A 1FEE50E0 41509208 41509120  802A4710 C19C9120 802B47E0 C1BED502  *......&\.&k..&j.....A.j....\A.N.*
00D60C20  8039C45B 4770C448 91848020 47E0C1BA  58E08000 BFAFE02C 4770C448 47F0C202  *..D$..D.jd..A..\.....D..0.0B.*
```

```
00D60C40  1FEEBFE7 802D9104 E00C47E0 C1E09140   802B47E0 C1DC91C0 80544770 C44847F0   *....X..j.\..\A\j ...\A.j{....D..O*
00D60C60  C2029140 802A47F0 C20291C0 80544780   C22241E0 000C1FAA 43A0300D 14AE19AE   *B.j ...\B.j{....B.\..........*
00D60C80  4770C448 41000034 4510C20A 0A0A1861   1FEEBFE7 802D58E0 E0001F55 BF538028   *;&\.K.-.D.K.-.D.K.-.D.j..\B k4*
00D60CA0  5E50E00C D2016000 C456D201 6002C473   D22B6004 C4759101 803D47E0 C24092F4   *-.n....B&k3-..OB*n...B*k5-..*
00D60CC0  6010950C 300D4770 C25092F3 6101047F0  C25C9505 40BC4770 C25C92F5 60101FEE   *.X..\\.K.-.\.K.-.\.K.-.&..X*
00D60CE0  BFE7802D 58E0E00C 58E0E00C D2076012   E000D703 601BE008 D2076024 5004BFE7   *&..B..X&.K.-.\.P-.-.o..o.-*
00D60D00  50114780 C2901FEE BFE75011 D202602D   E000D703 60306030 96046030 96206033   *........j...\B...C..OBB*
00D60D20  18160A23 41000034 18164110 10000A0A   9101803D 47E0C2BE 4110C306 47F0C2C2   *.B....i..h........i.......*
00D60D40  4110C2DE 0A234110 00018910 00148810   00084100 00808900 00181610 0AD00000   *............IEC020I NO SYNAD EXIT SPECIF*
00D60D60  00238000 C9C5C3F0 F2F0C940 D5D640E2   E8D5C1C4 40C5E7C9 E340E2D7 C5C3C9C6   *IED....IEC020I EROPT IS 'AB*
00D60D80  C9C5C404 00002000 002B8000 C9C5C3F0   F2F0C940 C5D9D6D7 E340C9E2 407DC1C2   *E' OR NOT SPECIFIED....a\....*
00D60DA0  C57D4DD6 D940D5D6 E340E2D7 C5C3C9C6   C9C5C404 00002000 18814A80 10005880   *.T..^\ ...X..j.\...C.K..*
00D60DC0  80045840 80444130 40C01FEE BFE7802D   9104E00C 4770C374 D2031008 30201FEE   *K.........X...\\.K..\.K..\.*
00D60DE0  BFE3803E 5FE04014 40E0100C D2011048   C46947F0 C37AD201 1048C46B 9240100E   *......V.;K..&..X&...D...X&.j.*
00D60E00  D221100F 100E1FEE BFE7802D 58E0E000   58E0E00C D2071032 E000D207 103BE008   *\..\C.K..D_0D...X&.j.\..\CWK.*
00D60E20  1F55BF53 80281EE5 185ED207 104B5004   BFE75011 4780C416 1FEEBFE7 50119180   *..D?.0D...X&.j.\..C.K..D..OD..*
00D60E40  E01247E0 C3CED201 1048C46D 47F0C406   1FEEBFE7 50119108 E01247E0 C3E6D201   *.k ....X&..X&.K...OD.K..D...*
00D60E60  1048C46F 47F0C406 92401049 50119120   E01247E0 C3FED201 1048C471 47F0C406   *..S<\D..DNK.$..S<\D..E.K.*
00D60E80  92401048 432040BC 18E24CE0 C45441AE   1044E00D 47F0C41C D2021044 C4661F22   *......P.).}.q.}..OD........*
00D60EA0  1054A000 D703D014 D01498EC D00C07FE   105BA000 18E24CE0 C45241AE C547D205   *......O..JESISOTAURDA..IEC020I O*
00D60EC0  00000008 00D60A76 D1C5E2E2 C9E2D6E3   47F0C448 0006000F 00300000 00000001   *01-1,                      ,*
00D60EE0  F0F160F1 6B404040 40404040 40404040   C1E4D9C4 C18000C9 C5C3F0F2 F0C940F0   *JES                           *
00D60F00  D1C5E240 40404040 40404040 40404040   40404040 40404040 40404040 40404040   *                              *
00D60F20  40404040 40404040 40404040 40404040   40404040 40404040 40404040 40404090   *                              *
00D60F40  40409080 4008B6D9 D6D5C740 D3C5D540   D9C5C3D9 C4D9C5C1 C440C5D9 D9D6D940   *.........WRONG LEN RECRDREAD ERROR*
00D60F60  40404040 E6D9C9E3 C540C5D9 D9D6D940   404040E6 D9D6D5C7 40D3C5D5 40D9C5C3   *......WRITE ERROR  WRONG LEN REC*
00D60F80  40404040 D9C4D9C5 C1C440C5 D9D9D6D9   40E6D9C9 E3C540C5 D9D9D6D9 40404040   *RDREAD ERROR   WRITE ERROR*
00D60FA0  D9C4D9C5 C9D55EC1 D3C9C440 D9C5D8E4   C5C1C440 40D9C5C1 C44040E6 D9C9E3C5   *INVALID REQUESTREAD READ WRITE*
00D60FC0  C9D55EC1 40C7C5E3 404040C7 C5E34040   404040C3 C8C5C3D2 40000000 00000000   * GET  GET  PUT  CHECK ....*
00D60FE0  40C7C5E3 90EBD00C 053047F0 301CC9C2   C240E5F2 4BD9F34B D4F0F1F2 61F1F061   *.}....0..IBMBOPB V2.R3.M012/10/*
00D61000  F9F04100 00805810 D04C1E01 5500C00C   47D03034 58F0C074 05EF58F0 D04890F0   *90....}<...{..}..0{...0}..0*
00D61020  104850D0 100418D1 9288D000 9200D001   5060D058 41620004 5060D078 5080D054   *..&}..Jkh}.k.}.&-}...&-}&&.}.*
00D61040  D703D07C 00085858 00085858 00001885   4C503AC4 1A575050 D0505080 D05C5860   *..&..j...&}.}.K.....z..&.}.*
00D61060  70105840 D07C4178 700D4778 3A958B00   600412BB 47703096 57A03AC6 58004008   *..&.}...j.}...K....o..m...*
00D61080  478030AA 5000D064 478030E6 9604700A   58A04008 56A0B000 59903ACE 58004004   *j.{...Wo..o..j.{...o..m...*
00D610A0  54A0B000 478030D4 9201700C 47F03A96   478030D2 58903ACE 14A916A0 50A0D064   *..r....j.}......j..*
00D610C0  5600B000 9140C000 478030E6 9604700A   5000B000 478030E6 9602700A 94FE700A   *.....o......o.....*
00D610E0  9140C000 478030FA 31084190 9601700A   9120C000 478030FA 0D644710 32644180   *............F...*
00D61100  5890400C 12994770 31084190 9601700A   00109101 D0644710 32644180 00809122   *......j.}...K....z..&.}.*
00D61120  D06547E0 32409138 90004770 313891FF   32409222 32409222 700C47F0 3A96950C   *..}..\.j.....k....0.on.*
```

```
00D61140  D064D203 C07F47B0 315C0700 45F03156 00D61154   00000000 C9C2D4C2 D6D7E9C1 0A0647F0  *("....*....O....O....IBMBOPZA...0*
00D61160  3E6A58F0 C25CD203 F050C268           D203F07C C2585010 F04C4110 F05450D0  *.........0B*K.O&B.K.0@B.&.0<..0.&*
00D61180  F00418DF 50001020 41E00008 50E01024   1BFF50F0 102C41E0 102041F0 10244100  *O...&..\..&\...&0...\...0...*
00D611A0  102890E0 100041E0 102C41F0 10304100   103490E0 100C41E0 103841F0 103C90EF  *....\...0...)<.)}..0...0B**
00D611C0  101858F0 D05005EF 58001030 5810D04C   58DDD004 18F005EF 41003E6A 58F0C25C  *K.0&B*K.0.B.&.0<..0.&}0..&...\**
00D611E0  D203F050 C26CD258 F074C258 5010F04C   4110F054 50D0F004 18DF5000 10184110  *K.0&B8K.0.B.&.0<..0.&}0...&...\**
00D61200  000850E0 101C1BFF 50F01024 41E01018   41F0101C 41001020 90E01000 41E01024  *.&\...&0...\...0...&..\...\.*
00D61220  41F01028 41001020 90E0100C 58F0D050   05EF5810 D04C58D0 D0049500 700C4770  *.0...\...0)&...)<.)}.n...*
00D61240  3A9647F0 32589140 90004710 329A9102   D0654780 32709180 90004710 35CE4108  *.o.0..j...j...j...*
00D61260  005841B0 3CC247F0 32A29102 D0659601   D0654780 008C9108 90004780 32889150  *....B.0.so.0..}...j...hj&*
00D61280  900647E0 32889150 D0654770 325817AA   4BA03ABC 41080064 41B03B72 47F032A2  *....\.hj&}...j...*
00D612A0  410800EC 41B03BD6 4A003ABC 5000D060   58F0C06C 05EF4121 00000680 44803AA8  *...O\...&.}-0{%...y*
00D612C0  41880001 D2032000 3B0E4122 00045020   70005810 D0604010 203E1B18 06104B80  *.h..K......&....)-....*
00D612E0  3ABC1A82 44103AAE 1B8A5080 201449A0   3AC04780 32F61AA8 502A0000 D2032024  *.b......&.....(..6.y&..K...*
```

JOB EXA7JHMX   STEP APP3   TIME 125832   DATE 94100   ID = 000   PAGE 00000116

```
00D61300  20106000 48104012 41B04014   91804014 4770331C 1A1441B1 00024811  *).K.-.....j......*
00D61320  000058A0 600812AA 4780334E 48FA0004   58EA0000 9180A006 47803344 D201D060  *...-...j...+....K.}-*
00D61340  E00048F0 06041EE 000212FF 47D0334E   181F18BE 06104910 3ABE4740 335C4110  *\..0}...j.+...*...*
00D61360  00074410 3AB49102 20244780 33F845E0   3A1612FF 472033F8 917F9000 47803396  *....j...8.\...8j".o*
00D61380  91409000 478033DC 91409003 47803396   58109024 58110000 461033DC 9108A063  *j...j...j.jf...j...o.*
00D613A0  478033DC 91409000 478033B6 91C0A064   477033DC 9102A065 477033DC 9602700D  *...j..j(...j...o.0*
00D613C0  5880D054 96408004 58F0C070 18124B10   3ABC4800 203E05EF D7037000 700047F0  *.oj...j.)..8o..*
00D613E0  3A9691FF 90004770 33EC9102 20254710   35CE9120 A05D4780 33F89608 700D1711  *.K...k..j...j".k...*
00D61400  1700D200 20299000 9200202A 91012024   4780341E 917F2029 4780353E 9222700C  *0.okA.*j...o.j...>j...*
00D61420  47F03A96 92C1205C 91089004 4710342E   9602202C 91022025 4780346E 91012026  *...k..0.o...kC.*k..j.*
00D61440  47803446 9227700C 47F03A96 41100004   58003B22 92C3205C 9218202A 91402029  *...Sk..kB.*...0...j.f.*
00D61460  478034E2 9214202A 92C2205C 41110006   47F0350E 58003B26 91402026 47803486  *k....0.j...kC.*...*
00D61480  9210202A 54003B2A 47F03462 91012026   478034B2 41100000 54003B2A 91042025  *...Bk..kC.*...o..0...*
00D614A0  478034C2 920C202A 92C3205C 4110001C   96042029 47F0350E 92C3205C 54003B2E  *kC.*k...j".o.0...kC.*k..j..*
00D614C0  92C3205C 9204202A 54003B32 917F2029   4780352E 92C3205C 9204202A 91202025  *...Sk..n...j&..*
00D614E0  478034E2 9208202A 95102028 47803506   47803506 41110006 91509006 47E03506  *j...k...j...*
00D61500  91222025 47703506 9218202A 41110006   4111000A 91042026 91042026 9680700A  *...j...o...0.j...*
00D61520  54003B3A 91082026 4780353A 9640700A   47F0353E 91042026 471035CE 54003B3E  *...j...o...0.j...*
00D61540  54003B42 42107008  *...*
```

At this point in the dump, SNAP now dumps the load modules currently in use. The first one will be the test program, APP3PGM1.

ACTIVE LOAD MODULES

LPA/JPA MODULE
NAME=APP3PGM1

```
00006900                                              B24000E0 18CF41D0   *      . .\...)DU&(D.....{......*
00006920 00000000 00000000 C4F450C0 C42C0700 4510C02C 10000000           *................\.............."*
00006940 4780C08A 4E70C3D8 00006B34 41000100 41101000 0A3C127F           *...(.+.CQo.C.3.(.CQ....(.....*****
00006960 5C5C5C40 960FC3DF C3D80700 4510C080 002F0000 5C5C5C5C           **** WAS RETURN CODE FROM ESTAE -*
00006980 40C5D5C4 E6C1E240 D6C4C540 C6D9D6D4 40C5E2E3 C1C54060           * ENDING.....E..0B....(m.0(.APP3*
000069A0 D7C7D4F2 C9D5C700 C2160700 4100C094 47F0C09C C1D7D7F3           **PGM2.......(.BRUINS ...A.....(.*
000069C0 47F0C0C0 1B110A08 D5E24040 4110C126 4A290700 4110C0BC           *.0{(..>..0{H.00........>.....*
000069E0 00000021 80006E38 000069EC 00000000 80006E3C 00000000           *.........................APP3PGM3.*
00006A00 00000000 41F0C0C8 D7C7D4F3 00000000 0A2A0700 4510C124           *...........................A..*
00006A20 C0034000 00000048 00000700 4510C134 8F006F94 0A134110           *.(....>..>!.w.........A..?m...*
00006A40 C68C9110 00006B52 80006F3C 0A134110 C6344B80 103E9110           **F.j..\B...A.<..?..F....j.*
00006A60 103047E0 C2180700 BFF71031 0EBFD201 C548C6F0 47F0C216           *..A..F..E...7...K.E.F0.0B.*
00006A80 47F0C180 C1784110 001058EE 030458EE 00A0B218 E00018A1           * .0A....0A@.\...........\..*
00006AA0 00001616 C68C4100 12FF40F0 C5484770 C2084110 C6344100           *.F...E...........0B...B..F..*
00006AC0 4100C538 180B58F0 7F000000 00802260 00006F3C 00009000           **E..."......A."....?..*
00006AE0 C5441FFF 45EF0004 BFF7F031 05EFD703 C1C8C1C8 4110C1C8           *.).&...0...70..P.AHAH..AH*
00006B00 00005DA0 40B10006 4510C214 00006F3C 80006F94 0A140101           *.\...7\..b....B..?..?m...*
00006B20 58E01008 1BFFBFF7 47F0C216 90ECD00C 2C0D0008 502D0008           *.F..E..7....0B..}..1.&...*
00006B40 4100C68C 18D21821 45E0C48C D207C463 C4CA4110 20054 5E0          **&K...K..{2...D..\D.K.D.D...\*
00006B60 50D20004 58C0F200 89100014 88100014 4E10C3D8 960FC3DF           *.D.K.D.D.k/D\...i...h..+.CQo.C.*
00006B80 C4BCD202 9261C44A BFF71031 05EF9260 C434D201 C548C6F2           *3.D.CQ..F...D...7...k-D.K.E.F2*
00006BA0 F337C44B C3D84100 C3C09204 10FC18F3 50F010F0 96801004           *o.........C\..C{k...3&0.0o..*
00006BC0 41F04000 96401141 11419604 11429102 F0014710 C2E01BEE           * .o...K...o...o..j.0...B\..*
00006BE0 55E0F010 4780C352 12EE4780 C3529602 11419680 11421FEE           **j.0..00..C.....0C...0\\.j.0.*
00006C00 9180F002 58F0F010 47F0C310 410000F0 41E0E008 9180F004           *.00...C..\...C.....0C......\C\*
00006C20 41F0F008 4710C326 06E01801 58101170 58101000 44E0C34A           *...o.....0C&K....0.4j.0..*
00006C40 41F00003 1BEF1A1E C350D200 1000F000 18F49102 F024780            *C...\0..C..\...\C.......C.o...0*
00006C60 C3B41BEE 55E0F018 58E0C00C 12EE4780 C3B49602 11425 8F0          *0..\0...}C.......}C...\.\C...0C.K...0.o..*
00006C80 F01848E0 F00012EE 19E047D0 C39018E0 18015810 11705810           *q.}.................*
00006CC0 98ECD00C 07FE0000 181047F0 C3B4D200 1002F002 960810FD           *.................&.,.o.F..*
00006CE0 00000000 0000000F 00005CE0 00000000 50006B96 00C65968           *.................&.,.o.F..*
```

```
JOB EXA7JHMX        STEP APP3        TIME 125832    DATE 94100    ID = 000                        PAGE 00000117

00006D00 00006D3C 00000000 00005660 00000000   00000000 00000000 00000000 00000000   *.............................*
00006D20 00000000 00000000 00000000 00000000   00006908 00006908 00000000 605C5C5C   *..........................-****
00006D40 C1C2C5D5 C440D6C3 C3E4D9D9 C5C47AF0   C3F261F0 F0F0F040 40D7D9D6 C7D9C1D4   *ABEND OCCURRED:0C2/0000   PROGRAM*
00006D60 40C2C5C7 C9D5E240 C1E37AF0 F0F0F0F6   F9F0F840 40404040 40404040 40404040   * BEGINS AT:00006908            *
00006D80 40404040 40404040 40404040 40404040   40404040 40404040 40404040 40404040   *                             *
      LINE 00006DA0  SAME AS ABOVE
00006DC0 40000700 F384C4CA 1000DC07 C4CAC3E3   07FEF0C3 F2F0F0F0 C6C658F0 F1F2F3F4   *...3dD.....D.CT..0C2000FF.01234*
00006DE0 F5F6F7F8 F9C1C2C3 C4C5C600 00000000   C6F1E2C1 00000000 00006E4C 00006F3C   *56789ABCDEF.....F1SA......><..?.*
00006E00 50006B0C 00D60548 00008E4C 00006AD0   00000000 009F1954 009F1930 009F9028   *&.,.O...><...}....*
00006E20 009D1FF8 00000000 009FF060 809DF510   00009000 00000000 00000000 00000000   *...8....0-.5.........*
00006E40 0001000C C1D7D7F3 D7C7D4F1 00040700   008C6D6D D6404040 404001C2 C1D96060   *...APP3PGM1....FOO    .BAR—*
00006E60 60606060 60606060 60606060 6E40D6D7   C5D540C5 D9D9D6D9 40404040 40404040   *————> OPEN ERROR        *
00006E80 40404040 40404040 40404040 00006EC0   40404040 40404040 40404040 40404040   *                             *
      LINES 00006EA0-00006EC0  SAME AS ABOVE
00006EE0 40404040 00000000 00000000 00000000   00000000 00000000 00000001 00004000   *...........................*
00006F00 00000001 00000001 54000000 C4E4D4D7   C4C44040 02000020 0000007D 00000001   *..............DUMPDD........*
00006F20 00000660 00000000 00000001 00000000   00000001 0000007D 00000001 00000000   *....-...,.........*
00006F40 00040000 046C0004 07F1D076 002EBB60   00000001 00000200 00005D28 02006B10   *....%..l}...-...)...,..*
00006F60 90000000 00542400 009DEE74 12C88D38   00D60548 0A000001 00002260 30013030   *.....H..O.....-..*
00006F80 00005D98 01DB36F0 00DB36F0 00000050   00DB4258 00000000 94000000 002C0050   *..)q..0..0..&....*
00006FA0 00000000 00000000 01008F78 00794000   00005F30 02000001 94000000 00005DE0   *......<......m...&*
00006FC0 009DB560 92C65968 00000001 00000001   08090079 00000000 00005DE0 00008FF9   *...-kF......)\..9*
00006FE0 00008FF9 00000079 00000001 00000000   00000001 00000000 00100008 00000000   *....9.............*
```

LPA/JPA MODULE
NAME=IEAVTRF4

This module won't be shown—it's an IBM-supplied dump formatting module.

LPA/JPA MODULE
NAME=IGG019DJ

This module is a standard IBM-supplied access method program and won't be shown. Its starting address, X'00C65940', is referred to in the SYSPRINT DCB.

```
LPA/JPA MODULE
NAME=IGG019BA
```

This module is a standard IBM-supplied access method program and won't be shown. Its starting address, X'00C88D38', is referred to in the SYSUDUMP DCB, which is at location X'009DAE68'. Refer to the subpool 230 dump immediately prior to the register areas to locate this. This is a BSAM support program, which is here because the SYSUDUMP data set was allocated to a disk data set to simplify publishing.

```
LPA/JPA MODULE
NAME=IGG019BB
```

This module is a standard IBM-supplied BPAM access method executor and will not be shown. Its starting address, X'00D60540', is referred to in the PDS DCB; refer to the formatted DCB listing earlier in the dump at offset +34.

```
00D60540     90B8D014 415F0000     0B5047F0 503020C9 C7C7F0F1 F9C2C2F0     *        .Y}.^...&.0&..IGG019BB0*
```

```
LPA/JPA MODULE
NAME=IGG0193B
```

This module is a standard IBM-supplied BSAM access method program and won't be shown. It's used by the PDS DCB. Note that the program's starting address isn't directly referenced in the DCB because the load module contains multiple CSECTs. Its address range in the dump is DA000 to DB4780; the PDS DCB refers to address DB36F0 at offsets +48 and +4C, and the address is inside the IGG0193B load module. The following program was brought into storage with the LOAD macro in APP3PGM1.

```
0LPA/JPA MODULE
NAME=APP3PGM2
09E00FA0 D4E5E240 C3D6D5E3 D9D6D340 C2D3D6C3   D2E240C1 D7D7C5D5 C4C9E740 F340D7D9   *MVS CONTROL BLOCKS APPENDIX 3 PR*
09E00FC0 D6C7D9C1 D440F24B 40E3C8C9 E240D9C5   D7D9C5E2 C5D5E3E2 40C140D3 D6C1C440   *OGRAM 2. THIS REPRESENTS A LOAD *
09E00FE0 D4D6C4E4 D3C540C3 D6D5E3C1 C9D5C9D5   C740D6D5 D3E840C4 C1E3C14B 00000000   *MODULE CONTAINING ONLY DATA......*
```

LPA/JPA MODULE
NAME=IEAVTRP2

This module is a standard IBM-supplied dump formatting program and won't be shown.

LPA/JPA MODULE
NAME=IEAVSSAF

This module is a standard IBM-supplied Vector Facility dump formatting program and won't be shown.

The User Subpool Storage part of the dump prints any storage in subpools 0 through 127. It includes both storage that the ABENDing program directly acquires itself, along with storage acquired in execution of other services, such as access method OPENs. The first storage area is acquired for the SYSUDUMP DCB itself, and includes an IOB at location X'00005620'.

```
00005540  00000000 009DD210 7F000000 00200000  009DAE68 000079A0 00005620 00000000  *......K.".......................*
00005560  00005548 009DAE68 00000000 00000000  00000000 50DF05F6 00D60548 009DD280  *....................&..6.O....K.*
00005580  00005548 00FD5118 000079A0 009DC9E0  00008000 04BE189A 009D0228 009DD470  *..............I\............M.  *
000055A0  00005548 00FD5118 7F000000 009DAE68  00005618 80005618 00005618 00000000  *........".......................*
000055C0  001D1700 00000000 009DE08C 009DAE68  00005618 000055A8 00005648 009DF348  *..........\...................3.*
000055E0  00F1D076 00C88D38 00F1D076 00000860  80DF074E 40DF033A 00005560 60C88EE6  *.1}..H...1}....-...+ ......--H.W*
00005600  00DB3828 00000000 00000000 00000000  00000000 00000000 41005618 7F000000  *............................"...*
00005620  02000000 00000000 00005650 0C000000  00005648 009DAE68 00000000 00000000  *...........&....................*
00005640  00000008 1A000405 1D0079A0 8000065D  081A0004 0600065D 00000000 00000000  *...............).......)........*
00005660  00000000 840C2000 FF850002 90006B10  FF850002 90006B10 00006E4C 00006AD0  *....d....e....,..e....,...><..|}*
00005680  00000040 009F1954 009F1930 009F9028  009D1FF8 00000000 009FF060 809DF510  *...             8......0-..5.   *
000056A0  00009000 00002260 00006908 00000000  00040002 009D9000 078D1000 00006B10  *.......-....................,.  *
000056C0  00006908 00000000 078D1000 00006B10  00040002 009D9000 078D1000 00006B10  *..............,...............,.*
000056E0  00040002 009D9000 00006E4C 00006AD0  00000040 009F1954 009F1930 009F9028  *........><..|}...            ...*
00005700  009D1FF8 00000000 009FF060 809DF510  00009000 00002260 00006908 00006DEC  *...8......0-..5.........-....._.*
00005720  50006B0C 00D60548 00000680 00000000  00006B10 000057F0 C1D7D7F3 D7C7D4F1  *&.,..O............,....0APP3PGM1*
00005740  00000000 00000000 40040001 00002000  00006B10 000057F0 00000000 04080000  *........ .........,....0........*
00005760  00000000 00000000 00000000 00000000  00000000 00000000 00000000 00000000  *................................*
00005780  03210000 00600400 00000000 00000000  00000000 00000000 00000000 000057A0  *.....-..........................*
000057A0  00600400 2FA0BF00 00000000 00000000  00000000 00000000 00000000 00000000  *.-..............................*
000057C0  00000000 00000000 00000000 00000000  00005AD8 00C00321 00000321 FFFF0005  *..................!Q.{..........*
```

```
000057E0 00000000 00000000 00000000 00000000  00FF0000 00000000 00000000 00000000  *................*
00005800 00000000 00000000 00000000 00000000  00000000 00000000 00000000 00000000  *................*
    LINES 00005820-000058C0  SAME AS ABOVE
000058E0 00000000 00000000 00000000 00000000  000000E2 C4E6C140 00000000 00000000  *.......SDWA.....*
00005900 00000000 00000000 00000000 00000000  00000000 00000002 00000000 00000000  *................*
00005920 00000000 00000002 00000000 00006B34  00000000 00000000 00000000 00000000  *................*
00005940 00000000 00000000 00000000 00000321  009DF348 05EF8200 00004510 C2140000  *.....3..b...B...*
00005960 00000000 00000321 046F307F 940C2000  5FB3EE40 046F307F 15485DC0 00C00321  *.70.?."m...?.")(.*
00005980 00F7F080 046F307F 940C2000 00000002  00000321 046F307F 00000000 00000000  *.?."m..^.?.")(..*
000059A0 00000321 258DA840 FE000000 046F307F  00000000 00000000 00000000 00000000  *..y..?".........*


JOB EXA7JHMX     STEP APP3     TIME 125832   DATE 94100   ID = 000        PAGE 00000147

000059C0 0378415B DF8A60AC 7F7550B0  00F7F080 00000000 00000000 00000000  *.$.?.-."..&.70..*
000059E0 00000000 00000000 00000000  00F7F080 00000000 00000000 00000000  *...........70...*
00005A00 00000000 860A9DC0 00010321  00F7F080 00000000 00000000 00000000  *....f..(...70...*
00005A20 00000000 860A9DC0 00010321  00000000 00000000 00000000 00000000  *....f..(........*
00005A40 15485F00 00000000 00000000  00000000 00000000 00000000 00000000  *................*
00005A60 00000000 00000000 00000000  06000000 00000000 00000000 7F7550B0  *............"..&.*
00005A80 00000000 00000000 00000000  00000000 00000000 00000000 00000000  *................*
00005AA0 00000000 00000000 00000000  00000000 00000000 00000000 00000000  *................*
00005AC0 00000000 00000000 00000000  00000000 00000000 0005AF0 000058F8  *..........10...8*
00005AE0 00000000 000005AB8 000005BF0  00000000 00000000 00000000  *.!y..$\.!..$0...*
00005B00 00000000 00000000 SAME AS ABOVE
    LINES 00005B20-00005CC0  SAME AS ABOVE
```

The following includes storage acquired during the OPEN for the PDS DCB, including the current IOB at location X'00005AD0'. Refer to the formatted data management control blocks to verify this.

```
00005D20          7F000000 009DCCF8  00005D98 80005D98 00005D98 00000000  *.......8..)q..)q.*
00005D40 00000000 00000000 00000000  00000000 00000000 00000000 00000000  *................*
    LINE 00005D60  SAME AS ABOVE
00005D80 00000000 00000000 00000000  00000000 21005D98 7F000000  *..........)q"....*
00005DA0 02000000 80006AD0 00005DD0 0C000000  00005DC8 00006F3C 00000000 00000000  *...}.).H.?...)q".*
00005DC0 04000004 6C000406 06009000 A0002260  00005DE4 00000000 00000000 00006F94  *...%.........)U..?m*
00005DE0 00005DE0 7F000000 00000000 00005DE4  00000000 00000000 00000000 00006F94  *.)".....)U.....?m*
```

```
00005E00  A000004C 00000000 00B38D80 52000000  00000000 00000000 4A940008 00000000  *....<.....................\m.......*
00005E20  00000000 00000000 02C0041 009DB560   92000000 00005D2C 00000000 00790079  *.................-k.....)......*
00005E40  00000000 00000000 00000000 C9C7C7F0  F1F9C1C8 00000000 0006CEC 00000000   *...............IGG019AH....%...*
00005E60  50C65E82 00000000 00000001 00005EA0  00005EA0 00005DE0 00006F94 0006D3C   *&F;b...........;...)\..?m.__.*
00005E80  00006D3C 0000000C 00000000 00000000  00000078 00C65E9C 00006908 00000000  *..................F.*.......*
00005EA0  0000014C 00000000 40000000 00000200  00000078 00006D3C 00005E00 00000000  *.......<.................*
00005EC0  00006D3D 00000000 20002000 00000000  00000079 00000079 00005E00 000212E0  *.....................\......*
00005EE0  06000001 00005EFC 00005DE0 00000000  00000000 00000000 00000000 00008F80  *.......;..)\...........*
00005F00  00000000 00000000 00000000 00000000  00000000 00000000 00000000 00000000  *..........................*
00005F20  00000000 00000000 00000000 00000000  08000000 00000000 04000000 00000000  *......;...................*
00005F40  00000000 00000000 00000000 00000000  00000000 00000000 00000000 00000000  *..........................*
          LINES 00005F60-00005FC0 SAME AS ABOVE
```

The following line shows the parameters passed to the program, which begins at address 00005FE8. See the first linkage stack entry to verify this.

```
00005FE0  00000000 00000000 80005FEE 0000000A  E3C8C540 D7C1D9D4 E2400000 00000000  *..........^......THE PARMS ......*
```

The following area was acquired for dump formatting and isn't related to program APP3PGM1.

```
000079A0  065D0000 007D0000 40F0F0F0 F0F5C5C3  F040F0F0 F0F6C4F0 F3C440F0 F0F0F0F0  *.)..'...00005EC0 00006D3D 00000*
000079C0  F0F0F040 F2F0F0F0 F0F5C5C5 40F0F0F0  F0F04040 40F0F0F0 F0F0F0F0 F0F0F0F7  *000 20002000 00000000   0000007*
000079E0  F840F0F0 F7F940F0 F0F0F0F0 4B4B6D4B  F0F0F0F2 F1F2C5F0 4040405C 4040405C  *8 00000079 00000000 0002012E0  **
00007A00  4B4B6D4B 4B4B6D4B 4B4B6D4B 4B4B6D4B  4B4B6D4B 4B4B6D4B 4B4B6D4B 4B4BBE0   *...-......;......;...)\.*
00007A20  5C007D00 0040F0F0 F6F0F140 F0F0F140  F6F0F0F0 F0F0F140 00000000 00000000  **.'... 00005EE0 06000001 00000000*
00007A40  40F0F0F0 F0F5C5C6 C340F0F0 F0F0F5C4  C5F04040 4040F0F0 F0F04040 5C4B4B4B  * 00005EFC 00005DE0   00000000 0*
00007A60  F0F0F0F0 F0F04040 F0F0F0F0 F0F0F0F0  40F0F0F0 40404040 5C4B4B4B E04B4B4B  *0000000 00000000 00000000   *..*
00007A80  4B4B6D4B 4B4B6B5D E04B4B4B 4B4BB5D   4B4B6D4B 4B4B6B5D 4B4B6B5D B5C007D   *...... )..........*../*
00007AA0  00040F0 F0F5C6F0 40404040 4040F0F0  F0F04040 F0F0F0F0 F0F0F0F0 F040F0F0  *..... 00005F00 00000000 00000000 00*
00007AC0  C6F0C6F0 F4F040C6 F0C6F040 F0C6F0C6  F0C6F040 40C6F040 4040F0F0 F0F04040  *F0F040 F0F0F0F0   F040F0F0 40F0F0*
00007AE0  C6F0C6F0 40C6F0C6 F040F0F0 40C4B4B  F4F0C6F0 40C6F0C6 F040F0F0 40F0F0F0  *F0F0 F0F0F0F0 F040F0F0  *...000*
00007B00  F0F5C6F0 F040F0F0 F040F0F0 7D000040  F0F0F0F0 40C5C00 7D000040 40F0F0F0  *05F00 00000000 00000000 00*.'..*
00007B20  F0F0F0F0 F7C1C3F0 40C3F6C6 C6F0F4F0  40C3F6C6 C3F640C6 F0C6F0C3 F6C6F0C3  *00007AC0 C6F0C6F0 F4F040C6 F0C6F*
00007B40  F0C3F640 C6F0C3F6 F040F4F0 40404040  F4F040C6 4C6F0C3F6 F6C6F0C3 F6C6F0C3  *0C6 F0C6F040   40404C6 F0C6F0C*
00007B60  F640C640 C3F6C6F0 F4F040C6 F6C6F040  F6C6F040 F4F0C6F0 40C6F0C6 F040F0F0  *6 F0C6F040 F4F0C6F0  *F0F040 F0*
00007B80  C6F0C6F0 C6F04040 4040C6F0 C6F0C6F0  F0C6F05C 007D0000 40F0F0F0 40F0F0F0  *F0F0F0 40F0F0*.'... 000*
```

```
00007BA0  F0F7C1C5 F040C3F6 C6F0C3F6 C6F040F4   F0C3F6C6 C6F0C3F6 C6F04040F4 C6F0C3F6  *07AE0 C6F0C6F0 40C6F0C6 F0C6F0C6*
00007BC0  40C6F0F4 F0C3F6C6 C2F4C240 40C6F4C6   F0C3F6C6 F040C3F6 C6F040F4 F4F040F4  * F040C6F0  F4F0C6F0 C6F04040 4*
00007BE0  F0F5C3F4 C2F4C240 F4F0C6F0 C6F04040   4040405C C6F0C6F0 40C6F0C6 F0C6F0C6  *05C4B4B 40F0F0F0F *F0F0 F0F0F0F*
00007C00  F040C6F0 F4F0C6F0 C6F04040 405C4B4B   40F0F0F0 5C007D00 0040F0F0 F0F0F0F0  *0 F040F0F0  *.. 000*'.. 00007B*
00007C20  F0F040C6 F0C6F5C3 F6C6F040 C6F0F4F0   C6F0C6F0 40C6F0C6 F0F4F040 F0F0F0F0  *00 F0F5C6F0 F040F0F0 F0F0F0F0 F0*
00007C40  C6F0F4F0 C6F04040 40C6F0F0            C6F0C6F0 F0F4F040                     *F040F0   F0F0F0F0 F0F0F0F040 F0F0*

JOB EXA7JHMX    STEP APP3    TIME 125832    DATE 94100    ID = 000                   PAGE 00000148

00007C60  F5C3F0F0 40F7C4F0 F0F0F0F4 F0404040   5CF0F5C6 F0F040F0 F0F0F0F0 F0F0F0F0  *5C00 7D000040  *05F00 00000000 *
00007C80  405CF0F5 C6F0F040 F0F0F0F0 F0F0F0F0   405C007D 000040F0 F0F0F0F7 C2F2F040  * *05F00 00000000 *... 00007B20 *
00007CA0  F4F0F5C3 C6F0C6F5 40C3F6C6 404040F4   F040C6F0 C6F0C6F0 40C6F0C6 F0C6F0C6  *405CF0F5 C6F0F040 F0F0F0F0 F0F0F*
00007CC0  F0C6C6F0 40404040 F0F5C3F0 F0F7C440   F0F0F0F0 F4F0C6F0 40C6F0C6 F0C6F0C6  *0F0 405C007D 000040F0 F0F0F0F*
00007CE0  F740C3F2 F0F5C3F0 F0F7C440 405C405C   C6F040F0 F040F0F0 F7C3C1F0 40C6F4C6  *7 C2F2F040  * *05F00 00000000 **
00007D00  4B7D4B4B 40F0F0F0 F0F7C2F2 F0405C00   7D000040 F0F0F0F0 F0F0F0F0 40C6F4C6  *.,.. 00007B20 *.. 00007CA0 F4F*
00007D20  F0C6F5C3 F340C3F6 C6F0C3F6 40C3F6C6   F0C3F3C6 F6C3F640 C6F0C3F6 C6F0C6F4  *.,.. 00007CA0 F4F*
00007D40  40404040 C6F0F4F0 C6F0C3F6 40C3F6C6   F6C3F640 F040C3F6 C6F0F4F0 40C6F0C6  *0F5C3 C6F0C6F5 40C3F6C6 F0C6F0F4*
00007D60  F0C3F6C6 F0C3F640 40405CF4 C6F0C6C5   F0C6F540 C3F6C6F0 C6F0F4F0 40C6F0C6  * F040C6F0 C6F0C6F0 C6F040C6 F*
00007D80  F0C6F0C6 F040C6F0 C6F0C65C 007D0000   40F0F0F0 F7C3C3 40C6F0C6 C3F6C6F0  *0C6F0C6  *405CF0F5 C6F0F040 F0F*
00007DA0  F4F040F4 40404040 405C007D 000040F0   C3F3C6F0 40C6F0C6 F7C3F4F4 F0404040  *0F0F0 F0F0F* *... 00007CC0 F0C6F0*
00007DC0  40C6F0C6 F0C6F0C6 F040405C F0C6F4C0   C6F040F4 F0C3F6C6 F0C3F640 F4F0C6F0  *40 404040F4 F0F5C3F0 F0F7C440 *
00007DE0  C6F0C3F6 4040405C F0C6F040 C6F0C6F0   F0F5C3F0 F0F7C440 40C6F0C6 F4F0C6F0  *FOC6  *0F0 405C007D 000040F0 *
00007E00  40C6F0C6 F0C6F0C6 5C007D00 0040F0F0   C5F040F0 F0C6F0C6 F7F4F0C3 F3C6F240  *FOC6  *0F0 405C007D F740C3F2 F0*
00007E20  C3F6C6F2 C3F6C6F0 40C6F4C6 40C6F0F0   F040F4F0 F5C34F0 40C6F0C6 4040C6F0  *C6F2C6F0 F4F04040 405C405C F0*
00007E40  C6F5C3F6 C6F040C6 F0F4F0C6 F0C6F040   405C5C40 5CF0F5C6 40C6F040 F0F0F0F0  *F5C6F0 F040F0F0 F0F0F0F0 F0F0405*
00007E60  C3404040 5CF740C3 F2C6F2C6 F040F0F0   C4F0F040 F4C2F7C4 F4C2C2C4 40F4F0C6  *C  *7 C2F2F040  * *05F00 00000*
00007E80  F0F0F040 5C5C007D 000040F0 F0F0F0F7   F0F4F0F5 C3F0F040 40404040 40F4F0C6  *000 **. .. 00007D00 4B7D4B4B 40F*
00007EA0  F0C6F5C3 F640C3F6 C6F0C3F2 C6F240C6   F0F4F0F5 C3F0F040 404040F7 C4F0F0F0  *0F5C3F6 40C3F6C6 F0C6F0F5 F0405C00*
00007EC0  F0C6F540 C3F3F040 405C007D 0040C6C6   F7F4F0C3 F4F0F5F4 40C6F0C6 F0F4F0C6  *0F5 C3F0F040 404040F7 C4F0F0F0 *
00007EE0  405CF0C6 F0C6F0C6 7D000040 405C7D04   40C6F0C3 F0F5C3F4 F040C3F3 C6F3C6F6  * *0F0F0 00007EC0 F0C6F6F540 C3F3C6*
00007F00  F0F05C00 C6F0C3F3 F6C6F040 F7C5C3F4   F0F0F040 C6F0C3F3 F040C6F0 F4F4040  *00*.. 00007EC0 F0C6F6F540 C3F3C6*
00007F20  C6F040C3 F6C3F3C6 F440C3F6 C6F0C6F4   40404040 C6F0C6F4 40405CF0 F040405C  *F0 C6F0C6F0 40F4F0F4 F0F4F0F0 *
00007F40  40C6F7F4 F0C3F3C6 F440C3F6 C6F0C6F0   40404C3 F6C6F0C6 F0C6F0F4 F0F4F0F4  * F740C3F4 C6F0C6F0 C6F04040 *0*
00007F60  C6F540C3 F3C6F640 F0F7C5C5 F040F4F0   F4F0C3F4 C6C6F0 C6F3C6F6 F040F4F0  *F5 C3F0F040 404040F7 C3F2C6F2 *
00007F80  007D0000 40F0F0F0 40C3F3C6 F440C3F6   F5C3C6F0 C3F6C6F0 F6C6F0C6 F440C6F0  *.,.. 00007EE0 405CF0C6 F0C6F6F040 *
00007FA0  C3F6C6F0 C3F6C640 40F0F4F4 F2C3F6C6   F2404040 40F4F0C6 4040405C 405CF0C6  *C6F0C6F7 C3F2C6F2  40C6F0F4 F0*
00007FC0  C6F5C3F3 C6F040C6 F0F4F0C6 F0F4F4F0   F4F0C6C6 F0C3F6C6 F440C6F0 405C007C  *F5C3F0 F0404040 40F7C4F0 F0*
00007FE0  F0C6F040 C6F0C6F7 C3F2C6F2 40C6F0F4   F0F5C3F0 F040405C C000000 5C000000  *0F0 F0F7C2F2 F0405C00   7D0*... *
```

```
00008F60
00008F80  00000000 00000000 00000000 00000000    00008F80 00010080    *................*
                                                   00000000 00000000    *................*
       LINES 00008FA0-00008FE0  SAME AS ABOVE
```

The following is the buffer area acquired from subpool 22 by APP3PGM1.

```
00009000  C1D7D7F3 D7C7D4F1 40E3C9E3 D3C5407D    D4E5E240 C3D6D5E3 D9D6D340 C2D3D6C3  *APP3PGM1 TITLE 'MVS CONTROL BLOC*
00009020  D2E240C1 D7D7C5D5 C4C9E740 F340D7D9    D6C7D9C1 D440F17D 40404040 40404040  *KS APPENDIX 3 PROGRAM 1'        *
00009040  40404040 40404040 40404040 40404040    5C404040 40404040 40404040 40404040  *                *              *
00009060  40404040 40404040 40404040 40404040    40404040 40404040 40404040 40404040  *                *              *
       LINE 00009080  SAME AS ABOVE
000090A0  5C404040 40404040 40E3C8C9 E240D7D9    D6C7D9C1 D47DE240 C6E4D5C3 E3C9D6D5  **       THIS PROGRAM'S FUNCTION*
000090C0  40C9E240 E3D640E4 E2C540E2 D6D4C540    D4E5E240 E2C5D9E5 C9C3C5E2 40E6C8C9  * IS TO USE SOME MVS SERVICES WHI*
000090E0  C3C84040 40404040 40404040 40404040    5C404040 40E6C9D3 D340C3D9           *CH          *        WILL CR*
00009100  C5C1E3C5 40E2D6D4 C540C1E2 E2D6C3C9    C1E3C5C4 40C3D6D5 E3D9D6D3 40C2D3D6  *EATE SOME ASSOCIATED CONTROL BLO*
00009120  C3D2E26B 40E3C8C5 D540C1C2 C5D5C440    E3D64040 40404040 40404040 40404040  *CKS, THEN ABEND TO              *
00009140  5C404040 40D7D9D6 C4E4C3C5 40C140E2    C1D4D7D3 C540C4E4 D4D74B40           **    PRODUCE A SAMPLE DUMP.    *
00009160  40C9E340 C4D6C5E2 40D5D6E3 C8C9D5C7    40D7D9D6 C4E4C3E3 C9E5C54B 40404040  * IT DOES NOTHING PRODUCTIVE.    *
00009180  40404040 40404040 40404040 40404040    5C404040 40404040 40404040 40404040  *                *              *
000091A0  40404040 40404040 40404040 40404040    40404040 40404040 40404040 40404040  *                *              *
       LINE 000091C0  SAME AS ABOVE
000091E0  C1D7D7F3 D7C7D4F1 40C3E2C5 C3E34040    40404040 40404040 40404040 40404040  *APP3PGM1 CSECT                  *
00009200  40404040 40404040 40404040 40404040    40404040 40404040 40404040 C3E34040  *                *              *
00009220  40404040 F2F44040 40404040 40404040    C1D7D7F3 D7C7D4F1 40C1D4D6 C4C54040  *                APP3PGM1 AMODE  *
00009240  F2F44040 40404040 40404040 40D7E4E340    40404040 F2F460C2 C9E340D4         *24             24-BIT M*
00009260  D6C4C540 C6D6D940 D7E4E340 40404040    40404040 40404040 40404040 40404040  *ODE FOR PUT            *
00009280  C1D7D7F3 D7C7D4F1 40D9D4D6 C4C54040    40404040 F2F440   40404040 40404040  *APP3PGM1 RMODE 24       *
000092A0  40404040 40404040 40404040 40404040    40404040 40404040 40404040 40404040  *                *       *
```

JOB EXA7JHMX   STEP APP3   TIME 125832   DATE 94100   ID = 000   PAGE 00000149

```
000092C0  40404040 40404040 40404040 40404040    40C2C1D2 D9404040 40404040 D9404040  *                BAKR    *
000092E0  D9F1F46B F0404040 40404040 40404040    C5E2C140 D3C9D5D2 40404040 D3C9D5D2  *R14,0           ESA LINK*
00009300  C1C7C540 40404040 40404040 40404040    40404040 40404040 40404040 40404040  *AGE             *       *
00009320  40404040 40D3D940 40404040 40D3D3D940    D9F1F26B D9F1F540 40404040 D9F1F540  *        LR  R12,R15      *
00009340  40404040 C3D6D7E8 40D7D9D6   C7D9C1D4    40C1C4C4 D9C5E2E2 40404040 D9C5E2E2  *   COPY PROGRAM ADDRESS  *
```

```
00009360  40404040 40404040 40404040 40404040 40404040 40404040 40E4E2C9 D5C74040  *                         USING  *
00009380  C1D7D7F3 D7C7D4F1 6BD9F1F2 40404040 40404040 40404040 C5E2E3C1 C2D3C9E2  *APP3PGM1,R12            ESTABLIS*
000093A0  C840C1C4 C4D9C5E2 E2C1C2C9 D3C9E3E8 40404040 40404040 40404040 40404040  *H ADDRESSABILITY                *
000093C0  40404040 40404040 40D3C140 404040D9 F1F36BC1 E2C1E5C5 40404040 40404040  *         LA    R13,ASAVE        *
000093E0  40404040 40404040 C7C5E340 C6D6D9D4 C1E360F1 40E2C1E5 C540C1D9 C5C140C1  *        GET FORMAT-1 SAVE AREA A*
00009400  C4C4D9C5 E2E24040 40404040 40404040 40404040 40404040 40E2D7C1 C3C540F1  *DDRESS                   SPACE 1*
00009420  40404040 40404040 40404040 40404040 40404040 40404040 40404040 40404040  *                                *
          LINE 00009440  SAME AS ABOVE
00009460  40404040 40404040 40E2E340 404040D9 F1F26BE2 E3C1C5E2 C1E5C540 40404040  *         ST    R12,STAESAVE     *
00009480  40404040 40E2C1E5 C540C2C1 E2C540D9 C5C740C6 D6D940C5 E2E3C1C5 40404040  *    SAVE BASE REG FOR ESTAE     *
000094A0  C5E7C9E3 40404040 40404040 40404040 40404040 40404040 40E2D7C1 C3C540F1  *EXIT                     SPACE 1*
000094C0  40404040 40404040 40404040 40404040 40404040 40404040 40404040 40404040  *                                *
          LINE 000094E0  SAME AS ABOVE
00009500  5C404040 40C9E2E2 E4C540C1 D540C5E2 E3C1C540 D4C1C3D9 D640E3D6 40C1D3D3  **    ISSUE AN ESTAE MACRO TO ALL*
00009520  D6E640E4 E240E3D6 40C8C1D5 C4D3C540 D6E4D940 D6E6D540 C1C2D5D6 D9D4C140  *OW US TO HANDLE OUR OWN ABNORMA *
00009540  D340E3C5 D9D4C9D5 C1E3C9D6 D5E2404D C1C2C5D5 C4E25D4B 40404040 40404040  *L TERMINATIONS (ABENDS).        *
00009560  40404040 40404040 40C5E2E3 C1C540E2 E3C1C5C5 E7C9E36B C3E36BD7 E4D9C7C5  *         ESTAE STAEEXIT,CT,PURGE*
00009580  7ED8E4C9 C5E2C3C5 6BC1E2E8 D5C3C87E D5D64040 40404040 40404040 40404040  *=QUIESCE,ASYNCH=NO              *
000095A0  40404040 40404040 40404040 40404040 40404040 40404040 40D3E3D9 404040D9  *                         LTR   R*
000095C0  F76BD9F1 F5404040 40404040 E3C5E2E3 40E3C8C5 40D9C5E3 E4D9D540 C3D64040  *7,R15       TEST THE RETURN CO  *
000095E0  C4C54040 40C2E940 40404040 E2E3C1C5 C4D6D5C5 40404040 40404040 4040C9C6  *DE   BZ     STAEDONE          IF*
00009600  40E9C5D9 D66B40C7 D640E3D6 40D5D6D9 D4C1D340 D7D9D6C7 D9C1D440 40404040  * ZERO, GO TO NORMAL PROGRAM     *
00009620  40404040 40404040 40404040 40404040 40404040 40404040 40E2D7C1 C3C540F1  *                         SPACE 1*
00009640  40404040 40404040 40404040 40404040 40404040 40404040 40404040 40404040  *                                *
00009660  40404040 40404040 40404040 40404040 40404040 40404040 40404040 40404040  *                                *
00009680  40404040 40404040 40404040 40404040 40404040 40404040 40404040 40404040  *                                *
000096A0  40404040 40404040 40404040 40404040 40404040 40404040 40404040 40404040  *                                *
          LINE 000096C0  SAME AS ABOVE
000096E0  5C404040 40404040 4040D7D9 C9D5E340 C1D540C5 D9D9D6D9 40D4C5E2 E2C1C7C5  **         PRINT AN ERROR MESSAGE*
00009700  C1D5C440 C5D5C440 C5E7C5C3 E4E3C9D6 D540C9C6 40C5D9D9 D6D940C9 D540C5E2  *AND END EXECUTION IF ERROR IN ES*
00009720  E3C1C540 40404040 40404040 40C3E5C4 40404040 40404040 40404040 404040D9  *TAE          CVD               R*
00009740  F76BC4D6 E4C2D3C5 E6C44040 40404040 40404040 40404040 40404040 40404040  *7,DOUBLEWD                      *
00009760  40404040 40404040 4040D6C9 40404040 C4D6E4C2 D3C5E6C4 4EF76BE7 7DF0C67D  *         OI    DOUBLEWD+7,X'0F'*
00009780  40404040 40404040 40404040 40404040 40404040 40404040 40404040 40404040  *                                *
000097A0  40404040 40404040 40404040 40E4D5D7 D2404040 40404040 40404040 404040E2  *             UNPK               S*
000097C0  E3C1C5E6 E3D64EF9 4DF55D6B C4D6E4C2 D3C5E6C4 40404040 40404040 40404040  *TAEWTO+9(5),DOUBLEWD            *
000097E0  40404040 40404040 40404040 40404040 40404040 40404040 40404040 40404040  *                                *
00009800  E2E3C1C5 E6E3D640 40E6E3D6 40407D5C 5C5C5C5C 5C5C5C40 E6C1E240 D9C5E3E4  *STAEWTO  WTO  '******** WAS RETU*
00009820  D9D540C3 D6C4C540 C6D9D6D4 40C5E2E3 40404040 40404040 40404040 40404040  *RN CODE FROM EST                *
00009840  C1C54060 40C5D5C4 C9D5C77D 40404040 40404040 40404040 40404040 40404040  *AE - ENDING'                    *
```

```
00009860  40404040 40404040 40404040 40E2E3C8  40404040 40404040 40404040 404040D9  *                     STH   R*
00009880  F76BD9C5 E3C3D6C4 C5404040 40404040  40404040 40404040 40404040 40404040  *7,RETCODE                    *
000098A0  40404040 40404040 40404040 40404040  40404040 40404040 40404040 40404040  *                             *
000098C0  40404040 40404040 40C24040 40C5D5C4  C5E7C5C3 F2404040 40404040 40404040  *          B     ENDEXEC2     *
000098E0  40404040 40C5D5C4 40C5E7C5 C3E4E3C9  D6D54040 40404040 40404040 40404040  *        END EXECUTION        *
00009900  40404040 40404040 40404040 40E2D7C1  C3C540F1 40404040 40404040 40404040  *                     SPACE 1*
00009920  40404040 40404040 40404040 40404040  40404040 40404040 40404040 40404040  *                             *
          LINE 00009940   SAME AS ABOVE
00009960  5C404040 40D6D7C5 D540C6C9 D3C5E240  40404040 40404040 40404040 40404040  **    OPEN FILES              *
00009980  40404040 40404040 40404040 40404040  40404040 40404040 40404040 40404040  *                             *
000099A0  40404040 40404040 E2E3C1C5 C4D6D5C5  40C5D8E4 4040405C 40404040 40404040  *          STAEDONE EQU      **


JOB EXA7JHMX        STEP APP3        TIME 125832     DATE 94100     ID = 000        PAGE 00000150


000099C0  40404040 40404040 40404040 40404040  40404040 40404040 40404040 40404040  *                             *
          LINE 000099E0   SAME AS ABOVE
00009A00  40404040 40404040 40E2D7C1 C3C540F1  40404040 40404040 40404040 40404040  *              SPACE 1        *
00009A20  40404040 40404040 40404040 40404040  40404040 40404040 40404040 40404040  *                             *
00009A40  5C404040 40404040 40D3D6C1 C440C140  40D3D6C1 C440C140 C440C1C0 C440C140  *                     LOAD A  *
00009A60  D7D9D6C7 D9C1D440 E3D640C3 D9C5C1E3  C540C3D6 D5E3C5D5 E3E240E2 E4D7C5D9  *PROGRAM TO CREATE CONTENTS SUPER*
00009A80  E5C9E2D6 D940C3D6 D5E3D9D6 D340C2D3  D6C3D2E2 40404040 40404040 40404040  *VISOR CONTROL BLOCKS         *
00009AA0  40404040 40D3D6C1 C440D6D6 D7F3D7C7  D4F24040 40404040 40404040 40404040  *          LOAD  EP=APP3PGM2  *
00009AC0  40404040 40D6C1C4 40C140D7 D9D6C7D9  C1D40D7D9 40404040 40E2D7C1 C3C540F1  *        LOAD A PROGRAM       *
00009AE0  40404040 40404040 40404040 40404040  40404040 40404040 40404040 40404040  *                     SPACE 1*
00009B00  40404040 40404040 40404040 40404040  40404040 40404040 40404040 40404040  *                             *
          LINE 00009B20   SAME AS ABOVE
00009B40  40404040 40C9C4C5 D5E3C9C6 E840C5D7  E8C2D9E4 C9D5E26B 40404040 40404040  *          IDENTIFY EP=BRUINS,*
00009B60  40404040 40C9C4C5 D5E3C9C6 E840C1D5  40C5D5E3 D9E840D7 D6C9D5E3 6B404040  *        IDENTIFY AN ENTRY POINT,*
00009B80  40404040 40404040 40E7E4D9 E2C14040  40404040 40C1D5C4 40C9E3E2 40404040  *       X                    E*
00009BA0  D5E3D9E8 7EE4D9E2 C1404040 40404040  40404040 40404040 40404040 40404040  *NTRY=URSA              AND ITS*
00009BC0  40D3D6C3 C1E3C9D6 D5404040 40404040  40404040 40404040 40404040 40404040  *  LOCATION                   *
00009BE0  40404040 40E2D7C1 C3C540F1 40404040  40404040 40404040 40404040 40404040  *              SPACE 1        *
00009C00  40404040 40404040 40404040 40404040  40404040 40404040 40C3D9C5 C1E3C540  *                             *
00009C20  5C404040 40C1E4C7 C88E3C9C6 5D40E3C3  C2404040 40404040 40C3D9C5 C1E3C540  *         A      *     CREATE *
00009C40  C140E2C5 D7C1D9C1 E3C5404D C4C1E4C7  5D40E3C3 C2404040 40404040 40404040  *A SEPARATE (DAUGHTER) TCB    *
00009C60  40404040 40404040 40C1E3E3 C1C3C840  C5D7F3D7 C7D4F36B 40404040 40404040  *          ATTACH EP=APP3PGM3,*
00009CA0  40404040 4040C1E3 E3C1C3C8 40C1D5D6  E3C8C5D9 40D7D9D6 C7D9C1D4 40404040  *ATTACH ANOTHER PROGRAM       *
```

```
00009CC0  40404040 40404040 40404040 40404040 40404040 40404040 40404040 404040D7  *                               P*
00009CE0  C1D9C1D4 7E4DE7C5 C3C25D6B E5D37EF1 6B404040 4040D6D5 C540D7C1 D9C1D4C5  *ARAM=(XECB),VL=1,     ONE PARAME*
00009D00  E3C5D940 D7C1E2E2 C5C44040 40404040 40404040 40404040 40404040 404040E7  *TER PASSED                     X*
00009D20  40C5C3C2 7EE3C1E2 D2C5C3C2 6B404040 40404040 40404040 40404040 40404040  * ECB=TASKECB,                   *
00009D40  40404040 4040D7D6 E2E3C5C4 40C2E840 D4E5E240 E6C8C5D5 40E3C3C2 40C5D5C4  *      POSTED BY MVS WHEN TCB END*
00009D60  E2404040 40404040 40404040 40404040 40404040 40404040 40404040 40E740E2  *S                            X S*
00009D80  C8E2D7E5 7EF3F340 40404040 40404040 40404040 4040E2C8 C1D9C540 E2E4C2D7  *HSPV=33               SHARE SUBP*
00009DA0  D6D6D340 F3F34040 40404040 40404040 40404040 40404040 40404040 40404040  *OOL 33                          *
00009DC0  40404040 40404040 40404040 40404040 40404040 40404040 40404040 40404040  *                                *
00009DE0  40404040 40404040 40E2D7C1 C3C540F1 40404040 40404040 40404040 40404040  *         SPACE 1                *
00009E00  40404040 40404040 40404040 C5D5D840 D6D54040 40404040 40404040 40404040  *            ENQ ON              *
00009E20  40404040 40404040 40404040 40404040 40404040 40404040 40404040 4040405C  *                               **
00009E40  E2D6D4C5 40C9D4C1 C7C9D5C1 D9E840D5 C1D4C540 E3D640C3 D9C5C1E3 C540C7D9  *SOME IMAGINARY NAME TO CREATE GR*
00009E60  D6E4D740 C3D6D5E3 D9D6D340 C2D3D6C3 D2E24040 40404040 40404040 40404040  *OUP CONTROL BLOCKS              *
00009E80  40404040 40404040 404040C5 D5D8404D C6D6D66B C2C1D96B C56BF36B E2E8E2E3  *           ENQ (FOO,BAR,E,3,SYST*
00009EA0  C5D45D40 40404040 4040C5D5 D840D6D5 40C6D6D6 60C2C1D9 40404040 40404040  *EM)       ENQ ON FOO-BAR        *
00009EC0  40404040 40404040 40E2D7C1 C3C540F1 40404040 40404040 40404040 40404040  *         SPACE 1                *
       LINE 00009EE0            SAME AS ABOVE
00009F00  40404040 40404040 40404040 40404040 40404040 40404040 40404040 40404040  *                                *
00009F20  5C40D7C5 D9C6D6D9 D440C140 E5C5C3E3 D6D940D6 D7C5D9C1 E3404040 40404040  ** PERFORM A VECTOR OPERAT       *
00009F40  5C40C9D6 D540E3D6 40C6D6D9 C3C540C3 D7E440C1 C6C6C9D5 C9E3E840 40404040  ** ION TO FORCE CPU AFFINITY     *
00009F60  E4D9E2C1 40404040 40C5D8E4 405C4040 40404040 40404040 40404040 40404040  *URSA     EQU *                  *
       LINE 00009F80            SAME AS ABOVE
00009FA0  40404040 40404040 40404040 40404040 40404040 40404040 40404040 40404040  *                                *
00009FC0  40404040 40404040 E5E3E5D4 406B4040 40404040 40404040 40404040 40404040  *        VTVM ,                  *
00009FE0  E3C5E2E3 40E5C5C3 E3D6D940 D4C1E2D2 40D9C5C7 C9E2E3C5 D9404040 40404040  *TEST VECTOR MASK REGISTER       *
0000A000  40404040 40404040 40E2D7C1 C3C540F1 40404040 40404040 40404040 40404040  *         SPACE 1                *
       LINE 0000A020            SAME AS ABOVE
0000A040  5C40D6D7 C5D540E3 C8C540D6 E4E3D7E4 E340D7D9 C9D5E340 40404040 404040C6  ** OPEN THE OUTPUT PRINT        F*
0000A060  C9D3C540 40404040 40404040 40404040 40404040 40404040 40404040 40404040  *ILE                             *
0000A080  40404040 40404040 40D6D7C5 D540404D E2E8E2D7 D9C9D5E3 6BD6E4E3 D7E4E35D  *         OPEN  (SYSPRINT,OUTPUT)*
0000A0A0  40404040 40404040 40404040 40404040 40404040 40404040 40404040 40404040  *                                *

JOB EXA/JHMX     STEP APP3     TIME 125832     DATE 94100     ID = 000          PAGE 00000151

0000A0C0  40404040 40404040 40404040 40404040 40404040 40404040 40404040 40404040  *                                *
0000A0E0  40404040 40404040 40D3C140 404040D9 F16BE2E8 E2D7D9C9 D5E34040 40404040  *         LA    R1,SYSPRINT      *
0000A100  404040C7 C5E34040 C1C4C4D9 C5E2E240 D6C640C4 C3C24040 40404040 40404040  *   GET  ADDRESS OF DCB          *
```

```
0000A120  40404040 40404040 40404040 40E4E2C9 D5C740C9  *            USING I*
0000A140  C8C1C4C3 C26BD9F1 40404040 40404040 40404040 40404040 C5E2E3C1 C2D3C9E2 C8404040  *HADCB,R1        ESTABLISH *
0000A160  40C1C4C4 D9C5E2E2 C1C2C9D3 C9E3E840 40404040  * ADDRESSABILITY *
0000A180  40404040 40E3D440 C4C3C2D6 C6D3C7E2 6BE77DF1 F07D4040 40404040  *     TM   DCBOFLGS,X'10' *
0000A1A0  40404040 40404040 E3C5E2E3 40C6D6D9 40E2E4C3 C3C5E2E2 C6E4D340 D6D7C5D5  *       TEST FOR SUCCESSFUL OPEN*
0000A1C0  40404040 40C2D5D6 40404040 40404040 40404040  *     BNO    B*
0000A1E0  C1C4D6D7 C5D54040 40404040 40404040 40404040 40D6D7C5 D540C6C1  *ADOPEN          OPEN FA*
0000A200  C9D3C5C4 40604040 40404040 40404040 D6C24040  *ILED - END JOB*
0000A220  40404040 40404040 40404040 E2D7C1C3 C540F140  *          SPACE 1*
0000A240  40404040 40404040 40404040 40404040 40404040  * *
0000A260  40404040 40404040 40404040 40D6D7C5 D540E3C8  *            OPEN TH*
0000A280  C540D7C1 D9E3C9E3 C9D6D5C5 C440C4C1 E3C140E2 C5E340C4 C3C24040  *E PARTITIONED DATA SET DCB *
0000A2A0  40404040 40404040 40404040 40404040 40404040  * *
0000A2C0  40404040 40404040 40D6D7C5 D540E540 C9D5D7E4 E3404040  *      OPEN  (PDS,INPUT)*
0000A2E0  40404040 40404040 40404040 40404040 40D3C140  *            LA  R*
0000A300  40404040 40404040 40404040 40404040 C5E340C1 C4C4D9C5  *                  GET ADDRE*
0000A320  F16BD7C4 E2404040 40404040 40404040 C5E340C1 C4C4D9C5  *1,PDS       GET ADDRE*
0000A340  E2E240D6 C640C4C3 C2404040 40404040 40404040  *SS OF DCB*
0000A360  40404040 40404040 40404040 D3C840C5 E2E2E340  *            LH  DCBBLKSI*
0000A380  40404040 40404040 40404040 C5E340C2 D3D6C3D2 40E2C9E9 C5404040  *            GET BLOCK SIZE*
0000A3A0  40404040 40404040 40404040 40404040 40E3D440  *            TM  D*
0000A3C0  C3C2D6C6 D3C7E26B E77DF1F0 7D404040 C5E2E340 C6D6D940  *CBOFLGS,X'10'    TEST FOR*
0000A3E0  E2E4C3C3 C5E2E2C6 E4D34040 D6D7C5D5 40404040  *SUCCESSFUL OPEN*
0000A400  40404040 40C2D640 C2D2C1E9 40C2D2C1 E8404040 C9D5E4C5  *      BO  GO*
0000A420  40404040 40D6D2C1 E8406040 C3D6D5E3 C9D5E4C5  *      OKAY - CONTINUE*
0000A440  40404040 40404040 40404040 40404040 40C4D9D6 D7404040  *            DROP  R*
0000A460  F1404040 40404040 40404040 40404040 C5D5C440 C4C3C240 C4  *1         END DCB D*
0000A480  E2C5C3E3 40C1C4D9 C5E2E2C1 C2C9D3C9 E3E84040  *SECT ADRESSABILITY*
0000A4A0  40404040 40404040 40E2D7C1 C3C540F1 40404040  *      SPACE 1*
0000A4C0  40404040 40404040 40404040 40404040 40404040  * *
0000A4E0  D540D6D7 C5D540D6 C640D74B C44BE24B 40604040 C9E2E2E4 C540C5D9 D9D6D940 D4  *N OPEN OF P.D.S. - ISSUE ERROR M*
0000A500  C5E2E2C1 C7C540C1 D5C440C5 D5C44040 40404040 C5D9D9D6 D940C940  *ESSAGE AND END    ERROR I*
0000A520  40404040 40D7E4E3 40404040 E2E8E2D7 D9C9D5E3 6BD6D7C5 D5D3C9D5 C5  *     PUT  SYSPRINT,OPENLINE*
0000A540  40404040 40404040 40404040 40404040 40404040  * *
0000A560  40404040 40404040 40404040 40404040 40D4E5C3 40404040 D9  *            MVC  R*
0000A580  C5E3C3D6 C4C56B7E C87DF1F6 7D404040 E2C5E340 C2C1C440 D9  *ETCODE,=H'16'  SET BAD R*
0000A5A0  C5E3E4D9 D5C0C3D6 C4C54040 40404040 40404040  *ETURN CODE*
0000A5C0  40404040 40C24040 40C5D5C4 C5E7C5C3 F2404040  *     B   ENDEXEC2*
0000A5E0  40404040 40404040 40C7D640 C5D5C440 C5E7C5C3 E4E3C9D6 D5404040  *        GO END EXECUTION*
0000A600  40404040 40404040 40404040 40404040 40404040  * *
```

```
0000A620  40404040 40404040 40404040 40404040  40404040 40404040 40D7D9C9 D5E340D6   *                 PRINT O*
0000A640  D56BC7C5 D5404040 40404040 40404040  40404040 40404040 40404040 40404040   *N,GEN                   *
0000A660  40404040 40404040 40E2D7C1 C3C540F1  40404040 40404040 40404040 40404040   *      SPACE 1           *
0000A680  40404040 40404040 40404040 40404040  40404040 40404040 40404040 40404040   *                        *
0000A6A0  40404040 40404040 40404040 40404040  40404040 40404040 40C4D640 E2D6D4C5   *                 DO SOME*
0000A6C0  40C961D6 40D7D9D6 C3C5E2E2 C9D5C740  40404040 40404040 40404040 40404040   * I/O PROCESSING         *
0000A6E0  40404040 40404040 40C5D8E4 4040405C  40404040 40404040 40404040 40404040   *      EQU  *            *
0000A700  C7D64040 40404040 40404040 40404040  40404040 40404040 40404040 40404040   *GO                      *
0000A720  40404040 40404040 40E2D7C1 C3C540F1  40404040 40404040 40404040 40404040   *      SPACE 1           *
0000A740  40404040 40404040 40404040 40E2D7C1  C3C540F1 40404040 40404040 40404040   *         SPACE 1        *
0000A760  40404040 40404040 40404040 40404040  40404040 40404040 40404040 40404040   *                        *
0000A780  40404040 ........ ........ ........  ........ ........ ........ ........   SAME AS ABOVE
          LINE 0000A7A0   SAME AS ABOVE
```

JOB EXA7JHMX   STEP APP3   TIME 125832   DATE 94100   ID = 000   PAGE 00000152

```
0000A7C0  5C404040 40C7C5E3 40C140E2 E3D6D9C1  C7C540C1 D9C5C140 E3D640E4   ** *   GET A STORAGE AREA TO U*
0000A7E0  E2C5C140 E2C140C2 E4C6C6C5 D96B40E2  C9D5C3C5 40E6C540 40C4D6D5 7DE340D2   *SE AS A BUFFER, SINCE WE  DON'T K*
0000A800  D5D6E640 E3C8C540 C2D3D6C3 D240E2C9  E9C540D6 C640E3C8 C540D74B C44BE24B   *NOW THE BLOCK SIZE OF THE P.D.S.*
0000A820  40C2C5C6 D6D9C5C8 C1D5C440 40404040  40404040 40404040 40404040 40404040   * BEFOREHAND                     *
0000A840  40404040 40404040 40404040 40404040  C5E3D6D9 C1C7C540 D6C2E3C1 C9D56BE2   *            STORAGE OBTAIN,S*
0000A860  D740F2F2 6BD3C5D5 C7E3C87E 4D11F17E  D7C1C7C5 6BD3D6C3 7EC2C5D3 D6E6      *P=22,LENGTH=(11),BNDRY=PAGE,LOC=BELOW*
0000A880  C5D5C7E3 C87E4D11 6BC2D5C4 D9E87ED7  C1C7C56B D3D6C37E C2C5D3D6 E6       *ENGTH=(11),BNDRY=PAGE,LOC=BELOW *
0000A8A0  40404040 40404040 40404040 40404040  40404040 40404040 40404040 40D3D9D6   *                          LR  R*
0000A8C0  F1F06BD9 F1404040 40404040 40404040  40404040 40404040 40D3D9D6 404040D9   *10,R1                     LR  R*
0000A8E0  C5E2E240 C9D540D9 C5C74040 F1F04040  40404040 40404040 40404040 C1C4C4D9   *ESS IN REG 10         SAVE ADDR*
0000A900  40404040 40404040 40404040 40404040  40404040 40404040 40404040 C5D1C5C3   *                          EJECT*
0000A920  E3404040 40404040 40404040 40404040  40404040 40404040 40404040 40404040   *                               *
0000A940  40404040 40404040 40404040 40404040  40404040 40404040 40C9E2E2 E4C540C2   *                     ISSUE B*
0000A960  D3C4D340 D4C1C3D9 D640E3D6 40D3D6C3  C1E3C540 E3C8C540 D4C5D4C2 C5D940E6   *LDL MACRO TO LOCATE THE MEMBER W*
0000A980  C540E6C1 D5E34040 40404040 40404040  C2D3C4D3 40D7C4E2 6BD4C5D4 D3C9E2E3   *E WANT      BLDL PDS,MEMLIST*
0000A9A0  40404040 40404040 40404040 40404040  40404040 40404040 40404040 40404040   *                               *
0000A9C0  40404040 40404040 40404040 40404040  40404040 40404040 40404040 40404040   *                               *
0000A9E0  F1F56BD9 F1F54040 40404040 40404040  40404040 40404040 40404040 40D3E3D9   *15,R15                    LTR R*
0000AA00  C7D6D6C4 40C2D3C4 D3404040 40404040  40404040 40404040 40E3C5E2 E340C6D6D9   *GOOD BLDL               TEST FOR *
0000AA20  40404040 40E2E3C8 40D9F1F5 6BD9C5E3  C3D6C4C5 40404040 40404040 40404040   *     STH R15,RETCODE           *
0000AA40  40404040 40404040 40404040 40E2C1E5  C540D9C5 E3E4D9D5 40C3D6C4 C540C6D6D9   *         SAVE RETURN CODE FOR *
0000AA60  40404040 40404040 C1E3C540 D9C5E3E4  ........ ........ ........ ........   *        LATE*
```

```
0000AA80 D9404040 40404040 40404040 40C2D5E9 404040C5   *R                     BNZ    E*
0000AAA0 D5C4C5E7 C5C34040 40D5D6E3 40E9C5D9 40404040   *NDEXEC               NOT ZER*
0000AAC0 D6406040 C7C9E5C5 40E4D740 40404040 40404040   *O - GIVE UP      SPACE 1     *
0000AAE0 40404040 40E2D7C1 C3C540F1 40404040 40404040   *           *                 *
0000AB00 40404040 40404040 40404040 40404040 5C404040   *                             *
0000AB20 40404040 40404040 40C9E2E2 E4C540C2 E3C8C540   *LDL MACRO TO LOCATE THE MEMBER W* ... ISSUE B*
0000AB40 D3C4D340 D4C1C3D9 D640E3D6 C5D940E6 D4C5D4C2   *E WANT                       W*
0000AB60 C540E6C1 D5E34040 40404040 40404040 40404040   *                             *
0000AB80 40404040 40404040 40D7D6C9 D5E340D7 C4E2BE3    *          POINT PDS,TTR       *
0000ABA0 40404040 40D640D7 D6E2C9E3 C9D6D540 E3D640E3   *     POSITION TO THAT MEMBER  *
0000ABC0 40404040 40404040 40404040 C3C540F1 40404040   *                      SPACE 1*
0000ABE0 40404040 40404040 40404040 40404040 40404040   *                             *

LINE 0000AC00  SAME AS ABOVE

0000AC20 5C404040 40C9E2E2 E4C540D9 C5C1C440 40D9C5C1   **              ISSUE READ MACRO TO REA*
0000AC40 C440C9D5 40E3C8C5 40C6C9D9 E2E340C2 D3D6C3D2   *D IN THE FIRST BLOCK       READ  D*
0000AC60 40404040 40404040 40D9C5C1 C4400C2D3 C140C2D3  *ECB1,SF,PDS,(10),(11)    READ A BL*
0000AC80 C5C3C2F1 6BE2C66B D7C4E26B 5D40040D9 C140C2D3  *OCK OF DATA                       *
0000ACA0 D6C3D240 D6C640C4 C1E3C140 40404040 40404040   *                                  *
0000ACC0 40404040 40404040 40E7C340 C2F14040 40404040   *             XC    DECB1,DECB1    *
0000ACE0 40404040 40404040 40404040 40C3C8C5 C3D240C4   *                        CHECK D*
0000AD00 C5C3C2F1 40404040 40404040 40404040 40404040   *ECB1                          *
0000AD20 40404040 40404040 40404040 40404040 40404040   *                             *
0000AD40 40404040 40404040 40404040 40404040 40404040   *           EJECT              *
0000AD60 40404040 40C5D1C5 C3E34040 40404040 40404040   *                             *
0000AD80 40404040 40404040 40404040 40D5D6E6 40D3C5E3   *                      NOW LET*
0000ADA0 7DE240C6 D6D9C3C5 40C1D540 C1C2C5D5 C44B4040   *'S FORCE AN ABEND.      *    *
0000ADC0 40404040 40404040 40404040 40404040 40404040   *          LPSW  0             *
0000ADE0 40404040 40D3D7E2 E64D40F0 40404040 40404040   *      SUPERVISOR-STATE INSTRUCTION *
0000AE00 40404040 40D3D7E2 E6D960E2 E3C1E3C5 40C9D5E2   *                             *
0000AE20 404040E2 E4D7C5D9 E5C9E2D6 D960E2E3 C1E3C540   *                   SPACE 1*
0000AE40 40404040 40404040 40E2D7C1 C3C540F1 40404040   *                             *
0000AE60 40404040 40404040 40404040 40404040 40404040   *                             *

LINE 0000AE80  SAME AS ABOVE

0000AEA0 5C404040 40C5D5C4 40C5E7C5 C3E4E3C9 D6D54040   **              END EXECUTION     *
```

```
JOB EXA7JHMX       STEP APP3        TIME 125832   DATE 94100    ID = 000                PAGE 00000153

0000AEC0  40404040 40404040 40404040 40404040 40404040 40404040 40404040 40404040  *                 *
0000AEE0  40404040 40404040 40404040 C5D5C4C5 E7C5C340 40C5D8E4 40404040            *        ENDEXEC EQU      *
0000AF00  5C404040 40404040 40404040 40404040 40404040 40404040 40404040 40404040  **                *
0000AF20  40404040 40404040 40404040 40404040 40404040 40404040 40404040 40404040  *                 *
0000AF40  40404040 40C3D3D6 E2C5404D D7C4E26B 6BE2E8E2 D7D9C9D5 E35D4040           *    CLOSE (PDS,,SYSPRINT)*
0000AF60  404040C3 D3D6E2C5 40C6C9D3 C5E24040 40404040 40404040 40404040           *   CLOSE FILES          *
0000AF80  5C404040 40404040 40404040 40404040 C5D5C4C5 E7C5C3F2 40C5D8E4 40404040  **       ENDEXEC2 EQU     *
0000AFA0  5C404040 40404040 40404040 40404040 40404040 40404040 40404040           **                *
0000AFC0  40404040 40404040 40404040 40404040 40404040 40404040 40404040           *                 *
0000AFE0  40404040 40D7D940 40404040 40404040 40404040 40404040 40404040           *  PR ,            *
0000B000  404040D9 C5E3E4D9 D540E3D6 40D4E5E2 40404040 40404040 40404040           *  RETURN TO MVS   *
0000B020  40404040 40404040 40404040 40404040 40E2D7C1 C3C540F1 C3C540F1 40404040  *          SPACE 1*
0000B040  40404040 40404040 40404040 40404040 40404040 40404040 40404040           *                 *

    LINE 0000B060  SAME AS ABOVE

0000B080  C2C1C4D6 D7C5D540 40C5D8E4 4040405C 40404040 40404040 40404040 4040405C  *BADOPEN  EQU    *       *
0000B0A0  40404040 40404040 40404040 40404040 40404040 40404040 40404040           *                 *
0000B0C0  40404040 40404040 40404040 40404040 40404040 40D7E4E3 404040E2           *           PUT  S*
0000B0E0  E8E2D7D9 C9D5E36B D6D7C5D5 D3C9D5C5 404040C4 C9E2D7D3 C1E840C5 D9D9D6D9  *YSPRINT,OPENLINE DISPLAY ERROR*
0000B100  40D4C5E2 E2C1C7C5 40404040 40404040 40404040 40404040 40404040           *  MESSAGE         *
0000B120  40404040 40C24040 404040C5 C5C3F240 40404040 40404040 40404040           *  B      ENDEXEC2 *
0000B140  404040C5 D5C440C5 E7C5C3E4 E3C9D6D5 40404040 40C5D1C5 C3E34040 40404040  *   END EXECUTION  EJECT  *
0000B160  40404040 40404040 40404040 40404040 40C5D1C5 C3E34040 40404040           *           EJECT  *
0000B180  40404040 40404040 40404040 40404040 40404040 40404040 40404040           *                 *

    LINE 0000B1A0  SAME AS ABOVE

0000B1C0  E2E3C1C5 C5E7C9E3 40C5D8E4 4040405C 40404040 40404040 40404040 4040405C  *STAEEXIT EQU    *       *
0000B1E0  40404040 40404040 40404040 40404040 40404040 40404040 40404040           *                 *
0000B200  40404040 40404040 40404040 40404040 40404040 40D7E4E2 C84040E4           *           PUSH U*
0000B220  E2C9D5C7 40404040 40404040 40404040 40404040 40404040 40404040           *SING             *
0000B240  40404040 40404040 40404040 40404040 40404040 40404040 40404040           *                 *
```

We now come to the last major section of the dump: the trace table. The trace table is very large. This job was run on a very lightly loaded system and there were no other tasks to record entries and compete for the trace buffers. As a result, a large part of the trace table will be omitted. However, all the omitted elements will come either from events that precede the start of APP3PGM1 or some events within SVC calls. All events relating to actions of the APP3PGM1 program are included.

```
------------------------------ SYSTEM TRACE TABLE ------------------------------
--                             -----------------                             --
--                             -----------------                             --
PR ASID TCB-ADDR  IDENT CD/D PSW----- ADDRESS-  UNIQUE-1 UNIQUE-2 UNIQUE-3  PSACLHS- PSALOCAL PASD SASD TIMESTAMP-RECORD
                                                UNIQUE-4 UNIQUE-5 UNIQUE-6  PSACLHSE

01-0321 009F9028  SVCR    B 070C0000 80E2E7C6  00000000 00F7F1B0 00000004                          A91BE6437B51F00
```

This is the first entry in the trace table. It demonstrates how to determine the time duration covered by the trace table, which is useful for figuring out if a wait for a specified period of time (i.e., the STIMER macro) is covered in the trace table or not. All subsequent trace entries are omitted up to the point that APP3PGM1 starts to get control. The following shows the GETMAIN request for the storage into which APP3PGM1 was loaded.

```
04 0321 009DF348  SSRV   78   8108FCBE 0000FB10 000006F8 00006908                                 A91BE6449D49281
                                        03210000
```

A number of events related to loading in the program are omitted here.

```
01 0321 009DF348  SVCR    0 078D0000 00006908  00006908 FD000012 00005FE8                          A91BE6644BE29405
```

The program just got control for the first time. Notice the address of X'00006908' in the PSW.

```
01 0321 009DF348  SVC   3C 078D0000 0000693E  00006908 00000100 0000691C                          A91BE6644BE30485
```

This results from the ESTAE macro, which generates SVC 60 (X'3C'), as shown here:

```
ESTAE STAEEXIT,CT,PURGE=QUIESCE,ASYNCH=NO
```

The code generated by this included the following lines (not all the generated lines are shown):

```
000010 4510 C02C          0002C    22+            BAL   1,*+28          LIST ADDR IN REG1 SKIP LIST
                          00014    23+IHB0001     EQU   *
- - - - (lines omitted) - - - -    24+            DC    AL1(16)         FLAGS FOR TCB, PURGE,        X
00002C 4100 0100          00100    33+            LA    0,256(0,0)      CREATE & PARMLST EQ 0
000030 4110 1000          00000    34+            LA    1,0(0,1)        MAKE REG1 POS.  XCTL=NO
000034 0A3C                        35+            SVC   60              ISSUE STAE SVC
```

Note that you can compute the offset in the program to find the statement that caused an interrupt by subtracting the starting address of the program (X'00006908') from the PSW address of the interrupt (X'0000693E'). This gives you a result of X'0036' (X'693E' – X'6908' = X'0036'), which is the location counter value after the SVC 60 instruction. The register contents from the trace entry are:

Register 15 = 00006908.   Since R15 isn't modified by the ESTAE macro expansion, this is just whatever R15 held at the time of the ESTAE macro; in this case, it was the starting address of the program.

Register 0 = 00000100.   This comes from the LA 0,256(0,0) instruction and is an internal parameter for ESTAE. See the *MVS/ESA Diagnosis: System Reference* manual for a description of the values in register 0 and 1 for the ESTAE SVC.

Register 1 = 0000691C.   This comes from the BAL 1,*+28 instruction and is the address of the parameter list that follows it (X'691C' – X'6908' = X'0014').

```
01 0321 009DF348    SVCR    3C 078D0000 0000693E   00000000 00000000 00000000 0000691C          A91BE6644BE3C585
```

Return from the ESTAE macro. Note that register 15 now contains zero.

```
01 0321 009DF348   SVC    8 078D0000 000069A8   00000000 0000699C 00000000                A91BE6644BE40585
```

This trace entry was generated by the LOAD macro:

```
LOAD    EP=APP3PGM2              LOAD A PROGRAM
```

The code generated by this includes:

```
00008C 4100 C094      60+    LA    0,*+8          LOAD PARAMETER INTO REGISTER ZERO
000090 47F0 C09C      61+    B     *+12           BRANCH AROUND CONSTANT(S)
000094 C1D7D7F3D7C7D4F2 62+  DC    CL8'APP3PGM2'  ENTRY POINT NAME
00009C 1B11           63+    SR    1,1            SHOW NO DCB PRESENT
00009E 0A08           64+    SVC   8
```

The register contents are:

Register 15 = 00000000. Not changed by the LOAD macro expansion.

Register 0 = 0000699C. Address of the module name to be loaded from the LA 0,*+8 instruction.

Register 1 = 00000000. Set to zero by the SR 1,1 instruction.

```
01 0321 009DF348   SSRV    78   8117FEFC   0000FD72 00000078 7FFFC018                     A91BE6644BE5D485
                                           03210000
```

This is the first in a series of trace entries defining the processing of the LOAD request. The SSRV request represents a system service request; 78 is the identifier for the various request types, see *MVS/ESA Diagnosis: Using Dumps and Traces*.) The parameters for this request are very similar to those for a normal GETMAIN or FREEMAIN. In the previous information, FD is the subpool requested (subpool 253). The 72 value represents a flag byte; the right-most bit is 1 for a FREEMAIN and 0 for a GETMAIN, which makes this a GETMAIN request. The next word (X'00000078') is the length requested, and the next word (X'7FFFC018') is the address of the storage. Refer to *MVS/ESA Diagnosis: Using Dumps and Traces* for further details.

```
01 0321 009DF348   SSRV   78        8111D4CA   0000FF12 00000020 009FD000                           A91BE6644BE65105
                                                03210000
```

Another storage request; try decoding this one.

```
01 0321 009DF348   SSRV   78        84BAA6C4   4000E600 000011C8 7F74FE38                           A91BE6644BE93505
                                                03210000
01 0321 009DF348   PGM    011 070C2000 84BAA6E6  00020011 7F750000                                   A91BE6644BE9D105
                                                00000001 00000000 0321 0321
```

This program check entry is for interruption code 011, a page translation exception, and represents a page fault. Note that the format follows that in the RTM2WA Summary, i.e., the fourth word (X'7F750000') represents the translation exception address. Note that the preceding trace entry is a GETMAIN request for subpool 230 (X'E6'), and storage is obtained at address X'7F74FE38'. From this, you can assume that the requestor is probably clearing the storage area it just obtained.

```
01 0321 009DF348   PC     ...    0        84BA1B24   00C04                                           A91BE6644BECB205
01 0321 009DF348   SVC    78 070C0000 84EBE6B0  0000E672 000002B8 00000000
```

The preceding entry is a regular GETMAIN macro. The format of the first word is as described for the SSRV entries previously shown. The subpool is 230 and the length requested is X'000002B8' bytes. Note, however, that the address where the storage was obtained isn't presented until the SVCR entry, which follows.

```
JOB EXA77HMX        STEP APP3         TIME 125832    DATE 94100    ID = 000                PAGE 00000188

01 0321 009DF348    SVCR      78 070C0000 84EBE6B0  00000000 000002B8 7F74FB80                A91BE6644BED3B85
01 0321 009DF348    SVC       12 070C2000 84EBE9A6  00000000 7F74FDE0 009FD060                A91BE6644BEDC885
```

The preceding trace entry is for a BLDL macro issued as part of the LOAD macro processing. You'll see another example of this later within APP3PGM1, which will match a source statement with the trace entry. BLDL is used to build a list of library member information. To do this, it must read in a block from the PDS directory. This trace entry is for a conventional (old-style) PDS rather than a PDSE.

```
01 0321 009DF348    SVC       78 070C0000 8106E5E4  0000FD50 00000286 00000000                A91BE6644BEE8105
```
BLDL gets some storage.

```
01 0321 009DF348    SVCR      78 070C0000 8106E5E4  00000000 00000288 009DF018                A91BE6644BEF1A85
01 0321 009DF348    SVC       0  070C0000 8106EDCE  00FE2FB0 01000800 009DF210                A91BE6644BF15105
```

SVC 0 is an EXCP macro. Register 1 in the trace parameters (X'009DF210') is the address of the IOB for the I/O request. Note that it's within the storage acquired in the preceding trace entry.

```
01 0321 009DF348    SSCH   2CA 00   02   00F1922C  00F24D90 0000F000 00FF7D20                A91BE6644BF6C105
```

The EXCP results in a Start Subchannel instruction. The device number is 2CA.

```
01 0321 009DF348    SVCR      0  070C0000 8106EDCE  00000000 810AC900 009DF210                A91BE6644BF71305
```

Return from the EXCP macro.

```
01 0321 009DF348    SVC     1 070C0000 8106EDE0  00000000 00000001 009DF20C                                     A91BE6644BF75105
```

The BLDL macro code now issues a WAIT macro (SVC 1), waiting for the I/O to complete. For a WAIT, register 0 contains the number of events to wait for, and register 1 contains either the address of the ECB if the count is one (which is the case in this example) or the address of a list of ECBs. Note that the ECB address (X'009DF20C') is also within the storage area acquired by the four BLDL trace entries earlier.

```
01 0321 009DF348    SVCR    1 070C0000 8106EDE0  809FF7B0 00000001 009DF20C                                     A91BE6644BF7FC85
```

The SVCR entry normally indicates that the program that issued the corresponding SVC is receiving control again. In this case, it really isn't since the related I/O event hasn't completed. Note that the R15 entry holds the address of the RB that's waiting.

```
01 003B 009C0CF0    I/O   2CA 078D1000 89FB4922  00004007 00FF7F68 0C000000  00000080 00000000 003B 003B A91BE6644C5DA805
                                                  010000B 00F24D90            00000000
```

The I/O completes. Note that there's a different ASID—003B instead of 0321—because the job was waiting instead of running when the I/O event finished. The status in the third unique fullword is X'0C000000', which indicates status of channel end and device end; this is normal I/O completion status.

```
03 0321 009DF348    SRB     070C0000 8100F960  00000321 00F19200 00F1922C                0321 0321 A91BE6644C647683
                                                           80                        00
```

The SRB dispatch is used to signal that the I/O has completed. Notice that the system has gotten momentarily busier; the SRB is dispatched on processor 03, which implies that 01 and 02 are busy.

```
03 0321 00000000   SSRV     2        80FEE79E  009DF20C 7F000000 00000000    A91BE6644C66F103
                                                00000000
```

The SSRV 2 entry records a branch entry to the POST macro routine. Since SRBs can't issue SVCs, SRB code must use branch entry (and thus generate SSRV trace entries) for many services. The first unique fullword (X'009DF20C') is the address of the ECB, which was specified in the SVC 1 trace entry four entries earlier. The second unique fullword (X'7F000000') is the ECB completion code; X'7F' is used to represent normal I/O ending status.

```
04 0321 009DF348   DSP               070C0000 8106EDE0  00000000 00000000 00000001 009DF20C  00000000 00000000 0321 0321 A91BE6644CE84B81
```

The Dispatch entry indicates that the TCB is restarting. Note that the PSW address is the same as was recorded for the SVC 1. Note also that you've been dispatched on processor 04.

```
04 0321 009DF348   SVC      78 070C0000 8106F118  0000FD03 00000286 009DF018    A91BE6644CE91581
```

Having completed the I/O successfully, the BLDL code can now release the work area it got earlier. One side effect of this is that, if you want to look at the ECB or IOB in the dump, the area might have been reused by the time the dump has printed.

```
04 0321 009DF348   SVCR     78 070C0000 8106F118  00000000 00000286 009DF018    A91BE6644CEA9101
04 0321 009DF348   SVCR     12 070C2000 84EBE9A6  00000000 00000000 009DF018    A91BE6644CEAF101
```

Return from the BLDL. Register 15 holds condition code zero. In the interests of brevity, a number of trace entries related to the rest of the program load operation aren't shown.

03 0321 009DF348   SVCR   8 078D0000 000069A8   00000000 89E00FA0 0000000C   A91BE66451962103

The LOAD macro finally ends, after about 100 trace entries.

03 0321 009DF348   SVC   29 078D0000 000069BA   00000000 800069AC 00006A2E   A91BE6645196F03

The above trace entry is generated by the IDENTIFY macro:

```
66          IDENTIFY EP=BRUINS,         IDENTIFY AN ENTRY POINT           X
                     ENTRY=URSA         AND ITS LOCATION
```

The code generated by this includes:

```
0000A0 4500 C0AC           000AC      67+          BAL   0,*+12          LOAD EP SYMBOL ADDR
0000A4 C2D9E4C9D5E24040               68+          DC    CL8'BRUINS'     EP SYMBOL
0000AC 4110 C126           00126      69+          LA    1,URSA          LOAD PARAMETER REG 1
0000B0 0A29                           70+          SVC   41              ISSUE IDENTIFY SVC
```

You should be able to work out the parameter addresses in registers 0 and 1 at this point.

03 0321 009DF348   SSRV   78   84BD2A64 0000FF12 00000020 009FE008   A91BE6645199 3C03
                                       03210000

The IDENTIFY code acquires storage for a minor CDE, which will be used to record the new entry point name (BRUINS). Go check location X'009FE0008' in the LSQA dump at this time to see what it contains. Refer to the IHACDE mapping macro if necessary.

03 0321 009DF348   SVCR   29 078D0000 000069BA   00000000 00000020 7F743EB8   A91BE6645199E183

Return from the IDENTIFY SVC.

```
03 0321 009DF348   SVC   2A 078D0000 00006A1A   000069D0 00000020 000069C4          A91BE664519A1F03
```

The next macro to cause an entry in the trace table is the ATTACH macro. This is coded as:

```
ATTACH EP=APP3PGM3,         ATTACH ANOTHER PROGRAM              X
       PARAM=(XECB),VL=1,   ONE PARAMETER PASSED               X
       ECB=TASKECB,         POSTED BY MVS WHEN TCB ENDS        X
       SHSPV=33             SHARE SUBPOOL 33
```

Some of the generated code from this macro includes:

```
0000B4 4110 C0BC          77+          LA   1,IHB0011              LIST ADDRESS
0000B8 47F0 C0C0          78+          B    IHB0011A               BYPASS LIST
0000BC                    79+IHB0011   EQU  *
0000BC 80000530           80+          DC   A(XECB+X'80000000')
0000C0                    81+IHB0011A  EQU  *
0000C0 41F0 C0C8          82+          LA   15,IHB0008             SET UP LIST ADDRESS
0000C4 47F0 F048          83+          B    72(,15)                BRANCH AROUND LIST
0000C8                    84+IHB0008   DS   0F                     SUP. PARAM. LIST
0000C8 000000E4           85+          DC   A(*+28)                ADDRESS OF SYMB NAME
- - - - (lines omitted) - - - - - -
000106 00000000000000000  105+         DC   XL10'00'               RESERVED BYTES AT END
000110 0A2A               106+         SVC  42                     ISSUE ATTACH SVC
```

The contents of registers 1 and 15 are parameter addresses for this ATTACH macro.

```
03 0321 009DF348   SSRV   78      84BD50FC   4000FF10 000000F8 009F9388          A91BE664519B1583
                                  03210000
```

The ATTACH processing begins by getting storage for a TCB, which is returned at location X'009F9388'.

```
03 0321 009DF348 SVC   A  070C2000 84BD5032 00000000 FD000198 FFFFFFFF           A91BE664519BD103
03 0321 009DF348 SVCR  A  070C2000 84BD5032 00000000 FD000198 009DF108           A91BE664519C9403
03 0321 009DF348 SVC   3C 070C1000 84BD54FC 00000000 00000102 009F93F4           A91BE664519CF503
```

Note that ATTACH creates its own ESTAE routine here.

```
03 0321 009DF348 SVCR  3C 070C1000 84BD54FC 00000000 00000000 009F93F4           A91BE664519DAF03
03 0321 009DF348 SVC   78 070C2000 84BD4406 0000FD02 000000F0 00000000           A91BE664519DF603
03 0321 009DF348 SVCR  78 070C2000 84BD4406 00000000 00000080 7F743BC8           A91BE664519E9603
03 0321 009DF348 SVC   78 070C2000 84BD4442 0000E102 00000080 00000000           A91BE664519EC03
03 0321 009DF348 SVCR  78 070C2000 84BD4442 00000000 00000080 7FFFBD10           A91BE664519F8403
03 0321 009DF348 SVC   78 070C3000 84BD446E 0000E101 00000030 7FFFBD10           A91BE664519FD503
03 0321 009DF348 SVCR  78 070C3000 84BD446E 00000000 00000030 7FFFBD10           A91BE6451A08103
03 0321 009DF348 SVC   78 070C1000 84BD448C 0000E101 00000010 7FFFBD80           A91BE6451A0B983
03 0321 009DF348 SVCR  78 070C1000 84BD448C 00000000 00000010 7FFFBD80           A91BE6451A15703
03 0321 009DF348 SSRV  78    810F37E2       0000E102 00000030 7FFFBD10 03210000  A91BE6451A24283

03 0321 009DF348 SSRV  78    810F388C       0000D702 00006000 7F74B000 03210000  A91BE6451A4CA83

03 0321 009DF348 SSRV  78    810F38A6       0000D703 00001000 7F74B000 03210000  A91BE6451A62C03

03 0321 009DF348 SSRV  78    84BD4868       0000E502 00000060 7F754FA0 03210000  A91BE6451A83C03

03 0321 009DF348 SSRV  78    8109FFCE       0000FF02 00000158 7F743A70 03210000  A91BE6451A90103

03 0321 009DF348 SSRV  78    810A01F8       0000FF03 00000158 7F743A70 03210000  A91BE6451AB9203

03 0321 009DF348 SSRV  78    84BD4B38       0000E501 0000005C 7F754FA0 03210000  A91BE6451ACAC03

03 0321 009DF348 SVCR  2A 078D0000 00006A1A 00000000 00000020 009DF128           A91BE6451ADDC83
```

Receive control back from the ATTACH macro. Register 1 contains the address of the TCB you just created.

```
03 0321 009DF348   SVC   38 078D0000 00006A2E   00000000 00000020 80006A20                    A91BE66451AE1883
```

The next trace entry comes from the following ENQ macro, coded in APP3PGM1 as:

```
ENQ   (FOO,BAR,E,3,SYSTEM)      ENQ ON FOO-BAR
```

The code this generated includes:

```
000114 4510 C124        00124   112+              BAL   1,IHB0013            BRANCH AROUND AND ADDRESS LIST
- - - - (lines omitted) - - - -
000124                          119+IHB0013 DS    0H                        OBJECT OF THE BAL
000124 0A38                     120+              SVC   56
03 0321 009DF348   PC   ...  0      811249BC      00101
```

Since a great deal of Global Resource Serialization takes place in the GRS address space, the ENQ SVC processing immediately transfers control to that with a Program Call instruction.

```
03 0321 009DF348   PT   ...  0      81123DEC      0321                      0321 0321
```

The Program Transfer records the return back from GRS.

```
03 0321 009DF348   SVCR  38 078D0000 00006A2E   00000000 00000000 00C00321                    A91BE66451B17F03
```

Receive control back from the ENQ.

```
03 0321 009DF348  *PGM   019 078D0000 00006A2E   00040019 7F60D000          00000000 00000000 00000000 0321 0321 A91BE66451B38103
```

The previous program check is as a result of the VTVM instruction:

```
VTVM ,              TEST VECTOR MASK REGISTER
```

This is at location 000126 in the program listing. Because vector support requires so much work to set up and so few installations use it, MVS runs with vector operations disabled until a program tries to use the vector instruction set. When this happens, a program check arises, which is the previous trace entry. Program interruption code X'0019' is the vector operation exception code. Since this program was run on a machine that included the Vector Facility, MVS will set up the control blocks (VSSA, etc.) needed to provide vector support. This involves about 200 trace entries, which I won't print due to volume.

```
02 0321 009DF348  *PGM  019 078D0000 00006A2E  00040019 0000E000    00000000 00000000 0321 0321 A91BE66453B10F01
                                                                    00000000
```

Finally receive control back after the vector environment is established.

```
02 0321 009DF348  SSRV  78       81258050  000DFD00 00006000 7F73D000                        A91BE66453B8A381
                                            03210000
02 0321 009DF348  SSRV  78       81258150  000DFD03 00001EC0 7F73D000                        A91BE66453BB0101
                                            03210000
02 0321 009DF348  SVC   13 078D0000 00006A3E  00000000 00000000 80006A38                     A91BE66453C42901
```

This entry is as a result of the following OPEN macro:

```
OPEN (SYSPRINT,OUTPUT)
```

Code generated for this macro includes:

```
00012C 4510 C134          00134  129+        BAL   1,*+8          LOAD REG1 W/LIST ADDR.
000130 8F                        130+        DC    AL1(143)       OPTION BYTE
000131 00068C                    131+        DC    AL3(SYSPRINT)  DCB ADDRESS
000134 0A13                      132+        SVC   19             ISSUE OPEN SVC
```

The trace entries for the OPEN continue for about 13 pages in the original dump. They won't be shown here. Now I'll list a few of the trace entries generated by OPEN because, while the OPEN processing was occurring, the APP3PGM3 task started up.

```
02 0321 009DF348  SSRV  78          860A9F74  0000E612 00000920 009DA358                                A91B66455B9B601
                                              03210000
02 0321 009DF348  PT  ...  0        8540D132  0321                                   0321 0321
02 0321 009DF348  PC  ...  0        8540D754  01600
```

Notice that the processor changes to 00 from 02 on the next entry. Also note that the TCB changes from 9DF348 to 9DF128, the TCB address for the subtask. There will be some setup for the new task before it receives control. The two TCBs are alternatively suspended, waiting for the local (LOCL) lock.

```
00 0321 009DF128  SRB        070C0000 8100F960  00000321 00FC19D4 00FC1968           00          0321 0321 A91BE66455BC9602
                                               80
00 0321 00000000  SSRV 10F            00000000 00F7F080 009DF128 009F93B0                                  A91BE66455BDB182
                                               00000000
00 0321 009DF128  DSP        070C0000 81070EA8 00000000 00000000 00FA7600   00000000 00000000 0321 0321 A91BE66455BEA102
00 0321 009DF128  SSRV 78             8108FD72 0000F501 00000098 00FC1968                                  A91BE66455C36782
                                               03210000
00 0321 009DF128  SSRV 78             8108FD72 0000FD01 00005000 009CC000                                  A91BE66455C85702
                                               03210000
00 0321 009DF128  SSRV 78             80CD95C2 0000E603 000003E8 009DEC18                                  A91BE66455CA5102
                                               03210000
02 0321 009DF348  SUSP       860A9F0C          009FF7B0 LOCL     00000000   00000000 00000000             A91BE66455CA6201
                                               00000000
```

```
00 0321 009DF128  SSRV 78           84BA73B0  0000FD03 00000604 7F7432E8                                              A91BE66455CB7C02
                                               03210000
00 0321 009DF128  SSRV 78           84BAA77C  4000E603 000011C8 7F747E38                                              A91BE66455CE2102
                                               03210000
02 0321 009DF348  DSP      070C0000 80FDEC80  00000000 00000000 060A9DA0 00000001 00000000 0321 0321                  A91BE66455CF1101
00 0321 009DF128  SUSP              8111ECFC  009F93B0 00000000 LOCL     00000000 00000000                            A91BE66455CF9102
02 0321 009DF348  SSRV 78           860A9F9C  0000E603 00000920 009DA358                                              A91BE66455CFCA01
                                               03210000
02 0321 009DF348  PT    . . . 0     8540D754  0321                                            0321 0321
02 0321 009DF348  PC    . . . 0     8540D132  01600


JOB EXA7JHMX     STEP APP3          TIME 125832     DATE 94100     ID = 000                              PAGE 00000208

02 0321 009DF128  DSP      070C0000 80FDEC80  00000000 00000020 009DF0E8 00000001 00000000 0321 0321                  A91BE66455D0CB02
02 0321 009DF348  SUSP              860A9F0C  009FF7B0 00000000 LOCL     00000000 00000000                            A91BE66455D12F01
                                               03210000
00 0321 009DF128  SSRV 78           8114E17C  0000FD03 00000074 7FFFC018                                              A91BE66455D32682
                                               03210000
00 0321 009DF128  SSRV 78           8117F440  0000FF12 00000088 009DD548                                              A91BE66455D3F202
                                               03210000
00 0321 009DF128  SSRV 78           80FF7694  0000FF01 000000F8 009F9388                                              A91BE66455D59982
                                               03210000
```

Eventually the APP3PGM3 program receives control.

```
00 0321 009DF128  SVCR   0 078D0000 89E00F30  89E00F30 00000020 000069C4                                              A91BE66455D5D282
```

The first thing the APP3PGM3 program does is issue an STIMER macro. This generates SVC 47 (X'2F'), and will wait for the time period specified in the STIMER BINTVL= operand. In this case, the time period is one minute (60.00 seconds), so this is the last you'll see of the APP3PGM3 TCB in the trace table.

```
00 0321 009DF128  SVC   2F 078D0000 89E00F4A  00000000 91000000 09E00F98                                              A91BE66455D65102
00 0321 009DF128  SUSP              81263806  009FF8A8 00000000 LOCL     00000000 00000000                            A91BE66455D74F02
                                               03210000
```

In the meantime, the APP3PGM1 task is still merrily—OK, stodgily—completing the OPEN processing. Several more pages of OPEN processing are omitted. One of the OPEN trace entries that merits discussion is the following, which is the entry for a DEBCHK SVC. DEBCHK validates a DEB, ensuring that no one slyly adds his own DEB into the chain. The code byte of X'81' indicates the access method—in this case, the job entry subsystem (JES2).

```
                                             00000000
02 0321 009DF348   DSP        070C0000 80FDEC80   00000000
                              00000000 06A9DA0 00000000   00000001 00000000 0321 0321 A91BE6645D78901

01 0321 009DF348   SVC    75  078C3000 00DE1796   00000002 81000000 00005E00     A91BE6645749110 4
01 0321 009DF348   SVCR   75  078C3000 00DE1796   00000000 81000000 009DB560     A91BE66457 4A1404
```

Return from DEBCHK. The DEB address is in register 1. OPEN next loads the access method executors—the programs that get control when your program does a GET or PUT, for example. SVC 8 is a LOAD macro.

```
01 0321 009DF348   SVC     8  075C3000 00BEEACA   00BEE9D0 009DC754 00FD8564     A91BE6645752C104
```

LOAD issues a GETMAIN to obtain storage for an LLE. In this case, the LLE is for module IGG019DJ.

```
01 0321 009DF348   SSRV   78      8114C892 0000FF12 00000010 009DF008           A91BE6645755340 4
                                          03210000
01 0321 009DF348   SVCR    8  075C3000 00BEEACA   00000000 00C65950 000000D6     A91BE6645755890 4
```

On return from the LOAD, the module address (00C65950) is in register 0.

```
01 0321 009DF348   SVCR   13  078D0000 00006A3E   00000000 00000948 009DC6B8     A91BE6645769 0D04
```

Eventually the OPEN ends.

```
01 0321 009DF348   SVC    13  078D3000 00006A56   00000000 00000948 B0006A50     A91BE664769 5904
```

The next thing in APP3PGM1 is another OPEN macro. The generated code for this is:

```
                    139          OPEN  (PDS,INPUT)
000142 0700         140+         CNOP  0,4            ALIGN LIST TO FULLWORD
000144 4510 C14C    141+  0014C  BAL   1,*+8          LOAD REG1 W/LIST ADDR.
000148 80           142+         DC    AL1(128)       OPTION BYTE
000149 000634       143+         DC    AL3(PDS)       DCB ADDRESS
00014C 0A13         144+         SVC   19             ISSUE OPEN SVC
```

As before, I'll omit most of the OPEN processing. The following are three LOAD macro trace entries generated by the loading of the access method routines for the PDS DCB. I'll explain these in some detail, because they're referred to previously in the explanation of the LLEs.

```
04 0321 009DF348  SVC    8  075C1000 00DB0B44  00FD50C8 009DB754 00FD8564                    A91BE6645A1FEA05
```

LOAD gets storage for an LLE. Note that the address is 009DF0C8, one of the LLE addresses formatted earlier in the dump.

```
04 0321 009DF348  SSRV  78     8114C892  0000FF12 00000010 009DF0C8                           A91BE6645A222685
                                          03210000
```

But which module is being loaded? Note that the address returned in register 0 is 00DAFA60, which is within the address range for the IGG0193B load module; hence, that is the program whose LLE is at 9DF0C8.

```
04 0321 009DF348  SVCR   8  075C1000 00DB0B44  00000000 00DAFA60 00000CF2                     A91BE6645A227905
```

The process repeats two more times. Try to work out each of the LLE and load module relationships yourself. Answers will be provided after the entries.

```
04 0321 009DF348  SVC    8  075C0000 00DB0B44 00FD50C8 009DB754 00FD8564   A91BE6645A22D405
04 0321 009DF348  SSRV  78     8114C892 0000FF12 00000010 009DF0B8         A91BE6645A248C85
                                  03210000
04 0321 009DF348  SVCR   8  075C0000 00DB0B44 00000000 00C88D38 00000059   A91BE6645A24D905
```

LLE is at 9DF0B8, and refers to module loaded at C88D38; this is IGG019BA.

```
04 0321 009DF348  SVC    8  075C0000 00DB0B44 00FD50C8 009DB754 00FD8564   A91BE6645A251905
04 0321 009DF348  SSRV  78     8114C892 0000FF12 00000010 009DF0A8         A91BE6645A26E105
                                  03210000
04 0321 009DF348  SVCR   8  075C0000 00DB0B44 00000000 00D60548 000000A5   A91BE6645A273285
```

LLE is at 9DF0A8, and refers to module loaded at D60548; this is IGG019BB.

```
JOB EXA7JHMX      STEP APP3        TIME 125832   DATE 94100   ID = 000     PAGE 00000219

04 0321 009DF348  SVCR  13  078D3000 00006A56 00000000 00000948 009DB6B8   A91BE6645A38A385
```

The OPEN macro finally completes.

```
04 0321 009DF348  PC   ...  8  00006A9F  0030B
```

This previous entry was generated by the following macro:

```
STORAGE  OBTAIN,SP=22,LENGTH=(11),BNDRY=PAGE,LOC=BELOW
```

Unlike GETMAIN and FREEMAIN, which generate SVCs in the normal case, the STORAGE macro generates a Program Call (PC) instruction. Generated code includes:

```
000192 B218 E000    00000    180+    PC    0(14)              .PC TO STORAGE RTN
```

The address in the trace entry (6A9F) minus the starting address of the program (6908) gives a difference of hexadecimal X'0197'. The expected value for this would be X'0196' (location 000192 plus the length of the PC instruction, which is four bytes). However, remember that the PC instruction sets the last bit of the PSW address to indicate the previous problem state bit setting of the PSW; you're in problem state, hence it's a one.

```
04 0321 009DF348   SSRV   132    00000000   00001616 00002260 00009000                A91BE6645A3AF705
                                            03210000
```

You get X'2260' bytes of storage at location 9000.

```
04 0321 009DF348   PR   ...   0    00006A9F   8128B828                     0321
```

The STORAGE macro returns control to us. Note that the address is odd due to the problem state bit.

```
04 0321 009DF348   SVC   12 078D2000 00006AB0   00000000 00006E40 00006F3C           A91BE6645A3B5805
```

Next is the BLDL macro BLDL PDS,MEMLIST that generates the following code:

```
000198 4110 C634   00634   185+   LA    1,PDS               LOAD PARAMETER REG 1
00019C 4100 C538   00538   186+   LA    0,MEMLIST           LOAD PARAMETER REG 0
0001A0 4111 0000   00000   187+   LA    1,0(1)              CLEAR HIGH ORDER BYTE
0001A4 1FFF                188+   SLR   15,15               FOR NO OPTION
0001A6 0A12                189+   SVC   18                  LINK TO BLDL ROUTINE
```

```
04 0321 009DF348  SVC   78 078C0000 8106E608  000E650  00000286 00000000                            A91BE6645A3C0405
04 0321 009DF348  SVCR  78 078C0000 8106E608  00000000 00000288 009DAD78                             A91BE6645A3DB705
```

BLDL starts by getting a work area. It next issues an EXCP to read the PDS directory:

```
04 0321 009DF348  SVC    0 078C0000 8106EDCE  00FE2FB0 01000800 009DAF70                             A91BE6645A3FD705
```

IOS receives the request and issues a Start Subchannel to the appropriate device.

```
04 0321 009DF348  SSCH  2CA 00  02  00F1562C  00F24D90 8000F000 00323220                             A91BE6645A440805
```

Control returns from the EXCP processor.

```
04 0321 009DF348  SVCR   0 078C0000 8106EDCE  00000000 810AC900 009DAF70                             A91BE6645A445805
```

BLDL now has to wait for the I/O to complete, and issues a WAIT macro (SVC 1).

```
04 0321 009DF348  SVC    1 078C0000 8106EDE0  00000000 00000001 009DAF6C                             A91BE6645A449105
04 0321 009DF348  SVCR   1 078C0000 8106EDE0  809FF6B8 00000001 009DAF6C                             A91BE6645A453885
```

(Don't believe the SVCR.)

```
:00 002E 009DC348  I/O  2CA 078D2000 00037CEC  80004007 00323468 0C000000  00000080 00000000 002E 002E A91BE6645AA73C02
                                               0020000A 00F24D90  00000000
```

Eventually the I/O completes. Note that you can compute how long the I/O took by subtracting the SSCH time stamp (A91BE6645A440805) from the I/O time stamp (A91BE6645AA73C02). The result is in the same format as the STCK instruction, i.e., bit 51 represents one microsecond.

```
04  0321  009DF348  SRB    070C0000 8100F960  00000321 00F15600 00F1562C  00          0321 0321 A91B6645AA92905
04  0321  00000000  SSRV   2        80FEE79E                              80                     A91B6645AAAD285
                                              009DAF6C 7F000000 00000000
04  0321  009DF348  DSP    078C0000 8106EDE0  00000000 00000001 009DAF6C  00000000 00000000 0321 0321 A91B6645AAD4C85
```

The DSP entry signals that the WAIT is finally satisfied.

```
04  0321  009DF348  SVC   78 078C1000 8106F134  0000E603 00000286 009DAD78    A91B6645AADCB85
04  0321  009DF348  SVCR  78 078C1000 8106F134  00000000 00000286 009DAD78    A91B6645AAFC205
04  0321  009DF348  SVCR  12 078D2000 00006AB0  00000000 00000000 009DAD78    A91B6645AB01105
```

The BLDL SVC returns control to you; note condition code zero in register 15.

```
04  0321  009DF348  SVC   72 078D0000 00DB3D26  00DB3828 00000000 F49DCCF8    A91B6645AB0F105
```

The next trace entry is from a BSAM module rather than the program. The code to read the block of data is:

```
0001C4                              203          READ  DECB1,SF,PDS,(10),(11)   READ A BLOCK OF DATA
0001C4 4510 C1DC                    204+         CNOP  1,*+24
0001C8 00000000            001DC    205+         BAL   1,*+24                   LOAD DECB ADDRESS
0001CC 00                           206+DECB1    DC    F'0'                     EVENT CONTROL BLOCK
0001CD 80                           207+         DC    X'00'                    TYPE FIELD
0001CE 0000                         208+         DC    X'80'                    TYPE FIELD
0001D0 00000634                     209+         DC    AL2(0)                   LENGTH
0001D4 00000000                     210+         DC    A(PDS)                   DCB ADDRESS
0001D8 00000000                     211+         DC    A(0)                     AREA ADDRESS
0001DC 50A1 000C          0000C     212+         DC    A(0)                     RECORD POINTER WORD
0001E0 40B1 0006          00006     213+         ST    10,12(1,0)               STORE AREA ADDRESS
0001E4 58F0 1008          00008     214+         STH   11,6(1,0)                STORE LENGTH
0001E8 BFF7 F031          00031     215+         L     15,8(,1)                 LOAD DCB ADDR
0001EC 05EF                         216+         ICM   15,B'0111',49(15)        LOAD RDWR ROUTINE ADDR
0001EE D703 C1C8 C1C8 001C8 001C8   217+         BALR  14,15                    LINK TO RDWR ROUTINE    @
                                    218          XC    DECB1,DECB1
```

This macro branches to IGG0193B. The module, in turn, issues an EXCPVR macro—essentially an EXCP with real addresses. This follows the typical pattern of an I/O request.

```
04 0321 009DF348   SSCH  2CA 00 02   00F15D2C  00F24D90  0000F000  00323B20          A91BE6645ABAA605
04 0321 009DF348   SVCR  72 078D0000  00DB3D26  00000000  810AC900  F49DCCF8         A91BE6645ABAFA05
04 0321 009DF348   SVC   1 078D0000  00D607B0  00D60548  00000001  00006AD0          A91BE6645ABB5105
```

The SVC 1 is due to the CHECK macro:

```
                              219          CHECK DECB1
0001F4 4110 C1C8    001C8     220+      LA    1,DECB1                LOAD PARAMETER REG 1
0001F8 58E0 1008    00008     221+      L     14,8(0,1)              PICK UP DCB ADDR
0001FC 1BFF                   222+      SR    15,15
0001FE BFF7 E035    00035     223+      ICM   15,B'0111',53(14)      LOAD CHECK ROUTINE ADDR
000202 05EF                   224+      BALR  14,15                  LINK TO CHECK ROUTINE
```

As with the READ macro, it branches outside the program before issuing the WAIT SVC.

```
04 0321 009DF348   SVCR  1 078D0000  00D607B0   809DF2C0  00000001  00006AD0                                 A91BE6645ABBD885
00 002E 009DC348   I/O   2CA 078D1000 00037CD4  00004007  0035FF68  0C000000  00000080  00000000  002E 002E  A91BE6645B67DD02
                                                 00100013  00F24D90                               00000000
04 0321 009DF348   SRB   070C0000  8100F960      00000321  00F15D00  00F15D2C  00                       0321  A91BE6645B68D105
                                                 80
04 0321 00000000   SSRV  129  80DAF6B8           00006AD0  7F000000  00000000                               A91BE6645B6A4F05
                                                 00000000
04 0321 009DF348   DSP   078D0000  00D607B0      00000000  00000000  00000001  00006AD0  00000000     0321  A91BE6645B6D3105
```

The I/O has completed. We now come to the final instruction of program APP3PGM1:

```
000204 8200 0000    00000     227      LPSW  0                      SUPERVISOR-STATE INSTRUCTION
```

Since APP3PGM1 is executing in problem state, the LPSW instruction generates a privileged operation exception, or an 0C2.

```
04 0321 009DF348 *PGM       002 078D1000 00006B10  00040002 009D9000   00000000 00000000 0321 0321 A91BE6645B6DA805

04 0321 009DF348 *RCVY PROG                                                                      00000000

04 0321 009DF348              940C2000 00000002 00000000   00000000 00000000 0321 0321 A91BE6645B748405
                                       00000000                      00000000
04 0321 009DF348 SSRV 12D     8103FFDA 009DF348 000C8000 00000000                               A91BE6645B77B185
                                       00000000
04 0321 009DF348 SSRV 12D     8103FFFA 009DF348 000B8000 00000000                               A91BE6645B788605
                                       00000000
04 0321 009DF348 DSP     078D1000 810420A4  00000000 00006E4C 00006AD0   00000000 00000000 0321 0321 A91BE6645B7AE405
04 0321 009DF348 *SVC  D 078D1000 810420A6  00D60548 00006E4C 00006AD0                               A91BE6645B7B3485
```

This previous instruction is the ABEND SVC that ends the execution.

```
04 0321 009DF348 SSRV 78      84C523F0 0000FF50 000000C8 009F93B8                               A91BE6645B7CAC85
                                       03210000
04 0321 009DF348 SSRV 78      84C5241A 0000FF70 00000F70 7F752090                               A91BE6645B806605
                                       03210000
04 0321 009DF348 SSRV 78      81260F70 0000E540 00000130 7F74BED0                               A91BE6645B8C4885
                                       03210000
04 0321 009DF348 PC  ..  0    81261116 00506
04 0321 009DF348 SSRV 78      89E061D6 0000FF70 000001C0 7F7A1E40                               A91BE6645B8E8285
                                       00040000
04 0321 009DF348 SSRV 78      89E06604 0000E574 000A2000 7F671000                               A91BE6645B9A8985
                                       00040000
```

JOB EXA7JHMX   STEP APP3   TIME 125832   DATE 94100   ID = 000   PAGE 00000220

04 0321 009DF348   SSRV   78   89E06916   0000E370 00000510 07D6AF0   A91BE6645C3F4B05
                                                  00040000
******** TRACE DATA IS NOT AVAILABLE FROM ALL PROCESSORS AFTER THIS TIME.

The preceding message indicates that, while there might be further trace entries, the trace can't be considered complete after this point. This is a typical end to a trace table.

JOB EXA7JHMX   STEP APP3   TIME 125832   DATE 94100   ID = 000   PAGE 00000221

The last page of a SYSUDUMP lists the page numbers in the dump for the various sections printed in it.

```
                                 DUMP INDEX
                                 ----------


DATA AREAS                                                 PAGE NUMBER
----------                                                 -----------

AREAS RELATED TO TCB AT: 009DF348/.........                 00000001
ENQ/DEQ CONTROL BLOCKS.....................                 00000026
DATA MANAGEMENT CONTROL BLOCKS.............                 00000027
IOS CONTROL BLOCKS.........................                 00000028
RTM CONTROL BLOCKS.........................                 00000029
PCLINK STACKS / SAVE AREAS.................                 00000034
INSTALLATION/SUBSYSTEM AREA................                 00000034
LSQA.......................................                 00000082
SP229/230..................................                 00000084
REGISTERS..................................                 00000094
SUMMARY STORAGE............................                 00000116
MODULES....................................                 00000116
   APP3PGM1................................                 00000136
   APP3PGM2................................                 00000144
   IEAVSSAF................................                 00000117
   IEAVTRF4................................                 00000117
```

```
IEAVTRP2.......................  00000137
IGG019BA.......................  00000120
IGG019BB.......................  00000121
IGG019DJ.......................  00000119
IGG0193B.......................  00000122
IOSVFMTU.......................  00000141
USER SUBPOOLS..................  00000146
TRACE TABLE....................  00000153

END OF DUMP
```

Glossary

ABEND Abnormal End macro instruction used to terminate a task. Also used as a verb.

ACB Access Method Control Block, a user-created control block for the VSAM and VTAM access methods. Represents one cluster or path (VSAM) or an application or logical unit name (VTAM).

AIA ASM I/O Request Area. Represents a single-page I/O operation to ASM.

ANSI American National Standards Institute, U.S. national standards-making body. Described the ASCII character code or terminals that use it.

AQAT Address Queue Anchor Table, VSM control block that points to free-space entries for a subpool with entries in order by address. *See also* DFE and SQAT.

ASCB Address Space Control Block, the primary MVS control block for an address space.

ASM *See* Auxiliary Storage Management.

ASTE Address Space Second Table, a cross-memory/data space hardware-defined control block used with PC instruction and access register mode storage access.

ASVT Address Space Vector Table, an MVS Supervisor control block that holds addresses of all ASCBs in an MVS system.

ASXB Address Space Extension Block, a swappable LSQA-resident address space control block.

ATTACH Macro instruction to create a subtask, sometimes used as a verb. *See also* TCB.

Auxiliary Storage Management MVS component responsible for paging services (compare to RSM and VSM).

CCW Channel Command Word, an eight-byte data area that contains one instruction (command) for an I/O device, an I/O controller, or the CSS itself. Generally defined in the *S/370 Principles of Operation*.

CDE Contents Directory Entry, an MVS contents management control block that describes loaded programs. *See also* XTLST.

CPU Central Processing Unit, term for the arithmetic and control units of a computer in the architecture defined by John Von Neumann in 1946 (compare to processor complex).

CSCB Command Scheduling Control Block, a communications task control block created to pass an operator console command to an address space; commands processed in this way include START, MODIFY, and STOP.

CSD Common System Data, a control block used in multiprocessor management; *see* chapter 1.

CSS Channel Subsystem, that part of a processor complex responsible for initiating and controlling I/O requests and channel paths; *see* chapter 8.

CTC Channel-to-Channel adapter, an IBM processor feature that provides a control unit within the processor that can then communicate with other processor complexes running separate copies of MVS. Sometimes abbreviated CTCA and used by VTAM, GRS, and other MVS components.

CVAF Common VTOC Access Facility, a feature of the MVS/Data Facility Product providing services to read MVS VTOCs; macros start with CVAF*xxx* or ICV*xxx*. An interface to DADSM.

Cell pool Facility supported by VSM that provides faster storage acquisition and disposition than the GETMAIN/FREEMAIN/STORAGE macros.

Channel Program A series of CCWs intended to be executed in sequence.

Communications Task The MVS component responsible for displaying messages (from the WTO macro), processing or forwarding commands, and generally controlling consoles; *see also* CSCB and WTO.

Contents Supervision (also called *contents management*) The MVS component responsible for loading, deleting, and overall management of programs; newer macros start with CSV*xxx*.

DADSM Direct Access Device Space Management, the MVS component responsible for allocating, extending, and freeing disk space, VTOC services, etc.; *see also* CVAF.

DAE Dump Analysis and Elimination, an MVS component that operates with RTM to avoid producing additional dumps for specified known problems or problems for which a dump is usually of no value.

DASD Direct Access Storage Device, an IBM term for a disk drive.

DAT Dynamic Address Translation, an IBM term for virtual storage; the term *DAT-off* describes a state where only real storage and real addresses are being used. DAT also describes the process of converting virtual addresses to real storage addresses.

DCE DASD Class Extension, an IOS control block that defines model-specific characteristics for a DASD device and its associated controller.

DDR Dynamic Device Recovery, an MVS component responsible for recovering from I/O errors by allowing movable media to be moved to another device during execution. Provides the SWAP command.

DDT Device Descriptor Table, an IOS control block that contains the addresses of device-dependent routines used in processing I/O requests, such as ERPs and MIH routines. The characteristics of attached devices.

DEB Data Extent Block, a control block created by the OPEN macro to represent files to MVS; it contains extent information for specific data sets and concatenations.

DECB Data Event Control Block, a control block created within READ or WRITE macros representing an I/O request at the application program level. Contains an ECB, various addresses, and flag bits.

DFE Double Free Element, a VSM control block used to track SQA/LSQA free space; *see also* SQAT, AQAT.

DFP Data Facility Product, a program product of MVS that includes most access methods, data utilities, etc.

DOM Delete Operator Message macro instruction, used to remove WTO messages from console displays.

DQE Descriptor Queue Element, a VSM control block that describes allocated pages.

DSECT Dummy Section in assembler language, essentially a description of data outside a program.

Dispatcher The MVS component responsible for giving control to tasks, i.e., letting them run. The prototypical traffic cop.

ENF Event Notification Facility, A facility added to MVS 4.3 to monitor certain system events, e.g., devices varied offline.

ENQ Enqueue macro; used to request shared or exclusive control of a resource. *See also* resource.

ERP Error Recovery Procedure. A program, usually IBM-supplied, that runs under control of the MVS I/O Supervisor to analyze and attempt recovery from I/O errors.

EVENTS A special form of the WAIT macro, offering better performance for many situations.

External Data Controller Older name for Channel Subsystem.

External interrupts An architectural feature of the IBM System/370 design that provides a separate class of interrupts for outside events; now it's mostly associated with timer supervision.

FBQE Free Block Queue Element, a VSM control block that describes CSA or free private-area 4K blocks.

FQE   Free Queue Element, a VSM control block that describes CSA or free private-area blocks less than 4K in size.

GDA   Global Data Area, a VSM control block that holds information about SQA and CSA storage.

GRS   Global Resource Serialization, the MVS component that supports the ENQ, DEQ, and GQSCAN macros.

HASP   Houston Automatic Spooling Program, an OS/360 forerunner to JES2.

Hot I/O   A term describing an I/O device that repetitively sends I/O interrupts to the External Data Controller, in excess of the actual host-requested I/O operations.

I/O   Input/Output, but you knew that already.

I/O Supervisor   The MVS component responsible for scheduling and starting I/O along with handling I/O completion, processing errors if needed, and notifying the requestor of completion.

IEFSDPPT   Program Properties Table. Holds special module information for contents management.

IOB   Input/Output Block, a user-created control block for use with the EXCP macro instruction; it's created by access methods in response to I/O macros (READ, GET, etc.).

IOCOM   I/O Communications Area. Contains addresses of IOS routines and selected data areas.

IOS   See I/O Supervisor.

IOSB   I/O Service Block, the control block that represents an I/O operation to IOS. Used with the STARTIO macro instruction.

interrupt   Generic term for an event, either external or internal, that causes current processing to be stopped and special nucleus code (the interrupt handler) to be given control.

JES   Generic term for the IBM MVS Job Entry Systems (JES2 and JES3).

JFCB   Job File Control Block, a control block that contains selected information about a data set specified by a DD statement.

Job Management   MVS term for the process of reading in a batch job, interpreting the JCL, preparing it for selection by an initiator, and producing printed output—generally all done by JES.

LCCA   Logical Configuration Communication Area, a control block that holds information about MVS status on a specified processor within a processor complex. Compare to PCCA.

LDA   Local Data Area, a VSM control block that holds storage management information for an address space. Compare to GDA.

LLE   Load List Element, a Contents Supervision control block that defines a loaded program.

LPDE Link Pack Directory Entry, a contents supervision control block representing a program loaded into the Link Pack Area.

LSPACE A DADSM macro to retrieve disk space information.

LSQA Local System Queue Area, a part of private address space storage that holds address-space-related control blocks, e.g., TCBs.

MLWTO MultiLine WTO. A WTO macro, or the message generated by it, that forms a multiple-line message.

Master Scheduler An address space used by MVS proper.

Media Manager A component of MVS that performs I/O for 4K blocks. It uses the same IOS driver ID as VSAM.

MIH Missing Interrupt Handler, a service of the I/O Supervisor that tracks I/O operations and issues warning messages for those that haven't completed within a predefined time limit.

O/C/EOV Open/Close/End of Volume, a term used to refer to these services in the DFP component supplied by SVC 19, 20, and 55, respectively.

ORB Operation Request Block, a hardware control block that holds information needed to initiate an I/O request to the Channel Subsystem. Used with the Start Subchannel (SSCH) instruction by IOS.

ORE Operator Reply Element, a communications task control block related to a WTOR macro instruction.

OUCB SRM User Control Block. Holds address space status information.

OUSB SRM Swappable Control Block, an LSQA-resident control block that holds address space status information.

OUXB SRM User Extension Block. Holds information about an address space that's swapped out.

PARMLIB Slang for the SYS1.PARMLIB data set.

PCCA Physical Configuration Communication Area, a control block that holds status information for a specific processor within a processor complex. Compare to LCCA.

PDS Partitioned Data Set, a library.

PSW Program Status Word. An eight-byte data area, defined by System/370 architecture, that contains the status of a processor.

PVT Page Vector Table, an RSM control block that holds system-wide RSM routine addresses and counts.

POST A macro that signals that an event has completed. Also used as a verb.

Program Properties Table Holds special contents management module information.

PURGE A macro instruction to intercept or stop an I/O operation. For example, SVC 16.

RACF Resource Access Control Facility, an IBM program product for computer security.

RB *See* Request Block.

RD Region Descriptor, a VSM control block that defines the starting address and length of a region.

Request Block Generic term for the PRB, SVRB, and IRB control blocks; RBs represent a transfer of control through MVS from one program to another.

Resource Generic term used in ENQ/DEQ or lock processing; a resource can be anything for which access or modification must be serialized.

RNLE Resource Name List Entry, a GRS control block that defines resources to be included or excluded from global serialization.

RPL Request Parameter List. Represents one I/O request in the VSAM and VTAM access methods.

RSM Real Storage Manager, a component of MVS that controls real memory allocation (compare to ASM and VSM).

RTM Recovery Termination Manager, a component of MVS that handles errors (either through ABEND or program checks), controls recovery from these, and processes termination of tasks and address spaces.

SADMP Stand-Alone Dump Program, a program that dumps an MVS system after it has failed completely, e.g., following a wait state.

SAF Router MVS feature that provides an interface to security products.

SCVT Secondary CVT, a logical extension to the CVT that holds system-wide routine addresses.

SDWA System Diagnostic Work Area, a control block created by RTM following an ABEND. Provided to ESTAE recovery exit, it can also be written to the SYS1.LOGREC data set.

SNAP Macro that produces dumps. There's also a SNAPX form for data spaces.

SPQA Subpool Queue Element (Anchor), a VSM control block that describes a series of free elements in a specified subpool.

SPQE Subpool Queue Element, a VSM control block that describes a free element within allocated space for a specified subpool.

SPT Subpool Table, a VSM control block that holds coded subpool characteristics.

SQA System Queue Area, a commonly addressable storage area used for selected, often short-duration fixed control blocks, e.g., IOSB.

SQAT Size Queue Anchor Table, a VSM control block used to track free storage in SQA and LSQA; *see also* AQAT and DFE.

SRM System Resources Manager, MVS component responsible for workload performance management.

SSCVT Subsystem Communications Vector Table, a control block that represents a subsystem to MVS.

SSIB Subsystem Input Block, one of two control blocks used when making a request to MVS subsystems. Used with SSOB.

SSOB Subsystem Option Block, *see* SSIB.

SSVT Subsystem Vector Table, a control block that defines the types of SSIB/SSOB requests to be processed by a subsystem and provides the addresses of the routines to perform the processing.

STCB Secondary TCB, extended TCB located above the 16MB line in ELSQA.

SWA Scheduler Work Area, storage used for control blocks related to initation and termination of jobs or steps, e.g., Step Control Table.

SYSEVENT Macro used to interface to SRM that uses SVC 95 and notifies SRM that specified events occured or conditions have arisen.

SYSGEN System Generation, the process of creating a new MVS system from scratch.

TCB Task Control Block, dispatcher control block that's the basic unit of work for MVS.

UCB Unit Control Block, an IOS control block representing a specific I/O device (or alternate path to an I/O device).

UCM Unit Control Module, a communications task control block that represents a console.

UCS Universal Character Set, a character set image table used in certain IBM printers.

VRF VTOC Recovery Facility, an implicit DADSM service that attempts to recover from various disk space allocation errors in the VTOC.

VSAM Virtual Storage Access Method.

VSM Virtual Storage Management, the component of MVS responsible for storage management.

VSSA Vector Status Save Area, an MVS dispatcher control block used to save information related to a task's use of the Vector Facility.

VTOC Volume Table of Contents, a DADSM data set kept on all disks that holds information about each data set on the disk.

WAIT Macro instruction that causes a TCB to stop executing until a corresponding POST macro is issued.

WPL WTO/WTOR/MLWTO/WTP Parameter List, A control block used with these macros that contains the message text, options, and so forth; refer to the IEZWPL macro.

WPX WPL extension. *See* WPL, and refer to the IEZWPX macro.

WQE WTO Queue Element, a communication task control block created for each WTO or WTOR request.

XCTL Macro used to transfer control from one program to another in contents management.

XTLST Extent List, a contents management control block that defines the starting address and length of a program.

Index

ABOUT THE AUTHOR

Hank Murphy was born in Lexington, Kentucky, and first learned assembler language in 1968 at the University of Kentucky, without which he might currently be in the horse business. He has been programming in assembler in OS and MVS environments ever since. He taught assembler language (IBM and VAX) at the Los Angeles Pierce Community College from 1981 through 1994, and taught advanced MVS topics as part of the UCLA Extension's mainframe systems programming certificate program from 1984 to 1993. His previous book, Assembler for COBOL Programmers, was published in 1990. Currently a contract programmer, his clients have included IBM and Candle Corporation. Hank Murphy lives in Agoura Hills, California, with his wife of 15 years, Barbara, and their three tykes, and uses his writing as an excuse to never clean off the dining room table.